Textbook of Psychotherapy in Psychiatric Practice

For Churchill Livingstone:
Publisher: Georgina Bentliff
Editorial Co-ordination: Editorial Resources Unit
Production Controller: Nancy Henry
Design: Design Resources Unit
Sales Promotion Executive: Hilary Brown

Textbook of Psychotherapy in Psychiatric Practice

Edited by

Jeremy Holmes MA MRCP FRCPsych
Consultant Psychiatrist/Psychotherapist, North Devon District Hospital, Barnstaple

CHURCHILL LIVINGSTONE
EDINBURGH LONDON MELBOURNE NEW YORK AND TOKYO 1991

CHURCHILL LIVINGSTONE
Medical Division of Longman Group UK Limited

Distributed in the United States of America by Churchill
Livingstone Inc., 650 Avenue of the Americas, New York,
N.Y. 10011, and by associated companies, branches and
representatives throughout the world.

First published 1991

ISBN 0-443-04197-0

British Library Cataloguing in Publication Data
A catalogue record for this book is available from the British
Library.

Produced by Longman Singapore Publishers (Pte) Ltd
Printed in Singapore

Preface

Scene 1. A seminar at a medical school. A group of bewildered clinical students are awed, initiated, empowered by a distinguished psychoanalyst who tells them they have a secret gift unavailable to anyone else in the hospital: time to *listen* to the patient...

Scene 2. A professorial ward round at a famous postgraduate psychiatric institution. The trembling SHO presents the case. The professor interviews the patient, skillfully, but with great detachment. A long and erudite discussion about diagnosis and psychopathology follows. A conclusion is reached. The professor departs, accompanied by acolytes. A nurse, the SHO, and a social worker who is trained as a psychotherapist remain behind. They ask, 'How then shall we set about trying to *help* this patient...?'

Scene 3. A newly appointed consultant is worried by his inability to persuade an anorexic patient, who is getting thinner and thinner, to eat. He arranges supervision with a psychoanalytical colleague who asks 'Now, what do you really *feel* about this patient ...?'

These vignettes, taken from my own development as a psychiatrist, may help to explain the background which led to the conception of this book. A psychiatry without psychotherapy is severely handicapped. Given the complexity of the subject there can be a tendency to retreat into academia or oversimplification. But the interaction of patient and psychiatrist of whatever persuasion inevitably creates an interpersonal field: psychiatrists are perforce psychotherapists. The aim of this book is to provide students of psychiatry of all ages, stages and disciplines with the understanding and skills needed to make use of this field for the benefit of their patients.

Learning to do psychotherapy starts with the 'taking on' of a patient, in that special sense that differs from medical management or the partial contribution to a multidisciplinary team. Case examples of such psychotherapeutic relationships form a central part of the organisation of the book, and I would like to express gratitude to the patients who have contributed in this way, not just to improved care for their fellow patients, but also to their therapist's self-understanding.

It has been exciting and pleasurable for me to work on this book with so many friends, colleagues and former teachers as fellow contributors. I also owe an immeasurable debt to those teachers, supervisors and colleagues who have not contributed directly, but who have created the philosophy of an integrated psychiatry and psychotherapy which informs its purpose. In particular, I would like to mention Michael Balint, Dorothea Ball, Egle Laufer, Jonathon Pedder, Henri Rey, Charles Rycroft, Neville Symmington, Rosemary Wiffen and Heinz Wolff. They have inspired (and continue to inspire) several generations of students of psychiatry and psychotherapy. I hope that this book can be seen as one of the many fruits of that inspiration.

Barnstaple 1991   J.H.

Contributors

Pamela M. Ashurst MB ChB FRCPsych
Consultant Psychotherapist, Southampton and South-West Hampshire
Health Authority; Honorary Clinical Teacher, Southampton Medical
School, Southampton

Mark Aveline MD(Lond) FRCPsych
Consultant Psychotherapist, Nottingham Health Authority; Clinical
Teacher, University of Nottingham, Nottingham

Anthony Bateman MA MRCPsych
Psychoanalyst, Consultant Psychotherapist, Friern Hospital; Honorary
Consultant Psychotherapist, Tavistock Clinic, London

Donald Campbell
Psychoanalyst; Principal Child Psychotherapist, PORTMAN Clinic,
London

Christopher Dare MD FRCPsych MRCP DPM
Senior Lecturer, Department of Psychiatry, Institute of Psychiatry, De
Crespigny Park, London

Ian Falloon MD DPM MRCPsych
Director, COMMEND Training Project; Honorary Consultant Physician
in Mental Health, Aylesbury Vale Health Authority, Buckingham

Patrick Gallwey MB FRCPsych DPM
Associate Member British Psychoanalytical Society; Consultant Forensic
Psychiatrist, Devon and Cornwall Forensic Psychiatric Service

Caroline Garland BA(Cantab) MA
Clinical Psychologist, Adult Department, Tavistock Clinic; Senior
Clinical Tutor, Maudsley Hospital, London; Member, British Psycho-
Analytical Society

Sandra M. Grant BSc MB ChB FRCPsych
Honorary Clinical Senior Lecturer, Gartnavel Royal Hospital; Honorary
Lecturer, Department of Psychological Medicine, University of Glasgow,
Glasgow

Robert Hale FRCPsych
Consultant Psychotherapist, Tavistock Clinic, London; Psychoanalyst

Sophia Jane Hartland MA BM BCh MRCPsych
Senior Registrar in Psychotherapy, Nottingham Psychotherapy Unit, Nottingham

Jonathan Hill BA MB BChir MRCP MRCPsych
Senior Lecturer in Child and Adolescent Psychiatry, Royal Liverpool Children's Hospital, Liverpool; Formerly Consultant Psychotherapist, The Cassel Hospital, London

Michael Hobbs MA MB BChir MSc MRCPsych
Member of the Institute of Group Analysis; Consultant Psychotherapist, Warneford Hospital, Oxford

Jeremy Holmes MA MRCP FRCPsych
Consultant Psychiatrist/Psychotherapist, North Devon District Hospital, Barnstaple

Murray Jackson MB FRCP FRCPsych
Emeritus Consultant Psychotherapist, Maudsley Hospital and King's College Hospital, London

Marc Laporta MD FRCP(C)
Assistant Professor of Psychiatry, McGill University, Montreal

Frank R Margison MB ChB MSc MRCPsych
Consultant Psychotherapist, Manchester Royal Infirmary, Manchester

Malcolm Pines FRCP FRCPsych
Member British Psychoanalytic Society; Member Institute of Group Analysis; Former Consultant Psychotherapist, Tavistock Clinic, Maudsley Hospital and Cassel Hospital, London

Ruth Porter FRCP FRCPsych
Member Guild of Psychotherapists; Member Association for Psychoanalytic Psychotherapy in the NHS; Former Senior Lecturer, Department of Medicine, Royal Postgraduate Medical School, Hammersmith Hospital, London

Anne Read MB BS MRCPsych
Consultant Psychiatrist, Westbourne Unit, Scott Hospital, Plymouth

Anthony Ryle DM(Oxford) FRCPsych
Consultant Psychotherapist, St Thomas' Hospital, London

William A Shanahan MRCPsych
Senior Registrar in Psychiatry, Charing Cross Hospital, London

Peter Shoenberg MA MRCP(UK) MRCPsych
Consultant Psychotherapist, University College Hospital, London

Richard Tillet MB BS MRCPsych
Consultant Psychiatrist with special responsibility for psychotherapy, Exeter Health Authority

Peter Wilson BA DipAppSocStud MACP
Director, London Youth Advisory Center, London; Consultant Psychotherapist, Peper Harow Therapeutic Community, Surrey

Contents

SECTION FOUR
Psychotherapy with special groups

The psychotherapies and their application to psychiatry

1. Introduction: analytic psychotherapy

J. Holmes

PART I   OVERVIEW

INTRODUCTION

The main purpose of this book is to show how psychotherapy can inform, illuminate and improve the everyday practice of psychiatry. It is divided into four sections. The first two consider how the principal psychotherapeutic methods can be applied in psychiatric settings, while sections three and four take the major psychiatric disorders and situations and show how they may be approached from a psychotherapeutic point of view. The aim is to produce a textbook which will be of practical use to psychiatrists and psychotherapists alike.

This introductory chapter is divided into three parts. The first stakes out the definitions and philosophies which inform the book, and looks at issues, such as the evaluation and delivery of psychotherapy, which are of general relevance, but which do not form the book's central focus. The detailed study of case histories lies at the heart of psychotherapeutic work, and, in keeping with the chapters which follow, the second part consists of two paradigmatic psychiatric cases presented from a psychotherapeutic point of view. Based on these cases, the third part considers the contribution of psychoanalysis to psychiatry, looking at assessment, formulation and diagnosis from the viewpoint of psychoanalytic psychotherapy.

Like an individual, a book has an unique identity but is also a product of its time and place. A multi-author text runs the danger of presenting a multiple personality lacking in coherence, but has the advantage that the historical and geographical circumstances from which it arises are clearly visible. What is the common thread that unites its co-authors? All work in the British National Health Service or are closely allied to it, using psychotherapeutic ideas and methods to treat patients with psychiatric disorders; all train psychiatrists and other mental health workers in psychotherapy; most are consultant psychotherapists or psychiatrists; the background of most, but by no means all, is that of psychoanalysis or psychoanalytic psychotherapy.

The relationship between psychiatry, psychoanalysis and psychotherapy is one of continuing debate and exploration (Pedder 1989, Wallerstein 1989). Psychoanalysis took North America by storm in the 1920s and 1930s and, despite recent redefinitions, remains firmly within the mainstream of American psychiatric culture. The acceptance of psychotherapy within British psychiatry has, by contrast, been much more cautious. This is partly a result of the militant empiricism of the dominant Maudsley school, whose legitimate scepticism about the wilder claims of psychotherapy has turned at times into destructive dismissiveness (Shepherd 1979, Will 1984). This resistance has been mirrored by a reluctance on the part of psychoanalysis to integrate with psychiatry, for fear of being assimilated or marginalised (see Ch. 2).

The climate of mutual suspicion has abated in recent years: this book is both a product of, and a contribution to, this rapprochement. In the background have been sociological and economical changes which have affected psychiatry and psychotherapy alike. A purely medico-biological approach in psychiatry is no longer acceptable: patients also need and expect the understanding and interpersonal skills which psychotherapy can offer in response to their distress. Another important change has been the development of community psychiatry, which means that psychiatrists are no longer in a position of hegemony, but share their power and influence with psychologists, community nurses, general practitioners and social workers, all of whom need psychotherapeutic skills and understanding if they, and their clients, are to survive the fragmentation of the post-institutional era (Holmes 1990). At the same time, psychotherapy can no longer afford to remain insulated from scientific evaluation. In an era of limited resources and rising expectations, the pressure for widely applicable, cost-effective and briefer forms of therapy grows ever more insistent.

The distinction between the biological and psychotherapeutic approaches in psychiatry can be traced back to the two great strands of European thought: that represented by the Enlightenment, with its valuation of reason, order and stability; and Romanticism, with its emphasis on individuality, and the importance of the emotions and of change. Psychotherapy is perhaps closer to the romantic impulse in its valuation of individual experience and biography, its recognition of the power of the imagination, and the need to find a meaning and purpose in life (Holmes & Lindley 1989). But there have been changes in philosophical perspective that blur these once clear demarcations between reason and imagination, science and art. It is clear, as Freud believed, that scientific methods can be brought to bear on human problems without necessarily being reductionist or dehumanising. It is also accepted that science itself is a system of meanings that cannot be value-free or absolute in its approach to the truth, and, when reduced to scientism, becomes a way of avoiding rather than revealing reality. A biomedical approach which sees depression simply in terms of an illness for which the appropriate drug should be prescribed, and ignores the part played by adverse life experience, is as obtuse as a psychotherapy which denies the relevance of genetics to schizophrenia. The emphasis in contemporary philosophy of science is on the *duality* of disease-causative and biographical-teleological models (Wallace 1989). Rorty (1989) argues for tolerance and pluralism, seeing science and poetry as 'alternative modes of adaptation to reality'. Given the dominance of science in contemporary culture, this duality is inevitably unequal; psychotherapy has gained some measure of acceptance, but is often relegated, as Freud (1926) antic-ipated, to 'one of many forms of treatment in psychiatry'. One aim of this book is to redress this imbalance.

CLASSIFICATION AND DEFINITION OF PSYCHOTHERAPIES

The plea for pluralism is equally applicable within psychotherapy itself, which has at times been riven by conflict between competing models and techniques. This lack of unity has itself contributed to the marginalisation of psychotherapy. This book is firmly wedded to the view that only the full *range* of psychotherapies can meet the varying needs of psychiatric patients, and that the psychotherapies themselves can only benefit from mutual influence and cross-fertilisation. Once the plurality of psycho-therapies is accepted, two problems arise. Firstly, an overall definition of psychotherapy is required that encompasses the great variety of approaches; secondly, there is a need for a classification that will differ-entiate and distinguish the main psychotherapeutic schools.

A possible overall definition of psychotherapy is as follows:

Psychotherapy is a form of treatment based on the systematic use of a relationship between therapist and patient – as opposed to pharmacological or social methods – to produce changes in cognition, feelings and behaviour.

The advantage of this definition is that it emphasises the essentially *interpersonal* nature of the psychotherapeutic relationship, from which much of its power derives; technique, although of no less importance, can only be effective if a good therapeutic alliance is established. This defi-nition is also wide-ranging enough to include most of the varieties of psychotherapy currently practised. Given this overall definition, the psychotherapies can be classified according to *theory, technique, setting, mode, length* and *level*, although none of these distinctions are entirely clear-cut.

Classification according to *theory* distinguishes between the Analytic (See below and Ch. 2), Behavioural-Cognitive (Ch. 4), Systemic (Ch. 5) and Experiential-Humanistic (Ch. 6) approaches, but even within these broad categories there is much common ground. Most psychotherapies contain ingredients from more than one theoretical approach; a good

Table 1.1   The psychotherapy 'matrix'

Theory	Technique	Mode	Setting	Timing	Level
Psychoanalytic	Interpretive	Individual	General practice	Very brief	Self-help
Behavioural	Directive	Group	Outpatient	Brief	'Level 1': counselling
Cognitive	Expressive	Couple	Day hospital	Time-limited	
Systemic	Supportive	Family	Inpatient	Indefinite	'Level 2': non-specialist psychotherapy
'Humanistic'	Paradoxical			------------	
				> one/week	'Level 3': specialist psychotherapy
				weekly	
				< one/week	

example is Cognitive Analytic Therapy, which combines psychoanalytic and behavioural theories in a novel way (see Ch. 11).

Therapists' interventive *techniques* can be divided into those that are directive, interpretive, supportive, paradoxical, challenging and expressive (see Ch. 7); most therapies contain a combination of techniques, although the proportions vary greatly. Psychotherapeutic *settings* also vary widely from in-patient units to mental health centres and day hospitals, from psychotherapy departments to general practitioners' surgeries. Therapy can be in individual, group or family/marital *mode*. The *length* of psychotherapeutic treatment varies from one or two sessions to several years, although the average therapy within the National Health Service takes probably no more than a few months (see Ch. 8). Finally, classification by *level* of training and sophistication of the practitioner (which arouses much passion among therapists about their position within the psychotherapeutic pecking-order) ranges from the 'level 1' of basic counselling, through an intermediate 'level 2' practised by many psychiatrists, social workers, psychologists and nurses, to specialist 'level 3' treatments such as psychoanalysis (Cawley 1977, Pedder 1989).

PSYCHOTHERAPEUTIC PSYCHIATRY

While this book addresses all three levels, it is predominantly focussed at 'level 2' practitioners, that is, at psychotherapeutically-minded psychiatrists and other mental health workers who wish to bring psychotherapeutic methods and ideas to bear upon the patients and problems encountered in general psychiatric work. Psychotherapeutic esotericism is eschewed, but the difficulties posed by attempting psychotherapy with the mentally ill are not underestimated. Several excellent textbooks of psychotherapy now exist (Brown & Pedder 1979, Storr 1979, Malan 1979, Thoma & Kachele 1986), but none are specifically concerned with the role of psychotherapy within psychiatry. This book attempts to describe a *psychotherapeutically-informed psychiatry*, or a *psychiatric psycho-therapeutics* relevant to the patients who are treated in psychiatric departments, and to those who work in such units.

Psychotherapy has a dual role within psychiatry, both as an overall approach which takes account of the interpersonal and psychological aspects of any clinical situation, and a set of specific methods of treatment. This book is concerned with psychotherapy in its adjectival as well as its substantive form; with being psychotherapeut*ic* as well as practising psychotherap*y*. It is just as important for a psychiatrist to understand the psychotherapeutic implications of routine practice – prescribing drugs, compulsorily detaining patients, or even making referrals for psychotherapy – as it is to be skilled in specific psycho-therapeutic techniques. From this perspective, psychiatry should be practised psychotherapeutically always, should use psychotherapeutic methods as an adjunct often, and provide formal psychotherapy whenever necessary.

OUTCOME AND THE 'MATRIX PARADIGM'

A textbook of psychotherapy is predicated on the assumption that psychotherapy *works*. Critics have claimed that psychotherapy is no more than, or no more effective than, placebo-treatment (Shepherd 1979) and that psychoanalysis in particular is a non-scientific closed system of thought (Eysenck 1983). The details of these charges and their rebuttal are exhaustively discussed elsewhere (Bloch 1982, Garfield & Bergin 1986, Holmes & Lindley 1989). Their value has been to sharpen the debate and to force psychotherapists to examine their work more critically.

Psychotherapy research is a difficult and uncertain field; nevertheless, certain conclusions can confidently be stated. Firstly, psychotherapy is unquestionably effective. A standard method for evaluation of therapies is the measurement of 'effect size'; this is a comparison of the treatment and control group means on standard outcome measures. The method of meta-analysis, based on averaging large numbers of studies, has consistently shown that the effect size for psychotherapy is around 1 standard deviation (SD) unit. This means that the average psychotherapy patient does better than do 85% of control subjects. Put another way, 70 % of psychotherapy patients improve significantly, while 30% do not; 30 % of controls improve spontaneously, while 70% remain the same (Karasu 1986). These figures are comparable with the results for anti-depressant therapy, where the effect size is also around 1 SD.

Secondly, these outcome studies are based on a 'drug metaphor' (Stiles & Shapiro 1989) which, although useful, should not be taken too far. Placebo psychotherapy can never be delivered blind as it can be in a drug trial. Psychotherapy is concerned with people, not physiologies, so expectations and assumptions make an inescapable contribution to outcome. It is important to note that 'placebo' treatments *do* produce change (with effect sizes of around 0.5), supporting the view that 'non-specific factors' as well as specific techniques, are important in psychotherapy.

A third conclusion concerns the differences between varying therapeutic approaches. The meta-analytic studies combine the results of many different types of therapy; behavioural, cognitive and analytic. On the whole, no consistent differences in outcome have been demonstrated for the different therapies, although some studies (e.g. Shapiro & Firth 1987) suggest slightly better results for cognitive-behavioural than analytic methods, which may partly reflect the greater ease with which treatment-goals can be specified in cognitive-behavioural therapies. This apparent equivalence of outcome between therapies has led to Luborsky's (Luborsky et al 1975) celebrated 'dodo-bird' verdict: 'everybody has won and all must have prizes'.

The discrepancy between different techniques yet similar outcomes has been called the 'equivalence paradox' (Stiles et al 1986) for which a number of different explanations have been put forward. Frank (1986) emphasises the common factors in all therapies (see also Ch. 8). These include 'positive involvement' with a therapist who possesses empathy, genuineness and non-possessive warmth; the development of new perspective on previously intractable problems leading to 'remoralisation' and a new 'assumptive world'; and the opportunities for exploration and trial-learning made possible by the security of the therapeutic situation. Ryle (1982) has suggested elegantly that, since behaviour is organised hierarchically, from basic assumptions through phantasies and plans to overt behaviour, with reciprocal feedback between different levels, change at one level will eventually produce effects at all the others and should therefore lead to similar outcomes. A third possible explanation for the equivalence paradox is that it is a research artefact, produced by averaging large numbers of therapies, therapists, and patients, and that, if teased out, different therapeutic methods would indeed be found to be effective for different clinical problems. (See Ch. 8 for a further discussion of outcome research in psychotherapy.)

This latter possibility can be related to Paul's (1986) idea of a 'matrix paradigm' in psychotherapy. Paul suggested that for each clinical situation the therapist should ask the question:

'*What* treatment, by *whom*, is most effective for *this* individual, with *that* specific problem, and under *which* set of circumstances.'

This might be adapted for psychiatric patients as follows: 'What form of psychotherapy, delivered by which member of the multidisciplinary team, is most effective for this personality, with that specific disorder, and in which setting?' Paul's paradigm suggests that an open-minded, evenhanded attitude is needed within psychiatric psychotherapy if the full range of patient characteristics and difficulties is to be met; this patient with schizophrenia needs a skilled family therapist if he is not to relapse when he returns home (see Chs 4 and 13); this patient with an acute episode of depression will do better if he is offered cognitive analytic therapy as well as anti-depressant drugs (see Ch. 11); this patient with recurrent relationship difficulties and episodes of self-harm needs an analytic approach if her life is to take a more positive turn and the negative pattern is to be broken (see Chs 12 and 14).

THE INDICATIONS FOR DIFFERENT PSYCHOTHERAPIES; ECLECTICISM

If every psychiatric patient can benefit from some form of psycho-therapeutic consideration and intervention, the question of the indications for psychotherapy becomes not *whether* the patient can benefit from psychotherapy, but rather *which type* of psychotherapeutic intervention is likely to be most appropriate, and at what *level* (see Table 1.1).

Various attempts have been made to refine criteria for the different modes and models of psychotherapy. Malan's criteria for brief analytic therapy (Malan 1979; see Ch. 8) include: good initial motivation; evidence of reasonable previous adjustment; the absence of exclusion criteria, such as psychosis, substance abuse or acute suicidal feelings; and the capacity to respond effectively to a trial interpretation. These criteria have been confirmed and extended by subsequent studies (Orlinsky & Howard 1986) showing that good outcomes from *all* forms of psycho-therapy are associated with three main factors: a strong therapeutic alliance, in which the patient sees the therapist and the therapeutic process in a positive light; some degree of educational achievement; and evidence of motivation, as shown by the ability to remain in therapy for at least 10 sessions.

Despite Malan's finding that severely disturbed patients could achieve good outcomes in brief psychotherapy, there is undoubtedly a research trend suggesting that the less severely ill and less socially disadvantaged a patient is, the more likely he is to benefit from therapy of whatever type. As much as 50% of the variance in psychotherapy outcome is related to patient characteristics such as these, rather than to features associated with the type of disorder or the personality of the sufferer (Karasu 1986). Modifications of technique are necessary if the undoubted benefits of psychotherapy are to reach the more severely ill and the socially dis-advantaged (Holmes & Lindley 1989, Lorian & Felner 1986, see Chs 15 and 20).

Paul's 'matrix paradigm' implies an ideal in which psychotherapeutic intervention is matched with patient need, in terms of both illness and personality. Proven examples of this include: the efficacy of family and behavioural interventions in schizophrenia (see Ch. 4); of cognitive therapy in depression (Blackburn et al 1986); and of brief therapy, analytic and behavioural, in anxiety/depression (Shapiro & Firth 1987). Research tends to confirm the clinical impression that introverts do better with analytic forms of therapy, while extraverts fare better with behavioural treatments (Bloch & Crouch 1985). Despite these certainties, the application of the matrix paradigm remains elusive. Most treatments contain a variety of therapeutic elements, are broad-spectrum rather than highly specific, and most studies have failed to find major differential outcomes between the different therapies. Certainly, a narrow-minded or sectarian psychotherapeutic stance will never be adequate to meet the range of client needs (Beitman et al 1989).

Most psychotherapists, however, are by training and persuasion wedded to a particular school or approach. This raises a fundamental dilemma within psychotherapy: despite the clinical need for even-handedness, in order effectively to conduct (or perhaps even write about) psychotherapy, a particular theoretical viewpoint and technical stance is required. Eclecticism is beneficial to the patient in the sense that no one form of psychotherapy can possibly meet all psychotherapeutic needs; but eclectic approaches in clinical practice can be confusing, and therapists, while retaining flexibility, get better results by practising one clinical method in depth rather than trying to master them all (Luborsky et al 1975). It is better to be able to play one instrument in all keys, than to play many instruments in only one (Carvhallo 1988). This volume is firmly committed to the need for variety within psychotherapy on practical grounds, but also for the theoretical reason that the individuality which psychotherapy aims to foster cannot result from a procrustean therapeutic stance. Some bias is unavoidable, however, and the overall balance of the book is more psychoanalytical than behavioural.

DRUGS AND PSYCHOTHERAPY

If psychotherapy is to establish itself as an integral part of psychiatry, it will, in the present climate, have to be justified on economic grounds. Cost-effectiveness will have to be demonstrated to those responsible for 'third-party payments' (the State, or insurance companies). A balance sheet for psychotherapy can be drawn up comparing 'offset costs' resulting from successful psychotherapy – reduction in drug use, fewer ineffective psychiatric and general practitioner contacts, reduced dependence on welfare payments, the economic benefits resulting from a return to work – with the cost of providing the therapy (McGrath & Lowson 1986). A good example is the Cassel study (Rosser et al 1987), a 5-year follow-up of 28 patients admitted to a unit offering long-term in-patient psychotherapy, which found that a net saving to the exchequer of around £0.5 million resulted from their admission.

But the rationale for psychotherapy cannot be based on economic grounds alone. Antidepressants and psychotherapy produce roughly similar effect sizes (around 1). A recent major study comparing drugs, 'general psychiatric management' and psychotherapy in depression (Elkin et al 1989) showed that all three were equally effective in mild depression, and that a differential effectiveness for drugs *or* psychotherapy over placebo-type general management only emerged for the more severe cases. Psychotherapists claim that psychotherapy produces *qualitative* improvement in patients' lives, such as increased autonomy, greater integration and maturity, which, although hard to measure, may significantly reduce relapse rates, as well as being in themselves ethically desirable (Holmes & Lindley 1989).

In clinical practice, many psychiatric patients receive a combination of psychotherapy and drugs. There is a naive view that drugs and psychotherapy are mutually incompatible, because drugs 'dampen' emotions while therapy evokes them. This can be refuted both theoretically and practically. Psychotherapy requires the patient to become more open to feared or unwanted feelings, whether this comes about through transference or de-sensitisation. While this process is impossible if feelings are completely inaccessible, it is equally so if they are overwhelming. For psychotherapy to work, there has to be an intact 'observing ego', detached enough to report on feelings, understand them and, where necessary, modify or accommodate to them. Drug therapy (or even ECT) can help restore this observing ego.

This theoretical argument is supported by empirical studies (Aveline 1988) which show, for example, in depression (see Ch. 11) and heroin withdrawal (see Ch. 18), that psychotherapy and drug therapy together produce better results than either alone. Nevertheless, drugs are frequently prescribed inappropriately or excessively, often in response to dynamic pressures such as the patient's demandingness or the doctor's counter-transferential anxiety or aggression; these pressures need to be understood rather than acted upon.

THE ORGANISATION AND DELIVERY OF PSYCHOTHERAPY

The availability of psychotherapy, within both statutory services and the private sector is very variable. Psychotherapy is provided by psychologists, psychotherapy departments led by consultant psychotherapists and some psychotherapeutically-minded psychiatrists, and by private psychotherapists, as well as in a number of social service and voluntary agencies. For a particular patient with a particular problem, the type of therapy offered (if any) is likely to be determined as much by geography, income and the availability of therapists and trainings, as by clinical need. To some extent, this diversity is healthy, and is consistent with the emphasis in psychotherapy on the variety and uniqueness of individuals, but it conflicts with

Table 1.2 Organisation of psychotherapy services (based on Grant et al 1991)

Level of Organisation	Population	Description	Level of Training	Staff Numbers	Organisation/ Structure
Health centre/ Community	Less than 50 000	1. Based in primary care. 2. Offering counselling and some other therapies, e.g. behaviour therapy of simple phobias; bereavement counselling etc., often as an adjunct to other treatments. 3. Refer difficult patients to District.	1. GP-Practice-based counsellors, CPNs. 2. Additional training and supervision available from District Psychotherapy team. 3. Some District staff working on sessional basis.	1. Number variable and determined by local circumstances. 2. Sessional input. 3. Close links with voluntary and local authority sectors.	1. Informal, dependent on local circumstances. 2. Advised as necessary by District Planning Team for Psychotherapy
District	150–300 000	1. A wide range of therapies offered including individual short- and long-term dynamic psychotherapy, plus group, family and marital therapies. 2. Part of departments of Psychiatry/Psychology. 3. May be based in Day Hospital.	1. Specialist staff mainly full- and part-time. 2. Supported by non-specialist staff.	1. Specialist staff approx. 5 WTE, e.g. 3 full-time plus 20 further sessions. 2. At least one of 'core team's should be a Consultant Psychotherapist.	1. Multidisciplinary organisation with 'core staff group'. 2. District Planning Team for Psychotherapy.
Region (Sub-Regional)	1–4 million	1. Specialised service to own District plus care of some 'difficult cases' from other Districts. 2. Offering a wide range of types and levels of training for the Region.	1. Multidisciplinary specialist team covering all major methods of psychotherapy.	1. Specialist staff from Psychiatry, Psychology. 2. Staff for basic District plus additional Regional staff. 3. At least two Consultant Psychotherapists.	1. Regional Planning group for Psychotherapy. 2. Advise Districts and Regions 3. Co-ordinate training, service and other needs, e.g. library.
National		1. Academic and training resource. 2. Specialist provision of library and training resources.			

the view that people have a right to an equitable provision of psycho-therapy services, no less valid than their right to medical, psychiatric or social provision (Holmes & Lindley 1989).

The executive of the Psychotherapy Section of the Royal College of Psychiatrists, of which many of the contributors to this volume are past or present members, has consistently advocated policies – on *manpower*, *training* and *service* – aimed to overcome this uneven and inequitable distribution. Firstly, it has argued that there should be at least one full-time consultant psychotherapist for every 200 000 of the population, approximately one for each health district. Secondly, it has established guidelines for the psychotherapeutic training of general psychiatrists, although, unlike the situation in Australasia, these are not yet mandatory; it is still possible to qualify as a psychiatrist in Britain with little or no psychotherapeutic knowledge or skill. Thirdly, it has described possible models for a psychotherapy service within the National Health Service (see Table 1.2).

Although these patterns vary greatly according to local conditions and the size of population served, all contain three basic elements: a specific treatment service for particular groups of patients: training and super-vision for psychiatrists and other members of the multidisciplinary team: and a liaison service which includes consultation and staff support for mental health workers (Grant et al 1991).

PART II   CLINICAL BIOGRAPHY

At the heart of psychotherapy rests the individual, with his own unique biography or 'case history', forming the bedrock upon which all theorising and psychotherapeutic practice is based. As examples, two patients will now be presented – both psychiatric rather than purely psychotherapeutic cases – suffering from severe depressive illnesses. In one, failure to appreciate psychodynamic issues may have contributed to a tragic outcome, while in the other, psychotherapeutic understanding may have made a significant contribution to recovery.

Case study 1.1   Depression and the dynamics of non-compliance

Mr A, a 40-year-old teacher, became profoundly and suicidally depressed in the face of, as he saw it, mounting pressure at work and 'an inability to cope with the demands being made of me'. He was strongly suicidal, and was admitted to hospital where anti-depressants were started. In hospital, he made himself useful to the nurses and spent much of his time looking after the other, more helpless patients. His depressive symptoms apparently soon lifted, and after leaving hospital he discontinued his anti-depressants, saying that he wished to solve his own problems and not to be drugged and befuddled. He was offered psychotherapeutic sessions which were characterised by long intellectual battles between him and his therapist.

After a while, he discontinued these too, saying that he preferred to seek co-counselling where he could work more collaboratively on his problems.

He was an only child; when he was eight years old, his father developed a progressive and crippling illness. Mr A admired his father's fortitude in the face of this illness, and felt that he could never possess similar courage. Because of the family difficulties, he was sent away to boarding school where he dealt with his feelings of loneliness and exclusion by deciding to 'go it alone' rather than bother his already burdened parents with his anxieties. He experienced his mother as rigid and controlling, and had never felt particularly close to her. He married a warm and supportive woman whom he idealised but whom he felt he was letting down by his illness, as he did his eight-year-old son. Some weeks after his discharge from hospital, despite close supervision from his general practitioner and psychiatrist, at a time when he was apparently doing well and preparing to return to work, he killed himself. It was clear from his notebooks that he had been planning suicide for several months.

This history illustrates how important it is to grasp the dynamic aspects of a case as part of general psychiatric management. Just as Mr A had felt alone in his teens, had felt that he *had* to be self-sufficient, that his own needs were insignificant in comparison with those of his father, just as he experienced his longing for intimacy and holding as shameful, so in his illness he experienced 'help' as humiliation, admission to hospital as a punishment analogous to being sent away to boarding school, and having to take medication as controlling rather than helpful. Consciously, he felt that he should be able to cure himself, meet his own needs, as he had done in his teens; unconsciously, he felt deep unsatisfied longings, and rage when they were not met.

While some of this was apparent to the psychiatric team, much was not. This was particularly true of the relationship with his mother which was *enacted* rather than *understood* by the staff, as they tried vainly to insist that he took his medication and stayed in hospital, rather as his mother had insisted that he wear warm clothes as she packed him off to boarding school. Had the staff appreciated this, a management strategy might have been devised that took more account of the fragility of his sequestered inner world, so at variance with his external show of competence, and they might perhaps have been more alert to the ever-present possibility of suicide.

This sad case illustrates how psychodynamic forces are inevitably brought into play in any psychiatric encounter. Through *transference*, the patient's day-to-day relationship with the hospital staff is coloured and shaped by earlier relationships of which he and they are often unaware, in this case experiencing them as controlling and contemptuous of what he felt to be his 'weakness'. Under the *regressive* effects of illness, the normal balancing effect provided by the ego is lost, and the influence of false assumptions becomes exaggerated. If transferential forces are not appreciated by the staff, they are likely, under the sway of counter-transference, to enact them in a way that may be counter-therapeutic (Langs 1976, Margison 1989).

The next case shows how an understanding of these process can lead to dynamic change and contribute to recovery.

Case study 1.2   Depression and the need to regress

Ms B was a 20-year-old who left home for the first time to work as a nanny in a distant town. There she met a young man of whom she become very fond. Their relationship was platonic; she spent a lot of time 'mothering' him – washing his clothes, cooking for him and helping him with his career. Her profound depression was precipitated by the discovery that he already had a girl-friend. She felt deeply ashamed of her 'mistake', and returned home to her parents, unable to continue with her job. She became more and more depressed, mute and retarded, while her parents – especially her mother, who had herself experienced depression while Ms B was young – became frantic with worry. She was treated with anti-depressants, lithium and phenothiazines with little improvement. Admission to hospital for a course of ECT was considered, and the suicide risk seemed very high. Her parents, especially the mother, were opposed to hospital admission and felt that the hospital staff could never offer the level of vigilance and concern which she had achieved, her mother having given up her job to be with her daughter 24 hours a day. Any suggestion that separation from home might be beneficial was met with intense anxiety and anger in the mother, who felt that she was being criticised and judged. Meanwhile, the psychiatrist who was seeing the patient for supportive therapy felt increasingly worried and hopeless, that his contributions were irrelevant, and that all important communication was between the patient and her mother, and not with himself.

Eventually, the patient was admitted briefly to hospital for a course of ECT, and then started to attend as a day patient. There was a perceptible though slight improvement, but the situation remained stuck and worrying. With the help of a family therapist, a new formulation and management plan was made. The patient's depression could be seen in terms of separation-individuation. Separation from her family had activated feelings of defective self-esteem and negative assumptions about herself possibly linked to her mother's depression when she was young; she lacked an inner sense of inexhaustable value and importance. Her awakening sexual feelings and the rejection confirmed her feeling about herself as unacceptable, mirroring her feelings about the inaccessibility of her very hard-working and slightly emotionally aloof father (described by his wife as 'absolutely brilliant at everything – except psychotherapy!'). Under the regressive influence of a depressive illness the patient returned to a symbiotic state of fusion with her mother, the ultimate expression of which were her suicidal wishes (see Ch. 12).In addition to the patient being seen individually, the family were offered family therapy sessions in which, rather than trying unsuccessfully to separate mother and daughter, their intense mutual involvement was encouraged, on the principle of *reculer pour mieux sauter*. The mother was seen as a necessary 'auxiliary ego', and was offered 'supervision' in her vital work of keeping her daughter alive. At the same time, the importance of the parents as a couple was emphasised through discussion about their courtship and life before becoming parents. Evidence of differences between family members was encouraged, aimed at helping them to see how it was possible to remain together yet healthily separate.

The patient began steadily to improve, and material emerged in the individual sessions which seemed to confirm both psychodynamic and systemic formulations. Encouraged by the therapist, the patient remembered a favourite fairy story. This was Hans Anderson's 'Little Mermaid', who fell in love with an earthly prince and was allowed to leave her watery home and join him, in return for abandoning the power of speech. Eventually, he tired of her silence and sought a wife. Overcoming her murderous jealousy, the little mermaid returned to the sea. But she had lived on earth so long she was now unable to swim: neither fish nor flesh, her only hope was death. This fairy tale seemed to encapsulate Ms B's experience of falling in love; the perilous transition from water to land which went so wrong symbolized all her own fears and inhibitions about moving from attachment to her mother to finding a man, from being a child to womanhood. Later, as her improvement continued, she dreamed of an older man who was trying to provoke her and her family into anger, while a depressed girl who was almost out of sight watched from afar. Her associations to the dream were that her father was sometimes obstinate and her relief that the depressed part of her was now almost out of sight. Following this dream, she said that a most unusual family row had broken out at the dinner table, in which, to her surprise, she had joined in. The row came to a successful end when the family started to think of what the neighbours would say about all this noise coming from a normally quiet house, and at this they all dissolved into helpless laughter.

Finally, 18 months after her breakdown began, she was fully recovered and ready to leave home once more. At her last session, she described an incident from the start of her illness in which she had been driving home with her mother in the dark. Due apparently to her mother's carelessness, the car engine had suddenly blown up. Her father rescued them, but 'it took him a very long time to get the engine clear and working again', she said, wiping away a parting tear.

In this case, a common enough psychiatric occurrence – a patient's refusal to come into hospital – was understood in terms of an unassuaged wish to remain symbiotically linked to her mother, and the therapeutic arrangements took account of her further need to negotiate an 'oedipal' (three-person: male-female) stage of development by offering individual and family therapy, and by seeing the mother *and* the 'official' therapist as of equal importance in her treatment. The transferential references to the therapist as an 'obstinate' father, who took a long time to get things clear, were noted but not interpreted.

These cases illustrate the three levels at which psychotherapy can contribute to psychiatry. Firstly, it provides a general framework for understanding the patient and her illness. Secondly, it can act as a guide to the management of the patient, taking into account not just the illness itself, but also the reactions of the staff, and the milieu in which treatment is conducted. Thirdly it is a specific mode of therapy, either on its own, or in collaboration with other forms of treatment.

PART III   THE ANALYTIC CONTRIBUTION

At its most simple, the psychoanalytical approach consists of a theory of *personal meaning* and a theory of *development*. As Frank (1986) has pointed out, in one sense *any* theoretical conception of illness or personal difficulty, including the purely bio-medical, contains a theory of meaning. If depression is viewed as a disturbance of cerebral amine metabolism, this attributes meaning to previously inchoate experience and this is both valid and valuable to the patient. Mr A's guilt towards his wife and son was partially relieved by understanding that his perceptions were distorted by his illness. Much of the practice of biological psychiatry contains informal cognitive challenge and restructuring of this sort. The psychoanalytical viewpoint is qualitatively different from this in that it seeks a *personal* meaning for the illness in terms of individual biography, and because it assumes a level of *unconscious* meanings which influence the behaviour of both patients and therapists. Mr A's guilt could be linked with his experience of feeling let down by his parents, due mainly to his father's illness, when he was at a similar age to that of his son. He was aware of the guilt, but not, apparently, of the feelings of anger and disappointment which lay beneath it, nor of the *transfer* of these feelings into his relationship with the staff: they in turn were unaware of their enactment of the role of a coercive but ineffectual mother. Seen in this light, the psychotherapeutic task consists of decoding personal, often unconscious, meanings (Hill 1954, Rycroft 1985). This interpretive viewpoint can be traced back to Freud's method of seeing a symptom, like a dream, as a compromise between a wish and a defence, a covert message whose meaning needs to be unravelled (Freud 1905a).

Seeing psychotherapy as a hermeneutic or narrative (Spence 1982) discipline, whose aim is to help the patient make personal sense of his problem or illness, leaves open the question of how the *truth* of any particular interpretation or meaning is established. At a clinical level, this is usually based on the affective response of a patient to an intervention (Malan 1979), but the fact that an interpretation feels 'right' does not establish its external validity: false beliefs may, at least in the short run, be as satisfying as true ones. The scientific underpinning of the psycho-analytic viewpoint lies in its account of psychological growth and development (Bowlby 1988). The meanings that are established in psychotherapy are often arrived at intuitively, but not arbitrarily; they are based on a theory of psychological maturation – of attachment, loss, differentiation, the establishment of an inner world – no less real than that of physical development. Ms B was vulnerable to depression because of hypothesised developmental difficulties in her early years. Her mother had herself been depressed and may possibly have been unable fully to respond to her daughter's emotional needs. This may have left Ms B with an internal 'depressed mother', rather than a 'mother who delights in my mere existence' (Storr 1983), and therefore with a fragile store of self-esteem. She remained emotionally dependent on her mother at a point in her life cycle at which separation was expected. So long as she remained emotionally close to her mother, the internal shared 'depressed mother' remained concealed. The move away from the mother entailed in the 'oedipal shift' towards the father was inhibited, so avoiding the experience of rivalry and ambivalence and anger, all of which are needed later for the establishment of autonomous relationships and object-choice. These themes then became realised as phantasies (or 'automatic thoughts'. Beck et al 1979): 'my father does not want me, he really belongs to my mother', 'my boyfriend belongs to his proper girlfriend', 'the hospital can't look after me properly, they are so weighed down with the other patients'.

The analytic contribution to psychiatry comprises three distinct elements. Firstly, it contains of a series of speculative hypotheses about the *aetiology* of psychiatric disorder, about how early environmental influences, together with biological factors, predispose to illness in later life. Secondly, it provides a language for *understanding* mental life that, by taking account of the internal world, makes sense out of the experience of mental illness, whatever its scientific explanation. Thirdly, it consists of a

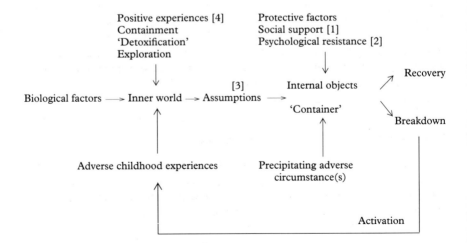

Fig. 1.1 Psychotherapeutic models of breakdown and intervention points.

method of treatment, which in some forms is of proven effectiveness. These could be seen as the *scientific, ethical-hermeneutic,* and *pragmatic* dimensions of psychotherapy.

Figure 1.1 attempts to summarise the models of mental illness used by psychotherapists. At least three causative hypotheses can be identified. Firstly, there is a simple 'linear' theory, in which adverse childhood experience is internalised and predisposes to breakdown in later life. This simple model is applicable to the sequelae of severe trauma (see Ch. 22), but needs to be supplemented by more complex interactional 'circular' models. Here adverse childhood experience, rather than being seen as 'causative', is activated by illness – whether biological or interpersonal in origin – and so colours and shapes the content, but not necessarily the form, of the illness. Thirdly, intrapsychic and interpersonal factors may produce either 'deviance amplification' (Hoffman 1981), or resilance in the face of adversity (Rutter 1987b). Psychotherapeutic intervention has an impact at a number of different points, as shown in the diagram. It may reduce the amplification of illness by providing appropriate support [1]; it may offer the patient methods of combating illness [2], as in cognitive therapy, where the patient learns to ward off negative assumptions [3] and thought patterns; or, in analytic therapy, it may, through the therapeutic relationship, offer a new experience [4] in which early adversity can be reworked and modified, while previously warded-off painful feelings are assimilated into a more integrated personality structure.

LINES OF PSYCHOANALYTICAL THOUGHT

The *object-relations* approach (Greenberg & Mitchell 1983) which informs much of this book, sees the individual as fundamentally object-seeking (as opposed to pleasure-seeking) and views action, thoughts and phantasies, including symptoms, as taking place within an inner 'representational world' containing the self and his objects. Four distinct lines of psychoanalytical thought will now be considered, each of which, although overlapping with the others, has made its own unique contribution and is relevant to a particular set of clinical problems. They will be considered in decreasing proximity to the mainstream of Freud's ideas.

Ego psychology: adaptation and defence

Ego psychology is particularly associated with the work of Freud's daughter Anna (1937), and with the American psychoanalyst Heinz Hartmann. It is derived directly from Freud's 'structural model' of the mind (Freud 1923), in which the ego is seen as mediating between the demands of the instincts on the one hand, and the restrictions imposed by reality and enforced by the internalised parents or 'critical agency', the superego, on the other. This model evokes a picture of accommodation, adaptation, compromise and dynamic equilibrium that are compatible with common-sense notions such as that of coping mechanisms. It can be compared with medical metaphors like that of cardiac decompensation occuring in a susceptible individual when faced with the increased circulatory demands imposed by pregnancy or infection. Perhaps because of these parallels, the ideas of ego psychology, especially that of defence mechanisms, have been quite widely accepted within psychiatry.

Valliant (1977) has systematised the analysis of defences, dividing them into three main groups: immature (e.g. splitting, projection), neurotic (e.g. repression, intellectualisation), and mature (e.g. sublimation, humour). According to this model, personality structure can be understood in terms of the habitual use of defence mechanisms to maintain equilibrium in the face of internal or external threat. Mr A tried to defend against feelings of failure, anger and emptiness by using the obsessional defences of intellectualisation, isolation and control. Illness results if defences are too rigid or inflexible (Reich's 'character armour'; see Ch. 6), or stress too overwhelming (see Chs 21 and 22), for equilibrium to be maintained.

Freeman (1988) has used the ideas of ego-psychology in his attempt to understand schizophrenia as a defective or absent ego state, but they are perhaps most useful in considering neurotic disorders, where three-person oedipal themes predominate. Many patients suffering from neurotic depression or anxiety face problems in their relationships of ambivalence, rivalry, anger, fears about separation, and feelings of sexual inadequacy and failure. Freud tried to relate these to the oedipal stage of development, in which the child needs to be able to love the parent of the opposite sex, and at the same time tolerate feelings of rejection and anger associated with the realisation that this parent is not his exclusive property, but has to be shared with the same sex parent (with whom identification has to occur despite this rivalry), and with siblings. In an era in which children are increasingly growing up in one-parent families, these ideas need modification. The contemporary child's deepest longing is often for an intact mother-father couple, rather than the exclusive possession of one or other parent. Split families may still be understood in oedipal terms, however, and the trauma of a 'reality which confirms the phantasy' (Symington 1986) makes such family disruption doubly painful. Ego psychology also recognises that healthy development requires a balance between a nurturing intuitive 'feminine' aspect, and a boundary-setting, protective 'masculine' function. This applies just as much to looking after patients as it does to bringing up children. Pedder (1989) has discussed the damaging separation between a 'feminine' intuitive psychotherapy and a 'masculine' scientific psychiatry; one of the aims of this book is to overcome this stereotype.

Kleinian theory: splitting and containment

Despite its relevance to psychotic states, the impact within psychiatry of the work of Melanie Klein (1950; 1957) and her followers such as Bion, Rosenfeld and Steiner (Spillius 1988), has been limited. Nevertheless, Kleinian theory has a great deal to offer in psychiatric practice. It provides a convincing account – whether or not it is an accurate reflection of the mental life of infants, upon which it is supposedly based – of the envy, destructiveness and splitting which characterises the behaviour and inner world of the psychotic (see Ch. 13) and borderline personality-disordered (see Ch. 14) patients who form a major part of psychiatric work. Also, through the theory of psychological *containment* (see Ch. 13), as opposed to physical restraint, it provides a basis for the therapeutic response needed to help such patients which is relevant to the era of community psychiatry. The concept of *projective identification* and the Kleinian emphasis on counter-transference illuminates the difficult feelings engendered in mental health workers by disturbed patients, and shows how these feelings can, if understood, be put to good therapeutic use.

Seen from a Kleinian perspective, Mr A had split his world into a good, caring, but unattainable 'mother-wife', and a controlling, dominating woman towards whom he felt intense anger. This split was repeated in relation to himself: an over-conscientious self, and a secret, hateful self who planned his suicide. The apparently inexplicable anger which some staff members felt when in contact with him, despite their liking him as a person and their otherwise professional attitudes, was an example of projective identification: unacceptable or feared aspects of the self are projected into those with whom the person is in contact, who then experience those feelings as if they were their own. The staff's anger and feeling of being controlled were reflections of *his* unacknowledged anger and powerlessness. The acceptance by the staff of the patient's decision to leave hospital and to stop anti-depressants – to 'go it alone' – confirmed the patient's sense that his fear and anger could not be contained, and so transmuted or detoxified, but had to be 'sent away'.

Attachment theory: security and loss

The work of John Bowlby (1969; 1973; 1980) is notable for its combination of rigorous empiricism with a psychoanalytic perspective emphasising the importance of early childhood experience for subsequent health or illness. For Bowlby, the origin of healthy development is the secure and responsive attachment of the infant to the primary care-giver, usually the mother. This enables the infant to explore both his own feelings and the outside world, and this forms a basis for self-confidence and curiosity in later life. *Anxious attachment* may result if the mother is physically or emotionally unavailable, and this in turn predisposes to subsequent dependency and anxiety. The premature loss of a care-giver may make an individual vulnerable to later depression, especially if grief is unexpressed.

Parkes (1986) has studied the role of unexpressed grief in psychiatry, and Brown & Harris (1978) have used Bowlby's ideas in their model of depression, vulnerability to which depends partly on childhood experience of loss, and partly on the presence or absence of attachment-figures with whom an individual can confide when faced with pain or difficulty. Pedder (1982) has combined these ideas with an object-relations view of an inner world in which, as development proceeds, the physical attachment to the parents is replaced by an internal 'good parent' providing feelings of security and self-esteem. The breast is lost, but is 'reinstated in the ego' (Klein 1957); the individual achieves autonomy but can receive nurturance from within and without when needed. Where this internalisation of the good object is impaired, the individual will be vulnerable to depression, as may have happened with Ms B. The task of therapy then becomes that of providing a secure attachment from which healthy separation can eventually, and with appropriate grief, take place; all being well, the patient will have built up a reservoir of good therapeutic experiences on which to draw when faced with subsequent difficulties and losses.

The interplay between attachment, loss and grief continue throughout life, and one advantage of Bowlby's ideas is that they are applicable to the whole life cycle, rather than viewing infancy and childhood as the sole determinants of later events. Influenced partly by Bowlby, and also by the ideas of Erikson (1968), psychotherapists now see adulthood as a continuing developmental process, a series of stages and crisis points each with its own potential for growth, stasis or breakdown (Nemiroff & Colarusso 1985; see also Chs 19 and 20).

Self-psychology: Kohut, Winnicott and others

The term 'self-psychology' is usually associated with the American psychoanalyst, Heinz Kohut (1977). It is also relevant to a rather disparate group of British analysts, notably Winnicott (1971), Rycroft (1985), Laing (1960) Symington (1986) and Casement (1985), whose work is characterised by: an emphasis on an experiencing self rather than a mechanistic ego; a reaction against the obscurities of psychoanalytic jargon, which Bettleheim (1982) claims is based on mistranslation; an emphasis on meaning rather than metapsychology; and an insistence that the real relationship with the therapist is as important as his technical skill. Both Winnicott and Kohut are concerned with how the developing infant 'comes alive' psychologically through the creative nurturance of the mother. The basis of this, for Winnicott, is the mother's capacity to act as a temporary container for the infant's fears and hatred, until the child is mature enough for them to be re-introjected and integrated into his developing self. Winnicott describes a 'transitional space', an overlapping realm that is not-quite-baby, and not-quite-mother, in which the infant learns to play and to develop a sense of creativity and relational autonomy. Transitional space is inhabited for Winnicott by transitional objects such as teddy bears and security blankets, but the mother herself can also be 'transitional' in this sense. Kohut (1977) proposes a similar view of the mother and later care-givers (including therapists) as 'self-objects': neither self nor objects, but an overlapping combination of both, extensions of the self without whom the individual feels depleted and lacking in self-worth.

These ideas have several important implications for psychiatry. Firstly, they help in the understanding of certain schizoid individuals who, behind the carapace of a false self, lack an inner sense of aliveness and creativity. Secondly, the emphasis on the real presence of the therapist as a curative factor in therapy links with research showing how Rogers' (1951) common factors in therapy, such as genuineness, empathy and warmth, contribute significantly to good therapeutic outcomes (see Chs 7 and 9). Thirdly, Winnicott's emphasis on therapy as 'learning to play' links with active therapies (see Ch. 6) which emphasise creativity and child-like exploration as legitimate and valid therapeutic activities. Ms B was helped by remembering the little mermaid fairy story that so poignantly encapsulated her situation in late adolescence – a fish out of water – (see Ch. 19) which, like a transitional object, both provided some distance from her overwhelming feelings, and was a creative expression of them.

DIAGNOSIS AND ASSESSMENT IN PSYCHOTHERAPY

According to Osler (Stoller 1984) it is more important to know what kind of patient has a disease than to know what kind of disease a patient has. This contrast between disease and individual lies at the heart of the problem of diagnosis and formulation in both psychotherapy and psychiatry. A medical diagnosis implies the assignment of a set of symptoms to a disease-category that reliably predicts pathology, response to treatment and prognosis. A psychotherapeutic formulation also attempts to summarise and systematise a set of disparate phenomena, to indicate appropriate treatment and to have prognostic value, but differs from medical diagnosis in a number of significant ways. Firstly, it almost always contains theoretical assumptions, for example, about the influence of childhood experience on adult life (for a contrasting view, see Ch. 4), while psychiatric diagnosis tries to be theory-free. Secondly, it focuses on interpersonal themes and relationship difficulties rather than symptoms alone. Thirdly, it concentrates on the *particular* circumstances of the patient and his unique biography, rather than on general classes of disease. Finally, it is arrived at partly by intuition, based on the therapist's subjective response to the patient, rather than relying exclusively on objective data.

A diagnosis – whether medical or psychodynamic – is a tool, and cannot be divorced from its purpose. The discussion that follows will consider: firstly, the psychodynamic formulation as part of the general understanding of any psychiatric patient; secondly, the systematisation of these formulations into diagnostic schemata; and thirdly the use of these schemata to indicate and guide different psychotherapeutic treatments.

The assessment interview

The word, 'assessment' contains two very different etymological implications. One derives from *assidere*, to sit beside, with its warm overtones of empathy and intuition. The other is associated with the idea of fiscal investigation for the purpose of taxation: a cold reckoning of assets, debts and deficiencies. The psychodynamic assessment combines both elements. Consider this account by the psychoanalyst Robert Stoller (1984):

'Let us imagine we are with a patient who we sense is sad. You cannot deny there are circumstances when the patient's welfare and what we do next depend on our distinguishing whether he is sad, very sad, regretfully sad, agonizingly sad, tragically sad, deeply sad, sad/dreary, sad/dull, sad/troubled, sad/strong, bitter/sad, bitter-sweet/sad, sad/wretched, sad/rueful, genuinely sad, exhibiting sadness for masochistic effect, sad as the character structure remnant of a manipulating mother, glad to be sad, sad without grief, sad after a heterosexual loss, sad after a heterosexual loss mitigated by unconscious homosexual relief ... or depressed rather than sad. If you were the patient – even a back ward schizophrenic patient – wouldn't you hope your doctor could tell the difference?'

The clinician uses his empathy and intuition to translate symptoms into interpersonal terms, based on the reactions evoked in him by the patient. Psychotherapeutic skill depends to a great extent on the capacity of the therapist to allow this internal resonance to take place, while at the same time remaining detached enough to observe the process as it happens. It is important to note the attention to detail implied in Stoller's account. The dynamically-minded clinician is not content to be told that the patient is 'depressed', or 'anxious'; he wants to know what the feeling of depression is *like*, what thoughts come into the patient's mind when he feels depressed, what precise circumstances provoke depressed feelings, how he sets about combating them, whether they are felt to be located in a particular part of the body, and so on. In this, the psychotherapist is doing no more than any good clinician, a point encapsulated in Winnicott's (1971) aphorism 'psychoanalysis is an extended form of history-taking'.

A patient's expectations, assumptions and difficulties, both conscious and unconscious, will be manifest from the start or even before the start of the initial interview. Ms B, at her first appointment, was sitting very close to her mother in the waiting area, and looked poignantly back as she was led away to the interview room – obvious evidence of her deep attachment to her mother. Less obvious were the feelings aroused by this in the therapist, who unwisely suggested that the best thing would be for her to go back to work as soon as possible; here he was enacting (rather than understanding) the patient's feeling that men would threaten to separate her from her mother, and expose her sense of vulnerability and inadequacy.

Psychotherapy is not all softness and empty. Information about un-conscious mental life is elicited by conventional history-taking, including enquiries about early memories, early and current daydreams, dreams and phantasies. There will be an attempt to assess the quality of significant relationships in childhood, any major separations, losses or traumata, and a detailed account of the patients psychosexual development. The circumstances of the onset of the illness are important, because they reveal the precipitating factors and point to an underlying dynamic constellation evoked by the precipitating stress. Mr A's depression was partly triggered by his son's learning difficulties, for which he felt responsible, just as he had felt responsible for his father's illness when he was a child. Ms B's unhappy love affair triggered feelings of shame and inadequacy that could be understood in terms of her inhibition of anger and unresolved rivalry in childhood.

Diagnostic systems in psychotherapy

The most widely used diagnostic systems in psychiatry are ICD-9 and DSM-III, or DSM-III-R, both currently in the process of revision. ICD-9 presents considerable shortcomings for the psychodynamically-minded clinician (Sharp & King 1989) being a uni-axial, atheoretical set of categories. DSM-III is more relevant, in that it is multi-axial, emphasising not just psychiatric diagnosis (axis 1), but also personality (axis 2) and stressors (axis 4). However, the concept of personality embodied in axis 2 is that of personality *disorder*, rather than personality *organisation* which the psychodynamic formulation tries to encapsulate. A sixth axis was originally proposed for DSM-III, defining 'defence or coping style', but was eventually dropped, due to lack of general agreement among psychiatrists about how this could be defined.

There are several systematised diagnostic methods currently used by psychotherapists, mainly for research or teaching rather than routine clinical practice; none are without methodological shortcomings. Four will now be considered.

Defence style

Valliant's hierarchy of defences provides an obvious starting point for a dynamic diagnostic system. Their validity is supported by a 40-year follow-up (Valliant 1977), in which mature defence styles were correlated with good subsequent adjustment. Defence styles can be realiably assessed by questionnaire, and correlate well with other general measures of 'neuroticism', but attempts to link particular defences with particular psychiatric diagnoses, e.g. splitting and projection with borderline personality disorder, undoing and isolation with obsessive-compulsive disorders, have proved unsuccessful (Andrews et al 1989).

Level of object-relations

Freud, and later Abraham (1924), proposed a developmental schema of libidinal maturation. Psychiatric disorder was conceived as correlating with developmental arrest at, or regression to, a particular level. Schizophrenia was associated with auto-eroticism, hysterical disorders with the oral phase of development, obsessive-compulsive disorders with the stage of sphincter control, and neurotic disorders, such as anxiety and panic, with the oedipal stage of castration anxiety.

This simplistic model has been superseded, partly for lack of objective evidence, and partly because libido theory has generally been replaced with an object-relations view of development (Greenberg & Mitchell 1983). The notion of levels or stages of development remains, however, and at least three can be defined:

Level 1: symbiotic stage. This is the symbiotic phase, where the patient is not fully differentiated as a person and seeks relationships characterised by merging and adhesiveness. He lives in a solipsistic world, seeing others as extensions of himself, whose primary function is to meet his needs. Anxieties associated with this phase are those of primitive dread, fear of non-being, and disintegration.

Level 2: part-object stage; 'paranoid-schizoid position'. Here, the individual is more aware of others, but relates to them as 'part-objects' rather than whole persons. This corresponds to the Kleinian paranoid-schizoid position, where the world is split into good and bad, and in which unwanted parts of the self are expelled into others by projective identification. Anxieties associated with this stage are those of abandonment and loss of control.

Level 3: whole-object stage; 'depressive position'. This is the Kleinian 'depressive position', or Winnicott's 'stage of concern', in which the individual inhabits a three-person world of separate, caring and cared-for objects, but is subject to rivalry, competition and doubts about sharing and acceptance. Fears associated with this stage are those of inadequacy and loss.

The attempt to assign a person to any one stage of development is difficult, especially as, under the regressive pull of illness, earlier and more primitive levels may be uncovered. Ms B revealed in the depths of her depression a level 1 symbiotic link with her mother; as her recovery progressed, level 2 issues of intense self-criticism (projected into others whom she saw as despising her) emerged; later, level 3 questions of comparison of herself with others predominated.

Conflict analysis

Freud's dynamic view of neurosis was based on a conflictual model in which illness arises when contradictory wishes or impulses become irreconcilable, for example feelings of aggression towards those upon whom one depends, or between sexual wishes and fears of rejection. Ryle (1982; see Ch. 11) has systematised this approach into a series of statements ('traps', 'snags' and 'dilemmas') which encapsulate such conflicts. For example, a common dilemma is that of 'too near – too far': 'Either I get too close in relationships and feel smothered or trapped, *or* I get too far and feel lonely and unwanted'. Traps are of the 'if but ...' type: 'If I am more independent my husband won't like it', or 'If I do what I want I run the risk of failing'. Snags are circular snares of the type: 'I feel unacceptable, so I placate; placation leads to exploitation; exploitation makes me feel angry; anger is unacceptable; therefore I placate, etc'. Patients can readily identify with pre-existing statements of this sort, which form a basis for therapy in which the assumptions which underlie them are examined and challenged. Luborsky (Luborsky et al 1989) has developed a similar research tool, the Core Conflictual Relationship Theme, which assigns patients' problems to a predetermined list of wish-fear-consequence themes. An example would be 'I wish to feel attractive; I fear rejection; therefore I feel inadequate'. These themes are repeated in the patient's everyday life, in the transference and, it is hypothesised, occurred also in childhood. To this extent, conflict analysis overlaps with the next category, dynamic focus.

Dynamic focus

The idea of a dynamic focus around which therapeutic efforts should be concentrated is particularily important in brief therapies (Malan 1979; see Ch. 8), but Thoma & Kachele (1986) see psychoanalysis itself as a focal therapy with an ever-shifting focus. The concept of focus in an extension of Strachey's (1934) idea of a 'mutative interpretation' which brings together at one nodal point the external relationship difficulty, the transference, and the hypothesised underlying childhood constellation. An important feature of focus derives from Freud's dictum that an interpretation should be aimed just near enough the surface of consciousness for the patient to able to grasp it, but far enough below to enable the overcoming of a resistance (Freud 1913).

The dynamic formulation

The dynamic formulation consists (Perry et al 1987) of a summarising statement that starts with the *psychiatric diagnosis:* proceeds to consider the *dynamic precipitant* of the illness, the *maintaining factors,* and the *childhood origins* or vulnerabilities: it considers the patient's *strengths and weaknesses* and *defence-styles*; proposes a *focal theme* which brings together the preceding elements; and goes on to suggest a possible form of *therapeutic intervention,* including a *prediction* about issues likely to arise in therapy, and possible outcome.

As an example, we will take Ms B. The psychiatric *diagnosis* was severe depression with endogenous features. The *precipitant* was the failed relationship, and the resulting feelings of shame and inadequacy. The *maintaining factor* was the symbiotic relationship with the mother and the illness itself, which made further exploration or social contact impossible. The *childhood origins* included possible difficulties in infancy, perhaps associated with her mother's depression and her sometimes rigid and inaccessible father. The assessment interview suggested a strong theme of loss and separation: several deaths were preoccupying the patient, and there was a counter-transferential pull to separate her from her family, either by sending her back to work, or by admission to hospital. The *focal theme* thus concerned the difficulty in making an oedipal 'move' from mother to father without feeling that what she had left behind was irretrievably lost. Her *strengths* included good academic achievement; her *weaknesses*, inhibition of assertiveness and aggression. Her *defence styles* were predominantly mature-neurotic: sublimation, altruism, repression and intellectualisation. The severity of her illness, together with her tendency to intellectualise, and the close involvement of her family meant that the chosen methods of *treatment* were drugs and ECT, supportive individual therapy and family therapy. *Predicted themes* were those of dependency on the therapist, and repressed anxiety and anger about separations and breaks in treatment.

CONCLUSION

In 1954, Dennis Hill, later to become professor of psychiatry at the Maudsley, wrote: 'My wish is to see a psychiatry which is one and undivided and... which is fundamentally psychologically oriented' (Hill 1954). Then, as now, that wish may have been utopian. Since it was written, there have been enormous developments in both the bio-medical and psychological aspects of psychiatry. Molecular genetics is beginning to make visible the biological substrate of psychiatric disorder, while psychotherapy, no longer confined within a narrow psychoanalytic or behaviourist credo, has established the psychobiological reality of an inner world based on attachment, exploration, loss, grief and belief.

As differentiation and specialisation have proceeded, the tension between the biological and psychological approaches has decreased. Hill's call for unity seems a less necessary idealisation. There is a movement away from a paranoid-schizoid era, in which opposing sides belittle and dismiss each other, to a climate more akin to the depressive position, in which each recognises the other's value and where rivalry is a stimulus to greater understanding rather than destructiveness. The tensions between the different branches of psychotherapy can also now more easily be contained, leading to creative competition and clarification. This unity of opposites can be seen metaphorically in terms of male and female (Pedder 1989), 'left' and 'right' brain functions, or as the entwined strands of a DNA helix. At each nodal point within psychiatry and psychotherapy, there are rational and intuitive elements; the creative tension between them often generates the most fruitful progeny.

Psychiatry at its best is a vigorous hybrid, combining science and art, reason and imagination, the biological and the psychological. The central reference point for psychotherapy is the individual, with his unique intrapsychic, familial and social experience. While psychotherapy remains part of a wider psychiatric whole, that pivotal vision will not be lost.

FURTHER READING

Brown D, Pedder J 1979 Introduction to psychotherapy: an outline of psychodynamic principles and practice. Tavistock, London.
Garfield S L, Bergin A E 1986 Handbook of psychotherapy and behaviour change. Wiley, Chichester
Holmes J, Lindley R 1989 The values of psychotherapy. Oxford University Press, Oxford
Perry S, Cooper A M, Michels R 1987 The psychodynamic formulation: its purpose, structure and clinical application. American Journal of Psychiatry 144: 543–550.
Symington N 1986 The analytic experience. Free Association Books, London

2. A history of psychodynamic psychiatry in Britain

M. Pines

In this chapter, the history of psychodynamic psychiatry in Britain will be traced. Not identical to, though closely linked with the psychoanalytic school, psychodynamic psychiatry has the characteristically British features of eclecticism, empiricism and individualism.

SOME OUTSTANDING PIONEERS

The Morrison lectures of 1915, given at the Royal College of Physicians in Edinburgh and entitled 'The New Psychiatry' (Stoddart 1915) will be taken as a starting point. They caused a furore, as described by Isabel Hutton (Hutton 1960), a young Scottish psychiatrist working with Professor George Robertson, the first Professor of Psychiatry at the University of Edinburgh. She described how senior Scottish psychiatrists left the hall in fury and disbelief, shaking their heads at the outrageous ideas put forward by the lecturer. However, George Robertson himself became a convert to psychoanalysis, and stoutly declared himself to be a Freudian from then onwards. Who was this lecturer and what was he laying before his distinguished audience? The man responsible was William Henry Butler Stoddart, Professor of Psychological Medicine to the Royal Army College, former superintendent of Bethlem, pupil and colleague of Hughlings Jackson and author of one of the most important contemporary text books in British psychiatry, *Mind and Its Disorders*.

Described as placid, apparently lazy, fat, affable and always well dressed, a man who enjoyed good food, good wine and idle days on the river (Rickman 1950), Stoddart laid down the first major challenge to British psychiatry arising from the slow arrival of psychodynamic thought to this country. In his lectures, later published as a book (Stoddart 1915), Stoddart outlined the psychoanalytic theory of mind, and the psychopathology of the neuroses and the psychoses. It was couched in the libidinal terms and topographic theory of those days, and one can understand how this was strong beer for an audience almost totally unaccustomed to psychoanalytic thinking. Yet Stoddart, who later became Physician in Psychological Medicine to St Thomas Hospital, London, was not a person to be ignored, for he was a significant establishment figure.

31

Of the early psychoanalysts, he was the most well-established, far more so than Ernest Jones, who had failed to gain entry to the higher realms of British neurology and psychiatry. In 1920, the third edition of his text book, *Mind and Its Disorders*, was reviewed in the Edinburgh Medical Journal. The reviewer attacks 'the extreme Freudian view presented in a manner which suggests that no-one has any scruples or doubts about its full acceptance.'(Edinburgh Medical Journal 1920). The book was described as confused, and the author as having a father complex towards Freud. The review ends: 'with regret it must be said that this book is one which will do much to retard the use of psychological methods in the treatment of disease'. However, it was said that attacks bounced off Stoddart; he assumed that they would come, and he assumed that they would cease in time – he could wait. Meanwhile, life was pleasant, and his attackers were, after all, good fellows but mistaken.

The first paper on psychoanalysis given publicly was in 1911, by David Eder at the British Medical Association neurological section, and described a case of hysteria and obsessionality treated by Freud's psychoanalytic method. 'When Dr Eder had finished speaking the chairman and the entire audience, numbering about nine, rose and strode out without a word,' (Hobman 1949). But Eder, like Stoddart, was a stout character and not to put off by such a rebuff. Indeed, he was a powerful and colourful personality whom Freud valued highly, as shown by the letter, he wrote at the time of Eder's death in 1936, to the analyst Barbara Low, Eder's sister-in-law. A member of a middle-class Jewish family, first cousin of the novelist Israel Zangwill, Eder was an early socialist who bore a scar on his head from the Bloody Sunday riot in Trafalgar Square of 1887. After graduating from St Bartholomew's Hospital in 1895, he became a general practitioner in Johannesburg, a medical officer in his family coffee and rubber plantations in Colombia, was caught up in South American revolutions, fell ill amongst cannibals and voyaged three thousand miles up the Amazon.

When back in England, Eder was active in socialist medicine, worked at the Margaret McMillan clinic for children in the East End, and promoted the new movement for school hygiene. He became interested in psychoanalysis just before the 1914–18 war, during which he was a medical officer in Malta and had much to do with what he called 'war shock' on which he wrote a significant book. In 1913, he visited Freud in Vienna, had a brief analysis with Victor Tausk and then, with Ernest Jones as President, he became Secretary of the London Psycho-Analytical Society. He also had a brief analysis with Jones, with whom he afterwards fell out for some years, being attracted to Jung. However, after eight months' analysis with Ferenczi in Budapest in 1923, he rejoined the British Psycho-Analytical Society and remained a prominent member for many years. He was active in developing the Institute for Scientific Treatment Delinquency, which later became the Portman Clinic. Eder was a much admired man who mixed in artistic and left-wing circles, and it was through the esteem in which people held him that psychoanalysis became acceptable to these circles. It is possibly through Eder that D H Lawrence became involved in psychoanalysis.

In his own writings, Ernest Jones (Jones 1959) plays down the significance of Stoddart and Eder as major figures in early psychoanalysis. Jones likes to portray himself as the father figure of British psychoanalysis and, with his combative nature and intellectual brilliance, he did indeed play the most significant part in the British psychoanalytical movement for many years. However, there were negative aspects to his contributions. He drew tight boundaries around the Psycho-Analytic Society, more or less dictated who would be accepted as a psychoanalyst and excluded from the Society many people who had contributed significantly to the widening knowledge and acceptance of Freud's ideas before, during and after the First World War.

Probably the most influential proponent of Freud's view was Bernard Hart, physician in psychological medicine at University College Hospital. Hart did become an Associate Member of the Psycho-Analytical Society, but never played an active part in it and always maintained a critical, objective view of Freud's work. However, he was probably its most accomplished expositor, through his book *The Psychology of Insanity* (Hart 1912, 1927), which went through many editions and was the most widely read introductory book on psychoanalysis.

PSYCHIATRY AT THE TURN OF THE CENTURY

To understand the beginnings of the psychodynamic movement, it is necessary to glance briefly at the position of psychiatry at the turn of the century, and at those individuals who began to introduce the psychological aspects of mind into an area then dominated by an organic and materialistic approach. This was the position of Henry Maudsley and of the great majority of well-established psychiatrists. The great input of Hughlings Jackson had convinced British psychiatrists that the only relevant approach to the neuroses and psychoses was through a study of the brain and of the dynamic functions of the central nervous system.

Jackson had shown how the higher levels of the central nervous system act to maintain the lower levels in suppression, and that a lesion of a higher level would release the actions of the lower level. Freud, who knew Jackson well, later incorporated this into his view of repression, in which the ego controls the manifestations of the id, which, however, re-emerge in the form of symptoms when the higher levels are not able to maintain their control (Dewhurst 1982).

Whilst British neurologists were pioneers in dynamic functional neurology, British psychiatrists were isolated from, or in opposition to, the far more advanced European psychiatry. The re-emergence of a psychology that opposed Jackson's materialism came from the Victorian 'other world' search for a spiritualism, an alternative system of belief that could replace religion. Dominated by Cambridge academics, the Society for Psychical Research investigated spiritualism, possession, dual personality and hypnosis. F W H Myers declared his opposition to Maudsley, emphasising unconscious mental processes with his concept of the subliminal self, although it did not have the dynamic qualities of the Freudian unconscious. At the same time, Havelock Ellis, who had qualified in medicine though he did not practice as a doctor, was knocking down cultural barriers to the recognition of the power of sexuality.

British psychiatry at this time was custodial and therapeutically somewhat nihilistic. However, signs that this intellectual monopoly was breaking down came in the movement to establish both outpatient clinics and hospitals for the treatment of the neuroses. The slow acceptance of psychodynamic psychiatry was due in part to the resistance of the mechanistic approach to psychiatry, in part also to the isolation of the early psychoanalysts.

Pioneers

One such pioneer was Dr Helen Boyle, who founded a small outpatient dispensary in Brighton in 1905, when the Lady Chichester Hospital was also founded (Boyle 1922). Psychotherapy was the main basis of treatment, though Helen Boyle herself was not close to psychoanalysis. The dynamic alternative to psychoanalysis in those days was the French school of Janet, Dubois and Dejerine, where persuasion and suggestion were the main methods, together with the hypnotic approach of Bernheim and the school of Nancy. T A Ross, the first medical director of the Cassel Hospital, declared his support of the French school, though he later became more of a convert to psychoanalysis, writing influential books on the subject (Ross 1923, 1932).

Another major pioneer before World War I was Hugh Crichton-Miller (1877–1959), who in 1911 opened Bowden House in Harrow on the Hill as a nursing home for functional nervous disorders. He had qualified as a doctor in Edinburgh, and had practised in both Italy and Scotland as a fashionable general practitioner; however he became increasingly fascinated by the functional nervous disorders. In his early years, he was assisted by Maurice Nicol, another significant early figure in psychoanalysis, who later moved to Jung and then, finally, to the spiritual movement of Gurdjief. But during World War I, Nicol was one of a significant group of psychiatrists and neurologists led by the psychologist, C S Meyers, who persuaded the army establishment that shell-shock cases should be treated with psychotherapy, and not be subjected to the practices of some eminent neurologists, who used electric shock and other pain-producing methods to force patients to give up their symptoms (Stone 1985).

In 1920, Crichton-Miller founded the Tavistock Clinic, and remained its director until his resignation in 1934. He was an eclectic psychotherapist and was eventually to be displaced by the more hard-line psychoanalysts of the 1930s; but without Crichton-Miller's enthusiasm, organisational abilities and capacity for clear communication, the Tavistock Clinic would have had a different and less influential development (Stone 1985).

WORLD WAR I AND SHELL SHOCK

It was the impact on psychiatry of the so-called 'shell-shock of World War I that led to the downfall of the dominant neurological approach. Such distinguished neurologists and physicians as Henry Head, Farquahr Buzzard and Langdon Brown, all later Regius Professors of Medicine at Oxford and at Cambridge, supported the new functional approach. Important figures such as William McDougall, William Brown and J A Hadfield worked in this area, and Maghull Hospital, Liverpool became for a while the central training ground for psychodynamic psychiatrists under the direction of R G Rows. It is regrettable that the history of Maghull Hospital over this period is not yet fully available.

W H R Rivers

One of the most interesting psychotherapists of this period was the experimental psychologist and anthropologist, W H R Rivers (Slobodin 1978). Rivers was an establishment figure of even more prominence than Hart and Stoddart. He was the director of the first experimental psychology laboratories in the Universities of London and Cambridge, and became a Fellow of the Royal Society. Rivers qualified from St Bartholomew's in 1882, in 1888 became MD, FRCP, and in the 1890s worked at Queen Square with Hughlings Jackson and Victor Horsley before going to study in Germany. In 1898, he was a member of the famous Torres Straits Expedition, the pioneering expedition that established modern British anthropology, in which he was accompanied by C S Myers, William McDougal and Charles Seligman. This turned him towards anthropology for several years, although during this period, in 1903, he co-operated with Henry Head in the famous Head-Rivers experiment on peripheral sensory mechanisms, that led to the subsequently influential theories of protopathic/epicritic sensations.

This division of sensation into the lower, primitive form and the higher, more differentiated form can now be seen as analogous to Freud's division of the mind into the higher and lower forms of organisation, and both are related to Jackson's doctrine of levels of the central nervous system. In

1915, Rivers, who was already familiar with the works of Freud and Jung, was introduced, at Maghull, to psychotherapy of the war neuroses. His work became famous through the autobiography of Siegfried Sassoon, whom he treated at Craiglockhart Hospital, near Edinburgh. Sassoon had mutinied against the slaughter in France and would have been court-martialled had not his friend, the poet Robert Graves, succeeded in persuading him that he was suffering from a nervous breakdown. (Sassoon and Graves called the hospital 'Dottyville'.) Sassoon was forever grateful to Rivers for his help at this crucial period, and ascribed his mental maturity to his contact with the mind of Rivers.

Rivers became the first President of the Medical Section of the British Psychological Society, and wrote a book, *Conflict and Dream* which described many of his own dreams and in which he both agreed and disagreed with Freud on dream mechanisms. Rivers brought his anthropological approach to bear on the study of mental life, unable to accept what he saw as Freud's limited view of the Western family, to which he had given universal significance. Tragically, Rivers died in 1922 from a strangulated hernia, but he had left his stamp on the 'new psychiatry,' a psychodynamic view of mind and its disorders. However, Jones, Edward Glover, John Rickman and other pioneer analysts vehemently opposed the work of people such as Rivers, who they saw as purloiners of Freud's ideas, without being true disciples. It was this intransigent view held by Jones and his followers that helped to maintain the longstanding isolation of psychoanalysis from the mainstream of British psychiatry.

The Brunswick Square Clinic

An example of this intransigence is the fate of the first London Clinic for Psychotherapy, a medico-psychological clinic, later known as the Brunswick Square Clinic, founded in 1912 by Dr Jessie Murray and Miss Julia Turner (Boll 1962). Murray had attended Janet's lectures in Paris, and conceived of a clinic to treat functional nervous disorders with new eclectic therapeutic methods influenced by, but ranging much wider than psychoanalysis. The clinic changed its name on its move to Brunswick Square, had departments for medicine, psychology, psychotherapy, physical exercises and education. One of the clinic's early physicians was Dr Hector Munro, but the best known of its early staff was James Glover who was Director of the clinic. James Glover was later joined by his brother Edward and other students who later became prominent as psychoanalysts, including Sylvia Payne, Ella Sharpe, Susan Isaacs and Marjorie Brierley. However, this clinic was to be short-lived. When James Glover went to Berlin for analysis with Karl Abraham, he returned determined to oppose eclectic psychotherapy and suggested affiliation with the British Psycho-Analytical Society. This amalgamation took place in 1922, and little acknowledgement has ever been paid to the pioneering eclecticism of the Brunswick Clinic.

War neuroses

After World War I, the Ministry of Pensions opened up outpatient clinics to treat the thousands of ex-combatants with severe functional symptoms. This, indeed, was the route that led to the establishment of outpatient clinics using psychotherapy. Many psychiatrists who had become converted to psychotherapy did not become psychoanalysts but established outpatient clinics at hospitals in London and in the provinces, such as at Littlemore, Oxford (Good 1930).

The Cassel Hospital was founded after World War I in response to demands that had been placed on psychiatry by the war neuroses.

MAPOTHER AND THE MAUDSLEY

The history of the postwar years must give prominence to the Maudsley Hospital under Edward Mapother (Lewis 1979). In addition to an offer he had made in his lifetime, Henry Maudsley had left money to the London Country Council in his will for the establishment of a hospital that would end the isolation of psychiatry from general medical knowledge and research, and which would admit only voluntary patients. Building was begun in 1913, but between 1915 and 1919 the hospital was used for the care of neurotic patients in the services, with Maudsley's consent.

Mapother, born in Ireland in 1881, entered psychiatry in 1907 at Long Grove. There, the Superintendent was Hubert Bond, who had gathered around him a group of brilliant young psychiatrists, including Bernard Hart. There was interest in Janet and Freud, and Mapother's contact with psychodynamic ideas was increased during his training at Maghull Hospital in 1917.

In 1919, Mapother went to the Maudsley, and in the early 1920s visited advanced European centres for psychiatry. In his first annual Maudsley report, Mapother wrote that he encouraged unprejudiced trials of every form of treatment, and that he was extremely glad that there was 'a considerable proportion of definite adherents of psychoanalysis amongst the clinical assistants and that there was no doubt of great advances introduced by these schools in our understanding of cases'. Mapother continued to advocate the provision of psychotherapy at the Maudsley, and to provide facilities for it, but he became increasingly opposed to the Tavistock Clinic, particularly to the Christian approach of Crichton-Miller, Hadfield and others, dubbing it 'the parson's clinic'.

J R Rees, who remained a personal friend of Mapother's thought that he had strong feelings of jealousy towards the psychotherapeutic strength of the Tavistock Clinic. However, at the Royal Society of Medicine's memorial meeting for Freud, he wrote that 'Freud brought to psychology and psychiatry more of the imagination of the great artist than of the solid objectivity and rigid logic of the scientist' (Lewis 1979). It is noteworthy that Mapother had written a paper with R D Gillespie from the York Clinic, in which they demonstrated the process of Freudian mechanisms such as unconscious homosexuality in cases of paranoia. Perhaps this was in anticipation of his later, somewhat paranoid, attitude towards psychoanalysis as represented by the Tavistock 'parsons clinic'. However, psychoanalytic psychotherapy did continue at the Maudsley under Mapother, represented in particular by W L Neustatter who wrote on the results of 50 cases treated by psychotherapy at the Maudsley in 1935 (Neustatter 1935). Later developments at the Maudsley, particularly after World War II under Aubrey Lewis, will be referred to later.

OPPONENTS OF THE PSYCHODYNAMIC MOVEMENT

'It is true that psychoanalysis is past its perihelion and is rapidly retreating into the dark and barren depths from which it emerged'. (Mercier 1916)

'Freudism, notwithstanding the diligent efforts made to acclimatise it, will, I feel sure, never take root in this country.' (Crichton-Browne 1920)

'I have now completed a task which, in spite of its repugnant nature, I have felt it my duty to perform. That the invidious poison, which is being instilled into the minds of the young by countless psychoanalysts, is doing untold harm is known to many and should be known to all.' (Bolton 1926; J Shaw Bolton was the first Professor of Psychiatry in England, holding the chair at Leeds.)

These extracts give a flavour of the strongly emotional opposition to psychoanalysis aroused in some prominent psychiatrists. Two Fellows of the Royal College of Physicians, Sir Horatio Bryan Donkin, a criminologist, 'a sociable man and prominent at the Saville Club,' and Sir Robert Armstrong-Jones, a former superintendent of Claybury Hospital and a Visitor in Lunacy, attempted to censure other FRCPs, presumably Stoddart primarily, for practising psychoanalysis, but the move was blocked by other Fellows.

The British Medical Association set up a committee to report on the status of psychoanalysis in 1927, after allegations had been made of patients being harmed. A young lawyer's suicide had been attributed to psychoanalytic treatment, but his therapist, Dr Millais Culpin, a distinguished member of the early psychoanalytic circle, was able to satisfy the coroner that the lawyer had in fact not been in psychoanalytic treatment. After many deliberations, the BMA decided to acknowledge psychoanalysis as a recognised form of training and treatment associated primarily with Freud's work (British Medical Association 1929). Although the committee would go no further in its support for psychoanalysis, this acknowledgement was seen by Jones and Glover, who had been active in giving evidence on that committee, as a triumph for the movement, as it gave recognition and respectability to psychoanalytic training. Thereafter, opposition to psychoanalysis became less raucous and extreme but was still steadily maintained by Mapother and other leading figures.

PSYCHOANALYSIS AND PSYCHIATRY PRE-WORLD-WAR-II

It was the intransigent attitude of Ernest Jones that blocked the development of a psychoanalytic influence in general psychiatry. Until World War II, Jones actively forbade psychoanalysts to work at the Tavistock Clinic, as he saw this as a dilution of the pure gold of psychoanalysis. Thus, developments at the Tavistock Clinic until after the war were spearheaded by eclectic psychotherapists who represented the 'new psychiatry'. J R Rees, assisted by H V Dicks, succeeded Crichton-Miller as Director, with J A Hadfield in charge of training. Hadfield practised what he considered to be psychoanalysis, but one of his analysands, W R Bion, many years later referred contemptuously to Hadfield as 'doctor put it into the past'.

However, Jones' embargo had positive as well as negative results. It allowed for a freshness of thought for psychiatrists such as Ian Suttie and John Bowlby, who were not caught up in the powerful controversies between the 'English school' of psychoanalysis, headed by Ernest Jones and much under the influence of Melanie Klein, and those Freudians who adhered more closely to the teachings of Vienna and Berlin.

Newcombe & Lerner (1982) have written about the historical context of Bowlby's attachment theory, looking at the psychological and social changes that followed World War I. They suggest that as well as the impetus given to psychotherapy by the treatment of shell-shock, there was the postwar atmosphere of bereavement and the change in mourning customs. Freud wrote *Mourning and Melancholia* during World War I and later, in *Beyond the Pleasure Principle*, struggled with the phenomenon of recurrent battle dreams. The impact of bereavement was enormous: roughly three-quarters of a million Britons died in the war, and about one-third of the dead were married, leaving about 248 000 widows and 381 000 fatherless children. The funeral and mourning customs that had signified loss before the war became impractical due to the enormous number of dead and the comforts of religion generally became less significant to the bereaved. When Bowlby was working at the Maudsley in 1933–34, he apparently became aware of bereavement as a fact in psychosis. This sensitised him to the significance of early separation, which he then studied in his analysis of a series of 44 cases of juvenile thieves seen at the London Child Guidance Clinic in 1936 and 1937.

Bowlby had been alerted to the significance of early attachment and the consequences of its disruption by the work of Ian Suttie. In his book, *The*

Origins of Love and Hate (Suttie 1988), Suttie took issue with Freud and contemporary Freudian instinct theory. He stressed what would now be called object relations, the prime significance of the early attachment of infants to mothers, and the trauma of separation anxiety that antecedes later generators of anxiety. Suttie was widely read in anthropology and sociology, and he brought this knowledge to bear on his outline of a form of psychology broader than Freudian psychoanalysis, a move from individual to social psychology.

It seems likely, as Dorothy Heard (1988) writes in her introduction to the reissues of *The Origins of Love and Hate*, that Suttie was influenced by Ferenczi. Suttie's wife, Jane, had translated many of Ferenczi's papers, and in the preface to the translation Ferenczi writes, 'it gives me great pleasure to lay my work once more before Anglo-Saxon readers, particularly because I have found that with their broad-mindedness, they often strive to view such opinions as mine without prejudice, whereas elsewhere these are turned down on account of their novelty or their boldness.' Much more than did Freud, Ferenczi emphasised the clinical aspect of psycho-analysis, the love between therapist and patient and the patient's need to find in the therapist a secure attachment in order to relive and recover from early conflicts and deprivations in the mother-infant relationship.

The Hungarian school of psychoanalysis had emphasised attachment almost from the start, and Ferenczi's pupil, Michael Balint later brought this development to British psychoanalysis. Suttie described the infant as having from birth an innate need for companionship which is the infant's only way of self preservation, and showed how the infant and child always tries to restore harmonious relationships with care-givers. He believed that a psycho-biological framework needed to be developed, with a language that would comprehend the individual and social phenomena of infancy. This viewpoint, later developed by Bowlby, clearly leads on to the work of Fairbairn, Winnicott and the Independent Group of psychoanalysts in the British Psychoanalytic Society. Suttie's early death, shortly after the publication of his book, prevents us from knowing how he would have developed his theories and his technique. The book was thoughtfully received within psychoanalysis, and may have influenced the work of W D Fairbairn, who was working in relative isolation in Edinburgh and who in his later papers advocated the replacement of the theory of libidinal drives by the theory of object relations.

W Line (1934–1935) a Canadian psychologist, provides an interesting viewpoint on British psychiatry in the 1930s in his article 'Some impressions of British psychiatry'. He affirms that the story of British psychiatry is essentially one of individuals, rather than of schools and systems, and that each outstanding personality drew more from the setting in which he worked than, for example, from any university tradition, which would have a particular philosophical culture and outlook. Thus, he tactfully underlines the fact that British psychiatry had not penetrated into the universities. Of the psychoanalysts, he writes 'they constitute the only group manifesting an easily recognised point of view, concerning which evangelical enthusiasm and energetic defence must be displayed. But, the main influence of psychoanalysis in Britain is not to be sought in the work of such extremists as Ernest Jones, but rather in the attitude toward the analytic system of thought reflected in the psychological trends of the country'. He contrasts the 'near-analysts', like McDougall, Hart and Yellowlees, all termed 'subjectivists,' and who adhered to the European emphasis on the individual, with the 'objectivists', such as R D Gillespie and Aubrey Lewis. Of Mapother, he writes 'the critical genius of Mapother appears to be a pertinent example; for his discussions of the weaknesses – systematic and practical – of analysis, and his penetrating descriptions of disordered mental states, reflect not a little the influence of process psychology' (i.e, the work of the psychologist, Spearman).

Line poses the question of why the psychoanalytic approach of McDougall had had so strong an influence in Britain. He compares the reception of psychoanalysis in the 1930s in Britain and America, and suggests, (contrary to commonly held view), that psychoanalysis has had a somewhat *more* cordial reception in Britain than in America. He attributed this to the greater emphasis on experimentation in American psychology; British psychologists had considerably less confidence in experimental psychology when applied to complicated problems of personality.

It seems that British psychology and psychiatry adapted psychoanalysis in a way that is characteristic of British thought, tending to appreciate the value of systematic thinking but not to formulate systems. As Line saw it, the 'British mind', with its interest in life and events as they are, seeks the aid of whatever systematic formulation seems most pertinent, and does not hesitate to import many systems, conflicting though they may be, when radically different problems demand solution. British thought retains a certain mobility, and British philosophers have always applied their ideas to the nature of society and its problems rather than developing purely abstract philosophical systems, as in France and Germany. The empiricism of Locke is typical. Systems tend to isolate thinkers, forcing them to defend a particular point of view and preventing their partici-pation in matters of social policy, where breadth of purview is essential. (This well describes the position of Ernest Jones and the Psycho-Analytical Society.) Application must be eclectic, and the British use any system as long as it works; they import systems but then proceed to compromise them by adding a great deal of common sense! Line thus convincingly outlines the setting that enabled Suttie and Bowlby to integrate social psychology with psychoanalysis in their ideas.

In the 1930s, a variety of articles appeared on the application of psychodynamic methods to inpatient and outpatient clinics. T S Good (1930) of Littlemore Hospital described how, after 1922, using wartime experience, it was possible to run a mental hospital almost entirely on the

open door system, using psychology to understand delusions and hallucinations. He emphasised that 'mental analysis' is the most certain of all
methods, as it reveals to the patient the causes of breakdown which he can
avoid in future. Ian Skottowe, Lindsay Neustatter and, later, James Flynd
all wrote on the early treatment of the neuroses by psychotherapy in the
outpatient clinics.

The only centre for serious inpatient psychotherapy in the 1920s and
1930s was the Cassel Hospital under its Director, T A Ross (1923, 1932).
Ross was a general practitioner who turned to psychotherapy during
World War I, and had the confidence of powerful figures both in the army
and in medicine. R D Gillespie was on the staff of the Cassel from
1925–26 after working with George Robertson in Edinburgh and, later,
Ronald Hargreaves, an important wartime figure in psychiatry and, for a
short while, Professor of Psychiatry at Leeds; W C M Scott, a pioneer
psychoanalyst in the psychotherapeutic treatment of psychosis, spent some
years at the Cassel. The respect in which Ross was held by psychiatrists
was important in maintaining a psychotherapeutic influence in psychiatry,
but it was not until after World War II that the Cassel reached eminence
under the dynamic leadership of T F Main (1989).

Another important centre of psychodynamic influence was the Institute
for the Scientific Treatment of Delinquency (ISTD). The Institute was
given this name in 1932, but had begun to form in 1931 under the
influence of Grace Pailthorpe, a psychoanalyst who had researched on
women prisoners at Birmingham prison under the guidance of Dr
Hamblyn Smith. Later, Pailthorpe continued her research at Holloway
Prison in London, and it was this work that led to the formation of the
ISTD. In 1933, the Institute opened the 'Psychopathic Clinic', the
forerunner of the present day Portman Clinic. The most active workers in
the early years were Edward Glover, Emmanuel Miller and Dennis
Carroll. Glover is the best known of these today, but Miller, a pioneer in
child psychiatry and family therapy, and Carroll, a psychoanalyst who had
an international reputation in the field of delinquency, were equally
important.

Thus, the direct influence of psychodynamics on British psychiatry
before World War II was apparently limited to a few small centres, such as
the Tavistock Clinic and the Cassel Hospital. However, its influence
diffused out into many areas of general psychiatry and, in particular,
shaped the development of outpatient clinics, where psychotherapy was
able to help in the treatment of war shell-shock and other neuroses for
which organic psychiatry had little to offer.

THE PSYCHOANALYTIC SCENE IN BRITAIN BETWEEN THE WARS

Despite being isolated from the mainstream of British psychiatry, the

British Psycho-Analytical Society became an important contributor to the international world of psychoanalysis. Under the leadership of Ernest Jones, who was joined by Melanie Klein in 1926, British psychoanalysis developed a form distinct from that of Vienna. Melanie Klein, who had been analysed by Ferenczi and later by Abraham, came to England at the suggestion of James and Alix Strachey. Alix Strachey had been living in Berlin, undergoing a second analysis with Karl Abraham, after a not very successful analysis with Freud. She had become friendly with Melanie Klein and was impressed by her ideas. Alix and her husband, James, arranged a lecture tour for Klein, who was eager to find a new platform for her ideas. Jones took to her and invited her to work and teach in London and also to undertake the analysis of his own children.

The leading British psychoanalysts, amongst them Jones, Edward Glover, John Rickman, Joan Riviere, Sylvia Payne, and, later, Winnicott and Bowlby, were all significantly influenced by Klein's work. Through her analysis of young children, Klein outlined her ideas on the early development of mind, suggesting that Freud's four libidinal phases of development (oral, anal, phallic and genital) be replaced by what eventually she termed the schizoid-paranoid and depressive positions. She outlined an elaborate system of phantasy structures of the infant in relationship to the mother's body; suggested that oedipal phantasies developed much earlier than Freud had proposed; and emphasised the great strength of infantile sadism and destructiveness, the latter concept deriving from her insistence on the importance of Freud's death instinct, an idea which she espoused from the start and maintained throughout her life (Grosskurth 1986).

Klein, a strong and ambitious character with a great drive for power, in many ways dominated the British psychoanalytical scene until the arrival in Britain of Sigmund and Anna Freud and the Viennese refugee analysts in 1938. It is sad to note that Melanie Klein, in a letter to Ernest Jones, accused him of 'having done much harm to psychoanalysis' (Grosskuth 1986, p.255) by inviting Freud and his daughter to this country. This revealed how much she feared that her influence would now be diminished and that she had come to equate psychoanalysis in Britain with her own work.

The arrival of the Viennese analysts led to a vigorous struggle for power within psychoanalytic society. The new arrivals were shocked at Klein's influence, and regarded her work as constituting so radical a break as no longer to be recognisable as psychoanalysis. During the war, this struggle led to a series of 'controversial discussion', in which a number of important issues were clarified, and which later led to the British compromise of three Independent but interdependent groups within the British Psycho-Analytical Society – the Freudians, the Kleinians and the Independent Group – which agreed to share and to divide training procedures (King & Steiner 1990).

Klein's explorations of the early mechanisms of mind, which she likened to psychotic phenomenon as shown in manic depression and schizophrenia, were important because they led to pioneering efforts by Bion, Rosenfeld, Winnicott, Little, Segal and others to treat the psychoses with psychoanalysis in the post World War II period (see below).

THE IMPACT OF WORLD WAR II ON BRITISH PSYCHIATRY

Just as World War I was a turning point for psychotherapy through the treatment of shell-shock, so World War II was a turning point for the application of a psychodynamic social psychology to institutions. Ahrenfeldt has described in some detail the application of such thinking in the British Army during the 1939–1945 War (Ahrenfeldt 1968). J R Rees, Director of the Tavistock Clinic, became Director of British Army Psychiatry, aided by Ronald Hargreaves, and under his leadership, psychoanalysts found themselves actively involved with others in the fashioning of new forms of organisation for the treatment of the war neuroses, and for the selection and training of officers and other ranks. W R Bion, John Rickman, A T M Wilson, J D Sutherland, S H Foulkes, Harold Bridger and T F Main are amongst the most significant of these workers. Eric Trist, a historian of these times and a close wartime associate of Bion's, has called these Tavistock members 'the invisible college', in that they maintained collegial links with each other throughout the war years.

This group achieved striking success through significant innovations in military psychiatry but also in army policy. How was this achieved? Sir Ronald Adam who became Adjutant General, the second highest post in the British Army, supported these innovations largely through his relationship with Ronald Hargreaves. The psychiatrists took part in social model building: (1) to identify problems; (2) to look for new solutions when old ones had failed; (3) to collaborate with military personnel in the structure of the models; and (4) finally to hand back the innovations to the military. These innovations included a method for the selection of officers (W R Bion and the War Office Selection Board) and the concept of a 'command' psychiatrist, in which a psychiatrist with a roving commission was attached to each of the five army commanders in Home Forces and later overseas. Another innovation (by Bion, Rickman and Foulkes) was the concept of therapeutic community. Psychiatrists were also used to prepare propaganda and analyse the mentality of enemies. Henry Dicks was prominent in this field.

In these and other ways, dynamic psychiatry showed itself useful to the military and became an effective part of modern military administration. Psychiatrists were involved with: the intake of soldiers and finding appropriate tasks for them; the promotion and training of officers; treatment of psychiatrically disturbed soldiers; the rehabilitation of such soldiers when possible; and returning them to active duty. Later, they became concerned with the rehabilitation of prisoners of war returning from the Far East, who had to be helped to overcome the enormous physical and mental traumata to which they had been subjected, to enable them to return to civilian life. Psychiatrists were involved in the study of the creation, maintenance and breakdown of morale; for example, T F Main was asked to investigate the background of the Salerno mutiny.

Therapeutic community

British psychiatrists generally were not well equipped to organise rapid rehabilitation for the psychiatric casualties of war. The first steps towards this new methodology came from Wilfred Bion and John Rickman. Rickman was a senior psychoanalyst who was deeply interested and well informed on sociological and anthropological matters; he and Bion, his former analysand, were responsible for the setting up of the 'First Northfield Experiment' (de Mare 1983, Main 1989). Northfield, a large military psychiatric hospital near Birmingham, was not meeting the wartime needs of the Army for the identification and treatment of recoverable cases of mental breakdown, and the discharge of the unrecoverable. Bion and Rickman were put in charge of a wing of the hospital, where they introduced a radical and psychodynamic treatment regime; discipline was restored, and the patients treated as soldiers on active service. The main technique adopted was group discussion. Neurosis was treated as the enemy; soldiers had to be taught to turn and to face this enemy and to develop the courage to do so successfully. Bion's experience as a young tank officer in World War I stood him in good stead, both through his practical experience and because it meant he was accepted by the military as a fully-fledged fighting man himself (Bion & Rickman 1943).

The experiment lasted only six weeks, possibly because Bion and Rickman did not fully understand the effects of change on a whole social system, but during that short time they managed to revolutionise the structure of a ward, and laid foundations upon which others were to build. The next more lasting phase, the Second Northfield Experiment (Foulkes 1948), was based on the work of Foulkes, Bridger, Main and others, and laid the foundations of the study of a hospital as a therapeutic institution, as described by Main (1989) in his pioneering papers.

While these innovations were taking place in military psychiatry, Maxwell Jones, who originally set out to study psychosomatic conditions leading to fatigue and exhaustion in soldiers, was working under the auspices of the Maudsley. His work was important in the development of the social psychiatry movement exemplified by his work at Henderson Hospital and, later, at Dingleton in Scotland. Jones did not come from a psychoanalytical background; his work relied more upon the concept of a 'living-learning environment' and concentrated on the examination of roles in relationship to work tasks.

Another important development during World War II was Anna Freud's residential nursery. Together with a devoted band of psychoanalytic co-workers, she cared for homeless and separated children and began the systematic observations of children for which the postwar Hampstead Child Psychotherapy Clinic became justly famous.

Anna Freud carried on her father's work and added to it her own contribution to child analysis which, in contrast to Melanie Klein's work, was based upon the systematic observation of children in different circumstances such as nursery schools, the care of wartime children in residential settings, and the observation of children with physical deficits such as blindness. The systematic analysis of this data was greatly aided by the construction and development of the Hampstead Index, a method for the systematic classification and analysis of the clinical data of the many children in treatment. This was systematised under the direction of Joseph Sandler. Anna Freud herself contributed the concept of the *developmental line*, the observation of the way in which the child progresses within certain defined areas of behaviour. Thus, one such developmental line is from emotional dependency to independence, from dependency on others for bodily care and gratification to self-sufficiency in this respect. This concept of developmental lines has proved very helpful in the study of children, adolescents and, eventually, of adults. Anna Freud's considerable contributions to the systematic development of psychoanalysis and its impact on child psychiatry are well brought out in the recent biography by Young-Bruhl (1988).

THE POST-WAR TAVISTOCK CLINIC

The 'invisible college' gathered together in the post-war years under the leadership of W R Bion. This group took control of the Tavistock and eventually ousted the pre-war members, in particular those who did not accept the psychoanalytic approach. Most undertook psychoanalytic training, as hardly any of them had begun or attempted a training in the pre-war years. The isolation of the Institute of Psycho-Analysis and the Tavistock Clinic began in this way to break down, but some problems arose directly from this. The Tavistock psychiatrists, despite their psychoanalytic training, were imbued with enthusiasm for a social psychiatric model. The training analysts, particularly Melanie Klein, saw these moves as resistances to a true psychoanalysis and therefore discouraged group therapy and associated explorations in social psychiatry. However, the enthusiasm of the staff maintained a great impetus in the field of group therapy for many years. They adopted the model of W R Bion and, later, that of Henry Ezriel. The latter in particular applied a strictly psychoanalytic object-relations model to the group phenomena, attempting to establish the nature of the group's transferences to therapist, and to examine both the anxieties that these evoked and the defences against them. Though this produced a number of significant papers, Ezriel (1950) was unable to complete his research, and a follow-up study of group therapy at the Tavistock Clinic by David Malan did not appear to support the clinical relevance of this approach.

Research into social psychiatry at the Tavistock became split off into the Institute of Human Relations, partly as a result of the changes that had to be made when the Tavistock Clinic entered the National Health Service. The Rockefeller Foundation gave a large grant to the Institute to enable it to continue the work begun in wartime conditions on the application of psychodynamic models to organisation and to social issues.

The Tavistock Clinic itself began to be well known through the work of John Bowlby in the Department of Children and Parents, and it was largely through Bowlby's work and the films made by his collaborator, James Robertson, that the world of medicine and of psychology, and later the wider community, began to understand the importance of the early mother-infant bond and the dangers of its disruption through hospitalisation (Robertson 1958).

R D Laing

Probably the best-known Tavistock figure of the post-war years was Ronald Laing. He wrote *The Divided Self* (1960) whilst still in training both at the Tavistock and at the Institute of Psychoanalysis, and he became the central figure of a significant movement. Laing brought the European existential and phenomenological approach to bear on psycho-analysis and this had an immediate appeal both to psychiatrists and to the lay public. Propelled into instant fame, he abandoned formal psycho-analysis and became involved in the Kingsley Hall Experiment, in which psychotic and borderline patients and a whole variety of disturbed personalities lived together with the therapists in a new form of community. Many claims were made for their clinical successors, inspired by their early enthusiasms.

Laing's writings, together with those of collaborators such as Esterson, Cooper and others, became linked with the 'anti-psychiatry' movement, which challenged the authority of psychiatrists to diagnose and treat patients, especially with drugs although psychotherapy and psychoanalysis were also targets for a while. It was at this time that the humanistic psychology movement was challenging psychoanalysis as the most significant model in psychotherapy.

Laing's writings have remained popular, although he never repeated the impact made by his first book, *The Divided Self*. His lasting contribution may be that psychology, psychiatry and psychoanalysis are now much more in the public domain, and the boundaries of psychiatric influence more open to community pressures.

The Balints

Another important innovation which spread the reputation of the Tavistock very widely was the introduction by Michael and Enid Balint of discussion groups for general practitioners, in which all aspects of the doctor-patient relationship could be examined. This had a profound effect on general practice, and the model of the 'Balint group' has now been widely applied to many groups other than general practitioners, for example psychiatrists, paediatricians, health visitors and occupational therapists (Balint & Balint 1961).

Group analysis

The work of Foulkes and of his collaborators at Northfield Hospital – de Mare, James Anthony and others – led to the formation of the Group Analytic Society and, later, of the Institute of Group Analysis. Foulkes carried on his research and clinical activities firstly as St Bartholomew's Hospital, and later at the outpatient department of the Maudsley where he trained generations of psychiatrists in the elements of group analytic psychotherapy. Foulkes' model differed significantly from the strictly psychoanalytic, and in some ways more limited, viewpoint of Bion and Ezriel. He devised a new framework based not only on his psychoanalytic training but also on his understanding of social psychology and Gestalt psychology, the latter through his work with Kurt Goldstein in the treatment and rehabilitation of brain-injured German soldiers of the First World War. Foulkes holistic, organismic model, which gave a comprehensive theoretical framework to the practice of group analytic therapy has proved fruitful and enduring.

Brief therapy

In the post-war era, some analysts began to see the need for effective forms of short-term psychotherapy that could be based upon psychoanalytic principles. The work of Michael Balint's short-term psychotherapy workshop, its staff drawn from the Cassel and the Tavistock, was described by David Malan (1963) and this led to a brief psychotherapy research programme at the Tavistock Clinic. This further enhanced the international reputation of the Tavistock.

The staff at the Tavistock taught the principles of psychoanalysis and of dynamic psychotherapy to a very wide range of disciplines, especially doctors, psychologists, and social workers. Much of this programme was coloured by the predominantly object-relations and Kleinian orientation that characterised the post-war Tavistock. This again, rather like the fate of the British Psycho-Analytical Society before the war, led to a certain separation and isolation of the Tavistock from mainstream psychiatry. Many psychiatrists regarded the Tavistock as an elite group who were not prepared to modify their attitude or their techniques to bring them more into line with their psychiatric colleagues – an unfair accusation, especially if the work of Balint, Bowlby and Malan is considered. In recent years, the Tavistock has made attempts to become much more in touch with developments in psychiatry and other forms of psychotherapies, to extend its work into the community, and to learn from others as well as trying to teach.

THE NATIONAL HEALTH SERVICE AND PSYCHOTHERAPY

Since the war, psychoanalytic psychotherapists have helped to develop training in psychotherapy throughout the country. Through their work on the committees of the Royal College of Psychiatrists and on the Committee of the Joint Higher Committee for Psychiatric Training, they helped to fashion and to implement a network of psychotherapy services and training in most parts of the British Isles. Senior Registrar posts are now available in many regions, and the psychoanalytic monopoly on training for future psychiatrists specialising in psychotherapy no longer holds. Senior registrars who are often alone or in very small numbers in regions distant from London can yet obtain a fairly comprehensive training. Psychotherapists within the NHS have come together to form the Association for Psychoanalytic Psychotherapists, which now publishes its own journal and has created a platform for psychotherapists within the NHS.

Changes in mental hospital practice

The work of Maxwell Jones and Tom Main was influential in bringing about many changes in hospital practice. The move away from custodial practices was accelerated by the creation of ward discussion groups, and the attempt to create therapeutic communities in parts of psychiatric hospitals or in small specialist units characterised the first two decades after the war. Though these experiments were not uniformly successful, they did help to change the climate of mental hospital psychiatry. Some units attempted the difficult task of a psychotherapeutic approach to psychoses, notably at Shenley Hospital and at the Maudsley. The programme at Shenley was controversial, and was eventually much toned down, and the programme at the Maudsley, carefully fostered by Henri Rey and Murray Jackson, seems to have come to an end with their retirement.

Research and practice into the psychotherapy of psychosis, carried out in America within institutions such as Chestnut Lodge, has not had the same opportunities in this country. There have been no facilities set up for intensive psychoanalytic therapy of schizophrenia and therefore the work has largely had to be done within the realm of private practice. Pioneers such as Bion, Rosenfeld, Segal and others, largely drawn from the Kleinian group, have greatly enlarged our understanding of psychotic mechanisms, though their clinical results have not been systematically evaluated (see Chs 13 and 14).

The most careful systematic psychoanalytic work in psychosis is that of Thomas Freeman (1988). Trained in the classical tradition of Anna Freud, Freeman has worked in the relative isolation of Scotland and Northern Ireland and has combined the career of psychoanalyst with that of consultant psychiatrist. His work with chronic schizophrenia, with delusions and hallucinations and with borderline patients is an important contribution. Together with his colleagues, Yorke and Wiseberg, Freeman has recently co-authored a book which links the developmental aspects of psychoanalysis with the phenomena of clinical psychiatry (Yorke, Wiseberg & Freeman 1989).

BRITISH PSYCHOANALYSIS

This section will briefly review some of the outstanding contributions made by British psychoanalysts to international psychoanalysis. These come from the Kleinian school, the Independent Group and, as outlined above, from Anna Freud's group. The achievements of the Independent Group are well set out in Kohon's *The British School of Psychoanalysis, the Independent Tradition* (1986). An interesting synthesis of British contributions to psychoanalysis, unfortunately excluding that of Anna Freud, is that of Hughes (1989), *Reshaping the Psychoanalytic Domain, the Work of Melanie Klein, W R D Fairbairn and D W Winnicott*.

The English school of psychoanalysis had already started to develop along its own lines in the 1920s, before Melanie Klein arrived in 1926. This can be related to the geographical distance of London from Vienna, to some of the cultural features that have been alluded to above in discussing the work of Suttie and Bowlby, and also to the particular character of the early generations of British psychoanalysts. Those with a medical background were mostly well-established neurologists and psychiatrists who were attracted to psychoanalysis because they saw it as a sound development within psychiatry, and a liberation from dogmatic neurological materialism. There was also a significant number of lay analysts and they, like most of the psychiatrists, came from the British upper-middle class. Some came from, or had close links with, the group of Cambridge intellectuals who formed an important part of the Bloomsbury Group, and who were well connected socially and were part of a progressive intellectual elite. James Strachey, the translator of Freud, was the brother of Lytton Strachey; Adrian Stephen, the younger brother of Virginia Woolf, and his wife Karen, a philosopher who had studied under Bertrand Russell; both qualified in medicine to become psychoanalysts; Joan Riviere was a member of the distinguished Verrall family of Cambridge intellectuals; John Rickman came from an upper-middle-class Quaker family, and the Glovers from Scottish Presbyterian families. The British group – solid, progressive and professional – thus contrasted greatly with the rather polyglot collection of early Viennese analysts, many of whom came from rather Bohemian and artistic circles, were highly neurotic though talented and, as a group, were often rent with conflicts and rivalries.

The very fact that Melanie Klein was invited to Britain and received the attention and support that she did, shows that the British group was ready to explore her radical approach to the child's mind. Reflecting the influence of Ferenczi and Abraham, Melanie Klein's work emphasises: the importance of very early object relations; the importance of projection and subsequent re-introjection under the influence of the child's instinctual drives, in particular of destructive aggression; and the very early establishment of oedipal relationships. The significance of the real relationship with the mother seems at times almost to have disappeared under the power of projection, although Klein does maintain that good mothering experiences are important in enabling the child to survive the very painful and dangerous early experiences of infancy, when the infant has begun to conceive of, and to perceive, the mother as dangerous and bad.

W R D Fairbairn, much influenced by Klein's work but working in isolation in Edinburgh, moves further from Freud than had Klein, in that he discards the concept of the libidinal drive altogether. For Fairbairn, the libidinal aim is the establishment of satisfactory object relations, and the prime need is not the release and relief of libidinal tension but living out a gradual consciousness of emotional dependency. Fairbairn's developmental line is from immature dependency to mature dependency, that is, he regards the person as always engaged in dependent relationships, by which he primarily means the dependency upon internal objects. For Fairbairn, the concept of the impulse, the instinctual drive, is replaced by a dynamic structure, and thus he is able to dispense with Freud's theories of mental energy which, for Fairbairn, represents an outmoded and irrelevant scientific model (Hughes 1989).

Although Fairbairn sees the mother as being the essential object of the child's needs, he devotes relatively little attention to the actual behaviour of the mother and the way in which she significantly affects the child's development. It was Donald Winnicott, a paediatrician who had moved to psychoanalysis, who placed the mother into a central position in the developmental situation. How the mother handles her child, how she responds to the child's needs and how she adapts herself actively to the child's development is at the centre of Winnicott's contribution (Hughes 1989). The mother is both environment and object. She is that which surrounds the child from birth, replacing the intra-uterine environment with an extra-uterine one in which all the child's biological and physiological needs have to be met by her. She is also the object mother, the person who has to be found and subjectively created by the infant, the 'subjective-object' who gradually becomes an 'objective object' as the child's capacities to deal with reality develop. She is also the object who has sensitively to begin to 'fail' her child, that is, gradually withdraw her ministrations so the child can begin to take over from her and meet his own needs. Naturally, Winnicott links his ideas about the significance of the mother's holding of the child in the maternal setting to the analytic situation. For him, the setting of analysis, the constancy and reliability of the analyst, his presence and his way of being with his patient are of the greatest significance in the analysis, particularly in the analysis of patients who have regressed to very early developmental stages. Winnicott's work is full of stimulating paradoxes, such as his statements that when he interprets to a patient, it is basically to show him that he does not understand him! By this, Winnicott means that the analyst has to show his patient that he is not omnipotent and omniscient.

This developmental line of Klein, Fairbairn and Winnicott characterises the British school of object-relations. Much of this work has been accepted by the followers of Anna Freud, although considerable differences still exist, such as the Freudian rejection of the Kleinian concept of the death instinct, and of seeing the transference situation as being based almost entirely upon the patient's projections, and in the nature and timing of interpretations.

ANALYTICAL PSYCHOLOGY (Fordham 1979)

There was little in the way of an organised school of analytical psychology in the 1920s and 1930s, although Jung had a considerable influence in Britain and made several visits. In 1914, he was invited to address the annual general meeting of the British Medical Association in Aberdeen. In 1919, with William McDougall in the chair, Jung addressed the section of Psychiatry of the Royal Society of Medicine, to whom he spoke again 20 years later in 1939. He held two seminars, one in 1923 and one in 1925, and in 1935 gave five seminars at the Tavistock Clinic. In 1938, Jung chaired a conference of the International General Medical Society for Psychotherapy, in Oxford.

Jung's principal disciple and exponent was H Godwin Baynes. An Oxford rowing blue and an important member of Rupert Brooks' circle of friends, the 'neo-Pagans', Baynes both translated Jung's work and represented it stoutly. Before the war, the Analytical Psychology Club and the Society of Analytical Psychology were formed; the latter was the training organisation and consisted originally of medical analysts. The predominance of medical analysts is built into the structure of the Society, of which Michael Fordham has been the leading member for many years. Fordham, who worked in child analysis as well as adult analysis, has made many important contributions to both theory and technique. Jungian ideas were represented at the Maudsley by E A Bennet and by Robert Hobson, but Jungian thought is conspicuous by its absence at the present day Tavistock Clinic.

There are interesting similarities between many aspects of analytical psychology and the object-relations school of British psychoanalysis, particularly the work of Klein, Winnicott and Fairbairn. Samuel, in *Jung and the Post-Jungians* (1985) has sought to demonstrate a steadily increasing approximation of Jungian and psycho-analytical ideas.

Psychoanalysis and psychiatry

Psychoanalysis in Britain has a good international reputation and is probably more recognised abroad than it is within this country. Academic psychology and psychiatry has maintained a distance and a resistance to psychoanalysis, though it has absorbed and integrated many psycho-analytic concepts without fully acknowledging them. Whereas before World War II psychoanalysis was isolated from mainstream psychotherapy and psychiatry, there has since then been a useful diffusion across the boundaries of the discipline.

Psychoanalysts are now much more engaged in the practice and teaching of psychiatry and of psychoanalytic psychotherapy, although this work does remain concentrated in London. Psychoanalysts have contributed to the development of a psychotherapeutic service within the NHS in the areas of individual, group and family therapy. Psychoanalytic theory has been greatly revised under the impact of the British school of psychoanalysis, and this work has led to interesting prospects for the understanding and treatment of the more severe personality disorders and the borderline and psychotic states. Child analysis has flourished in this country under the rival influences of Melanie Klein and Anna Freud. General practice has been greatly influenced by the work of Michael Balint and his followers, and the Balint-type discussion group has been adopted in many other areas of medicine and psychiatry. The British Psycho-Analytical Society has become much more open in recent years, and its influence should grow as a result.

CONCLUSION

Seventy years ago the psychodynamic approach began strongly to influence psychiatric practice in Britain through the experience of World War I, when large numbers of patients had to be treated and quickly rehabilitated. The British psychodynamic approach was largely based on Freud's ideas, but the influence of the small number of psychoanalysts was limited by their need to maintain a separate identity and only to practice psychoanalysis which of necessity took place entirely in the private sphere.

The outpatient clinics, such as those at the Tavistock and the Maudsley, and the York Clinic at Guy's Hospital, and the inpatient units, such as at the Cassel and some of the progressive mental hospitals, were staffed by psychiatrists who utilised some psychoanalytic and psychodynamic principles and practices and combined them with an empirical approach, using counselling, suggestion and persuasion.

Changing social attitudes to the mentally ill in the 1920s and 1930s allowed more optimistic and more liberal forms of treatment to take place in the mental hospitals, and the staff of these hospitals began to establish outpatient clinics for the diagnosis and early treatment of psychoses and neuroses. However, psychoanalysts and psychiatrists remained relatively isolated from one another until World War II, when they came together as teams for the first time. Psychodynamic and sociodynamic concepts, inspired mainly by the former staff of the Tavistock Clinic, were then accepted, tried and made their impact in military psychiatry. These psychiatrists and their pupils became a significant force over the next two decades, accelerating the pace of change in the mental hospitals and pressing for the acceptance of, and training in, psychotherapy for general psychiatrists. In this respect, there have been significant changes, and psychiatric training now has a definite psychodynamic component.

The post-war years have also seen the emergence of the new profession of clinical psychology, which now seeks autonomy and parity with psychiatry. Many clinical psychologists are analytically trained, and treat and teach in geographical areas where psychoanalysts, who still largely cluster in and around London, do not practice. Psychologists who have subscribed to behavioural methods are often in practice combining psychodynamic and behavioural principles.

Group psychotherapy has emerged as a strong force, and clearly has an important and growing place in the National Health Services and Community Psychiatry and in the sphere of the Social Services.

Psychoanalysts and analytical psychologists have contributed significantly to the National Health Service psychiatry, and the pre-war isolation of psychoanalysts from psychiatry no longer pertains. However, few academic positions within psychiatry are filled by psychoanalysts, and at the time of writing there is only one chair in psychotherapy in Britain, in sad contrast to the situation that exists both in other European countries and in North America. It is to be hoped that this will not for long continue to be the case.

In retrospect, psychodynamic psychiatry has a good record in Britain. There is much yet to be done, but progress cannot occur faster than society will accept and foster. The great social changes of the past two decades – much greater awareness of mental health issues, the closing of the large mental hospitals and consequent need for improved community health resources, the changes in social consciousness which have both allowed for and been stimulated by the rise of feminism – bode well for the psychodynamic approach in contemporary psychiatry. Public recognition that psychiatric needs cannot be met solely and simply by pharmacotherapy should exert considerable pressure on the psychiatric profession and their masters to improve the provision of psychodynamic services, despite the real difficulties that exist in practising psychotherapy or using psychodynamic approaches within the setting of the National Health Service.

FURTHER READING

Main T F 1989 The ailment and other psychoanalytic essays. Free Association Books, London
Suttie I D 1988 The origins of love and hate. Free Association Books, London

3. Group processes in psychiatry

M. Hobbs

INTRODUCTION

An awareness of group processes is essential to psychiatry.

The use of group methods in the *treatment* of psychiatric disorder, as in group psychotherapy, is only one particular example of the operation of group processes in psychiatric settings. An understanding of such processes is necessary in many areas of mental health practice other than in treatment itself.

Each person can be considered in a social context, and has a history of relationships with others. Similarly, each psychiatric disorder has an interpersonal and social dimension, and this may contribute to the disorder (as when family conflict contributes to a neurotic breakdown) or may be the product of it (for example, the social withdrawal which is a common feature of depressive illness). A holistic approach to mental health practice requires that we do not view the individual as an isolate, but as a member of a family and a wider social group. Failure to do so may well limit the effectiveness of treatment. For example, the treatment of a schizophrenic patient is undermined by the continuation of high levels of expressed emotion in his social or family environment; or a woman's depression may be maintained by persisting conflict with her husband.

In the practice of psychiatry, every activity is undertaken in a group context or against a backdrop of the group; and this reflects the fundamental natural relationship between the individual and his social context. The individual patient is treated in the group setting, even when the prescribed treatments are exclusively physical. The inpatient is treated in the social environment of the ward and hospital; the day-patient, in the group milieu of the day hospital, but in conjunction with the family or social context to which he returns each evening; and the outpatient in his natural social context. Similarly, the team, the ward and the hospital within which a staff member works are all groups which have their own particular and characteristic dynamics.

It is for these reasons that an understanding of group processes is fundamental to the good practice of psychiatry, whether or not the practitioner actually uses group methods directly in the treatment of patients. Group psychotherapy is a direct application of group methods to the treatment of patients with psychological problems; but other treatments are conducted in a group context, drawing more or less on the psychological processes of the group for their therapeutic effect. Because most psychiatric disorder derives from, and gives rise to, interpersonal difficulties and social problems, the group is the necessary context in which to treat patients.

GROUP DYNAMICS

Primacy of the group

We are all born into, and grow up in a natural group, the nuclear and extended family. We are educated in groups, and most of us go on to work and play in group settings. Recreational and social activities define our membership of groups in adulthood, and most of us proceed to reproduce the family group through sexual partnership and procreation.

Although much human energy is devoted to the finding, development and sustenance of relationships with one other person, as in a sexual partnership or close friendship, this dyadic relationship, when healthy is set firmly in its group context, in the family or among other friends.

Psychological maturation can be thought of as a continuous process of development from 'individual-ism' to 'social-ism'. There is a tendency in our present materialistic and individualistic society to view the individual in isolation, sometimes as if more important than the groups of which he or she is a member. It is this author's view that this trend towards individualism is both group destructive and anti-social, and a potent cause of both social and psychological disorder.

Individual and group: intrapsychic and interpersonal processes

The relationship between the individual and the group is fundamental to our understanding of the human, in health and in illness. This understanding is enhanced by psychological theories which construe the individual as a social being or group member.

Freud, in his earlier work, elaborated a metapsychology which emphasised *intrapsychic* processes, and which viewed the human as essentially pleasure-seeking and individualistic. Even so, Freud identified the primary impulses, or instincts, which motivate humans as *interpersonal* in nature: loving and hating others (or objects, in psychoanalytic terminology).

Object-relations psychology is a later development of psychoanalytic theory which is associated particularly with the 'British School' of Balint, Winnicott, Fairbairn and Guntrip (Sutherland 1980). According to object-relations psychology, the human is not motivated primarily by pleasure-seeking or destructive impulses, but by a need for closeness and intimacy with another person. As Fairbairn (1949) put it, 'libido is not primarily pleasure seeking, but object seeking'. Winnicott (1960) said that 'there is no such thing as an infant', meaning that an infant cannot exist in isolation. Whenever one finds an infant, one finds a mother (or alternative care-giver); and without maternal care there can be no infant.

Object-relations theory proceeds from a relational definition of the individual to an elaboration of the process by which, through experience of relationships, the individual develops an *internal* psychic world which is populated by internalised images of formative relationships. These *internal object relationships* act as blueprints or templates for the perception and development of later relationships. Collectively, they constitute an *internal group*, which is an inner representation of the history of relationships of which the individual was part.

Thus, there is a dynamic relationship between intrapsychic and interpersonal processes, between the individual and the group. Foulkes & Anthony (1957) wrote: 'there can be no question of a problem of group versus individual, or individual versus group. These are two aspects, two sides of the same coin'. Ashbach & Schermer (1987) re-iterate this anti-reductionistic viewpoint, observing that 'person and group exist in a complementary relationship'. They go further, asserting that 'the individual and the group emerge from a primal unity through the creation of a boundary which distinguishes one from the other'. Indeed, Ashbach & Schermer suggest that the individual and the group are complementary and inter-related configurations, derived from different positions in a hierarchy of object relations.
positions in a hierarchy of object relations.

Projection and transference in the group

Each person tends unconsciously to recreate the constellations and dramas of earlier relationships, especially those within the family.

Each person's perception of, and relationship to the groups of which he is part, will be mediated and potentially distorted by his internal world of object relationships. Put another way, each person has *transference*s to the group, its individual members and subgroups.

Case study 3.1   Projection in a member of staff

Jim, a staff nurse on an acute psychiatric ward, tended to view the ward generally, and its community group meetings in particular, as a hostile and unproductive environment; but he valued highly his relationships with individual patients and colleagues. The intensity and polarisation of his feelings surprised both Jim and his colleagues, until he was helped in a staff group meeting to realise the connection with his bewildering and frightening early childhood experience of being removed from his mother and taken into care in a children's home. Jim *projected* onto the ward his internal representations of that earlier group experience.

Case study 3.2   Splitting and transference

Anne, a severely neurotic young woman, formed a clinging attachment to the senior (female) nurse on the ward, but viewed the (male) consultant with contempt and was utterly dismissive of the junior staff and other patients. These processes were examined in a ward group psychotherapy meeting, where it emerged that Anne had been mother's favourite among many siblings in a family which was abandoned by an aggressive and alcoholic father. Her transference to the patients and staff of the ward recreated the constellation of the relationships within her family.
Whether or not these dynamic processes are explicitly exposed and explored psychotherapeutically, an understanding of them facilitates good psychiatric practice. An appreciation by the staff of Anne's family experience prevented the ward sister and consultant from falling out over her management, and enabled them not to dismiss her clinging behaviour pejoratively as 'attention seeking' (a common mistake which is generally the product of ignorance of dynamic processes). It also prevented their allowing Anne to be *scapegoated* by the patient group, many of whom resented her dismissive attitude and were jealous of her apparently close relationship with the ward sister.

Scapegoating is a product of multiple projections by other group members of their own bad feelings onto one particular member who, like Anne, often unconsciously invites it. Unchecked, scapegoating can lead to the isolation and exclusion of the victim in a way that often repeats earlier patterns of experience, compounds their psychiatric problems, and inhibits therapeutic change.

Systemic perspectives

It can be helpful to view the psychiatric ward or institution as an organisational system according to the principles of General Systems Theory. An institution can be seen as an inter-related hierarchy of systems. The ward, for example, is a system within a suprasystem (the hospital) and is composed of a number of subsystems (the patient group, staff team, defined activity or therapeutic groups, etc.). Each individual patient or staff member constitutes a lower order subsystem. Each individual's internal world of object relationships represents the base level within this hierarchy of systems (Kernberg 1975).

Each component of a system is in dynamic relationship with every other component of that system, so that potentially a change at one level in the system can have an impact on each other level and on the system as a whole. For example, the suicide of a patient in hospital has a dramatic impact on the patients and staff on the ward of which he or she was a member; but also has an impact on other wards in the hospital and often on the institution itself. Conflict between two senior staff members has an impact on their respective teams and wards, on each individual member thereof (the subsystems) and, potentially, on the whole hospital (the suprasystem). Thus, events and processes at one level within a system have an effect on both higher and lower levels of that system. In general, the impact diminishes with increasing remoteness within the system.

Levine (1980) has suggested that the ward psychotherapy group functions as a 'biopsy' of the milieu of which it is part. It is for this reason that, apart from its inherent therapeutic potential, the ward group is a valuable diagnostic activity. The group will often display patterns of relating, and other dynamics, which reflect processes occurring within the ward as a whole (for example, interpersonal conflict, subgrouping or mourning) or within individual members of it. The group is influenced by, and gives expression to, the dynamic processes occurring within its suprasystem and various subsystems. The value of being able to observe such processes is that it permits accurate diagnosis of their source and potential impact on the ward and its individual members, and may allow pre-emptive intervention where the dynamic processes are potentially destructive.

Defensive processes in groups

There is a natural regressive tendency in groups, which results in the surfacing within each individual group member of processes which hitherto were unconscious. In this way, the individual's internal world of object relationships is exposed and magnified in the group, putting him in touch with the anxieties associated with earlier experiences and conflict. Unless the individual is attuned to his own mental experience, the emerging anxiety is often felt to be inexplicable and therefore is unconsciously resisted. At this point the individual's characteristic *defence mechanisms* come into play in the group.

For this reason, the group is a useful medium in which to identify and 'diagnose' dynamic processes within its members which otherwise would be obscured.

Defensive processes may operate solely within the individual, or may be subscribed to by some or all members of the group. Scapegoating, as described above, is an example of a 'group level' defensive manoeuvre.

Within institutions, group level defences may operate in the staff, either intermittently at times of crisis, or constantly if the nature of their work is inherently anxiety provoking. Menzies (1959) drew attention to the way in which defensive social systems and working practices are constructed within hospitals as a means of protecting the staff from the anxiety and distress which is inevitable when working with sick and dying patients.

Defensive processes, whether they operate within the individual or within the group or institution, characteristically have a depleting and restrictive effect on those who operate them. Thus, although defences serve to protect the individual from anxiety, they will inevitably also limit his or her effectiveness. At a group level such processes may also undermine the therapeutic effectiveness of a ward or institution.

THE GROUP AS A THERAPEUTIC ENTITY

Before addressing the specific therapeutic applications of groups in psychiatry, it is worth considering those general properties of groups which can be promoted to therapeutic advantage.

In order to do this, the point made above about the universal interpersonal dimension to psychiatric and psychological disorders will be developed further. All such disorders are associated with disruptions in the individual's personal relationships. Neurotic and personality disorders both *originate* in disturbances of relationships, and are almost always disruptive *to* social relationships. Seen another way, psychological disorder is group-disruptive, isolating or dislocating the individual within his social network.

The crucial aspect of this for treatment is that the individual's social dislocation is re-created and re-enacted in the context of the therapy group, as in all other group settings. Each member will demonstrate in the group, in vivo, the ways in which he obstructs free and productive interaction with others. Deriving from the inner world of object relationships, such obstructive processes are mostly unconscious. The individual does not realise he possesses, and cannot readily control, his socially unproductive and isolating attitudes and behaviours.

Foulkes (1964) saw such disturbances in interaction as unconscious communications of the 'symptom', or symbolic expressions of the individual's internal disorder. He suggested that, while unconscious and private, such disturbance is pathological; but that, when communicated publically in the group, the 'symptom' is available for scrutiny and change. The process of making hitherto unconscious processes public, defuses them of their pathological potential. For such communication to be therapeutic, however, it needs to be received consciously within the group. This implies that the group-, or socially-disruptive processes within the individual need to be perceived, acknowledged, and spoken about with others in the group.

The group-analytic view, then, is that the healing properties of the group derive from the opportunities for active re-creation of each individual's inner disturbance and the public articulation of hitherto unconscious processes. Foulkes believed that the group has a normalising influence on each of its members: collectively, the group constitutes the very norm from which, individually, each of its members deviates (Foulkes 1948).

Of course, there are other ways of conceptualising the therapeutic function of the group. For example, Stock Whitaker (1985) referred to the 'corrective emotional experience' which is afforded to each member of the therapy group. In the group, the individual has emotional experiences which repeatedly challenge and correct the habits and expectations derived from earlier interpersonal events. The old, dysfunctional patterns of behaviour and relationships can then be relinquished.

Empirical research suggests that patients conceptualise these therapeutic processes rather differently. By asking patients to identify the events and experiences in therapy which they found most helpful or curative, researchers have differentiated a number of therapeutic factors or processes which operate in groups. The permutations of therapeutic factors which are identified and valued by patients differ greatly from one type of therapy group to another.

Bloch & Crouch (1985) define a *therapeutic factor* as 'an element of group therapy that contributes to the improvement in a patient's condition and is a function of the actions of the group therapist, the other group members, and the patient himself'. Their own classification enumerated ten therapeutic factors. These are:

1. universality; the recognition that one's problems are not unique
2. acceptance; the sense that one is valued and belongs to the group, an experience which is associated with the degree of 'cohesiveness' of the group
3. altruism; the experience of being helpful and of value to others
4. guidance; the receipt of information or advice
5. instillation of hope; gaining a sense of optimism about the possibility of therapeutic progress
6. catharsis; the experience of relief through expression of feelings
7. self-disclosure; revealing personal information about oneself
8. interpersonal learning; learning from one's constructive and adaptive relationship with others
9. vicarious learning; learning about oneself through the observation of other group members, including the therapist
10. self-understanding; the generation of self-awareness and understanding of one's actions and motives.

It can be seen from this list that several of the factors described identify different facets of the *sharing* of experience in the group (universality, acceptance, altruism and instillation of hope); others refer to the *communication* of this experience (catharsis, self-disclosure); while yet others refer to what is *learned* from examining such communications (interpersonal learning, vicarious learning, self-understanding).

This list is not exhaustive, of course, nor are the factors differentiated mutually exclusive. A controversial additional factor is the corrective recapitulation of family dynamics, which may be important particularly in analytic group therapy. Nevertheless, this list does give some indication of the therapeutic process as experienced by the patient.

GROUP TREATMENTS IN PSYCHIATRY

Group processes are used in three discernible ways in the treatment of psychiatric patients. Although there is considerable overlap between the categories in practice, they can be differentiated as follows:

1. the group as a *medium* in which other specific treatments are conducted
2. the group as the *milieu* for treatment
3. the group as a specific *method* of treatment.

Medium

As indicated above, all treatment in a psychiatric ward or day hospital occurs in a group environment. Often, the group, comprised of the patients and the staff on the ward or unit, is simply the context in which various specific treatment activities take place.

Specific psychological treatments which are conducted generally on a one-to-one basis are sometimes undertaken with patients in a small group. This might be for reasons of administrative efficiency (more patients can be treated) or because the social dimension of the group facilitates the therapeutic work, such as in a social skills group. Although the treatment is conducted in a group format, the dynamics of the group are not addressed, and interaction between members of the group is fostered only in so far as it supports the primary treatment activity. That is, the group is secondary to the therapeutic activity between each patient and the therapist(s).

Examples of this approach include cognitive behavioural group therapy, and some active and creative therapies (e.g. art, music and dance therapies), though the latter merge into the category below of 'the group as a method of treatment' in the hands of many practitioners.

The principles of cognitive and behavioural treatments are described in Chapter 4. The application of these methods in a group context is described by Alladin (1988), who refers particularly to the group applications of cognitive therapy, anxiety management and assertion training, 'all of which have been developed as individual therapies and their application to a group format has been largely a matter of cost effectiveness'.

Alladin identifies four goals of cognitive behavioural group therapy:

1. to provide a safe social milieu in which patients can disclose their problems and experiment with different patterns of behaviour

2. to encourage social interaction through which members of the group obtain feedback from others with which to test their own impressions of themselves
3. to assist the participant's understanding of and application of behavioural and cognitive principles and methods
4. to promote 'de-medicalisation' of their problems.

In these forms of treatment, the inherent therapeutic potential of the group is implicit, but may not be acknowledged explicitly by its practitioners. It operates through such 'non-specific' factors as the experience of feeling accepted by others, of recognising that one's difficulties are experienced also by others, and the consequent generation of hope and optimism (cf. Ch. 1).

Milieu

In some wards, units and other institutions, the group setting itself has been fostered as a therapeutic milieu. That is, the therapeutic properties of the social environment are recognised and used to enhance other specific treatments which are carried out in the ward.

This process derived its impetus from the Therapeutic Community movement.

The Therapeutic Community is a model of therapeutic activity which draws on the inherent therapeutic potential of the *community* of patients and staff in a ward or other treatment setting. It's emphasis is on *social therapy*, the aim of which is the re-socialisation of patients who are socially dislocated, isolated or otherwise out of step with life in society.

The Therapeutic Community movement had its origins in military psychiatric practice in England in World War II (Whiteley & Gordon 1979, Kennard 1983; see also Ch. 2) The further development of Therapeutic Communities in the United Kingdom and North America in the 1950s and 1960s was stimulated by recognition of the negative effects of institutionalisation in mental hospitals (Goffman 1961, Stanton & Schwartz 1954) and the growing liberalism of psychiatry after the war. Other factors which promoted this development (Caine & Smail 1969) were: (1) the recognition by mental health workers of social influences in the aetiology and manifestations of psychiatric illness; and (2) growing dissatisfaction with the restrictiveness both of conventional psychiatric treatments and of classical psychoanalytic psychotherapy. Experimentation with a range of group treatments during this same period was stimulated also by recognition of the logistical problem of meeting the demand of large numbers of patients for psychological forms of treatment.

Therapeutic Community principles were employed in a variety of ways in a variety of settings. Clark (1965) differentiated those institutions which took on some of the attributes of the Therapeutic Community, for example the regular ward meetings of patients and staff, without incorporating its fundamental philosophy (the 'therapeutic community approach'), from the 'Therapeutic Community proper'. He identified some of the characteristics of the latter, including: (1) a size which permits each member of the Community to know and to be involved with every other member; (2) regular meetings of the whole membership of the Community; (3) adoption of a philosophy which construes the individual's difficulties as interpersonal, and therefore amenable to modification through social interaction; and (4) emphasis on examination of the roles and behaviours of the individual in the Community, with associated analysis of social events occurring in that context.

Rapoport (1960) identified certain principles which prevailed in, and seemed to define, the 'Therapeutic Community proper'. These were:

1. *communalism,* the recognition and emphasis of the shared aspects of experience in the Community, and the de-emphasis of hierarchical relationships.
2. *democratisation,* the expectation that each member in the Community, patient as well as staff, should exercise responsibility and power in the decisions made in the Community.
3. *permissiveness,* the tolerance by members of the Community of a wide range of 'deviant' behaviours, except where these threaten the very existence of the Community.
4. *reality confrontation,* the repeated challenge to and analysis of behaviours which demonstrate the individual's problem in relating to and living harmoniously with others.

In practice, the therapeutic activity in a Therapeutic Community is organised into several components. These are the Community meeting or large group, a vehicle for social therapy in which reality confrontation can occur; shared activities, both those which maintain the Community and its home (for example cleaning, shopping and cooking) and those which emphasise the creative and social aspects of the Community (for example, sport and recreational activity, as well as artistic and industrial production); and small group therapies, the principles and purpose of which will be explored below.

Case study 3.3   Modifying antisocial behaviour in a therapeutic community

The advantages of treatment in a Therapeutic Community can be seen when we consider the plight of Ken, a man in his mid-twenties who had a long history of disturbed interpersonal relationships and antisocial behaviour, including theft, drunkeness and violence. The youngest of six children, he had grown up in a deprived urban area and, throughout childhood, had been neglected by his depressed and alcoholic mother and subject to arbitrary punitive violence by his intemperate father. He was the focus for much resentment by his older siblings, apparently because he was perceived as the parental favourite; and Ken had spent several years in Care as a result of injuries inflicted by his father and brothers.

Previous attempts at outpatient treatment had failed, so Ken (who had no sustained employment) was admitted to a residential Therapeutic Community for young people with neurotic and personality disorders. In this context, although he claimed that he wanted to 'mend his ways' Ken proceeded inevitably to behave in a manner which provoked antagonism, resentment and rejection from other members of the Community. Grasping and belligerent, he was soon suspected of stealing money, and returned drunk to the unit on several occasions. Early in his admission, he courted discharge by threatening the patients and staff who challenged his behaviour.

Although his behaviour could be tolerated within the Therapeutic Community in a manner which would be impossible in most psychiatric wards, his antisocial actions were confronted in the community meetings and construed as threats to the Community which invited bad feeling, retaliation and rejection. Through repeated confrontation by his peers in the Community meeting, and by continued analysis of the unconscious motives for his behaviour in the small psychotherapy group of which he was a member, Ken came eventually to see that his behaviour maintained his lifetime experience of being a victim, disliked and rejected by others and thereby isolated socially. Gradually, over several months, he learned to anticipate the destructive social effects of his actions, and to modify his behaviours. He became more cooperative, and an active member of the Community. He developed close relationships in which mutual liking was sustained; and, in his turn, he became able to challenge constructively the antisocial behaviours of newer members of the Community.

Method

The category of group treatments in which the essential processes of the group itself are used as the primary tool of treatment is 'group psychotherapy proper'. The major therapeutic effect is obtained from the interactions between members of the group, as well as with the therapist. Indeed, in most forms of group psychotherapy, the relationships between the patients in the group have as much therapeutic potential as those between each patient and the therapist.

Group psychotherapy is practised in many settings, and with a number of aims. The author has found it useful (Hobbs 1988) to distinguish three aims of psychotherapy, which can be applied to group psychotherapy too: maintenance, restoration and reconstruction. Each will be considered in turn.

Maintenance

One aim of group therapy is the maintenance of an optimal level of psychological functioning in patients who function generally at a fairly limited or precarious level. Such patients, who may suffer chronic psychiatric illnesses such as schizophrenia or major affective disorder, or who are rendered vulnerable by chronic neurotic or personality disorders, are prone to breakdown of psychological functioning in the face of stress. Judicious support may reduce the patient's experience of stress, even in times of adversity, and may thereby reduce the frequency and severity of relapse.

Supportive group psychotherapy is the major example of a group treatment in which the primary aim is to maintain the patient's usual level of psychological functioning. All therapies are supportive to a degree, but supportive psychotherapies emphasise the use of supportive techniques, and do not promote processes which aim to change the patient. Change itself is stressful, and this population of patients generally lacks the capacity for understanding their problems in psychological terms, which is necessary for the success of most other psychological treatments.

In supportive group psychotherapy, as in other supportive psychotherapies (Ch. 9), a psychodynamic appreciation of the patient and his difficulties is helpful for the therapist both in order to maintain therapeutic relationships in the group, and to facilitate the active therapeutic process. The patients concerned are inclined to generate feelings of frustration, helplessness and even hostility in those around them in the group, including the therapist, and a psychodynamic understanding of these dynamics may prevent bad feelings from obstructing the progress of treatment. The therapist uses such understanding, without generally making interpretations in the group of the dynamics which he perceives. This covert psychodynamic work is of particular importance when the patient seems to test and exhaust the goodwill of the other group members and the skills and resources of the therapist.

The major technical components of supportive psychotherapy are as follows:

1. *Empathy.* The capacity of the therapist and other group members to communicate to a patient that they understand something of his experience is perhaps the most supportive aspect of the relationships which can develop over time in a group.
2. *Encouragement.* The therapist and the group encourage each patient to recognise and use his own strengths and capabilities, thereby combating demoralisation and promoting the patient's self-esteem.
3. *Explanation.* This can be helpful, particularly when a patient appears to be ignorant of the potential consequences of a particular event or

course of action. This may come from the therapist or from other patients.

4. *Guidance.* Generally given in the form of suggestion or advice, guidance may be necessary when a patient faces certain problems which he does not have the resources to overcome. Where possible, each patient is taught a method of problem solving with which to approach his difficulties (Pekala et al 1985).

5. *Practical support* may sometimes be essential in order to modify disruptive factors in the patient's life. The therapist might offer this support himself or, more often, might arrange for another group member or someone else to do so if the patient has been unable to organise such assistance himself.

In supportive group psychotherapy, much of the therapist's activity is devoted to facilitating mutual support between the patient members of the group. This has the advantage, when compared with individual supportive psychotherapy, that each patient derives benefit both from the support of the other group members and from being able to offer support to them reciprocally. The opportunity for *altruism* is often cited by patients as helpful in the whole range of group psychotherapies.

In view of the chronic nature of the psychopathologies of this patient population, the attendance by a patient of a supportive psychotherapy group tends to be prolonged. Such groups, typically, are conducted in day hospitals and similar settings to which patients with chronic illness have access during periods of remission in their illness and at times of stress. Generally, a supportive psychotherapy group is conducted by more than one therapist, and it may be an active policy to change the therapists fairly frequently, so that no one member of staff remains responsible for conducting the group for very long. This policy is advocated in order to limit the degree to which any patient in the group may become dependent on an individual member of staff, and to promote instead the patient's dependence on the group itself.

In this respect, supportive group psychotherapy offers a marked advantage over individual supportive psychotherapy, in which, even if patient and therapist meet relatively infrequently, the opportunity for the patient to become dependent on the therapist is great. Some practitioners suggest that the patient's dependence on the therapist is a problem which should always be avoided, and it is true that dependency may sometimes generate insurmountable difficulties for the therapist and the therapy. However, dependency is inevitable and unavoidable in many of the patients for whom supportive psychotherapy is indicated. From a psychodynamic viewpoint, it is likely that the emotional needs of these individuals were not satisfied in early life, and it is therefore both inevitable and perhaps appropriate that they should seek a consistent figure upon whom to depend in adulthood. Unfortunately, the dependency which is expressed is often complicated by conflicts and hostility which derive also from the failures of early relationships.

There is a pejorative tendency in psychiatry to view any expression of dependence by a patient as pathological and to be combated. By re-formulating dependence as an *attachment need*, Mackie (1981) has provided a theoretical understanding of such behaviours. However, many psychiatrists and other mental health workers are not comfortable with the dependency or attachment needs of their patients, and the structure of many training schemes and established posts is such that frequent staff changes undermine the attachment by patients to an individual member of staff. For these, as well as economic, reasons, there is a real advantage in the patient developing an attachment to a supportive psychotherapy group, rather than to an individual therapist. The patient members often meet outside of the group, thereby maximising the availibility of support. It is also found that the patients often develop an attachment to the day hospital or institution itself, a process which is helpful in maximising the patient's sense of obtaining support.

Case study 3.4   Dealing with demanding dependency in a day hospital

Gladys was a widow in her late fifties who had suffered a series of phobic, obsessional and dysthymic disorders throughout adulthood. She had no children, and had been unable to function independently since the death of her devoted husband 10 years previously. Her neighbours had quickly become exhausted by her complaints and demands, and had tended to avoid or reject her. Gladys' family doctor, towards whom she then turned for support, was unable to cope with her demands. She presented at his surgery frequently, with a succession of minor physical complaints. Recognising that Gladys could not function without emotional support, the doctor referred her to the local psychiatric day hospital.

Gladys' treatment contract involved attendance at the day hospital on three mornings each week. She was encouraged to join a supportive psychotherapy group, which was conducted by different members of staff each day. She derived benefit from being able to talk about her experiences, particularly the death of her husband and other emotional and practical problems which she faced. She obtained advice and encouragement from the therapists and other patients, and found comfort in their empathic support. More than anything, however, Gladys found relief in having a place where she felt she belonged and regular activities in which she could engage, demonstrating the importance of the day hospital as an attachment object for her.

Restoration

The aim of restorative group therapies is to restore effective psychological functioning in individuals who have been disabled by illness or events.

There are two main populations of patients for whom this treatment approach is applicable: (1) patients in crisis, whose usual coping resources have been overwhelmed by adverse experience; and (2) patients suffering acute psychiatric illness.

1. Crisis group therapy. The term 'crisis' refers to the psychological disruption generated when an individual's (or family's, or other group's) customary coping resources are overwhelmed by particular events or experiences (Hobbs 1984). The events which produce crisis include bereavement, physical illness and conflicts in interpersonal relationships.

The stage to which a crisis develops in an individual depends both on the nature of the adversity and other current circumstances, and on the pre-existing coping resources of the individual and those around him. Crises are manifested by states of psychological dysfunction ranging from brief episodes of psychological and physiological disorganisation (anxiety, restlessness, impaired concentration, insomnia) through to frank psychiatric breakdown or suicide.

Some crises are precipitated by events which would disrupt the normal psychological equilibrium of any person, such as the sudden death of a loved close relative or friend. In others, crises seem to be precipitated by relatively trivial events, such as seemingly minor difficulties at work or in relationships; but this is because adversity is superimposed on a specific or pervasive vulnerability in the individual. Thus, crisis is the product of the interplay between external events and internal dynamics.

Crisis in itself is a normal human experience. Everyone experiences crisis of some degree at intervals. Most crises are resolved by the individual with the support and assistance of those around him; 'I'll get by with a little help from my friends'. For example, most people, when bereaved, go through a period of grief (a particular form of crisis) which resolves eventually with the support of others and the passage of time. Such experiences of crisis are natural and inevitable. Their resolution can enhance the repertoire of coping resources, and promotes both psychological maturation and mental health.

Sometimes, however, because of the nature, severity or duration of crisis, an individual may require psychiatric intervention. Except in those patients for whom crisis has resulted in extreme dysfunction (perhaps the emergence or relapse of a serious mental illness, or a determined attempt at suicide), when intensive psychiatric care will be necessary, crisis intervention aims to assist the patient's own resolution of his crisis. The treatment process involves recruitment of support and assistance from family and friends, practical advice, and counselling to promote the patient's own problem-solving and decision-making ability.

Generally, crisis therapy is undertaken with individual patients, both because of the way in which psychiatric services are organised, and because of the acute onset, intensity and idiosyncratic expression of crisis in each patient. Sometimes, however, crisis therapy is undertaken in groups (Aguilera & Messick 1978). This approach is particularly useful for the individual in crisis who lacks social support. For such people, the group offers support and guidance while the patient tackles his own crisis, and he may learn from the experience of others. A group approach may also be applied when it is possible to bring together a number of patients who face a common problem. For example, crisis group therapy has been employed beneficially with groups of people who have been bereaved (Yalom & Vinogradov 1988), groups of patients who have undergone mastectomy or other amputations, groups of victims (e.g. of physical or sexual assault), and for professional teams (e.g. ambulance crews and hospital accident department staff) who have been exposed to particular traumas in their work, such as in the course of a major disaster (see Ch. 22).

The purpose of group therapy for people in crisis is to provide a forum in which, by virtue of their shared experience, each member of the group can gain from mutual support, mutual acceptance, catharsis and the opportunity to test out strategies for dealing with his own personal crisis. The task for the group conductor is to promote this mutual interaction and support in the group, while still attending to each member's particular experience and distress.

Case study 3.5   Crisis support for ambulance crews after a major disaster

Following a particularly horrific road accident in which a number of people died, including children, several members of the ambulance crews who attended the scene reported sick, became withdrawn at work and home, or complained of stress. A psychotherapist, who acted as a consultant to the ambulance service, brought together the personnel involved to meet in a group on three occasions. In this context, the men and women who had been directed to the accident were able temporarily to relinquish their usual competence and effectiveness, and shared their personal emotional reactions to the tragedy which they had witnessed. Some cried, others expressed this anger, and all were united by their revulsion at the injuries sustained by the victims. Through the group meetings, these personnel were able to support each other in an honest and realistic appraisal of their experience and their responses to it. As a consequence, their symptomatology subsided and all were able to resume their usual duties very quickly.

---

2. Inpatient group psychotherapy. Group psychotherapy is undertaken by patients suffering acute psychiatric disorders either as a primary treatment or, more commonly, as an adjunct to other treatment methods, including pharmacotherapy, behavioural therapy and individual psychotherapy. In either case, the aim of the group psychotherapy in this context is to promote restoration of the individual's pre-morbid level of psychological and social functioning.

Since many patients with acute psychiatric disorders are admitted to hospital, this treatment approach is usually known as 'inpatient group psychotherapy'. Of course supportive and reconstructive group psychotherapies are also practised in the inpatient setting; so it is necessary always to establish the model of treatment to which the term is applied. In this chapter, the unqualified use of the term 'inpatient group psychotherapy' will refer to a restorative model.

With the move towards community treatment, group psychotherapy with patients suffering acute psychiatric illnesses is undertaken increasingly in day hospitals and other day treatment centres. Obviously, the setting has an influence on the practice of group psychotherapy, but the way in which a group is conducted should be tailored to the needs of the patient population, rather than the institutional setting.

As noted above, acute psychiatric disorders always have an interpersonal dimension. For many patients, the psychotic or neurotic breakdown is precipitated, or even caused, by interpersonal factors such as friction, rejection or loss. The psychiatric illness itself places a severe strain on the individual's relationships with family and friends; and may sometimes fracture certain relationships completely. For these reasons, group psychotherapy is always a valuable adjunct to other methods of treatment.

There are other reasons why group psychotherapy is useful for psychiatric inpatients. The process of hospitalisation itself threatens the patient's self-image. Apart from the effects of the illness itself, the need for hospital admission is damaging to the patient's self-esteem, and hospitalisation also removes the patient from his familiar environment and, therefore, threatens his usual defenses and identity. Put another way, hospital admission 'takes away the social structures that reinforce our personal and inter-personal boundaries and that help to clarify the differences between our internal and external worlds' (Rice & Rutan 1981). It is also true that hospitalisation offers a supportive environment in which the patient can relinquish his everyday responsibilities and defenses. The combined effect of these processes is that admission to hospital is often followed by a period of *regression*. As Kernberg (1981) observed, hospitalisation tends 'to bring about an immediate regression toward the activation of defensive operations and inter-personal processes that reflect primitive internalized object relations'. The regressive process serves a useful diagnostic purpose in that the patient's internal world is exhibited; and, of course, this exposure and unsettling of the internal world facilitates the therapeutic process. The inpatient psychotherapy group offers a forum in which the patient's dynamics are displayed and observed, and in which therapeutic processes may be brought to bear on the patient's problems (Rice & Rutan 1987).

For the patient, the inpatient psychotherapy group serves to promote resocialisation and the restoration of more effective psychological functioning. The patient can learn something about his illness and himself, leading to an eventual improvement in self-image.

By virtue of the patient population and the context in which the groups are conducted, inpatient psychotherapy groups have certain specific characteristics. Compared to outpatient groups, the meetings of inpatient psychotherapy groups tend to be shorter (45 or 60 minutes) but more frequent (three, four or even five times per week). Each patient's attendance of the group will be limited generally by the duration of his admission to hospital. In an acute unit with a high patient turnover, the membership of a group will be changing rapidly; and this may be disabling for the therapeutic function of the group (Klein 1977). One of the most disabling consequences is that the group may not progress beyond an early developmental stage in which it remains preoccupied constantly with issues to do with formation and cooperation, and beset by conflicts over dependency and trust. As Rice & Rutan (1981) described it, the group is 'forever beginning'.

In this environment, the group conductor needs to work with aims and methods which are consonant with the nature of the group if its members are to achieve anything productive. Yalom (1983) has advocated a 'single session time-frame' to take account of the high patient turn-over. Although this may be unduly conservative in most British inpatient units, there is value for this kind of group work in conducting each session as if it were the only occasion on which this patient population is going to meet together. The implication is that therapeutic business which is started must be completed within the frame of the session, such that, for example, all emotions which are uncovered and all interpersonal issues which are exposed must be brought to some satisfactory and containing conclusion.

This is a difficult task for the staff conducting the inpatient group, who commonly are junior and unsupervised. All too often, the inexperienced therapist colludes unconsciously with the fantasy role created for him by the primitive dynamics of the group (Kernberg 1978), and he may become 'so involved in the group's internal life that he is no longer able to preserve the necessary boundary between himself as an individual and the group as a whole' (Turquet 1974). For example, instead of challenging and analysing the group's hostile projections onto senior ward staff, he may lead the group's members into a destructive confrontation with his own colleagues.

Furthermore, it is not unusual for the conductor to be working with the inpatient psychotherapy group simply because it is an expected responsibility of the post which he holds. Reluctance and scepticism about the value of this therapeutic activity, in conjunction with his own unresolved conflicts and his inability adequately to process the more malignant projections to which he is subject in the group, may lead to his adoption of a persecutory style of leadership (Meares & Hobson 1977).

Case study 3.6   The persecutory (and persecuted) therapist

A new psychiatric registrar, antagonistic to psychological methods of treatment, assumed responsibility for conducting a ward psychotherapy group with one of the nurses. He was always 'too busy' to attend supervision sessions, and did not make time to talk with his co-therapist or to read about inpatient group psychotherapy. At first, he behaved in the group in a very prescriptive and authoritarian manner, ignoring and over-riding his co-therapist. The group members, sensing his ambivalence and lack of confidence, alternated between silent withdrawal and dismissive challenges to his leadership. Having failed to recognise the anxiety inherent in the patients' behaviour, he construed it as 'obstinacy'. After several sessions, frustrated by their passivity and lack of progress, he accused the group members of sabotaging their treatment and refused to attend the group any more.

Some of the difficulties for the conductor of an inpatient psychotherapy group derive from the complex boundary phenomena which characterise it. These have to do both with the dynamic relationship between the therapy group and the ward and institution of which it is a functional part, and with the fact (unlike in the outpatient group) that there is contact between patients and, often, between each patient and the therapist between sessions of the group. Contact between patients outside of group sessions is inevitable in the inpatient setting. It may generate difficulties for the small group (e.g. defensive pairing, subgrouping, and group 'secrets'), but it may confer advantage. In the hospital setting, the therapist can learn about each patient's problems from observation of his behaviour outside of the group sessions as well as within them. Perhaps more importantly, the continuity of social life on the ward offers an opportunity for extended mutual support, sharing and altruism between the patients.

Several models of inpatient group psychotherapy have been proposed which take account of the special needs of inpatients, who may be severely disorganised and relatively inarticulate. Farrell (1976) described an active experiential approach in which self-discovery and self-determination was promoted by the use of active Gestalt and psychodramatic techniques as adjuncts to verbal communication. Klein (1977) described a treatment approach which employed active exploration of the patient's current concerns in order to promote reality testing and a sense of responsibility in the patients. Maxmen (1978) presented an 'educative' model, the goal of which was modification of the symptoms and problematic behaviours which were the reason for the patient's hospitalisation. His model, like many others described, recommended promotion of the patient's cognitive appraisal of the causes and consequences of their illnesses. In each of these models, the group conductor works in an active and directive manner, promoting interaction between the patients and focusing on current concerns and behaviours.

Yalom (1983) has suggested that more than one 'level' of group psychotherapy is necessary in the inpatient setting, in order to meet the needs of patients with widely disparate degrees of psychopathology. The most severely psychotic, depressed or hypomanic patients may not be able to make constructive use of any group activity. As the patient's recovery from the illness proceeds, generally as a result of physical treatments, the patient becomes emotionally available for interaction with others. At this point, the patient becomes able to benefit from group work which is oriented towards the promotion of social interaction, though perhaps in the context of a shared activity. This is the basis of much group work undertaken by occupational therapists with acutely ill patients, and it serves to encourage resocialisation and reality testing. Later in treatment, the patient recovers enough healthy ego-function to make use of a more ambitious restorative group psychotherapy, in which a degree of self-examination and learning can be encouraged, as in the models described above.

Although many inpatients have mixed feelings about participation in psychotherapy groups, there is evidence to confirm that they both value and benefit from the experience if the group is conducted appropriately. Studies of the therapeutic factors valued by patients in inpatient group psychotherapy demonstrate that, compared with outpatient groups, inpatients tend to rate more highly such factors as universality, acceptance, altruism and instillation of hope (Maxmen 1973), rather than interpersonal learning and self-understanding (Yalom 1985). Such findings confirm the importance of the conductor's active attention to the promotion of mutual support, trust and open communication in the group, rather than a detailed analysis of each patient's problems.

Reconstruction

Reconstructive group psychotherapies aim for recomposition and rebuilding of internal psychic structures through the individual's experience of interaction in the group.

Although ambitious, this aim of psychic 'reconstruction' follows from recognition that long-standing disorders of self-concept, of behaviour, and of relationships with others are the products of structural 'faults' in the individual's internal world. Reconstructive approaches to treatment aim to correct the lasting effects of deficits and distortions in early relationships, which have been internalised structurally within the individual's psyche. They aim to promote lasting changes to the internal order, diminishing the fixity and potency of destructive dynamics and enhancing, instead, the fluidity of healthy regulatory function.

Reconstructive group psychotherapy provides each patient with an opportunity for self-examination and change through open interaction with others. This process is intrinsically anxiety-provoking, and is not suitable for those patients who decompensate psychologically under stress (i.e. vulnerable individuals, for whom a supportive treatment is preferable) or who already experience an incapacitating level of arousal (e.g., patients in crisis or suffering acute psychiatric disorders, for whom a restorative treatment approach is necessary).

Reconstructive group psychotherapy is indicated for those patients whose psychological problems are of long standing, but who retain a capacity for observing and acting upon their interactions with others. In practice, the patients who derive most benefit from this treatment model are those who suffer from neurotic, personality or certain behavioural disorders, but who possess some effective ego function. Sometimes, it is possible for a patient to progress on to reconstructive group psychotherapy after recovery from an acute illness or crisis, perhaps as a progression from a restorative psychotherapy group.

An individual's *ego strength* is a measure of his personal effectiveness, and is, therefore, predictive of his capacity to make effective use of psychotherapy (Lake 1985). Certain personal attributes are indicative of ego strength, and therefore offer useful prognostic criteria when assessing an individual's capacity to benefit from reconstructive psychotherapy, including this form of group psychotherapy. These are generally enumerated as follows:

1. evidence of achievement in study, work and life generally
2. a history of mutuality ('give and take') in relationships
3. a capacity to tolerate anxiety and frustration, and to control impulses
4. psychological mindedness, i.e. a willingness to examine one's experience and difficulties in psychological terms
5. a capacity to express and verbalise feelings
6. motivation for self-examination, insight and change.

It has often been suggested that group psychotherapy is indicated exclusively for people with interpersonal problems; but, as elaborated above, it can be argued that all psychological and psychiatric disorders are associated with interpersonal problems, which may be more or less overt. Most psychiatric patients can benefit from group psychotherapy, providing that a group is selected which affords a level of therapeutic activity which is appropriate for the patient's current state. In the de-repressive atmosphere of a reconstructive psychotherapy group, the individual's interpersonal difficulties, themselves external manifestations of covert intrapsychic processes, will become apparent. In this way, all layers of the individual's psychological problem become available for scrutiny and modification in the group.

There are a number of models of reconstructive group psychotherapy, including Gestalt and psychodrama; but two models in particular are practised widely in psychiatry in this country – interpersonal and analytic group psychotherapies.

*1. Interpersonal group psychotherapy.*The interpersonal model of group psychotherapy, developed in the United States and promoted particularly by Yalom (1983, 1985) has been well described by Ratigan & Aveline (1988).

The interpersonal model of psychotherapy derives from an existential philosophy which is predicated on the following assumptions:

1. our actions are *not pre-determined*
2. we can exercise *choice* over our actions
3. we are *responsible* for our actions
4. death is an inevitability faced by us all, and our *mortality* offers potential meaning to our lives
5. we are engaged in a constant search for the *meaning* in our existence.

Existential philosophy contrasts markedly with the fundamental tenets of psychoanalysis, which emphasises the ways in which human actions are powerfully influenced by unconscious processes.

Interpersonal psychotherapies, therefore, emphasise the concepts of freedom, choice and responsibility, and promote the individual's attempts to define the meaning of his experience. In contrast to the analytic model, to be described below, the interpersonal model of group psychotherapy is essentially ahistorical (Ratigan & Aveline 1988). There is exclusive emphasis in the group on the '*here and now*' of current interactions and functioning, and little attempt is made to explore the historical origins of each member's difficulties.

Accordingly, the group conductor's tasks are to promote interaction between members of the group, and then to encourage their examination of their interactions in order to identify and modify the patterns of perception and behaviour which obstruct free and productive relationships.

Inevitably, this process requires that the group members take risks in disclosing their thoughts and feelings, especially those for other group members, including the conductor. The reward for each member is that, through this process, he obtains *relief* from his *expression* of hitherto pent-up feelings and thoughts, from the experience that others can still accept him, and from the sense of *belonging* which is thereby generated in the group. Furthermore, he learns about himself from the *feedback* obtained from other group members, and can proceed then to try out new, more constructive ways of relating in the safety of the group.

At its most powerful, the group can offer a *corrective emotional experience* to its members. Instead of responding to an individual's dysfunctional attitudes and behaviours in ways which repeat that person's destructive experience with others, the group provides a new experience which both contradicts that individual's expectation and enables him to recognise his unwitting invitation of destructive responses from others. From this point of enlightenment, having recognised his contribution to interpersonal problems, he can choose to modify his own pattern of relating.

Case study 3.7   The impact of group 'here and now' on a persistent pathological pattern of relating

In an outpatient group conducted on interpersonal psychotherapeutic lines, Simon began to get into difficulties repeatedly with the other group members. He tended to invite protective concern and advice, particularly from the women, but he always rejected and ridiculed their contributions in a most hostile manner. The group conductor understood that this had much to do with his relationship in early life with his mother, who was an intrusive and controlling woman who undermined his attempts to assert his own identity and will; however, in the context of this group, the therapist made no attempt to encourage exploration of the historical aspects of Simon's interpersonal difficulty. Simon had been referred for psychotherapy because he had become intensely depressed and suicidal following the breakdown of his marriage, the relationship having failed after only three years amidst acrimonious and sometimes violent argument. Simon's therapeutic experience in the group began when one of the women suddenly exploded with anger after being rebuffed by him yet again. The other members of the group were able to stand back from this confrontation, and then to point out to Simon how repeatedly he provoked anger and rejection by his contemptuous dismissal of the interest and concern which he evoked from them. They proceeded to suggest that this might have been the source of difficulties in his marriage.

Initially, Simon rejected this suggestion contemptuously, but the other members of the group stuck to their convictions and persisted in their challenge to Simon. Eventually, the validity of what they were saying began to dawn on him and, perhaps for the first time in his life, he began to look at his own contribution to interpersonal conflict and to assume responsibility for it. Inevitably, his behaviour did not change immediately for he often slipped unwittingly into his old patterns. Through the persistent efforts of the group, encouraged actively by the group's conductor, he became gradually more able to anticipate and modify his response to others. Eventually, he was able to report a positive shift in his relationships outside the group, and his progress was very evident within the group.

In summary, then, interpersonal group psychotherapy promotes self-awareness and permits experimentation with new ways of relating. It produces new freedom and responsibility in personal actions and interpersonal relationships.

The therapeutic power of these processes is confirmed by empirical research. Yalom (1985) reported the therapeutic factors identified by twenty successful long-term group therapy patients using a Q-sort. The items identified as most helpful by the patients included 'discovering and accepting previously unknown or unacceptable parts of myself', 'being able to say what was bothering me instead of holding it in', and 'other members honestly telling me what they think of me'. In terms of the therapeutic factors which these items represented, Yalom's study found that interpersonal learning, catharsis, acceptance and self-understanding were rated most highly by this group of patients. Yalom's conclusion was 'that therapy is a dual process consisting of emotional experience and of reflection upon that experience'.

2. Analytic group psychotherapy. Analytic group psychotherapy has been developed in Britain, and the group-analytic model (Foulkes 1948, Hyde 1988) is now particularly influential in this country.

The philosophy of analytic group psychotherapy assumes that the individual's functioning in general, and his characteristic patterns of relating in particular, are influenced by inner blueprints or templates which are established throughout life by the internalisation of images of formative relationships. Although the philosophy emphasises the essential *history* of the individual, analytic group psychotherapy actually resembles interpersonal group psychotherapy in the emphasis placed on examination of each member's *current* experience in the group. Analytic group psychotherapy differs from the interpersonal model in that the interactions in the group are also examined for the formative historical antecedents within each individual which are thereby displayed. Thus, in analytic group psychotherapy, examination of the 'here and now' experience in the group is used to reconstruct the legacy of the past as it is evidenced in the present.

One of the most potent sources of information about the individual's formative experiences and current internal world derives from examination of his *transferences* within the group. Transference can be defined as the transfer onto a person, or other entity, of feelings, attitudes and ideas which derive from earlier experiences in relation to another person. This 'transfer' is a process of displacement and projection. In the regressive and de-repressive environment of a relatively unstructured group, each member reveals patterns from his internal world of object relationships through the transferences which he develops to other individuals within the group, including the conductor, and to the group as a whole.

The group is perceived often as a maternal object, which has a containing *matrix* (Roberts 1982) into which the individual projects many elements of his internal world, just as an infant or child communicates his inner experience both consciously and unconsciously to the mother (James 1984). If the group is *receptive*, communications are encouraged and take on an increasingly deep nature. Accordingly, the material which becomes available for *analysis* derives from progressively deeper layers of the group members' unconscious experience.

At times, the individual's transferences to the group can be seen to re-enact early constellations of relationships within the family. One member may be perceived and related to as an older brother, another as a younger sister and another (not necessarily, but often, the group conductor) as a father or mother, and so on. Through examination of his interaction with others in the group, each member is helped to recognise, own and disclose intimate and painful aspects of himself which previously were split off and located unconsciously in others. From the analysis of these patterns of relationships in the group, the individual is enabled to recover formative memories and to reconstruct his own history. Thereby he becomes able to appreciate how and why he has perceived himself, acted and related to others in the manner which he does.

Analytic work in the group does not proceed by each member having a turn at talking about himself, with all the other members listening and then contributing to analysis of his material. This does happen at times, of course, but analytic group psychotherapy involves much more the generation of *free-floating discussion* amongst the group members, interrupted sometimes by a collective reflection on, and analysis of, their pattern of interaction and each member's contribution to it.

The group conductor's task is to facilitate open and honest communication in the form of discussion and dialogue, and then to encourage examination of this interaction for clues to each member's idiosyncratic contribution. Each member is enabled thereby to take responsibility for hitherto disowned aspects of himself, and for his characteristic obstructions to dialogue and relationships with others. Through this process, analytic group psychotherapy promotes integration of the individual's mental functioning and personality.

Case study 3.7 (contd)   Transference in group therapy

Let us imagine that Simon, the patient described above to illustrate the application of interpersonal group psychotherapy, was to become a member of an analytic psychotherapy group. In many ways, the therapeutic work would proceed similarly, for Simon's characteristic pattern of relating would emerge similarly and eventually would be recognised and challenged by the group members. In the analytic group, his characteristic way of relating to the women members of the group would be seen as giving expression to his formative experience of relating with a woman, and particularly his mother. The analysis of this element of his behaviour might illuminate for Simon his unconscious need to retaliate punitively against his mother for her intrusive control. The therapeutic process might enable Simon to recognise that the women members of the group were not being intrusive or controlling, but genuinely concerned and helpful; and he might come to see that the qualities of intrusiveness and rejection did not derive from them, but were disowned aspects of himself which he had projected into them. Thus, through recognition of the relationship between his transferences in the group, his marital relationship and his early formative relationship with his mother, Simon might become able to understand and take responsibility for his behaviours, and thereby to modify them. Initially, he could experiment with more aware and constructive ways of relating in the relative safety of the psychotherapy group.

Applications of reconstructive group psychotherapy

Interpersonal and analytic group psychotherapies are conducted, with patients selected for reconstructive group psychotherapy, in a number of formats, including:

1. long-term outpatient group psychotherapy
2. medium-term inpatient group psychotherapy
3. short-term focal group psychotherapy.

*1. **Long-term outpatient group psychotherapy.*** This is the classical model of group psychotherapy about which most has been written (Rutan & Stone 1984, Yalom 1985).

Six to nine patients, previously strangers to each other, are selected to compose a group heterogeneous in terms of psychiatric diagnosis, personal features and interpersonal styles. There is some experimental evidence to confirm that specific preparation of the patients for this form of group psychotherapy improves their subsequent engagement in the group, and it may thereby influence outcome positively.

The patients meet together with one or two group psychotherapists on a regular basis, generally weekly for one and a half hours. The group is either *closed*, starting with a patient membership which is maintained without change throughout the finite life of the group (usually eighteen months to two years); or it is *slow open*, in that the original patients graduate successively from the group, to be replaced by new members throughout the open-ended life of the group.

Long-term outpatient group psychotherapy is a specialised activity for selected patients, primarily those with certain neurotic and personality disorders who possess also some of the criteria necessary to ensure good outcome (see above). Typically, the group is composed of patients who suffer dysthymic disorders, disorders of self-concept, and clear-cut interpersonal difficulties. It may also be appropriate as a later continuing treatment for patients who have suffered acute psychiatric illnesses or psychological decompensation in crisis, particularly if these acute states had exposed long-standing psychological problems.

On a more specialised basis, outpatient reconstructive group psychotherapy is undertaken with homogeneous groups of patients suffering particular problems which are amenable to this treatment approach. Group psychotherapy is a common part of the treatment programme for alcoholics, drug abusers, and certain categories of mentally abnormal offender, particularly those manifesting personality disorders.

2. Medium-term inpatient group psychotherapy. Some patients admitted to psychiatric wards in states of acute psychiatric disorder are able to progress to inpatient reconstructive group treatment after partial recovery, perhaps by graduating from a 'lower level' inpatient group. For this reason, a hierarchical network of group activities is sometimes constructed in admissions units so that it becomes possible for patients to make use of a succession of therapeutic group activities during their admission and after discharge (Yalom 1983). The aim of the reconstructive group is both to assist the patient in the later stages of recovery, and to enable him to tackle in a lasting way the long-standing psychological problems which preceded, and may have predisposed him to, his acute psychiatric breakdown.

Reconstructive group psychotherapy is also undertaken in specialised inpatient units. Patients are selected for admission on the basis of their capacity to make use of therapeutic group activities. Reconstructive psychotherapy in small groups is part of the treatment programme, which might also include large-group or socio-therapy, other group activities, and sometimes individual psychotherapy in addition.

The patients for whom this intensive group-based approach to treatment is particularly indicated are those with pervasive neurotic problems or personality disorders, especially those with a history of destructive patterns of relating and of self-harm. In effect, many of the patients who are selected for treatment in inpatient psychotherapy units are those who attract a psychodynamic diagnosis of borderline personality functioning (Kernberg 1984). Although group work with borderline patients is difficult, especially when their psychopathology is severe, success has been reported providing that the psychodynamics are understood and certain therapeutic principles are adhered to.

Borderline patients who do not display marked acting-out can be treated successfully in weekly out-patient analytic group therapy. Pines (1980) recommends inclusion of no more than one or two borderline patients in an outpatient group. He suggests that the therapists work to emphasise the similarities between patients, and to combat the borderline patient's habitual tendency to isolate himself through antagonising and alienating others.

Borderline patients who demonstrate serious compulsive self-destructive behaviours or psychotic functioning require inpatient or day treatment, for this can afford a greater degree of structure. In unstructured settings, such patients tend to regress rapidly and dramatically. Marked swings in mood and attitude within relationships are common. Often, they form close dependent attachments to members of staff or other patients, but the frustrations inevitable in these relationships provoke rage and hostility in the patient, with attendant acting-out. Common staff counter-transferences are counter-hostility, labelling (the patient is 'bad', 'manip-ulative', 'attention-seeking') and rejection, so that a persecutory spiral ensues. The therapist's capacity to achieve and maintain a working relationship with the patient is thereby tested repeatedly to an extreme. Caparotta & Marrone (1981) argue therefore that a therapeutic alliance is a *goal* of treatment with borderline patients, and not simply a pre-requisite for therapy.

For this goal to be achieved, borderline patients require some degree of structure and tolerant limits in the therapeutic setting in order to contain their internal emotional chaos. The therapy group can itself afford containment and support, for other patients demonstrate remarkable degrees of acceptance and understanding. In the context of the group, the borderline patient's transferences are diluted, and some spontaneous challenge to his destructive behaviours may be accepted. Nevertheless, the patient will need to find his own level of interaction within the group, maintaining his own safe distance by perhaps participating silently or by coming and going. Such 'valve' action seems to be necessary sometimes for the patient to deal with intolerable internal pressures.

Macaskill (1980) has suggested that it is valuable for the therapist to identify the patient's destructive defenses and transferences through empathic interpretation of the past emotional insults and injuries which gave rise to his psychic pain. Challenging or invasive interventions by the therapist may threaten the patient's tenuous sense of self, leading to psychological disintegration and hostile acting-out; but 'soothing' interpretations of destructive patterns can lead to increased reality testing and self-understanding (Macaskill 1982). Over time, the patient comes to learn something about his sensitivities and his characteristic distorted interactions with others; and by internalising the healthy experiences of interactions in the group, he develops a more substantial and integrated internal object world.

One or two Therapeutic Communities specialise in work with patients manifesting sociopathic disorders (Whiteley 1986). In this context, through intensive therapeutic work in small and large group formats, sociopathic patients are helped to recognise and modify the antisocial aspects of themselves which have brought them repeatedly into conflict with others. Because of the depth of the psychopathology of these patient populations, the intensive group psychotherapeutic work needs to continue for a prolonged period, and so admission to a Therapeutic Community is generally for a period of several months or a year.

3. Short-term focal group psychotherapy.   Reconstructive group psychotherapy generally has broad aims, tackling substantial flaws in self-concept, pervasive problems in relationships, and fundamental disorders of personality; and for this reason treatment is generally prolonged. However, relatively short-term reconstructive psychotherapy is undertaken in groups when patients are selected to work on a particular focus or area of psychological malfunctioning. In particular, groups of three to six months duration have been found to be effective for patients with specific post-traumatic disorders, certain eating disorders and some specific psychosexual problems.

The purpose of reconstructive group psychotherapy with these populations is firstly to promote the patient's self-disclosure and sharing of experience, thereby overcoming his disabling sense of isolation and stigmatisation. When this has been associated with the earlier experience of a specific trauma, particularly childhood sexual abuse, rape or some other assault, the patient's disclosure of the traumatic experience is often helpfully associated with the expression of hitherto pent-up emotions associated with the experience. The group work proceeds with examination of the ways in which the traumatic experience or habit disorder continues to get in the way of the patient's healthy functioning, particularly in relationships. In this way, he is enabled to overcome the habit or outgrow the traumatic event, thereby permitting improvement in self-concept and the growth of a more outward, assertive and constructive outlook. The benefits of a short-term group approach to treatment are well exemplified by their application to women who were sexually abused in childhood (Hobbs 1990a; see Ch. 21) and those who suffer bulimia nervosa (Hobbs et al 1989).

The therapeutic factors identified by patients in focal psychotherapy groups vary, but tend to emphasise the importance of universality, acceptance and instillation of hope, as well as the self-understanding which derives from the therapeutic experience (Hobbs et al 1989).

OTHER APPLICATIONS OF GROUPS IN PSYCHIATRY

The T-group

The T-group, or training group, is a means of learning about group dynamics from participation in a group. Developed in the 1940s and 1950s at the National Training Laboratories in the United States, T-groups are still a common and valuable component of the education and training of staff in the mental health and other professions.

The T-group has an *experiential* emphasis. That is, its members experience what it is like to be in a group in which there is no set agenda or activity to disguise the emergence of characteristic patterns of communication and interaction. As well as learning something about the dynamics of groups from the inside, the individual in the T-group also learns something about himself in a group, that is, the way he feels, thinks and functions in the group context. The task of the T-group, promoted by its conductor, is to permit the development of association, interaction and dialogue in the group; and then, on occasions, to stand back from this spontaneous process in order to examine the dynamics which were thereby exposed.

This is not an easy task. The member of a T-group is required to oscillate between involvement in the free-floating discussion of the group, and then dispassionate observation and analysis of the process in which he had been involved. In this, it therefore resembles reconstructive group therapies.

At a practical level, membership of a T-group generally involves attendance at weekly sessions of one and a half hours duration, typically through a term or academic year. Intensive attendance of a T-group in the course of a weekend or week-long conference is a common alternative.

The staff sensitivity group

Most staff working in psychiatric settings are familiar with the notion of the staff sensitivity group. Not many have been members of an established staff group, however, and many myths (many of them persecutory) surround this activity.

The purpose of the sensitivity group is to support and assist the staff's effective therapeutic work with patients through enhancing their sensitivity to the psychodynamic processes inherent in it. The psychotherapist who conducts the sensitivity group aims primarily to enable the staff to make use of themselves, that is, *their selves*, to the full in the treatment of the patients (Hobbs 1990b). This task is achieved by the creation of a forum in which staff members can acknowledge and deal with the powerful emotions, conflicts and other dynamics generated by close contact and therapeutic efforts with very distressed and disturbed patients. The group can also assist in dealing with certain external constraints which otherwise might have a deleterious impact on morale and therapeutic effectiveness, such as new working practices which are imposed from outside of the unit. Through the work of the group, the staff's sensitivity to a variety of inhibitory and disruptive dynamics is enhanced.

Why should mental health staff, including qualified and highly experienced practitioners, need to be supported and assisted in their work with patients?

Working with psychiatric patients is often stressful. Some patients are unpredictable, aggressive or rejecting of our efforts to treat them. Some harm themselves or harm others, and continue to do so despite our professional interventions. Some patients succeed in killing themselves while in our care. All of this generates an emotional reaction, even in seasoned staff members.

At another level, some patients have a disruptive impact even though their apparent behaviour is unremarkable. Particularly in the inpatient setting, some patients demonstrate a capacity to generate powerful and conflicting attitudes and emotions in the staff treating them, and they may provoke antagonistic divisions between members of staff (Main 1957). This dynamic, *splitting*, is particularly associated with patients whose personality functioning is borderline.

A common occurrence in psychiatric units is that a staff member becomes stirred up emotionally by a particular patient, usually because the patient's distress or pathogenic experience resonates with some aspect of that staff member's experience.

Because of the stresses inherent in working with patients, who are themselves disturbed and disturbing, distressed and distressing, unconscious defensive systems tend to emerge collectively in the staff (Jaques 1955, Menzies 1959). Offering protection from distress, such defense systems sometimes become institutionalised in the organisation and running of a ward or unit. As noted above, however, such defensive processes are usually obstructive to effective therapeutic practice.

The staff sensitivity group, if it works well, can serve to identify disturbing processes within the staff of a ward or unit, and can promote constructive ways of dealing with these, without resort to defensive practices. Staff can derive mutual support from the examination of their work together, can express the feelings generated by events within the unit, and can examine their responses to patients and to each other. When conflicts between members of staff are generated or fuelled by dynamic processes deriving from the patients, the sensitivity group's work may be necessary to protect the therapeutic effectiveness of the team. When a patient is violent or commits suicide, an urgent meeting of the staff group may enable the staff involved to give expression to their own sadness, fear and pain.

Case study 3.8   Splitting and explosiveness in a staff sensitivity group

Tensions emerged between staff members following a dispute about the management of a young woman who had been admitted after taking a series of major overdoses. Having observed the patient on the ward for several days, the medical staff argued that she was neither clinically depressed nor suicidal, and that she should be discharged. Some of the nursing staff concurred with this view, because the patient was unco-operative and provocative. Other nurses argued that the patient was deeply distressed, and found that she was prepared to talk if approached sympathetically.

In one such exchange, the young woman confided to a nurse that she had been abused sexually and violently by her father during childhood, and that her mother had refused to believe this when the patient had summoned the courage to disclose her ordeal. The nurse had been abused herself in childhood, and her unresolved feelings about this may have contributed to her decision not to relay the information to her colleagues.

From the discussion about this patient in the next meeting of the staff sensitivity group, the effects of her splitting were evident immediately to the conductor of the group. Some of the staff, including most of the men present, adopted a very negative attitude towards her, and used terms such as 'manipulative' and 'sexually provocative' to describe her. Other staff demonstrated a supportive attitude, but were unrealistic in their acceptance of her destructive behaviours.

As the dispute proceeded, the nurse in whom the patient had confided suddenly exploded into a furious attack on the critics, accusing the men of violating the patient, and her women colleagues of betrayal. A bitter argument ensued. With difficulty, the group conductor pointed to the splits evident in the group and invited its members to examine their present conflict as an external expression of internal tensions within the patient.

At this point the nurse at the centre of the argument blurted out that the patient had been raped repeatedly in childhood, and then dissolved into loud sobs. The men present were very quiet, while some of the women consoled their colleague. She disclosed then that she knew what the patient was going through because she had also been abused in childhood; but she stated clearly that she did not wish to talk more about her own experience in this group.

From this point, the staff were united in concern for their colleague and for the patient. The group conductor pointed out that the patient's behaviour was a product of defences which she had erected to protect her fragile core self, and that she tended unconsciously to invite repetition of the traumatic ordeal of her childhood. Having achieved a more informed and dispassionate understanding of the patient, the staff were able to examine her problems and later evolve a constructive treatment plan without dispute.

The staff sensitivity group is not a therapy group, yet it deals implicitly and sometimes explicitly with the feelings, attitudes and conflicts of the staff in relation to their work. Without such an opportunity, individual members of staff may develop stress-related physical or psychological disorders, and the morale of the staff as a whole may suffer.

There are certain important features of the staff sensitivity group, and of its conductor. The membership of the group is not selected, but is defined by the staff membership of the ward or other unit for which it is created. Ideally, staff members should attend the group regularly. Problems occur if particular staff members do *not* attend the group, especially if these are senior staff. This is because all staff contribute to the effective functioning of a team. Promotion and maintenance of sensitivity to dynamic processes cannot be delegated by senior staff to their junior colleagues. The staff member who does not participate in the sensitivity group (and who may well not join in other group activities) is inviting negative attitudes and projections from his colleagues, and may become a target for much ill feeling in the unit.

Full attendance of a staff group is problematic, of course, particularly in an acute unit where some nurses will have to remain in the clinical area at all times. Nursing shifts hinder regular attendance too. In practice, staff groups can work well if timed to coincide with the hand-over period between shifts, and if there is a general spirit of active participation rather than avoidance of the group's meetings.

The sensitivity group meeting does not have an agenda because this can be used to obstruct or defend against the emergence of more distressing material. Yet it has a task, to come to a better understanding of the mutual interactions between issues to do with one's self, one's colleagues, one's patients and the institution in order to improve job performance (Bramley 1990). This task needs to be understood and agreed by all who participate in the group.

Like the therapy group, the effectiveness of a staff sensitivity group develops over time if the membership is relatively constant. In its early stages, when the staff are apprehensive about disclosure and challenge, and when collective defences may be prominent, the conductor will need to work hard to foster a supportive environment. At this stage, the group may earn its common appellation of the 'staff support group'. Later, as trust and risk-taking increases, the group may become more challenging to its members and thereby will operate at a deeper dynamic level. Early on, the focus tends to be patient-related; but later, the group becomes more 'self-related'. By this means, the sensitivity group *builds* cohesiveness and effectiveness in the staff team.

There are particular problems, of course, when staff turnover is high. This can be the case particularly when there are significant numbers of students attached to the unit for short periods. The solution here may be for the students to have their own group meetings, and for there to be a sensitivity group exclusively for qualified staff or for staff who will be working in the unit for more than a minimum period, perhaps six months.

Certain qualities are required of the psychotherapist who conducts a staff sensitivity group, in addition to general competence in working with groups. Firstly, he must know something about the dynamics of teams and institutions. He needs to be sensitive and respectful to the culture of the units, and to its ways of working (Hobbs 1990b). There is no point in trying to conduct a staff group if one does not know about or agree with the work they undertake. Secondly, but of importance, he needs to have the authority and confidence to work with and to inspire trust in staff of all disciplines and grades, including those who are the most senior and experienced. Lastly, in order to preserve his neutrality and objectivity, the group conductor should come, if possible, from outside of the unit and needs to maintain an analytic stance of relative detachment and curiosity. It is for these reasons that specialist psychotherapists are often called upon to undertake this work with staff of psychiatric units.

CONCLUSION

The group is powerful. It has a natural anti-repressive effect and can expose the tensions and conflicts within and between its individual members. At the same time, the group has a natural healing capacity, which can be promoted and harnessed if the power of the group is understood and sensitively developed.

Many groups operate in the psychiatric setting, some as background to the therapeutic endeavours of the staff, but others organised and conducted for their therapeutic potential. None of us can function independently of the groups of which we are part, even if we do not wish to be group therapists. We are members of teams, and of institutions. We are concerned about our patients' social functioning, as well as the complexities of their internal worlds.

For these reasons, an understanding of group processes is essential to all who work in mental health services.

FURTHER READING

Aveline M, Dryden W (eds) 1988 Group therapy in Britain. Open University Press, Milton Keynes
Foulkes SH, Anthony EJ 1957 Group psychotherapy: the psychoanalytical approach. Penguin, Harmondsworth
Menzies Lyth I E P 1988 Containing anxiety in institutions. Free Association Books, London
Rice C A, Rutan J S 1987 Inpatient group psychotherapy: a psychodynamic perspective. Macmillan, New York
Stock Whitaker D 1985 Using groups to help people. Routledge & Kegan Paul, London
Yalom I D 1985 The theory and practice of group psychotherapy, 3rd edn. Basic Books, New York

4. Behavioural psychotherapy

I.R.H. Falloon, M. Laporta, W. Shanahan

DEVELOPMENT OF BEHAVIOURAL PSYCHOTHERAPY

John B. Watson is considered the father of modern behavioural psycho-therapy. In 1920, he published a description of a case where he was able to condition a fear response in an 11-month-old child named Albert. This was achieved by pairing the appearance of a furry white rat with a loud noise. Every time little Albert touched the rat a loud noise sounded. After a number of pairings the infant began to cry when he saw the rat. The fear response could be elicited without the accompanying noise. In addition, it was induced by stimuli other than the rat, such as white hair or cotton wool, that were similar in appearance. Mary Cover Jones was a pupil of Watson, who, at his suggestion devised methods of deconditioning anxiety responses by presenting the feared object while a child was engaging in a pleasurable activity, such as eating, or playing with other children who did not respond to the object with fear (Jones 1924). Unfortunately, it appears that Albert did not manage to benefit from these deconditioning experiments. Watson lost touch with him.

This early work and the associated animal models of conditioning that were developed in laboratory settings, focused much early behavioural psychotherapy on the treatment of anxiety disorders, especially specific phobias. This led to refinements in deconditioning strategies by Wolpe, Lazarus, Marks, Rachman and Meichenbaum. Wolpe developed a strategy he called *systematic desensitisation*. Phobic patients were taught deep muscle relaxation, and then imagined fearful scenes arranged in an increasing heirachy of anxiety (Wolpe 1958). Lazarus, a close associate of Wolpe, introduced behaviour rehearsal to enable patients to practice anxiety-producing social interactions in role plays with the therapist (Lazarus 1966). He incorporated the social learning principle of vicarious learning (Bandura et al 1963) into the development of modelling – a strategy where the patient was encouraged to imitate the non-anxious responses of the therapist. These approaches enabled socially phobic patients to be treated by a method known as *assertiveness training*. In this context, deconditioning was achieved by pairing the anxious response with anger. Marks found that anxiety could be extinguished in a more direct manner, without the need for accompanying relaxation. He advocated direct exposure to the feared object, in graduated steps. This approach was termed *exposure in vivo* (Marks 1975). Rachman applied deconditioning principles to obsessional rituals. Patients were encouraged to expose themselves to the stimuli they feared most, usually dirt, without engaging in any anxiety-relieving rituals until the fear response subsided. This was termed *exposure with response prevention* (Rachman et al 1971). Meichenbaum introduced specific cognitive strategies of *self-verbalisation* to assist the phobic patient to prepare for exposure to a feared situation, to confront the situation and to review the confrontation in a constructive manner (Meichenbaum & Cameron 1973). A more recent refinement has involved the association between hyperventilation and physiological changes that appear to increase the vulnerability to panic attacks in anxious persons. A strategy that involves slowed breathing has led to improved management of anxiety disorders (Clark et al 1985).

While the development of therapeutic strategies for anxiety disorders has been one of the major successes of behavioural psychotherapy, it has led many practitioners to follow a rather traditional medical model. Methods that have developed from an *operant conditioning* framework have contributed to an alternative approach to psychiatric disorders. B F Skinner (1938) introduced the notion of the experimental analysis of behaviour. This enabled any behaviour, normal or abnormal, to be examined in terms of the context in which it occurs. The antecedents and consequences associated with that specific behaviour were examined along scientific lines similar to those employed in animal experiments. Maladaptive responses to environmental stimuli could be learned if those responses were reinforced by pleasurable consequences, or the removal of unpleasant consequences, such as a reduction in depressed or anxious mood. This approach to the analysis of abnormal behaviour was later refined by Kanfer & Saslow (1965) as an alternative to psychiatric assessment; details of this will be provided later in this chapter.

Operant conditioning strategies have been employed widely in behavioural psychotherapy. Perhaps the best known applications have been in shaping non-institutional social behaviour in long-stay hospital wards (Allyon & Azrin 1968, Paul & Lentz 1977) and the training of speech and social behaviour in mentally handicapped and autistic children (Lovaas et al 1967; Howlin 1981). In a much wider sense, operant conditioning principles have alerted therapists to the fact that lasting behaviour change can only be accomplished when the modifications of behaviour patterns are more rewarding overall than those patterns that they seek to replace. In simple terms, people do more of the things that induce pleasurable consequences, and less of those things that induce unpleasant results.

The fears that behaviour modification could enable therapists to manipulate behaviour patterns in a Machiavellian manner are groundless

when considered according to these principles. Under institutional reinforcement contingencies, behaviour can be rewarded and punished in
such manner that stereotyped patterns develop. However, in most
community settings not dominated by repressive political regimes, the
individual is able to choose alternative behaviour patterns according to his
or her specific perceived needs at any moment in time. This has led to one
of the main basic assumptions that underlies behavioural psychotherapy:
*that at any time every individual performs the behaviour that he perceives to be
the best choice to produce a pleasurable result, limited by the resources of
physical and intellectual capacity, interpersonal skill, and materials available at
that moment.* Apparent self-destructive behaviour is viewed as the best
coping response for the person at the time it was deployed. This analysis
suggests that the main thrust of therapeutic endeavours should be the
interpersonal problem-solving skills of individuals. This approach
incorporates training in problem solving and interpersonal skills, and has
formed the basis for many of the strategies that have gained prominence in
the past decade. These have included *cognitive restructuring, social skills
training, behavioural marital and family therapy, sex therapy and behavioural
group therapy.* All have aimed to provide alternative strategies for assessing
and responding to specific situations perceived as problematic for each
individual. All these methods were devised by clinicians seeking to extend
the range of treatment strategies beyond the anxiety disorders that had
been the targets for so much of early behavioural theory. The specificity of
each approach to the individual and his or her problem behaviour, made
evaluative group research less applicable. Single-case design methodology
was developed to enable the scientific basis for behavioural psychotherapy
to be maintained.

The links between emotional states and physiology were first made in
ancient medicine. Modern physiology has begun to clarify the biological
substrates of emotional responses. The early theories that attempted to
link specific emotions to specific physiological responses have been
discarded in favour of more general stress responses. Each person appears
to respond to perceived stressors with a physiological response that is
specific to that person. The nature of this response appears to be
determined more by constitutional factors, such as genetics, than by the
precise emotion invoked. These links between stress and bodily function
have been exploited in the field of behavioural medicine. A simple
application has been the development of biofeedback as an aid to
conditioning physiological responses. The inextricable link between
psychological and physiological systems is a major part of behavioural
psychotherapy practice.

Behavioural psychotherapy has often been caricatured as a reductionist
approach concerned only with modifying behaviours considered inappropriate by the therapist. This misunderstanding derives from the fact that
almost all behaviour therapy publications occur in the scientific literature

and concern studies of specific components of treatment strategies tested under the constraints of controlled experimental conditions. Descriptions of the therapist-patient relationship and details of practical difficulties encountered in the application of these strategies are edited from such presentations. The landmark study of R Bruce Sloane, Fred Staples and colleagues at Temple University in the early 1970s is a notable exception (Sloane et al 1975). This study examined the therapist-patient relationship in a controlled study that compared behavioural with psychoanalytic psychotherapy. The results showed that behavioural therapists were imbued with the same humanistic qualities as their analytic counterparts, and that their patients considered the relationships they had with their behavioural therapists to be crucial. This area of research is extremely difficult and has tended to be neglected in the behaviour therapy literature.

An even more difficult area is that of sociological systems. Most behavioural psychotherapists view the responses of their patients within the context of their natural habitats, including their cultural mores. Indeed, the importance of conducting treatment in the actual environments where the difficulties arise has been a major development in this field in recent years. This has led to a greater emphasis on working with patients' families and friends (Falloon 1988). Pioneers in the field such as Skinner (1971) and Krasner (1965) have examined the potential for the application of behavioural principles within broader social and ecological systems than the traditional therapeutic context.

It may be concluded that behavioural psychotherapy is a broad-based approach to the resolution of personal problems and the achievement of personal goals for persons with mental disorders. While the main therapeutic strategies have derived from the experimental analysis of social learning theories, the context of the assessment and intervention is one that involves all systems of human ecology, integrating the biological, psychological and sociological factors involved in the development and maintenance of maladaptive response patterns. The subsequent sections of this chapter will examine specific aspects of the application of behavioural psychotherapy within psychiatry.

THE ASSESSMENT PROCESS: BEHAVIOURAL ANALYSIS

Perhaps the most distinctive feature of the behavioural approach to psychotherapy is the central role played by problem-oriented assessment, not merely in defining the treatment intervention, but also in continually providing feedback that is used to modify the intervention procedures until the problem is completely and permanently resolved. Time-limited research with goals of achieving statistically significant reductions in symptoms is far removed from the clinical practice of behavioural psychotherapy, and has led to much misunderstanding of the methods employed outside the research laboratory. Fred Kanfer and George Saslow (Kanfer & Saslow 1965) outlined a method of assessment that has formed the basis for behavioural assessment. This entails precise problem definition followed by a detailed analysis of the biopsychosocial systems that maintain the problem despite the patient's best efforts to resolve it. The steps include the following:

1. pinpointing the exact problem(s)
2. pinpointing the environmental factors that trigger or maintain problem behaviours
3. defining effective coping behaviours already deployed by the person and his social network
4. defining current levels of everyday functioning
5. defining expected levels of everyday functioning
6. defining the person's realistic everyday goals
7. defining all assets and deficits that may contribute to the efficiency of problem resolution and goal achievement
8. formulating an intervention plan, including continuous assessment and review procedures.

Behavioural analysis is similar to skilled detective work. In some cases, the problems seem obvious and it is tempting to jump to the obvious conclusions without completing a thorough assessment. Many seemingly straightforward treatment planned has foundered because the course charted has failed to notice the rocks just beneath the surface.

Case study 4.1   Agoraphobia and marital difficulties

A woman with agoraphobic symptoms responded well to straightforward exposure treatment, but this created marital tension when her insecure husband found her spending more time with friends and less time with him. Marital therapy was offered, but the husband was upset that he had been consulted only as an afterthought, and refused to co-operate in the treatment. His wife failed to achieve her goals of everyday functioning, and despite considerable relief of her anxiety symptoms, showed no benefits in terms of the quality of her life. If the therapist had spent a few minutes asking the wife how her husband might respond to the resolution of her anxiety and the achievement of her main goal of developing a close friendship with a person other than her husband, a more optimal outcome might have been achieved.

With complex cases, the need for this detective work is clear. There may be no obvious clues as to why the person has developed a particular problem, and why it has not been resolved. Factors that trigger episodes of mental disorders and maintain them are extremely varied. The behavioural psychotherapist sifts through the dust in search for plausible clues. The hope is that one or two straightforward factors may emerge that enable the therapist to place a finger on the precise intervention strategy that will produce rapid, complete and lasting problem resolution. In practice, this is seldom achieved, as many problems are not analysed until they have become chronic and are the endpoint of several factors that have become interwoven with time.

Unravelling this tangled net may not be achieved in the initial behavioural analysis. Instead, the behavioural psychotherapist may have to determine the factor most likely to provide a major contribution to the problem, and initiate a strategy most likely to resolve the impact of that factor. Behavioural analysis is a continuous process, and the outcome of the initial intervention plan may provide further clues to guide the therapist to formulate the next strategy. In order to clarify the process, efforts are made to add one specific strategy at a time, to the intervention plan, so that the relative effectiveness of each strategy can be evaluated and the most effective components of the overall plan can be determined. If a depressed person is started on an antidepressant medication, cognitive restructuring, activity scheduling and marital therapy at the same time, and shows dramatic improvement within a fortnight, it is impossible to know the relative contributions of the strategies. Indeed, we cannot tell whether the person would have responded without any of these specific strategies. However, if a behavioural analysis suggested that the depression seemed to have been triggered by inactivity associated with recent unemployment, which had in turn led to marital stresses due to financial difficulties, then the initial strategy might involve enhancing those constructive activities that would contribute to relieving the family's financial crisis, such as seeking a new job, signing on for benefits, etc.

It is evident that the skillful behavioural psychotherapist is one who can readily pinpoint the vital clues and pick the strategies most likely to produce rapid resolution of each person's unique problems. Often, it is more efficient to spend several hours conducting a detailed behavioural analysis and then only an hour or two of highly specific treatment, than to conduct a superficial behavioural analysis followed by months of frustrating, poorly understood treatment.

The analogy of the detective has been suggested, but perhaps a more appropriate model, (with a more positive connotation!), is that of the skilled scientist. The behavioural psychotherapist is attempting to employ a scientific, experimental model to his clinical work. He observes and collects facts, formulates straightforward hypotheses, tests each hypothesis with his treatment interventions, evaluates the outcome and reviews the additional facts he has deduced; he then repeats the process until he has found the answers and resolved the problem. A description such as this tends to portray the therapist as a cold, calculating boffin or, worse, as a threatening interrogator and brain washer. Nothing could be further from the truth. The skilled behavioural psychotherapist aims to develop an intimate, confiding partnership with each patient as they work together solving problems and achieving goals.

Collecting the facts

The basis of behavioural analysis is a series of interviews with the patient and close associates. Guidelines for these interviews are often provided, but a semi-structured approach is used at all times, not a rigid, interrogatory method. Interview reports are seldom accurate reflections of actual behaviour patterns, and it is always helpful to get corroborative evidence of 'facts' by employing multiple 'witnesses'. However, distortion of even very recent events is usual, particularly when the 'witness' is emotionally involved in the behaviour observed. Thus, a clearer assessment is obtained through naturalistic observations of behaviour patterns. This may involve getting a person to reproduce his anxiety symptoms, observing a mother disciplining a disturbed child, watching a family discussing how they might resolve a problem. Such observations are termed *behavioural tests*. There are many ways of conducting such observations, including therapist observation in the home, behind one-way screens, with audiotaped or videotaped recordings, sometimes activated at random to capture samples of interactions. A less accurate, but often more practical, method involves training persons to carry out their own systematic observations of their own behavioural patterns and those of others, and charting these in a specific manner. A husband may record the number of times his wife initiates affectionate contact, a parent may record the number of times a child throws a tantrum, a depressed person may observe their thoughts and feelings associated with a range of daily activities. Such observations may reveal the contingencies that surround problems, and correct misperceptions, such as 'she *never* shows any affection to me'; or 'he is uncontrollable... he throws tantrums anytime, for no reason at all, and there is nothing we can do about it!'; or 'I feel miserable all the time'!

Of course, behavioural tests have their own limitations. Often problems are associated more with perceptions and emotional responses to behaviour patterns, than with the overt behaviours. Perceptions and emotions are largely private events, difficult to assess in a reliable manner. However, attempts to do so often reveal surprising information. For example, the coping responses of persons to hallucinations and delusions usually reveal well-developed patterns that reduce the impact of the psychotic phenomena. Providing training in the systematic use of these strategies, which are often deployed without thinking and in an inefficient manner, often assists the patient to cope more effectively in cases where drugs have shown only limited benefits. Depressed mood states may be revealed as varying with the particular activity that the person is engaged in; some activities, including thought patterns, making the mood state worse, while others consistently improving the state. Once again, this provides information which helps the therapist to devise a programme for modifying a problem.

It may be noted that behavioural analysis of this kind is likely to suggest a wide range of therapeutic strategies, each tailored to the specific contingencies that surround each particular problem. Such an assessment differs substantially from the prescriptive approach associated with much behaviour therapy research, and much criticised by clinical behavioural psychotherapists (Wolpe 1977).

Behavioural observation is not the only method of assessment that is employed. Standardised questionnaires and rating scales are used widely. However, wherever possible, measures are employed that are specifically targeted to the unique problems of each patient. This may involve devising a rating scale specially to measure a target problem. For example, a person with an eating disorder may have his daily calorie intake charted, or a person with persistent hallucinations may have recorded the amount of time he hears hallucinatory voices during a 10 minute period when he is reading a newspaper in his therapist's office.

Systems analysis

Behavioural analysis examines the manner in which a person's problems interact with all biopsychosocial systems to provoke distress and dysfunction. This systems analysis is often called 'functional analysis'. Simple examples of this are: the manner in which eating certain foodstuffs may produce allergic responses in a hypersensitive individual; the way parents responses to a child's temper tantrums may contribute to an increased likelihood that such behaviour will recur in the future; the association between environmental stress levels and recurrent episodes of major mental disorders; the manner in which responses that are adaptive in one cultural setting may prove maladaptive in a different setting, (for example, giving clear instructions in a firm tone may be effective in business management but may upset a spouse when addressed in a similar way); the manner in which previous traumatic experiences may be triggered by apparently trivial antecedents, (for example, a car backfiring may trigger a response pattern in a former soldier similar to that experienced when he had been ambushed). All are simple illustrations of the way in which the behavioural psychotherapist analyses problems in a contextual framework.

The assets people display in dealing with problems are considered as important as their deficits. Assets may include problem solving skills, interpersonal communication repertoire, past experience of resolving similar difficult problems, support from close associates, self-image and personality attributes, as well as practical assets, such as availability of material resources. Therapeutic interventions can then be tailored to the unique assets and deficits of each person and his social context. For this reason, behavioural psychotherapy has few limitations in terms of applications to disadvantaged persons, and can be adapted to meet the special needs of the physically and mentally handicapped, and across the broad spectrum of social and ethnic groups.

The manner in which patterns of behaviour are influenced by the responses they elicit, is an important factor in behavioural analysis. Conditioning research shows strong evidence that people tend to adopt behavioural patterns that produce desirable consequences for them, and to reduce the performance of behaviour patterns that do not achieve pleasurable goals. Such principles seem to be contradicted by evidence of persistent antisocial behaviour patterns in certain individuals. However, when carefully analysed, it emerges that such individuals tend to achieve short-term rewards from apparently self-destructive behaviour, which outweigh the aversive responses that are often applied in a highly inconsistent manner and are perceived as relatively non-threatening by the recipient. Again, the perceptions of individuals are crucial in under-standing human behaviour patterns, and generalisations based on normative data cannot be applied to the analysis of individual behaviour and the factors that trigger and maintain each person's problems.

A simple method of surveying a person's reinforcers involves inviting that person to describe the activities, people, places and material object with which they spend most of their time on a day-to-day basis. Regardless of the constraints placed upon an individual, he will tend to adopt patterns of behaviour that ensure that he maximises his positive reinforcement and minimises his unpleasant experiences. In addition, the behavioural analysis seeks to identify discrepancies between the time a person currently spends engaged in patterns of behaviour, and his perceived ideal patterns or unfulfilled wishes of how he would like to spend his time. A woman experiencing agoraphobic symptoms, who appears very content with a lifestyle that revolves around family and friends visiting her and accompanying her on journeys from the home, is unlikely to throw herself wholeheartedly into a therapeutic programme that would enable her to become more independent. In contrast, another person with a similar complaint, who expressed strong wishes to engage in a wide range of activities outside the home in an independent manner, may be eager to seek alternative ways of coping with her anxiety responses.

Goal setting

The behavioural psychotherapist endeavours to formulate intervention plans that are directed towards goals of improving the quality of life of the patient and of others in his or her intimate social network, not merely eliminating symptoms of mental disorders. While, in most cases, relief of symptoms is associated with the changes in the quality of life that the patient desires, there are instances, such as the one above, where resolution of the symptoms may result in an apparent deterioration of the person's lifestyle, or in the lifestyles of those people associated with him or her. The primary problem that is targeted for intervention may change from that of the presenting symptom to the person's goals. In this case, it may be seeking alternative means of achieving daily intimate social contacts. Regardless of the nature of the problems that the person presents for treatment, behavioural psychotherapy aims to assist the person to achieve objective goals that are clearly related to enhancing the quality of his or her life. These goals are pinpointed carefully by the patient, with assistance from the therapist, particularly in developing a highly specific description, for example, 'meeting with a friend of the same sex for one hour each week to engage in a sporting activity of my choice'. The specificity of this goal may be contrasted with the initial description provided by the patient of 'getting some friends'. To achieve any significant step forward towards life goals, a range of problems need to be resolved. However, the primary aim of behavioural psychotherapy is to assist in achieving goals, by resolving the specific problems that are considered to be impeding progress towards those goals. The behavioural analysis facilitates this process by identifying the key roadblocks, as well as the key strategies that may lead to efficient removal of those blocks. No more than two goals should be tackled during one course of treatment, but further treatment courses may be contracted after successful completion of the initial objectives.

Assessing social network support

Throughout this discussion, the involvement of persons in the patient's social network has been mentioned. Intervention programmes invariably involve the patient's immediate associates, such as key relatives, close friends and work associates, in some aspects of the treatment or assessment process. The precise nature of this involvement will vary, from providing alternative perspectives on problem issues, education about effective coping strategies, assisting the patient in his homework assign-ments, to conjoint therapy. The aim of such involvement is not merely to assist the index patient, but also to achieve improvements in the quality of life of the close associate. Thus, at least one associate is assessed as part of each behavioural analysis. This assessment may be as detailed as that of the index patient, and explores the manner in which target problems are coped with, the person's understanding of the nature of the target problems (particularly when these are features of mental disorders), and mutual conflicts and stresses. Personal goals are set in the same manner as for the patient, and care is taken to ensure that these are independent of the patient. For example, 'I would like to get a cleaning job near home for eight hours a week', as opposed to 'I would like to help Jack get better'.

Measuring progress

This chapter has discussed some of the methods that are employed to define problems in an objective manner. The value of specificity has been stressed. A further advantage of such methods is that they allow progress to be measured on a repeated basis throughout periods of intervention. Thus, a depressed person, who has a target problem involving low levels of constructive activity is considered to have progressed when the time he spends in daily constructive activity increases from a weekly average of 35 minutes to a weekly average of 150 minutes.

The problem of whether changes in targeted measures are specifically associated with the treatment intervention that is being applied, is a special concern for behavioural psychotherapists. Efforts are made to define the specific relationship between a person's progress and the intervention applied. When such associations can be reliably defined, progress may be expedited by focusing therapeutic input on the specific component of the intervention package that is contributing to the observed benefits, and reducing resources devoted to aspects of the intervention that appear to have minimal therapeutic efficacy. Every case is considered a single-case experiment. Ideally, a multiple baseline ABAB design is employed. An initial period of baseline observation (A), when the target problem is merely assessed, is followed by a period of the same duration (B), when a specific therapeutic strategy is applied to the problem. The experiment is then replicated, with a further period of assessment only (A) when the intervention is stopped, and a further period of active intervention. When significant benefits are observed during *both* periods of active intervention, but are absent during assessment periods, it can be concluded that the intervention has a specific effect and benefits are not merely an effect of time or contact with therapists.

In practice, it is often difficult to adhere rigidly to such principles, but AB designs are usually feasible, as are ABCD designs. In the latter, an intervention plan is developed in clear phases, with intervention strategies being added sequentially, rather than a complex package of different interventions initiated that make it impossible to know which strategy is contributing to which effect. The use of multiple drugs is a good example of this problem. The behavioural psychotherapist targets drugs to specific symptoms, adding new drugs one at a time. This enables the additive benefits of the combination to be assessed, albeit in an interactive manner that contributes little to our understanding of the relative merits of the drugs when ingested on their own.

Assessment is a continuous process, with measures repeated at regular intervals. In addition to the day-to-day measures used to monitor progress towards resolution of target problems and personal goals, a range of other measures are employed. These include measures that reflect generalisation of treatment benefits to other problems that were not specific targets of the intervention. For example, sleep disturbance may have been the target of treatment for a person suffering from a depressive disorder; improvements in sleep may be associated with a more general improvement in depressed mood and activity levels, which may be assessed by changes on a Hamilton Rating Scale for Depression. Generalisation to the natural habitat of improved functioning in the clinical setting cannot be taken for granted. Thus, many of the gains noted in a hospital setting are not evident when the person returns home and attempts to replicate behaviour patterns under different circumstances. Finally, improvements may not be sustained over time, and problems may recur. Thus, comprehensive assessment should provide evidence that benefits occur in all relevant settings, and are stable during long-term follow-up.

Behavioural analysis may need to be reviewed at regular intervals, usually after 10–12 weeks of intervention. Problems that are not responding to therapeutic strategy may need to be reappraised, new problems targeted and new goals set. The impact of resolution of problems and the achievement of goals on interpersonal relationships and social systems, may give rise to further difficulties, particularly when the initial behavioural analysis failed to recognise the likely ramifications of the initial intervention programme. An example of this was a man who became extremely jealous when his wife's chronic depression was relieved, and developed panic attacks whenever he found that she had gone out to visit friends on her own. Further assessment of such consequences of change is essential and should continue until stable resolution of the targeted problems and personal goals of all persons involved in the therapeutic plan has been achieved.

SPECIFIC STRATEGIES

Behavioural psychotherapy has often been characterised by the specific therapeutic strategies that are frequently employed. However, it is important to reiterate that the core component of behavioural psychotherapy is the behavioural analysis, and that the therapist attempts to devise therapeutic intervention strategies that are based upon the existing problem resolution efforts of the patient and his close associates. If such efforts appear to have minimal efficacy, even when applied with a high degree of consistency, the therapist may then choose to introduce a strategy that has been shown to be consistently beneficial with similar problems in controlled research studies. In this section, a number of widely employed strategies will be discussed. They include desensitisation, exposure treatment, interpersonal skills training, problem-solving training, contingency contracting, operant conditioning, and cognitive restructuring.

Desensitisation strategies

Methods aimed at desensitisation were pioneered by Joseph Wolpe (Wolpe 1958) for the treatment of specific phobias. They have since been refined considerably and now form the most common strategy used in the treatment of all phobic, and most obsessive-compulsive, disorders. The principle involves exposing the person to the precise situation that he or she fears in such a manner that the fear diminishes. Wolpe's approach involved devising a hierarchy of feared stimuli of gradually increasing intensity. The person was trained to achieve a calm state through deep muscular relaxation, and then invited to imagine that they were experiencing the stimulus they feared least. The fear responses they then experienced where further dampened down by relaxation, until they were able to experience the feared situation without their usual fear responses. Once this response had been desensitised, they were invited to tackle the next situation in the fear heirachy. Eventually, the person was able to remain in a calm state even when imagining the situation they feared the most.

This method can prove quite protracted, and fear reduction in imagination does not always transfer to fear reduction in real-life settings. In a series of studies, Isaac Marks (1987) found that, in many cases, real-life exposure to the situation that the person feared most could achieve desensitisation rapidly, particularly if the person remained in the feared situation long enough to enable habituation to occur. Relaxation and other means of dampening fear responses proved helpful in encouraging the person to enter the feared situation and to remain there long enough to experience significant fear reduction. At times, this would require a period of exposure of at least two hours. This meant that therapy sessions needed to be extended beyond the traditional one hour, and that therapists would need to accompany persons into real-life settings, often outside the confines of the clinic.

Specific anxieties associated with the compulsive drive to perform obsessional rituals, such as hand-washing associated with a fear of contamination, or checking associated with fears of catastrophic events, can be desensitised by coaching the person to expose himself to the anxiety he experiences when he feels the compulsion to carry out the ritual, but to prevent himself from responding to that urge until the anxiety and the associated compulsion dissipate.

The practical difficulties associated with implementing in vivo exposure can be overcome by conducting treatment in groups (Hafner et al 1976), training relatives and close friends to assist in exposure sessions (Mathews et al 1981), and the use of computer-aided session guides (Ghosh et al 1988). The value of concomitant drug therapy is disputed, but may assist many people to expose themselves to feared situations that they would otherwise avoid without the partial relief achieved by drugs. Tricyclic drugs appear most effective, and to interfere least, with fear habituation processes. However, their benefits are reduced by a high incidence of unpleasant side-effects. Similar benefits may be obtained by relaxation training that focuses on applying the relaxation techniques immediately prior to entering a feared situation, and maintaining their application during the exposure. Cognitive strategies that counter the panicky thoughts that are a major part of the fear response may also facilitate more frequent, longer and above all, less distressing exposure to feared situations (Meichenbaum & Cameron 1973, Beck et al 1979). Research into the precise value of these adjuncts to desensitisation is still at an early stage, and no one approach can be claimed to have universal superiority.

Case study 4.2   A case of phobias and checking

Ruth was a 31-year-old teacher, married to James, an accountant. They had no children. Ruth developed anxiety symptoms around the age of 18, when she left home to attend university. Her main problems were a fear of eating in public, fear of sex and repetitive checking behaviour in her home. She managed to cope with these problems by avoiding feared situations until shortly after her marriage, when she found she could not engage in sexual behaviour without experiencing full-blown panic. She went to her GP and was given diazepam, which partially relieved her anxiety. Her husband was extremely understanding, and avoided placing any demands for sex or social activities that involved eating in public. After five years she became worried about the long-term effects of diazepam, and asked her doctor to help her to stop this treatment. She was referred for behavioural psychotherapy.

Her behavioural analysis revealed that her key fear was of vomiting in public. Her concern about sex was associated with a fear of morning sickness. Her husband continually reassured her when she become anxious, and reinforced her avoidance behaviour. At times he would attempt to help by collaborating with her checking rituals, which now involved spending up to one hour checking that lights, gas and taps had been turned off before retiring to bed. This behaviour tended to blunten their sexual desire and to support avoidance of sexual activity.

Both partners agreed that the first problem to tackle would be the eating in public. This would enable them to socialise more with friends and workmates, as well as to go on holidays. They set a mutual goal of going away to a hotel for a weekend in eight weeks' time. Therapy began with a session of education about the nature of anxiety and the principles of clinical management. James was taught alternatives to reassurance, which he rehearsed with Ruth in the session. During five subsequent sessions, Ruth constructed a hierarchy of steps towards eating in a hotel restaurant. These included: phoning the hotel and enquiring about the restaurant; having a drink in the bar and watching others eat in the nearby restaurant; having coffee in the restaurant; and eating a meal in the restaurant. James accompanied Ruth on these assignments and was taught to provide her with praise and support for her efforts. He practised how to coach her to stay in the situation when she became anxious and to remain there until the anxiety reduced, and to avoid reassuring her. She was taught a range of strategies to assist her when she experienced high levels of anxiety. These included, brief relaxation, respiratory control, coping self-talk and monitoring of anxiety levels. She found that slow, shallow breathing seemed most effective in controlling her anxiety levels.

Ruth and James booked a weekend in a seaside resort. This led to Ruth experiencing higher levels of general anxiety as she worried frequently about this anticipated event. A session was spent problem solving, deciding how they would cope with the worst possible scenarios that might occur during the weekend. Ruth rehearsed these coping strategies whenever worries about the weekend trip arose. The two-day trip was relatively successful. Although Ruth did not experience any actual pleasure during the trip, she was pleased and relieved that she had coped effectively throughout. James expressed his delight and appreciation of her efforts.

Progress was reviewed, and it was agreed to work next on anxiety about sexual contact. A similar desensitisation approach was employed, incorporating relaxing body massage (non-genital sensate focus) and other aspects of the Masters and Johnson approach. The risk of pregnancy was reduced by changing contraceptive strategies from diaphragm to oral contraceptives. This was associated with further fear reduction. Ruth rehearsed ways she could cope with morning sickness, even if it was persistent throughout her pregnancy. After four weeks, they had engaged in sexual intercourse on several occasions. Ruth remained anxious before and after, but reported the experience as moderately pleasurable.

The strategy of response prevention was employed in management of Ruth's checking problem. She was instructed to go to bed leaving one light on and a tap dripping, and to remain in bed until her anxiety had dissipated. Then she could turn the light and tap off, return immediately to bed and remain there until any further anxiety reduced. James was prompted to avoid reassurance, and to support Ruth's anxiety management strategies. This strategy proved less successful, resulting in a 50% reduction in checking behaviour. Both partners agreed that this was sufficient to improve the quality of their lives substantially, and sought no further improvement in this.

During therapy, it was noted that whenever Ruth experienced additional stress, her anxiety became worse. Her problems in managing stress appeared to be: (1) a tendency to withdraw from James and other social contacts when under stress; and (2) an unassertive approach to people who were provoking stress. For example, when her head teacher asked her if she would like to organise a school trip, she said she would, but had wanted to say no. Three sessions were devoted to stress management that focused on enhancing communication and problem-solving between Ruth and James, and rehearsing assertive responses with friends and workmates. After six months, considerable progress had been made and Ruth felt confident that she could continue to work on her problems with the support that James was giving her. He was delighted that he could now assist her in a useful way. Sessions were reduced in frequency to six-weekly to monitor their progress.

Interpersonal skills training

Deficits in interpersonal skills are a frequent problem for people with a wide range of mental disorders. Establishing friendship is highly dependent on a repertoire of conversational skills; intimate relationships demand competence in expressing feelings and in sexual behaviour; success in work may depend on good interviewing skills, problem solving ability and assertiveness; and parenting skills are by definition a crucial determinant of successful child-rearing. Many of those who present to mental health services have problems that result directly from a lack of these skills. Others may be inhibited from using an adequate repertoire of skills by anxiety or depressive feelings of inadequacy. Schizophrenic symptoms may interfere with the perceptual processes that enable a person to decide the most appropriate response to use in a specific interpersonal context.

Interpersonal skills training employs an educative approach that includes the follows steps:

1. Pinpointing the behaviour that is functionally deficient. This is achieved by a detailed behavioural analysis, that includes observations of the person attempting to respond to the situation either in real-life or in a realistic role-play.
2. Constructive feedback to the person on the strengths and major weaknesses of his or her performance.
3. Providing the person with alternative responses that he or she may consider more effective. This may be achieved through instructions, or through demonstrations of the responses (modelling).
4. Repeated rehearsal of alternative responses to the target situation by the person, with supportive coaching and guidance from the therapist, until the person feels comfortable with one or more alternative responses.
5. Where rehearsal is conducted in a role-played setting, it is crucial to ensure that further practice is provided in the real-life setting. This may be achieved through therapist-aided practice, assigned homework tasks, or with the assistance of friends and relatives.
6. All small steps towards the goal the person has set are rewarded in an appropriate manner, usually by praise from the therapist and significant others. In addition, inappropriate negative self-evaluation is countered by encouraging accurate perception of achievements and other cognitive restructuring methods.

In addition to the use of cognitive restructuring to overcome negative self-image, anxiety management strategies may assist in overcoming interpersonal anxiety. Interpersonal skills training has proven as effective as desensitisation procedures in the clinical management of social phobias (Trower et al 1978), and has been employed in groups of socially inadequate outpatients (Falloon et al 1977), in the community management of schizophrenia (Hogarty et al 1986) and depression (Bellack et al 1983), and as a major component of behavioural family and marital therapy (Falloon 1988).

Case study 4.3   Social skills training for schizophrenia

Jean was a 22-year-old woman with a three-year history of schizophrenic illness characterised by auditory hallucinations and thought interference. The florid psychotic symptoms lessened whenever she took adequate doses of phenothiazine medication, which was infrequent owing to her poor adherence to the prescribed regimen. She lived at home with her parents and 18-year-old brother. Her mother reported that Jean had always had difficulties getting along with her peers and preferred to stay at home, apart from weekly visits to her elderly grandmother. Since leaving school, she had become even more isolated. She had worked briefly at several jobs, but had lost them after a week or two, when she had stormed off in a rage after being criticised by a supervisor. She also lost her temper with family members, particularly her mother, with whom she argued and became physically violent almost daily.

An analysis of her present behaviour, her patterns of reinforcement, specific assets and deficits, and above all the functional handicaps that she wanted to overcome was carried out in a series of interviews with Jean and her family. One area that she was particularly keen to improve was her interpersonal skills. Her social deficits included the following:

1. *Reception of social clues*. Jean had difficulty discriminating social cues. Much of her difficulty was attributed to her florid symptoms of auditory hallucinations and thought insertion, which constantly interrupted her attention and reduced her ability to process external social stimuli. At times she heard 'voices' discussing her, which she believed to belong to her parents. This infuriated her, as she believed that her parents were going to kill her. She was unable to recognise social cues that indicated a person felt positive about her, and believed that everybody she knew wanted to avoid her company.
2. *Repertoire of skills*. Jean had always lacked fluent conversational skills. She spoke very quickly in a barely audible whisper, sat in a hunched-up manner, and avoided eye contact when speaking with people. When frustrated, she would throw violent tantrums. The content of her speech was frequently inappropriate, with abrupt, unrelated changes of topic.
3. *Performance of social skills*. When she was with her family, and people she knew well, Jean chatted adequately. She became very anxious with people in new situations, particularly groups.
4. *Reinforcement of adequate performance*. Jean felt she was a total failure, and constantly thought negatively about herself even when her performance was clearly competent. Her mother was overprotective, and did not encourage Jean to seek friends or work. Mother involved Jean in helping in the household chores, but was critical of her lack of persistence with them. Father criticised Jean's lack of sociability and her aggressive outbursts.

A comprehensive treatment plan was drawn up aiming to (1) improve reception of social cues by reducing florid schizophrenic symptoms with a major tranquilliser; (2) teach basic conversation skills; (3) teach alternatives to tantrums for handling frustration; (4) practice skills in group, family and community settings; (5) elicit positive feedback from self and others on performance in these situations; and (6) train more effective family communication. Because of previously noted poor compliance with tablets (despite extensive compliance training), depot fluphenazine was administered every two weeks. Within a week, Jean's florid symptoms had been reduced and her aggressive outbursts decreased dramatically. Her concentration was better and she initiated several conversations with her family. The content of her speech was more appropriate and coherent, and she stayed on one topic for a longer period.

Basic conversational skills were taught in twice-weekly sessions, one individual, the other in a small group. Initially, Jean practised talking more slowly, then more loudly. Because of her current difficulties with the content of speech she did not role-play conversations initially, but merely counted aloud from 1 to 20. Her parents were instructed to help her conduct these exercises at home, and to reward her by praising slower and louder speech. As she became more relaxed in the sessions, she pinpointed several situations in which she tended to lose her temper – when frustrated or criticised by a parent or authority figure. Group members discussed and demonstrated several ways of handling such criticism. She also practised these responses in the family sessions and at home.

Jean next worked on initiating contact with friends and sustaining conversations, as well as improving her range of topics of conversation. She was coached in more effective non-verbal skills, such as looking at her conversational partner and sitting in a more relaxed manner. She was taught to ask questions, and to use head nods and brief verbal prompts to encourage the other person to talk more. After each session, she set herself a specific homework assignment to complete before the next session. The group members commented on her progress. She befriended another woman in the group and went shopping with her on two occasions.

In addition to allowing practice of the behaviour learned in the individual and group sessions, family meetings were used to teach the family members to provide a more supportive environment for Jean. Mother was trained to shape Jean's independent behaviour, while Father was encouraged to adopt more realistic expectations of his daughter's performance. Modelling and role-playing were employed to rehearse more effective methods of family communication. All family members, including her younger brother, were coached. Three sessions were devoted to a description of the nature and course of schizophrenic illness and the rationale for continuing medication after the remission of symptoms. At a later point, Jean's tranquillising medication was changed to tablets, after strategies for supporting her adherence to the prescribed regimen had been worked out in the family sessions.
(Falloon 1988)

Problem-solving training

A structured approach to problem solving has wide-ranging applications throughout psychiatry. It was introduced by D'Zurilla & Goldfried (1971) in the rehabilitation of chronic patients, and has since been employed in crisis intervention (Bancroft 1986), including management of suicide attempts (Hawton & Catalan 1987), perceptual skills training (Wallace et al 1985) and marital and family counselling (Falloon 1988).

This strategy epitomises the emphasis that behavioural psychotherapy places on the resourcefulness of patients and their social networks. Patients are trained to structure their attempts to resolve their problems and achieve their goals, so that overwhelming issues can be tackled in a constructive manner. One of the most widely used methods involves six steps:

1. identifying the exact nature of the problem or goal
2. brainstorming as many solutions as possible without judging their potential effectiveness
3. highlighting the advantages and disadvantages of each proposed solution
4. choosing the solution that provides optimal benefits to resolve the current problem with resources that are currently available, i.e. the 'best fit'
5. formulating a clear plan for implementing the chosen solution
6. reviewing the efforts made to implement the plan, and making further adjustments and plans until the desired result has been achieved.

Whenever feasible, the problem-solving approach is taught to patients using a skills-training format, with the therapist coaching the participants rather than entering discussions as an active participant. Therapist interventions focus more on training persons to employ structure in their problem solving, than on issues of content. However, in crisis situations, the therapist may participate in an active manner to assist in the problem definition, seeking of an optimal solution and careful planning.

This problem-solving approach can be used as a method for dealing with therapeutic resistance. The therapist identifies a problem in the therapeutic process that is preventing him from achieving his own goals, and invites the patient to collaborate in seeking an optimal solution. This open style of therapist-patient collaboration characterises most behavioural psychotherapy, and contrasts with the image of the omnipotent behaviour modifier that has been promoted by detractors of this approach.

Case study 4.4   Enhancing marital problem-solving in bulimia

Elizabeth was a 28-year-old hairdresser, married for five years, without children. She was a well-built woman with a muscular frame. She had felt self-conscious about her large figure since puberty. Her mother had prevented her from dieting, and insisted on feeding her with cream cakes and cookies throughout adolescence. After Elizabeth left home at the age of 18, she began dieting and her weight dropped from 150 pounds to 130 pounds. However, despite constant efforts to lose more weight, she was unable to achieve any further reduction. This frustrated her and made her feel miserable and suicidal. When Elizabeth felt depressed she would visit her mother, who would feed her fattening treats. Although she found solace in the food, this mood elevation was short-lived; on returning to her apartment she felt guilty and ashamed of her behaviour. She learned that she could induce vomiting, and this provided a partial solution to her problem of coping with visits home.

Elizabeth met her husband at the age of 22; they dated for a year before getting married. She avoided premarital sex because she feared her husband would see her body as grotesque. After marriage, they had a satisfactory sexual relationship, but Elizabeth continued to cover her body as much as possible. Throughout the courtship, Elizabeth had desperately tried to lose weight through dieting and using laxatives. However, no stable weight reduction was achieved. She continued to induce vomiting after visits to her mother and occasionally after excessive food intake at restaurants and parties.

She was very keen to have children and went to a gynaecologist for a checkup. She was told to lose weight in order to have a healthy pregnancy; this advice caused her considerable distress. She began to worry constantly about her weight. She continued to diet but was again unsuccessful. At times when she felt very depressed and suicidal, she would visit an ice cream parlour or coffee shop and eat excessive quantities of high-calorie foods. On returning home, she relieved her guilt by induced vomiting. She began to induce vomiting after most meals and became increasingly depressed when she was unable to get her weight below 125 pounds.

Elizabeth consulted her family practitioner for advice on weight reduction. He observed that she appeared depressed and explored her problems. She told him about her self-induced vomiting and her concerns about not being able to get pregnant because she was overweight. After several counselling sessions, the family practitioner consulted the mental health service for further advice on Elizabeth's management. It was suggested that he involve the husband and conduct conjoint marital counselling. After three sessions, during which Elizabeth disclosed her eating behaviour and concerns about pregnancy to her husband, some relief of her depression was noted. However, her bulimic behaviour remained. She was referred for behavioural psychotherapy.

A behavioural analysis revealed that Elizabeth's husband cared for her deeply, shared her eagerness to have children, and found her body extremely attractive. He had found her depression difficult to cope with, largely because she had refused to discuss it with him. Husband and wife both appeared to have good communication skills, but avoided discussion of emotionally charged issues. It was agreed to provide five sessions of behavioural marital therapy to improve mutual problem solving. The couple were trained to express their feelings of pleasure and displeasure to each other. Elizabeth initially had great difficulty expressing unpleasant feelings to her husband. However, after telling him that she worried most about her weight when he was away on business trips, they successfully established a plan that he would telephone every night when he was away. Elizabeth felt much greater confidence in expressing her fears and concerns to her husband after this. After training in the six-step problem-solving format, the couple then worked out a strategy for preventing bulimic behaviour. This involved Elizabeth speaking with her husband or a close friend, who knew about the problem; this led eventually to a sustained elimination of the habit.

The couple planned a holiday in Greece and decided that they would begin their attempt to start a family. They returned two weeks later in good spirits, despite both having gained several pounds. Elizabeth employed a straightforward weight reduction programme over the next month and, with the support of her husband, began to accept that 130 pounds was her best weight. Six months later, she was half-way through her pregnancy, appropriately concerned about her weight gain, and very happy. She had told her mother about her difficulties and had requested her mother not to push food at her during visits. Elizabeth and her husband continued to convene weekly meetings, at which they discussed problems or future plans. Over a year later, after the birth of their son, Elizabeth appeared to be coping well, with no recurrence of bulimia or depression despite weighing 142 pounds. She was attending a new mother's group and using a diet and exercise programme to achieve her pre-pregnancy weight. Her husband had managed to change his work habits to enable him to spend more time at home and enjoy his role as a new parent. (Falloon et al 1988, pp 399–400).

Operant conditioning strategies

Strategies derived from operant conditioning principles include contingent reinforcement, shaping, extinction and time out. *Contingent reinforcement* involves providing specific rewards for performance of targeted behaviour patterns. *Shaping* entails reinforcement of behaviour patterns that gradually approximate the desired responses. *Extinction* procedures involve the removal of positive reinforcers that are often contingent upon inappropriate behaviour. These approaches form important ingredients in skills training procedures, both in the promotion of appropriate social skills and in the management of inappropriate behavioural responses.

The best known application of such strategies is the '*token economy*' approach to community rehabilitation (Paul & Lentz 1977). This involves persons residing in an institutional setting, where behaviour appropriate to community living is rewarded with tokens that can be exchanged for tangible rewards of chosen food, recreational and leisure pursuits. Inappropriate behaviour results in a loss of tokens and a subsequent loss of reinforcing activities. Attempts to institute such programmes for an entire group of patients are fraught with difficulty, and appear most successful where contracted on an individual basis with the full collaboration of the target individual. *Contingency contracts* of this nature have been widely used in child, adolescent and adult psychiatry, as well as in marital and family therapy. Specific positive reinforcement is a valuable component to basic training in effective interpersonal response patterns and instrumental role skills (e.g. grooming, work, parenting). In addition, continued reinforcement of competent behaviour performance, increases the likelihood that such performance will continue.

Time out is an effective strategy for reducing the frequency of targeted inappropriate behaviour, such as aggression, sexual acting-out, or other antisocial acts. Rather than rewarding the individual with interpersonal contact and attention, he is removed from all sources of reinforcement, usually into an unfurnished room. In households, this is seldom feasible, but a bathroom or spare room may be used in this manner. Again, the need to specify the contract in an exact manner, as well as obtaining the express consent of the target individual is crucial to the success of such strategies.

Another version of time out that has been used in family therapy, involves the individual learning to excuse himself when experiencing high levels of stress, and remove himself to a less stressful environment, for example walking outside, going to his bedroom. Other self-control procedures have been used for anger and stress management. These include the ability to use self-reinforcement for successful coping with potentially difficult situations.

It may be noted that almost all these procedures form part of the interplay of interpersonal discourse in the community. Behavioural psychotherapy serves to make these processes more clearly explicit and introduces greater consistency in their application. Such specificity enhances the learning that is associated with reinforcement procedures. However, continued performance of this behaviour is contingent upon lifestyle changes that ensure that newly acquired response patterns continue to receive adequate reinforcement once the specific therapeutic input is withdrawn. The involvement of family, work and other social systems in this process is vital to its success.

Case study 4.5   Modifying negative symptoms

Freddy was a 24-year-old single man, who lived with his parents and had suffered persistent symptoms of schizophrenia for five years. His behavioural analysis revealed that he spent 8–10 hours every day lying on his bed, that he smoked at least 40 cigarettes a day, enjoyed his meals, particularly desserts, and drank six mugs of coffee. He fed the household cat on a daily basis, and occasionally walked to a nearby park with the dog when asked by his mother. These activities were the only constructive activities recorded by the patient and his family during a two-week period and averaged 20 minutes a day.

Freddy identified his lack of activity as a problem, and set a goal of spending two hours a day engaging in constructive activity of his choice associated with the family household; he hoped to achieve this goal within 10 weeks.

Freddy and his parents concluded that a programme of incentives might assist him in overcoming the lack of motivation and inertia that were considered major limitations in achieving his goal. With the therapist's assistance, they devised a programme that provided Freddy with a range of desserts and food treats that he specifically enjoyed as reinforcers for his engaging in a range of constructive activities for specified periods of time. A contract was drawn up (see Table 4.1) that was taped to the refrigerator door.

Table 4.1   Work contract between Freddy W. and Jack and Dorothy W. Freddy agrees to carry out activities from the list below on a daily basis. For every 10 minutes of constructive activity, Jack and Dorothy agree to provide Freddy with one of the specific rewards listed below.

Constructive activity	Reward
Feed the cat	1 Mug of coffee
Watch TV for 10 mins	1 Ice cream treat
Walk dog for 10 mins	1 Large slice of cake
Take a shower	1 Chocolate bar
Mow lawn for 10 mins	Dessert of choice
Vacuum carpets for 10 mins	Video of choice
Have a chat	
Dry dishes	
Clean bedroom	

After a fortnight, Freddy had progressed to spending 30 minutes a day in constructive activity. The increase was attributed to his taking the dog on one long walk. Both Freddy and his parents were discouraged by this very modest improvement. The therapist reviewed the programme and helped them to see that some progress had been made, no matter how small, and prompted them to reinforce the efforts they had made. The major deficit in the programme was thought to be the relatively long periods (20 minutes) of constructive activity that were required before Freddy received any reward. These periods were halved during the next fortnight, and resulted in Freddy engaging in a number of household chores, including mowing part of the back lawn, assisting his father with a barbecue, and buying some groceries at the nearby store. His activities averaged 45 minutes per day during this period.

Over the next six weeks, the programme was further modified, and slow progress resulted. At the end of the 10-week period, Freddy was averaging 105 minutes a day in constructive activity. Both he and his parents felt pleased that he had made a small step towards a more satisfying life.

Cognitive restructuring

Behavioural psychotherapy employs a wide range of cognitive strategies in adult psychiatry. These include: education about mental disorders and their management, problem solving, self-verbalisation, covert rehearsal of behaviour, and modification of negative thoughts. An educative component is employed in the behavioural treatment of all major psychiatric disorders. The phobic receives explanation about the nature of anxiety, and of how exposure to the object he fears will expedite fear reduction; the person with schizophrenia receives education about the association between his florid symptoms and environmental stress; and the depressed person is taught to recognise the links between performance of specific activities and changes in his mood. Enhanced understanding of this kind is a major part of the therapeutic alliance between patient and therapist and assists in engaging the patient in therapy. However, such rudimentary explanations are seldom therapeutic in their own right, and cognitive strategies are more commonly associated with the methods devised by Albert Ellis, Aaron T. Beck and Donald Meichenbaum.

These researchers recognised that behaviour change could be enhanced by training patients to restructure their thought patterns, from maladaptive distressing thoughts of a catastrophic nature to more realistic appraisal of the difficulties that confronted them. An anxious person may be trained to recognise the features of anxiety that accompany a panic attack, and to contrast them with those of a heart attack, which he fears; he learns to tell himself that his palpitations, sweating and lightheadedness are most likely to be features of a panic attack that will improve with time, especially if he relaxes and slows his rapid breathing by counting. A depressed person may be trained to recognise the negative manner in which he automatically responds to everyday stresses, and how this amplifies his feelings of worthlessness and hopelessness. Training persons to challenge their negative thinking and to consider alternative rational explanations often succeeds in breaking the cycle of repetitive negative thinking that is a key feature of depressive phenomenology. Beck has devised an extensive range of strategies to assist in the application of this self-control procedure (Beck et al 1979). They include devising behavioural experiments to test negative predictions, keeping diaries of dysfunctional thoughts, verbal challenging of distorted thoughts, and modifying dysfunctional basic assumptions (see Ch. 11).

CONCLUSIONS

It is vital to recognise that strategies outlined in this section are merely those that are currently most widely used in behavioural psychotherapy. Very few have been specifically validated as the strategy of choice for any one disorder or problem. The choice of the strategy is made after extensive behavioural analysis, and may include all or none of the approaches mentioned above. Whatever strategies are chosen to initiate clinical treatment of a case, they are based upon specific hypotheses and goals, and are subject to revision as the results of their application are analysed from session to session. The reader is again reminded not to confuse this clinical approach with that associated with controlled research studies, where protocol demands restrict the therapist to rigid selection of one or more strategies applied for a specified number of sessions. Because the vast majority of publications on behavioural psychotherapy have concerned such research endeavours, it is easy to see how basic assumptions about the nature of its practice have crept into the common lore!

Research validation of behavioural psychotherapy

In common with most psychotherapeutic approaches, controlled group research on comprehensive behavioural psychotherapy programmes is exceedingly difficult. Rigid adherence to research protocols prevents adequate behavioural assessment and targeting of individualised goals and deficits. Despite these constraints, controlled studies have demonstrated the effectiveness of behavioural psychotherapy approaches in the treatment of adult phobic anxiety disorders, panic disorders, generalised anxiety, post-traumatic stress disorder, obsessive compulsive disorder, non-psychotic depressive disorders, schizophrenic disorders, rehabilitation of institutionalised cases, parasuicide, anorexia nervosa and bulimia, chronic pain, reduction of cardiovascular risk factors, stuttering, myalgic encephalitis, social inadequacy, alcohol misuse, sexual dysfunction and marital and family distress.

Comparisons with other psychotherapies have been relatively few. However, where they have been conducted, the behavioural approaches have tended to show advantages (Sloane et al 1975, Shapiro & Firth 1987). In addition to any clinical benefits that may be claimed for these methods, the highly specific nature of the approach facilitates reliable training of therapists from various professional backgrounds, and is associated with excellent cost/benefit ratios. These features should facilitate the widespread use of this approach, particularly in publically funded services. However, it is evident that this promise is not fulfilled, and that few psychiatric training programmes in Europe or North America provide more than an introduction to this approach. Further work needs to be conducted in the development of comprehensive training programmes in behavioural psychotherapy, similar to those now available in other fields.

Acknowledgements

Thanks are due to Mark Laporta and William Shanahan for help in the preparation of this chapter.

FURTHER READING

Beck A T, Rush A J, Shaw B F, Emery G 1979 Cognitive therapy of depression. Guilford Press, New York
Falloon I 1988 Handbook of behavioural family therapy. Unwin Hyman, London
Marks I M 1987 Cure and care of neurosis. Wiley, Chichester
Mathews A M, Gelder M G, Johnston D W 1981 Agorophobia: nature and treatment. Tavistock, London
Trower P, Bryant B, Argyle M 1978 Social skills and mental health. Methuen, London

5. Family therapy

J. Hill

INTRODUCTION

No single theory can encompass adequately the elements to be considered under the heading of 'family therapy'. Historically, it developed out of a recognition by clinicians of the need to work with the actual – as opposed to internalised or remembered – families of patients, and from the availability of theories that could be applied to interpersonal processes. Most emphasis has been placed on interpersonal processes within the family, but this is not required by the theory nor has it been an exclusive interest of those working within the 'family therapy' field. Indeed a crucial 'ecological' strand within the tradition has examined the wider social context, including that of professional networks and institutions. Thus, the subject matter of this chapter is the theory, the specific treatment approach, and the position of the patient, the family, and the clinician within the practice and organisation of psychiatry and allied disciplines.

THEORY

Whilst psychoanalytic and behavioural theories have been influential, much of the theory adopted within family therapy has come from outside psychiatry and psychology, for example, from sociology (Maruyama 1988), and biology (Hardin 1969). One of the most influential thinkers was Gregory Bateson, an anthropologist and biologist, who worked with a group of psychiatrists in the 1950s and focused particularly on the origins of schizophrenia (Bateson et al 1956). Bateson is best known for the double-bind theory of schizophrenia which, ironically, is only a single item within a rich framework – the irony being that he argued against looking at bits of frameworks out of context (Bateson 1972). His writings influenced all the major figures in the development of family therapy, and still have the capacity to inform and refresh the reader who may be new to the area. Three key aspects of his thinking are considered here.

Firstly, he argued that, whilst our language tends to lead us to name things or entities, biological systems deal in comparisons, differences and relationships. This happens in order to represent a state of affairs either in the physical world or in relation to other organisms, and this representation is of the form: Condition A exists as opposed to condition B'. When an Englishman greets another in the street and says, 'Warm for the time of year', even if he says simply, 'It's warm', he is referring to a comparison with, or difference from, another condition that might be expected.

This exchange in the street illustrates a further point made by Bateson both in his anthropological writings and his application of these to family functioning. This is that social interactions are rule bound, and the rules are constantly restated. These social rules are of the form, 'This interaction follows rule X as opposed to rule Y', and they work because the participants share expectations about these rules. The English preoccupation with the weather illustrates this. Frequently, the exchange about the weather defines the distance between the speakers, indicating that the exchange will be kept superficial, or it may provide a familiar opening that establishes rapport before going on to other issues. The way it defines the rules has to do also with where it is said, the tone of voice and the accompanying gestures. Thus, all communications contain both a message (e.g., about the weather) and a 'metamessage' or 'metacommunication', which specifies how the communication is to be understood as part of the interaction or relationship. If the content of what is said refers to the relationship, and it differs from the metacommunication (about the relationship), then the grounds for confusing or 'double-bind' communications are laid.

The third element arising from the work of Bateson and his colleagues is the proposal that interactions, such as those concerning the weather, occur within a wider social context or system that is governed by rules which tend to maintain stability. The extent to which the rules are adhered to is monitored by the participants. Behaviour that follows the rules is 'permitted', and departure from these rules is 'corrected'. The metaphor of cybernetics, that is to say of feedback loops which maintain homeostasis or dynamic equilibrium, has been extensively invoked within family therapy. It follows from the theory that some apparent changes within social systems, including families, may occur without a change in the underlying rules, and that profound change (which Bateson termed 'second order change') is achieved only when the underlying rules change. Whilst this might appear at first sight to be a relatively simple idea, its implications are quite complex and puzzling, and the reader should be warned that the area of systems theory and cybernetics has led to disputations in the literature more akin to those of medieval theologians than of practitioners in the area of mental health. A clear and more extensive discussion of systems theory as applied to family therapy is to be found in Hoffman (1981).

The importance of these three elements of Bateson's theory for psychiatry is that they lead us to ask clinical questions in a different way from the usual. Firstly, a question such as 'Is this depression?' or 'What causes depression?' becomes 'What is the depression to be contrasted with?'. The answer may be in terms of 'not depressed, less depressed or more depressed', or one might consider a greater range of possibilities that do not refer to depression, such as 'angry, potent, manic or sad', and so on. This form of reply goes back much further than Bateson, at least to Freud, who argued that defensive activity leads to symptoms which are both related to and different from something else. In his theory, that 'something else' was forbidden incestuous feelings. The analyses of both Bateson and Freud represent a marked departure from the concept of illness as a breakdown for which a cause is sought (Hill 1982). Instead, symptoms are viewed as systematically related to other possible mental states or behaviour that are not currently seen.

A second consequence of the Batesonian perspective is that all behaviours, whether verbal or non-verbal, both define and enter into interactions and relationships. Taking the example of depression, the question becomes, 'How does depressed behaviour enter into this person's key relationships and contribute to the definition of their ground rules?'. If symptoms may enter into definition of relationships and these relationships form part of a system that favours stability, then symptoms can perform a 'function' in terms of that stability. If the system is destabilised in such a way that a new set of rules apply, then there is no longer the 'need' for the symptom. This, in summary, comprises the clinical application of systems theory and cybernetics to psychiatric disturbance. The application in this way of the third Batesonian element to clinical practice, leads to the construction of hypotheses about the way symptoms may contribute to the stability of the family system. Thus, symptoms of depression may be seen to provide the conditions for continuing closeness between family members, to provide others in the family with caring roles, or to decrease the likelihood that a family member (for instance the youngest child) will leave home.

Two points should be made here. Firstly, whilst both the theory and the evidence (e.g. Patterson 1982) support the idea that family life tends to promote order and repetition, equally the development of each family member requires that families change. Events such as the birth of children, the move of children into the wider social setting of peers and school, puberty, the menopause, retirement, illness and death, all promote change. Symptoms which appear at such transition points may be seen as part of an attempt to slow down the process or conserve aspects of the family's life which might be lost if major change did take place.

Secondly, claims have been made that these theoretical proposals amount to a new (and superior) epistemology the acquisition of which '... means to put oneself 'over' or 'higher' in order to better observe something. To do this we must abandon the causal-mechanistic view of phenomena which has dominated the sciences until recent times, and adopt a systemic orientation.' (Selvini Palazzoli et al 1978). Whether we must abandon anything in order to take advantage of this framework, is a question that can be answered only with reference to complex conceptual and clinical issues, and the question remains open as to whether it represents such a 'paradigm shift' or a useful tool.

Bringing the theory into practice

A number of manifestations of the theory can be seen in the different 'schools' of family therapy, and these are discussed in the next section. However, one application of theory in practice permeates most of the different styles of the therapy, and merits separate consideration. This is the 'gentle art' (Watzlawick et al 1974) of *reframing*, whereby the therapist takes advantage of the concepts described earlier to look at the problem in a different way. As Watzlawick et al put it, 'to reframe, then, means to change the conceptual and/or emotional setting or viewpoint in relation to which a situation is experienced and place it in another frame which fits the "facts" of the same concrete situation equally well or even better, and thereby changes its entire meaning'. If the prevailing view of the problem is in terms of individual psychopathology, the therapist may reframe it in terms of relationships. If the frame that preoccupies the thinking of the family screens out some events or perceptions that do not fit, the reframing may include unnoticed aspects of behaviour, often strengths which have been unused. Reframing may simply turn around the perception of the same behaviour. Bad behaviour may be seen as evidence of liveliness, or anorexic symptoms as a form of defiance. Such reframing may form part of what is *said* to the family. Equally, it may be used as a way of *thinking* by the therapist and then may inform the therapist's action's without being spelt out. For example, when the therapist presses the parents of their anorexic daughter to take charge of her, and ensure that she eats, there are metamessages that reframe the situation both within the family and in relation to the professionals. The patient's refusal to eat is seen as a challenge to authority rather than as illness, and is therefore something about which the parents can do something rather than watch helplessly, and the domain of expertise and potency is identified as that of the parent rather than of the doctors or nurses.

Whilst reframing may play a crucial role in the planning of an intervention with a family, it is also a mode of thought and an orientation that is repeated throughout the therapy. It is manifest in simple acts such as the invitation of a spouse or of the children to a session, indicating an interest in the family; in the way the therapist listens to the views of each family member; or in the taking of a history that places symptoms in a developmental and family context.

SCHOOLS OF FAMILY THERAPY

Too much and too little can be made of the different schools of family therapy. It is important to bear in mind that, whilst there is a value in emphasising their differences, each has been influenced by the other, and rivalry or hostility has not been a significant factor in maintaining the differences between them. The value to the practitioner of knowing about the different approaches is that it provides a range of styles or strategies when thinking about a family. The principal features of each 'school' will be described briefly, and this description will be further amplified in a consideration of forms of family assessment and intervention.

The 'Milan Method'

The 'Milan Method' or 'Systems Therapy', as represented by Selvini Palazzoli et al (1978, 1980), seeks to elucidate the family system through a series of questions. The therapist is neutral in the sense that he or she sets out not to become emotionally involved with the family processes nor to align his or herself with any particular family members. A form of questioning termed 'circular questioning' is used, in which the perspective of each family member is examined in order to elaborate a circular or systemic hypothesis. These questions address differences or comparisons, and relationships. The focus may be historical; the therapist asks about differences in relationships before and after the onset of symptoms. It may concern the future; the therapist asks family members to predict the consequences for family relationships if a certain behaviour were no longer present. It may be current; for example, the therapist asks family members to compare the levels of anxiety about the problem shown by each parent. These questions, which utilise the first two elements of the theory described earlier, are used to formulate an hypothesis in terms of the third element. Frequently, the hypothesis highlights a conflict between the demands within the family for relationships to change – for example as children leave home, or following the death of a family member – and processes which are tending to oppose this. Symptoms are seen as an attempted solution to this dilemma. As described in its original form, this process of questioning is not intended to be therapeutic, although some of the original Milan group have come to believe that this approach may lead to change. In the classical description, the systemic hypothesis is used to formulate a message to the family which reframes the symptomatic behaviour and often includes a paradoxical injunction, i.e. an instruction that the patient should, to a greater or lesser extent, continue to show the same problem. Such a 'paradoxical' intervention is, however, only one of a range of possible messages which are designed to introduce difference to the prevailing family patterns, thus creating the need for the establishment of a new pattern – one that does not include symptomatic behaviour.

Structural family therapy

The structural approach pioneered by Salvador Minuchin (represented in Minuchin 1974, Minuchin & Fishman 1981) provides a marked contrast in style to that of the Systemic, whilst coming from essentially the same theoretical origins. The assumption is that, in order to function, families require a *structure* in which the separate and different functions off the marital relationship, the parental relationship and the sibling relationships are maintained. This ensures that the children are provided with the space to develop without the burdens of sharing the intimacies or difficulties of their parents' relationship, or of taking responsibilities that are the problems of adults. The approach is developmental in that it assumes that, whilst structure is maintained, the manifestations of it change as the family members age. The purpose of the structure is primarily to maintain stability whilst the children are young, but to accommodate considerable change, especially when the children reach adolescence and young adulthood. It is assumed that many of the psychological difficulties of late adolescence and young adulthood are related to the issue of the move from the family and the establishment of new relationships.

In contrast to the Milan therapist, the Structural family therapist is interested primarily in the processes that take place between family members in the room. Any particular sequence is taken to be indicative of interactions that are repeated in relation to many issues and over long periods of time within the family. These, then, are the primary sources of information for hypotheses about family functioning, and the interventions are designed to change what goes on between family members in the room with the therapist. The therapist is therefore active, and may become quite emotionally involved with the family, or form alliances temporarily with particular members. However, the idea is not that the therapist moves in to solve the family's problem for them, but rather that he moves in and out again, leaving the family with the possibilities of change.

The 'Strategic Approach'

The terms 'Strategic', 'Brief', or 'Problem Solving' all refer to a therapy in which the focus is on devising an intervention to fit the problem. Such an approach is represented in a number of key works, including Watzlawick et al (1974), Halcy (1977) and Madanes (1981). In contrast to the Milan and Structural approaches, no attempt is made to arrive at a formulation of family functioning in general. The emphasis is on problem solving, and so therapy is done with those who are interested in change, which may be only part of the family. Nevertheless, the theoretical underpinnings discussed earlier lead to a reframing of the symptomatic behaviours in interactional or systemic terms, and to interventions derived from that process. The therapist asks about the problem and the interactions centred on it, paying particular attention to the attempted solutions. The assumption is that there is a fit between the symptomatic behaviour and the efforts of other members of the family which promotes the continuation of that behaviour.

The focus of change in the therapy is behaviour, often defined as the least change of behaviour that the family members would regard as significant, and the intervention is in the form of a task to be carried out between sessions. The direction may be simply that the family members who are closest to the patient should respond differently to, or cease their attempts to prevent, the symptomatic behaviour. The rationale for this is to be found in the reframing of the problem. Alternatively, the reframing may form a basis for instructing the family members to intensify their behaviours, and the rationale for this is the same as that for the paradoxical injunctions of the Milan group.

FAMILY THERAPY IN PRACTICE

So far, family therapy has been discussed as if it were a therapeutic item that might or might not be added to the repertoire of the psychiatric team. However, family therapy is a particular manifestation of the Batesonian theory described earlier, and this theory has a range of possible applications in clinical practice. It may, for example, be used as a tool to examine the place of the patient within an institutional or interprofessional network and hence may help to clarify a therapeutic strategy quite independently of any consideration of family processes or therapy. Furthermore, an assessment of family processes may inform clinical management without leading to family therapy. When a psychiatric team has included an assessment of family processes in its thinking, then the admission of a patient is seen not only as the entry of an individual into hospital for treatment, but also as an encounter between the family and the team and the institution. Seen in this light, apparently ordinary and inconsequential events, such as the visit of relatives to the ward to talk to the doctor or nurses, may be seen as a crucial part of the family processes. This may influence the way such events are handled. Both the impact of the theory for practice in general, and the role of the assessement of family functioning within an overall treatment approach are considered further later in this chapter.

Indications for family therapy

Four principal considerations are relevant to the decision making about whether to offer family therapy.

Firstly, what research evidence is there that family therapy might be of value in this case? Here, the crucial issue concerns the use that may be made by the clinician of the available evidence, and this will be considered with reference to two areas. Perhaps the clearest evidence for the role of a family intervention in the treatment of major psychiatric disorder comes from studies of the effectiveness of family interventions in schizophrenia. There is good evidence that where a close family member shows a high level of expressed emotion, as evidenced by critical or hostile comments or over-involvement, the relapse rate is reduced by a family intervention which is designed to lower the expressed emotion. This finding is particularly salutary in the context of this chapter, as in some key respects the family interventions used in these studies differ from those described in this chapter (Goldstein et al 1978, Falloon et al 1982, Leff et al 1982, Anderson et al 1981). In particular, the approaches start with the assumption that the *presence* of an illness can be defined independently of interactional and family processes, even though its *course* may be influenced by them. Thus, all four studies have included education about the illness as part of the package, and have not sought to reframe symptoms. On the other hand, many of the issues addressed within these interventions have features in common with the forms of family therapy described here (Berkowitz et al 1984, Leff 1985). Russell et al (1987) carried out an evaluation of family therapy in anorexia nervosa, and found that compared to an individual supportive approach, family therapy was more effective in leading to maintenance of weight and regular menstrual cycles in girls with onset at 18 years of age or younger, and with duration of symptoms of less than three years. However, it was no more effective than an individual approach where symptoms had been present for more than three years, or where they had started after the age of 18.

How may such well-conducted research studies be of value in clinical practice? Firstly, as is the case with all experimental studies, they involve a comparison of a family intervention with one or more alternative forms of treatment. Similarly, in clinical practice the question always centres on a choice between two or more approaches, or on a combination of approaches. This means that unless clinical choice is close to that explored in the studies, such studies can act only as a factor in clinical decision making, rather than a straightforward indication for or against a particular intervention. Furthermore, the studies demonstrate the utility and limitations of family interventions in relation to particular questions. In the first example (that of schizophrenia) the question concerned relapse rate, and in the second (anorexia nervosa) maintenance of body weight and menstruation. If the clinical problem to be solved is different, then the research findings do not provide a direct guide. For example, the issue may be that the young person with schizophrenia is not supported by his parents in attending a day centre, or that the young person with anorexia nervosa is not establishing a life independently of her parents. A family intervention may be considered in order to solve such particular problems. The general point is that whilst research evidence is of considerable value it must be integrated into the therapeutic strategy which is designed for the particular case. A further point, which can be made in relation to all studies of psychotherapeutic intervention, is that it is difficult to determine which is the 'active' ingredient of the treatment. For example, the interventions designed to lower expressed emotion included (in different proportions) education, improving problem solving, improving communication, firming up intergenerational boundaries, and expanding social networks. Furthermore, a considerable body of literature has shown that the qualities of the therapist influence outcome irrespective of the form of psychological intervention used (see Ch. 1).

A second consideration which may sway clinicians in their choice of therapy is the availability of the clinical accounts of family therapy. Clinical papers frequently contain detailed accounts of exchanges between therapists and family members, and videotapes showing the work of prominent family therapists are available within training institutions. Such open demonstrations of techniques can be of great value, but these compelling and dramatic representations of processes within family therapy should not lead to a loosening of critical facilities. Sequences are usually chosen where they illustrate the theory, rarely where they appear to detract from it. Cases are described generally where the outcome has been favourable, and rarely where they represent therapeutic failure or frustration. Generalisations regarding the use of family therapy in a particular condition will be limited where there has been a lack of adequate specification of the condition, and biases introduced from patterns of referral to specialist or private clinics.

The third consideration concerns the details of the particular case. Information may be derived from other professionals, individual family members, a family assessment or a combination of these. It is important, especially within the context of a treatment strategy which may have several components, to identify which problems might be addressed if a family approach were used. The identified problem may be the presenting symptoms, and the task may be to find a therapeutic approach which leads to a lessening of these. Alternatively, the problem may be specified in developmental terms, along the lines of, 'The young person is not developing his life separately from that of his mother'. Alternatively, it may be a very specific issue, such as that the patient's father is repeatedly criticising him towards staff. Consideration of the extent to which the symptomatic behaviour appears to be related to the family processes may further aid decision making. For example, how intense and frequent are the family interactions in relation to the symptomatic behaviour? How committed does the family appear to be to the lifestyle based on this behaviour? The theory leads one to look not only at factors maintaining the status quo but also to alternatives within the family. Does the family have ways of being together other than that centred on the symptoms? Often, therefore, it is important to consider the strengths of the family members which may be used to bring about change. The strength may be quite clear, for example in the form of courage, persistence or humour, or may be apparent only after activities currently seen in a negative light have been reframed. Thus, the overall question is, 'To what extent does a formulation based on the theory described in this chapter make sense of the clinical problem?'

The fourth issue to be addressed is whether the use of family therapy would complement or contradict other forms of treatment. In the context of adult psychiatry, this may include admission to hospital, medication or even detainment under the Mental Health Act. It could appear confusing and unproductive to offer a form of therapy that seeks to redefine symptomatic behaviour in terms of relationships and the responsibility of each family member for their lives, whilst also offering treatment that identifies the 'patient' as unwell. This is, however, not inevitably the case, as both biological and interpersonal factors may operate simultaneously.

A related consideration concerns the professional network in which family therapy might be considered. Family therapy may, especially in the setting of adult psychiatry, be seen as an 'alternative' therapy that might be offered by staff who are disaffected or discouraged with the impact of conventional psychiatric treatment on a patient. For reasons that will become clear later in the chapter, it is crucial that the authority that is taken for the family therapy is the same as the authority that is taken for the case as a whole.

Finally, family therapy, to no greater or lesser extent than any other psychological treatment, depends on the quality of relationships between professionals and the patient and his or her family. Since several individuals have to be engaged for family therapy to proceed, and some members may be seen within the family as more powerful than others, the task of engagement is often quite complex. Without a therapeutic alliance, family therapy, however 'indicated', will fail; if it is achieved, the basis for useful work may have been established.

Setting up a meeting with the family

Much of the family therapy literature assumes that a family has agreed to family therapy and proceeds from that point. In practice, much of the skill lies with enabling a family meeting to take place. Members of families frequently assume either that the implication of a family meeting is that some or all of them will be blamed for the patient's condition, or that they will be given advice on how to handle the patient's illness. The aim is *never* to do the former, although the treatment might involve some tough talking, and it is *usually* not to do the latter. The initial aim is to bring the members of the family together to investigate the way the family functions, although any meeting with family members also has therapeutic possibilities.

The invitation to the family can be put in many ways, for example in terms of a need to understand the views of all of the members of the family, in order to utilise strengths, or pool ideas. It is crucial for the intending therapist to anticipate that the family process is likely to be activated around the invitation to the session, especially if the symptom is performing an important function.

Case study 5.1   Secrets in the family

A 24-year-old woman with a long standing history of repeated and severe cutting, periods of depression, and overdoses, was receiving inpatient therapy at a specialist unit. She had revealed whilst in the unit that she had been sexually abused by her elder brother over several years, but said that only one of her two sisters knew about this. Her father had been repeatedly violent towards her mother, and had left the family when the children were very young. Since then, her mother had brought up the children, and the brother had taken up many of the roles of 'man of the house'. A family session was held shortly after her admission; for a number of reasons it was decided to delay the offer of further sessions. In the first session, mutual protection within the family had been a very clear theme, with the implication that keeping secrets was part of this process. After several months it was decided to invite the family for a series of further sessions. The therapist (who was also the consultant) wrote to each member of the family and received first a phone call from the sister to whom the patient had confided regarding the sexual abuse, in which she proposed a meeting with the children only, as she was worried about the possible effect on her mother of further family meetings. She thought that her mother might collapse especially if the sexual abuse came up. The therapist told her that he understood her concern very well, especially the need to protect her mother, but that he thought also that if he took up her idea it would lead to a repetition of the family dilemma in which something secret went on with the children. He said also that perhaps the children underestimated the strength of their mother who, for all her frailties, had brought up the four of them single-handed. A day or so after this, the mother rang the therapist to say that she did not think a meeting should be held because of her fear of what her daughter (the patient) might do if she (the mother) said certain things. By this, she meant that her daughter might cut herself or take an overdose. His reply was to say that he understood her wish to protect her daughter but also that she could not take responsibility for what her daughter might or might not do.

The phone calls illustrated the circular tangle in which the family found itself. The children tried to look after their mother as if she were a child, the mother took responsibility for her daughter as if for an infant, and each was attempting to read the other's state of mind in anticipation of disaster. The therapist was being invited to agree that this was the only way things could be. In order to set up the session, it was important to convey that the current way of functioning had value and was respected, whilst insisting that the session would go ahead with the implication that things could be different. It is important to note, here, the process rather than the outcome. Under different circumstances, the decision might have been different. For example, it would have been reasonable to see the mother on her own, with the knowledge of the adult children, as a way of highlighting the boundary between her and the children. The crucial element is that the therapist's response was guided by an idea about the way the family functioned and about the way he was being asked to take part.

The meeting with the family – the setting

Ideally, the family will be seen in a room which conveys that their arrival as a family has been anticipated and is welcomed. It will be sufficiently large, but not so big as to overwhelm them; there will be the right number of chairs arranged approximately in a circle, perhaps with a small table at the centre; and if there are children in the family, there will be toys and drawing materials readily available. It is common practice for the room to have a one-way screen, so that one or more people can watch and listen and take part in discussion with the therapist. The people behind the one way screen may be able to phone the therapist during the session, or speak to him using an earbug. Almost always, the therapist will take a break to talk with the team. These procedures have several purposes. Firstly, processes in families are complex, and the therapist frequently does not notice events that might be relevant, such as the unsuccessful efforts of a child to interrupt or short circuit arguments, or non-verbal communications between family members that have not been focused on by the therapist. Secondly, families frequently induce the therapist to behave in particular ways, often without the therapist recognising what is going on. Minuchin (1978) describes the attitude of the family of the anorexic patient to the therapist as being one of 'grateful opposition'. The behaviour of the family members is consistent with the family rule that conflict should be avoided, and the therapist is pressed to avoid confrontation or intensity. This is manifest, for example, when the therapist goes into the session planning to take a particular line but finds himself doing something quite different, usually something rather polite and apparently pleasant. This process is likely to be much more apparent to those behind the screen. Thirdly, quite simply, it is much easier for those behind the screen to think. Even the experienced therapist who is continually developing new theories as he or she questions, often does not have the time to reflect on how to fit them together within the session.

Whilst this arrangement represents common practice, and to a certain extent has become part of the folklore of family therapy, it is not essential. If the facility of the one-way screen is not available, at least one member of a team may sit in the room with the therapist to perform a similar function. Equally, whether or not such a screen is available, the therapist may proceed in different ways, for instance with a co-therapist and without a team, or using a form of supervision which is separate from the session. Attention to the process is more important than obedience to a method.

The therapist and the family

What happens when a therapist sits down with the family? Clearly, this varies depending upon the family, but often there will be a struggle in which the principal issues are authority, space or separateness, and safety. In essence, these will echo the preoccupations of the family. Thus, in the family where members telephoned twice prior to a session, authority had in the past been confused and uncertain, the members were anxious about separateness, and they had not experienced safe or benign family processes. There was a question in the telephone calls and in the sessions about the authority of the therapist, his separateness, including his capacity for separate thought, and his potential dangerousness. To a greater or lesser extent, there is a pressure on the therapist to take so much authority that the family will abandon its own, or to take so little that the family's demands become overwhelming; to be so separate that the family does not feel that the therapist is available, or so close that he becomes a family member; and to be so benign that he can only agree with all that goes on, or so intrusive or dangerous that the family is threatened. Sometimes, the therapist will succumb to the pressures without realising it, sometimes he will choose to go along with them, and sometimes he will decide to oppose them. There is no perfect route, although if therapy becomes dominated by any one of these processes it is likely that help will be needed from an authoritative, thoughtful and helpful team of colleagues.

The style of the therapist informs the family about the sort of activity he is engaged in. He sets out to be active, natural, curious and emotionally straightforward. However, he clearly has a business that he wants to pursue in the session, and what this consists of will depend upon the principal influences on his style. These influences will be both personal, in the form of the therapist's own personality and life history, and professional. These professional influences will also be diverse, and will include the effect of the particular profession from which the therapist comes (psychology, medicine, social work and so on) and the styles of family therapy to which the therapist has been exposed.

Family assessment

The assessment of the family will have much in common with any assessment for psychiatric treatment or psychotherapy. Here, the focus is those aspects of the assessment that are relevant to a family formulation and intervention. The three key points of theory described earlier are central to the assessment. They are seen in the investigation of alternatives to symptomatic behaviour, the exploration of symptoms and their alternatives within family interactions and relationships, and in the identification of the role of symptomatic behaviour within the life of the family.

Different approaches to assessment are considered here in relation to a case example.

Case study 5.2   A depressed woman and her elderly mother

The patient was a 65-year-old woman with a longstanding severe retarded depression that had been resistant to conventional inpatient psychiatric treatment. She was seen together with her husband and her 93-year-old mother. Her mother had been widowed early in life and the daughter had been her only companion through her childhood. The patient had first married a man who had been violent, and the relationship had soon ended, whereupon the daughter had resumed her intimacy with her mother. In her subsequent marriage, to the current husband, the patient had maintained her closeness to her mother, to the extent that she had accompanied the couple on their honeymoon and on all subsequent holidays, and the husband and wife had had little independent life together.

The therapist who uses the Milan approach will examine the issue of difference in a number of ways; for example, by inquiring either about conditions prior to the onset of symptoms compared to those following their onset, or about what would happen if the symptoms were no longer present. In this case, the therapist asked about the state of affairs preceding and following the onset of symptoms, and it emerged that the depression started at the time of the husband's retirement, when the decision was made, mainly by the patient and her mother, that all three would move out of London to live together in the countryside. It seemed possible that the husband's retirement had introduced a possible difference to the family, with its implications of increased time and intimacy with his wife, and that the depression had introduced a countermove which had enabled there to be continuing closeness with both the mother and the husband. Thus, each of the elements of the theory were addressed through the questioning. The symptoms were part of the delicate balance of relationships which had been threatened by the retirement; by implication, if symptoms were *not* present there might be a profound change in family relationships.

A therapist using a Structural approach might well gather historical information in a similar way but would have a different focus. He would notice, as did the therapist in this case, that when the patient was asked a question she looked at her mother and her mother answered for her. Her mother repeatedly helped her daughter out in a way that maintained her as less competent and, by implication, unwell, whilst the patient's husband became increasingly distanced. Thus, the impression gained from the Milan-style historical questioning – that the symptomatic behaviour promoted closeness between mother and daughter at a time when her husband became more available for intimacy – was consistent with the sequences seen in the session. A further manifestation of the theory discussed earlier is seen in the way the family system is 'probed' to examine the way it responds to the introduction of difference. Having identified the repeated patterns of interaction in the room, the therapist acts to promote a different sequence. This is, of course, potentially the start of an intervention; but, more importantly at the outset of therapy, it is a probe to see how the family responds to the possibility of a different way of interacting. For example, the therapist might have waited until there was an appropriate moment and then asked the couple to talk together. The most likely outcome would have been that they might have achieved this for a few seconds before the grandmother interrupted. It would be crucial to notice how this was achieved. Did the husband signal the interruption with a glance or a movement of his body, or was it the patient who gave the signal? A further crucial point to be noticed would be whether the patient became even briefly more animated when talking with her husband, or whether she remained withdrawn and apparently unable to manage. The latter might also act as a cue for her mother to intervene.

The Strategic therapist would focus his attention on the behaviour which could be identified by the patient and other family members as a problem. 'Being depressed' would not be accepted, but 'not going out' or 'not doing the cooking' might be, provided each of those involved agreed about it. This process might lead to the identification of behaviour of the husband or of the mother which might be changed, and these would also become a focus of the intervention. The next step would be to enumerate the solutions which had been attempted. In this case, both the husband and the patient's mother had attempted to overcome her inertia by repeated persuasion, buying her items which she might use if she became less depressed, and taking her out on trips. The question of alternatives to problem behaviour is addressed not in terms of historical or future differences, nor in terms of different possibilities within the session, but in the form of different behaviour which might be negotiated with the therapist. Usually, the therapist establishes with the family members what would be the smallest change of behaviour that they would take as clear evidence of progress. In this case, the answer might be that the patient would cook the vegetables for one meal at the weekend. The family members might have been happy with this, but often it is necessary also to reframe the current situation in such a way that they can cease their attempts to get the patient to do more. Thus, in this case, the therapist might have said that with the retirement of the husband this was an opportunity for a reassessment of the roles of everyone in the family, and it would therefore be premature to assume that the patient should resume her previous duties in the house. Until they had each reassessed their roles, they should not encourage her to do more than the agreed task. The reader will have noticed that the description of the 'family assessment' has included a possible intervention. The hallmark of the Strategic approach is that what is assessed is the scope for the negotiation of clear goals for therapy, of possible differences or alternatives, and of the task, which often includes a reframing of the current position. Assessment and intervention are indissolubly linked.

Interventions

A variety of forms of intervention are to be found in family therapy, but most of them have common origins. Firstly, many of the early and influential family therapists had previously been psychoanalysts who had been frustrated by the slowness of psychoanalytic work. They were looking for a therapy that would be effective and relatively quick. It is characteristic of family therapy interventions that the therapist looks for rapid and tangible change. Secondly, clinical experience showed that whether problems were treated individually or with the family, the commitment to continuing the same way is often enormous. Thus, a form of 'strong medicine' was needed. But the family or individual who does not want or is afraid of change is not likely to accept an intervention with that label on it. So many family therapy interventions have in common a playful or paradoxical element that is of the form, 'change but stay the same', 'become what you already are', 'give up in order to go on'. Thirdly, if symptomatic behaviour can be seen as one of a set of alternative ways of being in relationships, and is therefore at the centre of forms of intimacy between family members, any invitation to change must include a recognition of what is valued and valuable in the way the family is working now, and an acknowledgement of existing strengths and energies that need to be preserved.

Paradox

Within the Milan approach, the primary form of intervention is through a message which defines the symptomatic behaviour in terms of the way the symptoms enter into relationships, the alternatives available to the family, and the role of the symptoms in preserving family life. This will be done at the end of the session after lengthy consultation with the team. This brings us to the concept of the counterparadox, which has been central to this approach, and which follows from the theory discussed earlier. If symptoms enter into family life just like the everyday currency of 'please', 'thank you' or 'would you like a hot water bottle?', then there is clearly a good reason for them to continue. Equally, the family members come to therapy with a wish that the symptoms should cease. This means that the family members are simultaneously doing something which promotes the continuation of the symptoms, and something to stop them; but only the efforts to stop them are declared. The vehicle for this undeclared wish for the symptoms to continue is the metamessage or frame given to the interactions. Thus, in Case study 5.2 the symptom could be seen to maintain the intimacy between the mother and daughter centred on the daughter's needs to be looked after, and the intimacy of the husband and wife was defined by the symptoms as one of carer and patient, rather than husband and wife. The implication of this was that if the couple were to define themselves as husband and wife, the wife and her mother could not be as close. The family is therefore seen to present the paradox that change is both wished for and feared. The message to the family containing the counterparadox would present the team's view about the relationship of the symptoms to family life, and advise the patient to continue with the same behaviour, at least for the time being.

There are several ways in which this technique may bring about change (Cade 1984). Firstly, the counterparadox or paradoxical injunction makes plain the undeclared component of family relationships. Secondly, the message places the symptoms in a new context, whereby it is seen as one component of the fit between members of the family. The third aim is particularly associated with the question of how to deliver 'strong medicine' in a form that can be swallowed. The therapist aligns himself completely with the tide of family life that pushes for things to stay the same. There are then two possibilities: either (1) the family accepts the therapist's view that things should fundamentally stay the same and thus, implicitly, accepts his authority, and change can be made within that context; or (2) the family believes this is 'strong medicine' and therefore it should be opposed, which can be done only by changing. Fourthly, there is an element of surprise; the light touch of the wrestler who uses the momentum of his opponent to unbalance him. Fifthly, there is the implication that if a patient and family can choose to continue the status quo, including the symptoms, then at some stage they can choose to change them. What appeared to be uncontrollable is defined as subject to their control.

Several members of the original Milan group no longer use paradoxical techniques, and Selvini Palazzolli et al (1989) now regard them as ineffective. However, they remain of interest partly because they capture something of the essence of many family therapy techniques, and partly because they have potential when used alongside other techniques. In this case, the patient's depressed behaviour was reframed in terms of her competing loyalties to her husband and her mother, and the family was told that she may need to maintain this state until the future shape of the family could be negotiated. The therapist also said that, on the other hand, if there were other ways of ensuring that these issues were sorted out, this might not be necessary. Thus, there was a paradoxical element which was included as part of a presentation of alternative possibilities.

Structural interventions

We will look next at the form of interventions used by Structural family therapists. Let us assume that the therapist introduced the 'probe' and saw that the patient and her husband did not sustain a conversation beyond a few words before the grandmother interrupted. He may seek to increase the intensity of his input so that the family can experience a more sustained period of difference. For example, he might ask the husband and wife to sit next to each other and face each other and talk; each time the wife turns to cue in her mother, the therapist might ask the husband whether this is what he wants, and challenge him to make sure that his wife talks to him before talking to her mother. If the husband cues in his mother-in-law, the therapist might use a similar approach in reverse. Alternatively, he might seek to strike up a conversation with the depressed woman that rekindles some old fires. For example, he might talk to her about what she did before she was married.

In this case, the woman had had considerable success as an athlete. When the therapist talked to her about this, she became quite animated in contrast to her usual demeanour. Depending on the therapist's judgment, he might either continue to talk to the wife, providing a rivalrous and flirtatious challenge to the husband, or move the conversation on to what it was that had brought the husband and wife together, bringing in the husband to the conversation and addressing the two of them. A further possibility would be for the therapist to talk to the patient's mother about her life, both in the past and currently, this time ensuring that neither the daughter or son-in-law are able to join in. As he attempts to undertake any of these approaches, the members of the family will undoubtedly try to re-establish the old shape, and the therapist has to be prepared to be just as stubborn. He delivers his strong medicine with a mixture of tact, toughness and humour. He will take advantage of the fact that he has recognised the strengths of the family, and has reframed much of what they do, perhaps with reference to their commitment, love or protection of each other. He will also insist that each is separate and each has a voice and this must be heard. Whilst the therapist using a Structural approach focuses primarily on detailed interactions, he will have ideas about possible more general themes that are being enacted. For example, with the history of an absent father, and then a violent spouse, there was a question of whether a man in the family could have a potency that could be enjoyed without it being dangerous. Bearing this in mind, the therapist might have talked to the husband about how he 'caught his wife the athlete'.

It is important to emphasise that, whilst there is a simplicity to these interventions, judgement and caution is needed in their application. The aim is not to empower some members of the family at the expense of others, but to promote the strength of each of them. In this family, the therapist had good evidence that the patient's mother was robust, and so an approach that addressed the couple and temporarily excluded the mother would be unlikely to lead her to be unable to cope. On the other hand, the readiness of the husband to break into a lively exchange between the therapist and his wife was not so clear, and so the therapist would be more cautious about this approach.

Strategic interventions

As we have seen, the assessment for a Strategic approach leads directly to the intervention. Once the groundwork has been done, much of the ingenuity of this approach resides in the devising of tasks. These may be of the form described earlier, whereby the participants are asked to agree to give up the attempted solution to the problem. However, the task may involve intensifying the behaviours, or turning them into something more playful or dramatic. Thus, in a family where there are many arguments, the therapist may talk about this as an indication of the capacity of each family member to put their point of view, but also suggest that they do not do it well enough or bring it to a proper conclusion. The task, therefore, is to set aside time to practise arguing better. Madanes (1984) sets tasks with playful or symbolic elements. When symptoms are episodic, for example, in panic attacks, it might emerge that the patient's partner is particularly physically demonstrative during an attack. The task might be set that the patient is to pretend from time to time that he or she is having an attack, and that the spouse is to comfort the patient during these 'attacks' in exactly the same way as during a real attack. The conditions under which the patient and spouse are physically close can then be established without the presence of a real attack.

Case study 5.3   Catholic candles

A task with a strong symbolic real content was set for a Roman Catholic couple, where the problem was the wife's repeated outbursts of violent and destructive behaviour. She had been physically and sexually abused as a child, and was in general extremely volatile, whilst her husband, who had come from a family in which there were 'no arguments', was extremely placid. The task consisted of lighting candles each evening before they went to bed, two of which were identified as representing their relationship, and two representing each of their families of origin. They were instructed as to who should light each candle and who should blow each candle out. The task was consistent with their strong religious faith, it was symmetrical (in marked contrast to other aspects of their relationship), and it contained a symbolic respect for, and leaving behind of, their families of origin.

Here again some words of caution are necessary. Whilst there is an apparent simplicity to strategic interventions, and an appeal, in that they may be devised without extensive assessment of individual and family functioning, they have nevertheless been developed by experienced clinicians. Elements of clinical judgment, and a wider assessment of family functioning, are frequently used in framing strategic interventions, although these are not made explicit in the theory.

FAMILY THERAPY IN GENERAL PSYCHIATRY

The emphasis in this chapter has been on the application of family therapy theories and techniques with psychiatrically ill patients. Whilst consideration of different schools has been necessary in order to indicate a range of approaches to gathering information and formulating inter-ventions, it should be borne in mind that none of these has evolved within adult psychiatry. There is therefore a danger that family therapy may be seen as a treatment that can be introduced without attention to the institutional and therapeutic context. If this were to happen, it would be an ironic legacy of Bateson whose main preoccuption was the examination of context; indeed this is where family therapy has much in common with individual and group analytic ideas. Two cases will illustrate some of the points.

Case study 5.4   Institutions as 'families'

The first was of a 20-year-old woman referred for in-patient psychotherapy. She had a long history of delinquency, alcohol and drug abuse, bingeing and laxative abuse leading to electrolyte imbalance, self-injury and serious overdoses. During the four months prior to admission, she was given intensive psychiatric care on an adult psychiatric ward because of the anxieties of the staff about her suicidal intentions. She had engendered very powerful emotions on the ward, where some nurses had formed special relationships with her, spending hours talking to her and staying late after their usual duties. The patient conformed both diagnostically and in terms of interpersonal and psychodynamic processes to the description of the 'borderline' personality organisation. The potential for a breakdown of authority and structure in these cases is usually very great, and so it was important to promote the definition of these within the institutional 'family' of the referring and receiving team. A meeting was set up with both consultants and senior nurses present, together with the relevant junior members of staff. The meeting was set up so as to reflect the differing institutional structures. It might be that the role of the patient within the referring team had served a useful function; it would have been disrespectful to attempt to discuss that, and so the task was not to question the previous management, but to highlight the fund of knowledge of the patient possessed by the referring team, and to ask for support in the proposed approach. In particular, specific ground rules were established between the two consultants and the two senior nurses. This turned out to be crucial, for, as predicted, once the patient was transferred she bombarded the previous unit with complaints about her treatment at the hospital, and one of the junior nurses from the referring team organised visits to the patient without reference either to her seniors, or to the nurses at the psychotherapy unit. Both of these issues were taken up by the senior professionals at each institution and the authority structures were maintained.

Here, family therapy perspectives informed the way in which the institutions handled the patient and each other, leading to suggestions about how things might be done differently, in a way that respected and valued the work done so far. In this case, formal family therapy was not considered appropriate.

Case study 5.1   Secrets in the family (contd)

In the case of the 24-year-old woman with a long history of self injury described on page 127, family therapy was offered. In many respects, the work with the family employed techniques that have been described earlier in this chapter. However, it was important that the family approach should be consistent with the rest of the work that was undertaken within the hospital. Tasks or messages that conflicted with it would have been contradictory and unhelpful. Furthermore, it could be argued that the admission of the identified patient to the unit had reasserted the idea of an identified patient with an individual condition. In as much as the approach of the unit was to reframe the patient's 'illness' in terms of intrapsychic and interpersonal processes, there was no contradiction; nevertheless, an admission lasting one year contains a strong a message about individual psychopathology. Family therapy did not attempt to move from the idea of an identified patient, but incorporated it as a facet of the individual differences among all the family members. In setting up the sessions, attention was paid to the family structure and to the institutional structure. In this case, authority and structure within the family had been lost. The team in turn encountered repeated efforts by the patient to undermine its organisation, and she particularly distrusted male members of the staff, especially those in authority. As the only member of the team with family therapy experience, it was clear that I should see the family. How would the fact that I was a man relate to: my function as a consultant for the case, and my role as joint leader of the team with the senior nurse; to the family's history of a violent and unpredictable father and older brother, who had sexually abused his younger sisters; and a family where secrets were kept? Ideally, perhaps, the consultant would have seen the family with the senior nurse, representing a couple with authority, but that would have belied the difference in their levels of experience. Therefore, the family was seen by the consultant with the senior nurse, the patient's therapist and key nurse all behind the screen. The presence and importance to the family's therapist of the team was made very clear to the family.

CONCLUSION

These examples bring us back to the starting point of the chapter, namely that 'family therapy' is a term that refers to a theoretical perspective with general utility, and a specific form of treatment. Family therapy perspectives are of value in the treatment of psychiatrically disturbed adults because they lead to questions about the place of pathology within family and professional systems. This may influence the treatment without leading to family therapy. Furthermore, they provide a framework for thinking about professional roles and a way of thinking about change. In these, they are respectful to the current ways of working and also present opportunities for alternatives. Finally, where family therapy is used it is essential to examine how it fits into the total therapeutic picture. The counter-therapeutic possibilities for mirroring family processes, or acting out institutional agendas by doing therapy that is different from that which prevails, is considerable. Frequently, symptomatic behaviour in a young adult is evidence of problems in the parents' relationship; an attempt by junior staff to do family therapy can be evidence of a similar process within a team. Conversely, the introduction of outrageous behaviour by an adolescent within a family can be a source of life; so can the introduction of an 'outrageous therapy' within a team. It all depends on how it is done.

FURTHER READING

Bateson G 1972 Steps to an ecology of mind. Ballantine Books, New York
Hoffman L 1981 Foundations of family therapy. Basic Books, New York
Minuchin S Fishman H C 1981 Family therapy techniques. Harvard University Press, Cambridge, Mass.
Madanes C 1984 Behind the one-way mirror. Advances in the practice of Strategic Therapy. Jossey Bass, San Francisco
Selvini Palazzoli M, Cecchin G, Prata G, Boscolo L 1978 Paradox and counter paradox. Jason Avonson, New York

6. Active and non-verbal therapeutic approaches

R. Tillett

INTRODUCTION

Most psychotherapies have at their heart a dialogue between patient and therapist. A number of approaches, however, extend beyond the conversational model to include the use of active or non-verbal techniques. These include psychodrama, sociodrama, drama therapy, art, music and the other creative therapies, Gestalt therapy, bioenergetics and other neo-Reichian approaches. Active techniques are also used in strategic and structural family work and behaviour therapy (see Chs. 4 and 5). All share the use of active experimental or non-conversational techniques, although beyond this they differ widely. Some are theoretically sophisticated, others essentially practical; some make direct use of the therapeutic relationship, others scarcely attend to it; some can be used only in groups, others in a variety of settings; some can be used for prolonged intensive treatment, others are more suited to less intense, shorter-term work. All make explicit suggestions for action, and may be termed prescriptive.

This chapter starts by examining the role and limitations of conversation as a medium of therapy, and outlines the history and development of the major schools of active and non-verbal therapy. The second section of the chapter explores the techniques they use, and the third section examines their application in specific clinical settings.

Conversation as a method of therapy

Words have been used as tools of human communication throughout man's history. Words are used to communicate both ideas and feelings; to convey concepts, descriptions, speculations, explanations, commands, flattery, accusations, love. Words are particularly good for conveying ideas, yet can also be used to communicate affect. When feelings are strong, however, words are often inadequate and increasing use is made of non-verbal communication – crying, shaking fists, smiling, grimacing and touching. In highly civilised societies, there is often an implicit bias which favours verbal descriptions of feelings as opposed to their direct expression or demonstration. But some things need doing, not discussing; there is a time for action, not words. Most people have had the experience of trying to convey sympathy to a grieving person and finding words inadequate; an arm around the shoulders may be the best way to communicate such feelings. Important human interactions, whether inside therapy or beyond it, include both verbal and non-verbal communication.

Modern psychotherapy, as a product of a developed society, can be seen essentially as a form of conversation – albeit a highly specialised one with its own particular characteristics and rules.

The function of conversation in therapy depends partly on its flexibility as a medium for exchanging ideas, and also on the very limitations which have caused some people to explore alternative approaches. A conversational exchange sets limits which may be important to both therapist and client, either of whom may fear the development of greater affective intensity. The use of words acts as a safety valve; when powerful emotion prevents further speech, the therapeutic dialogue is suspended while the client regains sufficient composure to resume talking. This boundary-setting function of conversation helps both client and therapist maintain equilibrium and to survive the experience. Conversely, non-verbal approaches may be useful when emotional intensification is desired.

Both therapists and clients vary in their preference for verbal as opposed to non-verbal forms of communication. Therapists are usually intelligent and articulate people skilled in the use of concepts and language. Research suggests that psychotherapists tend to prefer clients who are culturally similar to themselves, and also that well-educated people do significantly better in analytic forms of therapy than do people with poor academic backgrounds (Garfield 1986). The development of non-verbal approaches makes psychotherapy available to a much wider client population; dramatherapy, for example, has a great deal to offer the mentally handicapped, whose ability to use formal psychotherapy is limited; equally, experiental approaches can be helpful with people who are prone to intellectualise unproductively.

Despite the growth of interest in active and non-verbal approaches, conversation remains the bedrock of psychotherapy, and most approaches which extend beyond conversation continue to use words as part of the medium of treatment. Neo-Reichian therapists who specialise in body work, psychodrama practitioners and art therapists all use words as part of their approach. Though verbal dialogue may no longer be central to therapy, it is still part of it.

Writing about active approaches in therapy is clearly a paradoxical activity; these approaches have in common a wish to get beyond words, to action and expression. Their creative vigour, spontaneity and immediacy are hard to convey in print.

The development of non-conversational approaches

Sigmund Freud (1856–1939) is generally acknowledged as the founder of contemporary psychotherapy. Clearly, therapeutic conversations and encounters occurred previously, but Freud was the first to attempt a coherent synthesis of ideas and practices into a method of treatment. Like many other brilliant and charismatic figures, however, he inspired both devotion and rebellion, and many of the more active approaches to psychotherapy were developed by people who reacted against Freud's teaching and broke away from it. These approaches are therefore characterised both by their similarities as progeny of the Freudian tradition, and by differences which exemplify the personalities and beliefs of their developers. The use of active approaches in psychotherapy has been a focus for continuing discussion since Ferenczi coined the term 'active psychotherapy' in the 1920s. Freud appears to have disapproved of attempts to extend psychotherapy beyond conversational limits; he warned both Ferenczi and Reich of the dangers of doing so, and active approaches are still regarded with suspicion and mistrust by many psychodynamic therapists.

Not all the active approaches show such a direct line of descent from the Freudian tradition. Behaviour therapy, Systemic therapies and, more recently, Neuro-Linguistic Programming derive more from learning and communication theories, and are based on a different tradition and theoretical approach. They tend to focus on present attitudes and behaviours without exploring their historical origins, pay less attention to unconscious process, and on the whole ignore the transference relationship.

Psychodrama

Psychodrama was developed during the 1920s and 1930s by Jacob Moreno (1882–1974), a Rumanian who studied philosophy and then medicine in Vienna, where he subsequently founded the 'theatre of spontaneity' in which he encouraged young actors to explore current events through improvised drama. From his observations of the therapeutic benefits of play both in children and in adults, he developed psychodrama as a therapy, making extensive use of dramatic technique. Classical psychodrama is a group approach which focuses on the situation of one of the group members (the 'protagonist') who is encouraged to recreate and enact his difficulty or conflict using improvised dramatic techniques.

Moreno believed passionately in the value of creativity, spontaneity and play as approaches to human difficulties, and essentially developed a method of therapy rather than a theoretical exposition. Underlying his work were a number of assumptions. Firstly, that present interactions are contaminated by previous experiences and impede the ability to achieve what he defines as 'tele'; that is, the ability to relate accurately, empathically and without transference projections (related to Bion's (1962) 'alpha function' and Langs' (1976) 'type A communications'). Secondly, he believed that painful memories of past experiences and fearful fantasies about future events could be resolved by enactment in the therapeutic situation, often accompanied by catharsis, and leading to insight. He believed that people become 'role-bound', and that this inhibits their flexibility and spontaneity. In Moreno's view, discussion is inadequate to resolve this; action is required to explore new behavioural possibilities.

Moreno advocated the use of three clear phases in therapeutic sessions; the 'warm up', during which active exercises are used to promote spontaneity and cohesion and to identify possible protagonists and themes; the 'action', when the director helps the protagonist to explore and enact the material; and 'closure', during which the protagonist receives feedback from other group members who are encouraged to share their own feelings related to the enactment.

Sociodrama. This describes the use of psychodramatic technique to explore group issues. In sociodrama, all members of the group are involved in a common enactment which explores themes relevant to group, rather than individual, process.

Dramatherapy. The term, 'dramatherapy' refers very widely to any application of dramatic technique in therapeutic practice. Although clearly related to psychodrama, there is no single classical approach in dramatherapy. The Langleys (1983) and Jennings (1987) provide excellent accounts of the nature and use of dramatherapy in psychiatric practice.

Art and music, like drama, can be used both as vehicles for self expression and for formal psychotherapy. Art in particular has been increasingly recognised as a valuable medium for psychotherapy. Dalley (1984, 1987) describes this in detail.

Gestalt therapy

Gestalt therapy was developed by Frederick Perls (1883–1970), together with his wife Laura and other associates, as a synthesis of ideas from Freudian psychoanalysis (in which Perls was originally trained), Gestalt psychology, the teachings of Wilhelm Reich, ideas from existentialism (especially those of Martin Buber), and semantics. Perls was by nature active, extroverted and avowedly anti-intellectual, but he did articulate a theoretical foundation for his therapy which is characteristically active, experiential and experimental (Passons 1975).

Perls saw neurosis in terms of the restrictions and limitations which people impose upon themselves to fit in with their environment (physical, biological and social), and believed that successful adjustment required the employment of a person's full potential, both emotional and physical. One aim of therapy, therefore, is the identification, recovery and reintegration of parts of the self which have been split off and disowned.

As in psychodynamic therapy, the Gestalt approach presumes that a person's characteristic patterns of thinking, feeling and behaviour will be exemplified in the therapeutic situation, and that change occurring in therapy will generalise to the client's ordinary life. Moment-by-moment events in therapy are attended to in great detail but, in contrast to other dynamic approaches, interpretation is used sparingly if at all; clients are encouraged to develop their own understanding as therapy proceeds. The therapeutic relationship is seen as real and creative in itself, and not simply as a replay, via transference, of the past. The therapist may act as a projection object for the client, choosing whether to cooperate with or challenge the client's perceptions and demands; at other times, the therapist will divert the client's attention to external events (past or present), often by using dramatic enactment to recreate the external situation in therapy for re-examination and re-working. At times, the therapist will deliberately seek to frustrate the client in the therapeutic relationship, in order to promote both awareness and new behaviour. An example would be the refusal to offer explanations or interpretations, so as to intensify anger and/or provoke the client into thinking for himself.

Gestalt therapy explores the relationship between emotions and their physical expression; in therapy, attention is paid not only to the content of ideas and feelings expressed, but also to the physical process of the client – posture, breathing, facial movement, gestures, etc. Evidence of physical discomfort, distortion or imbalance are seen as clues to related difficulties in emotional process; such phenomena are commented upon but not interpreted.

The Gestalt approach was originally developed as an individual therapy, but Perls subsequently demonstrated its use in groups, usually working with an individual client in the group setting rather than attending to group process. This model has been widely assumed to represent the paradigm of Gestalt therapy, which can in fact be used effectively in individual, marital and family therapy as well, and in groups which focus on collective rather than individual process.

Neo-Reichian therapies

Bioenergetics, biosynthesis, biodynamic therapy, postural integration and other 'bodywork' approaches all derive from the teachings of Wilhelm Reich (1897–1957) (Rycroft 1971, Lowen 1975). Reich, like Moreno and Perls, trained originally as a psychoanalyst, then broke away to develop his own ideas. He shared with Freud a belief that human problems have their origin in the difficulties of early life, and that neurotic symptoms are frequently the result of repression of painful early life experiences. Reich believed that the physical expression of psychological trauma is represented physiologically by muscular tension and disturbances of posture, the so-called 'character armour'.

Neo-Reichian approaches work from these basic assumptions and seek to correct the client's disturbance by attending to the body as well as to the mind. Use is made of a variety of techniques, including exercises and remedial massage to relieve muscular tension and to correct posture. Patients may be encouraged to express their experience either verbally or non-verbally, and considerable attention is paid to the use of breathing and the voice. Some of the theoretical explanations given by neo-Reichian practitioners conflict with orthodox medical thinking, yet their undoubted contribution has been to focus attention on the possibility of two-way interaction between mind and body, so that bodily change can lead to mental improvement, as well as vice-versa. Although some of the techniques used by neo-Reichian therapists may be questionable in NHS practice, relaxation and fitness training, postural and breathing exercises are all firmly established therapeutic tools.

Primal therapy

Primal therapy assumes that major neurotic problems result from early infantile or even pre-natal experience, which must be re-experienced to achieve resolution. Primal therapy draws on a range of awareness-heightening exercises and neo-Reichian techniques, and actively encourages the client to regress to the 'primal' experience to allow the cathartic release of repressed emotion. In *rebirthing*, a related regressive approach, clients are encouraged to re-experience their own birth process.

These approaches to therapy are characterised by extreme regression and the exhibition of primitive behaviour. As in psychodrama, time is required afterwards for the re-establishment of contact with everyday realities. The primal approach was originally promoted vigorously in America by Arthur Janov, while in Britain interest was stimulated by Dr Frank Lake.

Psychosynthesis

Psychosynthesis derives from the work of Roberto Assagioli (1975) (1888–1974) an Italian psychiatrist who was influenced by Jung, with whom he shared an interest in the spiritual dimension of therapy as well as a belief in collective unconsciousness and the importance of archetypal myths and symbols. Assagioli was concerned with failure of integration, both within an individual and in the wider context of society and international relations. He developed the term, 'psychosynthesis' to indicate his belief in the importance of recognising, accepting, owning and integrating all aspects of the self. Related to this is the concept of subpersonalities; Assagioli suggested this term to represent a series of semi-individuated roles between which a person may shuttle according to the perceived needs of the moment. Therapy is directed at the recognition and integration of these different subpersonalities into a coherent whole, using a mixture of conversational and dramatic methods.

Neuro-Linguistic Programming

Neuro-linguistic programming (NLP) has no direct line of descent from the Freudian tradition, having been developed in the early 1970s by two Americans: John Grinder, a linguist and Richard Bandler, a mathematician turned therapist (Bandler & Grinder 1979, Robbie 1988). They studied, amongst others, Fritz Perls, Virginia Satir and Milton Erikson both in person and by using video recordings, and sought to establish a model of therapy which could replicate these talented therapists' achievements. The practice of NLP rests on three fundamental assumptions. Firstly, that it is essential to 'join' the client as accurately as possible. This involves the conscious adoption of the client's language patterns, physical and mental experience and cognitive habits. Secondly, NLP assumes that historical exploration and working through is not necessary to achieve behavioural change or problem resolution (an assumption shared with behaviour therapy). A third assumption is that the expectation of change is itself a powerful tool in achieving progress; there is an unashamed use of the 'magic' potential of therapy, and some techniques seem mainly intended to harness the client's expectation of progress. Much of NLP has links with communication theory, with behaviour therapy and with cognitive approaches, and there are also similarities to hypnotherapy. The technique focuses on the client's inner representation of external events, both past and present and seeks to change this. NLP's main aim is the relief of symptoms; it pays little attention to transference or to the promotion of insight. Although much of the approach is conversational, extensive use is also made of practical exercises, guided imagery and physical techniques.

SPECIFIC TECHNIQUES

Structured games and exercises

Structured games and exercises can be used for a variety of purposes, usually in groups, but occasionally with individuals. They can be used for introductory purposes, to establish and enhance trust, to promote contact and group cohesion, and to explore conflict. Exercises can be used to provide an opportunity for members of a group collectively or in subgroups to explore concentration, awareness and sensitivity, fantasies and projections about other group members, roles and interactions within the group, and non-verbal expressions of feeling. Dance, movement, massage and boisterous games can be incorporated.

A number of references contain detailed descriptions of a variety of structured games and exercises (Langley & Langley 1983, Brandes & Phillips 1978, Brandes 1982). As in cookery, these rather simplistic 'recipes' are for the guidance of the beginner; experienced therapists can concoct their own exercises from first principles.

Given that creativity is a central pivot of active approaches in therapy, slavish adherence to a recipe is undesirable; it is essential for the therapist to modify the technique or exercise to suit the individual situation.

Experimentation

Experimentation within therapy is common to all the active approaches and takes a wide variety of forms. Most experiments are created by the client or therapist in the immediate moment of therapy to heighten awareness or to explore alternative behaviour or solutions. Occasionally, experimentation can be useful to reinforce the status quo in the hope of leading to change by paradox. Many of the basic techniques of Gestalt therapy represent simple experimentation: for example, the suggestion that the client should repeat or exaggerate a particular word, phrase or gesture, experiment with saying or doing the opposite, or make simple changes in language (such as altering 'I cannot' to 'I will not'), or posture (such as, standing up if one wishes to assert oneself). More complex experimentation might include, for example, the suggestion that a client leaves the therapy room and then returns choosing a different style of behaviour or approach to see if this leads to fresh understanding. Group work offers opportunities for experimentation involving other members of the group or the whole group itself; an example would be 'doing a round', in which an individual group member tries out an existing or new behaviour on different members of the group in turn to explore the experience or to attract feedback.

There are some general rules about experimentation, common to all active approaches to psychotherapy. Experiments must be appropriate to the client, to the therapist and to the context. Ideally, an experiment will grow out of the immediate moment of therapy process, and will be couched in the client's own language, preferred sensory modality, themes and symbols; often, an experiment is suggested by the client's use of metaphor or simile. Therapists should avoid suggesting experiments which they themselves would be unwilling to do if challenged; there is always a danger of manipulating the client into doing work vicariously for the therapist. One should be wary of suggesting an experiment whose outcome is totally uncertain; both therapist and client must be able to contain what happens. Experimentation must be conducted with respect for the context in which therapy takes place, both literal and cultural. Many NHS premises are unsuitable for extremely noisy work, and it may be unwise to encourage participants to explore behaviour which is beyond prevailing social norms. An experiment needs to be difficult yet feasible. If it is not difficult, its successful accomplishment will give little feeling of achievement and therapeutic gain will be small. If, on the other hand, it is not feasible it will clearly fail, usually confirming the worst fantasies of the client and, therefore, reinforcing his or her problem. The skill of the therapist lies in creating experiments which are appropriate in the immediate moment of therapy, graded accurately to facilitate the client's accomplishment.

Dialogue

The use of dramatic dialogue has roots both in psychodrama and Gestalt therapy and is now widely used as a therapeutic technique. The client is invited to engage in spoken dialogue either with a part of himself or with an absent person to whom he has something to say, using an empty chair or some other object to represent the person or part of self to whom he is speaking. A dialogue can then be promoted with the client playing both parts, changing chairs as appropriate. Some people find this difficult, but many find it extremely helpful and the dialogue often achieves considerable emotional intensity. Sometimes this technique can be used simply to permit the expression of feelings to an absent person: ('Imagine your father is sitting in the chair over there – what would you like to say to him?'). More often, it is desirable for the client to experience both parts of the dialogue and to participate in turn from either chair, so as to integrate whatever has been split or projected. By personifying both halves of a dilemma, dialogue can be valuable in resolving intrapsychic conflict at a variety of levels from the superficial to the serious (for example, 'I want to stay with the group' versus 'I want to go home'; or 'I want to live' versus 'I want to die').

A second major use of dialogue is the completion of interpersonal 'unfinished business'. This refers to feelings about a past event which are still present in or out of awareness, especially where the other person is absent or dead.

It is also possible to use dialogue to work on marital issues in individual therapy, with the client gaining a surprising amount of insight into the spouse's views and feelings, thus mitigating some of the potentially disruptive consequences of only one member of a married couple being in therapy.

Dialogue can be used to resolve unfinished business with parents; these dialogues are often very intense and may be accompanied by cathartic release of very strong feelings, often hatred and yearning. Successful resolution is usually a major event in therapy. In the management of unresolved grief, a dialogue with the deceased person may permit the expression of feelings (positive or negative) which have been buried for years. Dialogues with parents and with deceased spouses frequently conclude with a benedictory statement from the 'absent' person; these moments are often extremely moving for both client and therapist.

The use of dialogue can be extended by the addition of more chairs to include other family members, or to allow the exploration of subpersonalities. It can be helpful to have chairs and other objects of different sizes, colours and shapes in the room to allow the client to select one which is 'just right'. A cushion, for example, may be suitable if the dialogue is with a young child or baby (for example, a dialogue with oneself as a child or between a woman and a baby whose life was terminated by abortion). A consulting room full of clutter can in these circumstances be a positive advantage.

Guided fantasy

Freud referred to dreams as the 'royal road to the unconscious'; guided fantasy is certainly a worthwhile alternative route. Fantasy work can be done at a variety of levels, but tends to be revealing and provocative and needs to be used carefully. Most therapists use some form of induction technique, usually similar to those used in relaxation training and sometimes borrowing from hypnotic induction techniques. It is important to be aware of the depth of induction achieved, as this will determine the reaction to the fantasy itself.

Unstructured fantasies can be done with or without induction; the client is encouraged to concentrate on fantasies and images (rather than thoughts), and to follow his imagination wherever it may go. Music can also be used to facilitate certain types of affect; well-known pieces tend to promote recall, while less familiar pieces and specially produced abstract tapes enhance the development of fantasy.

Structured fantasies require some facilitation and can be offered with a greater or lesser degree of specificity. An example would be to imagine being a tree; the simple, rather non-specific, image acts as a projective screen which is then embroidered by fantasy to provide material for exploration. The power of the tree-image can be developed by imagining its detail, its surroundings, its development, growth and eventual decay, the progress of the seasons, the proximity of animals and other living things, and so on. It is important that the facilitator introduces a minimum of specific information to allow maximum scope for the client's imagination.

Structured fantasies can be created around almost any subject or theme, reality-based, or archetypal. The depth and power of a fantasy experience will depend on the level of induction and on the theme or topic chosen, as well as on the client's ability and willingness to use their imagination. People who have little apparent access to their own unconscious process may make surprisingly powerful contact with it using guided fantasy, which must therefore be used with great respect.

Exploration of dilemmas and conflict resolution can be promoted by the use of fantasy dialogue; the participant is invited, as part of their fantasy, to make contact with a person (real or imaginary) from whom they may obtain wise guidance. They are asked to imagine the dialogue between themselves and the other person and to note carefully the advice they are given. The 'wise person' may offer them a gift which may be literal or symbolic, and which they may either accept or refuse.

Fantasy experiences may not be immediately intelligible to the participant; some knowledge of archetypes and symbolism is helpful for the therapist, who must decide whether or not to offer interpretation, and whether to promote discussion and sharing or private reflection.

USING ACTIVE APPROACHES

General principles

Active approaches tend to attract enthusiastic support, sometimes from people whose enthusiasm exceeds their discretion or experience; this can lead to the indiscriminate use of methods which are provocative, powerful and dangerous if used unwisely. The emphasis on experience rather than thinking can promote a culture in which 'anything goes', and in which all emotional expression is seen as desirable. This is naïve; for some patients, these approaches can be profoundly liberating, but for others they only invite further agitation and confusion.

Active approaches should not be used unless the practitioner has an explicit formulation of the problem and can state clearly – at least for himself – the aims of therapy. Active approaches can be used in three main ways; for pleasure, recreation and entertainment; for skills and awareness training; and, more specifically, as a method of psychotherapy, either alone or in combination with other techniques.

Pleasure, recreation and entertainment

The use of active approaches for these purposes needs to be prudent, especially with people who are emotionally vulnerable. It is all too easy for something which appears to be an innocent exercise or game to turn into a much more significant and emotional event, generating anxiety both in staff and clients. In general, exercises for this purpose should be concrete, non-symbolic and keep participants' attention directed outwards, away from their inner experience. For example, a therapist helping a newly formed group to develop some feeling of trust and confidence may notice a general anxiety within the group about the expression of hostility. An exercise which permits this to be expressed collectively and non-specifically (for example, a group shout) may allow the issue to be raised, expressed and shared, promoting the development of trust and group cohesion. The aim here is not to promote insight or change, nor to develop fresh skills, but to enhance awareness, contact, self-esteem and even joie de vivre.

Awareness and skills training

Many active approaches focus on experience rather than cognitive process, and as such are useful for experiential training both of staff and clients. The purpose of these exercises is to develop sensory awareness and flexibility. Many people, both staff and clients, are oblivious of much of their sensory input, and overlook their potential for consciously directing their attention to a particular sensory modality, internal or external. Contact with others, with inner emotional experience or with a person's own body can all be facilitated in this way.

Structured activities can also offer the opportunity to try out new behaviours and interpersonal skills in a safe environment; again, these can be used with a wide variety of clients as well as in staff training. Rehabilitation of people with limited social skills, for example, especially those re-entering the community after many years of institutional care, can be helped by the use of role-play and drama therapy.

The use of active techniques in the training of therapists is now widely accepted with extensive use of role-play, including role-enactment and role-reversal, and of learning through experimentation in training groups. Training in any of the active approaches involves participation, just as psychoanalytic training requires personal analysis. Practitioners intending to use active approaches should be exposed to them as participants, at least to the level of their intended use.

Psychotherapy

The active approaches can be used specifically for therapy at a number of different levels and with a wide range of client groups. Each approach can be used as a method of therapy, but many therapists make use of active and non-verbal techniques as part of a wider eclectic approach.

ACTIVE APPROACHES WITH PARTICULAR CLIENT GROUPS

Ideally, the use of active approaches will be determined by client need rather than therapists' enthusiasm ·or preference. It is difficult, however, when one has trained in a particular approach, to resist the temptation to use it on all clients, assessing new referrals for their suitability for the method rather than vice-versa. In general terms, the active approaches are suited to those whose problems can be worked through relatively briefly. They are particularly useful for people who need to develop their spontaneity and creativity, and for those who use intellectual discussion to avoid change. They have been used extensively in private groups offering personal growth, and in staff training and development, and are increasingly being used with more conventional client groups.

Mental handicap/learning disability

The variation of ability among patients with a mental handicap or learning disability is so wide, that generalisations are difficult. An appreciation of the particular difficulties of this group is necessary if therapy is to be offered appropriately; physical disability and concurrent mental illness may complicate the situation, and it is easy to forget that mentally handicapped people also have neurotic problems.

The use of creative arts therapies in mental handicap is well established, both at the 'fun and games' level and with more serious intentions. It is important to maintain a balance between skills training and self-expression, either of which can be used to avoid the other. A thoughtful account of drama therapy in mental handicap is provided by Brudenell (1987).

In general, regressive and cathartic therapies are unnecessary in mental handicap, and the more sophisticated approaches are less relevant. Bodywork, however, can be especially useful in the treatment of movement disorders and postural dysfunction. Massage and simple bioenergetic exercises can be both helpful and pleasurable, and can be used to develop skills and physical communication.

The elderly

Difficulties with mobility, concentration, hearing and sight are common in the elderly; psychological flexibility is reduced, and there is less urge towards insight, growth and change. But it is important not to generalise too far; many elderly people can make effective use of active therapy, for example to express their feelings about increasing infirmity or to work through losses from bereavement.

The most extensive use of active approaches with the elderly is probably in the area of life enhancement, providing enjoyment, entertainment, stimulation and contact without any specific therapeutic purpose beyond this. But elderly people can benefit from social skills training, role-playing and classical psychodrama, as well as more orthodox psychotherapy; motivation and flexibility are more important than age itself as criteria for selection. Elderly people enjoy reminiscing, which can be facilitated effectively by enactment on a participant or non-participant basis (Langley & Langley 1983). Singing, dancing and games can be used not only as entertainment but as physical therapy. Bodywork (especially massage) providing both physical contact and comfort is often much appreciated.

Chronic mental illness

In recent years, there has been an increasing emphasis on rehabilitation and community care, with social skills training using behavioural and dramatherapy techniques being widely used. People with chronic mental illnesses for whom further rehabilitation is unlikely to produce benefit can make enjoyable use of many games and exercises used by other groups. The use of more provocative techniques, especially those involving close physical contact, regression and catharsis, needs to be approached cautiously. Therapists working regularly with the chronically mentally ill can make effective use of art, music or drama as well as simple bodywork techniques. The wish to do powerful therapy with the chronically mentally ill may say more about the therapist's enthusiasm than it does about the client's needs. There is, however, an equal danger of failing to see and respond to the potential of a person with chronic mental illness, and the use of creative therapies can help to explore this.

Children and adolescents

Active techniques are especially suited to young people, whose high level of anxiety, short attention span and physical restlessness make conventional psychotherapy difficult. Young people instinctively use art, music, drama and dance to express their feelings, although they may overlook the therapeutic potential of these activities. A mixture of activity and discussion is ideal.

Acute mental illness

Psychiatric admission units are often unstable, tense communities with periods of disturbed behaviour, emergency admissions, visits by relatives, high population turnover and a wide range of clinical problems, ranging from acute psychosis to domestic crisis. There is little homogeneity or calm and, in general, provocative techniques are unhelpful. Attention needs to be devoted to the enhancement of trust and safety and, perhaps, a little fun. Regular lightweight groups making use of a variety of bodywork techniques or the creative arts can provide a safe forum in which people can explore their environment and encounter their fellow patients and the staff. Less actively disturbed patients can be encouraged to take part in more provocative exploratory techniques using projective exercises, guided fantasy and role play. Those able to tolerate a higher level of conflict can make effective use of more intensive art therapy, psychodrama, Gestalt therapy and regressive techniques. While patients in crisis are certainly susceptible to these approaches, the effects may be more powerful than either staff or patients expect. It is often wiser to restrict the use of more potent techniques for day patient or outpatient work once the acute crisis has settled.

Patients attending community mental health centres and day hospitals on a regular basis can often make effective use of active psychotherapy either on a sessional basis or as part of a continuing programme. The combination of experiential group work with individual or family insight-oriented therapy can be especially productive, but it is important for the different therapists to respect each others' work and communicate closely.

Formal psychotherapy

Although many of the active approaches can be used as specific methods of psychotherapy in their own right, there is a trend towards the use of active techniques in combination with more conversational approaches. This eclectic approach diminishes therapeutic purity, but enhances flexibility and range. Eclecticism can be used as a cover for inadequate training, and clients can be confused by a therapist's use of 'a little bit of this and a little bit of that'. But the judicious use of different techniques by an experienced therapist, based on proper assessment and formulation, can offer a client a wider range of therapeutic possibilities than any one approach allows.

In general, active and non-verbal approaches are helpful in heightening emotional and physical awareness, facilitating catharsis, developing spontaneity and creativity, and promoting behavioural change. They can also be invaluable in situations where clients find it difficult to express themselves effectively in words. This commonly happens at the extremes of the intellectual spectrum, as well as in people who habitually suppress their feelings.

The active approaches are generally suited to those whose problems can be worked through relatively briefly. People who have experienced grossly defective parenting or other major childhood deprivation usually require a more sustained therapeutic relationship which some active approaches fail to provide. Such people have intense emotional needs which are often unmanageably aroused by the 'I-thou' encounter preferred by most active practitioners. People with hysterical personalities are frequently attracted to experiential and active approaches all too easily producing superficially impressive emotional performances without much real gain. This is usually evident to the therapist, however, and the use of dramatic technique can help such people to distinguish 'performance' from real feeling.

The culture of many of the active approaches encourages therapist disclosure, and this will significantly affect the transference relationship; to some extent, the therapist has to choose whether to remain a transference object or to emerge as a participant in the continuing action. The use of dramatic dialogue, for example, will deflect the client's engagement away from the therapist towards the object of the dialogue; this can be useful in exploring the inter-relationship between the transference, relationships with significant others in the client's present life, and relationships with parental figures – Menninger's 'triangle of insight' (Menninger 1958, Malan 1979). Active participation by the therapist and transference analysis are not necessarily mutually exclusive; therapist participation makes issues of transference and counter-transference more complex, though possibly less intense. Certainly, the use of active techniques does not 'prevent' transference, a point which some inexperienced therapists learn to their chagrin.

The eclectic use of active techniques in continuing psychotherapy, therefore, requires continual decision making by the therapist, who must balance the relative merits of interpretation and experimentation, of transference and contact. The judging of pace and intensity is also important; active techniques, especially those involving physical activity, promote emotional arousal, and the therapist has to decide how far to pursue this in the continuing moment of therapy. Active and non-verbal techniques can be very useful when clients appear stuck, but can also avoid the potentially useful experience of frustration for both client and therapist, and the recognition of transference issues. In short, active approaches can be used as a defence against transference, just as interpretation can be used as a defence against experience or action.

Different situations require a variety of techniques; much of the skill of the active therapist depends on choosing the appropriate suggestion for a particular situation, grading an experiment up or down according to the needs of the moment. The use of structured exercises in psychotherapy is questionable; by and large, it is desirable to allow the process of therapy to flow naturally from the client, and the use of planned structures is in conflict with this. Using a mixture of conversational and active approaches, it is common in outpatient therapy for a session to develop some of the characteristics of a classical psychodrama with a period of 'warm-up' followed by enactment or experimentation, with or without subsequent discussion. In continuing psychotherapy, the use of active technique *without* subsequent discussion is particularly potent, allowing the client to retain the undiluted experience, possibly for discussion in the next session.

Many 'active' therapists use physical contact as part of their approach. This is clearly a contentious issue and raises serious ethical problems, particularly in individual therapy. Great care is needed with clients who are vulnerable, lonely and emotionally needy; an intense erotic transference may easily develop. A useful discussion of this issue is provided by Woodmansey (1988).

Most therapies encourage clients to experience their inner world and to express it. The active approaches are particularly useful in developing experiments through which the client can explore alternatives to existing fixed patterns of thought, feeling or behaviour. The following examples may serve to illustrate the use of active technique in continuing therapy.

Case studies from individual psychotherapy

Case study 6.1   A relationship problem

A young man in continuing individual therapy referred frequently to his mother from whom he was estranged, but found it difficult to talk in any depth about his feelings about her either in the past or the present, demonstrating in therapy the alienation which he experienced in real life. His attempts to talk about his relationship with his mother were usually accompanied by physical restlessness, particularly in his arms and hands. On one such occasion, he was asked to imagine that his mother was present in the room and what he would like to say to her. His agitation increased markedly, his fists clenched, and he looked scarcely able to cope with the situation. The therapist suggested, therefore, that he should remain silent, simply noticing what he wanted to say and what he was feeling. The client settled, and then discussed his experiences with the therapist and expressed relief at being able to do so. At the next session, the client indicated a wish to continue this exploration, and this time – through dialogue – angrily confronted his mother, though the therapist sensed that the confrontation was not entirely resolved. At the following session, the client was able to confront his mother with murderous wishes, enacted by a physical assault on the empty chair. As the attack subsided, the client became rapidly aware of another side to his feelings, and became tearful as he expressed his yearning for the love which his mother had failed to provide. At this point, he was encouraged to 'become his mother', and explained why she had been unable to do better. The session ended with a very touching reconciliation between mother and son.

Case study 6.2   Unresolved grief

An elderly widow was referred by her general practitioner having failed to recover from the death of her husband three years previously. After two exploratory sessions, she was encouraged towards a dialogue with her dead husband, during which she became extremely agitated. After a short period of extremely tense silence she blurted out the details of a secret love affair which had taken place many years previously, of which she had never told her husband. When she had finished, she was encouraged to exchange chairs, to 'be' her husband. She was asked to carefully watch and listen to the content of the session so far, and then to speak as the husband. She did so and offered understanding, forgiveness and absolution.

Returning to her own chair the woman was clearly very moved and subsequently said she had found the session extremely helpful. She began to renew social contacts and at follow-up continued to do well.

Case study 6.3   Depression after termination of pregnancy

A young woman was referred with depressive symptoms following a termination of pregnancy 18 months previously. It became clear that she had a number of problems, including difficulty in making and sustaining relationships, with an episode of deliberate self-harm prior to the pregnancy. During one session, she began to focus on the termination and, in particular, on the lost potential of the unborn child. She was encouraged to use a cushion to represent the baby, and rapidly started to cry as she spoke about both the baby itself, and about her own experience of being mothered, which had clearly been inadequate. She was encouraged to hold and talk to the 'baby' until she felt ready to put it down and say goodbye. Having accomplished this, she went on in further sessions to explore her feelings about her own childhood and began to understand how this had affected her in relationships with other people.

Case study 6.4   Phobic anxiety

An experienced teacher was referred with longstanding minor phobic symptoms. She herself recognised the link with introjected expectations from her parents. Her therapist considered the possibility of using dialogue with either one or both of her parents, but instead chose to suggest a dialogue with her husband with whom she had apparently not discussed her symptoms. Representing him, she provided a lot of very effective support and encouragement, including the advice 'you don't have to be everything to everyone'. It became clear that her wish for continuing therapy was part of her attempt to make herself as perfect as she believed her parents had wished her to be; it was suggested she should defer a decision about further therapy for the time being.

Case study 6.5   An existential problem

A young woman in individual therapy, with a long history of family bereavements, complained of listlessness. At the same time, her therapist noticed her physical posture which was slack and reflexive and that her breathing was shallow. It was suggested that she should experiment non-verbally with changing her physical posture and her breathing until she felt different. She sat up slowly, began to breathe more deeply, then rose from her chair and walked up and down the room obviously becoming increasingly excited until she stopped, turned to the therapist and said with immense conviction 'I am really alive'. This led quickly to an awareness of her anxieties about sexuality and the significance of the death of her father just prior to her adolescence.

A similar suggestion with a different patient elicited a slow and gradual unfolding, experienced by the patient as the emergence of a butterfly from its chrysalis.

Case study 6.6   Limited verbal ability

A rather inarticulate young man of limited intelligence was struggling to describe his feelings about members of his family and their relationships with each other. He was encouraged to draw his family, and quickly made a sketch which he was then able to use to talk more freely. His therapist was able to point out aspects of the sketch to which he didn't refer (for example, disparity in the size of the two parents).

Another example of the use of simple art work is given by Hobson (1985).

Case studies from marital and family therapy

Case study 6.7   Controlling unproductive dissent

A couple in continuing marital therapy repeatedly bickered and wouldn't or couldn't look at the origins of this. They were each provided with paper and pencil and asked to enumerate five problems which they believed the other would identify. Each was then asked to describe one way in which they themselves contributed to each of the problems and then the sheets of paper were exchanged. Both were surprised to discover how much the other recognised his or her views, and the rest of the session was spent discussing the contributions which had been offered without any further argument.

Case study 6.8   Role exchange

A couple in continuing marital therapy found it difficult to identify with each other; each came from a deprived background and had only limited ability to empathise. They were asked to exchange chairs and 'become' each other. Each was asked to speak in this new role while the other listened, without discussion. Both were surprised to discover they were understood better than they had expected, and the therapist was surprised by the level of empathic understanding displayed.

Case study 6.9   Sculpting

A family was seen as the result of a depressive reaction in the mother. Each member of the family in turn was asked to make a tableau of a typical family scene, arranging the family so as to express the situation as fully as possible. This provided a great deal of material for discussion and allowed each member of the family to assert their point of view.

This technique is also valuable in staff groups and other groups.

Case studies from group psychotherapy

Case study 6.10   Establishing trust

A therapeutic group was slow in developing trust, with few members contributing beyond a superficial level. One participant drew an analogy with hesitation before entering a swimming pool, and the therapist suggested a group exercise in which a 'pool' was constructed in the middle of the room and members of the group arranged themselves around it according to their perceived involvement. Gradually people began to play with the symbolism of the swimming pool, and in various ways all members of the group began to participate. Gradually, what had begun as a playful experiment developed a serious side as individuals began to recognise personal meaning in the symbolic activity. The mood of the group changed, rapidly became more serious and a number of people shared experience and insight.

Case study 6.11   Regression

A young man attending a continuing therapy group because of panic attacks expressed a sense of primitive terror which had troubled him for many years. He was encouraged to explore this, and became agitated before adopting a fetal position in the middle of the group. He asked to be enclosed and members of the group sat closely around him. He then became agitated again and expressed a wish to fight his way out. With the consent of other group members, he then did so while they resisted his progress. Much of his work was conducted non-verbally with a high degree of physical exertion. At the end, he was exhausted but quiet and peaceful, and subsequently referred to the experience as extremely valuable. No attempt was made to interpret what had happened, although a number of other group members reported their own associations.

Case study 6.12   Doing a round

A rather respectable young woman in a therapeutic group complained of her grey existence. Her therapist suggested that she should move around the group identifying each other member (including the therapist) with a particular colour. Having done this, she was asked to go back to each member in turn making a brief statement of how she would behave differently if she 'was' the colour associated with that person. In this way, she was encouraged to recognise and re-integrate aspects of her potential self which were projected onto others. She found the exercise difficult to do, but persevered and clearly began to enjoy herself. At the end she said 'I feel like a rainbow now' and, indeed, looked radiant. At a subsequent meeting of the group, she appeared more colourfully dressed and both her physical movements and speech were noticeably more fluid. Her feelings of well-being continued after the experiment.

Case study 6.13   Exploring tenderness

An earnest young doctor participating in a therapeutic weekend group for professionals was clearly having difficulty with the emotion expressed by other group members, preferring to ask 'intelligent' questions rather than sharing their experience. Challenged about this by another group member, he acknowledged his difficulty in accepting his own feelings, or expressions of tenderness from others. He was offered a 'group lift'; he lay on the floor of the room and was lifted to shoulder height by other members of the group and then rocked gently to and fro before being lowered gently to the floor. He clearly found this very moving and cried a little, apparently the first time he had done so for many years. Later in the weekend, he went on to explore his feelings about his parents both of whom had also apparently found it difficult to express tenderness. In a subsequent group, he showed less difficulty in contacting his own and other people's feelings.

Case study 6.14   Expressing hostility

A staff group was experiencing difficulty in acknowledging hostility. The group was divided arbitrarily into two subgroups which were asked to stand facing each other. One subgroup was invited to shout the word 'no' repeatedly, while the other group shouted 'yes'. The session quickly became extremely noisy, with a number of people clearly enjoying what they were doing, while others did not. As the noise died down, people were asked to sit down with a member of the opposite subgroup and to share their experiences. Subsequently hostility and conflict were expressed more openly.

Case study 6.15   Exploring behind the hierarchy

A staff group in a psychiatric unit seemed preoccupied with hierarchical relationships and power. The group leader suggested a 'blind walk', in which each member of the group was asked to lead another member of the group blindfold around the room, then exchanging roles. Group members were asked to pair up with someone of different perceived hierarchical status to their own. Some people clearly found the exercise difficult to take seriously, but many were impressed by their experience of their partner as a person, aside from hierarchical associations.

WORKING WITH STAFF

Staff sensitivity/support groups in the workplace

Staff sensitivity and support groups need to be handled with care. Psychiatric practice is emotionally stressful, and staff may have chosen this work because of a previously unrecognised emotional need. In addition, staff have a continuing working relationship with each other which should not be compromised by experiences within the staff group. In general, therefore, provocative, revealing and regressive techniques are unsuitable. Drama therapy exercises and games can be extremely valuable in promoting a safe forum in which people can explore their roles and relationships with each other; group or individual sculpting, interactional games, superficial fantasy work, trust and projective exercises can all be used. Structured games and exercises can be used as a defence against exploring tensions and conflicts within the group itself, and the group leader needs to guard against colluding unwittingly with this.

Therapeutic groups for staff

Therapeutic groups for staff are perhaps the easiest places of all to use active techniques. Participants in such groups are usually highly motivated, self-selected, willing to participate and in reasonable psychological health. Active techniques allow an appropriate balance of hard work and play, and can permit the expression of childish and anti-social behaviours, normally suppressed as part of professional self-discipline, to prevent their being acted out more destructively. In continuing regular groups of this kind, many of the decisions and issues will be the same as for an outpatient psychotherapy group. But staff, who are frequently in quasi-parental roles during their working life, can be more negativistic and rebellious than patient groups, and active techniques may allow these needs to be expressed. Some staff are over articulate and tend to intellectualise; non-verbal techniques can be especially valuable for them.

Many staff can make use of intensive short-term therapeutic groups, often organised on a residential basis for a weekend or longer (Tillett 1986). These events can explore a specific theme, or can offer an unstructured opportunity for professionals to work on their own problems and difficulties.

RESEARCH

The literature relating to active and newer approaches in psychotherapy is stronger on descriptions of method than on theory, and contains more anecdotes than objective scientific appraisal. Practitioners of the newer psychotherapies perhaps incline more to the artistic than to the scientific end of the psychotherapeutic spectrum, and the intrinsic creativity and unpredictability of these approaches obviously makes scientific comparison difficult. Comparative studies (Luborsky et al 1975, Smith et al 1980) have suggested that outcomes do not vary greatly between different approaches in psychotherapy, though behavioural and cognitive treatments produce slightly larger effect sizes than other approaches. There appear to be no adequate studies comparing active approaches with more orthodox treatment. A much quoted study (Lieberman et al 1973) reviewing American undergraduates who had attended encounter groups showed significant benefit but a worrying 'casualty rate' – 7.5% of participants deteriorated or even developed psychotic episodes. This was shown to be related both to client characteristics (low self-esteem, unrealistic expectations) and the personalities of the group leaders (charismatic, aggressive, overstimulating). Beutler & Mitchell (1981) suggest that experiential therapy may be especially helpful in patients who are likely to act out. The author's experience supports this, and suggests that both under- and over-inhibited patients can make use of active approaches.

Further research is clearly required to establish the efficacy of active approaches and to clarify the indications for their use.

CONCLUSION

It is difficult to do justice to the enormous variety of techniques which offer action in psychotherapy. Although the use of activity in therapy stems originally from the work of a small number of practitioners (Moreno, Ferenczi, Perls, Reich and others) there are now a bewildering number of choices for the therapist. Conversation and activity both have a place in psychotherapy, and each can be used as a defence against the other. Each therapist chooses an approach which is congruent with his or her experiences or values, and must choose between rigidity and eclecticism. The appeal of the active approaches lies in their immediacy, spontaneity and creativity; combined with conversation they offer an extended range of techniques to the psychotherapist. Active approaches have their dangers and limitations; they are powerful and potentially disruptive or dangerous. They sometimes attract therapists whose enthusiasm exceeds their experience, and are sometimes used indiscriminately. They are unconventional and hence appeal to the rebellious.

Used judiciously, they offer great potential both to therapists and clients in a wide variety of settings, not only in conventional psychotherapy but across the whole field of mental health practice.

FURTHER READING

Dalley T (ed) 1984 Art as therapy: an introduction to the use of art as a therapeutic technique. Tavistock, London
Langley D M, Langley G E 1983 Dramatherapy and psychiatry. Croom Helm, London
Passons W 1975 Gestalt approaches in counselling. Holt, Rinehart and Winston, New York
Rowan J, Dryden W 1988 Innovative therapy in Britain. Open University Press, Milton Keynes

Basic techniques

7. Learning to listen: teaching and supervising basic psychotherapeutic skills

F. Margison

INTRODUCTION

In teaching basic psychotherapeutic skills, the emphasis has often been placed on accurate and empathic listening, with relatively little account taken of appropriate types of interventions in different settings. This chapter begins with a review of the literature on some of the various methods used in teaching psychotherapy at a basic level, starting with listening skills and then covering basic training in psychotherapeutic interventions. A fuller account is given of the ways in which these techniques have been developed in Manchester, and of some practical difficulties encountered. The chapter ends with a brief account of recent attempts to provide a framework for supervisors and trainers who wish to extend basic skills through direct supervision of clinical work. The importance of recognising and helping trainees to take account of counter-transference is one of the most important areas of recent interest.

TEACHING BASIC PSYCHOTHERAPY SKILLS

Non-directive counselling : 'active listening'

Carl Rogers and his co-workers were able to confront directly the dilemma which troubles many psychotherapy trainers: how can systematic teaching of basic skills, often in a setting without the client or patient even being present, possibly help the enormously complex and personal task of therapeutic listening?

The basic task of 'listening' empathically from the other's imagined frame of reference brings about an internal transformation leading to a response which attempts to reflect accurately the feelings of the client – perhaps in a way they had been unable to express alone:

The most basic ingredient in the process dimension is considered to be the therapist's engagement in an empathic process, attempting to stay in the client's internal frame of reference and to sense the client's immediate awareness as if it were one's own, without ever losing sight of the 'as if'. Although there are many possible vehicles for expressing empathy, the 'reflective response' is the one most commonly found in client-centered

165

therapy. This consists of reflecting back to the client as accurately and sensitively as possible the awareness that he/she is trying to express, and asking, implicitly or explicitly, the client to check this against his/her own experience. (Rice 1980).

Supervisors from other models of therapy may be sceptical of this style of response, regarding it as a mere 'repeating back the last three words the client said'. This defensive repsonse merely parodies the style of non-directive counselling, but does draw attention to the Rogerian emphasis on the primacy of the client's experiential world. Laura Rice (1980) suggests that beginning therapists need a basic teaching programme which includes learning the following skills (1) 'attending behaviours'; (2) learning to distinguish the internal (client's) frame of reference from the external (therapist's or from the external world); (3) focusing on a 'feeling' level; and (4) learning to express what is heard in the therapist's own words.

Truax & Carkhuff (1967) and Ivey et al (1968) produced such training packages, which will be described in more detail below. Rice makes the point that such skills are related to the basic conditions of empathy, congruence, and non-possessive warmth, and provide a foundation from which accurate listening can occur. Great emphasis is placed on close attention to vocal cues in this method of teaching:

'One of the most useful indicators of liveness or poignancy is the voice quality of the client (Rice & Wagstaff 1967). There is a kind of voice quality that seems to indicate an inner focus on something that is being seen or felt freshly. Sometimes in the midst of a long client discussion expressed in a highly externalising voice quality one hears just a small blip of focused voice. The voice slows, softens without losing energy, pauses, and loses the 'pre-monitored' quality of the externalising voice. This should be an indicator to the therapist that this part must be heard and responded to. (Rice 1980)

As well as teaching the detection and recognition of vocal cues, the teaching programmes such as those designed by Truax & Carkhuff (1967) include an experiential approach in which the trainee therapists receive the same listening conditions as are being practised. Hence, the teaching approach combines two seemingly immiscible forms of learning: the experiential approach, similar in many ways to therapy, and the didactic skills-based approach. The two great contributions of client-centered therapy have been its emphasis on the importance of teaching basic skills and its demonstration that behavioural techniques of shaping and modelling applied to trainees are not incompatible with a human and personal approach to therapy.

Rice (1980) and others from this school imply that the therapist *only* needs to attend and reflect for discovery and change in the client to take place. This view of the process of therapy has been subject to considerable criticism; but even if the criticisms are accepted, the basic principles of teaching psychotherapeutic skills through the client-centered model have made an enormous contribution. One particular issue developed by workers in this school challenges the assumption about what is meant by 'non-directive'. Often, the therapist and, in turn, the trainer can be quite directive in pressing the client (or trainee) to stay with painful experiences. The therapy is non-directive in the sense that it assumes that the client or trainee will find his or her own solution if the right conditions (either in therapy or in training) are offered. The corollary of this, however, is that unconscious forces and unconscious resistance to conflict are given almost no emphasis in this model. Whether such an 'atheoretical' approach can be useful in teaching basic skills will be discussed in more detail later.

Micro-counselling

Ivey & Simek-Downing (1980) took the basic principles outlined above and made from them a serious attempt to provide a teaching package. They took into account key criticisms of the work of Truax & Carkhuff in teaching global conditions, such as the provision of 'empathy', to therapists in training. Critics (Matarazzo & Patterson 1986) had pointed out that such global skills or conditions do not truly reflect the moment-to-moment changes in therapy, and do not provide a framework for choosing particular interventions. Also, the outcome research literature (Lambert et al 1978, Luborsky et al 1971, Rachman 1973, Meltzoff & Kornreich 1970) does not convincingly show that these positive therapeutic outcomes can be generalised to other centres, nor the ability of the 'Truax & Carkhuff' factors significantly to predict outcome.

Ivey acccepted many of the principles of active listening, but concentrated his attention on achieving 'generative competence', that is, a sustained ability to produce particular types of specific intervention. The training, therefore, involved a systematic, step-by-step approach:

1. a commitment to learn one skill at a time
2. the skills needing to be modelled or presented (ideally with video tapes and descriptive manuals)
3. the trainees then needing to practise and monitor their own competence through self-observation
4. a need to master each skill so that the trainee can produce the desired interventions in an interview at will.

To the psychoanalytic critic, this approach may seem bizarre – as though a creature from outer space had decided to learn about making love and practised by learning, parrot-fashion, lines from Romeo and Juliet. This attempt by Ivey (and indeed other researchers following similar lines elsewhere) to isolate the ingredients of therapy are seen not just as misguided by many psychodynamic therapists, but intrinsically destructive to the essence of psychotherapy – the rhythm and flow of unconscious forces and their containment and understanding within a therapeutic relationship.

Certainly, the limits of the approach need to be acknowledged: the method is good at helping trainees to identify and unlearn maladaptive interventions, and can provide a framework of basic competence from which more detailed and clinically sensitive therapeutic practice might arise (Ivey 1980). The very helpful and thorough analysis of skills has been highly influential in the psychotherapy process – outcome research literature, but there are important deficits. For example, the taxonomy is weak in the crucial 'deep relective' or exploratory skills, where the therapist makes hypotheses which go beyond what the client has said. The crucial distinction is that reflective comments might provide a new descriptive phrase for how the client is feeling, but there is no attempt to bring into awareness the warded-off feelings which psychodynamic therapists see as part of 'the Unconscious'. Indeed, the whole taxonomy is weak in describing interpretations of unconscious impulses or conflicts. Also, there is an assumption made in this taxonomy that quality and quantity refer to different domains, whilst this is clearly not the case in clinical practice. Some low frequency interventions, such as the crucial mutative interpretations of psychodynamic therapy involving parental, outside and transference links, incorporating defence, anxiety and impulse (Malan 1979), are not easy to fit into this nomenclature, although they might form pivotal points around which a whole session is built. It is possible to describe them in terms of the quality of the intervention, but the taxonomy given here does not allow for this to be done effectively.

At its worst, the microskills training could identify the lowest common denominator for a particular skill and train people to do that frequently, which can end up with a 'production line' approach, producing identical therapists. In many ways, such criticism is unfair. Ivey is attempting to teach basic counselling skills quickly, and emphasises the therapist's ability to monitor their *own* quality in a systematic way. His attempt to delineate and describe the bread-and-butter·skills of therapy has been enormously influential, and has led to the development of sensitive and acceptable training programmes.

Ivey's approach is most effective in teaching what Cawley (1977) calls level 1 and level 2 skills. Cawley differentiates those skills necessary for all health practitioners and mental health professionals respectively, from the more specialised psychodynamic and behavioural skills described as levels 3 and 4. The looseness of some of the categories used by Ivey (1980) can be seen in his analysis of quantitative dimensions, which states that the category 'interpretation' is the most frequent intervention used not only in the psychodynamic school but also the existential/rational-emotive, and transactional analysis schools. It is clear that his conceptualisation of the higher level skills needed for specific psychodynamic training is incomplete.

In summary, it is perhaps worth bearing in mind the large numbers of professionals who might benefit from basic teaching of psychotherapy skills. The most important impact of Ivey's work has been in tackling this area, which includes the development of packages to improve the detect-ion of psychiatric morbidity, and to teach effective interventions for professionals who are relatively unskilled in the mental health field. For trainees wishing to specialise in a particular form of therapy, it seems likely that more focused training would be necessary, perhaps using quite different methods. The main contender for this is the apprenticeship-style supervision traditionally offered in psychodynamic therapy; this is discussed in more detail below.

Kagan's approach

So far the emphasis has been on teaching basic attentive listening and on simple teaching programmes to practise appropriate interventions. Kagan (1980) added to this by realising that trainee therapists bring into their training and supervision setting some fundamental anxieties which interfere with learning. These anxieties, he claimed, were susceptible to a systematic teaching programme, just as much as were the basic listening and intervention skills. He noted that trainees 'feigned clinical naïvete':

'In interpersonal recall sessions in which the counsellor alone is the focus of the recall process, the 'feigning of clinical naïvete' becomes clear.' I knew she [the client] was very unhappy underneath but put on a smile, but – and I know this is stupid – I was afraid she might cry if I told her I knew she was 'hurting', and then I would feel that I had made her cry.' (Kagan 1980)

This defensive pseudo-naivete was reinforced by the trainee at times completely 'tuning out' those difficult interactions. In traditional psycho-analytic psychotherapy supervision, this defensiveness is assumed to be present but is thought to be minimised by 'holding' and by the supervisory relationship. Kagan, shows clearly how significant these defensive oper-ations can be, and it seems likely that the supervision setting often pays inadequate attention to the degree of anxiety present in the trainee.

'Interpersonal Process Recall' is Kagan's model to deal with this. The best known component is the use of a videotape of clinical sessions to cue the therapist to how he or she was feeling at the time: 'the person is able to recall thought and feeling in amazing depth' (Kagan 1980). The trainee then seems able to overcome the show of naïvete and reveals a surprisingly sophisticated awareness of underlying blind spots, which can then be discussed subsequently in a safe setting.

The basic sense of safety is provided by attention to the setting in which the training is taking place. Their original model uses such tapes alone initially, and then in small group settings often with peers. One person takes the role within the group of acting as 'inquirer', that is, the role of facilitator for the self-discovery process taking place in the therapist.

These methods have been extended in clinical research (Elliott 1983) in a variety of ways, involving the client seeing the tapes and highlighting key events in the therapeutic process. In the context of this chapter, however, it is mainly the training implications of using videotapes which will be stressed.

Goldberg (1983) discussed the extensive resistance to the use of videotape amongst supervisors – primarily the way in which the videotape camera can act as a distractive 'other', hence making the situation tri-angular rather than two-person. The videotape also can interfere with the self-reflection and scrutiny that can take place in the supervisory space. Nevertheless, Goldberg points out the lost opportunities if videotaping is neglected. The same dilemmas were examined by Friedman et al (1978), who questioned residents and supervisors about their attitudes to videotaping and then introduced systematic videorecording for half of the trainees. They found little measurable destructive impact, but anxiety was provoked in the trainees who subsequently rated their experience less positively than they had expected.

It is in dealing with this potential anxiety and even narcissistic injury of residents that Kagan is most instructive. By using self scrutiny and peer evaluation, he was able to make good use of limited teaching resources and limit the threat of exposure experienced by many trainees (Margison 1989). Through Kagan's sensitive training methods, he became aware of substantial fears which distort communication, these fears being shared by client and therapist alike. He quotes the definition of a 'diplomat' :

'A diplomat is a gentleman who can tell a lie in such a way to another gentleman (who is also a diplomat) that the second gentleman is compelled to let on that he really believes the first gentleman, although he knows that the first gentleman is a liar, who knows that the second gentleman does not believe him. Both let on that each believes the other, while both know that both are liars.' (Kagan 1980)

Kagan points out that people do behave like this to a greater or lesser extent, even in the assumed openness of psychotherapy, therapist and client can choose to keep their interactions at a falsely superficial level. He postulates four basic fears which underlie this 'diplomatic behaviour': (1) a fear of being hurt by others; (2) a fear of being incorporated by others; (3) a fear of striking out against others ourselves; and (4) a fear of incorporating/seducing others. These complementary fears are set for particular individuals because of previous experience, in such a way that particular salience is given to one or more combinations. Individuals then behave 'diplomatically' to avoid such interpersonal risks as isolation, on the one hand, or loss of identity on the other. Here, the trainee is reflecting the core approach-avoidance dilemma which is often described by psychodynamic theorists (Hobson 1985, Ryle 1982).

To help the trainee learn more about these personal themes in a safe environment, Kagan developed techniques 'for coping with interpersonal nightmares' using a method called 'affect simulation'. 'Stimulus vignettes' allow the therapist to face fears such as being mocked or seduced. The vignette is in the form of a videotape of a 'patient' facing the camera, so that the trainee can imagine that they are in a private conversation. Examples include a woman licking her lips and telling the viewing therapist 'if you don't come over here and touch me I'll go out of my mind'! Such intensely threatening stimuli evoke feelings which are then explored systematically in a group setting.

The purpose of these methods is to encourage the trainees to examine difficulties that are likely to arise in real therapy. The method is intensive and can be quite anxiety provoking. It seems to provide some of the benefits of supervisory attention to counter-transference and some of the insights coming from personal therapy, but in a highly concentrated and specific form.

Dendy (1971), in an evaluation of these methods, showed that independent raters of interview skills after training found marked increases in affective sensitivity and no concomitant loss of other skills. Moreover, these trainees were then shown to be able themselves to train other undergraduates in these methods of counselling (Archer & Kagan 1973).

These impressive results were, as in psychotherapy itself, contingent upon high levels of motivation. In reports of failed interventions with trainee groups such as court workers (Heiserman 1971), who did not perceive any need for counselling skills, the intervention was ineffective.

In summary, these early teaching programmes gained prominence in North America in the 1960s and 1970s, and provided good empirical evidence that training in basic counselling skills could be provided simply and effectively using novel methods, drawn in a large part from the educational rather than the psychoanalytic literature.

DEVELOPMENTS IN BRITAIN

The climate in Britain during the 1970s was highly ambivalent towards psychotherapy. On the one hand, the dominant ideology within psychiatry was a combined biological/social model with relatively little emphasis on intrapsychic forces; against this, was a growing recognition of the importance and role of psychotherapy, seen for example in the recognition by the Department of Health and Social Security of psychotherapy as a separate specialty in 1975. In this context, several research groups developed training evaluation packages to develop the psychotherapy skills of psychiatric trainees.

Systematic description of interview behaviours

An important series of studies was carried out to determine the best interviewing style to encourage revelation of both feelings and fact in assessment consultations with mothers bringing their children to a child psychiatric facility (Cox et al 1988).

In the first phase, (Rutter, et al 1981) reliable measures of interview behaviours and responses from the informant were developed, and this was followed by a naturalistic study in clinical practice (Cox et al 1981a, 1981b).

In the next phase, interview styles were compared by systematically varying the interventions used. Emotional expression was encouraged by the interviewer responding to emotional cues, by a reflective style with few interrogative closed questions, by direct prompts about emotionally sensitive areas, and by the use of interpretation of feelings, expressions of sympathy and direct questions about feelings and emotions.

In the most recent study (Cox et al 1988), the systematic exploratory style (using interpretations, emotional reflections, sympathy and enquiries about feelings) was shown to be a technique which could be taught effectively, and could be distinguished empirically from a more structured style. The impact of the teaching was confirmed by the finding that the differences between systematically-structured and exploratory interviews increased as an interview progressed, suggesting that a qualitatively different atmosphere had been engendered.

These important studies confirmed that the basic techniques taught can have a significant and replicable effect on clinically important disclosures, at least in this setting.

It may or may not be justified to extend these findings in assessment interviews to a therapeutic setting, but the overall findings encourage an optimistic belief that training in basic psychotherapeutic skills can produce a significant effect on therapeutic interactions.

The grammar of psychotherapy

Cobb & Lieberman (1987) took a similar view that trainees could be helped by systematic basic teaching. These authors attempted to teach over 100 psychiatric trainees scattered across a wide area to the south west of London. Three levels of interactive skills were distinguished in this study. The basic level draws on the work of Maguire et al (1978), Ivey & Simek-Downing (1980) and Heron (1975), and teaches to an agreed level of competence the key interventions that a therapist might need, for example, in starting or ending an interview effectively.

These skills are supplemented at level two by emphasising the obvious but crucially important point that a given intervention might be based on different therapeutic *intentions*. The intentions might be expressed at the strategic level (for example, 'I am going to spend this interview gathering factual data' or 'I am going to assist this person to express blocked-off painful feelings about her child's death') or at the tactical level (for example, 'At this point my questions seem to block the flow, so I intend to express my emphatic understanding by guessing that he is feeling stuck with me').

The third level of interaction is a more global view of the interview as a whole, asking what was the therapist's understanding of the problem, what factors were influencing the relationship, and what hypotheses will be in the therapist's mind. This level leads on naturally to a deeper and ongoing study of the influences of transference and of unconscious conflict, which are not dealt with in detail within Cobb and Lieberman's course.

This essentially pragmatic and atheoretical approach has been popular in helping trainees and in providing an acceptable package which is also compatible with the more traditional 'general psychiatry' orientation of the trainees' other key teachers. The teaching uses systematic study of the trainees' therapeutic interventions, both from real clinical sessions and from role-plays.

The main teaching aids used by Cobb and Lieberman were called 'interactograms' (Table 7.1). These are simple-to-use tools which allow trainees to describe what they are doing in a systematic way. Interactogram I is essentially a microskills analysis which allows the trainee to

Table 7.1 Interactogram I: Microskills analysis of therapist behaviour (From: Cobb & Lieberman 1987)

Questions
Non-leading open
Non-leading closed
Leading (open or closed)

Facilitation
Silence (3 seconds)
Noises

Statements
Orientation/introduction
Reassuring
Encouraging/emphatic
Summarising
Checking/seeking clarification
Focusing/scanning/prompting
Self-revelation
Other (specify)

Play through a tape of your own and classify each of your interventions according to the above list. Think for yourself what impact your particular style of interviewing is likely to have on this patient.

describe *what* he is doing already, and to reflect on the impact of, say, an excessive use of closed questions.

The second interactogram (Table 7.2) uses Heron's (1975) six categories of intention – prescriptive, informative, confronting, cathartic, catalytic and supportive. The first of these three are described as 'authoritative' and the second three 'facilitative'. This interactogram encourages the trainees to say what they did, why they did it, what the focus was (therapist, patient or therapist-patient interaction) and what the immediate impact was.

Table 7.2   Interactogram II: Microskills analysis of impact of therapist behaviour on patient

Therapist intent	Microskill	Focus	Effect on patient
Prescriptive, informative, confronting, cathartic, catalytic, supportive)	Question, statement, etc.	Patient/therapist	Mild/moderate/strong, positive or negative
(e.g. Catalytic)	(e.g. Self-revelation)	(e.g. Therapist)	(e.g. Mildly inhibiting)

The third stage of the grammar of psychotherapy uses a simple flow diagram to elicit the trainees' views over a whole session under a number of headings (Fig. 7.1). Firstly, a trainee considers whether a hypothesis was present, and if so what the evidence was, whether it is patient- or therapist-focused, explicit or implicit, and whether it was acceptable to the patient. There is also space for a comment about whether the patient was primarily reality- or transference-based at that point in the session, and whether the therapist's view was likely to be reality or counter-transference dominated.

Evaluation of this model is so far limited (Lieberman et al 1989). The teaching seemed well received and popular: the amount of teacher time was reasonably low; and independent evaluation of the interviews confirmed the patient's own perceptions of the therapist, i.e. that improvement had occurred in the student group compared to a control group of junior psychiatrists who had not received the grammar of psychotherapy training.

The studies of Lieberman et al reflect teaching developments which have taken place in many centres, but the main strength of their approach is the assumption that psychotherapy teachers can take on a responsibility for teaching basic skills for the majority of trainees in a whole region, not just those keen trainees who actively seek supervision.

Developing a 'Conversational Model' of psychotherapy

Over the last 15 years, Hobson and his colleagues have carried out extensive research on the Conversational Model of psychotherapy. The

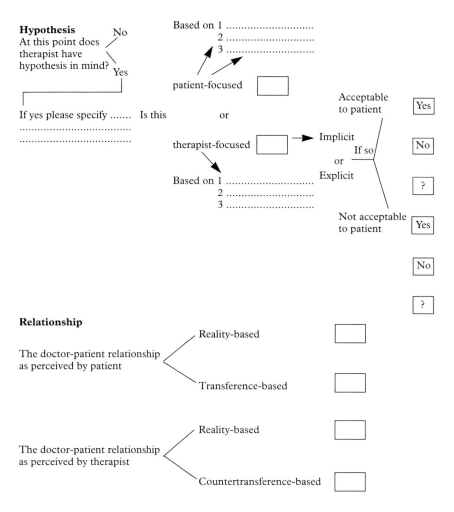

Fig. 7.1   Interactogram III: Macroskills

therapeutic method relies on the assumption that the 'here and now' interaction in a therapeutic conversation will reveal and repeat the very relationship difficulties which have led to the patient seeking help (Hobson 1977, 1985). In essence, therapy is thought to consist of interpersonal learning within a focused conversation.

The first stage of the research was an attempt to delineate the therapeutic behaviours thought to be characteristic of the model, and to develop a rating system sensitive to these techniques (Goldberg et al 1984). The ratings included measures of behaviours specific to the beginning and end of sessions; measures of cue recognition; therapist involvement; negotiation; the function of the intervention (question, information, advice, framework giving, understanding or linking hypotheses); content; and time focus. Every statement made could be rated simultaneously on these six rating scales.

The rating scales have since been compared (Elliott et al 1987) to five other systematic ratings of therapists 'verbal response modes', and have been shown to be reliable and to overlap with the key categories developed in other systems, whilst retaining specificity for the stylistic variables which were thought to be particularly associated with the Conversational Model.

In the next phase of the research, these skills were compared between a group of psychiatrists trained by Hobson and a further comparison group of eclectic psychiatrists of similar seniority, each of whom had had some psychotherapy experience but no contact with Dr Hobson. Many of the predicted features were found to occur in the untrained group as well as in the group which had been in direct contact with Dr Hobson, and were therefore re-construed as more basic psychotherapeutic skills. A further group of key behaviours, however, were described as highly distinctive. The key changes were shifts of style towards more negotiation, therapist-owned comments, focus on feelings, focus on the present 'here and now', an increase in comments which focus the therapy, and increases in content referring to relationships with others and with the therapist. This was confirmed by an analysis of the results showing that the Conversational Model therapists and Hobson himself had remarkably similar response profiles. This part of the study was carried out in a clinical setting with depressed patients referred to a psychiatric outpatient clinic.

In the next phase of the study, these key behaviours were used as the basis for preparing a teaching package based on the work of Ivey and others. Twelve trainees were shown the teaching material, and then joined an eight-week supervision group. Their interview style was measured before, during and after training. The teaching material consisted of a descriptive booklet accompanying three tapes. The first showed individual key behaviours, the second showed an assessment interview linking the skills together, and this was supplemented by a third instruction teaching tape, based on microskills training, which required the trainees to practise the skills out loud in response to a simulated clinical situation. The three videotapes were followed by a period of consolidation using role-play and clinical supervision in supervision groups of three lasting for eight weeks.

In essence, the study showed a great increase in many of the desired interventions following the videotapes alone – particularly in the stylistic measures such as use of negotiation, use of personal pronouns, and avoiding questions. These changes were consolidated by further changes after the supervision/role-play. Among the twelve trainees, there seemed to be some differences in response (one of the trainees actually worsened with the videotapes) but generally they showed consistent positive changes similar to those described from the first study. An important subsidiary finding was that attitudes to treatment and psychological-mindedness did not seem to predict the degree of change occurring. The magnitude of the changes with such simple training methods excited considerable interest, and the package (Margison & Hobson 1982) has now been used by psychologists and nurses (Paxton et al 1988), as well as psychiatrists, in several departments.

The work needs to be assessed with caution however. Many of the criticisms of client-centered therapy and of Ivey's work apply here – the teaching of simple skills is not necessarily reflected in better clinical outcomes. The trainees can be enabled to hide behind a plausible therapeutic mask whilst not really understanding the patient's communication. The results may not persist over time and may be specific to the teaching setting.

Some of these criticisms have subsequently been tested. Godbert (1989) followed up the trainees from the original study and found that the level of skills when the trainees were asked to respond to a similar simulated situation two years later, had declined only slightly from the results at the end of the teaching package, and remained much higher than those initially shown. This finding may not generalise to clinical settings, where conflicting demands may be present, but at least shows that the trainee has retained the skills in his or her repertoire of therapeutic styles. Godbert also asked the trainees what effect, in retrospect, the teaching had had, and all but one reported long-term positive effects despite the brief nature of the teaching.

A second study (Margison et al 1986) addressed the possibility that the promising results would only apply in a privileged, teaching hospital setting. In a replication study, they found that, if anything, greater gains were made in non-teaching hospital trainees, although admittedly these trainees started from slightly lower baselines. The study also showed no differences between overseas and British graduates in their ability to assimilate the Conversational Model, contrary to some critics' expectations of the cultural specificity of the Model. Also, the replication compared experienced with inexperienced *trainers*, and showed no differences between the groups, suggesting that detailed prior knowledge of the Model is not necessary. It seems that the trainers were functioning in some ways similarly to the peer facilitators in Ivey and Kagan's work – their effects coming from the general encouragement to stay with the teaching tape prompts, rather than in conveying specific skills. However, this interpretation has not yet been subjected to formal evaluation.

The encouraging results from this preliminary teaching package prompted the research group in Sheffield led by Shapiro (Shapiro & Firth 1987) to develop a 'manual' form of exploratory therapy based on the Conversational Model, which goes beyond the basic skills to show how the Model applies to a whole therapy with an agreed focus.

The results of the work in the Sheffield projects suggests that the effectiveness of this model of therapy in depressed and anxious patients is comparable to that of behavioural/cognitive prescriptive therapy (although some measures did show slight advantages for the prescriptive approach). More detailed process studies (Barkham & Hobson 1989, Hardy & Shapiro 1985, Stiles et al 1988a, 1988b, Elliott & Shapiro 1988) have shown that the mechanisms of change operating in exploratory therapy are profoundly different from those found in prescriptive therapy: the therapists use different interventions; their problem formulation is different; clients rate the experience of therapy differently; and the perceived therapeutic impacts seem to be different between the therapies. Briefly, it appears that therapeutic change depends upon a gradual gaining of insight, but that this process often involves the use of shared metaphors around which change is organised, as Hobson originally described in his phrase 'a common feeling language'.

Taken together, this suggests that the earlier pessimism about possibly teaching therapeutic 'tricks' may be unfounded, and that systematic teaching of a model of therapy might be clinically sensitive and effective. The basic skills approach is in some ways naïve, but it can lead fruitfully to the acquisition of a powerful model of exploratory therapy which can be used in brief and longer-term therapies in ways which allow a psychodynamic focus to be expressed in interpersonal terms.

Role-play

The limits of the videotape teaching methods described above are well recognised, and other methods relying on role-play and self-monitoring have been developed to teach trainees from several disciplines.

Role-play is an extremely powerful method by which basic therapeutic concepts can be introduced. A model of role-play has been developed which is very flexible and can be used for seminar groups of up to about twenty trainees for illustrative purposes, or in greater depth in closed groups of up to about six or seven trainees.

The method involves two volunteers for each role-play, interacting for a brief period (initially about three to five minutes but later up to about 10 minutes where appropriate). The trainee playing the patient says a few words to introduce the patient's problems, basing this on a patient they have seen in their previous clinical work, and the therapist is told whether this is an assessment interview or from ongoing therapy. A card giving brief instructions is then given to the patient or therapist or, occasionally, to both. After the role-playing, each participant is asked about their experience. Then the group as a whole are free to comment. A light-hearted atmosphere with non-critical comments is encouraged; the 'unnatural' effect of following role-plays distorted by the instruction card reduces the chance of the trainee feeling humiliated in public.

Ideally, a closed group of five to seven trainees meet together with the same trainer for approximately six weeks. The training groups may well be interspersed and supplemented with other exercises, such as role-plays of ward rounds, drawing up of geneograms or similar experiential training techniques. The role-plays themselves go through four levels of sophistication. The first set involve simple instructions to the therapist to alter his/her style in gross ways – such as avoiding eye contact or always making encouraging statements. The trainees then look at the enormous and wide-reaching impacts these alterations have on the conversation and, in the process of this scrutiny, learn some of the basic techniques and their possible misuses (Table 7.3).

Table 7.3   Example of role-play cards used in Manchester training

---

A Basic skills

Cards given to 'therapist' – assume a first session.
1. Avoid eye contact throughout.
2. Make very obvious eye contact.
3. Ask only direct questions to elicit factual information.
4. Comment frequently that you don't understand.
5. Make exclamations of surprise about what you are being told.
6. Lean forward in your chair.

B Negotiation cards

Cards given to therapist or patient – assume you are several sessions into therapy.
1. Say to your therapist that therapy is helping – could you meet more frequently.
2. You think your patient has improved and want to open a discussion about ending.
3. You will be away for three weeks in two weeks time and want to tell your patient.

C Dual experience cards

These cards show how persecutory spirals may develop.
1. Card to *patient* and *therapist* – be suspicious of everything the other says, do not accept things at face value.
2. Make comments about how the other person is dressed, but phrase them in an emotionally neutral way.
3. Translate what the other person says into a different jargon, e.g. 'learned helplessness'.

D Dilemma cards

1. You want to tell your therapist that you would like to meet in a different setting, e.g. the pub.
2. You feel unattractive and think the therapist is deliberately avoiding touching you – you wonder if he/she would be prepared to disprove this.
3. Behave in an increasingly hostile way; make personal comments about age, sex, race, dress, manner, etc.
4. Describe to your therapist your increasing impulses to smash things in the room.
5. Say in a matter-of-fact way that you have decided to kill yourself.

The second phase involves examining the emotional impact of limit-setting, contracts and boundaries. This allows the trainees to learn about the necessary structure of therapy, and the sensitivity of the patient to unintended emotional nuances, for example, when the therapist is discussing future missed sessions for holidays.

In the third phase, the role-play cards focus on the shared experience in the therapy of the patient and therapist – feelings such as suspiciousness or of being blocked.

The fourth stage involves the 'interpersonal nightmares' of Kagan which were described earlier. Trainees are encouraged to talk about their fears and fantasies or, indeed, their actual bad experiences in therapy when they felt seduced, attacked, humiliated or out-smarted. The trainees show remarkable courage and self-awareness, despite their previous lack of experience, when trying to understand difficult situations derived from their previous clinical work and from the role-plays.

One card, for example, asks the patient to demand of the therapist a reassurance that he/she is not talked about outside, after overhearing other therapists laughing about a patient in a public place. If the therapist is drawn into reassurance rather than exploration of this by saying that he never discloses anything outside the therapeutic situation, the role-play card prompts the client to express anxiety about the lack of supervision! Such well-laid traps leave the therapist bewildered, and most trainees express considerable relief that these are well-recognised clinical situations and that their anxieties are widely shared. The subsequent discussion also leads to examination of various ways in which sensitive setting of limits might be achieved to preserve the therapists' own boundaries and the necessary structure of the therapy itself.

Process narrative recording

To supplement the role-play work, the trainees are also encouraged to audiotape at least one patient on a regular basis. In addition to the usual supervision of that patient, they are asked to write up their sessions in a particular structured way drawn from the research techniques of 'process narrative recording'.

At the left hand of the paper, they put the tape counter reading so that they can play the correct bit in the subsequent supervision. In the next column, the trainee writes out a verbatim account of the therapist and patient statements from a segment of the session. At least as an exercise, they are encouraged to make precise verbatim recordings measuring the length of the pauses and accurately recording the dysfluencies and over-talking. This draws their attention to the ways in which the material taken to supervision is usually highly stylised and edited.

In a middle column, the trainees write the main 'chapter headings' of the therapeutic session (for example, 'introduction to the session', 'bullying theme begins', 'link from past with the situation with the therapist', etc.) so as to provide a structured overview of the narrative flow of the session. These headings are accompanied by a very brief statement of the core conflict being worked on at that particular time. A simplified version of Luborsky's (1988) Core Conflictual Relationship Themes may be used, i.e. the wished-for and the corresponding feared relationship. For more experienced trainees, an expression of the full potential mutative interpretation might be written down, as expressed in Malan's triangles of conflict and person (Malan 1979; see Ch. 1).

Trainees who are keen to develop their research skills can supplement this process recording using the right hand side of the page to plot a variety of different items. In one session, they might systematically record the types of interventions they used, and/or the intentions. This is very similar to the interactograms I and II described earlier, but directly link the categories to the session content. Trainees are then encouraged to experiment with their ability to listen using a variety of experimental methods. For example, in one session the therapist might systematically record *every* metaphor used – even 'dead metaphors', such as 'I don't see

Table 7.4 Taxonomy of therapist difficulties and coping strategies. (From: Davis et al 1987)

Therapist difficulties
(Coded by *experience* of therapist in the situation)

Therapist feels incompetent
        damaging
        puzzled
        threatened
        out of rapport
        stuck
        thwarted

Therapist's personal issues evoked
Therapist faces painful reality of situation
Therapist faces ethical dilemma

Therapist coping strategies
(Coded by source of support)

Therapist turns to self
      – re-appraisal
      – self management

Therapist turns to patient
      – shares difficulty or some aspect of it

Therapist turns to other
      – consultation
      – education
      – responsibility diffusion
      – gratification

Therapist turns to practice
      – technical intervention
      – non-technical intervention
      – change of tack

Therapist turns away from difficulty (avoids)
Therapist turns against the patient
Therapist turns away from patient (terminates)

---

the point' or 'I am in a mess', so as to detect any latent themes being expressed obliquely.

Drawing on Kagan's work with interpersonal process recall, more experienced trainees are also able to plot their key counter-transference responses, for example feeling bored, excited or sexually aroused at particular points in the session, and can then systematically link these feelings with other aspects of the narrative. A further technique which has been helpful for some trainees is to record the nature of their experienced difficulty at any point in the session, using the therapist difficulties rating manual (Davis et al 1987); this lists and briefly describes the key difficulties a therapist might experience, such as feeling threatened, blocked or in an ethical dilemma. In addition, the trainee then records in a systematic way his way of coping with that particular difficulty, and can compare this with the taxonomy of coping strategies developed by the same research team.

It is clear from the response of trainees that the options for active listening are almost endless, and this method can provide an exciting alternative to established teaching methods, particularly for trainees with an interest in research methods. However, there are significant disadvantages to this style of listening. Some critics have correctly pointed out that the technology can be used in a defensive way which actually avoids the trainee having to tolerate inactivity and uncertainty. Probably the optimal use of such teaching techniques is to supplement the basic therapeutic skills teaching described earlier, and to use these methods in conjunction with more conventional supervision, as described in the psychodynamic literature.

SUPERVISION SKILLS

In this concluding section, an alternative view is presented of the central importance of the supervisory relationship in developing basic therapeutic skills, in contrast with the more 'technology-based' approach described earlier.

So far, it would be possible to imagine the supervisor/teacher as essentially engaged in an educational process no different from learning any other skilled role. Pedder (1986) comments that supervision is better seen as lying at a difficult-to-define point on a continuum between education at one extreme and therapy at the other. He quotes Fleming's (1967) analogy of the supervision being comparable to a jug, potter or gardener: the jug model sees the supervisee as a passive recipient of knowledge; the potter model sees the supervisor acting like Prometheus forming an image in clay after his or her own likeness; and the healthier, gardener analogy sees the supervisor's task as to facilitate growth, with careful pruning where necessary.

The pruning model draws heavily on the work of Michael and Enid

Balint (Balint & Balint 1961, Balint 1957). Balint describes 'listening' as central to the doctors task. Gask & McGrath (1989), in their review of psychotherapy teaching in general practice, quote Balint (1957) on this, stating that:

'our aim is to help doctors become more sensitive to what is going on, consciously or unconsciously, in the patient's mind when doctor and patient are together... the events we are concerned with are highly subjective and personal, often hardly conscious, or even wholly beyond conscious control; also as often as not there exists no unequivocal way of describing them in words'.

This facilitative model is accepted widely in psychoanalytic settings, although it can be criticised in some general practice situations (e.g. Gask & McGrath 1989) for not being securely linked to positive therapeutic outcomes.

There is, however, yet a further dichotomy to consider. Supervision can be separated into two basic models based on the teaching of skills (didactic model), or a focus on the personal experience of the supervisee (counter-transference model) (Betcher & Zinberg 1988). These authors described the importance of privacy in the supervisory relationship and, again, the impact of audio-visual technology on that privacy.

The authors raise, but do not answer, many important questions, such as whether the supervisor should get to know the therapist personally, whether they should discuss matters other than the therapy, whether the supervisor should be clinically responsible for the patient, whether the supervisor should assess the therapist's competence. Their general point is that any intrusion on the privacy and the boundaries of supervisory work may interfere with the necessary rhythm set up between the supervisor and therapist, which in turn might usefully reflect the rhythm of the therapist-patient interaction.

The style of supervision which focuses on counter-transference experiences has become one of the dominant models in the last decade or so. As recently as 1976, Goin & Kline commented that only 12 of 24 supervisors in their study commented on counter-transference, and four of these only indirectly. They comment on the fear of supervisors that they might intrude or cross the boundary into therapy.

Lakovics (1983) successfully clarified and made researchable the elusive concept of counter-transference in his classification of counter-transference manifestations. He described concordant and complementary identification, referring respectively to a feeling in the therapist mirroring that experienced by the patient, or a situation where the therapist's feeling can be seen as a *response* to the patient's unacknowledged feelings (for example, fear in response to the patient's rage). This work draws on the concepts of Racker (1968), but he also added interactional reactions, life events, institutional counter-transference and classical counter-transference. This very practical paper helps the supervisor to decide which types of counter-transference are legitimately linked with the therapy itself; which might be temporary manifestations of a current crisis interfering with the therapy; and which require attention in a broader context in the institution or through the trainee's own therapy.

Eckler-Hart (1987) points out the ways in which therapists themselves develop a 'false self' – a professional way of relating which defends self-esteem. He quotes trainees who see supervision as 'like a complete evaluation of the self.' Book (1987) describes the ways in which a 'teaching alliance' can overcome the potential threat to self-esteem by encouraging 'introspective curiosity'. He suggests that the supervisor can legitimately use clarification and confrontation, but not interpretation of counter-transference phenomena, if the necessary distinction from therapy is to be preserved.

This final theme brings us back to the initial point of the chapter. It is possible to delineate and teach basic psychotherapeutic skills, but here the emphasis is on *supervisory* skills. Judkins & Margison (1988) have extended the techniques previously used to foster basic psychotherapeutic skill acquisitions (microtraining, role-play, etc.) and applied these to the basic listening skills needed by the *supervisor*.

The teaching exercises were designed to help the supervisor to delineate and recognise certain characteristic types of supervisory intervention. For example, the 'supervisory style' exercise distinguished: a didactic style which was formal; an interpretive style which was similar to therapy; and a 'laissez-faire' style which had a colleague-like atmosphere. A further exercise helped supervisors to distinguish the degree of control they exerted (at one extreme, seeing the patient as 'on loan to the therapist' – an over-concerned style – and at the other extreme with an under-concern verging on complacency). A further overlapping dimension of 'intrusiveness' ranged from the invasive supervisor, to one who remains frozen in formal roles. Another exercise looked at skills to deal with regular patterns of resistance in the supervisee. These included: structural avoidance by the over-reliance on verbatim transcripts; interpersonal defences, such as generating confusion; and active defences, such as the refusal to disclose information for apparently plausible reasons.

These training techniques have not been fully evaluated, but it is hoped that their impact will be to encourage supervisors to take a similar attitude to supervision as they do to their therapeutic work.

SUMMARY

The last three decades have seen a huge expansion in the methodology and applications of teaching in basic therapeutic skills. Well-established methods of teaching initially developed in North America, such as the use of role-play and microskills teaching, have found an important niche in the United Kingdom.

The impulse behind the major developments in this country – interviewing skills to elicit feelings, the 'grammar of psychotherapy', and research in the Conversational Model – has been a determination to produce effective methods of psychotherapy teaching which can be generalised to other settings, but which also retain a sense of perspective and humility in the training methods used. None of the authors of the studies quoted claim to do more than teach the basic listening and intervention skills which can provide a foundation for a style of practice which may be initially unfamiliar to psychotherapeutically naïve trainees. This then forms an important foundation on which more systematic teaching of psychotherapy can build. At this more sophisticated level, the analogy of the gardener becomes more appropriate than that of the teacher. For more advanced practice, the supervisor's task may be to disentangle some of the undergrowth of counter-transference manifestations, and so help the trainee to understand and value his or her own personal contribution to the therapy. The didactic element is always there in the background, providing a structured framework of descriptions. Once mastered, they allow the supervisor to proceed in a way that fosters growth of therapist and patient alike.

FURTHER READING

Hobson R F 1985 Forms of feeling: the heart of psychotherapy. Tavistock, London
Ivey A E, Simek-Downing L 1980 Counselling and psychotherapy: skills, theories and
    practice. Prentice-Hall, New Jersey

8. Brief psychotherapy

Pamela Ashurst

Most of the psychotherapy available within current psychiatric provision in the National Health Service is brief psychotherapy. It is, or should be, one of the cornerstones of psychiatric practice, and is therefore of great significance, both medical and social.

It has been shown that most attenders at psychotherapy departments have short-term psychotherapy, and only a relatively small proportion have long-term psychotherapy. Despite this, because the majority of clinical time is spent on a small number of patients, a 'clinician's illusion' (Cohen & Cohen 1984) exists that the typical psychotherapy patient is in long-term therapy. A recent study of a clinical setting oriented towards long-term therapy demonstrated that half the patients seen had fewer than 13 sessions of treatment, and that less than one-third of the total were seen for more than 26 sessions, although the vast majority of professional resources were concentrated on the relatively few patients who engaged in long-term treatment (Howard et al 1989). A similar situation probably exists in British NHS psychotherapy practice, regardless of the background training and orientation of the therapist.

There is a widely held assumption among psychotherapists that long-term treatment is better than brief therapy, and that patients having brief treatment are less likely to be 'cured' and more likely to need further help than patients who have prolonged therapy from the outset.There is, however, much evidence to show that a substantial percentage of patients treated with both brief dynamic psychotherapy and with lengthy psychoanalysis seek further treatment. Bennett (1983) suggests that patients (unlike therapists) view psychotherapy as valuable and useful at times of need, but not as a definitive process. He argues that episodes of focal therapy offered at times of need within the framework of an enduring but latent therapeutic relationship may be more appropriate for individual developmental transitions and life events than either short- or long-term traditional approaches.

In theory, briefer treatment should enable more people to benefit from limited resources; but 'quicker is not necessarily better' – a point easily overlooked in a climate in which performance indicators and cost-accounting are the vogue, and instant cures are in tune with the mentality of our age. Efficiency is important, but quality of treatment should remain a central concern of the clinician.

The scope of brief psychotherapy is broad, and many practitioners of differing philosophies and theoretical persuasions have contributed to its development. This chapter will be devoted to brief dynamic psychotherapy, derived from psychoanalytic understanding. Consideration will be given to the historical development of brief psychotherapy, recent trends in practice, its scope and underlying theory, the technique of its application, the indications for its use, the limitations of treatment, and outcome. Central to dynamic psychotherapy is the relationship between the therapist and the patient; paradoxically, this is of particular importance in brief psychotherapy precisely because the therapeutic relationship is time-limited – a uniquely privileged and personal relationship between two people constrained within an impersonal, containing and well-boundaried framework.

There are still those who regard the development of short-term techniques of dynamic psychotherapy as regrettable, believing that it represents a deviation from 'real' psychotherapy, and that it can lead to only superficial and temporary change. There is now a considerable body of evidence to refute these contentions, and it is clear that brief psychotherapy can be the treatment of choice for many conditions which cause considerable distress. In suitable cases, brief psychotherapy may be preferable to longer-term treatment, and there is evidence that brief intervention is capable of stimulating long-term personality change.

Recognition that mental structures are not closed systems, but that change or modification of one area of conflict can lead to an alteration of the entire internal psychodynamic system, is an underlying principle of brief psychotherapy. If a patient is enabled to function more effectively in one aspect of his life, he may experience an improvement in self-esteem and this in turn leads to more rewarding feedback from his environment.

Psychotherapy always involves learning, and once a patient has learnt to benefit from his experiences through therapy – however brief – life can be relied upon to promote further maturation. The increase in self-esteem from overcoming something which has previously been avoided, from being able to handle an irrational fear, from getting praise in the working environment, from engaging in relationships with others, all have the potential to create and reinforce change, both from within and from without.

THE DEVELOPMENT OF BRIEF DYNAMIC PSYCHOTHERAPY

Historical perspective

It is a common held misconception that short-term dynamic psychotherapy has been developed relatively recently, because increasing demands for psychotherapeutic help have outstripped the resources available. In fact, the earliest forms of psychotherapy – including Freud's earliest treatments – were brief, lasting weeks or months, successful in promoting change or cure of troublesome symptoms, and often lasting in their effect. The longer forms of psychotherapy, notably psychoanalysis, were a later development, but Freud continued to use brief psychotherapy when it was indicated. A single consultation, lasting four hours and conducted whilst walking around the town, is said to have cured the impotence of the composer Gustav Mahler; the conductor Bruno Walter wrote in his autobiography of the benefits he had derived from a six session therapy with Freud. 'Dora', the patient from whom Freud learned so much about transference, was in treatment for only three months, and many of Freud's didactic analyses lasted for a few months only.

There is evidence that Freud himself was troubled by the increasing length of the psychoanalytical process (Freud 1937) and its implications for treatment. By today's standards, most of the analyses conducted by Freud early in his career would be described as short-term, and Freud tended to be apologetic about the length of analyses, even when they lasted only a few months. He was aware that many of the cases which became famous through his writing were not lasting successes, and was frequently dissatisfied with the therapeutic outcome of his work. The uncovering of infantile neuroses in lengthy analysis did not necessarily lead to a more satisfactory outcome. Freud was certainly aware that longer and more intensive treatment is not necessarily more effective.

In 1918, Freud presented a paper in Budapest proposing that in certain cases of phobia or obsessional neurosis, it is sometimes necessary to institute 'active measures' to induce the patient to face the phobia or anxiety if therapy is to be successful (Freud 1918). Freud also experimented with setting a termination date for therapy in his analysis of the 'Rat Man' in 1912, published six years later as *From the History of an Infantile Neurosis* (Freud 1918). Freud clearly recognised the usefulness of this technique, but did not adopt it generally with his therapy.

Freud's pupils Sandor Ferenczi and Otto Rank independently began to experiment with modification of psychoanalytic technique with a view to shortening treatment and making it more effective by actively focusing therapeutic work. They eschewed the classical passive stance of psychoanalysis and were attacked for their disloyalty in deviating from Freud's theories. They published a joint work *The Development of Psychoanalysis* in 1925, in which, to a greater extent than other colleagues, they emphasised the importance of current events and life situations and the use of here-and-now transference interpretations, rather than historical reconstructions, in the therapeutic process. Rank emphasised the importance of setting a time limit to the analytic process, and the issue of separation became the central focus of his psychotherapeutic work. He also stressed the importance of the desire to change, if therapeutic endeavour was to be successful.

In the 1930s, Alexander (1946) began to question the traditional beliefs of psychoanalysis, recognising that intellectual insight alone is not a sufficient prerequisite for change, and that only through actual emotional experience in the transference relationship with the therapist would a patient learn to deal with an unbearable situation in a new way. Alexander also believed that the therapist should adapt his technique to the needs of the individual patient, and sought flexibility in the therapeutic approach.

Freud himself regarded intellectual insight alone as insufficient for the therapeutic task. He noted that even if the analyst has uncovered a resistance and shown it to the patient, this in itself will not cause the treatment to progress. 'One must allow the patient time to become more conversant with this resistance with which he has now become acquainted, to work through it, to overcome it, by continuing, in defiance of it, the analytic work according to the fundamental rule of analysis.' He went on to observe that this working through of resistance may be an arduous task for both the patient and the analyst but that: 'Nevertheless, it is a part of the work which effects the greatest changes in the patient and which distinguishes analytic treatment from any kind of treatment by suggestion' (Freud 1914b).

Towards the end of his professional life, Freud recognised that psychoanalysis could not guarantee a permanent cure, and that further episodes of treatment might be necessary if life circumstances led to new problems or precipitated a recurrence of ones previously assumed to be cured.

Contemporary influences

During the 1950s and 1960s, several groups working independently on both sides of the Atlantic began to experiment with changes in their practice of short-term therapy. Foremost among them were Balint and Malan at the Tavistock Clinic, and Sifneos in the United States. Mann and Davanloo came to attention a little later, with their respective highly individual approaches, but all these workers are representative of the current trend towards developing time-limited therapy based on psychodynamic principles.

Basic theoretical concepts: Malan

David Malan (1963, 1976c, 1979) developed his basic theoretical concepts of brief psychotherapy as a result of his work and research at the Tavistock Clinic. The 'Universal Technique' which he described is much more active than the traditional psychoanalytic technique, and uses the language of everyday human interaction, free from jargon, and much of the therapist's own personality in the service of the patient.

Neurosis (internal conflict) is seen as the end result of maladaptation resulting from early experiences which evoked feelings that were too powerful or frightening or exciting to be expressed or dealt with appropriately. The real feelings are repressed and not available to conscious recall (hidden feelings or impulses, I), and the neurosis is a defence (D) against them, usually accompanied by inappropriate anxiety (A) which increases markedly if the defences are challenged. The feelings will be re-experienced in the transference which develops spontaneously during dynamic psychotherapy.

Malan (1979) demonstrated the therapeutic principles in diagrammatic form as two triangles – the triange of conflict and the triangle of person – to illustrate both the conflicts and the relationship or context in which the conflicts are experienced, and to make visible the links which are the basis of the transference interpretations. Understanding the relationship between the patient's internal conflicts and the people in his life is the shared task of therapist and patient, and is central to any emotional readjustment promoted by brief psychotherapy.

The triangle of conflict is the first area to be explored in relation to the current life problem of which the patient complains. Exploration progresses from the defence (D) which is manifest, through the anxiety (A) to the hidden feeling (or impulse, I). It is important that the defence is weakened so that the hidden feeling (unconscious) is able to rise up to the surface, but anxiety (conscious) is likely to increase as the defence is attacked. The nature of the conflict is clarified first in relation to the significant other (O) in outside life – frequently a partner or colleague either current or in the recent past. Only after the conflict has been clarifed are transference links made (the triangle of person), either with significant figures from the past (P), usually parents (O-P link), or in the here-and-now of the therapy situation with the therapist (T) as the transference intensifies. The therapist will be variously an important current (O-T link) or past (T-P link) figure in the transference, but these feelings will be unconscious and may be sensed as a resistance or defence in the transference.

Real therapeutic progress with a deepening of rapport often follows interpretation of a T-P link, and Malan's work (1976b) suggests strongly that working through such links is associated with a successful outcome of therapy. The therapist in short-term dynamic psychotherapy actively pursues the two triangles, intuitively seeking the corners and making the links, using rapport as a guide.

The Tavistock Group: brief focal psychotherapy

Brief focal psychotherapy is a form of applied psychoanalysis which was developed by Michael Balint (1964, 1972), David Malan (1963, 1976c) and others in their workshop at the Tavistock Clinic in the 1960s and 1970s. The importance of choosing a focal conflict to be explored in a brief, time-limited period of therapy is emphasised by selective attention and selective neglect on the part of the therapist, and setting a date for completion of therapy. Most of their therapies lasted between 14 and 26 sessions, with a mean of 20 sessions. The main features associated with a good therapeutic outcome in brief focal psychotherapy were the establishment of the therapist/parent link, the early development of a working alliance between patient and therapist, the capacity to deal with termination issues during therapy and the absence of exclusion criteria.

David Malan became pre-eminent in systematic outcome research in the field of brief psychotherapy. Although his research validated the theories of many of the earlier psychoanalysts interested in brief therapy, during his last years at the Tavistock Clinic, Malan promoted the technique developed by Habib Davanloo in preference to his own work, an approach which is less dependent on interpretation and relies more on an early confrontation of the patient's defences.

Davanloo: broad-focus, short-term dynamic psychotherapy

Working in Montreal, Habib Davanloo developed his technique of broad-focus, short-term dynamic psychotherapy (Davanloo 1980) for patients with a variety of neurotic problems, including longstanding obsessional and phobic neuroses. He recommends from five to 40 sessions depending on the conflict area and personality structure, more complex problems usually requiring 20 to 40 sessions of therapy. He does not set a specific termination date, but the patient is told that the therapy will be short. The initial evaluation consultation is an open-ended session directed at confronting patients' defences and exposing their true feelings; the ability to tolerate powerful negative feelings without becoming psychotic or suicidal is important. The motivation for change and willingness to engage in treatment are challenged, and the capacity to respond to transference interpretations and to establish a good working alliance with the therapist are important selection criteria.

The first aim of Davanloo's technique is to enable the patient to experience his true feelings as intensely and early as possible during the therapeutic encounter. The therapist relentlessly challenges the patient's resistance, intensifying the tension in the session in the service of understanding the true nature of the patient's problems. Many observers find viewing this technique extremely disturbing, since it appears that the patient is being bullied and subjected to unreasonable pressure. Davanloo claims that the pressure is directed against the patient's defences rather than the patient himself, and that although this pressure creates powerful feelings, usually of irritation and anger with the therapist, much of it is transference anger linked with past situations which needs to be exposed. Experiencing this 'healing anger' (Molnos 1986) and having the opportunity to express it gives great relief to the patient, and other feelings, such as sadness and warmth, may emerge at this point. When the patient feels that these have been understood, the therapeutic alliance becomes much stronger. There is an increase in spontaneity and in the ability to express feelings generally, and at this point much new material emerges, including memories and dreams which have not previously been available to conscious recall.

The therapist's first task has been confrontation of defences. The next task is for the therapist to help the patient understand the links between his defences, anxieties and underlying emotions in the session, and the way in which these patterns developed in the past as a result of feelings about parents, siblings and other powerful authority figures. Their influence on his current life and relationships with important people, such as his partner, friends and workmates is clarified. This phase of 'working through' consolidates an understanding of the old processes and defensive manoeuvres; but the experience of the feelings in the here-and-now – that is, in relation to the therapist in the transference situation – is of vital importance if they are to be a basis for change.

Sifneos: short-term, anxiety-provoking psychotherapy

Peter Sifneos, working with the Beth Israel group in Boston, also favours a very active technique and uses anxiety-provoking confrontations and clarifications early on in short-term, anxiety-provoking psychotherapy or STAPP (Sifneos 1972, 1979). His emphasis is on active systematic problem solving and the development of new attitudes, both to enhance insight and to teach the patient how to use these new problem-solving skills after the end of therapy. As its name implies, his unorthodox technique gives rise to a great deal of anxiety and resistance on the part of the patient. Unlike Malan and Davanloo, Sifneos interprets conflictual material by using the patient's statements verbatim, before analysing the patient's defences. He has focused his work and research on patients who have unresolved conflicts in their relationships with their parents, usually the parent of the opposite sex (unresolved Oedipal conflicts), and prefers to leave the length of therapy flexible – between eight and 20 sessions over a period of two to six months. He has systematically investigated the cognitive components of STAPP, and acknowledges the contribution of learning theory and behavioural modification.

Mann: time-limited psychotherapy

James Mann, also working in Boston, allows no variation in his Time-Limited Psychotherapy (Mann 1973), limiting treatments to a total of 12 hours distributed according to the patient's needs. Twice-weekly, hour-long sessions for six weeks, or half-hour sessions for 24 weeks may be prescribed, although in practice most patients are seen at weekly intervals for twelve 50-minute sessions. There are usually between two and four hours of evaluation before the psychotherapy contract begins, during which a central issue is selected as the focus for therapy. He chooses a recurrent problem of developmental relevance, and characterises it as a preconscious element, which is described as the patient's 'present and chronically endured pain'. The therapist's formulation of this central issue includes an image of the self, a statement about feelings, the therapeutic contract and the therapeutic goal, and is intended to provide a clearly recognisable exposition for the patient to hold on to. Mann views time as a specific operative factor in psychotherapy, as well as an important curative feature. However, he sees the resolution of issues of separation and termination as critical to the success of the brief psychotherapy, and keeps the interventions and interpretations close to the patient's conscious preoccupations; unlike Davanloo and Sifneos, he does not engage in confrontation.

Ryle: Cognitive Analytic Therapy

Anthony Ryle in the United Kingdom developed Cognitive Analytic Therapy (CAT) to combine the therapeutic strengths of a brief, pragmatic, structured approach with the formulatory power of psycho-analytic theory (Ryle 1982, 1990; see Ch. 11). The central task of CAT is to help the patient revise patterns of thought and feeling which prevent new learning. The patient is given a rationale of the treatment, the Psychotherapy File, which removes some of the mystery of the therapeutic process. The basis of treatment is the 'CAT reformulation', undertaken as a joint task by the therapist and the patient, and written down. Diagrammatic reformulation is also used. Active cooperation and homework is expected from the patient throughout. Avoidance and self-defeating manoeuvres are constantly challenged and reformulated. Ryle has drawn freely from various sources which have influenced his technique: the short-term dynamic psychotherapists (particularly Mann), and cognitive behavioural approaches. His technique differs from that of other short-term dynamic psychotherapists, especially in the emphasis on collaborative empiricism. Transference is used, since invariably the patterns identified in the formulation occur within the therapeutic relationship. The clear structure makes it relatively easy for inexperienced therapists to feel confident about this technique. In more experienced hands, patients with poor motivation, severe problems and borderline personality structure, who may be unsuitable for psychoanalytical psychotherapy, can make impressive gains from the 16-session treatment which persist at follow-up (Ryle 1990).

CURRENT PRACTICE

When a patient presents with neurotic disturbance in psychiatric practice, the choice facing the psychotherapist lies between reinforcing defences or opening up change. In brief psychotherapy, the commitment is to the prospect of change, and the foregoing outline of various approaches in short-term dynamic psychotherapy reflects some of the similarities and differences between leading practitioners in the field.

The scope of brief psychotherapy

Brief psychotherapy is generally understood to be therapy of limited duration, lasting between one and 50 sessions in total. This would include: the therapeutic assessment consultation, usually between one and four hours in length, offered as one open-ended session or a limited series of consultations over a period not exceeding one month; and crisis consultation work, which is usually of between one and five sessions in a concentrated period, related in time to the precipitating crisis. Most brief psychotherapy is offered for between six and 40 sessions, depending on the nature of the presenting problem, the personality structure and life experiences of the patient, and the particular approach of the therapist. Short-term dynamic psychotherapy is often assumed to be synonymous with brief psychotherapy, but is in fact only one of a range of brief psychotherapeutic methods which have been developed over recent years to make effective psychotherapeutic treatment more readily available for patients with a broad spectrum of neurotic disorders.

The brevity of short-term therapy necessarily affects its scope and influences its techniques, goals and priorities. It may be primarily supportive, or insight orientated. It may be superficial or deep and exploratory, depending not only on the needs and capacities of the patients but also on the skills, preferences and characteristics of the therapists. The need to adhere to the time limit and the corresponding necessity of keeping the central issues of therapy clearly in focus require much activity on the part of the therapist.

However, the therapist's conscious and realistic reactions to the patient are particularly influential in brief psychotherapy, leading to expectations and perceptions which can either hinder or enhance therapeutic prospects to a greater degree than might occur in longer treatments (Strupp 1980). The therapist's personal reaction to the patient thus has major implications for selection, case management and therapeutic outcome (Frances et al 1984).

Common factors in psychodynamic therapies

Certain factors are common to all psychodynamic therapies:

1. A good *therapeutic alliance* – that is, the relationship between the patient and the therapist – which is based on the real qualities which both patient and therapist bring to the therapy, but also on the

unconscious factors governing their relationship, which are subsumed under the rubric of transference/counter-transference.

2. *Emotional catharsis* results from expression of feelings and a release of emotional tension in the safe and accepting environment created by the good working alliance.

3. A degree of *cognitive learning* occurs as a result of insight gained from interpretations; that is, the patient learns new ways of thinking.

4. The therapist acts as a *model* for the patient, much as parents will have done in early life, and either consciously or unconsciously the patient is likely to adopt some of the standards and behaviour of the therapist. It is said that imitation is the sincerest form of flattery, and in psychodynamic therapy, much of this is attributable to unconscious factors.

5. The *corrective emotional experience*, which Alexander (1946) regarded as the most important factor in promoting change in psychodynamic therapy, is generally acknowledged to be of major importance. However, it is not achieved by manipulation of the patient and the therapeutic situation, but by using the transference and the reality of the therapeutic situation, when the reactions of the therapist are more constructive, accepting and enabling than those of significant figures in the past. This may be viewed as a form of operant conditioning, where both overt and covert communications from the therapist are used in the service of the patient's healthy development.

6. The final factor common to all dynamic psychotherapy is usually called '*working through*'. This is an important aspect of the development and growth which takes place in psychotherapy, when the patient 'tries out for size', as it were, the new perceptions of the world and the possibilities that this affords, which have resulted from insights gained in therapy. The continuing support of the therapist, like that of a parent encouraging early independent exploration in a healthy child, is an important factor in promoting life-enhancing change, rather than a merely intellectual appreciation of the possibility of change.

Although dynamic psychotherapy, unlike behavioural psychotherapy, does not openly rely on instruction, advice, suggestion and persuasion, there can be little doubt that the patient receives powerful messages from the therapist, both overt and covert, which exert considerable influence.

Selection of patients

Selection of patients for short-term dynamic psychotherapy is of crucial importance, and the qualities required by the patient are similar to those for any form of dynamic psychotherapy. The most important qualities which are likely to ensure that the patient has the capacity to work with unconscious intrapsychic factors, and to tolerate the anxiety and stress involved in bringing these into consciousness, are:

1. Evidence of ego strengths. This will be indicated by sexual, social and occupational adjustment, intelligence and capacity to assume responsibility.
2. A capacity for meaningful personal relationships. Experience of at least one important relationship with another person in the past will be essential for the success of the relationship with the therapist.
3. A capacity to interact with the therapist, in order not only to establish a therapeutic alliance but also to ensure that transference feelings will be mobilised.
4. 'Psychological mindedness'. The ability for a person to be reflective and to think in psychological terms about the difficulties which he is experiencing will influence the capacity to use interpretations and to benefit from insight.
5. The ability to experience feelings. There are some patients, sometimes of high intellectual ability and academic achievement, who are fascinated by the philosophy of psychotherapy, but who use their intellect as a defence against feeling and who therefore resist the emergence of the powerful underlying emotions which are an essential accompaniment of change and progress in psychotherapy.
6. The existence of a core conflict to serve as a focus for therapy.
7. Motivation for change.

These last two factors are particularly relevant in selecting patients who are likely to benefit from short-term dynamic psychotherapy. Unless most of the patient's difficulties revolve around a central conflict that can be defined in psychodynamic terms, it is unlikely that short-term therapy will be helpful. The focus does not need to be on a specific life episode, such as bereavement with evidence of unresolved grief. It is, however, likely to be concerned with powerful feelings derived from important and anxiety-provoking relationships, such as sibling rivalry, early experience of separation and abandonment, and dependency conflicts. Sifneos (1972) believes that the focus must be of Oedipal origin, but other workers in the field do not share this view. This tendency to focus on Oedipal conflicts to the exclusion of other, often more powerful, traumatic experiences may be a result of the central position that the Oedipal theory occupies in psychoanalysis, since most of the leading short-term therapy practitioners are experienced psychoanalysts. There are many developmental crises which have a more traumatic effect than the classical Oedipal situation (see Ch. 1), and even very early traumas can often be worked on in short-term psychotherapy in suitable patients. People with 'transitional crises' (e.g. leaving home, marriage, parenthood, retirement) are often excellent candidates for brief focal psychotherapy, but a wide spectrum of perso-nality disorders and psychoneuroses may be suitable for short-term dynamic psychotherapy if the patient satisfies the other selection criteria.

The last and most important factor in deciding the suitability of patients for short-term therapy is motivation. Strong motivation to change, and to participate in the often painful and stressful work of short-term psychotherapy is an essential prerequisite for successful therapeutic outcome. It is not simply a wish to be rid of troublesome and disabling symptoms, but an acknowledgement of the need to make personal change and adaptation rather than to be the passive recipient of treatment. A sound therapeutic alliance in short-term psychotherapy is an active working partnership, with little room for idealisation on the part of the patient, or for omniscience and omnipotence on the part of the therapist.

Limitations and contraindications

The limitations and contraindications to short-term dynamic psychotherapy include psychosis; major character disorders with poor impulse control; chronic severe psychomatic illnesses; deeply depressed patients with persistent suicidal urges; schizoid patients, who are unable to form a relationship with the therapist; markedly dependent patients in need of long-term support; and those patients whose positive gains from their symptoms make them unlikely to part with them easily.

Technique

Four factors that are specific to short-term dynamic psychotherapy can be identified:

1. time-limited – usually between six and thirty sessions but not exceeding one year
2. active therapist
3. focus on a core conflict
4. face-to-face therapy.

Setting a time limit results in an emphasis on termination and the end of therapy right from the beginning. It promotes anxiety, and influences the entire therapeutic process; it will inevitably raise issues of previous separations. It does, however, encourage autonomy and individuation, since the patient knows that there is no question of unlimited therapy being available. The time limit serves to concentrate the attention of both patient and therapist on the work in hand.

Therapists working in short-term dynamic psychotherapy need to be extremely active, rather than maintaining a classical free-floating attention which encourages the discursive patient. Although the therapist should be non-directive, he must insist on maintaining the focus of therapy, which leads to a high level of therapeutic tension and interaction with the patient. Balint used the terms, 'selective attention' and 'selective neglect', to emphasise that the therapist must responsibly choose to focus therapeutic attention on matters which are relevant to the therapeutic focus, avoiding the digressions and deviations which might produce interesting material, but which are not apparently strictly relevant to the task in hand. Such digressions are frequently a defence against working with difficult and painful material, and often reflect a habit of avoidance which is deeply rooted and may be maladaptive.

The active but non-directive therapist must also engage in persistent confrontations and interpretations, not only to maintain the focus of therapy, but also to enable the patient to make conscious those links which reflect powerful experiences with significant persons – usually parents – in the distant past, that are reflected in relationships in the present. This relentless focus on transference interpretations, linking past with present, is a powerful discouragement to regression and to the development of a symbiotic dependency resulting from transference issues which is a central factor in long-term therapy, and particularly in psychoanalysis.

All this activity is enhanced by patient and therapist sitting face-to-face in chairs which are not too comfortable, and which discourage relaxation, fantasy and avoidance. The active therapist in short-term dynamic therapy needs to be alert to all the communications which his patient gives about his state of arousal and discomfort. Changes in the overall appearance, body posture, tone of voice, facial expression and avoidance of gaze are all signals that anxiety is being provoked, powerful feelings aroused, or defences marshalled. The therapist can deepen rapport with the patient by sensitivity to these cues, which often facilitates expression of material not previously accessible to conscious recall.

There is no place for social interchange in short-term psychotherapy, since this dissipates the tension which is essential in time-limited treatment. Likewise, the admission of material such as dreams and poetry has to be carefully considered, since it may contribute something powerful to understanding the patient's predicament, but may also be used as a defence against the discomfort of the therapeutic encounter. Be that as it may, the therapist can never know that his interpretations are correct, unless they have meaning for the patient. The highly motivated patient necessary for successful short-term therapy is less likely to block off and defend against interpretations because he is unready for treatment. The content of the interpretation may be of less importance than its timing – 'the propitious moment' (Stierlin 1968).

Interpretations in psychotherapy are concerned with making sense of the incomprehensible, with giving *meaning* to thoughts, feelings and behaviour which are a *response* to the situation, as well as making sense of the situation or predicament itself. The power of an interpretation depends on its acceptability to the patient, which is likely to depend in turn on the benefits which he derives from this new meaning. The best interpretations are those which the patient is led to discover for himself.

RESEARCH AND EVALUATION IN BRIEF PSYCHOTHERAPY

The brief dynamic psychotherapies outlined in this chapter may be regarded as forms of applied psychoanalysis. Whilst psychoanalysis is an excellent hermeneutic research tool, there are numerous methodological problems in mounting quantitative research into the process or outcome of classical treatment. Much of the psychoanalytic literature is devoted to hypotheses and individual case studies, although the work of the Mount Zion group demonstrates that hypothesis-testing is possible within psychoanalysis (Sampson & Weiss 1986). The most notable exception to the case study approach is the Menninger Project (Kernberg et al 1972) (see Ch. 9) which for many years combined an extensive treatment programme with concurrent research. This project, albeit interesting as a rare example of research on long-term therapy with adequate follow-up, does not allow conclusions about the effectiveness of treatment, due to many design problems including lack of a control group, systematic biases in patients excluded, small and unrepresentative sample and psycho-dynamic measures of inadequate reliability.

Meta-analysis of psychotherapy research has suggested that psy-chotherapy produces positive change (Smith et al 1980; see Ch. 1); short-term therapy studies also report substantial improvement rates (Muench 1965, Reid & Schyne 1969). How do short-term therapies compare in effectiveness with longer-term ones? In general, it has not proved possible to demonstrate any superiority of long-term psychotherapy over short-term dynamic therapy, although this absence of evidence is from relatively few good studies (Luborsky et al 1975, p 1001). Dose-response studies of therapies do suggest that up to a point (somewhere between 10 and 40 sessions) the more the therapy the better the outcome, but there is also a law of diminishing returns operating so that relatively more therapeutic benefit derives from the early sessions (Howard, Kopta, Krause & Orlinsky 1986).

Comparison of single psychological therapies of any kind tends to lead to equivalence of outcome – indeed, Luborsky et al (1975) gave the dodo bird's verdict that 'Everyone has won and all must have prizes'. No one therapeutic approach has been shown to be clearly superior to any other, but therapy is demonstrably better than no therapy. Bergin & Lambert (1978) estimated that about 10% of outcome variance is attributable to variations in technique, less than can be attributed either to patient or therapist factors.

More recently, this apparent equivalence has been challenged by those pointing out that the use of global measurement and random assignment to groups is likely to obscure more potent effects of specific techniques which could be revealed by more precise measurement related to specific treatment goals and alternative research strategies (Stiles et al 1986, Howard, Krause & Orlinsky 1986)

Within meta-analysis of psychotherapy research, the ways in which outcomes have been measured may favour behavioural interventions at the expense of psychodynamic therapies. It has been repeatedly shown that the correlation of outcome assessments by patients, therapists and independent clinicians is only moderate, although Mintz et al (1979) present powerful evidence from the Penn psychotherapy project that despite these differing viewpoints, a meaningful consensus is possible between measures. The use of psychodynamic vs symptom assessment could give more favourable estimates of outcome, but produce major problems of reliability of assessment (Mintz 1981).

Perhaps more worrying is the lack of adequate follow-up data in psychotherapy research, since the immediate effects of treatment may differ from the longer-term effects. It is quite possible that examining only short-term outcome produces spurious evidence. For example in the behavioural field, Kingsley & Wilson (1977), comparing two treatments for obesity, found the relative outcomes reversed when a long-term follow-up was made. The reluctance of researchers to report follow-up data is understandable, given the cost of obtaining such information and the statistical problems caused by patients dropping out or receiving further help in the interim.

Following Malan's work at the Tavistock Clinic (1963, 1976b), great emphasis was placed on the importance of predictive factors at initial assessment for deciding on the focus and course of psychotherapy. There is a contradiction between different accounts of research findings about whether or not the outcome of therapy can be predicted from patient factors in the way suggested by Malan. For example, Henry (1986) believed that 'the selection criteria are more theoretically elegant than pragmatically useful', and Bachrach (1980) claimed that 'no controlled, empirical study of psychoanalysis or psychotherapy has ever appeared in which outcomes were more than marginally predicted from initial patient characteristics.' In contrast, however, Bergin & Lambert (1978) conclude from an extensive review of psychotherapy research that 'The largest variation in therapy outcome is accounted for by pre-existing client factors, such as motivation for change, and the like.' They found no need to revise this opinion in a later version of this review (Lambert et al 1986).

How can these apparently contradictory viewpoints be reconciled? It seems to hinge on what one means by a 'marginal' prediction. Patient factors generally account for around 25% of the variance in outcome due to psychotherapy, and this size of effect could be dismissed as modest. However, using the method of displaying effect size (see Ch. 1) recommended by Rosenthal (1983), one finds that an effect of this size would increase the success rate of therapy from 25% to 75%, which clearly is of clinical and practical significance.

An example of an interactive effect between patient characteristics and therapy type which would be obscured in a simple group comparison is provided by Horowitz et al (1986). In comparing insight-oriented brief dynamic therapy following bereavement with supportive psychotherapy, they found that for patients with relatively high ego strength, greater benefit was obtained by the former, but that some patients actually deteriorated after the insight-oriented approach. Where such interactions exist, if only overall effectiveness is examined, equivalence of outcome could have been demonstrated, but this would have been highly uninformative of what was really happening in the process of change.

For these reasons, a new generation of psychotherapy researchers are seeking alternative paradigms in which to examine the mechanisms of change in psychotherapy (Rice & Greenberg 1984). The new paradigm methods are labour intensive, but can be adapted to the requirements of routine clinical practice for a non-intrusive, inexpensive research technique (Parry et al 1986). These methods rely on the intensive analysis of session-by-session data, particularly with regard to significant change events and the process by which therapist and patient arrive at them. Short-term dynamic psychotherapists have exposed themselves to peers and critics by not only attempting systematic research and evaluation of their work, but also by allowing themselves to be videotaped during therapy sessions. This has enabled their technique and the interaction with the patient to be subjected to close scrutiny, resulting in a better understanding of the process of psychotherapy, and has allowed evaluation by independent observers. Although some workers are reluctant to allow such intrusion into the confidential therapeutic space, the open attitude reflects a marked change from the previous practice of psychoanalytic psychotherapy and psychoanalysis, which was regarded by many as unduly secretive and defensive.

A number of research programmes have been undertaken which are relevant to brief psychotherapy, including the Sloane study (1975); work at Massachusetts General Hospital continued at the Beth Israel Hospital in Boston (Sifneos 1972); the Vanderbilt project (Strupp 1979); the Penn psychotherapy project (Mintz et al 1979); research at the Langley Porter clinic in San Francisco (Horowitz et al 1984) and the Sheffield UK project (Shapiro & Firth 1987). The results from these studies have influenced practice more than is credited in some quarters, although the degree to which the findings generalise to realistic clinical practice is limited.

There is clearly a need for evaluation of therapy in service settings to complement the findings of research designs which ensure statistical conclusion and internal validity at the expense of external and construct validity (Shapiro 1989). However, lack of resources to assist evaluation, audit and research, the reluctance of some practitioners to subject their work to scrutiny and a lack of research skills in clinical practitioners has limited the reciprocal influence of research findings and modified practice.

Psychotherapy service evaluation has a different focus and purpose from that of psychotherapy research. In providing health care of any kind, it is a painful truth that the provision of therapy is influenced by resource constraints. In a cost-conscious climate, there may be a tendency to focus on treatments (e.g. drug treatment) which superficially seem cheaper. If this is done without a systematic assessment of the psychological health needs of the population or evaluating the quality and cost-effectiveness of treatments, very serious mistakes may be made. Surgical analogies spring to mind; there is no use removing an ingrowing toenail while the abdominal tumour grows unchecked, simply because the toenail procedure is quicker and cheaper and can be carried out by an inexperienced operator. Similarly, there is no future in stopping halfway through a cholecystectomy because the waiting list is long.

It is easier to see the indications, contraindications and correct procedure for surgical treatment, and to evaluate the results of inter-vention; psychotherapy is much more complex, not least because the personality of the therapist is a variable which is difficult to quantify, impossible to standardise, and which greatly influences treatment. Many of the measures used in psychiatric research seem simplistic and irrelevant to psychotherapy evaluation. There remains a serious challenge to those delivering psychodynamic therapy within the National Health Service (or any third-party payment system) to demonstrate the need for, and the quality and cost effectiveness of the treatments provided. This issue is not addressed by psychotherapy outcome research. The challenge has not yet been taken up, but cannot be ignored much longer.

SHORT TERM DYNAMIC PSYCHOTHERAPY IN PSYCHIATRY: THE SOUTHAMPTON MODEL

The Southampton Department of Psychotherapy has had a longstanding interest in short-term dynamic psychotherapy within a broad range of treatment approaches, including behavioural and cognitive analytic therapies. The influence of David Malan's work on both practice and teaching has been of fundamental importance. Over the past eight years, Malan's advocacy of Davanloo's work has affected both the scope and technique of practice at Southampton.

Very brief treatment

Very brief treatment usually lasts between one and five sessions and is a form of brief psychotherapy in its own right. It has particular value in crisis intervention work, when it is directed to restoring the status quo following an acute disturbance to the patient's equilibrium. The cathartic effect of being able to share powerful and distressing feelings with another person who is attentive, respectful and non-judgemental can be of great value. It can be difficult to share acute distress, and friends and relatives may be unable to cope with someone who is presenting a very different face from the one with which they are familiar. Patients may themselves feel overwhelmed by this unfamiliar state, and feel the need to protect others from the destructive, although potentially transformative, forces which they are experiencing. They are likely to be greatly relieved at the availability of unconditional help offered by professionals for whose feelings they need take no responsibility.

Case study 8.1   Post-traumatic stress disorder

This case demonstrates the value of a three-session intervention in post-traumatic stress disorder. A young man had been involved in a car crash in which he received multiple fractures and other serious injuries. He eventually recovered after many months in hospital, but lost his driving licence and with it his highly paid job as a sales representative. He returned to his former work as a hospital technician, but felt undervalued and bitterly resented his changed life style. He sought help for terrifying dreams in which he would wake inside a refrigerator in the hospital mortuary, unable to move and frozen stiff. He would try to cry for help, but found the noise of the refrigerator motor deafening, and would wake screaming in panic.

At consultation, he was seriously depressed and admitted to actively planning a violent suicide. He was troubled not only by his nightmares, but by intrusive obsessional thoughts involving mutilation, and he feared that he 'might cut up (his) wife'. Prior to his accident he had never been troubled by such symptoms.

Careful exploration of the details of his crash revealed that he had been trapped in his car and released by firemen with cutting gear. He remembered feeling very cold, trapped and unable to move; he thought that he was dying and could not cry out to let people know that he was still alive. He remembered looking down at his trapped body from outside himself, and thinking that he would have to leave it. As he recounted this story in detail, he began to feel very cold and to be deafened by noise. For the first time telling of his 'near death' experience, he was able to connect his nightmares with it, and understood that the cold body in the refrigerator was his own cold body in the metal box trap (the car); the deafening noise of the refrigerator motor was the noise of the cutting equipment. He wept, talking of the fear and subsequent pain of that terrible event. He had been given excellent physical care, but nobody had talked to him about his feelings and what he had gone through, concentrating rather on his good fortune and his 'lucky escape'.

Following this initial consultation (two hours) the nightmares ceased, as did his intrusive and distressing thoughts of mutilation. He used two more 50-minute sessions to explore the realistic losses which he had sustained – status, money, job prospects, occupying the driving seat – and his suicidal preoccupations gave way to sadness as he acknowledged his anger and grief. He stopped the anti-depressants which had been prescribed before his referral, and mourned his losses without further disabling symptoms.

Case study 8.2   Single session catharsis

A single session may achieve a great deal. In this example, the focal event occurred several years before consultation. A woman had lost her 11-year-old Down's syndrome daughter. She had been a frail child and her death was not unexpected, but several years later her mother was still troubled by dreams in which she experienced her daughter's presence but could not see her face. She talked in detail about her daughter and her dying at the first consultation, and returned the next week to say that she had seen her daughter's face in a dream the night following the previous session. She had achieved what she needed, and had no wish for further therapy.

Crisis work always has an obvious focus, and there will be no need for therapist and patient to create one, since the circumstances of the presentation usually make it immediately clear. The crisis results from the loss of control which the patient experiences in relation to the situation or the symptoms. Making sense of it by exploring it with a perceptive and non-involved other, can re-create a sense of mastery in a very short time. Disabling symptoms become manageable once they are understood.

Transference links and interpretations may be of importance in very brief therapy, even in a single session, but the therapist's contribution as a real person with real empathic qualities will be of much greater importance than transferential issues. There is no place for encouraging dependence and neurotic transference in such work, nor for exotic interpretations which explore phantasy at the expense of neglecting the real trauma of actual experience. However, the significance of the experience may only become clear in the light of an individual's personal history and vulnerability, or of his phantasies which have been triggered by the crisis.

If the crisis has disturbed an equilibrium which was maintained by precarious defences, and there is a much deeper underlying problem previously unrecognised because it was not obviously disabling, crisis intervention work will be insufficient, and therapy will be required to deal with the underlying disorder.

Short-term dynamic psychotherapy

All psychiatric trainees on the rotational training scheme are expected to gain experience of psychotherapy under supervision throughout their general professional training in accordance with the Guidelines of the Royal College of Psychiatrists. With close supervision, trainees can feel safe in trying out new skills, and rapidly gain confidence as they discover how effective they can be. They learn vicariously from their peers in the supervision group, and use their newly acquired psychodynamic insights in work with other patients. Psychotherapeutic skills become a valued part of their professional therapeutic armamentarium and help them in decisions concerning patient management.

Diagrammatic representation of the therapeutic process is an excellent aid to understanding the process of brief psychotherapy. Malan (1979) developed his two triangles – the triangle of conflict and the triangle of person – to illustrate both the conflicts and the relationship or context in which the conflicts are experienced. It further allows a clear demonstration of the therapeutic principles of short-term dynamic psychotherapy, by making visible the links which are the basis of the transference interpretations; Malan's research had shown these links to be of major importance in relating problems to the relationship in which they occur, if they were to be of more than intellectual interest and to promote emotional readjustment. Angela Molnos has further developed these triangles in order to make the relationships and the process of dynamic brief psychotherapy clearer for the beginner. She created her diagram, the four triangles (Molnos 1984), as a visual aid to clarify the process of brief psychotherapy and the relationship between the patient's internal conflicts and the people in his life.

The following case study is typical of the therapy carried out at an early stage in training by a psychiatric registrar under supervision. He was present at the assessment consultation conducted by the consultant using Davanloo's approach of confronting defences. The therapy identified a core problem which linked the onset of the patient's breakdown, his relationship with his mother and his relationship with the therapist.

Case study 8.3   Brief therapy brings years of panic and depression to an end

Mr H was a 54-year-old married former schoolmaster with a 25-year history of neurotic depression. For three years, he had suffered acute anxiety attacks with hyperventilation. His overwhelming symptoms of panic were kept in check by the numbing effects of large doses of antidepressants. For five years, he had attended as an inpatient, outpatient and day-patient with a diagnosis of depressive neurosis. He experienced remissions and relapses related to alterations in medication, and he was retired from his work on health grounds. Mr H presented as a large, tense man with a jovial facade. His early life had been overshadowed by a critical, controlling and unpredictable mother; his admired father had died suddenly when Mr H was 20. There was evidence of unresolved grief at this loss, but the core problem clearly related to the relationship with his mother, which had been replayed in his working life, with a newly appointed headmaster. He described the critical episode which precipitated his breakdown in 1984, when he had been publicly humiliated. 'I felt as if the ground was falling from under me ... I was so scared, I ran away.'

Persistent confrontation of his defences (genial, placatory, humble) increased his anxiety considerably until he was unable to avoid his anger with the assessor. He was able to link this with the murderous rage which he felt towards his mother (Past) and towards his superior (Current) but which he had never previously acknowledged (X – hidden impulse/feeling).

He was offered short-term dynamic psychotherapy (16–20 sessions) with the registrar. Mr H failed the sixth session without warning. In supervision, the probable unconscious avoidance had been discussed and a brief letter of reminder was sent. This extract is from the beginning of the following session. Note that the therapist avoids any social interchange invited by the patient's apology and tale of his decorating.

H. 'Sorry I didn't come last week. I completely forgot. It was only when your letter arrived that I realised where I should have been last week! I was decorating and got carried away as it was going so well. I'm sorry I missed the session.'

Th. 'Sometimes it can be difficult to come to sessions when the talk has stirred up painful memories.'

H. 'Yes. I think you're probably right. It was maybe just me running away again.'

Th. 'Running away from what?'

H. 'That horrible scared feeling I get by going over these things. It brings it all back. That uptight feeling. Makes you want to run away. But from what? [Pause (15–20 seconds), hand-wringing and sweating] I've just had this sudden vision of a big red angry face. Really glaring at me. That's the sort of thing that brings on this feeling. I've got it now.'

Th. 'Tell me about the face.'

H. 'It's large and overbearing. I can picture it right now. Easily. It's twisted and angry. The sort of thing you'd want to run away from. Horrible!'

Th. 'Whose face is it?'

H. 'Mother's! It's her face all right. Her face and her fury.'

Th. 'How are you feeling now?'

H. 'Very unpleasant. I could run away right now. That feeling is all over. It's like a huge angry red sun from which you'd never be able to escape. Why it should be so big though, I don't know. It's huge.'

Th. 'Why might it be so big?'

H. 'Don't know. But I do know it'll scream at me, and I can practically anticipate the blow that comes afterwards.'

Th. 'Tell me about that.'

H. 'That's the way it always was with her. A furious face and argument over practically nothing, and then the back-hander to follow. That's when we'd have to run to get away. But this face seems too big to escape from. I'm quite amazed just how big it is.'

Th. 'Maybe to a child she would have seemed very big.'

H. 'Yes. I suppose that could be it. She was a big woman anyway. About five foot ten. Towered over us as kids. And when she got angry her face would go crimson. For any reason or not. If she got that way she'd wipe the floor with you. Maybe it's no wonder I feel this way now.'

Th. 'Were you worried I might be angry with you for not coming last week?'

H. I don't know. Maybe in a way. Not as much as I realise now.' [laughs] 'She's certainly got a lot to answer for.'

Th. 'How does that make you feel?'

H. 'Angry. Sometimes I think I never realised just how angry I must have been at that time. Looking back at what she did I guess there must be a lot of anger. But you couldn't let it out. She'd come down on you like a ton of bricks if you answered back. You bottled it up and kept it to yourself.'

Th. 'How do you feel about her now?'

H. 'Hate her. I can admit to that easily. I hated her, but at that age I was too small to do anything to get back.'

Th. 'What would you like to have done?'

H. 'Stuck that carving knife in her. Surprise myself in saying that but that's what it feels like. Kill her.'

Th. 'How does it feel to say that?'

H. 'Don't like saying it! Quite worrying in fact. Hate the idea of violence.'

Th. 'Maybe that's why releasing these feelings has been so difficult on these other occasions. Being afraid of what you might do if you lost control, you've run away instead?'

H. 'Hadn't thought of it that way. I suppose you might be right.'

The working hypothesis formed at assessment was re-confirmed and experienced in the session/in the transference with the therapist/in the here-and-now. Therapy ended as planned at Session 16.

Mr H was very optimistic about the future and planned to try to resume his teaching career. He needed no medication and was free of panics: 'I'm back in control again – the family agree – psychotherapy worked.' 'You let me see that I had that hate and anger and let me accept it ... and you didn't judge me on it ... you said it was OK and that recovered my equilibrium.' 'I feel as though I'm walking tall again.' A year after concluding short-term dynamic psychotherapy Mr H remains well.

Case study 8.4   Bereavement

Brief focal therapy is appropriate following bereavement where the process of grieving has been blocked. In this example, the patient's experience of anger in the relationship with the therapist allowed the grieving process to be resolved.

Mrs J, aged 56 years, had been widowed three years previously. She had continued to work as a district nurse until a month before her referral, when she had developed influenza. She was threatening suicide and felt she had nothing to live for, having become so depressed and bitter that she had recently severed contact with her only son, who lived some 200 miles distant with his wife and their baby. She was clinically depressed but had refused hospital admission, and her anti-depressant medication was not apparently achieving any improvement in her symptoms. She had lost two stone in weight, slept badly and woke early, and was hostile and hopeless.

She had had no recourse to psychiatric treatment before her husband's death, but two weeks after it had lost the use of her legs and had spent a month in the Unit, where she had recovered from her hysterical paralysis. It now seemed clear that the episode had been an unconscious identification with her husband in his sudden fatal illness; he had suffered a dissecting aneurysm of the aorta which had not been diagnosed before his death, but which had rendered him 'legless'. A diagnosis of morbid grief was made.

Mrs J agreed reluctantly to drive herself daily to the psychiatric ward from her nearby home, but was not prepared to participate in ward activities of any sort. She saw the doctor twice weekly for brief focal psychotherapy. Her idealisation of her dead husband was total, and she expressed rage that the hospital had not diagnosed his affliction and had sent her home, telephoning later to inform her of his death.

She had married against her parents' wishes and for several years they had cut off contact with her. Her mother was a controlling, unpredictable, critical woman and her husband had provided a placid, kindly, emotional haven – an escape from her harsh childhood. Mrs J's sister had refused to have anything to do with their mother, and was reported to have suffered throughout her adult life with neurotic depression and phobic problems, which had been attributed to her childhood experiences. Mr and Mrs J had nevertheless given her mother a home for some years in her old age, until her tyrannical and difficult behaviour had become intolerable and Mr J finally insisted that she went to live in an old people's home some distance away, only months before his death. Mrs J believed that her mother had 'broken his heart' and had refused to have any contact with her, being uncertain even that her mother was still alive.

Mrs J had kept the house exactly as it was when her husband died, and spent hours gazing at his photograph which stood on her piano. Although very musical, she had withdrawn from playing the organ in her local church because she had lost her faith in God since He had allowed her good husband to die and her hated old mother to live. She could not bear to touch the piano, since it brought unbearable pangs of grief.

The only thing which had kept Mrs J going was her work, but she now found it intolerable. She was full of rage at wives who found it burdensome to cope with sick or dying husbands, and felt particularly vindictive towards a woman whose husband had suffered a severe stroke which had robbed him of all independence and of his capacity to communicate. She longed to have had the chance to care for her own husband during his final illness, but had been robbed of the opportunity even to be with him at the moment of death. Her anger with his doctors spilled over onto the doctors with whom she worked.

All these issues and many more were discussed in detail during her twice-weekly therapy sessions. She made a good therapeutic alliance with her therapist, but was hostile towards anyone else who approached her. She steadfastly refused to acknowledge any negative feelings towards her late husband. In Session 8 (week 4) the therapist observed that it had clearly been too painful for her to make the transition from Mrs J, John's wife, to Anne J, widow, and that by avoiding 'burying' John, she was avoiding the reality of facing life without him. The anger was palpable, and Mrs J was literally 'lost for words'. She suffered a short-lived aphonia, but recovered her voice the next day and was able to tell the therapist how angry she was with her, and to link her fury with the aphonia. This proved the turning point, and she never looked back, using six more sessions at weekly intervals and coping with a two-week gap occasioned by the therapist's holiday. She tentatively joined some of the ward activities and began to plan to return to work. She visited her son and was relieved to find that her daughter-in-law bore no rancour (she had unconsciously attributed to her the qualities of her own mother) and that she enjoyed her visit to them. She was able to talk with them about her grief and was surprised to find them understanding and supportive.

Mrs J attended for her final session (14), 13 weeks after her initial referral. She had returned to work, and had arranged to practise on the church organ, having resumed her piano playing. She found it made her feel good and that she thought of John with appropriate sadness as she played his favourite music. She gave the therapist a small gift 'to remember me by'. The card inside read simply 'Thank you for helping me to live again'.

Some years later, the therapist received an airmail letter from Africa. Mrs J had decided to work there with Voluntary Service Overseas as a nurse tutor after her retirement, and was finding a full and satisfying new life. An unusual and unexpected follow-up confirming the lasting results of her brief therapy.

Case study 8.5   Episodic focal therapy

The next case illustrates Bennett's (1983) point that episodes of focal therapy at times of need may facilitate developmental transitions. Here, several brief interventions were made to good effect in relation to life events.

Mr M was a 33-year-old teacher who presented with disabling anxiety and neurotic depression following the break-up of a relationship with his girlfriend of several years. He was referred by his psychiatrist for a psychotherapy assessment, and experienced intense negative transference feelings towards the female psychotherapist, which evidently reflected his powerful ambivalent relationship with his mother. The youngest of her three sons, she had allied with him against her husband, and he had always had difficulty in asserting his own needs against her demands. He refused the suggested therapy, but contacted his psychiatrist eighteen months later, asking to see 'anyone except Dr A'. The psychiatrist wisely referred him back to Dr A, and the florid transference feelings were explored in a further consultation. Mr M accepted a place in an eighteen-month group conducted by Dr A and a male co-conductor. He used the group well, made major gains and was symptom-free at follow-up, with considerable insight into his own problems. During the course of the group, he reported that he had been found to have high blood pressure and was started on hypotensive drugs by a physician.

Two years after the group ended, he wrote to Dr A to say that he had angina and was awaiting investigations and possible heart surgery. Industrial disputes and waiting list delays increased his anxiety as he waited for the relevant invasive investigations, and he asked for more therapy so that he could talk about the fears for his life in this unexpected crisis. A girlfriend had left him, unable to cope with the situation. He had ten weekly sessions of brief focal therapy with another therapist (who had been trained in behavioural and cognitive therapy and was just starting brief focal therapy under supervision) which finished when he was admitted for coronary bypass surgery. He later wrote to thank Dr A for arranging therapy, and said that it had been extremely helpful. He had returned to work and was again enjoying vigorous sailing.

Some two years later, he wrote again to Dr A in some despair, saying that his chest pain had recurred and that the cardiac surgeon had told him there was no physical cause, since investigations revealed that his graft remained patent. At consultation, he was depressed, expressing hopelessness about his future. The therapist challenged his defences against his underlying anger, which was expressed through his pain. Mr M was frightened that experiencing the intensity of his feelings would literally 'break his heart' and that he would die. The therapist was expecting to be away for a prolonged period the following year, but felt that short-term dynamic psychotherapy would be helpful and offered 12 sessions, since there was no time for a longer contract, reasoning that the 'shared history' would enable short-cuts to be taken, and that if Mr M collapsed in a therapy session, the hospital emergency squad could be summoned!

The therapist's retreat into a detached, confronting role was experienced as a hostile attack by Mr M, and he became a pleading, frightened child, seeking reassurance and encouragement. His anxiety increased as the therapist probed his real feelings, until it became clear that the therapist was being experienced as his vicious bullying older brother, who had dealt with his envy of Mr M by hostile and sadistic treatment of him, reflecting the brother's own treatment by their father. Mr M had been protected from father's cruelty by his liaison with mother, which in turn had protected her from her husband's violence. Eventually, Mr M's long-repressed murderous feelings towards his brother erupted in the session, with some relief of the alarming chest pain that he was experiencing. He worked through much of his early life experience and current family relationships in the next six sessions, and related his own passivity and avoidance of conflict inside and outside the family to those childhood experiences. He saw that this anxiety and depression were linked to early threats to his security (his anxious, dependent attachment to his mother) which was repeated in his adult relationships. He decided to finish therapy at the tenth session, thus avoiding the therapist's abandonment and allowing him to take control of the ending which he acknowledged, although he also had a good rational reason for terminating early. He has remained well, although experiencing occasional chest pain, and has had no further need of therapy. His personal relationships within and without the family are under his control.

CONCLUSION

The indications for short-term psychotherapy, its scope and its technique are necessarily influenced by its brevity. If a patient's adaptive capacities are greatly impaired, it is unlikely that brief psychotherapy would be beneficial.

The therapist must be free of therapeutic over-ambition. If he regards brief therapy as 'second best', the therapist will not serve his patient well. Coleman (1949) has observed that often 'the patient contents himself readily with limited treatment objectives when the therapist can allow him to do so'.

Much working through, and continuing change, is accomplished by the patient after therapy has stopped. The major aim should be to enable the patient to use his own strengths and resources in the service of continuing change and development, not to rely on the therapist to hold the magical key; the patient must harness his own power and not project it into the all-powerful therapist.

Paradoxically, the practice of short-term psychotherapy requires the most complex therapeutic skills developed through extensive and intensive psychotherapeutic work with patients, yet it can be practised usually quite safely and often very effectively by the relative beginner – especially if there is close and skilled supervision available. Since it is clear that the bulk of psychotherapy practised within the NHS is brief psychotherapy, and simple logistics make it unlikely that more than very few patients would ever have the opportunity of long-term intensive treatments, it is important that we take brief psychotherapeutic approaches seriously, and learn to practise brief treatments as well as we can. Our patients deserve no less.

Acknowledgements

Thanks are due to Glenys Parry for help in the preparation of this chapter, and to Edward Komocki for the Case study transcript 8.3.

FURTHER READING

Malan D 1979 Individual psychotherapy and the science of psychodynamics. Butterworth, London
Parry G, Shapiro D A, Firth O 1986 The case of the anxious executive: a study from the research clinic. British Journal of Medical Psychology 59:221–233

9. Supportive psychotherapy

S. Hartland

Supportive psychotherapy has for too long been the least prestigious of the psychotherapies; it has attracted the least interest, has traditionally been practised by the most junior members of a health care team with little or no supervision, has lacked a unifying theory and has failed to excite the imaginations of researchers. Instead, it has been viewed as the mere propping-up of those patients who are unlikely ever to be able to function independently. In this chapter, I hope to show that these views are outdated, and that there are ample rewards for both patients and therapists prepared to embark on a journey of uncertain outcome and where the going will assuredly be difficult much of the time.

DEFINITION

There is no universally accepted definition of supportive psychotherapy. The term 'supportive' has been coined in an attempt to distinguish this form of psychotherapy from other forms; especially perhaps from 'insight-orientated' or 'dynamic' psychotherapy. Broadly speaking, behavioural psychotherapy concentrates on altering the patient's actions, cognitive therapy aims to change the person's thinking, and dynamic therapy, starting from the patient's feelings, aims to provide a new emotional experience which will lead eventually to the replacement of immature and inappropriate defence mechanisms by those which are more mature and appropriate. Supportive psychotherapy, having no clear-cut technique of its own, may include elements of all the above approaches. Bloch (1986) describes it as a therapy calling for 'an intricate blend of art and technique'. The name itself can be misleading, implying as it does that other psychotherapies are not supportive, and that support is all that is offered. Of course, all psychotherapy is, or should be, supportive; the point about supportive psychotherapy is that more emphasis is placed on the supporting or maintaining element, and there is less pressure put on the patient to change. Patients may indeed make profound changes in the long term, but the key feature of this therapy is that of providing an ongoing, consistent relationship in which the therapist aims to help the patient live as independently as possible in the outside world.

213

The term, supportive psychotherapy has sometimes been used to describe the short-term counselling offered to those who have been psychologically shaken by a recent crisis in their lives, but who are not long-term psychiatric patients. It has also been loosely applied to the supportive work of any psychiatric outpatient clinic concerned with the follow-up and management of patients. Neither of these are under discussion here.

A possible definition is as follows: supportive psychotherapy is a long-term psychotherapy aimed at maximising the patient's strengths, restoring his psychological equilibrium and acknowledging, but attempting to minimise, his dependence on the therapist. It does this by fortifying the patient's appropriate defences without attempts to restructure his personality, by enlarging his behavioural repertoire, by alleviating his anxieties and, most importantly, by providing a secure and trusting relationship with the therapist over a period of time.

THE PATIENT

How does one decide which patients are best suited to supportive psychotherapy? If this is a question of deciding between different types of psychotherapy, then Werman's (1984) definition is helpful: 'Supportive psychotherapy assumes that the patient's psychological equipment is fundamentally inadequate.' Inadequate to the task of independent living, that is. These patients are likely to require long-term help from professional carers in managing their own lives on a day-to-day basis.

Psychiatrists and general practitioners alike have a number of patients who they recognise may need ongoing support over an indefinite period. In the psychiatric hospital, the rotating junior member of the medical team tends to inherit from his predecessor a small population of outpatients who are seen at regular intervals, usually varying from one to six months, and who have often been attending the outpatient clinic over a number of years. They may or may not be on medication. They may have longstanding psychiatric histories, with repeated admissions to hospital. Their diagnoses will be varied: they may have had one or more acute psychotic episodes, or a less florid but progressive illness; they may have one of the neurotic disorders, in particular, chronic anxiety, depression or a tendency to somatise emotional problems; they may have any one of the personality disorders to such a pronounced degree that they are unable to cope with day-to-day living. People with a severe physical illness or who are mentally retarded may also come into this category.

Whatever the initial cause, they have not been able to manage on their own in the outside world and require help. Their lives in the community will tend to be impoverished; they often have difficulty making even superficial relationships with others, and may be extremely isolated individuals whose hospital appointments are the social highlight of their lives. Where closer relationships do exist, they may well have many deep-rooted pathological features; for example, a symbiotic relationship with a parent or child where there is intense dependence on both sides.

These patients are often obviously both fragile and exceedingly demanding; doctors, both senior and junior, are frequently at a loss as to how to help them once the crisis which initially brought them for help has been resolved, and what appears to be needed is an indefinite period of support. Such patients usually end up as candidates for supportive therapy not as a result of a planned treatment programme, but because attempts at rehabilitation or getting them to manage on their own, have failed, or because supportive therapy is seen as a convenient way of disposing of 'untreatable' patients. While it should perhaps be the aim with all patients to return them to a fully independent life in the community, there are always some for whom this will never be possible. Recognition of this fact can allow a planned approach to long-term treatment in which supportive therapy is likely to play a part.

In general practice, patients often present with a series of minor physical complaints in order to gain access to the doctor. They may form part of the group described as 'heartsink' patients by O'Dowd (1988): patients who 'evoke an overwhelming mixture of exasperation, defeat and, sometimes, plain dislike that causes the heart to sink when they consult.' Much time can be wasted by both doctor and patient in investigating the physical complaints, when it is unrecognised that what the patient requires is the space to discuss his problems with a concerned listener. In O'Dowd's study, meetings set up to discuss the reasons for the patients' discontent in reality lessened the doctors' discontent by the sharing of the negative feelings produced by the patients. Frequent but regular short appointments with the same doctor and with no fixed agenda, in which the person is free to talk about whatever is concerning him, may be the best way to help these dependent patients. They may continue indefinitely to need a modicum of medical support, but when they can rely upon having a regular time, even when the intervening interval is quite long, they are likely to feel less compelled to present with a physical symptom in order to get attention.

THE THERAPIST

Who should carry out supportive psychotherapy? As mentioned above, it is often the province of the least experienced staff members when practised in the hospital setting. Yet it can be argued that supportive therapy calls for a higher degree of skill on the part of the therapist than does insight-orientated therapy. The Menninger Foundation's Psychotherapy Research Project (Wallerstein 1989) compared the results of different psychotherapeutic treatments performed by therapists with varying degrees of skill on patients with a wide range of ego strengths. Ego strength was defined as a combination of:

1. the degree of integration, stability and flexibility of intrapsychic structures
2. the degree to which personal relationships were adaptive, deep and gratifying of normal instinctual needs
3. the degree to which the dysfunction of the intrapsychic structures was manifested as symptoms.

Patients with high ego strength were found to improve whatever psychotherapeutic approach was used, irrespective of the skill of the therapist. For patients with low ego strength, who are those under consideration in this chapter, the skill of the therapist was crucial in determining outcome. The concept of therapeutic skill included the therapist's experience, his mastery of technique, his knowledge of his own personality and his awareness of specific counter-transference reactions. The implication is that less skill is required when a standardised procedure, developed from a definite theory, is offered; dynamic therapy, based on psychoanalytic concepts and involving a focus on the transference, together with a stance of neutrality on the therapist's part, can be successfully carried out by relatively inexperienced therapists. Supportive psychotherapy, with a less clearly defined theoretical framework, and where the therapist is more of a real person for the patient, demands greater flexibility from the therapist. It is essential to be thoroughly conversant with the rules of psychotherapy and to have long experience of applying them before one can judge when it is appropriate to break them; supportive psychotherapy calls for a more intuitive choice of intervention than does dynamic therapy, and adherence to a standard technique may be detrimental to outcome. The therapist's personality and suggestive influence on the patient are of greater importance in supportive therapy, and the therapist must be even more fully alerted to transference and counter-transference issues than he is during dynamic therapy. Skill and experience are therefore both necessary in the therapist for an optimal outcome for the patient in supportive therapy.

Ideally, the therapist should have had enough of his own personal therapy to be aware of his own unresolved conflicts and vulnerable areas, as there is no doubt that patients, like children, are extremely quick at picking these up and playing on their therapist's weak points. The therapist needs to be prepared for this. If, however, the therapist has had no experience of personal therapy, he should at least be in supervision with someone skilled and experienced enough to deal with the pitfalls in therapy that are bound to arise.

The therapist also needs an inexhaustible supply of patience and optimism. Patients taken on for supportive psychotherapy will not give the quick rewards of the patient with a stronger ego. Change, if any, may be imperceptibly slow. The therapist may have not only the patient, but members of the patient's family, friends, and other professionals to deal with; this can be a daunting task for a junior member of staff to face, especially if he himself is not adequately supported.

Given the slow nature of the therapeutic process in supportive therapy, the question of the time commitment becomes very important. The therapist needs to be able to work with the patient long enough to see the results of his endeavours. The patient needs time to build up a trusting relationship on which he can rely. If sessions are short and infrequent, as is likely to be appropriate in order to limit the patient's dependence, the relationship will take longer to develop (the longer and more frequent sessions offered in other types of psychotherapy are contra-indicated here). Junior members of staff may find it difficult to commit themselves for a period of time sufficient to yield any satisfactions to either patient or therapist.

No therapist can manage adequately more than a small number of this sort of patient; they are too demanding and frustrating. Anyone embarking on supportive therapy should consider very carefully how many of these patients he feels he can handle adequately and restrict himself to this number. This, of course, is a counsel of perfection as it is often impossible to predict in advance how one will cope, and there may also be nobody else available to take on the patients.

Flexibility has already been mentioned as a desirable quality in the therapist undertaking supportive therapy. A variety of techniques from different types of psychotherapy may be used according to what the therapist feels is appropriate at the time. An ability to think laterally, or to use his imagination on behalf of his patient, is also a great advantage. Together, patient and therapist may come up with novel and ingenious solutions to the problems in the patient's life. This is half the fun of this type of therapy: the therapist will need to have recourse to all his own life experience, to his intimate knowledge of his patient and to his cognisance of cognitive or behavioural techniques, in order to help the patient deal with seemingly intractable problems and adapt more creatively to the external world.

THE THERAPEUTIC RELATIONSHIP

To support, says the Oxford English Dictionary, is to strengthen the position of a person by one's assistance, countenance or adherence. Although in all therapies the nature of the therapeutic relationship will vary over time and between sessions, in supportive psychotherapy there is more variation of role for both therapist and patient. This is true partly because of the use of a wide range of techniques, but also because the personalities of both patient and therapist will play a larger part than in other therapies. The vulnerability of the patient will mean that the therapist assumes more responsibility for the patient, and for the sessions, than he would do in dynamic psychotherapy, where the patient is assumed to be more autonomous. The therapist may act at different times as guide, teacher, advice-giver, as well as listening, empathising, clarifying and – sparingly and with discretion – interpreting. Because of the more active role of the therapist, the patient needs to be able to trust the therapist to act on his (the patient's) behalf if necessary, in much the same way as one would trust any professional whom one consulted. In dynamic therapy, the therapist aims to remain as neutral as possible towards his patient and to disclose little or nothing of his own feelings, in order to foster the development of the transference; the negative and positive feelings of the patient towards his therapist are interpreted and worked through. The therapeutic relationship will therefore undergo many vicissitudes as the feelings of the patient change. In supportive therapy, the therapist is setting out on a different journey; he is not aiming to bring about major characterological changes in the patient, but, rather, to help the latter develop better adaptive responses to daily living. If he is at times to take over some of the functions of the patient's ego on the patient's behalf, the trusting relationship should not be threatened.

Psychodrama introduces us to the role of the 'auxiliary ego' whose purpose is to assist and strengthen the ego of the protagonist; in much the same way, the therapist in supportive therapy may use his own resources to shore up the patient's ego and lend him support when this seems to be necessary. For this reason, the relationship between patient and therapist is kept as positive as possible, much as it would be in cognitive or behavioural psychotherapy. Although the therapist may be well aware of the patient's negative feelings towards him, he will, on the whole, not bring these to the patient's attention but strive to accept how the patient feels and to maintain an atmosphere of trust.

Real intimacy implies a knowledge and acceptance of the other's negative and positive feelings as well as of one's own. These patients have a limited, sometimes very severely impaired, capacity for intimacy, and may have few or no relationships outside the relationship with the therapist. The therapist must therefore be aware of the danger of the patient's becoming very dependent on him as perhaps the only person in his life who has offered him time, undivided attention and concern. To minimise this dependence, the therapist can encourage the patient to look for other sources of support; these will be mentioned later.

In summary, then, the therapeutic relationship should be one of trust, with fewer swings of mood than would be true of a dynamic therapy. The therapist may show more of himself as a real person at times if this seems appropriate, but will always work towards strengthening and maintaining the therapeutic alliance.

BOUNDARIES

Boundaries are important in all types of psychotherapy, and supportive therapy is no exception. They constitute the 'rules of the game' without which no effective therapy can occur. When breached, problems are likely to arise. They provide a place of safety within which therapist and patient can play, and establishment of boundaries constitutes one of the important differences between a professional and non-professional relationship.

Firstly, there is the problem of the sessions: how frequent should these be and how long should they last? There is no definite rule about this; some patients will need a session every fortnight, some may last several months between sessions, and use other sources of support in the meantime. The therapist will have to 'titrate', as Holmes (1988) puts it, the frequency of sessions against the need of the patient until he discovers the optimum balance. This will consist of the longest time between sessions that the patient can comfortably tolerate and that will still enable him to function at his best level in the community. When the patient is well, the length of time between sessions can be extended; on the other hand, when crises occur in his life or he becomes ill, he will need more intensive care, even possibly several sessions a week.

The length of each interview should generally be between 20 and 45 minutes. About half an hour has been found to be satisfactory for the majority of patients. This should allow enough time for the patient to describe how he feels and for therapist and patient to discuss strategies of coping and possible pitfalls. Again, flexibility is the key; some patients may need more time than others. What matters is that the person can be certain of a set period of time, at regular intervals, with the same person. In this way, a trusting relationship can be established. Just as in dynamic psychotherapy, the reliability and consistency of the therapist are what lay the foundations for trust to be built up. It follows that it is as important here as in other psychotherapies for the patient to be informed well in advance of any breaks in therapy, such as holidays, or unavoidable absences of the therapist. It is tempting for the therapist to underestimate his importance to the patient, particularly when they are meeting infrequently for only 20 minutes or so. Yet this time may represent a lifeline to the patient, especially if he lacks other sources of support and his relationships are generally unsatisfactory. The comfort of knowing he has a time set aside for him when he will be able to talk about what is worrying him to an understanding other, may enable him to tolerate stresses that would otherwise result in an increased use of medication or other services in the community. He can, as it were, carry the thought of his next appointment around with him like the bottle of tranquillisers he never needs to take because he knows that they are there. Junior doctors who are only in a post for six months before rotating to their next appointment may not realise the need to inform their chronic outpatient clientele of their impending departure; this can have a disastrous effect on the patients. Some patients may have become attached more to the institution than to the individual they happen to be seeing at the time, but others will have become very dependent on the person offering them support, and may become extremely upset by that person's leaving. They need time to accept and work through their feelings with the person concerned before the break occurs, and even then they may find it impossible to accept the loss.

WHAT HAPPENS?

Although change may well occur during supportive therapy, it is not the primary aim. Winston, Pinsker & McCullough (1986) argue that maintaining the status quo is the principal objective. These authors also point out that the emphasis in the past has been to say what supportive therapy is *not* rather than what it *is*, so that the therapist starting to practise this form of psychotherapy is still quite ignorant of what he should actually be doing during the course of treatment.

There are no definite rules about what should go on during the course of each session between therapist and patient. The aims of treatment are:

1. to acknowledge and face the real losses and deprivation the patient has experienced, but not to allow him to use these to prevent himself making progress in life
2. to prevent further breakdowns by monitoring the patient's current mental state
3. to act temporarily as an auxiliary ego in an attempt to strengthen the patient's own ego through identification
4. to encourage the patient to develop new and more satisfactory behaviour and ways of coping with life
5. to provide a source of comfort to which the patient can return for as long as he needs it.

With these ideas in mind, the therapist may listen, encourage, clarify, educate, reassure, suggest, acknowledge and accept. Many patients come to psychotherapies of all persuasions feeling demoralised and hopeless; none more so than those thought to need supportive psychotherapy. They may feel dependent on others for help, fiercely resent that dependence, and anticipate the future as bleak and the world hostile. They may lack any sense of control over their lives and be blind to their own potential, failing to use the coping mechanisms they already possess.

Even if there are no definite rules, it is possible to break down the process of therapy into different components to be considered separately.

Listening

Probably the most important component in psychotherapy is listening. To be listened to seriously (but not solemnly), respectfully (but not deferentially) and non-judgementally is something we all need. Alice Miller (1983) describes it well in relation to children: 'The child has a primary need to be regarded and respected as the person he really is at any given time, and as the centre – the central actor – in his own activity.' The adult is no different from the child in this respect; being listened to seriously means being seen as the central actor in one's own activity by another person.

For the most damaged patient, being listened to may constitute a proof that he actually exists. It may help to refute his own worst fears of not-being. This is not a fear of disintegration, because that assumes some sense of wholeness which could be shattered. Many patients have never experienced themselves as existing as a person in their own right. Being listened to seriously by another person offers a recognition of themselves as a separate person, with their own thoughts and feelings. A psychotherapist colleague once described 'just sitting' with a patient; this summed up her attitude of attentive quietness which facilitated the patient's unburdening. 'Being with' rather than 'doing to' the patient is the important distinction made by Wolff (1971).

Listening is not always easy for the therapist; it is made easier by the lack of outside distractions which are so common in the rest of our lives. Psychotherapy should be carried out in a private, quiet room where interruptions from people or telephones and other noises are avoided so far as is possible. The therapist should try to disengage his mind from other concerns so that the whole of his attention can be focused on the patient. While he is listening to the patient's story, he is working extremely hard at sifting out the important points, hearing the unspoken as well as the spoken, trying to make sense of what the patient is bringing both in terms of external reality and in terms of that individual patient's psychic reality. He will be aware of the relationship between himself and the patient and what is happening in it, and also be thinking of possible strategies for helping, and of the most acceptable way of presenting these to the patient.

Doctors and nurses are taught to listen, and then act. It can be hard for people in these professions to forego the second half of this injunction when they come to practise psychotherapy. Listening on its own is often undervalued, but being really listened to is a rare and supportive experience in its own right. Even the most inexperienced therapist can offer something of inestimable value to a patient if he is prepared just to sit and listen with his full attention.

Acceptance

Acceptance is often seen as a passive phenomenon, but like listening, is in reality very active. It implies a taking-in and digesting of what the patient brings, and an attempt to make sense of it for the patient. We speak of 'holding' or 'containing' the patient by analogy with the way a normal mother will hold or contain her baby. She will try to make sense of the baby's unmanageable feelings on his behalf; she will not be overwhelmed by the baby's anxiety but will contain it and hand it back to him in more manageably-sized portions. By tolerating what the baby finds intolerable, she will lead him to develop the resources to deal with his own pain, anxiety, isolation. So the therapist listens to what the patient has to bring and tries to understand how the patient is feeling. He may want to ask questions in order to clarify how the patient feels, or if he does not understand. If the patient feels that the underlying meaning of his words as well as the overt meaning of what he says has been understood, he is likely to feel accepted.

Case study 9.1   Acceptance of the 'unacceptable'

One patient felt intolerable anxiety over his secret activity of cutting out photographs of well-known people from magazines and reassembling them against appropriately chosen backgrounds into scenes of violent, sadistic attacks on the innocent. Once he had talked in detail about this and understood it in terms of his perceived helplessness in the outside world and his need to gain control over those he felt had damaged and abused him, his anxieties lessened, and the activity itself began to lose its compulsive nature.

Patients coming for supportive therapy often feel totally unacceptable, not only to other people but also to themselves. If they are sure of the therapist's non-judgemental understanding, or at least the therapist's best attempts at understanding them, they are likely to feel some measure of acceptance. This in turn leads to their feeling more acceptable to themselves, and to a raising of their self-esteem. Being accepted by one person may come as a completely new experience to the patient who has never felt wanted or loved for himself alone, and whose experience may have been of repeated rejections invited by his difficult behaviour or rebarbative personality.

Expression of feelings

Giving the patient permission to voice his feelings, whatever they may be, is of prime importance. Often, all the therapist need to do is to acknowledge those feelings. Sometimes, he may share the patient's distress at the havoc caused in the patient's life by a chronic illness, mental or physical.Sometimes his feelings will be very different to those of his patient. Although as a rule it is best not to make known one's own feelings directly to the patient, it may be legitimate at times to do so, especially in this type of psychotherapy. The patient may be much comforted to know that the therapist feels the same way as he does, and as a result be less tempted to class himself as abnormal or ill. He may value the therapist's honesty (honesty being a prime requisite in all psychotherapy), if nobody has dared tell him about some of his less agreeable qualities or habits. Inside a therapeutic relationship, where both parties have agreed to meet regularly over a period of time, both partners can be freed to look at the difficult feelings which it would not be possible to examine in a normal relationship, whether professional or social. This applies to feelings which belong inside the relationship as well as to feelings about external matters. For example, examining in detail how the patient approaches the therapist or other people, and the nature of the interchange that takes place, may enable the patient to understand why his relationships are unsatisfactory.

Education

Many patients who come for supportive therapy lack information about what is wrong with them, or about what they themselves might do in order to help themselves. Patients thought suitable for a dynamic approach may be quite capable of getting the necessary information they require, and it would be a mistake for the therapist to do it for them. In supportive therapy, where the therapist, when appropriate, assumes more responsibility for the patient, the giving of information can be extremely helpful.

The patient may need to know what the likely course of his illness will be, if he has a chronic problem, so that he can plan his life sensibly. The therapist may need to help the patient face the unpleasant reality either of irreparable damage that has occurred in the past, or of increasing restrictions and difficulties possible in the future. It is important not to gloss over painful truths, but equally important that the patient retains hope. If he is to be on medication temporarily or permanently, he is likely to need information about the drugs concerned, and will need time to come to terms with the psychological as well as the physiological consequences.

If the patient has lived a very isolated life, he may need educating in the broadest sense about social situations and human nature. His assumptions about these may be very much at odds with reality. His ideas will need to be voiced and examined in detail, but gentle encouragement to see things from another perspective is often helpful. For example, the patient who sees himself as the only person with problems, and assumes everyone else to be happy and untroubled, can have this unrealistic view questioned by the therapist. It may take months or years for a patient to revise his opinions, and he may never do so, but at least the possibility of viewing things in a different light has been given him. Very small shifts in how he sees things may enable him to start making significant changes in his outside life.

Reassurance

A dangerous word, reassurance, as all too often doctors and others are apt to reassure patients to satisfy their own needs rather than those of the patient. If the therapist is unable to bear his own aggression, suspiciousness, envy, hatred or fear of death, he is unlikely to be able to tolerate these feelings in the patient. He may be so uncomfortable when these feelings emerge in therapy that he hastily brushes aside the patient's communication in order to make himself feel more comfortable. Reassuring the patient by saying, for example, that he will feel better soon, that everyone has these feelings, that life is really much more pleasant or cosy than he thinks, is to reassure falsely. The patient needs to be allowed to experience the depths of despair or rage without the therapist intervening to 'make things better'. Only when he has been able to do this, will the patient start to see the positive side as well as the negative. If he has been interrupted in the process, he is likely to feel that there are some things too bad or dangerous to be talked about, since the therapist has shown himself unable to bear them.

So what reassurance *is* appropriate? If the patient has misplaced ideas, such as that he is going mad, that he will be forcibly admitted to hospital, that he has a serious or incurable physical illness, then the therapist can correct these ideas and in so doing reassure the patient. Of course, if the patient's fears are valid, for example, the schizophrenic patient who knows that he is 'mad', then the therapist should not tell the patient untruths but, rather, explore with the patient what his fears are about. Madness means different things for different people; it may mean that the patient fears he is no longer allowed to have any control over his destiny or that someone will take over every decision on his behalf; it may mean that he fears being permanently out of control of his behaviour or feelings; it may have to do with how other people will see him. Without talking over what the patient's specific fears are with him, it is impossible to guess what these are, and tempting to reassure the patient, falsely, that of course he is not going mad. This reassurance will relieve the doctor's anxiety but is unlikely to do much for the patient, especially if the latter's fears are all too well founded.

Patients who are dying may ask the doctor or nurse in great distress whether their illness is curable, or whether they are going to die. What is needed is for someone to allow them to talk about their fears, which may be of suffering and pain, of their family's distress, of things that they still need to do but may not live to complete or of any number of other concerns connected with death; in other words, to explore the meaning for that particular individual of his question. It is easy to make assumptions that one knows what it is that the patient is asking without really getting him to be specific. If the question frightens the doctor, as well as the patient, it is easy to collude in brushing away the fear as quickly as possible.

It is reassuring to have one's fears taken seriously and explored in detail, even when those fears cannot be removed. The sharing of doubt and uncertainty over major questions of life and death and human relationships can be helpful at times. If the patient learns that the therapist can tolerate uncertainty in some areas of life, that the therapist does not have to find answers to everything, he may feel surprisingly comforted. This is not intended to advocate confusion and uncertainty in areas where more enquiry or information can lead to clarity and certainty; it is more to suggest that some patients may be comforted by the therapist's ability to share with them the mysteries of the human dilemma, which will allow the patient to experience their common humanity. Other patients may desperately need the therapist to remain an authority, and become very frightened if he insists on divesting himself of this role: clearly, the therapist needs to judge what would be most appropriate at the time.

Talking over the patient's fears with him will relieve those fears to some extent. Talking about how he might manage those fears, and suggesting possible strategies of coping, will give him the feeling that he can cope. Permanently anxious patients may view the therapist as a source of the calm and quietness which they lack themselves; by retaining an inner image of the therapist outside the sessions, they may learn to develop some of that calm and tranquillity inside themselves. This will mean that in situations where they feel particularly anxious and out of control, they may be able to conjure up the image of their therapist and imagine what the therapist would say to them, and thence become able to soothe themselves. In the same way, we may imagine that a small baby whose mother comforts and soothes it when it is frightened gradually learns the capacity to comfort itself for increasingly longer periods of time in the absence of its mother. In other words, the baby internalises the comforting mother, who becomes a part of himself. So we hope patients learn to internalise and integrate into their own personalities the encouraging and comforting therapist, who can help them tolerate the stresses and uncertainties of life.

In dynamic psychotherapy, there is a distinction between therapists who believe in providing the patient with a new experience of being held and contained, and in responding to the patient's need for closeness, and therapists who believe that this would be to encourage the patient's dependence, will only lead to more and intensified demands, and is an avoidance of facing the painful realities of deprivation and loss. It can be assumed that patients coming for supportive therapy will have suffered more severe and earlier traumas than those for whom a dynamic approach is indicated. The therapist cannot undo what has been done, nor supply what has been absent or lost from the patient's early experiences. What he can do in therapy is to provide an experience of a relationship with a real person, in which the patient has a chance to learn a different way of relating to others. The opaque, aloof therapist has little or no place in supportive therapy; that the therapist is a real person is of supreme importance to the patient, so that a real relationship can be internalised and used in fantasy to help the patient outside sessions and after therapy has ended.

Advice and suggestion

Patients suited to supportive therapy may not be able to think their way through to a solution of their difficulties without more direct advice or suggestion from their therapists than would be given if the therapy were insight-orientated. The therapist assumes more responsibility for his patient than he would do in dynamic therapy, and acts as a prop to the patient's ego. The patient may be very unskilled at managing quite basic practical issues, such as applying for a job, renting a flat, acquiring information about leisure pursuits that interest him, or approaching people for help with financial matters, legal affairs and so on. The therapist will aim to help the patient become as self-sufficient as possible by developing the patient's skills in these areas. Patients who have difficulties handling their relationships may be given suggestions as to the ways in which they might deal with these, always bearing in mind that the patient should be encouraged to think for himself rather than merely relying on the therapist for advice. So, for example, a man with an intrusive and over-bearing mother who will not allow him to make decisions or lead his own life without interfering, could be encouraged to think of the various ways in which he could assert himself effectively without antagonising his mother permanently. A woman whose children refuse to do what she tells them and are permanently unruly, can be helped to see that setting appropriate limits will not destroy their affection for her and will make life more comfortable for all of them. In the future, the hope is that the patient will manage similar situations on his own, with the aid of what he has learned during therapy.

If the patient is following a path of action that is unproductive, dangerous, or likely to lead to unfortunate consequences for himself or others, the therapist may need to become more directive and use every tactic he can muster to prevent the patient pursuing that route. He may suggest, advise, cajole and point out the undesirable results of the patient's intended action. This should only be done when the therapist is clear that his own personal choices and prejudices are not clouding his judgement about what is best for the patient. Our patients frequently act in ways which we do not necessarily condone, but which are unlikely to be injurious to themselves; in these cases, it is usually best for the patient to learn from his own mistakes rather than the therapist trying to prevent these. The wise parent allows the child to experiment and learn from failure as well as success.

Suggestion is less forceful than advice and is given when there are a variety of possible alternative strategies that could be adopted. It can be a less directive way of conveying the therapist's opinion to the patient, such as 'I wonder if we should be thinking about cutting down on your tablets as you seem so much better', or 'Since you enjoyed the relaxation you did on the ward, had you thought of finding out about local evening classes in relaxation or yoga?' This gives the patient the opening to discuss what he feels about the idea, without feeling too browbeaten by the therapist into doing something he does not want to do.

Other sources of support

It is common practice in supportive therapy to try to help the patient engage in activities which can provide interest, social contact and comfort outside the therapeutic situation, and act as ongoing supports even when therapy comes to an end. According to the degree of skill the patient possesses in making contacts for himself, the therapist's efforts may range from merely suggesting possible avenues the patient could explore, to contacting other agencies on the patient's behalf and arranging for him to attend. It is the therapist's task to assess his patient's capabilities and help him choose the most appropriate paths to follow. These may be activities specifically provided for rehabilitation by the health authority, such as art, music or drama therapy, anxiety management courses, social skills groups or industrial rehabilitation units; or may be leisure pursuits available to the local community. Among the latter are yoga, meditation, relaxation, sports of all kinds, and a wealth of day and evening classes covering a variety of interests. In the community, too, there may well be self-help groups for depression, schizophrenia, eating disorders or anxiety, where the patient can find acceptance and support from people with problems similar to his own. He may find for the first time that he has something of value to offer others, and this is often a very potent source of self-esteem. Professional help may be valuable and necessary, but the patient is a patient in this setting and not allowed to forget it; more rewarding for him is to feel a valued member of the community, and the therapist's efforts should be directed towards helping him achieve this. The aims should be limited; success is crucial. It is no good expecting someone with poor social skills to negotiate the hurdles of an evening class when a more suitable goal might be to have a short conversation with the newsagent from whom he buys his daily paper.

Involving other people

Other people who may be involved in therapy include other professional helpers, both inside and outside the National Health Service, and the patient's family and even neighbours or friends. This involvement of other people is commoner in supportive therapy than in most other psychotherapies because of the nature of the patients, who are likely to be receiving support from a variety of different sources, such as their general practitioner, a social worker or community psychiatric nurse, the local vicar, the teacher of an evening class, or the staff at a rehabilitation unit. It is quite possible for all these individuals to be working at cross purposes to each other without knowing that this is what they are doing, because of the lack of communication between them. Some patients will seize the opportunity of playing one advisor off against another, if there is no consistent policy of care agreed upon and maintained by the carers. The patient's therapist may or may not be involved in the setting up of a therapy plan which includes contributions from a number of different professionals with a variety of skills. It is important that the functions of these people do not overlap unnecessarily, as well as that their advice and help is not contradictory. Each individual needs to know what he or she is trying to achieve with that particular patient, and to agree on the long-term goals. An established policy of treatment between the carers offers support to each of them, so that no one person feels that he is battling on alone in impossible conditions.

What is the role of the supportive therapist in this arena? It is likely that he will know the patient more intimately than do the other people involved. His first priority is to establish the most promising framework for this patient's growth, and to develop a trusting relationship with the patient within the session. Nothing should be done to forfeit that trust if possible. Confidentiality is of course of prime importance, and the therapist's first loyalty is to the patient. If the therapist feels that it would be beneficial to the patient to make contact with a third person, it is vital that the latter's consent is obtained before the therapist approaches that person.

The families of patients are often given less support, information and encouragement than they deserve. They may feel that they are excluded from help themselves and yet carry the greatest burden of caring for the patient. They may have been coping for years with impossibly difficult behaviour from the patient or, alternatively, be acting themselves in such a way as to encourage the patient to remain a patient and prevent him or her from taking steps towards a more independent existence. In insight-orientated therapy, the therapist would not attempt to solve these difficulties other than by working with the patient's fears, fantasies and accounts of other people in his life; in supportive therapy, the therapist is concerned with stabilising and maintaining the patient's equilibrium, and may feel it is appropriate to intervene more directly in his patient's world from time to time. In other words, supportive therapy is reality-orientated from the start, a feature it shares with cognitive and behavioural psychotherapies.

It may be of help to see the patient together with a family member in therapy for a specific purpose over a defined period of time. If marital problems predominate, the patient and his wife may be seen together for a set number of sessions specifically to work on their joint difficulties, after which the patient is seen on his own again. If the patient is agoraphobic, a family member might be asked to help with a behavioural approach of graded exposure. What is offered will depend on the particular skills of the therapist, what else if available locally, and on his judgement of what seems most appropriate at the time.

A third category of people whom the therapist may wish to contact is that of friends of the patient, or people with whom the patient has some important relationship such as the vicar of the church he attends. Again, this should never be done without the patient's agreement, and only when it is thought that it is in the patient's best interests. A minimum of contact with others is what is aimed at. However, a brief word of advice on, for example, limiting the amount of contact with the patient, or allowing him to take more responsibility for himself, may be helpful to an over-involved friend.

Medication

Many of the patients for whom supportive therapy is thought suitable may need to be on medication, either in the short term or for long periods of time. The therapist may well know the patient more intimately than does his general practitioner, and be in a better position to prescribe drugs. Full discussion with the patient is essential, and the patient should if possible be left to make the decision about whether he needs drugs, and how much he should take. This should not occupy more than a small proportion of the time available in the session, as drugs should only be an adjunct to long-term therapy. Close liaison with the general practitioner is necessary to inform him about what is being prescribed or, if the therapist is not medical, to talk about what medication the patient might require, and come to an agreed decision.

Interpretation

Interpretation is intentionally listed at the end because it is of low priority in supportive therapy. Even in dynamic therapy, the more experienced therapist probably tends to interpret less frequently, though more effectively, as his skill develops. If we see dynamic and supportive therapies as opposite poles of a continuum rather than as totally separate entities, then just as holding and containing may at times be the predominant feature in dynamic therapy, so supportive therapy may move towards a more interpretative approach if and when the patient is capable of using this.

Interpretation is often a rather pompous word for what can be described as the pointing out of similarities, or making links, between the patient's current experiences, his past experiences and what is happening in the relationship between himself and the therapist. The therapist should be aware of these links, but he may not feel it appropriate to mention them to the patient unless he judges that the patient is capable of understanding and using the information. Meares & Hobson (1977) draw an important distinction between making useful links (which approximate to helpful interpretations), and interventions which are derogatory, intrusive or which invalidate the patient's experience. Interpretation can also be construed by the patient as an attack or criticism, even when it has been offered in all good faith, by the fact of seeming to increase the distance between patient and therapist and failing to see things from the patient's point of view. Where the patient's ego is very fragile, the therapist may need, as mentioned earlier, to act as an auxiliary ego rather than as an observer; in other words, to accept what the patient says without offering another viewpoint, or seeking to explain it. The patient may not be capable of tolerating the therapist as a separate person in his own right with different opinions, and to insist on that separateness before the patient is ready to accept it is counter-productive to therapy. Until the patient has been allowed to undergo what Balint (1968) refers to as the 'harmonious interpenetrating mix-up', or what Rayner (1986) calls the 'state of non-differentiation', he will not be able to progress to an intimacy which involves the recognition of the other as a separate person.

On the other hand, if the patient is gradually coming to understand the reasons for his behaviour and feelings, a rightly-timed comment from the therapist can provoke a moment of real insight which will lead to greater flexibility in his attitudes. Perhaps the most important moments in therapy are when patient and therapist arrive at the same understanding at the same time after a period of puzzling together over some difficulty of the patient's; simultaneous enlightenment is very rewarding!

Case study 9.2   'Hopelessness' as a mark of abuse

A patient had been sexually abused in childhood over a number of years by two members of her family; she put on weight, became unable to leave the house and was unable to do anything constructive with her life. She was unaware, as was the therapist, that through her 'failure' and hopelessness she was unconsciously demanding a recognition of the damage done to her, and an admission of guilt by the abusing members of her family before she was prepared to countenance any change in herself. The session during which she and the therapist simultaneously understood this led to a profound shift in her attitude.

DIFFICULTIES

Patients in supportive therapy tend to be those with more extensive and earlier privations and losses in their lives, as has already been noted. They will lack many of the strengths of patients thought suitable for a more intensive, insight-orientated approach. These patients may remain dependent and needy, and any steps forward that they do make are likely to be imperceptibly small and to take place over many months or years. The strain that this places on the therapist should not be underestimated. It is frustrating and annoying to put in a lot of hard effort and see no result. Perhaps general practitioners are more accustomed to this role than are hospital doctors, since they are used to taking on patients for life and have not the satisfaction of being able to discharge patients for whom they can do no more. No therapist should have more than a few patients in supportive therapy at a time, and the rest of his caseload should offer him more immediate gratification.

However, most problems in therapy are caused less by the nature of the patients than by the failure of the therapist to acknowledge his true feelings towards them. In technical terms, it is the transference and counter-transference issues which may lead to breakdown of the therapeutic relationship, especially in inexperienced hands and when no supervision is available. Most professional carers choose their profession because it is rewarding to help people; perhaps most of us need to feel we have something of value to offer and need to see this received with gratitude by our clients or patients. It is hard to acknowledge our own dislike and aggressive feelings for a patient, our rage at feeling useless or rejected. Perhaps the closest parallel is that of the mother who comes close to battering her baby (and few mothers do not know that feeling). Here is this tiny creature dependent on you for sustenance and care; it screams and you try everything in your power to comfort it: cuddling, talking, food, baths, clean nappies. It refuses to be soothed and continues to scream ungratefully. One's best efforts are rejected and of no avail; the baby fails to appreciate how hard one is trying to help. Eventually, the mother becomes enraged, losing her patient kindliness and goodwill and feeling furious at the baby's repudiation of her efforts, which feels like a personal attack. A very similar picture can arise with patients who may be abusive, critical, rejecting, complaining and lacking in motivation to improve. The therapist, however well-intentioned, feels that his efforts to help are being flung back in his face by the ungrateful patient. Yet that patient may be in desperate need of a holding environment where he can voice the anger and despair he feels without being turned away. The result can be that therapy is abruptly terminated by one or other party, leaving both feeling rejected, angry and humiliated. If the therapist believes he should have only kindly feelings towards his patient, it will be shocking and painful for him to find that he feels totally enraged and full of punitive hatred. Professional standing is no armour against these feelings. The therapist may not even be aware that this is how he feels, and it is this failure of awareness that is potentially dangerous and can even lead to disaster.

The seminal paper by Winnicott: 'Hate in the counter-transference' (1949) is particularly helpful here, as it gives permission to the therapist to feel dislike and hatred of many aspects of his patient, and in so far as hatred and love are inextricably linked in relationships, suggests that there can be no genuine relationship with a patient unless hatred as well as love can be acknowledged by the therapist and both allowed to co-exist within him. There is less likelihood of an aggressive or punitive reaction from the therapist if these feelings are recognised and accepted. Negative feelings of which the therapist is unaware are likely to be far more powerfully destructive of the therapeutic relationship and even, occasionally, of the patient himself (see Ch. 12).

It is usual only for those who intend to practise psychotherapy full-time to have had their own personal therapy. These therapists will probably find it easier to come to terms with their feelings about their patients, and to sort out what rightly belongs to them, and what to the patient in the therapy session. It can be difficult to know, for example, whether the anger one feels is one's own, or whether it has been projected into one by the patient, i.e. one is feeling it on his behalf. Personal therapy and supervision are both of help in sorting out this type of confusion.

Another problem only briefly mentioned so far is that of dependence. Dependency can result from the inability to accept and integrate loss; that is, depression follows a denial of the possibility of loss and the continued need for the actual presence of the other person. If this is recognised from the start of therapy, then the importance of working with the patient's dependence as a central issue of the therapy can be addressed. The therapist does not want to encourage the patient's dependence upon himself or others, yet he must accept that the patient is likely to remain dependent for a considerable time. His aim should be to help the patient gradually learn to want and seek out more independence for himself. Some patients are too fearful to do this, and will continue to cling to the therapist or anyone else around for the rest of their lives. Others will start to learn, perhaps from the repeated and predictable experience of loss of the therapist at the end of every session (a loss which can be explored and discussed within the therapy), that they can have pleasure in functioning more independently than they thought possible beforehand, so long as they know that help is freely available to them when they are in need. Preserving the balance between providing a reliable, ongoing source of support, and gently encouraging the patient to move towards a position of more independence is a long and complex task. Premature loss of the therapist for whatever reason may undermine all the good work that has been carried out up to that moment by patient and therapist. This is why the therapist in supportive therapy ideally needs to be able to commit himself on a long-term basis to his patient.

If patients are seen over a very long time, they come to rely on their therapist and the time they are allotted, however brief and infrequent that time may be. It has already been suggested that encouraging involvement in other activities likely to prove therapeutic will help. Relationships with other people in the helping professions may dilute dependence on any one individual. Bloch (1986) describes the 'Wednesday Afternoon Clinic' model, where the patient is encouraged to become attached to an institution rather than a single therapist. The contact with other patients in the waiting room where refreshments are provided and there is space to sit and talk, a welcoming receptionist, and the rotation of therapists so that the patient sees a different therapist at each visit, ensure that the patient's eggs, so to speak, are in several different baskets. The benefits of this system, which is unlikely to be widely available in this country at the present time, need to be weighed against the advantages of having one steady, ongoing relationship with a single therapist. It may be a realistic approach to the problem posed by the numbers of patients requiring supportive therapy and the lack of therapists with sufficient skills to provide it.

SUPERVISION

There has been a notable lack of supervision (see Ch. 7) for those engaged in practising supportive therapy, whether inside or outside hospitals. Often, supportive therapy has been seen as a last resort after all other treatments have failed. The lack of a theoretical framework has meant that therapists have worked empirically and have had no forum in which to discuss with others their successes and mistakes. Support for the supporters has been absent.

If the status of supportive psychotherapy is to change, then supervision should be made available to those practising it. It has been pointed out that the transference/counter-transference issues are likely to cause considerable problems in supportive therapy, given the very early and extensive damage to their personalities that most patients have incurred. This means that supervision must be given by someone trained in recognising and handling these issues. Inevitably, supportive psychotherapy is practised now, and will continue to be practised in the future, by inexperienced therapists with little or no training in psychotherapy; supervision is essential if therapy is to succeed. It is a good way of dealing with the blind spots experienced by all therapists in the course of treating patients, and, in particular, offers an excellent opportunity for the therapist to explore and become aware of his negative feelings for his patient.

Supervision also offers a 'self-help' group to therapists, in which listening to the problems other members of the group are experiencing with their patients can greatly enlarge the individual experience; it may be the only place where members of a multi-disciplinary team can meet as equals involved in the same work. Contributions from different professionals may offer the opportunity to see the patient from various angles, which is more important the more damaged the patient.

CONCLUSIONS

Supportive psychotherapy is a long-term venture where cure is not the primary aim. Helping the patient function at his optimum level with the minimum of input from professional carers is the intention. The sessions themselves are more flexible in frequency, length and content than is the case in other types of psychotherapy, depending on the needs of the individual patient at any one time. Problems which should be anticipated are to do with the difficulty in maintaining a constructive relationship with a very damaged individual, and with dependence issues.

It should be said that following the growth of counselling and psychotherapy services in the community generally, patients referred to psychotherapy departments in the NHS are increasingly likely to be those with severe character disorders who have not been helped by a range of psychiatric treatments in the past. The result is that often a long period of purely supportive therapy may be required before any dynamic work can begin, assuming that the latter is possible at all. We are far from being able to apply the strict criteria of suitability for dynamic therapy thought appropriate at one time. Psychotherapists in the NHS are now having to broaden their approach in order to help these more severely disturbed individuals, and the boundaries between supportive and dynamic therapies are less distinct than they once were. Nor can we any longer profess to discriminate clearly between the types of change expected from different psychotherapies. Robert Wallerstein (1989) summarising the conclusions of the Menninger Foundation Research Project, points out that there was a 'substantial range of changes' in patients treated with supportive psychotherapy, and that these changes were in many cases indistinguishable from those brought about by dynamic or interpretative psychotherapy. It seems, he says, that supportive psychotherapeutic techniques achieve far more than has been expected of them in terms of major structural changes in the patient's personality. He concludes that supportive psychotherapy, or rather, the supportive aspects of any psychotherapeutic approach, deserve more respect that they have usually been given in the literature. Few, if any, psychotherapies exist in pure form in practice; most are a judicious blend of techniques from different modalities. Certainly, within the NHS there is a continuing challenge to rethink the basic psychodynamic principles and to introduce as much flexibility as possible into the service offered without allowing standards of work to deteriorate.

Patients referred to specialist psychotherapy services, however, are the privileged few. For the vast majority, there is still the difficulty of supportive therapy being practised by a wide variety of therapists without an adequate knowledge of the issues involved and with little or no support for themselves. In future, it is to be hoped that more psychiatrists with a specialised psychotherapy training will interest themselves in supportive psychotherapy and its techniques, both directly and through supervising trainees. Only in this way will supportive therapy gain a much-needed respectability.

FURTHER READING

Crown S 1988 Supportive psychotherapy: a contradiction in terms? British Journal of Psychiatry 152: 266–269
Holmes J 1988 Supportive analytical therapy: an account of two cases. British Journal of Psychiatry 152: 824–829
Waterman D S 1984 The practice of supportive psychotherapy. Brunner, New York

Psychotherapeutic approaches to psychiatric disorders

10. Anxiety and stress-related disorders

M. Aveline

INTRODUCTION

If human beings were machines and had no consciousness, there would be no experience of anxiety. Anxiety is a necessary part of the evolutionary progress of the species from organisms without consciousness to sentient persons. Feelings of anxiety are almost always disturbing and are often painful. As the title of the chapter indicates, anxiety and stress-related reactions may also be *disorders* whose amelioration is sought by patients asking for help. But first and foremost, anxiety serves adaptive purposes; sight should not be lost of this enabling function.

As clinicians, it is easy to reify the experience of anxiety into an abstract object, disconnected from its source and having no meaning. The anxiety-ridden patient may even wish this to be the case, as then there is no need to delve into origins with all their potential for emotional upset. Indeed, patients often prefer to see their anxiety as an alien encumbrance from whose grasp they hope that they will be easily released. It will come as no surprise in a text on psychotherapy in psychiatry that these positions are rejected. Instead, the contrary position is asserted. Frequently, anxiety draws attention to that which needs to be attended to if a person is to be in touch with the complexities of his individual nature and situation.

Anxiety and fear have much in common. Fear is a reaction to an external threat and in its degree is proportionate to the danger faced; Freud called this *realistic anxiety*. Anxiety is a disproportionate reaction to an apparently minor threat, but where the true source of the danger is usually hidden in a person's subjective inner world. For Freud, the source of anxiety is not an external but an *internal* threat – often a repudiated feeling, such as anger or sadness – of which the patient may be unaware. Thus, the anxiety does not concern the situation as it actually is, but how it appears to the individual and what it touches upon in the person's inner world. Although a qualification will be entered later to the following statement, let us for now accept what Epictetus, the Greek Stoic philosopher, said: 'Men are disturbed not by things, but by their view of them'. Hence, in any psychotherapeutic treatment, it is essential to tease out the meaning – conscious or unconscious – of the situation for that individual.

239

Anxiety signals a threat to psychological equilibrium. It is experienced as an unpleasant feeling of incipient helplessness, loss of control or, even, dissolution. These physiologically-mediated, often transient symptoms point to the interplay of personal meaning and psychological structure. Psychodynamically, the symptom of anxiety has a story to tell about what is psychologically difficult for that person, what intrapsychic conflict is active. At a higher level of abstraction, the character structure of an individual can be seen as embodying ways that he has evolved, however maladaptively, to deal with the repeated experience of anxiety in his or her life.

As a therapist, engaging with the patient on the level of character goes beyond the simple experience of anxiety to a consideration of the psychological motifs of the individual's life. This is the level that is advocated in this chapter, the level of long term interpersonal patterns as opposed to a narrow concern with the symptoms of psychiatric disorder. What is stressful for the patient and why? How does the patient habitually (habit being the precursor of character) attempt to deal with the stress, and with what consequences for personal relationships and the production of symptoms? How may the triad of stress, character and reaction be understood and modified with the benefit of less constrained and more fruitful living?

At each stage in life, there is a psychosocial maturational task to be achieved, eight in all in Erikson's (1965) epigenetic chart of development. In the first five years, the child needs to develop the ability to trust, be autonomous and take initiatives. These abilities are fundamental; they are the substrate for mature adult relationships. At each stage, anxiety has to be faced and overcome; the anxiety of being separate and the fear of being shamed or crushed. In these tasks, the constellation of the family is very important; to it, the child brings his constitutional and inherited characteristics. There is a dynamic interaction between these characteristics and the family constellation, which is shaped by the inheritance, events, set-backs and life-histories that each family member contributes to the whole. Beyond the family is the society which sets, through its form, events and phase of development, the cultural context for the family. In a chronology of a life, each stage has a potential for psychological growth or stasis. Facilitating experiences and the successful negotiation of later stages have some capacity to off-set adversity in the early years, but a good beginning is important. How an individual resolves each stage cannot be fully understood unless the dovetailing of all the elements – past and present – is seen. In practice, this full understanding is a rarely realised aspiration.

This chapter provides a framework within which some understanding may be gained of: (1) the genesis of anxiety; (2) the character patterns that develop in response to anxiety; (3) the reaction to severe stress; and (4) relatively brief treatment interventions suitable for psychiatric practice.

DESCRIPTIVE TERMS AND DIAGNOSIS

How does the psychotherapist's concept of anxiety relate to psychiatric diagnosis? Psychotherapists tend to see symptoms in a much more fluid way than do nosologists. Nosologists are concerned to define distinctive syndromes whose validity as disorders will be confirmed by family, treatment and outcome studies. (Note that the term 'disorder' supercedes the term 'disease' in the new version of the International Classification of Diseases (ICD-10) released in 1990.) Psychotherapists see symptoms as reflecting an underlying dynamic process, a disorder of dynamic structure rather than a free-standing illness entity with a definable course. Indeed, in the course of a psychotherapy, the presenting symptomatic picture is likely to vary substantially, with the patient manifesting a gamut of symptoms as the psychological exploration deepens. Nevertheless, psychotherapists recognise the importance of description and the value of using a common language for communication with colleagues.

In his early writing, Freud (1894a) introduced an important classification of anxiety and neurosis. His first distinction was between *psychoneurosis* and *actual neurosis*. Psychoneurosis was thought to result from psychological conflicts and past events in the person's life; subdivisions of this category are *conversion hysteria*, *anxiety hysteria* (now an outdated term for *phobic neurosis*) and *obsessional neurosis*. In contrast, actual neurosis stemmed from the physiological consequences of present disturbance in sexual function, either sexual excess in the case of *neurasthenia* or frustration in the case of *anxiety neurosis*. Neither the distinction between psychoneurosis and actual neurosis nor these aetiological theories are fully accepted now (Laplanche & Pontalis 1973). In *character neurosis*, psychological conflicts find their expression not in symptoms but in the structure of the personality. Gelder et al (1989) consider this term confusing, and argue against its use on the grounds that the subject may have no neurotic symptoms.

Freud saw anxiety and the defences against it as central factors in mental life. Threats to the ego itself – which he related to the development of psychotic states – he called *primary anxiety*, while his concept of *signal anxiety* related to neurotic disorders in which the *functions* of the ego, rather than its existence, are threatened. The former emotion accompanies the threat of dissolution of the ego and is to be avoided at all costs; the latter represents an alert to the ego, warning of an impending threat to its equilibrium (Freud 1926). Other forms of anxiety with clear aetiological overtones are described in the literature, namely *castration anxiety* arising from real or imagined threats to sexual function, *separation anxiety* from loss of objects with whom contact is felt to be essential for survival, *depressive anxiety* from fear of the destructive effect of the subject's hostility on his good objects, *persecutory anxiety* from the fear of being attacked by bad objects and, finally, *objective anxiety* where the fear is provoked by real, external danger (Rycroft 1972). How do these psychoanalytic descriptions of anxiety correspond to the categories in the major diagnostic classifications?

Under the heading of Neurotic, Stress-related, and Somatoform Disorders, ICD-10 (WHO 1988) recognises: phobic disorders of various types; other anxiety disorders including panic disorder, generalised anxiety and mixed anxiety disorder; obsessive-compulsive disorder; reaction to severe stress which includes acute stress reaction and the important new category of post-traumatic stress disorder; various forms of dissociative and conversion disorder; somatoform disorder; and neurasthenia. In the section on Personality Disorders, anxious (avoidant), dependent and paranoid types are to be found, among others.

In the American classification, DSM-III-R (APA 1987) greater weight is given to aetiology, when this is known, and the practice of assessing the patient on the multiple dimensions (Axes) of illness (Axis I), personality (Axis II), physical disorders (Axis III), severity of psychosocial stressors (Axis IV), and global assessment of optimal functioning (Axis V) is positively encouraged. This more idiographic approach comes closer to the individually constructed formulation of the psychotherapist. From DSM-III onwards, the term 'neurosis' no longer features, as it is thought to be too closely linked to psychoanalytic aetiological theories and thus to be inappropriate for a predominantly descriptive classification. The disorders identified under the heading of Anxiety are similar to those in ICD-10, but considerable interest has been generated by the category of post-traumatic stress disorder. This is shown by those who have experienced severe stress, as in war, torture and disaster (see Ch. 22). The clinical picture is dominated by recurrent, intrusive recollections of the traumatic event, sometimes triggered by stimuli, and an emotional numbing. DSM-III-R has a wide range of personality disorders, including dependent and avoidant personality disorder which have close aetiological links with anxiety and the means used to avoid it.

It should not be thought that firm boundaries exist around these anxiety-related disorders. Anxiety and depressive symptoms frequently co-exist; pure phobic and other anxiety variants are rare; and there is a marked association with particular personality features. For these reasons, Tyrer (1985, 1989) has proposed the category of 'general neurotic syndrome'. This syndrome has characteristic constitutional and natural history features, namely: (1) combined diagnoses at some time of agoraphobia, social phobia, panic disorder, non-psychotic depression, anxiety or hypochondriasis; (2) an episode of illness in the absence of major stress; (3) passive-dependent or anankastic personality features; and (4) positive family history in first-degree relatives. Over time, the person would develop, in addition to their baseline state of pathological anxiety, dysthymic, panic and agoraphobic symptoms in response to stress. Only by taking a longitudinal view would the clinician be able to see that this was all part of one disorder.

AETIOLOGICAL PROCESSES

Psychoanalysis

Instinct theory

Freud revised his theory of the aetiology of anxiety several times as new knowledge was presented to him in his analytic work. In this, he showed his strength as a courageous, scientific innovator. Freud bought to his invention of psychoanalysis the mind of a biologist. He was profoundly influenced by the mechanistic thinking of the 19th century. Man, he held, had two vital drives (instincts), one for self preservation, the other for procreation or preservation of the species. Life readily offers opportunities to satisfy the first drive, but the second may be blocked by the inherently repressive forces of civilisation. When the open expression of the drive for preservation of the species or *libido*, as Freud termed it, is blocked, the drive energy is not dissipated but continues to circulate in the closed energy system of the individual until it finds some expression, usually in symbolically significant symptons or a development arrest (fixation) in personality development.

As previously noted, in Freud's first formulation, anxiety was taken to be the result of the libido not being discharged in sexual activity (Freud 1894a). This led him to speak of an actual neurosis where there was no psychological conflict or use of defence mechanisms. Mechanistic remedies were initially proposed, but Freud soon realised that matters were not to be so simply resolved. In his series of papers with Breuer (Breuer & Freud 1893) on patients with conversion hysteria, they had stated the dictum 'Hysterics suffer mainly from reminiscences' (p.7). What they meant was that, under hypnosis, the patient gained access to hidden memories of pathogenic events from the past, and in so doing were relieved of the anxiety that underlay their symptoms; the past, while it remained hidden from the conscious mind, was still active in the present.

'Each individual hysterical symptom immediately and permanently disappeared when we had succeeded in bringing to light the memory of the event by which it was provoked and in arousing its accompanying affect, and when the patient had described that event in the greatest possible detail and had put the affect into words' (Breuer & Freud 1893, p.6)

What kept the memory of the event out of consciousness – and hence unable to cause psychological pain or distress – was the 'mental mechanism' of *repression*. This mechanism, which is central to psycho-analytic explanations, preserves the memory in all its freshness and power in the unconscious mind. Freud, in the face of Breuer's growing distaste for and repudiation of what was being discovered, noted that the repressed memories were often sexual in nature and featured childhood seduction. Initially, Freud believed that these were actual events which had to be repressed because they were too terrible to be faced, thus creating a psychic abscess that needed, as it were, to be lanced in therapy through abreaction. Later, he could not believe that childhood seduction was so frequent and, instead, came to see the accounts as fantasies and not realities. The fantasies represented the *repressed wishes* of infantile sexuality, and had the same power to disturb as real events (Freud 1914). This reversal of view has attracted the wrath of those who feel, with some justice, that the emphasis on fantasy has made it much harder for their histories of childhood sexual abuse to be taken seriously. Nevertheless, the discovery of the power of fantasy was of the greatest importance; it justified attending to the inner psychological world of the individual.

In the *topographical* model of the mind described above, three elements are noteworthy: (1) memories and wishes in the unconscious mind influence conscious thought and behaviour; (2) wishes, especially sexual and aggressive wishes, that are unacceptable to the conscious mind are repressed; and (3) anxiety signifies a failure of repression.

The topographical model of the mind later yielded to the *structural* model with publication of *The Ego and the Id* (Freud 1923). The psychic apparatus is made up of three agencies – the ego, superego and id – each with its own functions. The ego holds the ring in a three-cornered struggle between the primitive wishes or impulses of the id, the moral strictures of the superego and the demands of external reality. Anxiety, instead of being the result of the failure of repression, is now seen as the cause of repression. Anxiety originates in the ego, and is a psychological force in its own right; it motivates the ego to use repression and other defensive mental mechanisms to control primitive drives whose expression would be disruptive. As we have seen in the section on diagnosis, anxiety is a *signal* of threat to psychological equilibrium. The individual fears that ill consequences will follow unless the threat is controlled. Taking this proposition one step further, it is the nature of the consequence that determines the quality of the anxiety. Thus, in *superego anxiety* (anxiety that stems from the action of the superego), the person has a sense of having committed a wrong act, feels guilty and fears being found out. In 'castration anxiety', the fear is of some diminution of the person's capacities or of bodily damage, classically from retaliation by a harsh father in the oedipal struggle, (although current psychoanalytic thinking gives less emphasis to bodily damage and, instead, highlights the 'narcissistic' damage that results from feeling unloveable in the mother-infant phase of development). In *separation anxiety*, the person anticipates the loss of an important human relationship and in *id* or *impulse* anxiety, a fear of loss of control of aggressive impulses which may, but only may, result in the psychotic dissolution of the ego (Nemiah 1980).

What makes traumatic events traumatic? This is more than a tautology. Many lives have in their history terrible events and seemingly adverse conditions. Some people are traumatised or scarred by what they have experienced, but not all. Some, even, may gain a greater sense of purpose or be tempered in their character, as steel is when it is forged in the flame. Others falter or are thrown into panic.

Initially, Freud (1894b) held that no experience could have a pathogenic effect unless it appeared intolerable to the subject's ego and gave rise to efforts at defence. Freud doubted that a stress in adult life could be traumatic unless there was a pre-existing trauma with which the stress was linked. Anxiety, then, was the signal of a threatened repetition of the stressful moment (Freud 1933, Lecture 32). All traumatic situations are held to have at their core the experience of helplessness; the helplessness is physical when the danger that is faced is external and real, and psychical when the danger is instinctual and inner. With this formulation, Freud swept away his original distinction between realistic and neurotic anxiety; both sources of anxiety could be brought into consciousness and worked with (Freud 1926, Appendix XI). 'In the experiences that lead to a traumatic neurosis the protective shield against external stimuli is broken through and excessive amounts of excitation impinge on the mental apparatus' (Freud 1926, p. 130).

The idea of a protective shield and that which needs to be protected was taken further by Bion, a Kleinian analyst. In the mechanism of projective identification, a person places outside himself, in another person, disturbing feelings which are experienced by the recipient as if they were his own feelings. It is hypothesised that, in infancy, the mother needs to act as a 'container' for these projective identifications and, as it were, detoxify them while the child is building his mental apparatus, his own internal container.

Garland (see Ch. 22) found in her study of the survivors of an underground fire that this catastrophic stress appeared to fragment the survivors' 'internal container', and flooded them with primitive, psychotic anxiety of death and annihilation. The catastrophic stress also re-activated deficiencies in the relationships (with the primary objects) of early life and, to an important extent, gained its lasting force from resonance with those deficiencies. One saved her life by taking refuge in a cupboard but was aware of others outside, dying in the heat and smoke; she knew that her life would be forfeited if she tried to rescue them. This situation was terrible enough in itself, but it later painfully reminded her of her inability to protect her sisters from the abuse to which they and she were subjected in childhood and which culminated in her sister's death. The trauma of the past had been re-awakened by the trauma of the present. The combination of the two led to the development of a post-traumatic stress syndrome.

Object-relations and secure attachments

'Psychoanalytic theory is an "instinct" theory. That is, it is primarily concerned with how the isolated individual finds or fails to find ways of discharging his instinctive impulses' (Storr 1989, p.91). The view correctly represents classical psychoanalysis and is still the key construct for some analysts. However, more recent psychoanalytic thought has been radically re-fashioned, and re-fashioned for the better in the author's opinion, in what is oddly called 'object-relations theory'; it would be better termed human relations theory'. The development has been accompanied by increasing interest in the self, 'self-systems' and their operation in relationships.

In Britain, the innovative figures have been Fairbairn, Guntrip, Balint and Winnicott; in North America, Kohut and Kernberg. W R D Fairbairn and his follower and interpreter, Harry Guntrip, spent their professional lives working in relative isolation, the former in Edinburgh and the latter in Leeds. Perhaps this isolation freed them from the constraint to conceptualise within the psychoanalytic orthodoxy of the time. In any event, what they proposed was a major departure from what had gone before, the libido theory. Human beings, they asserted, are relationship-seeking from birth. In an idealised view, the infant is seen as being born with a pristine, unfragmented ego which becomes split and subdivided into various subselves or egos – the central ego, libidinal ego and anti-libidinal ego – as contact is made with an inevitably imperfect world and intrapsychic manoeuvres are deployed to try and cope with this reality. Aggression is not a primary instinct but a reaction to frustration. Frustration quintessentially results from the experience of the infant of not being adequately loved for himself, an unsatisfying experience of crucial importance in psychological development. In the libidinal ego resides the wish for love, and in the anti-libidinal ego the experience of unmet love which has been interpreted by the infant as having been actively denying and punishing; these subselves are similar in their structure to the good and bad objects of Kleinian theory, both being based on the mechanism of splitting. The central ego is the conscious self of everyday living that tries to establish good personal relationships. Depending on what the original experience was like, the anti-libidinal ego, operating from the unconscious mind, has greater or lesser power to sabotage during a person's life the efforts of the libidinal ego to find love (Sutherland 1980). What this difficult terminology means is that, within a person, there is a psychic replica of the original frustrating situation, a replica which ties the individual to their past, tends to recreate the past in the present and is ready to be activated when conditions are adverse. Here, we have another mechanism with which to understand what can make stress stressful.

In the Northern object-relations school of Fairbairn and Guntrip, the infant during the first year of life is held to encounter two important developmental states, the schizoid and the depressive. At this time of absolute infantile dependence, the young child has to make some sense of its world, that is, within the limits set by its narrow comprehension of being a self-aware ego, more than a collection of part-objects and separate from other persons. When love is wanted and not given; the infant may react in two ways. The infant may hate the other for not giving and then become depressed for fear that the hate will destroy the very person that is needed and loved, a fear that grows into guilt; this is the *depressive state* of 'love made angry'. Alternatively and more alarmingly, at an earlier stage of development, the infant grows ever more hungry for the total love that is not given and, then, begins to fear that its own love and need for love is so devouring and incorporative that it will destroy the other person. The result of this 'love made hungry' is the *schizoid state*, a state of aloof withdrawal in an attempt to do without external relationships. These two states, the depressive and the schizoid, are *basic* or ultimate *dangers* which need to be escaped from but which lie in wait ready to be awakened by bad external circumstance. Later in development, paranoid, obsessional, hysterical and phobic defences are used to protect the person from experiencing these inner terrors; this accounts for the previously referred-to pleomorphism in symptoms that are often manifested during the process of exploring inner feelings in psychotherapy. This model provides us with a more interpersonal frame with which to understand what anxiety may be about. Anxiety signals an emerging fear that our hate will destroy or, even worse, that our love will destroy the other from whom we seek love (Guntrip 1974a).

Explicit in Fairbain and Guntrip's formulation are two fundamental ideas. Firstly, that a secure sense of self is only developed in the context of good object-relations (i.e. personal relationships), and secondly, that this is an ideal, never to be achieved with perfect consistency. The first idea led Guntrip (1974b) in particular to emphasise the therapeutic importance of actual, good relationships in therapy, an emphasis with which the author wholly agrees. Kohut over-extends this formulation; he places primary responsibility for maintaining these good relations on the shoulders, firstly of the parents and secondly of the therapist who fail when they do not maintain empathic contact (for a good account of Kohut's self-psychology, see Baker & Baker 1987). Important though Kohut's ideas are, they neglect the interactive processes between parent and child – some children, for example, are less loveable than others – and burden parents and therapists in their parental role with impossible standards. Winnicott (1960) in the south of Britain sounded a reassuring and realistic note when he wrote of 'good-enough mothering', a less absolutist concept but an experience which gives the child a sufficient sense of being loved and enjoyed for himself so that a sense of wholeness develops; there is then little need to evolve a 'false self' which in its compliance covers over and stunts the 'true self' with its inherent capacity for relatedness.

Is there any research evidence to support the importance of secure object-relations in optimal development? Bowlby (1965, 1969, 1973, 1979, 1980, 1988), in a series of publications, has brought together impressive research findings made by him and other workers into a coherent model of development based on attachment behaviour. Much of psychoanalytic theory is based on retrospective, speculative constructions of the origins of adult psychopathology, illuminated by the form of the transference neurosis. Instead, Bowlby, himself an analyst, started with certain classes of childhood traumata and traced their sequelae. He began with the depression shown by infants separated from their mothers on admission to hospital, and the high incidence of severe personality disorder in children raised in residential homes that, as it turned out, offered insufficient opportunity for the subjects to form stable affectional bonds with staff in their roles as parental substitutes. His interest in ethology and systems theory led him to use in his prospective theory the then unfamiliar terms of control system rather than psychic energy, and developmental pathways rather than libidinal phase. At any moment, an individual faces an array of potential developmental pathways with his way being determined by the interaction of the person as he is then and the environment as it happens to be. 'Attachment behaviour' is what a person does to obtain or maintain proximity with figures to whom he is attached. Anxiety signals fear that this attachment will be broken.

Bowlby describes three types of attachment: secure, anxious resistant and anxious avoidant. The first is self-explanatory. In the second, the person fears losing his attachment figure and clings to him or her; this person is prone to separation anxiety or, perhaps, the anxiety that Rank (1924) ascribed to the 'trauma' of birth. In the third type of attachment, the expectation is of being rebuffed; attachment is avoided and a false self developed. This third pattern is similar in content to Fairbairn's schizoid state and, as we shall see in the next section, with Horney's 'moving away' solution to the anxiety of being alone and abused. In our consideration of this topic, we are moving towards identifying enduring *character patterns*, for this is what the continued experience of anxiety and the deployment of repetitive solutions results in. Subject to the proviso that genetic inheritance substantially contributes to personality, it is as Harry Stack Sullivan said: a person's character is his or her history.

Interpersonal processes

Karen Horney secured great popular appeal with her lectures and writings in the 1930s and 1940s in the United States. As is often the fate of popularists, and especially those who challenge the orthodoxy of the day, she was shunned in the latter part of her career by the analytic establishment. Expelled from the New York Psychoanalytic Institute in 1939, she founded the American Institute for Psychoanalysis two years later and was its Dean until her death in 1952. Her heresy – now an orthodoxy – was to question the primacy of the libido in development, especially in female psychology, and to stress the importance of cultural factors. She held that neurotic problems arise from specific cultural conditions which result in disturbed human relationships. Her therapeutic stance was optimistic; her focus was, firstly, on the here and now of the therapeutic relationship and, secondly, on manifestations of the person's neurotic pattern. The neurotic personality stands in his own way, showing rigidity rather than flexibility in reacting to different situations, and a discrepancy between achievements and potentialities (Horney 1937).

For Horney, the *basic anxiety* was a childhood feeling of being isolated or helpless in a potentially hostile world. This could arise from many kinds of adversity: indifference, domination, lack of respect for the child's individual needs, lack of reliable warmth, over-protection, injustice, unkept promises, and so on. To escape experiencing basic anxiety, human beings have four means at their disposal: rationalisation, denial, narcosis with sedatives or alcohol and avoidance, the last by *neurotic patterns* or *trends*. Neurotic patterns are developed as ways of keeping going in disturbing conditions, but become organising principles in a person's life. A person may predominantly *move toward* others. In so doing, he accepts his own helplessness and tries to win the affection and support of others, especially if they are powerful; the gain is a feeling of belonging and being supported. This pattern is clearly dependent or, in Bowlby's terminology, an example of anxious attachment. An illusion of security is bought at the cost of loss in individuality. When the predominant pattern is to *move against* others, the assumption is that the world is hostile and has to be fought against. Safety lies in strength, the strength to defeat others and to take revenge for past and present hurts. The pattern is paranoid. In the third pattern, the person predominantly *moves away* from others, a schizoid solution. Here nothing good or bad is expected from relationships. Feeling that he has little in common with others, the individual turns away into isolation and detachment, his only comfort being his inner thoughts and dreams.

Existential concerns

'Human memory is a marvellous but fallacious instrument', so begins the first chapter of Primo Levi's last book *The Drowned and the Saved* (1988) in which he remembers and bears witness to the horrors of the German concentration camps of World War II. He recalls his time in Auschwitz so that those of the human race, who can bear to listen, may not forget what was done and how it came to be done. It is a small insurance against repetition.

Levi's account is savage; most of the victims were killed. But what they faced puts us in touch with moral and humanitarian issues and, at a deeper level, with *ultimate existential concerns* which, in general, we do not like to consider and which, certainly, arouse anxiety. As T S Eliot (1944) wrote, 'Human kind cannot bear very much reality'. Existentially, the human condition is transient. While we live we exist, but inevitably we die, and from this fact there is no escape. The quotation from Eliot continues: 'Time past and time future, what might have been and what has been, point to one end, which is always present'. In a universe without meaning, we have responsibility for all that we do, our choices, actions and design. It is a fearful freedom. In life, we are essentially alone. 'No matter how close each of us becomes to another, there remains a final, unbridgeable gap; each of us enters existence alone and must depart from it alone. The existential conflict is thus the tension between our awareness of our absolute isolation and our wish for contact, for protection, our wish to be part of a larger whole' (Yalom 1980, p.9). In a universe without meaning, each human being has to find his own meaning in life. Of course, in religion, believers find a transcendent meaning.

The existential perspective is bleak. Man has great responsibility for his future, but also great freedom. The bitter-sweetness of life stems from an appreciation of a person's *Dasein* or Being-in-the-World, and their fear of non-Being, the ultimate source of anxiety (May 1958).

Psychotherapists and other people that enter into the emotional lives of their fellow man are constantly faced with the transient and mindless nature of existence. In the world as it is, there is so much injustice, cruelty and ill-fortune, and in individual lives, much sadness and tragedy. Fortunately, there is also hope which may be rekindled and new purpose that may be forged. Although, in existential terms, humans are solitary in their aloneness, they are sufficiently similar to be able to partially understand the concerns of others and to aid them in the process of living.

Cognitive processes in anxiety

Over the last three decades, there has been a fascinating shift in emphasis in behaviourism. From having an almost exclusive focus on the external determinants of behaviour, the role of cognitions has come to the fore to the extent that it is now rare to find a text on behaviourism without the suffix of 'cognitive' (Marzillier 1989). Skinner's black box of the mind has to be opened if the springs of motivation and attitudinal sets are to be discovered.

Beck is one of the most influential cognitive theorists. He sees anxiety and depression as the product of errors in logic. Anxiety, as Marks (1975) has also recognised, had phylogenetic value in the evolution of the species;

it served to protect humans from danger, as in the well-known *flight or fight* reaction. Now, anxiety reactions are largely counter-productive and maladaptive, being the product of (1) *selective attention* to threats to one's domain - specifically, to social attachments and sense of freedom and individuality (Emery & Tracy 1987) - and (2) *dysfunctional thinking*. In acute anxiety, an event is labelled by the person as dangerous and the autonomic nervous system is placed on alert. In generalised anxiety, there is anticipatory fear of losing self-confidence and personal security. In social phobias, this fear is focused on having inadequate social skills and being negatively evaluated by others, and in panic attacks on imminent physical or mental disaster. These reactions are preceded by *automatic dysfunctional thinking* whose nature the sufferer can be taught to identify and challenge. Dysfunctional thinking is essentially negative (Beck et al 1979). Examples of such thinking are *arbitrary inference, selective abstraction, over-generalisation, magnification* and *minimisation, personalisation* and *absolutist, dichotomous thought*.

Why a person should think so negatively about himself, his world and his future is not fully explained. Furthermore, altering his behaviour or current thoughts is held to be sufficient to effect change. And yet in the author's view, each person has his own story which needs to be told and re-told as new sense is made of everyday life. The concept of deep cognitive structures or *schemata*, some of which may lie outside consciousness, bridges the gap between psychodynamic and behavioural models. These schemata organise a person's world view. Guidano & Liotti (1983) and Liotti (1986) describe a complex system of self-knowledge which is in a continuous process of modification, depending on the perception of present events and the memories of past experience. Self-knowledge is elaborated through three structures: the *metaphysical hard core* of tacit self-knowledge with invarient rules for personality function, such as 'I have always to be careful', the *protective belt* which defines and maintains personal identity, for example 'I'm a weak person'; and *research plans* which sets rules for how experience is to be assimilated, for example 'Believe every danger or warning', or 'Get others to help you'. Applying these concepts to anxiety, Guidano & Liotti (1983) lay stress on dependent patterns of attachment in childhood in patients with agoraphobia. The parents are seen as being hyperprotective and inculcating feelings of insecurity about the outside world. A self-image of weakness in a hostile and dangerous world is developed; much effort has then to be expended in adult life in controlling the weakness.

Constitution

Man is not born as a tabula rasa ready to be written on as the environment dictates but, rather, with a constitution that, together with other inherited and acquired physical characteristics, forms the substrate with which the environment interacts. Important among these givens is temperament.

Temperament refers to simple, non-motivational, non-cognitive stylistic characteristics with high hereditability which appear early in childhood and show substantial stability (Rutter 1987b). Emotionality, activity, sociability and, perhaps, impulsivity are the best-validated dimensions in temperament (Buss & Plomin 1986). Temperament influences the way in which the child interacts with the environment, and contributes to the formation of personality traits which are dispositions to act in particular ways and which may cluster together to form personality types.

In the population at large, 3% show anxiety disorders but this rate is increased to 15% among the relatives of patients with anxiety disorders (Noyes et al 1978). Though it is difficult to separate the effect of nurture from that of nature, Slater & Shields' (1969) twin study showed a concordance of 41% for monozygous twins where the proband had an anxiety disorder, and only 4% for dizygotes. The evidence suggests that there is a genetic tendency to develop neurosis.

AETIOLOGICAL PROCESSES – A SYNTHESIS

Many processes have been adduced in this chapter as explanatory mechanisms for the genesis of anxiety. The explanations are by no means mutually exclusive. Rather, they often describe very similar dynamic mechanisms in different language.

Although genetic inheritance may contribute to a tendency to anxiously over-react in any situation, anxiety is first and foremost a *reaction*. The question, then, is a reaction to what and why? Why does one person react when another may not? What internal and external factors play a modifying part in the response? No uniform answer can be given to these questions, as the reaction that results in anxiety depends on individual persons and situations. Anxiety in all its manifestations belongs to a single class of experience, but it may be generated by different combinations of aetiological processes. The same signal has different causes. Thus, aetiological processes and factors increase or decrease vulnerability to stress, and may sensitise the individual to particular stress or emotionally-charged relationship configurations. Massive stress will be too much for the majority; minimal, overt stress may be too much for some.

Figure 10.1 depicts the operation of aetiological factors. Genetic inheritance lays an anxious foundation for some. Vulnerability or, its obverse, resilience is the interactive product of early experience. Difficulty in mastering the psychological tasks of childhood sensitises the child to certain situation *or* situations which may be about to happen and which have the same meaning as the original. These actualities or potentialities engender the different anxieties of separation, of being shamed and made guilty, of 'castration' and being rendered helpless and, at a deeper level, of

VULNERABILITY FACTORS

Genetic inheritance:	±	Sensitising childhood experiences:	→	Vulnerability:
Temperament		Love destroying object		Intra-psychic conflict
Physical characteristics		Hate destroying object		Negative automatic thinking
		Feelings inadequately contained by parent		Negative schemata
		Failure with maturational tasks		Character neurosis
		Of separation		Horney's patterns of moving toward, against and away from others
		→ insecure attachment		
		Of autonomy		
		→ shame and doubt		
		Of initiative		
		→ helplessness		

THE OPERATION OF STRESS

Stress	±	Vulnerability	→	Anxiety reaction
Which induces feelings of:				Depending upon **modifying factors:**
Incipient helplessness				Emotional support
Loss of control				Quality of close relationships
Dissolution				Disturbance in family system
Includes physical disaster and increased existential awareness				

Fig. 10.1   Aetiological processes in anxiety and stress-related disorders.

the child's hate and, worst still, his love being destructive. The revival of these anxieties is intensely frightening, and has to be defended against by repression, a fallible instrument of self-defence. With these beginnings, the child enters subsequent stages with, to use Jerome Frank's phrase, his *assumptive world* already drawn, with particular biases which structure his engagement with his family and others and shape that environment. In turn, the environment consolidates – or minimises – trends in the developing structure of personality. These trends may become organised, defensive patterns that find their definitive form in character neurosis. In Horney's model, three predominant trends are described – moving toward, against and away from others; each is maladaptive in its rigidity; each protects against experiencing once more the unsafety of the formative experiences and its consequent anxiety. Feelings of incipient helplessness, loss of control and dissolution lie at the heart of anxiety. It is these feelings that are directly created by external stress, especially when it is catas-trophic in severity. Severe stress in itself can be overwhelming. Also, it reaches back in the person to times in his history when he has felt helpless, out of control and split apart, and takes its meaning from the lessons that were learnt then. If that time in the past was traumatic, then the trauma of the present will be doubled; residues of past traumas will be activated.

In the interaction between person and situation, the mediator is meaning, while the moderator is the quality of the social and relationship matrix. Cognitive sets or schemata codify individual attitudes to self and others. Standing at the top of a slope of self-perception which reaches down out of consciousness into the unconscious mind, they organise the perception of events and, if negative, tramline the person towards anxiety, depression and loss of self-esteem. Negative ways of thinking and acting may be reinforced by the behaviour of others in the social network. Conversely, supportive relationships absorb the impact of stress, and structure the personal environment so that legitimate relationships-wishes are met.

Case study 10.1   Post-traumatic stress disorder

Let us see how these factors appear to have operated in a woman who was referred for psychotherapy some months after she had been raped. One night, a man had broken into her house and terrorised her, her husband and child for several hours. Ann, a woman in her late 20s, was repeatedly raped at gunpoint. Firstly the couple were forced to have sex, then the husband, now bound, had to watch while the rapist abused his wife. She was sure that she was going to be killed, especially when the rapist thrust the gun-barrel into her vagina. Her future was also put in jeopardy by the man threatening to infect her with AIDS. The man was arrested, tried and convicted. Her general practitioner was concerned about the apparent lack of reaction of both her and her husband after this appalling event, and referred them both; the husband declined to attend on the grounds that this was something for his wife to sort out.

Ann was inclined to dismiss the event, and seemed more concerned about the rapist's welfare than her own. Paradoxically, she worried about the rapist being sent to prison and felt guilty about the rape. The feeling was accentuated through having become sexually excited to the point of orgasm during the rape, a not uncommon but very disturbing feature of this kind of assault. She was grateful that her child had been spared, and felt that, in some way, she expected and deserved to be raped. She angrily resisted attempts to explore her inner feelings, preferring to be emotionally deadened with anti-depressants, and leaving her therapist at the end of the sessions full of the anger, despair and helplessness that she so obviously felt but could not face.

Ann was a victim thrice over. She had been violently raped; both she and her husband had been humiliated and had faced death. This in itself would have been terrible enough, but her reaction was powerfully influenced by her childhood experiences and her choice of husband. Twice as a child, she had been raped. On neither occasion was any support forthcoming from her parents, who blamed her for going into the woods and denied what had happened to her there. They did not defend her against sexual abuse by a neighbour and left her feeling unloved and unwanted. This she internalised as a belief that she was unloveable and that the best that she could do in life was not to assert herself and try and survive by being passive. This pattern was reinforced by her mother's constant criticism and her father's ineffectuality. She repeated this configuration by marrying a highly critical and demanding man whose violence, both verbal and physical, she passively accepted. Soon after the rape, her husband re-commenced his criticism of her, a guilt-inducing process which was reinforced, firstly, by the isolation that she encountered at work where colleagues, perhaps in embarrassment withdrew from her and, secondly, the shaming publicity in the newspapers. In her psychological reaction, she identified with her aggressor, thus protecting herself from her anger and hatred of him. This defence distanced her not only from facing how close she had come to death but, more importantly, from her anger and disappointment with her parents for their failure to nurture her as a child and, their lack of belief in her childhood rapes, and her hidden anger with her husband's criticisms and demands. The stress of the rape linked directly with her low self-esteem, and her profound conviction that she was and deserved to be a victim. Psychotherapy challenged this defence, aroused anxiety and was resisted for that reason. To be in touch with her repudiated wishes and feelings was to raise the whole question of how she had constructed her life and whether she was strong enough to construct a new one. Psychotherapy began with the impact of the stress, but very quickly broadened the inquiry into the place that the rape had in the story of her life. This broadening is a painful, difficult process but is a key feature of the psychotherapy of anxiety and stress-related disorders.

THE PSYCHOTHERAPY OF ANXIETY AND STRESS-RELATED DISORDERS

In general psychiatry practice, as in specialist psychotherapy, brief treatments are to be preferred to lengthy ones, patient preference should be taken into account, and purity of approach should not rule out the deployment of helpful procedures. It is against the criterion of effectiveness that the value of interventions should be judged. What psychotherapy especially contributes to the therapeutic field is, firstly, a broader perspective on the disorder than the symptoms alone and, secondly, a radical questioning of meaning and of the logic of the therapist's interventions and their consequences.

In this section, a brief form of psychotherapy suitable for psychiatric practice is described and a number of practice points identified.

Assessment

Assessment is the first step in responsible practice. In assessment, many elements need to be combined. The assessor must think *psychiatrically* in order to identify any co-existant or underlying psychiatric disorder which may either influence prognosis or be amenable to pharmacological intervention (see below, Pharmacotherapy and psychotherapy). Equally, it is important that medical conditions such as thyrotoxicosis or stimulant abuse presenting with anxiety are excluded. The assessor must think *psychodynamically*, identifying psychological processess in the past and the present that have lead to increased vulnerability, and teasing out their interaction with stress factors. Then there is the role of forecaster, in which the assessor thinks *psychotherapeutically* about the likely themes and course if the patient were to come into psychotherapy. Any plan for intervention must be *practical* and relate to the resources available, not to an ideal state. During the assessment interview, the assessor must take care of the *inverview* so as to create the conditions that will allow the patient to speak sufficiently fully about important matters so that the assessment may be properly made, and must take care of the *patient*. The assessment interview should not be traumatic; care needs to be taken that the patient's apprehensions are dealt with and that he leaves, in so far as is possible, in an intact, encouraged state (Malan 1979).

Among the key questions to be answered in the psychodynamic assessment are: (1) what the patient feels to be his main problems; (2) what influences have shaped this person and how does these problems seem to have come about; (3) what view the patient takes of himself and how he thinks others see him; (4) what patterns are formed typically in relationships; (5) whether there are others in the patient's social world who contribute to the problems and whether there is a wish that these persons be involved in the therapy; and, finally, (6) why is the person seeking help now?

The psychodynamic assessment takes a view of the patient as a whole, that is, as an individual person in relationship to a particular environment. Anxiety precipitating stressful events is identified and, as appropriate, married up with recurrent situations of similar psychological meaning in the history. Estimations of patient strength, severity of disturbance and the likely availability of family and community support are made. These findings are brought together in a *formulation*, which attempts to answer the question: why is this person at this stage in his life reacting to this stress in this way? (Aveline 1980).

Case study 10.2   Phobic anxiety, grief and dependent attachment

Let us see how Jane was assessed. Jane, a socially accomplished woman in her 50s, presented with phobic anxiety 18 months after the sudden death of her husband. Her acute fear was precipitated in social gatherings from which she could not escape back to the safety of her home. Closer examination revealed longstanding, generalised low-grade anxiety which had not been a problem to her while her husband was alive. With a partner, her husband had built up a small business in which Jane had a titular interest. She had positively taken no interest in the running of the business and been actively shielded from it by her husband. His attitude had been that he would provide financial security and she should care for their children; this was their pact. Now, she had lost her husband's support, her children, now grown up, were squabbling about the inheritance and she was financially embarrassed.

In all her married life, Jane had not contemplated being without her husband. Without him, she felt half a person. She was envious of other couples – seeing couples was a potent trigger for her panic attacks – and felt shamed by her incompleteness. She felt unable to make decisions, a life-long feature as it turned out. At home, she held imaginary conversations with her husband, kept his suits on their hangers and polished his shoes in anticipation of his hoped-for return.

Her family history was relevant. The only child of elderly parents, she had been brought up to respect and fear her autocratic father. He was a man not to be crossed; he kept his business affairs to himself and wanted his women to be decorative, home-makers. Her mother offered little opposition to these views and, indeed, spent much time in bed with ill-defined ailments.

In the assessment interview, Jane was reluctant to accept any link between her phobic symptoms, the social precipitants, the death of her husband and her childhood. She was, by turns, self-critical of her weakness and defended against experiencing any of her inner feelings. At the same time, she looked to the therapist to provide guidance and expected him to take away her troubled feelings.

Diagnostically, there was no evidence of an underlying biologically-based depressive disorder. In the language of psychiatric diagnosis, she had a grief reaction with phobic anxiety features in the setting of a dependent personality. Psychodynamically, she had suffered the loss of her husband, an attachment figure on whom she had been dependent and whom, it seemed likely, she had chosen for his Victorian male characteristics. These characteristics replicated those of her father, with whom she had an anxious attachment. Her interpersonal pattern was to move towards others, not causing offence, stifling any anger and hoping that someone would come to her rescue. These acts of self encouraged others to ignore her, and treat her, at least in financial matters, as if she were a fool. Cognitively, in her schemata, the integrity of her survival was based on being part of a married couple, a base she maintained through dysfunctional thinking of magni-fication and over-generalisation. Neither her children, nor her husband's partner were supportive. Her psychological defence was one of denial, im-mobility and a slender hope that her symptoms would spontaneously go away. Her phobic symptoms represented panic that she would not be able to cope and was helpless, that her grief would surface, and that she might get in touch with forbidden anger with her husband for the dependent role that she had with him and with her father before. Despite her ambivalence over psychotherapy, she wanted to resolve her difficulties, albeit as pain-lessly as possible.

She was suitable for psychotherapy. The first focus would be on her bereavement – the external stress – and helping her face her loss. The second focus would be on her anxious attachment, its genesis, the role it had played in her life-decisions, and how she might now take steps to alter the pattern. The therapist anticipated that she would resist the exploration in order to spare herself pain and to avoid making what were now necessary changes in the pattern of her relationships. In the transference in the first place, she would look to the therapist as a husband or a father to make decisions for her; in the second place, as she got closer to her anger, she would placate the therapist and fear his retaliation if she became challenging. He had some sense that she would perceive the exploration as an unwelcome intrusion. We return to her case in the next section.

Psychotherapy

Psychotropic medication, supportive psychotherapy, cognitive-behavioural therapy, and dynamic psychotherapy, probably in that order of frequency, are the common treatments for anxiety and stress-related disorders.

In dynamic psychotherapy: (1) the therapist strives to provide a relatively safe place in which self-reflection and personal change may occur; (2) he takes a sustained affirmative interest in the patient's well-being; (3) the therapy encourages the patient to feel more hopeful and less demoralised; (4) personal change is not achieved without taking risks; (5) successful experimentation, undertaken at the right time, enhances the person's sense of mastery and effectiveness.

Dynamic psychotherapy begins with the exploration of the presenting problem or surface difficulty, especially if there is an obvious external stress. Later, the inquiry can be broadened to discover the place of the symptom in the story of the patient's life. In post-traumatic stress syndrome, the stress will be clear. Its catastrophic impact needs to be recognised and the details of the event told and retold until they lose some of their overwhelming power. How vulnerabilities from the past may have been activated will need to be explored. More than words may be necessary; patients may find it easier to use painting or clay modelling. An active, abreactive approach such as psychodrama may be helpful; group therapy has been found to be especially useful (McFarlane 1989). Most anxiety reactions have less dramatic antecedents, although usually there will be an external stress which is stressful because it engages a vulnerability in the patient.

Psychotherapy requires committment on the part of the therapist. The patient needs to know that he can rely on seeing the same therapist at the same time each week for a set amount of time. An average therapy for anxiety and stress-related disorders would be for between 12 and 25 sessions, each of 45 minutes duration. There needs to be clarity about when the therapy ends but this should not preclude spacing out the sessions towards the end as the patient finds his feet, and having a planned reunion some months later. What does need to be considered is the meaning of these and other management decisions which break the frame of strict psychotherapy: Is a lack of faith in the patient's ability being conveyed? Is the exploration of negative transferences and termination being avoided? Is the patient's dependent wish being gratified for the therapist's narcissistic satisfaction? On the other hand, to take the image of parents and children, when the children grow up and leave home, they are not precluded from returning and sharing what is going on in their lives; they are sustained by the continued relationship with the parents who are there to be called on in time of need. The therapist has a professional job to do, but the human bond that develops between him and the patient is a crucial part of the therapy and should not be denied.

Sometimes, the patient's anxiety will be so disabling that direct measures to deal with it will be necessary. Patient preference may dictate a direct approach too. Psychotropic medication is dealt with in a later section. Cognitive-behaviour therapy offers a wide range of techniques, often under the heading of stress management and relaxation, which may be used either as treatments in their own right, or as a prelude to dynamic exploration (see Ch. 4; also Kanfer & Goldstein 1986, Dryden & Golden 1986, and Michelson & Ascher 1987). The language of behaviourism and psychoanalysis is very different, and their adherents are all too often in opposition, yet what effective therapists do in actual practice has many similarities. Strupp (1983) and Lazurus & Messer (1988) have provided two stimulating accounts of therapies, analysed from both perspectives.

Case study 10.2 (contd)   Phobic anxiety, grief and dependent attachment

Having delineated a number of practice points in psychotherapy, let us return to the case of Jane and see what transpired. She was seen on 15 occasions, initially at weekly intervals, over a period of 18 months. Throughout, she was resistant to exploring her inner feelings. Typically, she would recount a setback and note that she was feeling more anxious or phobic, but go on to deny that there was any link between the two. When pressed, she would say how distasteful she found it to be weak, by which she meant distressed. 'Cry and you cry alone, laugh and the world laughs with you', was her motto. Why she should hold to this position was not immediately clear. It certainly impeded the exploration of her grief for her husband.

To begin with, she blamed herself for his death. If only she had sought medical help for his angina, he might still be alive. 'Still present in your life to make you complete' the therapist continued, but she would have none of this, perhaps because of the note of implied criticism of her husband. It was as if there was in her words a 'closed door' inside her which she was not at all sure that she wanted to open; this metaphor became part of the language in the therapy. The therapist spoke of her bereavement being also the opportunity for personal growth; this she could not see. All she could see was that she had lost him.

Although psychotherapists are careful not to impose their solutions on their patients, the therapist soon formed an impression of what Jane would do if she were not so inhibited. She would face her grief and her anger, find in herself the strength to be decisive and develop the capacity to be more self-reliant, regardless of whether or not in the future, she formed another union with a man.

In the therapeutic relationship, Jane expected the therapist to take the lead. He was the expert; he should tell her what to do. Inwardly, the therapist felt a curious mixture of protectiveness and irritation. When he refused her request, she became angry. This was a turning point. It put Jane in touch with her irritation with her husband for leaving her with a mess for which he had not prepared her. He had not involved her in the business. Gradually it emerged that, in fact, Jane had had decided opinions on what should have happened in the business, but had not voiced them. The question then arose of why that should be, and this took the discussion back to her father. It had been dangerous for either Jane or her mother to stray outside their role and intrude on his business affairs. At best, they risked rebuff; at worst, rejection. He was intolerant of distress and weakness; it was important for Jane to keep his good opinion, as the vital force within the family seemed to rest with him as a male. Several features of her case fell into place: her need to conceal her distress, her choice of a husband who replicated her father's stance but who, it must be said, was much less punitive, and the therapist's counter-transference feelings which recreated an aspect of her relationship with her father.

Over the next few sessions, a course was steered between recognising the extent of her loss and her profound wish not to be single, and exploring the way in which her history handicapped her from taking necessary steps towards a more independent and self-determining life. It was acutely difficult for her to be at social gatherings where there were couples present. She was well aware of her shame in this setting, and less aware of her rage. *Significant action* was for her to go to a party. She managed this with the support of the therapy (and a dose of minor tranquilliser), and then went on to hold a 'thank-you party' for the friends who had rallied round after her husband's death, on this occasion enlisting the support of a male friend. Two more positive steps were taken; firstly, with great trepidation, she confronted her solicitor who was being dilatory in settling her husband's estate, and secondly, she dispensed with the attentions of a longstanding male friend who leant on her but was oblivious of her own need for support.

This was a successful therapy. Her phobic symptoms reduced in frequency and were less disabling when they did occur; she came off tranquillisers. She gained a sense that she could be a force in her own life and no longer sabotaged herself with thoughts that she was stupid and would be found out to be such. To the last, she found the process of unearthing her feelings distasteful, and was reluctant to accept the nature of the psychological link between events and her reactions. This ambivalence was perhaps shown in her not attending the second of two follow-up sessions. She continued to grieve for her husband, and regretted that she was without a partner. However, she felt sufficiently stronger in herself not to feel compelled to rush into a new relationship just because the opportunity was there. Therapy had begun with her phobic symptoms, translated them into a fear of being alone and helpless, related this to longstanding relationship patterns, and examined their source. Therapy could not provide her with a new husband, a proper wish for her. What it did do was to help her into a better position to lead a more autonomous life and make a more balanced choice of partner.

Case study 10.3   Panic, hypochondriasis and severe separation anxiety

Not all psychotherapies are successful. Often this is because the patient's ego-weakness is greater than was first apparent, or because insufficient time has been allocated for the therapy. The contrast between Jane's case and Matilda's is illuminating. Matilda, a spinster and clerical worker in her early 40s, presented with intense panic. She had been unable to work for the previous month, and was convinced that she was about to die, probably of heart disease. The precipitant had been the arrival of a new boss, thus ending many years of symbiotic relationship with her predecessor. The previous superior had been paternally supportive and had delegated to her much administrative work; she had felt appreciated and, on a deeper level, comforted. The new superior changed all this; she returned Matilda to work where her skill had atrophied and, at the same time, held her accountable for the running of the department for which she was not responsible. Looking back in the history, acute anxiety had surfaced on several occasions in the preceding two years when the boss had been more distant than usual. The youngest of two children, Matilda had always felt outstripped by her brother, who had gone to university, left home and married. Matilda, though intelligent, had never found a secure niche for herself. She ventured away from home for periods, only to return in defeat, to the increasing bewilderment of her aging parents.

A 20-session contract was established, but the work did not go well. She remained wedded to the idea that she was about to die, and could not accept a suggestion that her panic was to do with her feared death as a person, now that her father-boss had gone. Instead, she pressed her general practitioner for medical investigations whose negative findings supplied only transient reassurance. She felt that the therapist was holding her at a distance, and could not accept the finite number of sessions that they had together. Indeed, once the contract was complete, she wrote in bewilderment that she had never believed that the intense phase of weekly therapy would come to an end when it was planned to end, that the therapist had not meant what he had said, and that termination was his way of saying he hated her. Soon after, she returned to live with her parents and took a job below her level of ability. Matilda located her strength outside herself in others, especially in those with whom she could establish the role of approved child. The loss of her father-boss disclosed an inner emptiness of terrifying intensity which had been camouflaged by competence in her professional work, competence which was evident to others but never accreted into self-confidence. *Her love was made angry*, the more so as she came to see her old boss and then the therapist as *hateful deniers* who could give her what she wanted if they so chose. The world seemed hateful and persecutory, and safety lay at home with her parents from whom she expected so much more than they, now or in the past, could give her.

In her panic-driven flight, it was over-optimistic to expect her to change course so radically. What had not been apparent at assessment was that the change of course was so radical and that her personal resources were so slight. Superficially, there are similarities with Jane's case, in that both showed the pattern of anxious attachment. Although the balance of force between Jane's parents was skewed, Jane had shown little disturbance as a child. In contrast, Matilda had been a sickly child, had missed long periods of schooling and had been gathered up by protective parents. In adult life, Jane had trained as a physiotherapist, worked for a while, married, had children and sustained her marriage; in short, she had been able to love and to work. Matilda's achievements were much more tenuous. She qualified in her profession but held herself back from promotion to positions of responsibility. Her love relationships were disappointing; men used her for their purposes; she was never their first priority. For her, medication was palliative and supportive psychotherapy would be needed for a long time. Dynamic psychotherapy that might alter the direction of her life was too great a challenge. Matilda still exchanges letters with her therapist; it is to be hoped that one day she will find the strength to stop and redirect her path.

Pharmacotherapy and psychotherapy

Pharmacotherapy and psychotherapy are often portrayed as negative opposites; the former driving the real problem underground and the latter unnecessarily stirring up psychological conflicts. Neither position is wholly valid; both approaches have their place. What is important is to be aware of the implications of the therapeutic intervention. Psychodynamically, the process of prescribing and receiving medication will have meaning. It may represent a transferential tug into action – a plea for rescue – that would be better analysed than yielded to by the therapist. The therapist may be responding to the patient's fantasy that it is possible to resolve problems by living passively, without assuming responsibility for the choices that have been made and are being made in that person's life (Aveline 1988).

Pharmacological remedies for anxiety are readily deployed. However, the addictive potential of each set of compounds – the benzodiazepines being the latest – limits their utility, except for brief periods of treatment in acute situations. Generally, psychological interventions either in the cognitive-behavioural or psychodynamic form are to be preferred.

Pharmacotherapy and psychotherapy have different loci of action, the first affecting the patient's clinical state and the second the quality of his relationships, the one being rapid in its effect and the other slow. Karasu (1982) advocates an additive model in which the different contribution of each is recognised, rather than the essentially negative alternative models of pharmacotherapy as inhibitory to the psychotherapy process, or psycho-therapy as superfluous to pharmacotherapy. In the author's view, the psychotherapist should not neglect speedy biological remedies when these are indicated – indeed, pharmacotherapy may be an essential preliminary step in order to reduce anxiety levels to the point where the patient can cope with the exploration of psychotherapy – but the overall aim should be to help the patient manage his life without recourse to medication.

OUTCOME

In a community sample, about half the subjects aged 20–50 years and identified as having neuroses had recovered in three months (Tennant et al 1981). However, where generalised anxiety lasted for more than six months, 80% still had symptoms three years later (Kedward & Cooper 1968). These figures can be interpreted in many ways. They underline the transient nature of many anxiety reactions as, from the point of view of a psychotherapist, people face the stress in their lives and have inner vulnerabilities activated. When adaptive capacity is good, the anxiety soon subsides. In the lasting anxiety disorders, their persistence is likely to be underpinned firstly by deeply ingrained character patterns, and secondly, by adverse social situations. The psychotherapist can do little to alter adverse housing, employment and limited life-opportunities. What the therapist can do is to help the patient examine and alter his personal contribution to his life. This therapy in itself is bound to be anxiety-provoking, a difficult struggle to face that which the patient would often rather not face but which can lead to a freer, more robust life. Let T S Eliot have the last word: 'What we call the beginning is often the end and to make an end is to make a beginning. The end is where we start from'.

FURTHER READING

Bowlby J 1988 A secure base. Routledge, London
Freud S 1926 Inhibitions, symptoms and anxiety. Strachey J (ed) The standard edition of the complete psychological works of Sigmund Freud, Vol. 20. Hogarth, London
Kanfer F H, Goldstein A P 1986 Helping people change, 3rd edn. Pergamon, New York
Strupp H H, Binder J L 1984 Psychotherapy in a new key. Basic Books, New York
Yalom I D 1980 Existential psychotherapy. Basic Books, New York

11. Depression

A. Ryle

Depressed mood is experienced at some time by most people, and is present to some degree in the great majority of psychiatric patients, often as but one part of a spectrum of symptoms. As a diagnosis, depression is probably over-popular among clinicans, due perhaps to the availability of specific pharmacological and psychological treatments, and also among researchers because of the availability of relatively reliable and simple measuring instruments. In this chapter, the role of psychotherapy in the treatment of depressed patients will be discussed. This necessitates considering the varieties of depression and the varieties of psychotherapy, a task made difficult by the fact that neither are entirely satisfactorily classified at present.

PHYSICAL AND PSYCHOLOGICAL FACTORS IN THE AETIOLOGY OF DEPRESSION

A number of factors contribute to depression in humans, including: (1) genetic predisposition; (2) psychological factors such as infection or childbirth; (3) psychological predisposition due to early life experience; and (4) current life events. The symptoms of depression of whatever cause will include the central psychological disturbance of mood, marked by hopelessness about the world, the self and the future (Beck 1976), poor concentration and low self-regard and, to a varying degree, the well-known physiological disturbances of sleep, appetite, sexual desire and so on.

Genetic predisposition to depression, suggested by a family history, is common, being most marked in the bipolar affective disorders; but even when genetic factors are present, past and present psychological and social influences are important as precipitants and maintaining factors in the illness. As Brown & Harris (1978) have shown, a history of early adversity, and a current life situation which is marked by the social isolation, associated with lack of employment or of a confidante, are significantly associated with the development of depression; and a range of life events requiring adaptation to change, particularly if they involve loss, can provoke depressive episodes.

The role of pharmacological and psychological treatments

In deciding whether or not to use pharmacotherapy for the depressed patient, both the current symptoms pattern and the family history must be taken into account. The more marked the somatic disturbance, and the more severe the mood change, the more likely it is that antidepressants will be effective. Indeed, in the most severely depressed patients, psychotherapy is impossible because the patient cannot in any real way engage with it. In such cases, the role of the doctor is to support the patient through the illness and to maintain morale and co-operation with treatment. In some less severely depressed patients, who may have some evidence of major depression but who are reluctant to take medication, psychotherapy may be tried for a period of 3 to 6 weeks, but if no change is achieved within that period, antidepressants are clearly necessary (Simons et al 1984). In many such patients, combining antidepressant medication with psychotherapy is appropriate. In the less severely depressed patient, however, psychotherapy is the treatment of choice. In clinical practice, patients in the more severe categories are often under-medicated, particularly in primary care settings, while those at the milder end of the spectrum are often unnecessarily medicated. Depressed patients are typically under-investigated and under-treated psycho-logically.

Interaction of physical and psychological factors

An episode of depression may be provoked by any or all of the following factors: genetic predisposition; physical illness or childbirth; life events, either occurring randomly or as a result of the individual's personality and life procedures; and earlier life events resulting in vulnerability to adversity or loss. Once established, depressed mood and depressed thinking and impaired functioning can become self-maintaining. This mutual reinforce-ment, much emphasised by cognitive therapists, is a crucial factor in maintaining depression. There is good evidence to show that depressed mood is accompanied by a selective bias towards recalling and anti-cipating negative events, and is associated with impaired social and intellectual performance. This cycle can be broken by either pharma-cological or psychological interventions. In view of this, it becomes less difficult to understand how the changes resulting from treating mild depression with either cognitive therapy or with antidepressant medication have proved largely indistinguishable by researchers (Simons et al 1984, Blackburn & Bishop 1983), although this failure may also reflect the limited range of change-measures employed.

In considering the significance of life events in the provocation of an episode of depression, it is important to discriminate random life events, for which the individual bears no responsibility, from those in which his or her personality or life procedures have played a part. The majority of depressed people are living in relationships or in relation to themselves in ways which are stressful and unsatisfying, and their depression is therefore to some extent self-generated or self maintained. This being so, treatment of depression requires that attention be paid to different levels of psychological functioning. The initial requirement is to relieve the mood and break the depressed cycle either by antidepressant medication or by cognitive therapy or by a combination of the two (Rush et al 1977, Blackburn et al 1981). Once this is achieved, psychotherapy may be indicated to influence the personality and interpersonal factors which were antecedent to the depression and which, if untreated, are liable to engender further episodes. Such therapy is not always necessary since patients, as they recover from a depressed episode, may be able to solve their own problems without help. It is nevertheless important not to be satisfied with symptomatic relief as the only outcome measure. The more an individual has actively created the causes of his depression, the greater the indications are for a more transforming kind of psychotherapy. The range of psychotherapeutic methods available and the indications for them will be considered in more detail below; before this, however, some further attention to differential diagnosis is called for.

DIFFERENT KINDS OF DEPRESSION

Grief and mourning

Unhappiness in the face of loss, whether of a partner, parent, child, friend or of one's own health or employment, is a normal phenomenon. The response goes through recognisable stages of protest, denial, anger and, finally, acceptance. Although it can be severe, the normal grief reaction is of limited duration. The end state is one of acceptance of the fact of the loss, and a realistic evaluation of the real value of that which has been lost, relatively free from defensive idealisation or denigration. Failure to complete mourning leads to a general inhibition of feeling and is a common cause of depression. Patients presenting in this way have often experienced earlier similarly unmourned losses.

Treatment of abnormal grief reactions is an important psychotherapeutic task, the need being to help the patient experience directly the range of feelings which have hitherto proved unmanageable. As a loose analogy, one can understand the problem as one of 'phobic avoidance', not of particular external situations but of intense internal feeling states. Treatment involves supporting the patient's exploration of and exposure to these avoided affects.

Depression in personality disorder

Depression is common in patients with borderline personality structure. It is experienced in the context of unstable states in which sense of self, memory, and access to and control of affects all vary. These patients may experience extremes of self-hate, often accompanied by self-harm and self-neglect and sometimes by destructive attacks upon others. Antidepressant medication may have a part to play in the treatment of these patients, and the prognosis is better for those who show marked affective disturbances. It may be that individuals with fragile but more or less integrated personality structures decompensate in the presence of depression, but are able to reintegrate adequately when the depression is treated. In all cases, psychological management is essential although difficult, for these patients easily develop regressed, deeply ambivalent attachments to their care-takers. Their management requires considerable skill, especially as destructive acting out, for example overdosing on antidepressants, is common. All too often, these patients provoke unstable responses of either over-protection or rejection from the psychiatrists and others whose job it is to help them.

Despair

Despair may be the end result of adversity, of a life progressively restricted by impoverished patterns of relating, or of a long unrelieved depression from any cause. It may also be a manifestation of the emotional isolation and coldness of the patient with a schizoid personality. Such patients present when the isolation has become unbearable or when it has been breached by a relationship which has gone wrong, often due to idealisation followed by massive disillusion. The level of fear, hurt and anger and self-hate present in these individuals calls for skilled psychotherapeutic treatment.

Necessary depression

Individuals who have been unable to experience depression – or, more accurately, unable to experience sadness – as in the case of pathological grief reaction, or patients with schizoid personality problems who have persistant difficulties in experiencing a wider range of feelings, may respond to therapy with an apparent *worsening* of mood. The emergence of directly experienced depression and, more particularly, of frank grief, is in fact a sign of recovery, and the correct response to the appearance of such feelings should be to support the patient through the experience rather than to rush in with the intention of curing or suppressing it. Most patients at this point report relief as they realise that something is 'thawing' inside them. When the patient is recovering from severe depression, this thaw may also increase the chances of suicidal behaviour, and it is important to maintain or increase support through this phase. A similar, less intense experience of sadness may be provoked by any successful psychotherapy; as the patient recognises the restrictions and pains of his past life, he or she may actively grieve for the hitherto unrecognised loss of life and possibility.

PSYCHOTHERAPEUTIC APPROACHES

In the remainder of this chapter, a range of therapeutic techniques suitable for use in the context of psychiatric hospital and community practice will be considered. Firm research evidence for the general advantages of, or specific indications for, different approaches is lacking, so to some extent this account can only reflect personal preference. General psychiatrists are likely in any case to choose those particular methods with which they feel comfortable, and they can do so in the confidence that patients have the capacity to make good use of many different kinds of help.

The failure of psychotherapy research to demonstrate different effects of, or different indications for, the various therapeutic procedures is disappointing. One possible explanation for this failure is that outcome measures of change used in research are often crude (for example, symptom scores, self reports of social functioning), and such changes may reflect the non-specific effects upon morale achieved by any helpful intervention. The author's own view (Ryle 1984) is that while different therapeutic inputs aim to effect different levels of functioning, (for example, discrete behaviours, or overall strategies, beliefs or assumptions about the world or attitudes to the self) all such experiences are assimilated by patients into their own complex mental structures. Thus, a depressed patient taught behaviourally to increase self-rewarding behaviour is likely to become less guilty, while the patient whose guilt is explored and diminished by interpretative therapy may become more self-rewarding in his or her behaviour. According to this view, the therapist should be free to 'push where it moves' (a principle embodied in Cognitive Analytic Therapy, described towards the end of this chapter) but this should not be taken to imply that 'anything goes'. Therapists should develop a range of skills and a capacity to select methods according to their patients needs and capacities (see Ch. 1).

The remainder of this chapter will present the main features of supportive, cognitive-behavioural and psychoanalytic treatments, and will then describe the author's own model for an integrated framework for therapy – Cognitive Analytic Therapy – within which methods drawn from many sources can be combined.

Supportive therapy in depression

All depressed patients need care and support during the depressed phase. The aim is to counteract as far as possible the hopelessness and self-blame commonly encountered, to explain the nature of the illness and the appropriate extent of personal responsibility for it, to expound the treatment offered and ensure cooperation with it, and to offer an accurate prognosis. Reassurance on its own is not particularly effective; it needs to be offered repeatedly on the basis of an honest account of the situation. It is often helpful to offer the same explanation to relatives.

Support does not necessarily mean offering uncritical and unconfronting acceptance. As patients begin to recover, it often becomes evident that the depression has resulted from unexpressed anger or unacknowledged loss; that it is occurring in the setting of long-term personality factors such as perfectionism; or that it reflects current interpersonal difficulties. The continuation of uncritical and unqualified support and the simple definition of the depression as an illness to be endured, can induce in the patient a regressive dependency which undermines the return to normal life and prevents the recognition and change of these long-term predisposing factors. In most cases, one of the active treatments to be described below should be instituted as soon as the patient is able to participate. Long-term supportive therapy for patients with severe personality disturbance is a skilled treatment requiring a complex psychodynamic understanding in which the role of the supporting doctor needs to be carefully analysed and understood (see Ch. 9 and Werman 1984).

Behavioural and cognitive therapies

Behavioural and cognitive-behavioural therapeutic methods have developed rapidly over the past few decades (Ch. 4), with an increasing interest in cognitive therapy. Many clinicians are put off by the evident over-simplifications of human experience embodied in purely behavioural approaches, which can appear manipulative and diminishing of human dignity in their refusal to consider consciousness or self-awareness. It is, however, clear that these over-simplifications, whether acknowledged as such or not, have produced valuable technical tools for therapists and for patients. In recent years, the theoretical convergence between social learning theory and cognitive psychology, the developments in cognitive psychotherapy, and the growing interest in the emotions by cognitive psychologists (see, for example, Greenberg & Safran 1987) have closed the gap between these approaches and humanistic and psychoanalytic therapies.

Behavioural therapies are based upon the paradigm of the reinforcement or extinction of behaviours by their consequences, these consequences being, in humans, most frequently social. In depressed patients, diminished or absent positive reinforcement or persistently distressing or punishing consequences of behaviour are seen as the crucial targets for therapy. The plight of the depressed patient is seen to result either from a deficient environment or from a lack of individual skills. In assessing the treatment needs of a depressed patient, a careful analysis of the individual's behaviours and experiences in respect of positive and negative reinforcements is therefore essential; this involves patient self-monitoring and keeping detailed records of mood fluctuations. On the basis of such analyses, a range of techniques is available designed to initiate change. These include: (1) where possible, planning more positive and fewer negative events; (2) teaching assertion and other relevant social skills; and (3) recognising the behaviour-outcome links and hence being able to increase positive and diminish negative outcomes. Such programmes of change are carefully monitored and rated, intermediate goals being set at an achievable pace so that the recognition of success becomes itself a reinforcement of the new behaviour.

Additional techniques aiming to reduce distressing symptoms may accompany these procedures. Teaching physical relaxation (practice is usually helped by providing audiotape instructions) offers a non-specific but often helpful way of diminishing discomfort. Fear of failure due to the depressive predictions may be helped by rehearsal through role-playing or imagination, and by teaching self-management techniques. These approaches merge into the more formally cognitive methods to be described below.

The essential role of the behavioural therapist is that of a good teacher whose skills are those of analysing behaviour-outcome sequences, of designing appropriately graded programmes and of teaching a range of self-observing and self-managing skills.

Cognitive therapy (Beck et al 1979), while incorporating behavioural techniques, is concerned not only with the relation of behaviour to outcome but also, and more centrally, with the relationship between thinking and feeling. The depressed patient is seen to suffer primarily from the results of specific faults in his thinking. His beliefs and assumptions and interpretations of the world are seen as the cause of his depression, and therapy aims to identify, challenge and revise these faulty cognitions. The therapist, within the context of a collaborative relationship, will attend to the symptoms, moods and emotional life of his patient, with the aim of working out these links between thinking and feeling.

The early stages of cognitive therapy have the following components (Young & Beck 1982): (1) taking a full history of the problem; (2) identifying the centrally important issues to be worked on; (3) instilling hope, especially by starting work on a problem where change can be achieved early; (4) teaching patients to recognise how thoughts and feelings are linked, both in sessions and through patient self-monitoring between sessions; and (5) teaching patients to think in focused, rational ways about their difficulties. These various methods require recruiting patients to act and work between the sessions.

A particularly valuable cognitive-behavioural technique in the early stages of therapy is the use of patient self-monitoring. Patients are instructed verbally and in writing to observe and record the events, thoughts and images provoking and accompanying the onset or worsening of their depressed mood. These written accounts are retained by the patient, and at a later time are rated according to the degree to which the thoughts or images are felt to be realistic. Patients learn to identify inappropriate ('catastrophic') patterns of thought and imagery which operate rather like videos in their mind, and are able to recognise the inappropriateness of these images. Self-monitoring in this form, therefore, both identifies the inappropriate thoughts, and provides patients with some control over them. In further discussion with the therapist, these thoughts may also be linked with the underlying maladaptive beliefs (such as 'everybody should love me', or 'I must do everything perfectly'), or with forms of cognitive distortion. These distortions include the depressed person's tendency to discount good, and exaggerate bad news ('catastrophising'); to deny responsibility for success but claim it for failure; to over-personalise and over-generalise; and to take inappropriate responsibility for some events and deny it for others ('errors of attribution'). These processes are in turn identified and challenged by detailed discussion.

Another useful technique in depression is the use of a 'coping and pleasure' diary. A record of each part of the day is kept, each activity being rated according to the degree to which it was (1) managed and (2) enjoyed. Such records often serve to correct the depressed person's negatively biased recall, and also help indicate which activities may be encouraged and which should be discouraged or modified.

As therapy proceeds, the early emphasis on identifying behaviour-outcome and thought-feeling links will shift to a concern with underlying thought contents and processes ('basic assumptions') and this in turn will be replaced by a focus on initiating new ways of acting and thinking.

There is a reasonable body of research now available to show that cognitive therapy, according to the range of measures used, is as effective as anti-depressant medication in the treatment of minor depressive illness, but the evidence that subsequent relapse is less likely is equivocal (Blackburn et al 1986).

In conclusion, cognitive therapy is clearly satisfactory as a symptomatic treatment of minor depression. However, as argued earlier, psychotherapy should also aim to modify the antecedent interpersonal and personality factors that are usually present in such patients. Cognitive therapy may indeed do this, but researchers in the field have not yet demonstrated such changes. Personality factors relevant to depression are manifest in attitudes to self, in patterns of relating to others, in the various forms of restriction on awareness of self and others described in the psychoanalytic literature as ego defences, and in problems of unstable personality structures. The fact that a significant proportion of patients do *not* respond to the commonsense collaborative therapy offered by cognitive-behavioural therapy is, I believe, explicable in terms of the influence of these personality factors on the therapeutic process itself. This is an area which has only recently attracted attention among cognitive psycho-therapists, and to consider these questions we need to examine the contribution of psychoanalysis, where these factors are of central concern.

Psychoanalytic treatment of depression

Theoretical basis

It is difficult to summarise the essential features of psychoanalysis, due to the relative complexity of the theory compared to that of cognitive-behavioural approaches. This complexity is compounded by the difficult metaphoric language; internal debates and controversies within psycho-analysis (see Ch. 2); and by the isolation of psychoanalysis from the rest of psychology. It also reflects the ambitious nature of the psychoanalytic project, which alone has attempted to offer a comprehensive understanding of human experience. In particular, this approach embodies notions of how the early life of the infant shapes the adult personality and is reflected in the individual patterns of relationship; it emphasises the ways in which a person's knowledge of himself and of the world is incomplete, serving to protect him from unmanageable anxiety; and it recognises the conflictual and contradictory nature of human thought and action.

The classical understanding of depression is derived from the analogy between melancholia and mourning (Freud 1917) based on the idea that anger (largely denied) at a lost person or relationship is turned against the self (see Ch. 13). This view has been modified by later developments in the theory (see Pedder 1982), in particular in the emergence of object-relations theory as the dominant school. In the Kleinian view, the roots of depression are universal, being a reflection of the infant's realisation of its separateness from its mother, a separateness seen to be a source of ambivalence and guilt which constitute the 'depressive position'. Winnicott (1965) described this phase more optimistically as representing the emergence of a capacity for concern. Fairbairn (1949) differed from Klein in laying less emphasis on innate, universal forces and more on the infant's actual experience.

The crucial understanding offered by these theories is that *intrapsychic structure is interpersonally derived,* and hence that the adult personality bears traces both of the infant and of the internalised parent. The basis of healthy development is the internalisation of (in Winnicott's words) a 'good enough' mother. Defects or disruptions in early care leave the individual with a deficient capacity for self-care, reflected in low self-esteem and unsatisfactory patterns of relating to others. Where early care has been disrupted by the departure or death of the parent, losses in later life are liable to re-evoke the painful experiences of the early loss which the immature child is unable to assimilate.

Treatment

As a practical treatment, full scale psychoanalysis will always be unavailable to most people, but applying psychoanalytic understandings to less intensive forms of therapy is now well established practice (see Ch. 8).

The essence of applied psychoanalysis remains the use of the therapeutic relationship as an arena within which the patient's neurotic difficulties are made manifest and can be modified. In order to use the relationship in this way, many of the features of psychoanalytic practice are retained, notably the use of interpretation as a therapeutic method and the avoidance of direct suggestion, task setting or of any of the various procedures employed by cognitive-behaviour therapists. Although the patient will usually sit and be able to see the therapist, the therapist will be personally opaque and unrevealing and relatively silent; his comments are attempts to link the 'here and now' interaction with the patient's past family relationships and with his current difficulties. In time-limited, once-a-week therapy, the regression which develops in full scale analysis, in which earlier infantile patterns are expected to become manifest in the transference, is not encouraged and is less likely to occur. Nonetheless, intense emotional involvement with the therapist can occur and it is through this that the depressed patient may be helped.

From a psychoanalytical perspective depressed patients may seek therapy either (1) because their life-long avoidance of painful feeling and the consequent impoverishment or distortion of their life has led to severe restrictions on the quality of their existence, or (2) because a more recent loss has activated in an overwhelming way the feelings rooted in early losses. Therapy, in such cases, will require the patient to experience, in relation to the therapist, these unassimilated feelings, being helped to overcome longstanding defensive avoidance of them, and to experience their more satisfactory resolution. This resolution means that the patient must both allow the relationship with the therapist to develop and cope with the loss of it; the handling of the termination of therapy is therefore crucial. Such coping requires the 'internalisation' of the therapist as a 'good enough' figure who can provide the basis for the development of a more reliable, self-caring part of the personality.

Some psychoanalysts have developed strictly time-limited approaches (see Ch. 8). For example, Mann & Goldman (1982), in describing a 12-session psychoanalytically-based model of therapy, suggest that many patients, and this includes most depressed patients, have a sense of unmet need which leads them either to a constant frustrated search for perfect care or to the avoidance of closeness because of their fear of loss or of unmanageable dependency. The impact of a strictly time-limited therapy can be to free patients from this dilemma; saved from the frightening over-dependency which an open-ended or more intense therapy might offer, many patients can experience getting something important while suffering a manageable disappointment. Moreover, in experiencing the ending, with its anger, disappointment and sense of loss, they may be able to overcome their previous tendency to close off such feelings, a closing off which contributes significantly to the depressed mood.

Apart from helping patients overcome underlying long-term sources of depression, dynamic therapy can help patients to modify neurotic patterns of behaviour which are responsible for continuing restrictions on their experience, and for their repeated destructions or distortions of their important emotional relationships. Persistent neurotic mechanisms whereby, for example, others are provoked to be rejecting, or in which the terms of relationship are self-denying or harming, or in which self-control and self-care is harsh or neglectful can be identified and changed by dynamic therapy, enabling people to free themselves from the repeated experience of pain and loss which maintains depression. Moreover, if, in the course of the treatment itself, these neurotic mechanisms lead to non-cooperation or difficulty in the therapeutic relationship, such resistance and difficulty can itself become the theme around which therapy is conducted.

Psychodynamic psychotherapy, in contradistinction to cognitive-behaviour therapy, is aimed primarily at altering personality or, in its briefer forms, at the resolution of key conflicts. Relatively little attention is paid to symptomatic relief; indeed, during therapy, as patterns of avoidance or repression are revised, there is often a temporary increase in the level of symptomatology.

Outcome research into this kind of therapy is clearly more difficult than is a demonstration of behavioural change or symptomatic relief. A large body of research exists to demonstrate positive effects from psycho-dynamic therapy (see Ch. 1), as from other forms, but much of the research is methodologically unsatisfactory and it was out of the author's own interest in defining and describing psychodynamic change in less ambiguous ways that Cognitive Analytic Therapy (CAT), to be described in the next section of this chapter, evolved.

Cognitive Analytic Therapy

Cognitive Analytic Therapy (CAT) is a form of therapy applied primarily in brief time-limited work. It is fully described in Ryle (1982, 1990). It's theoretical base draws upon both cognitive and psychoanalytic sources; while the latter are the largest influence, the attempt has been made to restate key psychoanalytic ideas in a language compatible with current thinking in cognitive psychology. The practice of CAT also represents an integration of diverse therapeutic approaches.

An initial period of joint work with the patient culminates in a reformulation of the patient's problems. This is written down as a prose summary of the pains and solutions of the patient's past, and as a list of key problems and 'Target Problem Procedures' (TPPs). These describe how the patient is currently actively thinking and behaving in ways that maintain his difficulties. These descriptions may be supplemented by diagrams illustrating the sequences in need of revision, and depicting how different states of mind are related to each other and how transitions between them are triggered. The work of therapy consists in part in the patient learning to recognise and in due course modify these sequences, something that is done both through homework (TPP diary keeping) and by demonstrating the use of these procedures in the relationship with the therapist. These methods may be combined with cognitive or behavioural techniques or with other therapeutic devices, such interventions always being directed to the modification of one of the identified problem procedures.

The theory underlying CAT is called the Procedural Sequence Model. This describes how aim-directed activity is organised and effected and revised and how it is not revised in the case of neurosis. A 'procedure' is a repetitively used sequence of mental and behavioural events, the circular model including anticipation and feedback. Neurosis is understood as the repetitive use of ineffective or harmful procedures, and the task of therapy is to describe these procedures, identify why revision has not occurred and devise methods for changing them.

Common patterns of neurotic procedures, described as traps, dilemmas and snags (Ryle 1979; see Ch. 1) are listed in the 'Psychotherapy File' along with instructions in self-monitoring; patients are given the file to read at the first session and this contributes to the joint work of reformulation, which is usually completed at the fourth meeting.

The procedures of most concern to therapists are those which shape emotionally signficant relationships and those to do with self care and self control. These are called 'Reciprocal Role Procedures' (RRPs), to emphasise that, to relate to another person, requires that one both enacts one's own procedures and predicts or elicits the corresponding role procedure from the other. This aspect of the model represents a re-statement of object-relations theory, with some modifications. The infant, in his or her early interactions with the mother, will develop procedures for relating to aspects of the mother rather than to a whole person, for example: needy child to providing or depriving mother, or compliant or submissive child to controlling parent. In this process, a model of two sets of procedures, one infant- and one mother-derived, has been acquired, those of the mother becoming 'internalised' as part of the structure and repertoire of the self. The particular kind of parenting received will, in this way, influence personality. The further task is the integration of this range of discrete RRPs into a suitably complex array of interpersonal procedures and an effective self organisation. This integration is never complete, and everyone retains traces of unrevised childish procedures; in patients with borderline personality organisation, this integrating process is very imperfect and discontinuous, so that polarised and primitive feelings, thought and actions are manifest.

In the treatment of depression, CAT addresses the same range of issues as are considered in psychoanalytic psychotherapy, with emphasis being placed on the need to understand the role of past losses, the significance of the transference, and the importance of termination as offering an experience of manageable loss. However, the early work on identifying current procedures (which will include the procedures used to avoid anger or sadness) is likely to place more emphasis on the ways in which depression is maintained, as, for example, in the patterns of self-care or of relationships. In addition, the active participation of patients in self-monitoring, reading the Psychotherapy File, and in cooperating in the reformulation task, reduces the development of dependent transference attachments. CAT recruits the healthy capacity of the patient to think about himself, and provides him with new tools with which to do this. Some of the ideas of cognitive and behaviour therapists may also be of use. Contrary to the belief of most dynamic therapists, however, this active approach does not inhibit the development of emotionally significant attachments to the therapist, and treatment is usually accompanied by the return of lost memories and the re-contacting (or first encountering) of deep feelings from the past. In psychoanalytic terms, the 'ego' having been strengthened, the need for defence is diminished, with little emphasis being placed on the interpretation of ego defences.

Another feature of CAT – the extensive use of written material – is of particular value at the end of therapy with depressed patients. Termination is always of significance to the depressed patient, and in brief therapy (CAT is usually of 12 to 16 sessions only) there is always some disappointment or anger, and some grief, both reflecting the real loss of the therapist and echoing earlier losses. It is usual to write a 'goodbye letter' which is read out at the last or last but one session and which is given to the patient. As with the earlier written reformulation, the experience of receiving a clear account which names feelings directly is usually a moving one. In the goodbye letter, the problems redefined and addressed in therapy can be reviewed, the work achieved noted, and the unfinished business and painful feelings around termination described. Patients may also benefit by writing their own review of their therapy experience. In the period between termination and the follow-up interview (usually 3 months later), the goodbye letter reminds the patient of what was achieved and links the figure of the therapist (as, it is to be hoped, an ultimately benign figure to identify with and internalise), with a set of useful understandings and new ways of thinking.

The relation of CAT to cognitive and psychoanalytic psychotherapy

It is apparent that CAT owes much of its theoretical understanding to psychoanalysis, and much of its practice to methods drawn from cognitive psychotherapy. The defining characteristics of CAT are the level of active participation evoked from patients and the emphasis placed upon reformulation. This emphasis requires, from therapists, a level of precise thinking which is challenging but valuable. Reformulation guides the use of a wide range of therapeutic procedures but also represents a tool of direct use to the patient, offering a new perspective on his or her difficulties and a new basis for self-observation and control. In this way, the patient's capacity for autonomy is enhanced. The self-sabotaging and treatment-blocking procedures, which often make cognitive and behavioural therapies of limited impact, are overcome through the understanding of psychodynamic issues which is incorporated in the TPPs. The flexibility of the method means that morale is restored in the early stages through the reassurance offered by reformulation and through the use of cognitive-behavioural methods, such as self-monitoring, which give patients the experience of the possibility of change. These approaches are combined from the beginning with the effort to understand the wider picture and to set the episode of depression in the context of the patient's life. An example of CAT treatment of a depressed patient will now be given.

Case study 11.1   Cognitive analytic treatment of a depressed patient

Barbara, a 26-year-old landscape design student in her final year at college, was referred from a psychiatric colleague after nine months of only partially successful treatment for depression with anti-depressant drugs. Prior to this, she had been extensively investigated for severe headaches, (this included a CAT scan) but no cause was found. She had sought referral for psychotherapy for some time. Her major depressive symptoms had included sleep disturbance and weight loss. She was now partially improved, but her ability to work was still impaired.

Barbara was a rather tired-looking, attractive young woman who was precise but quite halting in telling her story, seeming anxious to avoid exposing her feelings. She said that she felt that the depression of the last year was only an increase in level of something which had been with her much longer.

Barbara was the second of two children. During her childhood, her father had been working abroad and her brother had been sent off to school and she had never formed much of a relationship with him. The father's job involved a good many moves. When she was eight, she was sent home to a boarding school in England where, some months later, she was visited by her mother to be told that her parents had separated. Both parents later remarried and thereafter she would spend her holiday with one or other, usually her mother. Frequently, often with little warning, she would find that the plans had changed or the parents had moved and there was only a relatively short period when she felt there was some stable place she could call home. The school did not encourage her to make a fuss. For example, her father used to send her tapes rather than letters, but she was not allowed to play them 'because nobody else had a tape recorder'. However, she coped well academically, and went on to a college of further education to complete her schooling. However, at this time, her mother died suddenly. She had no emotional support in dealing with this death. She then failed her exams and it was two or three years before she retook them. At the time of therapy, she was nearing the end of her professional training.

She had had boyfriends on and off since her late teens and was currently in the fourth year of a relationship with an older man; this was her longest relationship. She said he seemed unable or unwilling to understand the nature of the experience she was now going through and a joint meeting was arranged so that he could be given some idea of this. Barbara was offered a 16-session therapy and was given the Psychotherapy File.

At the joint session with the boyfriend, Nigel, the therapist felt that he was willing to hear what was said and it seemed possible that Barbara had contributed to his incomprehension by her own insistence on coping. This view was revised later in the therapy.

First session

Therapy started four or five weeks later. Barbara agreed for the sessions to be tape-recorded as part of a research project into therapeutic process. She started by talking about the joint session, and said that she felt Nigel had now categorised her as being similar to other friends he had known who had had therapy but she felt that he had not, in fact, understood anything personal to her. She went on to talk about a typical uncomfortable experience in their relationship. She was waiting for his return before eating and he came back more than an hour late. She offered to make some soup and a sandwich with the last two remaining slices of bread. She put the bread in the toaster, whereupon he went into the kitchen and ate the lot. She made some mild protest, felt guilty for doing so, and subsequently felt depressed.

She then talked about the college, where the requirement to present her work to groups of fellow students made her feel anxious; she was both competitive and vulnerable in this situation. She reported how she had found one of the tapes her father had sent her when she was in boarding school, and how she had been reminded of her strong sense of his anxiety to maintain contact and of her cheerfully reassuring him that all was well.

At this stage, the therapist's provisional understanding of the sources of Barbara's depression included the long-term emotional deprivation and losses in her childhood and adolescence, with the possibility of incomplete mourning for her mother. In her relationship with Nigel, she was feeling misunderstood and was being over-placatory. As a child, school achievement had clearly been the most secure source of self-esteem, and her anxieties around her college work could be seen to be linked with this, by way of unreasonably perfectionist strivings.

At the end of the session, the therapist suggested that she should monitor (1) any further headaches that she might have and (2) any further interactions with Nigel which were distressing.

Second session
In the second session, Barbara appeared quite tense. In the beginning, she
went through the Psychotherapy File with the therapist noting those parts
which she had identified as referring to her self. She had marked, in a
section comparing aggression with assertion, the passage; 'a fear of hurting
others can make us put our feelings aside or put our own needs aside'.
Under the section describing traps, she had marked, in relation to Nigel
only, the placation trap. She has also marked the social isolation trap. Under
dilemmas, she had identified two concerned with either keeping feelings or
plans in perfect order or fearing a mess; this was in line with the therapist's
impression of her perfectionist pressures, formed in the first interview. As
regards dilemmas in relations with others, she had marked a number
concerned with control in dependent relationships.

The therapist suggested that her anxious perfectionism might stem in
part from irrational guilt related to her parents divorce and to her mother's
death, to which she made a non-committal reply. She then reported an
occasion on which she had had a severe headache. This had occurred when
she had had to wait over five hours for an interview with a teacher at her
college. When he finally appeared, she had been unable to use the
interview because of the headache. She was able to see quite clearly how
this was a situation when she felt needy but over which she had had no
control, and she could see how her headache could have resulted from
unexpressed anger.

The other main issue discussed at this session was another episode
between her and Nigel. Following the discussion of the sandwich at the first
session, she had assertively demanded an evening out together at a
restaurant. He had again been more than an hour late and, by the time of
his arrival, she had sunk into a state of desolation. The therapist suggested
that although the occasion was in some sense minor, the feelings that she
experienced were those which were appropriate to the coping, abandoned,
eight-year-old child who had not, at the time, been able to experience the
extent of her anger and loss.

The session ended with a discussion of her college work, where she
thought many of the demands made of students were impossibly large and
ambiguous. There was quite likely some truth in this, but it was clear that
her own anxious perfectionism and her preference for tidy and precise work
was also a contributory factor.

In this session, therefore, the Psychotherapy File served to link Barbara's
depression with her perfectionism, and to recognise her pattern of feeling
out of control in close relationships. Her self-monitoring had served to
identify the emotional meaning of her headache; she had no further
headaches during therapy. The sandwich episode and her understanding of
her placation of Nigel had already produced some behavioural change, but
this had led to the direct experience of feelings of abandonment (rather
than inexplicable 'depression') which she could see, were linked to her
earlier childhood experience.

Third session
Barbara reported a difficult week. Having been upset, she had looked for

some kind of comfort from Nigel. When this was not forthcoming, she had been angry, whereupon he dismissed her for being childish. At this point, the therapist read to her the draft reformulation, which she accepted without revision. This read as follows:

Dear Barbara,

Here is the letter I promised – anyway a draft of it. My main impression of your childhood and early adolescence is of your having had to cope – cope with the moves around the world, with boarding school at eight, with the unsupported dealing with your parents divorce and with all the later moves of home, over which you had no control. Although you managed it all, I feel a forlorn little girl was there too. Your mother's death was one more pain you had to cope with alone.

Apart from coping, I believe you learnt to depend upon achievement and order as your main security. These are real qualities: for example, they were reflected in the way you were accurate and precise in how you studied the Psychotherapy File (and in how you are, I imagine, in your work). But I think there is also an element of keeping chaos at bay; both the risk of failure and the uncertainty of your deep mixed feelings kept you out of touch with your own experience and liable, at least with Nigel, to undervalue your own worth and needs in ways which lead you to accept terms which make you resentful and depressed (e.g. the sandwich). Also with Nigel, perhaps because this is a longer and more emotionally committed relationship, you have contacted your own needs and are aware of deep sadness (as in the wait in the restaurant) which is out of scale with the event, but in scale with the old losses it puts you in touch with. Perhaps your headache was from a similar unmanageable disappointment with your teachers. You do not value your sense of what you need and you switch to disappointed anger (echoing what you could not manage to feel as a child) or into debilitating symptoms, which at least in the past made doctors take you seriously.

So, I think therapy needs to help you deal with these issues:

1. *It is as if, if you care for someone, then you must give in to them. (This makes you depressed or headachey.) I hope that we can help you make proper self- and other-valuing terms for these relationships.*
2. *It is as if you must either keep tasks and feelings under tight control or be overwhelmed with chaos or unmanageable feelings. I hope therapy can help you enter the zone of scarey, powerful feelings so that in the future, you need not spend so much energy avoiding and controlling them.*

This reformulation was accompanied by a preliminary version of a diagram which was finalised at the seventh session.

Barbara brought to this session some relics from her early childhood and a photograph of her mother; as the therapist looked at this, although she remained contained, there was a strong sense of feelings below the surface.

Fourth session

Barbara reported another difficult week and a particular episode with Nigel in which she felt he had put her down in a social situation and treated her like a child and then abandoned her.

As in the last session, there was a strong sense of feelings nearing expression. This included some cautiously negative feelings for the therapist, in that she said that she feared that the use of the diagram and being tape-recorded would 'turn her feelings into things'.

Fifth session

In view of the comment last time, the therapist suggested that they stop recording and she was very pleased to do that. She reported yet another episode with Nigel. On this occasion, she had spoken her mind directly but subsequently had withdrawn and cried for several hours. She was deciding that the relationship was over and she would have to move out. The therapist looked at the diagram with her, in particular at the description of the core state (see below). The therapist suggested the need for her to develop a more caring and concerned part of herself. She went on to talk of a friend of hers (also called Barbara) with whom she had been on holiday the previous year and of her amazement at this friend's capacity to look after herself, i.e. to make proper meals when she was hungry, sleep adequately when she was tired and so on.

Sixth session

Barbara reported a more active week with more satisfaction at work. She felt more in control in relation to her fellow students and she felt more detached from Nigel and had increased her independent activities. In this session, she described some dreams. In one she was assertively telling off somebody at work whom, in fact, she wished to treat that way. In another, her mother was present although she knew that she was dead. In a third, a friend who was currently pregnant had a child with Down's syndrome. The therapist suggested that she could perhaps be envious of this friend and therefore wish to give her a painful experience. She acknowledged this possibility with some reluctance.

Seventh session

The seventh session opened with a discussion of an episode at work in which Barbara felt she had been criticised without justice or reason by one of her fellow students but had been unable to make any kind of reply. The therapist suggested that her own self-criticism (part of her core state in the diagram) made her vulnerable in this way. This was contrasted to a later episode in which she had been unreasonably brusque and angry with a waiter in a restaurant . The therapist linked this with earlier episodes with traffic wardens. She reported a dream which seemed a powerful representation of her order versus chaos dilemma – the first part being concerned with very pure rectangular spaces, the second with cars being driven around by men armed with dangerous implements. She went on to talk about her more general sense of danger in the world, and of her need to be vigilant always. She described how walking to the Psychotherapy Unit, located in the neglected and derelict parts of the hospital, made her feel unsafe, and how, to feel really secure, she needed to be in her own room with all access locked. Expecting attack, she could be aggressive towards those she saw as functionaries (traffic wardens, waiters) but placatory towards those she was emotionally exposed to. This distinction was incorporated into a diagram representing a *core state* in which a critical, uncaring part was in relation to a needy, guilty and covertly angry part. From this core, two sequences emerged. In one, she was anxiously vigilant and exhibited the dilemma 'either critical, looking down on others (e.g. traffic wardens, waiters) or feeling forlorn, of no value and being submissive and placatory, then resentful, headachey, hopeless and tearful'. The other sequence was initiated by perfectionist striving, leading on the one hand to real achievement, and on the other to over-control of feelings, rigidity, then exhaustion, self-criticism and, again, hopeless crying.

Eighth session
Session eight started by Barbara describing re-reading her adolescent diaries and feeling her father's pressure on her not to make a fuss. Her mother, she felt, had been much less constraining. She had, however, felt powerless in relation to her parents frequent moves, and always felt pulled between them; her mother, in particular, always wanted her to spend more time with her than she in fact did. She had had a dream filled with violence in which she had escaped to safety in the end.

Ninth session
The main points to this session were Barbara's continuing disillusions with and distancing from Nigel. From her descriptions, the picture increasingly emerged of an insensitive, self-preoccupied man. She also reported some more assertive behaviours at work.
    Between the third and ninth sessions, the agenda of therapy had been characterised by continuing revision of the relationship with Nigel, marked by her ability to state her position and her needs more clearly and by his apparent inability to hear what she was saying, and by some reflection and dreaming and return of memories concerning her early life.

Tenth session
Barbara reported an unfamiliar lightness of mood in which she kept finding herself laughing. She described a less absolute commitment to work; after taking some time off, she had been able to return and proceed. Some time was spent considering the final version of the diagram, looking at the changing relationship with Nigel and with work. It seemed from this discussion that although the familiar patterns were still operating, they were much less dominant and that there was some change in her core state in the direction of more acceptance and kindness towards herself.

Sessions eleven to thirteen
This lightness persisted, Barbara became less anxious about her studies and for the first time in her life was late in submitting a piece of work to her tutor. She had had a number of memories, both happy and sad, from her childhood, including a sudden shock of recognition of her own physical similarity to her mother. In the course of the twelfth session, discussing the end of her relationship with Nigel, the end of therapy and the many changes that were to occur in the next few weeks, she felt momentarily sad and then became quite blanked off. She described this as feeling like the onset of anaesthesia. Having noted this, she was able to experience some

sad and needy feelings in this session in a way which felt very fruitful and relieving.

Sessions fourteen to sixteen; the 'goodbye letter'
These sessions were spaced out, as they coincided with Barbara's successful completion of her final examinations. During this period, she moved into her own flat and began a relationship with a new man. Her lighter mood persisted. At the end of therapy, she was given a 'goodbye letter' from which the following are extracts:

'Although quite a lot of our time together has been spent on the relationship with Nigel, I feel that the more important task was dealing with those aspects of yourself which had allowed that relationship to take the course and form that it did. The famous sandwich which epitomised your deep expectation of not being cared for and your inability to make claims for yourself, the forlorn wait in the restaurant made manifest what I had already responded to, namely the prematurely coping but still needy little girl, concealed most of your life by efficiency and order. The repeated experience of having had to manage on your own... had combined to generate in you the two main strategies of personal survival which we described in the diagram; strategies which left largely unchanged the inner reality which was at once needy, covertly angry and guilty, and self–critical and harsh ... I think the power of these self-perpetuating loops has been significantly broken. You have learnt to recognise and claim your own feelings and needs, and you have been far less rigid both at work and with your feelings. These changes became manifest in the lightness of mood which occurred after the ninth session ... Your residual, irrational guilt about leaving Nigel, and your slight bewilderment at a possible new relationship with someone who cares for and even looks after you in some ways, are residues of the old regime but, I think, only residues...'

At this last session, Barbara did not bring a letter, but she read from some prepared notes. She had felt unable to write down how much better she felt and she linked this inability with a realisation of how extensively she avoided naming hopes or achievements as if to do so would mean that they were bound to go wrong. Her new boyfriend kept bewildering her by asking her what she would like to do and then agreeing to do it, and she found herself avoiding stating her preferences from the same magical dread. On one occasion, when she thought, wrongly, that he had failed an appointment with her, she experienced a wave of panic and anger and was reminded of her recurrent experiences with Nigel. She reported a much warmer relationship with her father, and she was allowing her friends, whom she had always seen singly, to meet each other for the first time. Looking back, she realised how little she had known about herself before; looking forward, she felt pleased and surprised to be at a point in her life when her own choices could determine what she did.

Comment on Barbara's case history

This case history illustrates a number of the points discussed earlier in this chapter. Barbara's antidepressant medication was helpful, but it is probable that psychotherapy could have been started some months earlier; the medication was discontinued gradually over the first three months of therapy. Despite her reserved nature, she was able to engage quickly and effectively in therapy; it is likely that her active participation (reading the Psychotherapy File, self–monitoring) and the sense of being understood conveyed by the reformulation contributed to this. The two identified procedures, described initially in words and elaborated in the diagram, made sense of her experience and led to some rapid behavioural change, so that her reinforcement of her depression was rapidly diminished. Simultaneously, she was able, within the safety of the therapeutic relationship, to recontact and revise feelings about her past and about both her parents. Transference feelings were largely positive. In one session, she brought a dream about the therapist making a tape recording, which could have been interpreted in terms of links with her father (who had sent her tapes when she was at school), but in his comments the therapist focused instead on an early part of the dream which illustrated her 'controlled versus overwhelmed' dilemma and on the presence and permissability of mistrust. Her brief, initially blanked–off experience of sadness in the twelfth session suggested that therapy had provided her with an experience of manageable loss. The reformulations and the goodbye letter summarising what had been understood and changed in the course of therapy were designed to link the internalisation of the therapist with the reminder that she had acquired a new capacity and new tools for self–understanding and self–care.

The cognitive components in the therapy were probably valuable but would not have been sufficient; Barbara did not need to learn new social skills or to identify maladaptive thoughts so much as she needed to understand how her inner state was in conflict and was manifest in damaging modes of relating; she also needed to be helped to feel directly and remember more fully her past experience. A psychoanalytic therapy might well have achieved this, by way of a more exclusive focus on transference issues.

Within the spectrum of depressed patients, Barbara represented a case of mild–to–moderate severity, and the historical adversities contributing to her depression were less extreme than is often the case. Time–limited CAT is nearly always an adequate intervention in such cases, and is often effective in patients with earlier and more severe disruptions. It is also effective in patients of low educational and socio–economic status. It is hence a satisfactory first intervention in nearly all cases; those who at termination or follow–up are not recovering satisfactorily (about 1 in 4 of the author's own outpatient sample) may be offered further treatment in the same or some other mode.

CONCLUSION

Psychotherapeutic responses to the depressed patient can be divided into three levels. Firstly, to offer support through the painful experience of depression; secondly, to revise behavioural and cognitive processes serving to maintain depression; and thirdly, to alter those aspects of the individual's personality and relationship paterns which predispose him or her to further episodes.

These three levels require increasing levels of skill from the psychiatrist. Appropriate supportive therapy and the use of cognitive and behavioural methods should, the author believes, be in the repertoire of all general psychiatrists. The use of cognitive approaches in inpatient settings, as described by Perris (1988) would also seem to offer a real advance on the benign caretaking or rather unfocused groupwork characteristic of many inpatient regimes. Dynamic therapy is more challenging because the psychiatrist, in using the therapeutic relationship as the focus of therapy, is called upon to examine and perhaps modify his own reactions. To do this will involve personal supervision and some form of personal therapy. The development of CAT as a time–limited dynamic therapy offers another way of extending the use and understanding of the therapeutic relationship. The jointly arrived–at reformulation provides both patient and therapist with a framework which explains and predicts both the patient's life problems and his relationship with the therapist. The strict time limit is of particular value in work with abnormal grief reactions. Trainees with little or no previous experience working within this framework under supervision are able to do effective therapy (Brockman et al 1987) and to make use of transference–countertransference interaction. For these reasons, CAT seems (as it was intended to be) a therapy particularly suited to National Health Service conditions, where depressed patients are numerous and trained therapists are few.

FURTHER READING

Beck A T, Rush A J, Shaw B F, Emery G 1979 Cognitive therapy of depression. International University Press, New York
Pedder J R 1982 Failure to mourn and melancholia. British Journal of Psychiatry 141: 329–337
Ryle A 1990 Cognitive analytic therapy: active participation in change. John Wiley, Chichester.

12. Suicidal acts

D. Campbell, R. Hale

Case study 12.1   An autobiographical account of suicide

A young woman, who had been in therapy for some years, wrote of her experience of suicide:

I am so afraid that nothing can really give any reader a sense of what I felt. I should have to write an entire book trying to explain the many desperate feelings over years which led up to it, this suicide attempt. It was in no way an isolated incident, but part of the very fabric of my life from childhood onwards. I had to struggle for a sense of worth and meaning and the basic hope which I only now understand are the norms for many people, but which were lacking in me.

I am frightened still – of this account somehow being rejected, going unheard, being discounted or disconfirmed, because these were all the things which I felt as a child and teenager within the family which were reactivated by any external rejections and which culminated in my suicide attempt. Although it is truer to speak of it as my suicide as I began to later, because it was a kind of death and then, very slowly over years of analysis, a kind of rebirth. I did not understand what I have just written of the feelings which led to my suicide at the time, of course. I did not understand myself what had wounded me to this degree. It is not so easy to understand the sources of your own pain, especially in the face of a concerted effort to deny it and to deny further that you have any reason, any right, almost, to such pain.

INTRODUCTION

As a consequence of their study and treatment of suicidal individuals, psychoanalysts are in a position to extend and also to challenge various assumptions and part-truths that other professionals and laymen have made about suicide. Suicide is commonly held to be part of a depressive state in which the person feels that life is not worth living and that death is preferable. Certainly, sadness and pessimism are often present, but they do not in themselves account for the major drive towards suicide. A

287

second assumption is that suicide is a cry for help. This is a view that is influenced as much by the professionals' need to help as it is by the patient's crying out for it. A third assumption is that suicide is a means of manipulating others. Again, this is in part true. A fourth assumption is that suicide can be a solitary or solipsistic act in which the person rationally decides to take leave of life. This has also been referred to as the rational suicide, or the suicide of anomie. Although both acts may occur, they are extremely rare. Each assumption is only partly true, and, if taken as the whole truth, is misleading because it fails to recognise the violence inherent in the suicidal act.

If a self-destructive act is examined superficially, the patient's conscious intentions may well confirm one of the popular assumptions about suicide. However, closer scrutiny of unconscious processes reveals the less acceptable face of suicide as an act aimed at destroying the self's body and tormenting the mind of another. The contradiction between a benign view of suicide and the perception of the act as violent will be apparent to the observer but not to the patient. Usually, aggressive wishes are so unacceptable to the patient that they are relegated to the unconscious by repression. The patient, therefore, continues to deal with the contradiction between his conscious view of the suicide attempt and unconscious wishes by resisting any attempt to bring aggressive intentions into consciousness.

A patient reported that he had taken 199 aspirins. One had fallen on the floor and he refused to take it because it might have germs on it. It would be potentially dangerous for a clinician to respond only to the patient's conscious wish to live, that is, to protect himself from germs, and not to pursue the intent behind swallowing the other 199.

Ambivalence is at the centre of the suicidal act. In the authors' opinion, therefore, to identify any self-destructive act as either suicide or parasuicide is both simplistic and incorrect. The most useful term is 'a suicidal act', with the outcome unstated. A working definition of the suicidal act may thus be proposed as 'the conscious or unconscious intention at the time of the act to kill the self's body'.

HISTORICAL ASPECTS

Suicide has for a long time been the focus of interest for psychoanalysts. In 1910, the Vienna Psychoanalytic Society organised a symposium entitled 'On Suicide with particular reference to suicide amongst young students'. Contributors included Sigmund Freud, Alfred Adler and Wilhelm Stekel. It represented a turning point in the study of suicide, which had previously concentrated on external factors, for example, Durkheim's monumental works relating the incidence of suicide to social and geographical factors. Attention was now directed to the inner fantasy world of the individual, where the destructive and vengeful nature of suicide was recognised.

In Stekel's paper to the conference, he stated, 'I am inclined to feel that the principle of Talion plays the decisive role here. No one kills himself who has never wanted to kill another or at least wished the death of another'. He went on to explore the nature of the relationship between the young person and his or her parent: 'The child wants to rob his parents of their greatest and most precious possession, his own life. The child knows that thereby he will inflict the greatest pain. Thus, the punishment the child imposes upon himself is simultaneously punishment he imposes on the instigators of his sufferings' (Stekel 1910). This paper laid the foundation for all subsequent psychoanalytic thinking on suicide.

Aggression turned against the self in suicide was taken up by Freud in his paper, 'Mourning and melancholia' (Freud 1917). Freud observed that in melancholia after a loss or a 'real slight or disappointment' coming from a person for whom there are strong ambivalent feelings, the hate originally felt towards the person may be redirected towards the self. He writes:

'It is this sadism alone that solves the riddle of the tendency to suicide which makes melancholia so interesting – and so dangerous. The analysis of melancholia now shows that the ego can kill itself only if ... it can treat itself as an object – if it is able to direct against itself the hostility which relates to an object and which represents the ego's original reaction to objects in the external world' (Freud 1917, p. 252).

In the suicidal individual, it is the body that is treated as a separate object and identified with the lost loved and hated person.

ACTING OUT

Suicide is a form of acting out. Freud used the term 'acting out' originally to describe the phenomenon of a patient, whilst in psychoanalytic treatment, carrying out an action which in symbolic form represents an unconscious wish or fantasy which cannot be experienced or expressed in any other way within the treatment. Over the years, the term has been broadened to describe a general character trait in which a person is given to relieving any intrapsychic tension by physical action.

Acting out is the substitute for remembering a traumatic childhood experience, and unconsciously aims to reverse that early trauma. The patient is spared the painful memory of the trauma, and via his action masters in the present the early experience he originally suffered passively. The actors in the current situation are seen for what they are now, rather than what they represent from the past. Furthermore, the internal drama passes directly from unconscious impulse to action, short-cutting both conscious thought and feeling. The crucial element is that the conflict is resolved (albeit temporarily) by the use of the patient's body often in a destructive or erotised way.

The person will implicate and involve others in this enactment. The others may be innocent bystanders or, as we shall see, have their own unconscious reasons for entering and playing a continuing role in the patient's scenario. The patient thus creates the characters and conflicts of his past in the people of his present, forcing them (by the use of projection and projective identification) to experience feelings which his consciousness cannot contain. He gains temporary relief, but as the players in the patient's play disentangle themselves from their appointed roles, they return to the patient his projected affects. Because he knows no other solution by which he can escape his inner conflicts, the patient is forced to create anew the same scenario in a different setting. This is the essence of what Freud referred to as 'repetition compulsion' (Freud 1914a).

In suicide, the unconscious fantasy often revolves around settling old scores from unfinished and unacknowledged battles of childhood. These are memories which reside in that part of the patient's mind of which he is unaware and of which he has no understanding. Freud described these memories as ghosts which compulsively haunt the patient. 'That which cannot be understood inevitably reappears; like an unlaid ghost that cannot rest until the mystery has been solved and the spell broken' (Freud 1914a).

Our way into this mystery is by viewing acting out as equivalent to a symptom. In a symptom, a fantasy finds symbolic expression in psychological phenomena (or, in the case of a psychosomatic symptom, in physical illness); in acting out, it is the action which is the symbol of the unconscious conflict. As with the symptom, the exact form of the action is precisely and specifically fashioned by the unconscious fantasies and conflicts.

THE SUICIDAL FANTASY AND THE PRE-SUICIDAL STATE

Behind every suicide there is a suicide fantasy. A suicide fantasy may or may not become conscious, but at the time of execution it has distorted the patient's view of reality and has the power of a delusional conviction. The fantasy is the motive force; killing the body fulfils the fantasy.

There are various resources for the detection and understanding of a suicide fantasy. The suicide fantasy is rooted in childhood, and may become apparent as it is enacted in the individual's behaviour or way of relating to others. The authors' data has come from two sources: (1) 500 interviews occurring within a four-year period with patients who were seen within 24 hours of a suicide attempt and after admission to the casualty department of a large metropolitan teaching hospital (Hale 1985); and

(2) comments made during psychoanalytic psychotherapy and psycho-analysis by 20 suicidal patients before or after suicide attempts.

Listening to the suicidal patients with a psychodynamic ear, it becomes clear that two aims coexist, a conscious aim and an unconscious one. There is in each patient a conscious intention to die, and it was their body they expected to die. There also exists a less conscious aim to survive. These patients imagine that another part of them would continue to live in a conscious, bodyless state otherwise unaffected by the death of their body. To paraphrase Freud's (1917) observation, when these patients reached the point at which they intended to kill themselves, they experienced their body as a separate object.

The suicide fantasy always includes a dyadic relationship, between a part of the self which will survive and the body which is identified with an intolerable object. Although killing the body is indeed a conscious aim, it is, in fact, a means to an end. The end is the pleasurable survival of an essential part of the self (Morse 1973, Maltzberger & Buie 1980) which we will refer to as the 'surviving self', a self that survives in another dimension. However, this survival is dependent on the destruction of the body.

THE CORE COMPLEX AND THE SUICIDE FANTASY

One half of the dyadic relationship embodied in the suicide fantasy is the body experienced as a separate object. What is the nature of this object now identified with the body, and why is it expendable?

Glasser (1979) has identified a constellation of childhood conflicts under the concept of the 'core complex' which has proved helpful in understanding the dynamics of physical assaults on others. The authors believe that this core complex also makes a major contribution to understanding the internal conflicts which the suicide fantasy aims to resolve.

The human infant is dependent upon a primary caretaker, usually the mother, for its survival. From the earliest period of development, the child develops complex and often subtle means of signalling its wishes to the mother, who usually responds appropriately to satisfy the child's needs. However, too much or too little gratification increases the child's pain, anxiety and aggression, which is defensively projected.

When the mother is unable to accept the child's aggression and relieve his fear and pain, there are a number of consequences. The mothering object may be perceived as ungiving, poisonous or untrustworthy. The child's body, which is the medium of the mother's care, may become identified through projective identification with the bad mother or seen as the cause of her rejection. The child faced with the reality of too much or too little gratification from its mother regresses to a more primitive idealised image of an omnipotent, all-satisfying mother, with which it then tries to merge so that all his needs can be gratified. However, this regressive move to merge with the mother is now accompanied by the child's anxiety about the consequences of any success in merging, namely the annihilation of its separate, independent and differentiated self. The child is now caught up in a pathological bind between the wish to satisfy its need by merging with the mother on the one hand, and the fear of its own extinction if it is successful on the other.

Only the most disturbed people fail to negotiate the core complex altogether. But in suicidal adolescents and adults, we believe there may be a significant unresolved residue of the core complex with a specific vulnerability to acts of betrayal. We have found that suicidal individuals experience even a minor rejection or disappointment as a catastrophic blow to their self-esteem and psychic integrity, which then dramatically undercuts their capacity to cope. As psychic defences are breached, the body is felt to be at extreme risk. There follows a regressive longing to merge with the primitive omnipotent caretaker. In this state, the individual is vulnerable to re-experiencing primitive anxieties of annihilation: either being engulfed by the object if they succeed in merging, or being abandoned to starve if they are unsuccessful in getting 'into' the object.

When adult relationships of people suffering from core complex anxiety are observed, it is seen to be necessary for them to hold conflicts which they experienced with their mother, now represented by a partner, at a safe distance. To get too close to the partner is to merge and be engulfed;

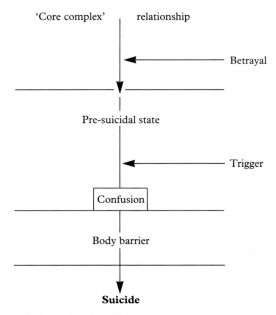

Fig. 12.1   The psychodynamics of suicidal acts.

to separate is to be abandoned to starve. The person thus lives in a narrow corridor of safety, controlling his or her partner by acts of cruelty or coercion, never allowing the partner to make his or her own choices. Very often, the partner in the relationship will share or mirror this pathology and thus the two become locked in mutual distrust.

As with every relationship, the two partners gradually establish the rules by which they can control one another. But eventually something will occur which will alter the balance of the relationship, and at this point it may enter a crucial, pre-suicide phase. Whatever the event, it is seen by the potentially suicidal patient as a betrayal of a fragile trust which has held the two in equilibrium, and is perceived as a direct attack on their psychological integrity. When psychological defences are breached, the body is also felt to be at extreme risk. The at-risk individual mobilises his aggression in a psychic self-defence. His aggression may be aimed at his own body or another's.

Figure 12.1 is a graphical representation of the process we are describing. This schema introduces three further elements – the trigger, the role of confusion and the body barrier.

The trigger

A trigger to violence may take any of three forms, and precipate the final breakdown into a destructive attack, either suicidal or violent:

1. An *actual physical attack*, however small. In the process of an extended argument, one workmate pushed his fingers into the ribs of Mr A to make his point more forcefully. In response, Mr A broke his mate's jaw.
2. An *attack by physical gesture*. The commonest gesture must be a V-sign, but it can be a look or a turning away. It can even be the click of a door.
3. *Words which have an intrusive, dismissing and sexualised character, which are felt as a physical assault.*

What all three things have in common is, firstly, that they are experienced as an assault, and, secondly, that the recipient/'victim' cannot assess them objectively so that they are felt to be overwhelming. It is thus the internal meaning of the trigger that matters. What is explosive to one person will be innocuous to another.

Case study 12.2   'You smell'

A 19-year-old girl killed herself. On a previous occasion, when she had thrown herself under a train, the provocation was that her mother had said, 'You smell', i.e. 'I don't like the way that your body smells'. Before the girl was born, her mother had tried to abort her and then had been extremely depressed throughout her childhood; although highly intelligent, she had been unable to care for her child both emotionally and physically. To the girl, therefore, her mother's statement confirmed what she had always unconsciously believed and yet not known, that her mother had never wanted her and that her existence was at her mother's expense, that she was a parasite on her mother. Her suicide also fulfilled her mother's original wish that she should not exist.

Confusion

Two observations substantiate the importance of confusion as an element in violent suicidal acts. Firstly, in general hospitals the commonest cause of violence is a toxic confusional state in which an innocuous stimulus is perceived as threatening – DTs are a good example. Secondly, about 35% of suicides, and a very large number of acts of violence occur after alcohol has been ingested. It is commonly suggested that 'alcohol dissolves the superego' and with it the conscience and a prohibition against violence. We would also suggest that intoxication impairs the ability of the ego to discriminate between threatening and non-threatening forces whether from outside or within. As a result, terrifying conjunctions of thoughts can occur which the ego in a confusional state is unable to keep separate.

Confusion has two elements. Firstly, the conjunction of two previously separated ideas, probably unconscious coming together into consciousness may be so unacceptable to the mind that they are fragmented into chaotic disorder. Secondly, this chaos is in itself terrifying for it represents the total loss of control which we all fear – that is, going mad. Thus, when more sophisticated ego defences fail, more primitive 'reflexive' physical defences are employed. The 'body barrier' is crossed.

Body barrier

The term 'body barrier' describes the resistance which exists in everybody to translating the fantasy now conscious – of the violence – into physical action. The state of confusion described above reduces this resistance. However, if this resistance has been once overcome it becomes increasingly easy to adopt this chosen pathway of discharging the intrapsychic tension.

The suicidal individual has withdrawn from others in favour of the cathexes of his own body, so that the primitive anxieties of annihilation are experienced in relation to his body which has become identified with the engulfing or abandoning object. Violent individuals attack an external object in order to break out of an engulfing state, with the self more or less intact. The suicidal individual leaves the external object intact and assaults an internal object, represented by the body, identified with the engulfing or abandoning mother who is perceived as someone who would kill by suffocation or starvation. The body must be killed if the self is to survive.

In intrapsychic terms, this is homicide, justifiable homicide. Just as there is a split between the good self and the bad body, there is a split between the hated and engulfing or abandoning primal mother, now identified with the body, and the idealised one with which the self will fuse once the bad mother/body has been eliminated.

SUICIDE FANTASIES

Suicide fantasies, which elaborate the relationship between the 'surviving self' and the body, take at least five forms which will be described briefly. Although one type of fantasy may dominate consciousness, suicide fantasies are interdependent and at an unconscious level not mutually exclusive. Within the patient, each fantasy is organised around a wish to gratify pre-genital impulses which are predominantly sado-masochistic or oral-incorporative in nature.

The suicide fantasy underpinning all of the other fantasies is a *merging fantasy*. Patients who harbour a merging suicidal fantasy imagine death as a return to nature, becoming one with the universe, achieving a state of nothingness, a passport into a new world, a blissful dreamless eternal sleep; or as a permanent sense of peace. These patients believe that in death the self will survive in a state akin to that of the sleeping infant. The dominant wish is to be fused 'with the image of the madonna of infancy. By becoming one with her, the suicidal patient hopes to taste again the omnipotent, timeless, mindless peace of his baby origins, far from the wearisome hostile inner presence of his miserable adulthood' (Maltzburger & Buie 1980).

However, as seen in the core complex, the wish to fuse with an omnipotent mother is accompanied by an anxiety about the consequences of fulfilling that wish, the annihilation of the self. In the psychotic state typical of those dominated by suicidal fantasies, splitting of the self from the body leaves these patients believing that the body is actually an impediment to the fulfilling of the merging fantasy.

The body is identified with the engulfing or abandoning mother and is then eliminated. This makes possible the fusion of the 'surviving self' with the idealised madonna-mother of infancy.

A second suicidal fantasy is the *revenge fantasy*. The revenge fantasy centres on the impact that the suicide makes on others. Here, a conscious link to a real object is maintained more strongly than in other suicide fantasies. The destruction of something precious to another person is a devastating attack. A son or daughter who takes his or her own life robs the parents of their dearest possession, knowing that no other injury could possibly be so painful to them (Menninger 1933). The often conscious thought in the revenge fantasy is 'They will be sorry'. The implicit message is that the parents have raised a child who hates himself because they did not love him enough. The threat of suicide to blackmail others may accompany the revenge fantasy.

This suicide fantasy has a markedly sadistic orientation, with the 'surviving self' often enjoying the role of the invisible observer of others' suffering, especially due to their feelings of guilt and remorse because of the suicide. There is a sense of retaliation, revenge and irrevocable, everlasting triumph.

A third fantasy is that of *self-punishment*. The *self-punishment* fantasy is dominated by guilt, frequently associated with masturbation which aims to gratify, in fantasy, incestuous wishes, and an erotisation of pain and death. Here, the surviving self is gratified by its sadistic treatment of its own body rather than that of others, as occurs in a revenge fantasy. Masochistic impulses are satisfied as well, in the self's identification with the helpless, passive, submissive body.

Case study 12.3   Self-punishment fantasy and erotisation in a completed suicide

This sado-masochistic dynamic is evident in the complexity of those sexually deviant practices that maintain a delicate balance between masochistic pleasure in self-torture and the risk of death, as in the dicing-with-death phenomenon (described later), and is illustrated by the suicide of a man who had broken off treatment two years prior to his death.

He was found hanged above a fallen chair and dressed only in a raincoat surrounded by burning candles. From the patient's earlier accounts of his elaborate ritual, it was clear that the 'surviving self' in his suicide fantasy was secretly identified with Joan of Arc, a woman who victoriously led men in battle and was martyred and reincarnated in a new dimension as a saint.

Underlying the risk-taking, sado-masochistic dynamic was an infantile wish to get inside a woman; he was naked inside the raincoat, thereby sharing her death. The sacrifice of his male body was the means to that end. The candles represented her execution pyre, the noose introduced excitement with the real risk of death. This tragic and extreme case illustrates the interplay between sado-masochistic and oral incorporative impulses and the coexistence of one or more fantasies during a pre-suicidal state.

This interplay of fantasies is particularly remarkable during the turbulent, fluctuating time of adolescence (see Ch. 18). Adolescents who are dominated by pre-genital needs and have had difficulty in separating from their parents may blame their sexual bodies for the incestuous guilt they feel over intrusive wishes. These adolescents believe that punishment of their body by killing it is the only way to relieve them of their guilt.

A fourth fantasy is the *elimination fantasy*. In the elimination fantasy, which is seen particularly in adolescence, there are similar conflicts between pubertal sexuality and the unresolved pre-oedipal needs. Laufer

& Laufer (1984) have drawn attention to the way in which adolescents, as well as adults, may experience their bodies as a source of madness when unacceptable regressive infantile wishes are felt to be located in their sexually maturing body which then seems confusing, alien, and threatening. The self in their suicide fantasies 'survives', paradoxically, by killing a body that is driving them mad. Although there are likely to be sado-masochistic aspects, the predominant feeling is relief that a threat has been disposed of, as a violent individual feels after beating off what he believed to be an attack on his life.

In the elimination fantasy, the body is experienced as a destroyer. In some cases, it threatens to destroy sanity, while in other cases the body threatens to kill the self. The mechanism is similar to that seen in paranoid cases, with its reliance upon splitting aspects of the self and projecting them into others. But for the suicidal patient with an elimination fantasy, a split-off body is the object upon which is projected murderous impulses in such a way that the 'me' self then feels that his 'not me' body is occupied by an assassin (Maltzburger & Buie 1980).

What distinguishes this suicide fantasy from others is that the surviving self is motivated less by malicious intent, as in the revenge and punishment fantasies, than by primitive self-preservative instincts. The body is not an object of sadistic attack by the self, nor is the self preoccupied with revenge upon others.

The internal dynamics are similar to those of the individual who feels ensnared in the core complex to the extent that he believes his life is at risk and reacts with self-preservative violence. In the psychotic life and death struggle contained in the elimination fantasy, the only thing that matters to the 'surviving self' is the elimination of the 'killer' body to avoid total annihilation. In this fantasy, suicide is conceived of as killing the 'assassin body' before it kills the 'me' self. Suicide is enacted in self defence.

Case study 12.4   An elimination psychosis

A 19-year-old boy was tortured by unacceptable perverse fantasies during a pre-suicide state. In a session, as the tension created by suicidal thoughts reached the breaking point, he shouted, 'I have got these thoughts. [He tapped the top of his head.] Up here. I can't get rid of them. They are driving me mad. I just want to get a gun, put it right here [he pushed his index finger into the top of his head] and blast it out. Pow!'

A fifth fantasy is the *dicing-with-death fantasy*. The patient who is compelled to dice with death actively puts his body, or a symbolic representative of it, at risk in order to both attract and attack the primary object. This may take obvious forms, such as compulsive gambling, or driving whilst drunk. It may be structured and socially sanctioned in activities such as parachuting and mountaineering or motor-racing, or involve various kinds of delinquency and sexual deviancy. Whatever the risk-taking activity, it should alert the clinician to the fact that the patient may enter a pre-suicide state, and careful attention should be given to the fantasies which are being gratified. Obviously, many risk-takers do not lose touch with reality and do not exceed the limits of their bodies, their equipment or their environment. Nevertheless, because they maintain a delicate balance between failure and triumph, changes in their internal state can alter that balance with fatal results.

Case study 12.5   The reckless driver

A patient who had numerous car accidents assumed that others should look out for him. He saw no need to drive within speed limits. He was, in Freud's terms, 'the exception'; that is, someone who had unjustly suffered enough as a child and felt he had a right to a fantasised mother he had never had – an omnipotent mother represented by fate and other drivers who would anticipate his behaviour and protect him from any danger. By putting himself at risk, he hoped to arouse anxiety in others, especially his analyst, and provoke them to rescue him and make him safe and secure. But this attitude towards his body, a body that he did not value enough to protect, represented an identification with the neglectful mother, as well as his condemnation of her. There is a strong sado-masochistic dynamic in both passive submission to fate, on the one hand, and actively flaunting the risk-taking, on the other.

IMPLICATIONS FOR THE THERAPIST

The principal danger for the therapist working with suicidal clients lies in minimising this pre-suicidal state or missing it altogether. The 'dicing-with-death' syndrome is built upon minimising the risk of failure and heightening the excitement at the prospect of triumph. The therapist may get caught up in the excitement of a gamble or of watching his patient 'have a go', and fail to see the more hidden excitement in the revengeful use of failure. On the other hand, in over-reacting to anxiety and taking responsibility for the patient's body, the therapist may gratify in the transference the patient's wish to shift the responsibility for his body from himself to the analyst, and thereby make the analyst the executioner (Asch 1980). The therapist's active intervention to prohibit risk-taking may also reinforce the patient's passivity and, as a consequence, raise his anxiety.

The central danger in every pre-suicide state is contained within the suicide fantasy. There are of course exceptions, but we are stressing the priority of understanding the suicide fantasy and of conveying this understanding to the patient as the principal way of defusing their need to act out the fantasy.

The ten danger signals

The case of a patient whom we shall call Mr Adams will serve to illustrate many of the danger signals which can be recognised during the pre-suicide state.

Case study 12.6   The suicidal businessman who 'got on with it'

Mr Adams had interrupted his analysis in an optimistic frame of mind to go to Edinburgh, his home town, to try to generate business for his failing company. Business had not gone well during the first two weeks. He could not face his old friends. On a Sunday afternoon, he felt lonely and suicidal and telephoned his wife in London, hoping she would express sympathy and fly out to join him. Instead she complained about his using suicide to blackmail her. She could not stand his threats any more and told him to get on with it if he was going to do it. At first Mr Adams felt shattered, hurt, rejected and totally alone. However, once he decided to kill himself he felt great relief and calm. He took seventy 10-mg tablets of diazepam and lay down feeling at peace. As the pills took effect he felt he was drifting off into another dimension. There was a sense of oneness in another kind of existence. He was found by accident and taken to hospital.

In retrospect, it was possible to identify a number of danger signals during Mr Adams' recent therapy. The first was *a previous suicide attempt*. Mr Adam had tried to kill himself about three years earlier. Those who have attempted suicide once represent a 27-fold greater risk of subsequent successful suicide compared with the general population (Hawton & Fagg 1988). Until the patient becomes aware of his original suicide fantasy, resolves the conflicts which were dealt with by an attempt to kill the body, mourns the psychic death of the body, and takes responsibility for the act in order to work through the guilt associated with having abandoned the body to a homicidal ego, the body will still be at risk to another lethal attack and suicide will remain a secret weapon, a trump card which may be played whenever the original conflicts re-emerge.

A second danger signal is the *propensity to deal with internal conflict via action*. Mr Adams played the horses whenever he became depressed. He sought to be the favourite son of fate. It was fate, not Mr Adams, which resolved problems. The patient who habitually deals with internal conflicts via external action will be more vulnerable to acting on a suicidal impulse when he is unable to make use of the activity that provides relief. In this case, Mr Adams had gambled away all of his money – half a million pounds. Loan sharks were pressuring him.

The third danger signal is a *recently experienced failure*. Mr Adams had recently lost several important clients. Many suicidal patients suffer from poor self-esteem, are severely self-critical and feel themselves to be failures. An actual failure, for example getting sacked or failing an examination, is a danger signal because it is experienced as confirmation by the outside world of what the patient has always felt about himself. Hope for rescue from outside is lost. The persecutory self has irrefutable evidence from outside of inner badness or worthlessness.

A fourth danger signal is the *withdrawal from others into the body*. When Mr Adams arrived for his first session, he was dishevelled, unshaven, withdrawn and lethargic. Mr Adams' withdrawal from others and neglect of his body point to a shift from acting out conflicts with others, to acting them out with his body.

A fifth danger signal is an *actual or attempted suicide by a parent or a close relative*. Two months before Mr Adams' suicide attempt, his mother had tried to kill herself by taking a massive overdose. Actual or attempted suicide by a parent or close relative may well precipitate a suicide attempt by a spouse, son or daughter. In Mr Adams' case, his mother's unsuccessful attempt on her life increased his guilt because he had ignored her explicit warnings that she would kill herself. His fear of her increased as well. He made a significant verbal slip when telling his analyst of his mother's suicide attempt: 'My mother tried to kill myself'. This was the mother/killer with which his body was now identified.

A sixth danger signal is the attempt to *blackmail with suicide*. Judging from his wife's response, it appears that there was at least an explicit suggestion of suicide to blackmail her into rescuing him. This is a danger signal familiar to all working with suicidal patients, but one that may not be taken seriously enough. A professional may well react negatively to the sadistic and manipulative aspects of the blackmail and dismiss the patient, as did Mr Adams' wife, with near fatal results.

In fact, it is difficult for therapists and relatives to avoid being placed in a double bind. Threats of blackmail may arise before a holiday break, when the patient is having to separate from his therapist and cope without his support. Paraphrasing Asch (1980), implicit or explicit blackmail has this message: 'Unless you see me more often or cancel your holiday I will kill myself. I will commit suicide because you failed me. It will be your fault. You will have driven me to it. You will have killed me'. The danger in giving in to this demand is that it will endorse the fantasy that someone else can completely take over responsibility for the patient's body, and in so doing sanction the abdication of responsibility for his actions. The worker will have to find ways of making this aspect of the fantasy clear to the patient, especially his wish to deny his own violence towards his body and the sadistic use of it against others.

On the other hand, the suicidal individual may experience the practitioner's *refusal* to satisfy these demands as a rejection, as though abandoning them to die. This is why blackmail must always be taken seriously. Beneath the sado-masochistic dynamic may lie a terror that the patient no longer feels safe in his own hands and is really asking for protection against himself.

A seventh danger signal is *consent or collusion between the patient and others in a suicidal fantasy*. An experience of rejection or a feeling of having been abandoned or dismissed, especially when it comes from someone who is valued, may be the precipitating factor in the actual attack on the body during the pre-suicidal state. It was after his wife refused to come to him, and in effect told him to get on with his plan to kill himself, that Mr Adams took an overdose. As Straker (1958) points out, 'A decisive factor in a successful suicide attempt appears to be the implied consent or unconscious collusion between the patient and the person most involved in the psychic struggle'.

Those working with suicidal individuals are vulnerable to being provoked or subtly led into attitudes and reactions which are experienced by the individual as rejection or collusion in the suicidal fantasy. This is what happened when Mr Adams told of his plan to go to Edinburgh. During his therapy, there had been signs of improvement in his appearance, attitude and life outside the session. Therapeutic work had focused on such danger signals as his gambling, his earlier suicide attempt, and his mother's attempt on her life. The therapist's mistake was that he let him go. Why?

It later became apparent that in Mr Adams' therapy the analyst had failed to recognise a shift in the balance of power between two suicide fantasies, with near fatal consequences. After his mother's attempt on her life, which he experienced as an attack on *his* life, Mr Adams developed an elimination fantasy. The aim of this first suicide fantasy was to escape the assassin-mother by identifying her with his body and then killing that body. The analyst was alerted to the existence of the elimination fantasy by its enactment in Mr Adams' neglect of his body, slovenly dress and poor hygiene. In this way, the analyst was able to bring Mr Adams' elimination fantasy into the analysis.

However, a second suicide fantasy that Mr Adams could merge with an idealised, asexual, omnipotently gratifying mother became a delusional conviction. Mr Adams believed that this fantasy of merging with his mother, which developed out of the first elimination fantasy, could be actualised once the assassin-mother, now identified with his body, had been killed. This belief motivated Mr Adams to plan his suicide. He became calm and optimistic because he now had a secret solution to his conflicts. The merging fantasy escaped detection because it was accompanied by apparent improvement.

As is well known, an eighth danger signal is the formation of a *suicide plan*. The wish to die and the accompanying suicide fantasy may wax and wane in the patient's consciousness. The formation of a suicide plan, that is, the scheme for carrying out the suicide fantasy, heralds the acute pre-suicide state. The suicide fantasy may include a method of killing the body, but the development of a suicide plan includes the details of time and place. Pills, a weapon or equipment may be collected. The attention to detail will vary, but any evidence of a plan should be taken seriously.

However, secrecy is often an important ingredient, and evidence of a suicide plan may be hard to discern. Attention to the patient's state of mind or feelings about himself may lead to an important clue. There is frequently a kind of inner peace that accompanies the formation of a suicide plan. Any sudden change in the patient's affective state towards a relaxation or calm, rather than necessarily being an indication of improvement, should alert the practitioner that the patient may have formulated a suicide plan. From a technical point of view, the worker should try to elicit the details of the plan and bring it into the open. These details will illuminate the suicide fantasy.

Mr Adams' depression lifted as he implemented the details of his suicide plan. He collected Valium tablets, returned to his birthplace and deceived others about his intentions by appearing more sociable and optimistic. He was, in fact, in the midst of a narcissistic regression sustained by the prospect of imminently fulfilling his merging suicide fantasy. As far as the patient is concerned, he is already at peace because he has crossed a rational barrier of self-preservation and now positively identifies the assassin (his body) and has no doubt about killing it. In a sense, a psychic homicide has already occurred.

Case study 12.7   The uncle and the rock

This critical stage in the pre-suicidal state was described by a 15-year-old boy who was with his uncle over the weekend before the uncle killed himself on the following Thursday. 'It was as though Uncle George was already dead on Sunday. He had tied his life to a rock with a piece of string. He threw his life out of the window on Sunday but the rock didn't hit the ground until Thursday'.

A ninth danger signal is the *loss of concern* both by the suicidal individual for others, and by others for him. One of the consequences of the suicidal individual's withdrawal from other people during a pre-suicidal phase, albeit behind a deceptive facade of sociability, is that the depressive affects, anxieties and fears are no longer communicated. As a result, those around the suicidal person may cease to respond to his needs and feelings as they ordinarily might do. Even if they have some intellectual awareness of the suicidal risk at this critical moment, the patient's narcissistic withdrawal cuts others off from any normal stimulus for empathic responses of alarm or concern (Tahka 1978).

A suicide attempt may now be imminent because the patient is emotionally cut off from his friends, relatives or professional helpers who would ordinarily protect him from himself. The signal for this danger is the sudden loss of subjective emotional concern for a depressed or suicidal patient by those most involved with him. For the professional, the loss of concern may manifest itself as a failure to recognise the importance of the therapeutic relationship in the patient's life. In letting Mr Adams interrupt his sessions, the therapist broke a cardinal rule of maintaining the centrality and reliability of the therapy. Thus, the therapist should carefully scrutinise any impulse to alter his interpretive stance or disrupt the consistency of the therapeutic structure unless, of course, hospitalisation is required.

A tenth danger signal is the appearance of *counter-transference reactions which may contribute to a loss of empathy or failure to perceive a psychic homicide*. This may manifest itself in many different ways. In Mr Adams' case, the therapist reacted to his narcissistic withdrawal by letting him temporarily leave his therapy and go to Edinburgh. Mr Adams then perceived the therapist as sanctioning and colluding with his suicide fantasies. The therapist's reaction, like that of Mr Adams' wife, was an essential ingredient in the fulfilment of the suicide plan.

A greater understanding of the danger signals may enable the therapist to play a more constructive role during a pre-suicide state. The danger is that if the signals are missed, the therapist may behave unwittingly as the hostile internal object from the past that the patient can only overcome through death.

THE ACUTE MANAGEMENT OF SUICIDE

It is hard to underestimate the value of the proper management of a suicide attempt. Even if the patient survives, it is a situation which offers the possibility of his either returning to the same vicious circle whence he came, or of helping him to move forward to something new. Whether or not the patient ends up in formal psychotherapy, the dynamics of this management bear careful study.

Many suicide attempts go undetected. The patient merely 'sleeps it off'. Sometimes relatives will allow this to happen. Their indifference may betoken their underlying animosity to the patient. When a general practitioner is called, even he too may decide that nothing needs to be done.

For the most part, however, the patient is referred to a casualty department where, with the exception of violent alcoholics, attempted suicides are among the least popular patients. Medical procedures, some of which are of very doubtful value, are accompanied by such comments as 'Why didn't you do it properly?' or 'Don't you think we've got better things to do with our time?' It is easy to condemn these attitudes, but in reality they represent a natural response to the patient's aggressive act. Some regard these procedures, particularly stomach wash-out, as a potential deterrent to future attempts, and certainly they are experienced by the patient as painful and humiliating, but it is doubtful if they do deter.

Case study 12.8   The stomach wash-out

A patient was reminded of a statement he had made when he took a previous overdose that he would not do it again because he could not stand a stomach wash-out. He was asked whether these thoughts went through his mind when taking the current overdose. His reply was that his intention had been that there would not be a wash-out this time. The stomach wash-out can be seen as an attempt by the staff to regain control of the patient's body, a control which the patient has taken from the medical profession in swallowing the tablets which usually his doctor had prescribed.

Where there is a medical reason for the patient to be admitted, he is fortunate. Having attacked his body, to be allowed, forced even, to regress and to have bodily needs placed first, may well be psychologically exactly what he needs. The hospital can act as a relatively neutral container for all of the patient's projections. What the patient does not need is contempt or disdain from the professional staff, hard as this is to avoid. Thus, supporting the staff of the acute medical wards who are dealing with suicide is an important part of the psychiatrist's work. Unfortunately, many patients are discharged or encouraged to discharge themselves without any psychological assessment, even though this is recommended by the Department of Health.

The assessment of the patient should take place as soon as possible after the patient has regained consciousness, because it offers an opportunity to begin therapy. If the therapist can be included in the original chaos and receives the basic raw projections immediately after the suicidal person regains consciousness, the need to repeat the suicidal act may be reduced. Once the process of repression and denial has started (possibly after the first night's dreamwork has been done), it will be necessary for the patient to recreate the same sado-masochistic relationship with the same vulnerability to suicide. Delay in identifying and owning suicide fantasies allows old defences to be re-erected, with the psychiatrist as an accomplice. As one woman put it, 'It is as though it was another woman who tried to kill herself last week'.

The assessment itself must have the following aims:

1. The identification of severe psychiatric illness in order to arrange appropriate treatment.
2. To let the patient know that his actions are taken seriously by the therapist, even if not by himself.
3. To establish the extent to which the patient can look inwards at the reasons for his actions. Surprisingly, this is often much easier for the patient in the disturbed state of mind immediately following a suicide attempt. A helpful technique to encourage this process is that of the 'action replay'. In this, the patient is encouraged to give a detailed

account of the events leading up to the day of the suicide, to the actual hour and then the minute. As the patient recalls each of these details of the acts, both he and the therapist are often given much more direct access to the affects and fantasies which motivated the act.

4. To encourage the patient to keep this access to unconscious processes open by offering both tentative interpretations and assuming that the patient will want psychotherapy. If the latter turns out not to be the case, little has been lost.

5. If possible, the patient should not be returned to the same sado-masochistic relationship from which he came. It is far safer to hand the patient over to the care of a willing neutral relative or friend. It is essential to impress upon this person the seriousness of what has happened. If no such suitable person can be found, it will be necessary to admit the patient to a psychiatric ward until such time as the therapist and patient feel it is safe to let him return to his partner or to living on his own. The general principle, as always, must be that the supportive matrix is sufficient to contain the patient's pathology.

Therapy should start as soon as possible. The appointment must be within a period of time that the patient can manage. It is crucial that the therapist stays alive in the patient's mind. In this acute phase, the promise of a session in two days may mean never: that is, too long for the patient to hold the therapist in his thinking. A central belief of the suicidal person is that he has the capacity to kill off all of his good objects. To offer him an appointment beyond his own time span, or with a person whom he has not met, will be perceived as both a further rejection and confirmation of his belief in his own destructiveness.

CONCLUSION

As to the outcome of therapy, let us return to the young woman whose personal account opened this chapter.

Case study 12.1   An autobiographical account of suicide (contd)

Any account of my life would have to place my 'suicide' at the centre. From childhood, everything led irrevocably towards this rapidly narrowing path, and everything since has led from it in an ever widening arch. If I was unlucky that nothing stopped the headlong momentum towards it, I was not lucky, but quite simply saved, because I had an interpreter to direct me from it. I hope this will not be a matter of chance for others.

FURTHER READING

Freud S 1917 Mourning and melancholia. Standard edition 14. Hogarth, London
Laufer M, Laufer M E 1984 Adolescence and developmental breakdown. Yale University Press, New Haven
Maltzberger J G, Buie D H 1980 The devices of suicide. International Review of Psycho-Analysis 7: 6-22

13. Psychotic disorders

M. Jackson

INTRODUCTION: CREDO, CAVEATS, PRINCIPLES

The subject of this chapter concerns an area of theory and practice which is so wide that very few people can write with authority on the whole field. Much of what we know about the psychopathology and psychoanalytic psychotherapy of psychotic patients derives from the work of psychoanalysts working in privately funded institutions in the United States and in private practice in Britain. A vast literature has arisen from such work in the United States, where there has long been considerable acceptance of the view that psychogenic factors play an important part in the aetiology of psychotic disorders; this is in contrast to the more biomedical approach that has prevailed in British psychiatry. Although the psychoanalytical approach is currently encountering difficulties in the United States, partly for economic and political reasons, it is generally accepted that this work has produced a rich legacy of experience and knowledge. In contrast, despite the fact that psychoanalysis has had a considerable (though not always acknowledged) impact on British psychiatry overall, it is widely regarded as having little relevance to the proper treatment of psychotic patients.

The contribution in this chapter is for those psychiatrists and other concerned health professionals working in the public hospital service who wish to understand more of psychoanalytic ideas about psychotic states; who may perhaps use such information to bring a more psychodynamic perspective to inpatient units caring for psychotic patients; and who may be considering undertaking the individual psychotherapy of such patients within an in-, day-, or out-patient setting.

This chapter is about the need to listen to and understand the psychotic patient, and to respond to him in a psychotherapeutic manner. Without psychotherapeutic understanding, the psychotic patient may receive only superficial attention to such basic issues as panic, destructiveness, security and containment. With such understanding, important psychotherapeutic work becomes a possibility, and individual psychotherapy within a psychotherapeutically oriented general psychiatric ward can be achieved, even where resources are inadequate.

The chapter is divided into three sections – principles, theory and practice.This division is intended to provide a clear demarcation between the three different but related ways in which analytic understanding can help in the management of psychotic patients. Firstly, such understanding makes sense of that which is otherwise incomprehensible, and this is intellectually satisfying and reassuring for the psychiatrist; secondly, a general understanding of psychotic thinking can often usefully guide management; and finally, in selected cases psychotherapy can be undertaken with these patients.

In institutions in the United States with the special provision already mentioned impressive psychotherapy has been done, and many psychotic patients have been successfully treated. Important results have been achieved by modified psychotherapeutic techniques, and the work of Sechehaye (1951) and Rosen (1962), using a technique of dramatically entering the world of the patient's experience, has been particularly influential in informing the approach of many subsequent workers. Such techniques as inducing regressive states in psychotic patients, or playing an active part in attempting to repair deficiencies of early emotional provision, have had undoubted success in experienced hands; but they can only apply to a small fraction of the psychotic population, and their use in unskilled hands is not without risk. Idealising the psychosis, blaming the family or society, and uncritically accepting the patient's experiential reality and internal object relationships as being literally true, can lead to a collusive and anti-therapeutic relationship between patient and therapist.

Having worked for many years in a short-to-medium-stay acute psychiatric unit, the author's own experience has mostly been with first-attack and recurring psychotic disorders and severe personality disorders. Although the discussion shall in general be confined to these areas of personal experience, it is hoped that the chapter will have relevance to complementary therapeutic activities, such as art, music, drama and body awareness work, group and family therapy, and to the vital topics of rehabilitation and community care. Psychotherapy in chronic schizophrenia will be touched on, but the interested reader will be referred to major contributions in the literature (see Freeman 1988).

General statements about psychotic patients are suspect, but a few personal generalisations are made here in an attempt to provide a framework at the outset for the reader who will find many conflicting and sometimes contradictory views expressed in the literature.

Psychotic patients in general need to be treated in a hospital-based psychiatric context, and psychotherapeutic treatment must be on the basis of shared care and responsibility between the psychotherapist and the psychiatric team. Medication is usually essential, and should be prescribed by someone other than the psychotherapist if the patient is being seen for individual psychotherapy. The therapist should offer the patient a commitment of at least two years' treatment, not less than once weekly, and preferably more frequently. The couch should not be used whilst the patient remains in a regressed state.

The therapist should in principle avoid physical contact with his patient, and should confine his interventions to talking. However, when regression is severe enough to require admission, the patient may respond more to tone of voice than to the content of words, and physical contact with nurses and other professionals may prove both inevitable and desirable. To understand the most helpful form this might take requires nursing skills of a very high order. The psychotic patient is frightened of emotional closeness and is often terrified of losing control of his explosive feelings, of losing his sense of bodily integration and identity as a person. His dread of separation and all the pain that this brings is so great that it releases wishes for fusion, but this leads to fantasies of invasion, and a consequent dread of being invaded. His capacity to form a stable ego in psychotherapy is therefore acquired only very slowly and painfully, and he easily becomes confused with other people. The psychotherapeutic transference may make it possible to resolve this confusion for the first time.

Because the psychotic individual uses projective defensive mechanisms to protect himself from the perils of attachment (which has proved to be so catastrophic in his experience in the distant past) he is profoundly distrustful, and, in the case of the clinically paranoid patient, intensely suspicious. He needs to discover in the therapist and therapeutic team, individuals who will remain consistent in their attitude of sympathetic enquiry and willingness to try to learn what are the mental mechanisms that he is using which would make his psychotic experience intelligible and meaningful.

Much has been written about the need to gain the patient's trust, to help him overcome his feeling of being a bad and dangerous person, and to help him feel accepted and acceptable. Such humane attitudes should be a normal part of all psychiatric practice, but the psychotic requires in addition a more profound understanding of mechanisms that have been used, possibly since infancy, to prevent the recurrence of catastrophe, and of the complexities of the secondary gratifications that may have arisen from adopting a psychotic way of thinking. To try to make good, without such understanding, what the patient (with or without justification) perceives as deficiencies of parental, particularly maternal, provision, can often lead to disappointment and failure.

The essential points made so far may be summarised as follows. Psychotherapy with psychotics must be on the base of shared care; there should be no deliberate induction of regression; patients are suspicious for good defensive reasons; smothering the patient with love won't work.

The advent of anti-psychotic drugs has transformed the lives of patients suffering from schizophrenia and related psychotic disorders, very largely to their great benefit. Biomedical research is beginning to identify the disorders of genetics, brain structure and chemistry that occur in a proportion of such patients, and to consider their nature, origins and relevance as causal factors. The contribution of psychoanalysis to the understanding and treatment of such disorders remains controversial, at least in the current climate of psychiatric opinion, and the introduction of psychoanalytic concepts into psychiatric practice remains problematic (see Lucas 1985, Freeman 1988).

Whilst the value of psychoanalytically derived treatment modes (such as group and family therapy and the principles of the therapeutic community) is widely accepted, no such consensus exists in regard to the place of individual psychoanalytically oriented psychotherapy. Segal (1981) is of the opinion that whilst formal psychoanalysis is the treatment of choice for the rare case in which all conditions are favourable, the main contribution of psychoanalysis in this sphere lies in research, understanding of psychotic mechanisms and even future methods of prevention. London (1983) has pointed out that psychoanalysis has made rich contributions to the understanding of schizophrenia, and conversely the study of schizophrenia has enriched psychoanalytic theory. However, he points out that very few psychoanalysts (including himself) have had much direct experience of long-term psychotherapy with schizophrenic patients, or have encountered the wide variety of psychotic patients familiar to the general psychiatrist. Conversely, very few psychiatrists have had much experience in applying psychoanalytic concepts to the study and treatment of hospitalised psychotic patients.

Many psychiatrists are of the opinion that psychodynamic psychotherapy has little or no place in the treatment of psychotic patients; others consider that it can be extremely harmful to such patients and is thus contraindicated. It is certainly true that inexpert psychotherapy in the wrong setting may harm some patients, and safeguards are required to avoid the dangers inherent in the experience. Such safeguards include a sufficiently thorough assessment of the case both from a general psychiatric and psychodynamic point of view; the provision of an appropriate hospital milieu with an understanding of the psychodynamic approach as a context within which the patient can be effectively contained and appropriately treated; and adequate supervision for the inexperienced therapist.

Some reading about the subject is probably essential, and many helpful texts are available (Arieti 1974, Kernberg 1980). Perhaps the most generally known and influential is the early work of Laing (1960, 1961), who conveyed the understandability and meaningfulness of the experience and behaviour of the psychotic patient at a time when the biological approach appeared to be threatening the psychodynamic. An account of personal treatment is described vividly by Green (1964); psychoanalytic contributions are to be found in Searles (1965), Segal (1964), Rosenfeld (1965, 1987), Schulz (1983), Pao (1979), Joseph (1986), Ogden (1980) and Grotstein (1983).

Although to undertake the psychotherapy of a psychotic patient is a major decision, it should be recognised that there is a very wide array of conditions included in the category of psychotic states, some of which are of good prognosis, eminently suitable for psychodynamic psychotherapy and entail no significant risk.

It must also be kept firmly in mind that the psychotherapist is in a particularly privileged position, in that if the patient is unable or unwilling to use his services, the psychotherapist need simply announce that he cannot help. The psychiatrist is in a much more difficult position because he is likely to have great pressure put on him to do something helpful for the patient. This can provoke both rational and irrational activity on the part of the psychiatrist. Rational responses lead to appropriate psychosocial and biological interventions that will actually help the patient. Irrational activity may be provoked when the psychiatrist becomes the recipient of the patient's projections. As will be discussed later, projective identification is a primitive form of defensive (and sometimes offensive) activity used universally, but particularly by psychotic individuals. When this mechanism is active, the psychiatrist and other carers may be put under great pressure by the patient, who is unconsciously attempting to recruit them into some inner drama. To understand the nature of this drama we must now turn to a consideration of theory.

THEORY

A comprehensive and convincing theory of schizophrenia does not yet exist, based either on biomedical or psychodynamic models. The most important contribution of psychodynamic theory to psychosis is the account provided by the *phenomenology* of the illness, which is seen in terms of a regression to primitive modes of thinking. It is important to emphasise that the psychoanalytical account of psychosis is not so much an aetiological theory as a descriptive account that makes it possible to understand the world of the psychotic and to communicate meaningfully with him about his experiences.

PSYCHOANALYTIC THEORIES OF SCHIZOPHRENIA

In 1898, Kraepelin divided mental illness into two main categories: dementia praecox, and manic-depressive psychosis. This work provided a basis for the attempt to understand the nature of the disturbance of thinking, affective life and contact with reality that characterises psychotic disorders. Bleuler, in 1911, coined the term 'schizophrenia', and described its psychodynamics in terms of ambivalence, loosening of associations, and autism of thinking processes. He investigated the disturbed view that the psychotic patient has of himself and others, for which he used the terms 'transitivism' and 'appersonation', phenomena that have since been superseded by the concepts of projective and introjective identifications.

Sigmund Freud

Freud made his first contribution to the study of psychosis in 1896, when he published an account of a case of chronic paranoia (Freud 1896). Later, he produced his interpretation of the autobiography of Judge Schreber (Freud 1911b), who suffered from a severe recurrent paranoid psychosis. Freud concluded that schizophrenia is a form of narcissistic neurosis, and that it is not amenable to psychoanalytic treatment, because the patient is unable to form a working transference with the therapist.

Adult mental disorders often show features that might be regarded as normal in a small child, such as denial of reality, regressive behaviour or the confluence of 'primitive' levels of function with more mature ones. Freud attempted to explain these processes in terms of a model of mental development based on the ideas of the neurologist, Hughlings Jackson. He applied Jackson's model of the heirarchical evolution of brain function to mental organisation, envisaging a series of developmental levels from the least to the most developed, an evolution that can be reversed under conditions of stress, leading to a dissolution of the more advanced mental functions and re-emergence of the less advanced ones. From this model, Freud developed his theories of fixation points in the course of development which, through regression, may be reactivated at a later period under stress. He saw in psychosis an extreme form of the regression seen in neurotic states, resulting in the domination of consciousness by the primary processes of thinking (as occurs normally in dreaming) over the secondary (rational) processes. The delusion, in Freud's view, is 'a patch over a rent in the ego'. The stresses that set the regressive process in motion are the anxiety and guilt generated by instinctual desires which cannot be accomodated by the fragile ego of the psychotic. The individual then turns away from the external world in an attempt to reduce these stresses, but then confronts an inner world filled with primitive feelings that are equally overwhelming.

Many of the features of psychosis are illuminated by this model, in particular the loss of ego boundaries with impairment of the capacity to differentiate self from other, inner world from outer reality, and cognitive disorder based on the revival of perceptual and sensori-motor precursors of mature conceptual thinking. Other ego functions may be lost in this psychotic regressive process, or 'de-differentiation of ego functions'. This includes loss of the capacity to distinguish between thought and perception, perception and memory, past and present, and conceptual thinking in general. Thoughts may be expressed in hallucinations and in actions, people may be mis-identified, the self confused with others.

Such concretely expressed preoccupations tend to refer to the person's mental representation of his own body (the 'body image').

Case study 13.1   Psychosis as a metaphorical statement

A young woman was found wandering in a public garden in a confused state, pouring perfume into flowers. Acutely psychotic, she was admitted to hospital where it soon became clear that the psychotic attack had been precipitated by sexual guilt, and her action was a metaphorical statement, as in a dream, although not recognisable by her as such, that (like Lady Macbeth) she was in despair that perfume could ever sweeten her feelings.

This sort of 'pre-verbal' thinking is action-centred, concrete, and spatially-oriented, as opposed to the thought-centred, metaphorical thinking of the adult, taking place in a non-Newtonian 'inner world'. Rey (1979), referring to the work of Piaget on the precursors of conceptual thinking in the child, describes the essential features of this schizoid mode of thinking as centred on the dominating framework of an inside and an outside, containment and container.

Freud's dictum that the ego is first and foremost a body ego is seen as most profoundly accurate, as in the following patient:

Case study 13.2   'The ego is a body ego'

A chronic schizophrenic woman was unable to deal with her sense of personal badness by verbal conceptual thinking. She experienced such feelings as being bad and persecuting 'things' inside her own body. When her feelings of guilt became active, she would suddenly swallow perfume or, if this was not available, liquid detergent.

When a psychotic patient appears to hallucinate for no apparent reason the answer is often to be found in his feelings about his immediate circumstances:

Case study 13.3   The psychotic's sensitivity to his environment

The author was asked to see a disturbed schizophrenic patient who had been seen by several psychiatrists in the previous days, without effective contact being achieved. The therapist arrived late, the patient was brought in and as he sat down he suddenly stared at the window. A little later he asked the therapist if he had seen the red aircraft flash past the window (which in reality opened onto a courtyard). Exploration made it possible to understand that this was a communication, in concrete psychotic terms, of his thought that the therapist would rush into his life, race through a brief interview (as he felt that the therapist's frustrated predecessors had done) and quickly disappear, leaving nothing of significance or help for him.

Melanie Klein

Klein's developments of Freud's theories were highly original, and though in some respects still controversial, brought new understanding about psychotic processes and a method of psychotherapy that is much more actively interpretative than, for example, that advocated by the 'Washington' school of psychoanalysis (Pao 1979, Searles 1965). Klein believed that a rudimentary ego of some sort exists from the beginning, an ego that relates at first only to parts of the mother, is capable of experiencing severe anxiety and that deploys primitive mental defence mechanisms (see Stern 1985). Beginning with detailed study of manic-depressive psychosis and schizoid conditions, on the basis of her work with very young children, Klein concluded that psychotic conditions are partly the expression of a revival of mental mechanisms that have been relegated to a minor role in the mental economics of the healthy adult, revived to deal with the intense anxiety that has its roots in the panic states of early infancy. She called these primitive states of mind and defences 'psychotic' anxieties and mechanisms, and regarded the transference processes that emerge in the course of psychotherapy as repetitions of real and fantasised experiences of infancy (for a contrary view, see Freeman 1988). Concepts such as splitting, projective identification, idealisation and the manic defences are indispensible to the understanding and treatment of psychotic states. Klein's model of progress from the paranoid-schizoid to the depressive position, and its use in understanding the schizophrenic and affective psychoses, has brought new treatment possibilities and further theoretical developments.

Projective identification

Perhaps the most influential of Klein's concepts is that of projective identification. This is a primitive mental defence mechanism, mobilised to deal with mental pain, and operative from early infancy throughout life.

Klein regarded projective identification as a universally held unconscious fantasy, an omnipotent belief that it is possible to deal with unwanted feelings ('parts of the self') by a form of primitive denial which attributes the rejected aspects to something or someone else. The primitive quality of this form of mental functioning determines that the process is conceived in spatially-oriented terms, of expulsion, projection or 'putting into' the object. The consequence is that perception, and conception, of subject and object is distorted, and the ego function of reality-testing and the structure of the 'ego boundary' is weakened. In normal development, these distortions are corrected ('transmuted', Bion 1962) by the *mother's* ego; she allows the small child to use her as a receptacle where painful and complex feelings can be differentiated and later integrated. Using this benign projective identification, the infant builds up a picture of a 'good' gratifying mother and a 'bad' frustrating mother which, as development proceeds towards the depressive position, will eventually be brought together. Klein saw in psychosis a persistence of untransmuted projective identification in which splitting implicit in the above account is excessive, and the patient lacks a secure identity or sense of ownership of loving and aggressive feelings. This may manifest itself as a psychotic transference, as Segal (1981) shows in her discussion of Freud's belief that the psychotic patient was inaccessible to psychotherapy because he could not develop a 'workable' transference:

'Far from not developing a transference, the psychotic develops an almost immediate and usually violent transference to the analyst. The difficulty with the psychotic's transference is not its absence but its character – the difficulty both to observe it and to stand it. The apparent lack of transference or its peculiar nature when it manifests itself is due to the fact that the psychotic transference is based primarily on projective identification. By projective identification, I mean here the patient's omnipotent phantasy that he can get rid of unwanted parts of himself into the analyst. This kind of transference is both violent and brittle. The psychotic tries to project into the analyst his terror, his badness, his confusion, his fragmentation and, having done this projection, he may perceive the analyst as a terrifying figure from whom he may want to cut himself off immediately; hence the brittleness of the transference situation. The violence of his projective identification gives rise to a variety of phantasies and feelings. The patient may feel completely confused with the analyst and feel he is losing such identity as he still possesses; he may feel trapped, or that the analyst may invade him in turn. His experience of the transference is very concrete, as is his experience of the analyst's interpretation. When he is in the state of projective identification, and the analyst starts interpreting, the patient is apt to experience it as projective identification in reverse, that is, to feel that the analyst is now putting into him, the patient, the analyst's own unwanted parts and driving him mad. This concreteness of experience, in which he feels he is omnipotently changing the analyst and the analyst concretely and omnipotently changes him, is a technical point of utmost importance. It is essential for the analyst to understand that, when he interprets anxiety, the patient may feel that he is in fact attacking him, or if he interprets a patient's sexual feelings, the patient may experience it concretely as the analyst's sexual advances, towards him or her.' (Segal 1981)

PSYCHOSIS, BORDERLINE, NEUROSIS: DIFFERENTIATING FEATURES

The neurotic person has acquired sufficient maturity to have a stable and continuing sense of self and a firm grasp of outer reality. His conflicts are those of incompatible wishes aroused within important relationships: his problems of guilt, of maintenance of self-esteem, of envy and jealousy are the daily concern of all psychotherapists. Life for the psychotic, although requiring him to master similar problems, is quite different and usually very much worse. Since his inner world of phantasy is constantly threatening to distort his perception of external reality, his whole existence and sense of self may be constantly at risk. His primitive mental defence mechanisms originally deployed early in life to make pain and anxiety bearable in the interests of survival, make him vulnerable, under certain stressful conditions, to confusion, disturbed sense of personal identity and body image integrity, severe anxiety sometimes amounting to terror, and a waking experience that normal people may experience only in nightmares or under the influence of certain drugs.

Case study 13.4 Psychosis as a waking dream

A patient admitted in an acutely agitated and confused state became extremely violent when approached by hospital staff. Physical restraint and forcible medication gradually relieved his confusion to a level where he was able to talk about his hallucinatory and delusional experience. He was being menaced by a giant rat that had been sent from the star Vega and he believed that the staff were handing him over to this monster.

Subsequent exploration made it possible to understand the nature of this experience, the meaning of the content, and of the conflicts and life events that had precipitated the psychotic attack. The episode demonstrated a temporary total loss of the ego function of reality testing and of cognitive abilities. His thinking was concrete, dream-like, and was expressed in a symbolic drama of crime and punishment which for him was a real event. He was visualising his thoughts which had become externalised and perceptualised, and using mechanisms of splitting, projective and introjective identification.

The hallucinatory rat could be thought of as the fantastic embodiment of a persecutory superego figure, created originally by the projection of his own unintegrated infantile aggressive attacks (oral-biting, anal-spoiling) on his 'bad' mother. This formulation threw light on his current conflicted life situation, in which he was faced with the fear that his wife had discovered his long concealed homosexual desires. The complexity of the confusion he was experiencing is illustrated by the observation that at times he wondered whether the Vega inhabitants may have sent the rat in order to test out whether he would decide that it was a real rat or a hallucination, a thought that could be considered as the projection of his sane capacity for reality testing.

This process of the transformation of the pre-psychotic preoccupations into the primary process expression of the delusional content of the psychotic phase has been described in detail by Freeman (1988).

Psychotic confusion is not always painful, as is the case in defensive, wish-fulfilling delusions.

Case study 13.5   Delusions as wish-fulfilments

A psychotic young man spent many days wandering about the ward with an expression of blissful contentment on his face. He was quite inaccessible to the ward staff and it was only on later exploration that it emerged that he believed that he was a beautiful young girl being looked at admiringly by an elderly woman. His mother had died in his infancy, and this provided a clue to understanding the complex psychotic identification that had overtaken him. He had unconsciously created a fantasy, a wishful delusion, in order to deny the pain of separation and loss, a state of mind in which his wishes for 'symbiotic' fusion with his mother as a beautiful young girl, had come true.

This primitive level of functioning does not usually overwhelm the whole personality, with total loss of contact with reality. Except in the case of profound regressive episodes, some degree of intact functioning is preserved, and what is observed clinically is a confluence or confusion of normal and pathological thinking. It is thus possible to conceive of a normal part of the personality in the psychotic individual and a psychotic part of the functioning of a less disturbed person (Bion 1957). This concept has proved extremely useful, involving a form of thinking described by Rey (1979) as 'the schizoid mode of being', and underlying the pathology of the 'borderline' (Jackson & Pines 1986, Jackson & Tarnopolsky 1990; see Ch. 14), or 'psychotic character' (Frosch 1964, 1983). It is the existence of the sane part of the personality that allows the psychotherapist to hope to do useful work with either borderline or psychotic patients, by inviting the borderline patient to take an interest in his 'madness' and the psychotic to discover his 'sanity'.

It is not always possible to differentiate the borderline from the psychotic except through a trial of psychotherapy. Frosch (1983) contends that the borderline patient may have the experience of disturbed contact with reality, amounting to derealisation and depersonalisation, but does not show the clear impairment of reality-testing characteristic of the psychotic.

Case study 13.6   Psychotherapy as a trial of reality-testing

A young man felt compelled to measure the height of his buttocks from the ground every morning on waking. He feared that he was changing into a girl of short stature.

Such a fear of changing gender is a not infrequent precursor to an acute psychotic attack, often associated with compulsive masturbation or sexual promiscuity as a form of reassurance. It is also encountered in young borderline patients, in the form of a fear of discovering that they are homosexual. Despite the ominous nature of the fear of the patient just mentioned, psychotherapeutic exploration confirmed that his capacity for

reality-testing was actually intact, and that he did not have a truly
delusional potential.

Psychotherapeutic exploration enabled him to recognise his fears of his
passive desires and the metaphorical nature of his preoccupations. His
feeling about reality had been disturbed, but his capacity to test it was
essentially intact, and his preoccupation could be identified as an
overvalued idea rather than a true delusion.

Such fears about identity can lead to stimulus seeking, which in the case
of the borderline typically takes the form of self-cutting or the ingestion of
stimulant drugs. This can be understood as an attempt to ward off
depersonalisation or, in the case of the psychotic, to allay the panic
associated with the experience of the impending danger of fusion with
another person, or of attempting to create a sense of distance from the
object who is felt to be threatening to invade and control him. Inexplicable
negativistic behaviour may sometimes prove to have the same significance,
i.e. a last-ditch defence against fears of invasion.

MANIC-DEPRESSIVE PSYCHOSIS

Freud's crucial discovery in his 1917 paper on psychotic depression
(melancholia) was the recognition that the self-reproaches of the
melancholic derive from aggressive wishes re-directed from their true
target, the 'bad' (frustrating, disappointing) object, onto the self. He saw
this process as an abnormal form of mourning, a pathological response to
loss, and constructed his model of the superego to account for the severity
of nature of the underlying guilt (see Pedder 1982). In mania, Freud
argued, through fusion of the ego and superego, the subject makes a
pathological escape from this inner persecution. Freud believed that, as in
schizophrenia, these 'narcissistic neuroses' were not accessible to
psychotherapy because the patient was so self-preoccupied that he was
incapable of forming a working transference. Abraham (1924), who
regarded the pathology as having its deepest roots in a developmental
failure in the weaning period of infancy (where 'hate paralyses love'), did
not share Freud's pessimism, and analysed a small number of typical, and
quite severe, manic-depressive patients with impressive results.

Klein developed Abraham's views, and in 1934 presented a definitive
paper, 'A contribution to the psychogenesis of manic-depressive states'
(Klein 1950), in which she formulated her concept of the depressive
position and the manic defences which are mobilised in the attempt to
relieve the guilt that is aroused by the destructive fantasies of the
melancholic. She later elaborated the concept of the depressive position as
a developmental stage evolving from the paranoid-schizoid position which
predominates in the first year of life. It represents a crucial maturational
advance to a 'position' where the child has come to recognise his mother

as a whole person, good and bad, feels guilt of a potentially constructive kind about his aggressive feelings towards the 'bad' frustrating mother, and begins to experience reparative wishes to make good the damage he fears he has caused her. Difficulties around the stage of the depressive position may predispose to depressive illness or mania later in life.

Mania

Mania results from a pathological identification with a powerful, idealised object in unconscious fantasy, bringing an essentially delusional state of mind, a psychotic identification allowing the subject to feel full of life, power and excitement. This defensive denial is associated with attitudes of triumph over the helpful and needed person: contempt, devaluation and control (see Rosenfeld 1965, Jacobson 1967, Freeman 1988). In psycho-dynamic terms, the manic-depressive has reached a higher level of development and maturity than the schizoid, and the powerful reparative wishes that can so often be encountered in such patients attest to a creative potential, sometimes outstandingly fulfilled, usually tragically miscarrying.

Two types of depression

Klein's recognition of the severity of destructive processes in these conditions was accompanied by the discovery that the guilt aroused in this state is of a very different, and potentially very constructive sort. The concern for the victim of the destructive attacks, and the associated reparative wishes, introduce a different and healthy form of depression akin to mourning. Winnicott recognised the momentous significance of these discoveries:

'Melanie Klein's work has altered psychiatric classification by separating out two kinds of depression the one from the other. One kind represents an achievement in emotional development almost synonymous with the acquisition of a capacity to be responsible, or a capacity to feel a sense of guilt, and the other (with depersonalisation and other features that could be referred to as "schizoid") represents a failure initiated at an early stage, before the establishment of what Melanie Klein calls the "depressive position" in emotional development'. (Winnicott 1965, p. 129)

Winnicott emphasised the essentially healthy nature of this potentially constructive and growth-promoting depression:

'The depression is a healing mechanism; it covers the battleground as with a mist, allowing for a sorting out at reduced rate, giving time for all possible defences to be brought into play, and for a working-through, so that eventually there can be a spontaneous recovery. Clinically, depression (of this sort) tends to lift, a well-known psychiatric observation.' (Winnicott 1965, p. 275)

Klein's model of progress from the paranoid-schizoid position to the depressive position allows comprehension of the dynamic nature of mixed, or schizo-affective states, of the not uncommon appearance of paranoid features in affective psychoses, and of the frequent change of clinical picture over time, an event that often requires a revision of diagnosis.

Rosenfeld's views

Klein's views (Mitchell 1985) have been consolidated and extended by her followers (Spillius 1988). The most significant contribution to the psychoanalytic understanding of affective psychosis has been that of Rosenfeld (1965) who gave a brief and concise account of the psychopathology and psychoanalytic treatment of depressive and manic-depressive patients. Acknowledging the important contributions of Fromm-Reichmann (see Cohen et al 1963) and Jacobson (1967), and drawing on his own wide experience, he made several observations which provide guidelines for the intending psychotherapist.

Rosenfeld pointed out that the manic-depressive patient forms intense transferences in the first session of psychoanalytic psychotherapy. These may at first be very positive, but are idealised and unstable; they quickly change when frustration is encountered, when the therapist may be regarded as bad, even persecuting, and dangerous acting-out or even suicide may ensue if this situation is not recognised. The patient's main anxiety is the intensity of his destructive impulses, of which he may have little conscious awareness, which threaten to damage or destroy the object on which he depends, originally the mother. These conflicts have their roots in early infancy, although life experience can have a negative or positive effect on subsequent development.

Rosenfeld contends that the more deeply depressed patient believes that he has killed and lost his loved object and that all attempts at restoration are useless, so that he gives himself up to complete despair. When therapy is undertaken, the patient may begin to have some hope, and uses methods of pressure and manipulation in order to invoke in the therapist, by projective identification, his anxiety about his destructive impulses and his despair. This can be understood as an unconscious attempt to test out whether the therapist can stand the feelings which he himself cannot stand, and help him understand and begin to deal with them.

In the manic phase, the patient ceases to try to make himself understood, and the therapist becomes the target of attacks with destructive motivation. The depressed patient may experience two essentially different mental states, both called 'depression', but with different dynamics and significance. The first state is characterised by guilt and despair. In the second he also feels guilty but tends to be paranoid. This is the melancholic state which Freud explained as reproaches towards the object turned against the self, the attack of a harsh and archaic superego. Subsequent development of superego theory has allowed more understanding of how the melancholic superego acquires such savage and relentless qualities, threatening the patient with death and destruction. Klein showed how the superego begins to form in early life, how it tends to be extremely severe, as the result of projection of the infant's own aggressive feelings into the frustrating 'bad' mother, and how it remains unmodified in the future depressive. The understanding and gradual modification of the melancholic superego is one of the main tasks confronting the psychotherapist.

Finally, Rosenfeld pointed out how in the manic phase there exists an identification with idealised objects, conferring a great sense of omnipotence. In this state, the patient triumphs over the needed object, both in outer reality and in his inner world, and acquires an exciting sense of superiority which tends to have an extremely sadistic quality. By treating the needed object with disparagement, depreciation, triumph and contempt, he overcomes his feelings of dependency and inferiority.

'CONTAINING' THE PSYCHOTIC PERSON

Prolonged contact with a psychotic patient is likely to arouse intense and conflicting feelings in the person trying to help and understand. Many psychotics have regressed to a more primitive level of functioning, understandable in part as a revival of levels of development in infancy and childhood where psychological growth has become distorted or arrested. When these primitive modes of functioning impair normal rational thinking, the psychotic person is exposed to severe anxiety, confusion and impulsiveness. Winnicott (1965) regarded this regression as an unconscious attempt to find a 'facilitating environment' which would give the patient that which had been missing in the first place, in order for psychological growth to be resumed.

'Container-contained': a key concept

The term, 'containment' is often used loosely, and it is important to be clear what it is referring to in a particular context. In the most general way, it refers to actions necessary to protect the acutely disturbed patient from harm to himself and others, usually involving admission to a suitable containing structure, typically a psychiatric hospital ward. Here, he will find helpful people who will try to 'contain' him, that is: to control his aggressive or self-destructive behaviour; to reassure him as far as possible by words and behaviour; to talk with him if possible in order to understand what he is experiencing; and, when these anxiety-alleviating attempts are insufficient, to administer appropriate tranquillising medication. When the acute disturbance subsides, another level of 'containment' becomes possible, provided by the understanding, with-standing, accepting and enquiring attitude already described.

A final sense of the word is to be found in the process whereby the helper may accept the patient's attempts to recruit the helper in playing a part in his own inner drama. This is 'containment' in the sense of accepting and 'digesting' the patient's projections in the service of understanding him, and of helping him recognise, tolerate, and ultimately integrate impulses and desires that he has never been able to acknowledge.

Case study 13.7   The need for 'containment' by the milieu

An example was provided by a severely obsessional patient who washed his clothes until they disintegrated. On one occasion when he threw them into the ward laundry bin, a nurse picked them out to examine them. The patient at once turned on her verbally with ferocious abuse, saying, 'You filthy little thing! Aren't you ashamed of yourself?'

It was possible to help the staff to see that he was giving the nurse an example of what it is like to be tyrannised by an inner parental figure that allows no investigative instinctual activity. In dynamic terms, the patient was projecting the tyrannised and submissive part of his self (one of several mental self-representations) into the nurse as container, who was then felt by him to be identical with that part, and then, in his outburst, himself identifying with an introjected persecutory internal parental figure.

The consequence of this process of projective and introjective identification was that his perception of the object (nurse) was severely distorted, and his sense of self equally so. This is one reason why these mechanisms are called 'psychotic', even though this particular patient was not clinically psychotic.

A similar process was observed in a disturbed psychotic patient:

Case study 13.8   Loss, projective identification, reversal

Psychotherapy had been started when the patient was an inpatient, and an attachment to the therapist had clearly developed. The therapist had to leave unexpectedly for a fortnight and the patient became acutely disturbed. Overactive, confused and excited, she shouted repeatedly 'I am God! I have the sacred heart of Jesus inside me, but Dr X [the therapist] is jealous of me and is going to murder me in order to get it for herself!'

In this case, a more complex fantasy is operating but with the same dynamic mechanism based essentially on a reversal. Incapable of containing in her own mind the feelings aroused by the sudden separation, the patient projects her murderous envy and jealousy of the sustaining object (the needed and valued mother-therapist) and identifies (introjectively) with the lost idealised mother-therapist (God) who contains the most precious and desired (part) object which is contained inside Jesus, whose complex meaning for her might include unconditional and infinite paternal love, succour and elimination of all suffering.

The theory of '*container-contained*' was developed by Bion (1962) to describe a process whereby a normal mother, capable of 'reverie', is able to think about her infant's distress by responding empathically to his communications and helping make his feelings tolerable to him. When this process fails, for whatever reason, the infant may then be unable to integrate frightening impulses into his sense of self, and proceeds to develop with a split-off area existing like a hidden foreign body in his mind, making him vulnerable to psychotic developments later in life (see Segal 1981, Hinshelwood 1989).

Containment and the family

Psychosocial research has shown that emotional overstimulation of the individual within his family or equivalent social context is often associated with the relapse of psychotic patients discharged home in a relatively stable state. This work has led to therapeutic interventions designed to help the families lower the level of 'Expressed Emotion' (EE) in order to help the schizophrenic patient maintain his stability (Leff et al 1982).

In terms of 'container-contained' theory, a 'high EE' environment will not only prevent the possibility that the parents or spouse might accept and 'process' the patient's projections, but may even greatly increase his persecutory fears. By contrast, a 'low EE' environment will not only help to keep the patient in a calmer and less excited state of mind, but will make it possible for the processing of projections to take place. The acceptance and tolerance by relatives of the patient's projections, achieved by calm and intuitive understanding, can have an immensely reassuring effect for the psychotic patient, and contribute greatly to his capacity for reality testing.

UNDERTAKING PSYCHOANALYTIC PSYCHOTHERAPY WITH PSYCHOTIC PATIENTS

GETTING STARTED

Assessment is the first step toward the decision to take the patient on for a trial of individual psychotherapy. Since success is never predictable at the outset, even with neurotic patients, all psychotherapy begins as a 'trial', and a decision may be needed about whether or not to formalise this as an agreement between patient and therapist. When the patient is already in hospital, assessment is likely to be less complicated, because the ward staff, and the intending therapist if he is working on the ward, have had adequate opportunity to assess the patient's psychological strengths and weaknesses.

Assessment of the patient

The search to delineate prognostic factors in schizophrenia has inspired a vast literature, only a small proportion of which is concerned with the *quality* of treatment resources and the influence of psychotherapy. The characteristics of the 'good-prognosis' patient are well known – first attack, previous personality not too schizoid, reasonable or superior intelligence, some previous achievement, obvious precipitating stresses, acute onset, affective features, awareness of being ill (Arieti 1974). These patients are likely to be suitable for psychoanalytic psychotherapy, but this does not imply that other types of patient are unsuitable. There are some factors that are not taken into account in conventional outcome studies. Alanen and his colleagues (1986) followed the progress of 100 successive schizophrenic and schizophreniform patients over eight years of 'case-specific' treatment, in which all treatment modes, including at least 80 sessions of individual intensive psychotherapy, were available and provided according to the individual need of each patient. They concluded that individual psychotherapy within a psychotherapeutically-oriented ward where skilled family therapy was also available was clearly the most favourable provision for these patients. This impressive work, which is still in progress, also revealed the great prognostic importance of the existence of at least one close relative with an empathic and understanding attitude.

The patient's motivation is obviously of crucial importance, a variable that Alanen's group extended in an interesting way. Impressed by the favourable prognostic significance of a patient having held on to hope for improvement in his life, they introduced 'a new psychosocial prognostic variable of *maintenance or loss of grip* in the efforts to reach the goals and modes of satisfaction ordinarily associated with adult life.'

Assessment of the milieu

As already indicated, the quality of the family background is of crucial importance. That of the ward milieu is equally so. Whether psychotherapy is to begin in hospital, or in a day centre or outpatient setting, the presence of a hospital ward with a psychotherapeutic orientation, and a reasonable level of psychodynamic sophistication is an almost essential requirement. In such a ward, all members of the interdisciplinary team will understand and approve of the psychotherapy, and their management of the patient will be complementary to it (Ugelstad 1979, Oldham & Russakoff 1987). In such a situation, the therapist is free to pursue psychotherapy, and the general management can remain the responsibility of the hospital staff. In practice, this level of skill, experience and sophisticated organisation may be very hard to find, and cannot thus be regarded as an indispensable requirement. It is, however, essential that the management be at least neutral towards the psychotherapy. If it is fundamentally opposed to such work, there is little chance that the psychotherapy will succeed.

Assessment of the therapist

The therapist needs to consider his own motivation, capacity for empathy and interest in the patient, and willingness to commit himself to the patient for a long time. Although it is not necessary for him to like the patient, a feeling of significant dislike requires self-examination, which may lead to the conclusion that that particular patient might be better suited to another therapist.

Therapy for the therapist

Psychoanalysts experienced in work with psychotic patients strongly recommend that the therapist should have a sufficiently thorough personal analysis to help him recognise his own 'normal' psychotic potential, and to cope with the demands that the patient will make on him, particularly by the use of projective identification. However advisable this might be, there would be very little psychotherapy available for psychotic patients if this were to be regarded as an essential condition for undertaking psychotherapy. On the other hand, some experience of personal psychotherapy, whether individual or group, might justly be regarded as an essential requirement for anyone attempting psychotherapy with any type of patient. In practice, good work is done by talented people who, for whatever reason, have no personal experience of psychotherapy. In fact, it often happens that the experience of helping a psychotic patient provides an incentive for the worker to seek personal therapy.

Supervision

The help of skilled supervision, individually or in a group, is also advisable. Even when this cannot be obtained, contact with colleagues, discussion groups or seminars may not be difficult to arrange, and can greatly support the therapist in his task.

The setting for therapy

The essential practical requirements, although perhaps obvious, may not always be easy to provide. These are: a room; two chairs (unless the patient is so disturbed that the session must be conducted in his room); a period of time that is uninterrupted and predictable (the bleeper must be left outside the room!); and a therapist who is punctual, interested and willing to listen and to try to understand. In the relatively uncommon event of a patient being actually or potentially violent, help must be immediately available, in the person of an experienced nurse inside or outside the room. The length of the session will depend on the conditions. The traditional 45 or 50 minute session is a desirable aim but may not be possible early in therapy. If the patient is first seen in an acute breakdown, the therapy should start at once if possible, and the therapist should see the patient every day, even if it is only possible for a short time. On the other hand, situations may arise when one or more prolonged sessions may prove invaluable.

Frequency of sessions

Most of the intensive psychotherapy reported by psychoanalysts takes place in private practice, which, at least in the United States, is supported by well-endowed private hospital facilities, where patients may be seen up to five or six times weekly if it is thought necessary. This is unlikely to be possible in the public sector of mental health care in the United Kingdom, although the experience of treating the right patient under the right conditions with such intensity can be invaluable for patient and therapist. Even very infrequent sessions over a long period of time can be helpful to many patients, but at a rate of less than once weekly it is unlikely that a coherent on-going process can be established. Twice-weekly sessions for a patient who is in a therapeutically active ward is a satisfactory pattern and may be as much close contact as the patient can stand, although when admitted in an acute state the patient should be seen daily if possible, however briefly.

Therapist expectations: how long? what result?

The psychotic patient may need some form of therapeutic support for many years, sometimes for life. This does not imply that the therapist is taking on such a commitment, which is more likely to be the function of the rehabilitation and community care services. However, he should prepare himself for a period of at least two years, and more if possible or necessary. Properly conducted therapy with the right patient is unlikely to do harm, and should certainly benefit him. This benefit may be modest but significant, such as the lessening of thought disorder, or a decrease in the level of medication required. In some cases, cure or complete remission may prove a realistic aim, but it is rarely possible at the outset of treatment to predict which therapist will prove to have the ability to provide, and which patient the capacity to use, such help.

The 'inaccessible' patient

Under existing conditions, many patients are clearly inaccessible to planned psychotherapy. However, as Schulz (1983) points out, a patient may be deemed 'inaccessible' not on good clinical grounds, but because the therapist is insufficiently experienced, does not have an adequate or coherent conceptual framework to guide his efforts, or is operating in a setting in which the philosophy of psychotherapy has not been properly understood or accepted.

Case study 13.9 An 'inaccessible' patient

A 26-year old woman had had recurrent episodes of confusion, delusional belief and catatonic immobility for 10 years. Hospital treatment with ECT and anti-psychotic medication relieved the symptoms, but she continued to relapse. Psychotherapeutic investigation beginning in an acute phase in a psychodynamically oriented ward revealed a system of delusional beliefs centring on the conviction that she was pregnant by oral means (she had a previous history of recurrent anorexia), and had to remain catatonic in order to protect the baby from destruction and herself from disintegration. Her first psychotic episode began with the hallucinatory experience of seeing the dead body of her brother (who was in reality alive and well) in a coffin. This brother was born a year after her, for her a fateful event that contributed to the development of massive defences of denial of aggressive feeling and a passive character structure.

After several months of individual and milieu treatment in the ward, she continued as an outpatient for two years. She had no further treatment after this but was followed up at long intervals for seven years, during which time she remained symptom-free, married and had two healthy children. She was still taking an occasional minor tranquilliser in times of stress, but is regarded as completely cured by her family and herself. This therapy was guided by the concepts of splitting, and projective and introjective identification. In the acute attacks, she regressed from object relationship to a primitive form of psychotic identification, in which she experienced herself in unconscious fantasy as being the mother with the baby brother inside, threatened from without and within by her long-forgotten and split-off murderous jealousy.

Concurrent milieu therapy in the early stages greatly helped her to recognise and deal with the aggressive feelings that she believed were omnipotently destructive. She became very much more self-assertive in an appropriate way and acquired a significant amount of insight into her mental functioning. Although she is probably still vulnerable and cannot be regarded as psychodynamically strong, she illustrates the three ways in which psychoanalytic understanding can be helpful with psychotic patients; by enabling bizarre and otherwise inexplicable features of her experience and behaviour to be understood; by enabling psychoanalytically informed management of her case by the psychiatric team who were able to help her overcome her fear of her own destructiveness and aggression; and by allowing it to be recognised that she was actually accessible to individual psychotherapy.

MANIC-DEPRESSIVE AND MIXED PSYCHOSES

The psychodynamics of the affective and mixed psychoses are different from those responsible for the confusion and disintegration encountered in schizophrenia, and such patients present particular difficulties, but also particular opportunities, for the intending psychotherapist. Although such patients are widely regarded as unsuitable for psychoanalytic psychotherapy, some experienced analysts (e.g. Rosenfeld 1987) do not share this general pessimism and believe that many are accessible provided that appropriate management is possible.

Because of the extreme risk of suicide in the depressive phase, the difficulty in making contact in the manic phase, and the abruptness with which dramatic events may occur within a patient who seems deceptively stable, the patient must be treated in hospital, or at least in the knowledge that he can be admitted immediately when necessary. However, Wynther & Sorensen (1989) have shown that with carefully selected patients, outpatient psychotherapy may well proceed without severe disturbance.

The formidable obstacles to psychotherapy must therefore not be underestimated, but they can be surmounted, as the following case illustrates.

Case study 13.10   Inpatient psychotherapy in manic-depressive psychosis

A young woman became depressed as the day of her wedding approached. She responded briefly to anti-depressants, but relapsed and was referred for assessment for psychotherapy. This was offered to her, but whilst waiting she made a serious suicide attempt. She was admitted to a general psychiatric ward where the full range of biological treatments brought little or only temporary relief. She soon developed severe and typical manic episodes, and cycled erratically over the next five years during which time she made repeated suicide attempts, and had some 70 electroshock treatments; leucotomy was finally being considered. As a last resort, she was admitted to a psychodynamically oriented ward for a trial of psychotherapy. The combination of milieu therapy and individual thrice-weekly psychotherapy led to fundamental progress, despite the difficulty of continuing it through severe manic and depressive phases when she was dangerously self-destructive and required maximum security nursing observation for many months. In the course of two years of inpatient psychotherapy, she showed many of the features outlined by Rosenfeld (1987).

The eldest of four children of a devoted but fragile mother and an unstable, probably cyclothymic father, she was sent at the age of 18 months to be cared for by her grandparents when her sister was born. Her mother found her withdrawn on return and never achieved the close contact with her that she did with her other children. She grew up in an atmosphere of violent parental discord which ended in divorce during her adolescence. Sociable and intelligent, she had an outstanding career as a medical student, which was cut short in her first post-graduate year. When contemplating marriage, she was required to perform termination of pregnancies and became acutely depressed. It became quite clear during the course of therapy that this event had mobilised long-repressed destructive feelings towards her younger sister, and that the threat of marriage and therefore the possibility of motherhood had completed the destabilisation.

After an initial period of very positive transference, she suddenly made a serious suicide attempt, the first of several during the following year. She remained withdrawn and semi-stuporose for several months, a state punctuated by brief episodes of typical manic psychomotor excitement and overactivity. It was possible to maintain contact with her through her dream life, which was vivid and revealing. She showed an intense negative response to help and understanding, but gradually began to realise how afraid she was that she would destroy the psychotherapeutic help, and that the therapist would be unable to stand her destructive attacks on his attempts to help her to acknowledge dependency, and confront her with long-denied envy and jealousy.

As her manic defences weakened, she became aware of feelings of intense pain, only gradually recognised as of an emotional nature, but eventually identifiable as a sense of loss, despair and guilt. By this time, her defences of denial, splitting and projective identification had lessened, and she had become capable of a much more integrated capacity to feel loss, a distinct progress towards the depressive position. She then embarked on what proved to be a final assault on the therapy, in the form of a determined attempt to convince the staff that the psychotherapy was making her much worse and should be abandoned. When this crisis was negotiated, she began to improve steadily, and was able to say, months later, that at that point she was finally convinced that the therapy and the therapist were stronger than her own self-destructive feelings.

Two years after admission, she was discharged solely on lithium medication, and continued psychotherapy with another psychotherapist. She had one relatively brief re-admission when she became depressed following a bereavement, but it was clear that this state was essentially a normal mourning process. At the time of writing, this psychotherapy has continued for two further years without severe disturbance.

This patient may yet have to work through serious personal problems, but there is no doubt about her increased stability. She illustrates features typical of the manic-depressive, in particular the extreme sensitivity to loss, and the extreme severity of the mental pain against which their manic defences are deployed. (Jackson 1989b)

TECHNICAL ISSUES

'Technique' refers to the specific things the psychotherapist should, and should not do in conducting psychotherapy with the psychotic patient. At the simplest level, the therapist could be advised to 'think Freudian, but think for yourself'. The rules of therapy with neurotic patients apply with some important modifications. The therapist might begin by inviting the patient to tell him what he thinks is the trouble, and in what way the therapist might help him. With some patients, this will be an appropriate start, but perhaps not with others who are mute, confused or deeply suspicious. A psychotic patient may begin with the fear that the therapist, far from wishing to understand and help him, is actually intending to harm him. There may be many reasons for such basic distrust and suspiciousness, and the therapist will need to come to understand them. He should first consider that the patient may be to some extent justified in his attitude, particularly if the therapist is laying claim to an understanding that he does not actually have at that moment. The therapist may then consider whether he is witnessing a schizoid character trait of distrust, which may also be understandable in the light of the patient's previous life experience. Finally, he may consider whether he is receiving a transference projection of some remembered figure realistically recalled, or unrealistically distorted ('internal object relationship').

It is characteristic of the psychotic to fear emotional closeness and to employ distancing manoeuvres to avoid the dangers of such psychological contact. His sense of self is at best precarious, and his sense of self-esteem, however much it is defended by omnipotent grandiosity, is fragile. To have to admit the need for the dependency on another person may be disastrously humiliating, and at a less rational level may threaten his basic sense of his own existence, including his experience of his bodily image. A manic patient may loudly proclaim that he is Jesus Christ or Mohammed, and feel devastated, when his mania recedes, to discover that he isn't and that the psychotherapist knew it; however, a more schizophrenic patient may have the terrifying experience of losing his sense of self, of being invaded or controlled by someone or something else, or of mysteriously and alarmingly having become somebody else.

To work with psychotic patients it is important to avoid deliberate attempts at being friendly or permissive; to maintain a firm professional attitude, focusing on the positive but being alert to the negative; to avoid responding to transference as though it were reality; and to be alert to counter-transference (Schulz 1983).

A major issue for the therapist is finding ways of understanding delusional material and dealing with it psychotherapeutically. Awareness of the psychotic's fear of emotional closeness and of destructive feelings, commonly of envy or jealousy, and the dream-like character of much delusional thinking, may give a lead to the patient's central disturbing conflicts. The following two cases illustrate these processes.

Case study 13.11   Sibling rivalry in a delusional form

In the throes of a paranoid psychosis, a young man became anxiously preoccupied with the subject of cot deaths of babies. He had heard that this might be caused by negative ionic radiation, and he became totally engaged in ideas about how he might invent an ionic shield to prevent such tragedies.

In this case, repressed oedipal conflicts in the form of wishes to destroy a rival sibling and at the same time to protect him assume a dream-like form, using primary process mechanisms of displacement and symbolisation (ionic radiation representing his destructive feelings).

Case study 13.12   Dread and the crumbling of defences

A manic and paranoid woman loudly proclaimed that she was the High Priestess of Osiris and began frantically warning others that the Venusians were invading the earth and that its protective cosmic shield was in danger of breaking down. This young lady had long been secretly in love with her elderly employer, an eminent and powerful man, and the threatened breakthrough into consciousness of her guilty oedipal desires was being expressed in the form of a symbolic drama. The patient had temporarily lost the capacity for recognising her symbolic thinking for what it was, had externalised her inner problems and was experiencing terrifying psychotic dread. By following the rules of dream interpretation, the therapist was able to decode the process and came to understand her experience. The cosmic nature of the delusional beliefs may reflect a grandiose state of mind, but also aptly expresses the magnitude of the anxiety that the patient is experiencing and the fact that any explanatory meaning is preferable to what Bion has called 'nameless dread'.

It is sometimes possible to recognise that the patient has significant awareness of his preference for delusional explanations over reality. Sometimes it is possible to point out to the patient that he prefers mad thinking to a painful reality which he cannot believe that the therapist can help him face. It may take a long time to help the patient acquire some insight into this preference.

Case study 13.13   The comfort of madness

A man in early middle-age had been compulsorily detained in a mental hospital for 10 years in a state of chronic paranoid psychosis. His central delusion, which had not changed since first admitted, was that the BBC had him under constant surveillance, were controlling his mind and broadcasting his thoughts and effectively intruding into his mental privacy night and day. This state of affairs led him to episodic violence, and he required large amounts of medication. He had a history of depression in adolescence following the death of his mother, and his psychosis had broken out 10 years later. In order to study for a degree in mathematics, he had rented an empty lighthouse on a remote Scottish island, where he lived and studied in total isolation. His delusional beliefs began after three months.

He was admitted for a trial of milieu and individual psychotherapy. It gradually became clear that the moment he began to feel any sense of dependency or need, or any feeling of painful isolation or depression, he would hallucinate and complain violently about the persecuting voices that would never leave him alone. In this way he filled up the 'potential space' in his mind where new and painful meanings might develop (Ogden 1985). He preferred constant delusional presence to isolation and depression. After six months it was possible to rescind the compulsory order, and after a year he had improved sufficiently to be referred back to his own hospital on a minimal dose of medication. He began a rehabilitation progress with no relapse, but a few months later died in his sleep of a massive myocardial infarction.

Decoding and interpreting

When the meaning of the delusional content begins to become clear, the therapist can consider how to convey this understanding to the patient. At times, it may be more important to explore the defensive purpose that the delusion may be serving, that is, to attend to the process rather than to the content. In the case of the neurotic patient, the psychotherapist is accustomed to the idea of working from the surface to the depths, of directing attention to the point of the patient's maximum anxiety at the particular moment, and to attending to defence before dealing with content (Malan 1979). In general, these guidelines also apply to the psychotic patient, but with the complication that the depths may be on the surface, and the point of immediate anxiety hard to discover (see Case study 13.3 above). It is a mistake to assume that a patient will necessarily be capable of understanding direct interpretations of symbolic material, and it is important to remember that an interpretation should be brief, unambiguous and presented at a level that the patient is capable of grasping. However, experience will strengthen the therapist's capacity to convey to the patient the meaning of his delusional beliefs and psychotic anxieties in a direct way. It should be remembered that an interpretation may be a process that needs to be worked at over a period of time, and that reliable and useful insight usually proceeds very slowly and in small steps. It must also be recognised that it is not the interpretation alone that helps the patient. The therapist's continued presence, his stable professional attitude of genuinely benevolent interest and impartial curiosity, and his dedication to seeking the truth are powerful therapeutic factors. Yet, however valuable this relationship factor may be, it is the therapist's knowledge of the mental mechanisms that the patient is using, and his ability to help the patient understand them that enables reliable progress to be made. Projective identification and other psychotic defences invariably lead to feelings of depletion and ego-weakness. As disavowed parts of the self are accepted and integrated with the help of the containing presence of the therapist's 'auxiliary ego', so the patient gains a strengthened sense of identity and wholeness.

The depressive position

When a patient begins to improve, it becomes possible to recognise more integrated responses to loss (as in Case study 13.10 above) or the emergence of constructive guilt and reparative feelings of regret and concern for the objects felt to have been ill-used or unappreciated in the past. In this phase, periods of silence, which are usually disturbing in the more schizoid phase and should rarely be allowed to continue for long, may assume a new quality of reflectiveness and sadness which may usher in a constructive capacity for grief and mourning.

Modifications of technique

The 'classical' approach advocated particularly by Kleinian analysts insists that the therapist should do nothing but sit, listen and talk when he has something helpful to say. This attitude does not imply a lack of recognition that a human encounter of profound significance to both parties is taking place, but, rather, implies deep reservations about approaches that advocate self-disclosure, particularly disclosure of counter -transferential feelings by the therapist. The same reservations apply to departures from standard technique, in the form of touching or holding the patient, or of inducing regressive states as a therapeutic procedure. In general, the beginner is advised to start off with a classical approach and to think carefully before departing from it. In the case of the acutely disturbed patient, however, the therapist may have no choice but to employ some physical contact, but even in this case should reflect on what it means to the patient.

Destructiveness in psychotic patients

Kleinian therapists tend to be alert to the manifestation of destructiveness in the patient, and to detect the presence of reparative wishes as the patient approaches the depressive position. This emphasis requires the careful differentiation of purely negative destructive processes from aggressive ones that are being used in the interests of self-preservation. When destructive processes are identified, their nature must be investigated. The gratifications of manic triumph, often of a sadistic character, are not identical to the pleasures of perverse sexuality, nor to the pleasurable aspects of omnipotent thinking (see Ch. 15).

A particular form of destructiveness in psychotic patients, described by Bion (1962), is known as 'attacks on linking'. In this view, much psychotic psychopathology can be understood as the patient's destructive attack on his own capacity to attach meaning to perception and to think about what he perceives. In such a patient, the conflicts are not between incompatible sets of meaning, as is the case of the more normal subject, but between wishes to maintain a psychological state in which meaning can exist, and wishes to destroy meaning and thought and the capacity to think and to create experience (see Ogden 1980). This deep division between constructive and destructive aspects of the self has been elaborated in great detail by Rosenfeld (1971), who introduced the concept of 'destructive narcissism' to explain a comparable process. This emphasis on destructive and reparative processes in the psychotic presents a sharp contrast to the view of schizophrenia as essentially a disintegration product of basic ego deficiency (Freeman 1988), and tends to lead to a more active technique.

CONCLUSION

Implicit throughout this chapter has been the view that psychotic phenomena are meaningful, and can be understood in terms of unconscious fears, feelings and wishes and the defences employed by an overwhelmed and defective ego to deal with them. This holds good whether the aetiology of psychosis is seen in terms of genetic abnormality, environmental failure or, as seems probable, both. While physical treatment is the mainstay in the acute phase of a psychosis, strengthening the ego through psychotherapeutic containment and self-understanding can produce long-term qualitative benefits in selected cases, and may help to prevent further breakdown.

The professional who decides to undertake the psychotherapy of carefully selected psychotic patients will thereby learn a great deal about deep mental mechanisms, and may profoundly help a group of severely ill patients whose psychic life is all too frequently neglected.

FURTHER READING

Arieti S 1974 Interpretation of schizophrenia. Basic Books, New York
Laing R D 1960 The divided self. Tavistock, London
Mitchell J (ed) 1985 The selected Melanie Klein. Penguin Books, London
Rosenfeld H A 1965 Psychotic states: a psycho-analytical approach. Hogarth, London
Searles H F 1965 Collected papers on schizophrenia and related subjects. Hogarth, London

14. Borderline personality disorder

A. Bateman

BORDERLINE PERSONALITY DISORDER

The concept of borderline personality disorder (BPD) remains both controversial and confusing even though the term has been used as a diagnostic category for over 50 years. Although there have been many attempts to discard the term altogether, its use is increasing and it can no longer be regarded as a vague 'dustbin' diagnosis into which patients are placed if their mental disorder is unclear. It seems likely that the persistence of the term is not merely a result of diagnostic ignorance, but that it reflects a real clinical phenomenon. As a result of the widespread use of the term in America, BPD was included as a diagnostic category in the DSM-III (1980) and in the DSM-III-R (1987). However, it is not in the ICD-9 and it seems unlikely to gain enough general acceptance to be included in the ICD-10. This variation in classification may reflect historical differences in psychiatric practice between the United States and Britain especially the greater acceptance of psychoanalytic views in the American compared with British psychiatry.

Unfortunately, the term, 'borderline' is nowadays used both by psychoanalysts and psychiatrists in many different ways. For example, it is used as a diagnostic category in the guise of 'borderline personality disorder', 'borderline personality organisation' and 'borderline schizophrenia', whereas at other times it becomes an umbrella term rather akin to the terms 'psychosis' and 'neurosis', or even a sub-category of the affective disorders. These various uses of the term will be discussed in more detail below.

HISTORICAL BACKGROUND

Although the concept of borderline personality has now, to some extent, been embraced by general psychiatry, it was originally a psychoanalytic concept. In 1938, Stern described a group of patients who had failed to respond to psychoanalytic treatment in the same way as did psychoneurotic patients. He termed this group of patients 'border line', and stated that they 'fit frankly neither into the psychotic nor into the psychoneurotic group'. The major clinical symptoms he enumerated were excessive narcissism, psychic collapse in the face of a painful experience, hypersensitivity, profound feelings of inferiority, masochistic trends, severe anxiety, the use of projective mechanisms and difficulty in reality testing, especially in the context of personal relationships. He considered that these symptoms were not necessarily peculiar to 'borderline' patients, but compared with neurotic patients, they were often more pronounced, persistent and difficult to influence by traditional psychoanalytic treatment.

In 1942, Deutsch, another psychoanalyst, used the term 'as if' personality to describe a similar group of patients who were outwardly normal but on closer scrutiny lacked a genuineness of emotional contact. Deutsch placed the 'as if' personalities closer to schizophrenia than any other diagnostic group, thereby tending towards the view that the 'as if' personalities may be on the border of a psychotic illness rather than allied to the neuroses. However, she felt able to distinguish them from psychotic patients by their capacity to retain a grasp on reality.

A large number of papers on borderline disorders have arisen from these early descriptions, and two overlapping trends have emerged. Firstly, there is a line of development which suggests borderline disorders are in fact a mild form of schizophrenia. For example, Zilboorg (1941) and Hoch & Polatin (1949) suggested terms such as 'ambulatory schizophrenia' and 'pseudoneurotic schizophrenia', respectively, as alternative, and in their opinion more accurate, terms for a similar group of patients to those described earlier by Deutsch. Patients suffering from pseudo-neurotic schizophrenia were said to show symptoms of severe generalised anxiety related to all aspects of their life (pan-anxiety), multiple neurotic symptoms such as conversion phenomena, phobias and obsessive-compulsive symptoms (pan-neurosis), and multifarious sexual preoccupations leading to difficulties with sexual identity and perverse sexual enactments such as sado-masochistic behaviour (pan-sexuality); these symptoms were associated with mild schizophrenic thought disorder such as concrete thinking, hence the term pseudo-neurotic schizophrenia. Some of the patients also suffered from frank psychotic episodes. Although the term pseudo-neurotic schizophrenia has disappeared from the nomenclature, the association between borderline disorders and schizophrenia, for example, in the Danish adoption studies of Kety et al (1968), remains.

The second line of development views borderline patients as a distinct group of individuals who function psychopathologically between neurosis and psychosis. Knight (1953) and Frosch (1964), for example, both view borderline patients as having a specific, stable personality organisation which is not covering a latent psychosis or neurosis, although both authors point out that transient psychotic symptoms may occur under the impact of 'stresses and strains'. In fact, Frosch suggests that the term 'borderline' is too vague and that it should be replaced by the term 'psychotic character', thereby emphasising the characterological aspects of the disorder and the propensity of the patient fleetingly to lose contact with reality.

More recently, both Kernberg (1967) and Grinker et al (1968) have developed the concept of borderline patients as being related to severe personality disorders rather than neurotic and psychotic states, and such a view has become more widely accepted.

Overall, the divergent bodies of opinion described above have given rise to two separate but overlapping diagnostic categories in the DSM-III (1980). Those patients thought to have a stable personality structure and who are neither neurotic nor psychotic are assigned to a category of borderline personality disorder; those thought to be genetically and symptomatically related to schizophrenic spectrum disorders are named schizotypal personality disorder. There is now general agreement that these two major diagnostic groups can be distinguished both clinically and for research purposes, although overlap clearly exists (Spitzer et al 1979). BPD is classified in the DSM-III under Axis II which subsumes both developmental disorders and personality disorders. In view of the multi-axial approach of the DSM-III, such patients may also develop an illness classified under Axis I, such as an affective disorder or schizophrenic disorder, and the DSM-III specifically notes that multiple diagnoses should be made when necessary. Despite this, the idea of BPD as a personality disorder is not yet fully accepted even though the name implies that patients should be classified along with the other personality disorders, such as hysterical, obsessional, psychopathic and so on; nor is there a general agreement that the disorder may make an individual susceptible to other psychiatric illness. In summary, there are at least four different conceptualisations of BPD in the literature. They are:

1. borderline personality as a specific category of personality disorder
2. borderline personality as a general category of personality disorder
3. borderline personality as a variant of affective disorders
4. borderline personality from various psychoanalytic viewpoints.

These will now be considered separately, although it should be mentioned that the sub-divisions are not mutually exclusive and depend to a large extent on the different theoretical backgrounds of the exponents of each viewpoint.

Borderline personality as a specific personality disorder

The view of borderline personality as a specific personality disorder is epitomised by the work of Gunderson & Singer (1975) and colleagues who define BPD in terms of symptomatology and behaviour patterns. Such an approach correlates well with the practice of general psychiatrists in the United Kingdom who see personality disorder in terms of persistent patterns of behaviour which lead either an individual or others to suffer. Gunderson et al (1981) have developed a semi-structured interview, known as the Diagnostic Interview for Borderlines (DIB) in an attempt to differentiate between BPD and other diagnostic groups. The DIB relies on the history of the patient as well as his current symptoms, and measures five main areas of functioning: social adaptation, impulsivity, affective state, psychotic symptoms and interpersonal relationships.

The social abilities of patients with borderline personality disorder may be reasonably good, especially if they are not under stress; they may be normal in appearance and behave appropriately in social interaction. When viewed over a period of time, however, this outer appearance crumbles repeatedly when under stress and their behaviour becomes impulsive and self-destructive. This self-destructiveness may be episodic, e.g. cutting themselves, taking overdoses, or breaking windows, or it may become chronic and part of a way of life, leading, for example, to drug dependence, sexual deviation and promiscuity. This in turn interferes with social function and may lead to loss of employment or academic failure.

Two affects dominate the clinical picture, namely anger and depression. Anxiety may also be present. The depression tends to be different from the typical guilt-laden, hopeless, remorseful type seen in depressive illness. Instead it takes the form of a sense of emptiness, isolation and loneliness with an inability to experience pleasure or satisfaction (see Ch. 13). This is occasionally described as existential despair.

Patients with BPD commonly develop psychotic symptoms. However, when psychoses do occur they are clearly stress-related, transitory, lasting a few hours or days only, and unsystematised. Stable delusions or hallucinations are not a feature. The question arises as to whether all patients with BPD develop psychotic symptoms at some point in their lives. There is general agreement that only a subgroup of patients actually develop full psychotic symptoms, but all patients with the disorder show impairment of reality-testing under stressful circumstances.

Interpersonal relationships are often superficial and transient. Closer relationships tend to become clinging and demanding and are marred by manipulation, devaluation and destructive behaviour. This is in contrast to neurotic patients who are able to develop stable close relationships, albeit often over-dependent, and schizoid personalities who are more withdrawn.

Such a clinical description of BPD has remarkable similarities to the features described in the earlier papers by Stern (1938) and Deutsch (1942), and overlaps with the diagnostic criteria in DSM-III. The DSM-III describes BPD as a 'pervasive pattern of instability of mood, interpersonal relationships, and self-image, beginning by early adulthood and present in a variety of contexts'. In order to make the diagnosis, five out of eight listed items have to be present; the items relate both to the individual's recent and long-term functioning, and include a pattern of unstable and intense interpersonal relationships, often described as 'stably unstable', impulsiveness, affective instability but with a predominant background mood of depression, inappropriate intense anger or rage, recurrent suicidal threats or gestures, persistent disturbance of self-image and sexual orientation, chronic feelings of emptiness and desperate efforts to avoid real or imagined abandonment.

Although these criteria are very similar to those put forward by Gunderson et al (1975), there are some major differences. For example, DSM-III makes no reference to the vulnerability of the borderline patient to transient psychotic episodes; conversely, there is an over-emphasis on the affective state of the individual. The problem with this omission of vulnerability to psychotic episodes is that it leads to diagnostic confusion between BPD and other personality disorders and, indeed, some neurotic disorders. Furthermore, DSM-III's emphasis on the affective state of the patient can result in overlap and confusion between BPD and the affective disorders (see below).

Borderline personality as an overall category of personality disorder

Kernberg (1967, 1975), an American psychoanalyst, considers BPD as an overall diagnostic group under which other personality disorders may be subsumed. BPD therefore becomes a superordinate diagnosis, much like that of neurosis or psychosis; other personality disorders may be noted as secondary diagnoses. However, he uses the term 'borderline personality organisation', as he considers the use of the term 'borderline state' to be confusing. The latter implies a transient or short-lived disorder, whereas 'organisation' more correctly indicates a specific, stable state of mind. This viewpoint has led Kernberg to put forward a particular psychoanalytic approach, based on a mixture of ego psychology and object relations, to define borderline personality. The term 'ego' is used to describe the more rational, reality-orientated and controlling aspects of the personality which are partly conscious and partly unconscious. They are concerned with the need to control the more primitive impulses arising from the unconscious and to adapt these to outer reality, in accordance with the demands of the social and cultural environment in which the individual finds himself. Kernberg suggests that the ego of the borderline patient shows characteristic weaknesses, namely difficulties in tolerating anxiety, lack of impulse control and an inability to develop and use sublimatory channels. These features may, to some extent, sound like those put forward both in the DSM-III and by Gunderson. However, Kernberg places a more dynamic emphasis, in contrast to Gunderson's descriptive account; he stresses that it is not solely the *level* of observable anxiety that is at issue but more the ability of the patient to *deal with* anxiety. In addition, the capacity to control impulsive behaviour is judged not only by the frequency of outbursts of aggression, but also the way in which the individual reacts to such impulses. Borderline patients are more likely to consider such outbursts as being appropriate or presentable and to deny their importance. The use of sublimation to defend against heightened anxiety and impulses may be difficult to assess, but in general the borderline individual shows a lack of consistency and achievement in the development of creative interests for enjoyment; if such sublimations are present, their usefulness crumbles when under acute stress leading to episodes of intense feelings of hostility or depression.

Kernberg considers the excessive use of specific primitive defence mechanisms to be a characteristic of borderline personality. These are *splitting* and its associated mechanisms of omnipotence and devaluation; *projective identification*; primitive *idealisation;* and certain types of *denial.* The mechanisms of defence play an important part in the healthy psychological functioning of all individuals, and help to shape character and personality; it is their failure or their excessive or inappropriate use that leads to a disorder in personality, or even psychiatric symptoms. In the borderline patient, evidence of excessive use of defence mechanisms may be suggested by the history of the patient's relationships and his ability to manage in stressful situations, and by observing how he copes with the anxiety engendered in a detailed interview.

The essence of splitting consists of keeping the good and the bad aspects of others and of oneself strictly separate, in order to avoid ambivalent feelings of love and hatred towards the same person. For example, this may emerge in an interview if the patient shows an excessive tendency to see everything in terms of either good or bad, white or black, and as a result idealise a former psychiatric treatment or psychiatrist whilst at the same time devaluing what is presently being offered. Extremes of splitting and devaluation are often associated with omnipotence.

A more detailed discussion of projective identification is to be found in Chapter 13; in this process whole parts of the personality may be split off and projected into another person or object who then represents and becomes identified with the split-off parts; attempts are then made to control these parts of the self by asserting control over the other person. The topic is well reviewed by Sandler (1988). This particular defence mechanism is important in the management of borderline patients, as staff may become the recipients of the projections and, as a result, enact a fantasy with the patient and become controlled, at least in part, by him. This will diminish their ability to make reasoned clinical judgements.

If these and other defensive maneouvres fail to diminish anxiety, Kernberg, in agreement with Gunderson but in contrast to the DSM-III, believes that brief psychotic episodes may develop. However, a more constant characteristic in his view is the tendency of the patient to use primary process thinking, in which logical and irrational thought become confused without necessarily reaching the level of a psychotic illness.

Finally, Kernberg describes pathological internal object-relationships as a feature differentiating borderline patients from both psychotic and neurotic patients. In brief, borderline patients have unstable, but divided self- and object-images, as exemplified by the excessive use of splitting, but when close interpersonal involvement occurs, self and object become confused. In contrast, psychotic patients show undifferentiated self- and object-images, and so experience such symptoms as thought insertion and thought broadcasting in which they are unable to differentiate between themselves and others; neurotic patients show a much greater stability and delineation between self and object, and are able to show concern for others and experience guilt. Such a capacity for empathy with others is lacking in borderline patients.

Kohut and his school of self-psychology have challenged Kernberg's approach. Overall, Kernberg's view is in keeping with most psychoanalytic views in that it postulates that very early disturbances in a child's development lead to the formation of primitive psychic structures which become fixed and prevent the attainment of independence. Self-psychology challenges this emphasis on the developmental move from a state of dependence on important figures to a position of independence and autonomy. Instead, self-psychology suggests that, throughout life, an individual uses aspects of other people as a functioning part of himself in order to provide a structure which enhances his self-cohesion and protects against fragmentation. Kohut (1977) uses the term 'self-object' to describe this use of others. In Kohut's view, the use of self-objects is universal. However, in borderline patients the search for others as self-objects becomes both predominant and coloured by desperation. Kohut describes three types of self-object: an omnipotent, idealised self-object, a mirroring self-object and a twinship self-object. Arising from this theoretical position is an advocacy of the creation of an environment within therapy which allows and encourages the patient to use the therapist as these self-objects. In this way, it is hoped there will be a greater emergence of a cohesive self. This has important implications for technique.

Borderline personality as a variant of affective disorder

The co-existence of affective illness and borderline personality is far greater than would be expected from the incidence of each disorder alone. Differentiating between the two disorders inevitably becomes difficult if affective features are part of the diagnostic criteria of borderline person-ality, as occurs in the DSM-III. However, Gunderson & Kolb (1978) were able to discriminate between BPD and neurotic depression on the basis of drug-induced psychotic experiences, paranoid symptoms and interper-sonal difficulties, which were more common in the borderline group. Affective features in borderline patients are qualities of emptiness and boredom and are associated with impulsive behaviour, rather than the sense of hopelessness, self-depreciation and despair that is found in depressed patients. Despite this, many studies (for example, Pope et al 1983, Akiskal et al 1985) have demonstrated an overlap between affective disorders and BPD. Bateman (1989) found that 80% of inpatients in a British psychiatric hospital who met DIB criteria for BPD, also met PSE criteria for a depressive disorder. However, a greater degree of anxiety, irritability and hostility at interview differentiated borderline from neurotically depressed patients.

The majority of studies mentioned above were based on inpatients, and it remains possible that depressive features, when present, result in borderline patients being admitted to hospital, but that depression is an associated feature of only a small subgroup of borderline patients, and is not a constant characteristic. In summary, a great deal of uncertainty still surrounds the overlap between BPD and affective disorder. The subject has been reviewed by Gunderson & Elliot (1985).

Borderline personality from the British psychoanalytic viewpoint

As mentioned earlier there continues to be a good deal of resistance to the concept of BPD in the United Kingdom. To some extent, this is because mainstream British psychiatry takes a predominantly biological or social approach, and psychoanalysis plays only a peripheral part (see Ch. 1). In view of the fact that BPD remains in the province of psychoanalysis, some further knowledge of psychoanalytic concepts is necessary in order fully to understand British psychoanalytic points of view, represented by the Kleinian, the Independent and the Freudian streams.

The work of Melanie Klein (1946) and her followers has been most influential in the area of BPD. She described two basic developmental positions in which different anxieties and different defence mechanisms predominate. In the earlier, paranoid-schizoid position, the defence mechanisms of splitting and projection predominate, and the leading anxieties are of persecution and are primarily concerned with the survival of the self, which is felt to be under threat. In the developmentally later, depressive position, the predominant anxiety changes to a concern for the object; feelings of guilt, loss and dependence are experienced as the threat to the self is lessened. An intermediate position, sometimes known as the borderline position, is considered to form the psychological core of the borderline patient (Rey 1975, 1977; Steiner 1979).

Rey describes borderline patients as experiencing themselves as neither fully sane nor quite mad, neither fully male nor completely female, neither homosexual nor heterosexual, neither a child or an adult, and so on, but always somewhere in between these states. Such a state of mind leads borderline patients to make fleeting contact with themselves and others, only to find that such an experience is so unbearably anxiety-arousing as to require either a massive retreat to the paranoid-schizoid position (which may result in transient psychotic states) or a wish to destroy the object (leading to outbursts of rage) or the self (leading to suicidal acts) which was capable of such feelings.

Clinically, such an internal state of affairs may be represented by a borderline patient who begins a relationship with someone only to find that the contact arouses such powerful feelings of dependency and need that retreat becomes necessary to ensure a feeling of survival. The part of the self which allowed the initial contact may then be attacked; this can become enacted in an orgy of self-mutilation. Sometimes, such a retreat may also be observable in an assessment interview. The interviewer may help the patient transiently contact depressive feelings only to find that he quickly moves away from them, sometimes even by having to walk out stating that, after all, no help is needed. This so-called 'claustrophobic-agoraphobic' or 'too-close-too-far' dilemma, is central to the borderline patient: he wishes to be close but finds that this leads to a terror of becoming engulfed; equally, he is terrified of distance, as it results in isolation, feelings of abandonment and acute loneliness. Both experiences lead to outbursts of aggression resulting in the clinical presentation of a chaotic life-style in which stormy marriages, promiscuity, multiple failed relationships and brief friendships abound. Sexual perversions or substance abuse may predominate in an attempt to avoid the dilemma altogether (Glasser 1979).

Winnicott, an Independent psychoanalyst, had a rather different approach and considered borderline pathology to represent an arrest in development which had resulted from particular maternal failures. His concepts of transitional objects (Winnicott 1957) and false self (Winnicott 1960) illuminate some of the problems posed by the borderline patient.

'Transitional' refers primarily to a state of mind which bridges an early infantile state in which baby and mother merge, and a later stage in which the infant has an inner sense of separateness and recognises, to some extent, an external reality. Often, the infant uses objects to guide himself through this stage of development and these are known as transitional objects. For example, a child may use a favourite blanket or cuddly toy, and, according to Winnicott, the child's treatment of this represents what is going on in his inner world. At one moment the blanket is his mother, at another it represents part of himself, whilst yet again it can be just a blanket. Thus, the object represents a state of mind in which the child does-and-does-not have his mother under his omnipotent control. It is this intermediate state of mind that becomes of importance in borderline patients, and to some extent corresponds with the view that borderline patients experience themselves as never sure of who or what they are.

Winnicott believed that it was an inability on the part of the mother to help the child negotiate the transitional stage of development which interfered with the child's quest for independence. The mother who continually impinges on the child's attempts to use his transitional objects both for creative play and security, will be experienced as intruding on his fragile state. This results in a persecutory state of mind in which the child can only be reactive to the world, and not truly interactive.

Just as maternal failures may interfere with the infant's movement towards finding a creative use of the transitional states, they may also allow the development of false self. Winnicott (1960) states:

'The false self sets up as real and it is this that observers tend to think is the real person. In living relationships, work relationships, and friendships, however, the false self begins to fail. In situations in which what is expected is a whole person, the false self has some essential which is lacking. At this extreme, the true self is hidden.' (Winnicott 1960, p.142)

Such a situation is often experienced in the practice of psychotherapy – a patient may present himself as highly organised, intelligent and insightful, but in treatment it becomes clear that the mind itself has become the location of the false self; affective experience and true intimacy are dissociated and lost to the self. In such patients, psychotherapeutic treatment may provoke intolerable anxiety leading to a retreat from feeling towards an intellectual and rational safety. Some borderline patients present to the psychiatrists in this way and only began to reveal the falsity of their self as treatment develops.

Winnicott suggests that the particular maternal failure which leads to the development of a false self is one in which the mother fails to respond to and 'implement the infant's omnipotence; instead she substitutes her own gesture which is to be given sense by the compliance of the infant'. In other words, an apparently compliant, understanding state of mind may cover an unmodified omnipotent structure in which the child, and later the adult, never has a clear identity or sense of himself. As a result, there is no feeling of inner security which can distinguish between what is 'me' and what is 'you', what is 'inside' and what is 'outside', and so on. The concept of the development of a false self and the use that is made of transitional states by an individual has important implications for treatment.

Contemporary Freudian psychoanalysts (Yorke et al 1989) also consider borderline disorders primarily in terms of development and early object relations, but take into account the faulty, disharmonious development of the ego, its vulnerability to frustration and its relationship to the superego and the id. In many ways, Contemporary Freudians do not view borderline disorders as a specific nosological entity, and prefer to think about 'non-neurotic developmental disorders' in an attempt both to take account of the heterogeneity of the conditions, and to underline the unity of such apparently disparate terms as borderline, schizoid and narcissistic, all of which are subsumed under this heading. The 'non-neurotic developmental disorders' can be contrasted with the neuroses and psychoses. The 'symptom-neuroses', such as hysteria, obsessive-compulsive disorders, phobias and so on, represent a high level of developmental pathology in which the psychic structures of the ego, superego and id have developed substantially. The ego, as previously mentioned, deals with the more rational, reality-orientated and controlling aspects of the personality. As well as adapting these aspects of the personality to outer reality, the ego also needs to control the more primitive id impulses. The term 'id' refers to the basic inborn drives, like self-preservation, sexual and aggressive impulses. Some of these impulses and their accompanying wishes and fantasies are conscious, but others are unconscious, either because they are repressed or because they are innate but have not yet reached conscious awareness. The term 'superego' is used to describe conscience and ideals; these are derived through internalisation of parental and cultural influences from childhood onwards, and vary from person to person and in different cultures. The ego has not only to try to adapt the instinctual demands of the id to outer reality, but also has to cope with the conflicting demands of the id and superego. Thus, the individual is to some extent viewed as being in a state of conflict, and the ability to adapt to such a state depends on the degree of psychological development that the individual has achieved.

In differentiating between the symptom neuroses, the psychoses and the 'non-neurotic developmental disorders', it is suggested that conflict can be partially resolved in the symptom neuroses but only through a compromise involving repression and the formation of symptoms, such as anxiety, hysterical conversion and so on. In contrast, psychotic states involve a global psychic dissolution, in which contact with external reality and object relations is lost. The ego is overwhelmed, and the formation of delusions and hallucinations may represent reparative efforts by the disintegrated ego to re-contact lost objects. In the non-neurotic developmental disorders, which include the borderline disorders, ego development has been halted at an early developmental stage, often before a phase of object constancy has developed, and as a result is fragile and continuously in danger of fragmenting. Such an arrest in development is thought to occur as a result of severe trauma at this early stage. Many authors (Horowitz 1986, Boyer 1987, Frosch 1988) emphasise that the early histories of borderline patients show evidence of aggression, violence and inadequate mothering. Such problems lead the only partially differentiated ego to become overwhelmed both by id impulses and by external dangers. As a result, the internalisation and subsequent iden-tification with love objects, such as mother, father and so on, is arrested. Thus, conflicts or unacceptable wishes, impulses and fantasies cannot be dealt with by repression nor by compromise, as in the neuroses. A detailed case history and the psychoanalytic treatment of a borderline patient illustrating these points is given by Fonagy (1989).

Although there are many areas of overlap between these three views, a major difference which has important consequences both for conceptualisation and treatment involves the question of differentiation of subject from object. From the Kleinian point of view, there is no such normal stage of development as a merging between mother and baby leading to a confusion or transitional stage, and Kleinian analysts emphasise instead the excessive use of projective mechanisms which leads to the apparently objectless state. The focus of interpretation is therefore on the processes of projection and projective identification in which unwanted feelings or parts of the self are 'evacuated' into objects. In contrast, both the Independent and Contemporary Freudian analysts tend to place greater emphasis on the development of the psychic structures and the role of the external environment in their formation, and the importance this has for self and object differentiation. Thus, in conceptualising the problem of borderline patients in terms of developmental arrest, the focus of the therapeutic task and interpretation is on providing a setting for the expression and re-working of transitional phenomena and helping to diminish the degree of intrapsychic conflict.

Faced with such a different array of theoretical viewpoints, it is difficult for the clinician to be sure about making a diagnosis of a borderline disorder, and, once the diagnosis is made, about how to proceed. Nevertheless, there are a group of patients who do not fit easily into a more familiar diagnostic category, and yet whose distress and behaviour cause considerable difficulty for the psychiatrist. It is amongst this group that a diagnosis of BPD should be considered. Often, such patients seem to develop a powerful attachment to a particular psychiatrist, institution or therapist, and to make constant, apparently insatiable demands.

CLINICAL FEATURES

Case study 14.1   A borderline patient presents in the casualty department

A junior psychiatrist received a telephone call when he was on duty about a patient who was well known to the hospital but not to himself. She was demanding admission and, quite rightly, he suggested that she should come to the department so that they could discuss things. On arrival, she was weeping and told him he must admit her immediately and do something to make her better. He, she implied, would know what had to be done. The psychiatrist judged her not to be psychotic or seriously depressed and so began to discuss ways other than admission to help her cope with her considerable distress. This increased her demands for admission as she began to realise he might not take her into hospital immediately. She began shouting at him, called him worthless, useless and inexperienced, and ordered him to call the consultant whom she claimed would have the experience to know that her admission was necessary. The psychiatrist continued the discussion as best as he could, but eventually the patient stormed out in a rage and a flurry of denigratory remarks. Some hours later, she was seen by another psychiatrist in a different hospital who also felt she did not need admission; after abusing this psychiatrist she disappeared, only to resurface some hours later in the arms of the police who had found her running along the central reservation of a dual carriage way. She was then admitted and soon became calm.

In many ways, these events are enough to make a presumptive diagnosis of BPD. Suggestive features are the urgency of the presentation, the overwhelming anxiety and excessive demands, the initial idealisation of the doctor who is 'to do something' or to remove the anxiety, and the rapid change of mood to one of anger and contempt. Finally, the outcome suggests that the physical containment by the police quietened the patient and relieved her distress. The doctor himself reported that the events seemed to have occupied most of his duty day and that when the patient was admitted she seemed somewhat triumphant, whilst he was left feeling he should have admitted her in the first place. As so often occurs when borderline patients are interviewed, a confusion had developed within the psychiatrist; he had been tempted to admit the patient but had then found himself not wanting to, believing it to be inappropriate. Eventually, feeling so controlled and ordered around by her, he was determined to stand up to her. Such feelings engendered in the psychiatrist are also important in making a presumptive diagnosis of BPD. Abend et al (1983, p. 186) have emphasised the importance of the countertransference response in the treatment of borderline patients. The most prominent feelings are those of being attacked, confused, frustrated, guilty and counter-aggressive on the part of the therapist. All these feelings are discernable in the brief clinical example given above.

After making a presumptive diagnosis of BPD, it is important to take a more detailed, longitudinal view of family relationships and a careful phenomenological history, for example, looking for brief psychotic symptoms, as only an overall picture can clinch the diagnosis.

Borderline patients may not present in such an immediate and dramatic way. At interview, no overt anxiety or distress may be evident, although a suicidal attempt, self-mutilatory act or impulsive gesture may have preceded the presentation to the psychiatrist.

Case study 14.1 (contd)   A borderline patient presents in the casualty department

The patient described above had in fact presented more calmly in the past, when she had impulsively resigned from her job when her immediate superior had asked, with genuine interest, how she was getting on with her family. She had become enraged, thrown the papers off her desk and walked out. Two days later, she visited the psychiatrist and appeared calm but became haughty when questioned about her resignation. She stated 'I can resign if I want to and it is nothing to do with anybody else'. She did not wish to reconsider her act and eventually closed the subject by saying,

'What is done is done, now shut up'. Such haughty negativism can easily create difficulties for the interviewing psychiatrist, who may be left feeling hopeless and impotent.

The background of this particular patient was also instructive. She was the daughter of a milkman who spent most of his income on gambling. Her mother was an office worker whom she described as over-anxious and over-protective. The patient's early memories concerned her father's drunken evenings in which he would whip her younger brother with the dog lead whilst she cowered in the corner. Her mother did nothing to prevent such incidents and they continued for many years. At the age of four, the patient had to go into hospital for a mastoid operation, and this resulted in frequent nightmares and vomiting attacks. It was characteristic of the family instability from which she came that these were dealt with by punishment and further violence. The patient's symptoms became worse during adolescence, and by the age of 18 she was suffering from anorexia nervosa, panic attacks, agoraphobia and spider phobia. She had done poorly at school despite being of above-average intelligence, and her employment career was peppered with sudden resignations, short-term assignments and menial jobs. At the age of 19, she was admitted to psychiatric hospital and described in the admission notes as appearing agitated and aggressive and having lost contact with reality. She was also suffering from visual hallucinations of insects and spiders. An initial diagnosis of schizophrenia was made. Because the symptoms subsided after a few days, the diagnosis was revised to one of agitated depression with obsessional ruminations and an associated spider phobia. However, doubt about the diagnosis remained and she was treated with major tranquillisers for four weeks. These were eventually stopped and a final diagnosis of neurotic depression, obsessive compulsive disorder and immature personality disorder was made.

Multiple diagnoses attached to a patient, or a rapidly changing diagnosis, is indicative of a BPD. To some extent, this may reflect an unwillingness on the part of British psychiatrists to make a diagnosis of BPD, but it also underlines the rapidly changing symptoms that characterise the disorder, especially around the time of hospital admission. When a patient is admitted to hospital and after only a few days different staff members have markedly different impressions of the same patient, a diagnosis of BPD should be considered. Bateman (1989) found that 50% of hospitalised borderline patients had received more than one diagnosis by the time of their discharge. The most common diagnoses were of neurotic depression and hysterical personality disorder.

METHODS OF TREATMENT

Drugs or psychotherapy?

Overall, the most commonly recommended form of treatment of BPD is psychoanalytic psychotherapy. Some authors propose that pharmacological treatment, for example with antidepressants, is also effective; however, there is no convincing evidence that this is the case, although anti-psychotic medication has been shown to be of some benefit (Soloff et al 1986). Whatever the merits or demerits of medication, the greater danger is that of over-medicating and thus suppressing the capacities of the individual to harness useful aspects of his ego, thereby increasing the likelihood of a severe regression. Arguments as to the relative efficacy of a pharmacological or psychotherapeutic approach are often ultimately rather sterile; it is not at all clear whether the aim of improving mood and mental function through the use of drugs can easily be compared with the aim of helping someone change their personality through psychoanalytic treatment. Furthermore, the two forms of treatment are not mutually exclusive; many psychiatrists use drugs to help ameliorate an acute crisis and only later embark on psychotherapeutic treatment (see Chs 1 and 10).

Inpatient treatment

Another aspect to the debate about the treatment of borderline patients centres on where the treatment should take place – as an inpatient, day hospital patient, or outpatient?

Initially, inpatient treatment may be necessary to prevent excessive self-destructive acts or impulsive behaviour. Unfortunately, admission to hospital may promote severe regression in any patient, and this is especially true in borderline patients who can rapidly develop a clinging dependency and become unable to function without a member of staff. They find themselves incapable of getting dressed, may be unable to organise their daily life, and occasionally become incontinent. Fortunately, such a malignant regression may be short-lived, but all staff members are likely to be caught up in it. A borderline patient behaves as if someone in the hospital has the answer to his problems, and the caring and warm attitude of sensitive staff can encourage such a belief. The borderline patient may be warm, friendly and appreciative of some members of staff, but irritable, fractious and complaining towards others. This can lead to splits amongst the staff, either setting one staff group against another, or causing intra-professional strife. Arguments on ward rounds about whether a patient should be discharged or merely warned about his or her behaviour are frequent, with some staff claiming that the patient is making good use of hospital admission whilst others insist that the stay has been abused, manipulated and devalued. At other times, conflict may occur about important clinical judgements as to whether a patient is seriously suicidal or merely attention-seeking.

Such conflicts of opinion between staff, and disputes about diagnosis, often reflect the internal conflicts of the borderline patient and their excessive use of splitting mechanisms; the conflicts and defensive manoeuvres are projected onto various members of staff who then become, to the patient, representatives of his earlier life. The patient responds to that member of staff as if he were not a nurse, doctor or therapist, but more to do with someone from his past life such as a parent or other important figure.

Such problems make it imperative to establish a detailed structured programme of treatment as soon as possible after admission. This must be a programme which is agreed upon and implemented by all staff, as any minor disagreements between staff will be used by the borderline patient to foster a split between them.

Case study 14.2   The 'absent' consultant

Ms A H was a 29-year-old architect who was admitted to hospital after cutting her wrists. She soon gained the caring attention of the nurses, who found her sensitive to their difficulties in running a busy acute unit. The senior staff nurse spent considerable time with her, and late one afternoon had to call the consultant as she felt the patient was seriously suicidal. The consultant could not come immediately but arranged to visit the ward after his outpatient clinic. During this telephone call the patient disappeared. The staff nurse was anxious that the patient had left hospital with the intention of killing herself, and so criticised the consultant about his late attendance and an argument ensued. In fact, the patient reappeared a few hours later saying she had gone home to collect a few clothes. The dispute between the nurse and the consultant seemed to be an enactment of the patient's past – namely a division between a caring mother and an absent, unreliable father.

Although this example is over-simplified, an understanding of such problem can help staff respond appropriately to a patient. The patient had known of the concern of the nurse and ignored it. It transpired that her mother had been idealised and her father denigrated to a degree that was out of proportion to reality. This idealisation had prevented painful experiences from entering consciousness about her mother's depression when she was three years old. The depression had left her mother unable to cope, and, at an important time in the patient's development, her mother had been distant, detached and unable to care for her. To some extent, the patient was taking revenge on her mother, in fantasy at least, through her lack of concern for the nurse's anxiety about her disappearance. The response of the nurse to the patient's attachment was also important. The nurse was flattered to be thought well of, and had allowed herself to become, in the patient's fantasy, an ideal 'mother'; when the nurse required advice from the consultant, she was experienced by the patient as someone who had seriously failed in her capacity as a carer. This sense of abandonment in the patient led to the retaliatory sadistic attack in the form of a disappearance whilst threatening suicide.

In the treatment of BPD, there is a risk that one or more members of staff will become 'special' to the patient, and the patient 'special' to them. Borderline patients rapidly stimulate omnipotent feelings in others. The mobilisation of omnipotence in others may become so powerful that objectivity and the capacity to recognise realistic goals for treatment may be lost. The staff may become involved in an enactment with the patient of heightened treatment ideals; when these fail, as they inevitably must, both patient and staff become engaged in a repetitive cycle of destructive struggles involving recrimination about failed treatment. Sometimes this can lead to staff abandoning the patient altogether, for example by discharge and refusing further admission. But such attempts on the part of the staff to control a deteriorating situation can arouse infantile aggressive feelings and acute paranoid reactions on the part of the patient, which only serve further to intimidate the staff and increase their fears. These fears often lead to statements such as 'the patient should be taught a lesson', or 'we have to stand up to such manipulative behaviour' or 'we must not allow ourselves to be pushed around'. These responses ignore the severity of the patient's distress. The patient's actions are often an attempt to support his collapsing ego, by at least trying to exert control over the staff. His hope is that the staff will help him prevent a total collapse; his behaviour often undermines and prevents this.

Effective psychological treatment of this most difficult group of borderline patients depends on an understanding of the necessity for the hospital to act as an 'auxiliary ego'. An auxiliary ego acts as an extension of the individual's ego and strengthens it. The hospital can do this by its physical structure and permanence. The borderline patient will gain strength merely by the knowledge that admission and subsequent protection and care are always possible if he feels overwhelmed by his fears of being unable to cope with everyday life. As the ego of the borderline patient begins to fragment, the hospital and the staff can take over some of its functions and help the patient retain a grasp on reality, much as a mother does with her child. The importance of this particular function of the hospital setting should not be underestimated for borderline patients. The institution should have an ability to go some way to meeting demands and to avoid excessive use of counter demands such as, 'If you agree to do X then we will do Y'. Such a capacity on the part of the staff will allow the patient to repair, at least in part, his own fragmented ego function. Continuity of care and a well-organised multidisciplinary team are equally important. Frequent staff changes and ward closures, for example, will inevitably precipitate a relapse in the patient. Similarly, the question of discharge of the patient from hospital needs careful consideration and preparation, especially if a successful treatment milieu has been developed. The possibility of discharge must be discussed with the patient some weeks before the possible date, and the staff should be prepared for a relapse. McCready (1987) has reviewed the literature on inpatient treatment of borderline patients and gives a useful account of staff responses and their relationship to the patient's intrapsychic conflict. Similarly, Rosser et al (1987) have attempted to assess the efficacy of psychotherapy as an inpatient.

Day-hospital treatment

Similar problems to those encountered during inpatient treatment tend to be present during day-hospital treatment. Under these circumstances, the patient requires the capacity to function outside hospital but he will only be able to do so if the separation at the end of each day and at weekends is carefully handled. Fortunately, the regularity of a day-hospital setting goes some way to overcoming this difficulty, as does the permanancy of the staff. But a general psychiatric day hospital may have to serve too many functions to develop a full treatment programme for borderline patients. A more specialised day hospital, running on psychoanalytic lines, may be more appropriate. Here, the conditions can be created which allow careful interpretation of the underlying conflicts of a particular patient. This is often best done initially in long-term groups which can provide support and understanding over a period of at least a year. The acceptance by both patient and staff of the need for long-term treatment helps to contain the mutual wish omnipotently to make everything better as rapidly as possible. A minimum length of stay is likely to be one year, and during this time the 'claustrophobic-agoraphobic', 'too-close-too-far' anxieties can be safely explored. Often, these anxieties will be expressed as overt behavioural actions on the part of the patient, such as staying away from the day hospital for a few days. The day-hospital team then need to decide whether to telephone the patient, thereby making contact whilst not being too intrusive, or to make a home visit which may be experienced by the patient as being 'too close'. There is no easy answer to such a problem but each case requires careful consideration.

Individual psychotherapy of borderline patients

Outside the hospital and day-hospital services, once-a-week psychotherapy, either individually or in a group, is the only treatment for borderline patients that is widely available in the NHS. Within that framework, there are many differing opinions about how borderline patients are best treated. The topic has been comprehensively reviewed by Waldinger (1987). Should the setting and structure of once-a-week sessions be modified, for example, by offering to see the patient for an extra session when his anxieties appear overwhelming? Or is it imperative to maintain the limits? What type of interventions bring relief to borderline patients?

Kernberg (1984) initially placed an emphasis on early confrontation about reality and interpretation of the transference in the treatment of borderline patients, but he has recently modified his views and recognises that a more flexible approach using supportive and expressive techniques may sometimes be necessary. For example, borderline patients often find the analytic setting terrifying, and develop persecutory feelings about the therapist. Kernberg warns that at these times it may be necessary for the analyst to stop interpreting and to clarify the immediate reality of the treatment situation, including asking the patient to sit up and to discuss with him in great detail everything that has led to his present paranoid stance. Rosenfeld has given a similar warning to that of Kernberg, and described a patient whom he eventually asked to sit up and tell him all about the criticisms and grudges he felt. No interpretations were given, and an entirely receptive empathic listening attitude was adopted. It seems possible that such a technique will be required especially if the therapy is in danger of breaking down as a result of a transference psychosis. On the other hand, many psychoanalysts and psychotherapists disagree strongly with such an emphasis on the use of clarificatory, supportive or empathic remarks. Some analysts advocate an adherence to psychoanalytic technique whatever the symptoms of the borderline patient and warn of the dangers of straying from an interpretive role.

A further area of disagreement concerns the role of aggression in the psychopathology of the borderline patient, and how it should be interpreted. Some analysts are more likely to place an emphasis on the destructive aspects of aggression, seeing it as representing the death instinct; whereas others are likely to emphasise those aspects of aggression that are secondary to frustration, thus being more concerned with the importance of separations, abandonments and other frustrations. An inappropriate emphasis on either theoretical view about the origins of aggression and destructive impulses is likely to cause misinterpretation at various times, with a resulting escalation of a patient's difficulties. For example, if a therapist emphasises the destructiveness that is present when a borderline patient continually interrupts other patients' sessions, marches into the building demanding to be seen and so on, the desperate frustration that the patient is experiencing in not seeing the therapist will be missed. This may result in a further deterioration in the patient's capacity to maintain the limits of treatment, as he increases his attempts to retain a link with the therapist between sessions. Paradoxically, self-destructive acts may be a desperate attempt on the part of the patient to confirm a feeling that he exists, and a therapeutic approach which only takes up the destructive component will be unhelpful. Conversely, an over-emphasis on pain and frustration resulting from separations will miss some of the hostility that is also present. Winnicott maintained the view that a focus on aggression may prevent the development of an empathic, nurturing relationship, which he thought to be essential if the borderline patient was to develop and change within psychoanalytic treatment. He suggested that interventions should sometimes be clarifications and reflections rather than deep interpretations. Macaskill (1982), in a discussion of transitional phenomena and the psychotherapy of the borderline patient, emphasises the need for an empathic stance on the part of the therapist to borderline patients as the only way of avoiding severe counter-transference difficulties of despair and helplessness. In many ways, the danger is in allowing an enactment of an earlier mother-infant relationship within the therapist-patient relationship, in which the therapist, like the original mother, finds himself unable to hold, modify and return the projections of the patient in a more acceptable form.

The view of the self-psychologists (Kohut 1977) is in some ways complementary to that of Winnicott. As previously mentioned, self-psychologists put forward a view that a patient must be allowed to use the therapist as a self-object. They see the acting out which is so often described during the treatment of borderline patients as occurring because of a failure on the part of the therapist to recognise the functional necessity of the self-object. They suggest that such a failure is likely to come about as a result of too strict an adherence to classical psychoanalytic technique. Instead, they emphasise that a therapeutic environment must be created in which the maturation of the self is facilitated by gradually decreasing the reliance on self-objects. Crucial to this approach is an empathic stance on the part of the therapist.

It seems probable that nearly all psychoanalysts and psychotherapists, whatever their orientation, make interventions which are not interpretative. It also seems likely that many of the differences about techniques used in the treatment of borderline patients would become more apparent than real if it was made clear which types of borderline patient are being described, or at least exactly what their state of mind was at the time of the intervention. For example, it is generally agreed that many of Winnicott's patients were obsessional and over-controlled, whereas those described in papers by Kernberg and Rosenfeld are more impulsive and self-destructive and thereby less likely to be able to adhere to a regular psychotherapeutic setting without the analyst invoking confrontational techniques and using deep interpretations to ameliorate profound anxieties.

In general, the individual therapist faces similar problems to those of the hospital. The therapist has to follow a thin dividing line between empathy on the one hand, and limit-setting on the other; between becoming an auxiliary ego and fostering regression; between offering structure and allowing flexibility; and between being 'real' and offering new experience and interpretation. Exactly which is uppermost at any particular time will depend largely on the patient and on the sensitivity of the therapist to his requirements at that time. Each patient will have different needs and require different techniques at various times during therapy. This is discussed in more detail by Pines (1989).

Rosenfeld (1978, 1979), after discussing various types of borderline patients, remarks that the one thing they do have in common, is that 'they are difficult to treat'. Yorke et al (1989), in a discussion on non-neurotic developmental disorders, concur with this view and point out that although superficially the patients may appear neurotic, if a large component of externalisation and projective mechanism are noticed this suggests a more ominous prognosis. They suggest that borderline individuals find it difficult to form treatment alliances, and enter into destructive transferences in which 'angry and complaining attachment is especially common. In the course of treatment their behaviour may deteriorate, often developing anomalies such as self-destructiveness or externally directed aggression'.

Such problems in the psychotherapeutic treatment of the borderline patient are in part a result of the excessive use of projective mechanisms. Almost any intervention by the therapist may be experienced by the patient as an attack or moral judgement, and this may lead to a serious impasse in the treatment.

Case study 14.3   No need equals no loss

A borderline patient whose mother had died when she was three months old had been in psychotherapeutic treatment for nearly a year when just such an impasse was reached. She was silent throughout most of her sessions, and whenever the therapist tried to take up the silence with her she would treat him with derision and deny there was any problem. She pointed out that the idea of therapy was that you could do what you liked and that you didn't have to say anything if you did not wish to. When she did speak, she told the therapist that she didn't really feel anything, nor did she have any thoughts, and she couldn't find any words to express anything. In contrast, the therapist felt an enormous fury and despair. It seemed that through the mechanism of projective identification, a wishful fantasy had been created and actualised in the analysis, so that the powerful feelings were all in the therapist whilst the patient could maintain an idealised state in which she had no such feelings. The patient maintained that she needed nothing from the therapist. During the last session before the therapist went away on holiday, the patient secretly tape-recorded the session. This only became apparent later, when it became clear that this was a reflection of her wish to avoid needing anything or anybody so that she did not have to tolerate any sense of loss or separation. To experience such feelings threatened an internal catastrophe for her, and the therapist was able to link this with the loss of her mother when she was three months old. She had attempted to deal with this loss, now being re-enacted in the transference, by embalming the therapist's voice and interpretations so that she could enact the fantasy that her mother had never died. Her difficulties about separations had also become evident when she revealed that between sessions she would lock herself in her flat, take the phone off the hook and swaddle herself in her bedclothes. At these times, she would feel safe, calm and comforted; in her flat she could recreate an internal world where everything was under her omnipotent control, and in her omnipotence she *was* her mother who thereby remained alive. To come out of this state only led to panic; for example, between sessions, she had found herself walking the streets not knowing what she was doing, only to find herself near the hospital. Terrified, she had rushed home and did not attend her therapy for a fortnight. When she returned to therapy, she told the therapist that she had no words left as they were now too 'old'. She asked the therapist if he had any words left. The therapist suggested that perhaps she wanted his words so that she would then know what to say. The patient responded by saying that she would only borrow his words. She then demanded that he should give her some words as she knew he had them all. She gradually became more insistent about this.

This brief clinical example illustrates the complexity of the mechanism of projective identification. In projective identification, parts of the self and internal objects are split off and projected into an external object, which then becomes possessed by, controlled and identified with the projected parts. In this example, the words are all in the therapist and the patient is without them. In projective identification, a wishful fantasy is created which involves the analyst; attempts are then made to actualise the unconscious wishful fantasy within the therapeutic situation to make them real. In this example, the therapist felt compelled by mounting anxiety to speak. He suggested to the patient that she believed that he *had* to speak in order to show that he was still alive, as she was terrified that she had 'borrowed' too much of her mother's life and that there was no longer any life left in her mother; just as she now believed that there was no life or words left in the therapy. The patient responded by saying that she was 76 years old, which the therapist immediately realised was the composite figure of the patient's age and her mother's age when she died.

This report from a psychotherapy session illustrates the level at which a therapist may have to work with a borderline patient, and shows the need, on the part of the therapist, transiently to be able to enter into the patient's psychotic world. Such attention to detail inevitably brings an intimacy that is likely to arouse claustrophobic-agoraphobic conflicts. As this patient's treatment developed, she began to fear that the therapist was an oral, greedy person who would eat up all her words, and so she began to avoid the sessions and ate large amounts of food instead. As she put on weight, she began to fear that in her own greediness she had in fact devoured her therapist and so, in panic, she returned. This oscillation, so often a striking feature in the borderline patient, needs sensitive interpretation on the part of the therapist if the patient is to be able to begin to move from omnipotence to a more realistic experience of the outside world. This is inevitably a long-term process.

Despite the areas of disagreement discussed earlier, there are a number of areas in the treatment of borderline patients which all therapists accept as basic requirements for safe and effective therapy. These include: the need for long-term treatment; a stable framework within which the treatment can take place; and an appropriate emphasis on reality in therapy, especially with regard to the dangers of self-destructive behaviour and outbursts of hostility. The therapist must set limits if self-destructive activity threatens to endanger either the patient or the therapy; he can do this by carefully attending to management issues before starting therapy and, if necessary, arranging for another staff member to deal with practical difficulties arising outside therapy, for example, housing problems or hospital admission. This leaves the therapist free to address the anxiety-provoking conflicts which are being expressed through the damaging actions.

All psychoanalysts are agreed that long-term treatment is essential, and Gallwey (1985) warns that: 'Any experience of being taken on, encouraged to become deeply attached, and then terminated suddenly may be catastrophic to patients who have managed to keep themselves going by avoiding precisely that type of hazard, which no amount of interpreting in the short term can possibly alleviate'.

It should be made clear from the outset both to the patient and his relatives that long-term treatment is indicated. The requirement for treatment to continue over a number of years raises some important practical issues due to the increasing tendency for psychiatric registrars and other staff to move jobs every 6–12 months. Registrars must make arrangements to continue seeing the patient throughout their rotation, preferably within the setting in which the treatment began. This may be difficult, and serves to emphasise the need for more specialist resources to be provided. The treatment of borderline patients by a general psychiatric team may become impossible as a result of their incessant demands on time. Hurried interviews, short outpatient appointments and rapid staff turnover all exacerbate the borderline patients' difficulties, leading them to make further demands on an over-stretched service. This leads to frustration on the part of the staff and gives little benefit to the patient. A specialised psychotherapy service can provide trained staff whose task is to provide a setting through which the patient's anxieties can be gradually explored. Unfortunately, such a resource is all too rare. Its provision will alleviate the work of the general psychiatric team, and enable appropriate treatment to be offered to this most difficult group of patients.

FURTHER READING

Pines M 1989 Borderline personality disorder and its treatment. Current Opinion in
    Psychiatry 2:362–367
Tarnopolsky A E, Berelowitz M 1987 Borderline personality – a review of recent research.
    British Journal of Psychiatry 151:724–734
Yorke C, Wiseberg S, Freeman T 1989 Development and psychopathology. Studies in
    psychoanalytic psychotherapy. Yale University Press, London

15. Social maladjustment

Patrick Gallwey

INTRODUCTION

By and large, people are remarkable for their capacity for positive social relating. Even though minor acts of dishonesty are very widespread, in a reasonably fair society it is only a minority of individuals who become either habitually maladjusted or behave in a seriously destructive antisocial fashion. Nevertheless, social maladjustment, whether or not associated with mental illness, represents one of the most difficult problems encountered in psychiatric practice. This is particularly so for inpatients, not only because bad behaviour in hospital threatens the treatment of other patients, but also because it often seems to get worse in institutions. This is partly because, in this situation, many individuals emotionally regress, which encourages both over-dependent and anti-authority attitudes. This tends to alienate staff, who in any case may be unsympathetic to patients who are not defined as properly ill and who have become subject to the pejorative psychiatric label 'personality disorder' (Lewis & Appleby 1988).

Over-dependent attitudes, however, can be used constructively to begin a working therapeutic alliance; and even some of the anti-authority attitudes, particularly if they can be understood within the context of the patient's history, can, if tackled sensibly and sensitively early on, lead to the appropriate setting of boundaries enabling some individuals to feel properly contained and more secure. In the face of harmful, dangerous, unpleasant and provocative behaviour, it is difficult to maintain a therapeutic stance, particularly if the behaviour is occurring within an environment of which the therapist is directly a part, such as the inpatient setting. Outpatient psychotherapies are less problematic from that point of view, at least during periods when the behaviour is simply being talked about. If the destructive behaviour enters the therapeutic situation itself however, as it is liable to do, particularly in transference based psychotherapy, then the situation can be even more difficult because of the lack of direct support for the therapist from other staff. It is very important to keep in mind the possibility of attacks occurring in sessions with any patient who has a problem of violence, and to have a fully worked out procedure for calling help if this becomes necessary.

In practice, psychiatric help is often sought in problems of persistent violence, particularly domestic violence, impulsive dangerous behaviour (such as fire raising) where there is no clear hedonistic purpose, and for sexual maladjustment. Where the criminal law is involved, the offending individual often initiates psychiatric contact by asking his solicitor or probation officer if he can see a psychiatrist when faced with prosecution. This produces the obvious problem of trying to determine whether the fear of the outcome of prosecution is the real determining factor in the request for psychiatric help, rather than a more genuine motivation to change. Even if this is in part the case, the shock of prosecution can also bring home to an individual his need for help. Nevertheless, self-referral by the patient through concern at his behaviour, or even as a result of pressure from family or friends, is a much clearer indicator of good motivation.

UNDERSTANDING BAD BEHAVIOUR

There is a tendency for theories which purport to explain delinquent behaviour to be far too general, and to take insufficient account of individual differences in the nature of the harmful behaviour, its frequency, and in the characteristics of the individual personality in relation to the behaviour. Some maladjusted behaviour is rather obvious in its origins. When individuals have been abused, humiliated and hurt in their formative years, it is understandable that they may live out revengeful feelings against others, particularly those associated with their bad experiences. Revenge is a powerful and commonly occurring cause of persistent bad behaviour and can be used as a focus for a therapeutic approach to severe offenders (West et al 1978). It is a very great handicap to have had a violent father and many problems of violence and antisocial behaviour spring both from identification with a violent father and from personality weaknesses which result, 'inter alia' from the inability to internalise good parental strength. Maternal deprivation, which has been much stressed by Bowlby (1951), is complex in its effects. Again, it results in impoverishment of personality resources with rapidly mobilised persecutory anxiety, both of which can lead to delinquent behaviour. It also leads (Bowlby 1973) to much neurotic symptomatology and poor capacity to manage stress.

The relationship between neurosis and delinquency is examined below. Winnicott's writings on delinquency (Winnicott 1984) are an important source for those wanting to develop psychotherapeutic understanding of the 'antisocial tendency', as he terms it. However, his theory that delinquent acts imply hope through a delayed testing out of the environment which has failed the individual at the appropriate age because of parental insufficiency (Winnicott 1984), is in a sense too benign. Not only does his theory fail to address fundamental psychic disabilities against learning in persistent delinquents (see below), but it also takes insufficient account of purely destructive, sadistic and revengeful feelings in much criminal behaviour. These feelings are central in mobilising punitive reactions and in justifying the retributive element in punishment. If they are ignored, then attitudes of revengeful retribution are increased within communities. Also, individual offenders may feel both more unsafe and more inclined to live out their dangerous impulses because the social response has not apparently recognised their gravity. If, however, punishment is overdone and psychological factors in the criminal behaviour are ignored, this leads to scapegoating by the community and to a perpetuation of the very kind of experiences that caused the problem in the first place.

PSYCHOTHERAPY WITH OFFENDERS

Winnicott's optimism has to be set against the fact that much adult bad behaviour derives from severely entrenched psychopathology, which results in a poor therapeutic response by offenders; socially harmful, destructive or dangerous behaviour is very resistant to psychotherapy of all kinds. There are two major reasons for this:

1. When individuals have a *persistent* destructive attitude, then a major prerequisite for engagement with any form of psychotherapy – positive motivation – is simply not present, and in the absence of a therapeutic alliance containment is probably all that can be achieved.
2. Where individuals suffer from *episodic* bad behaviour, even though, in their better phases, they may be able to engage positively with therapeutic work, the episodes of bad behaviour are usually characterised by loss of emotional contact with themselves. As a result, anything they may have learned in treatment disappears at the moment when they live out their psychopathology.

This latter phenomenon was first explored by Freud in his theory on acting out (Freud 1914a), which states that in order to avoid conscious awareness of conflict, some individuals avoid contact with difficult feelings through unthinking action. Freud (1911a) saw thought as an experimental form of action, but thinking requires management of the often conflicted and turbulent emotions which underlie it. Management of emotional stress, whether it be from the frustration of instinctual needs or the imposition of psychological trauma, has more recently been explored in terms of very primitive defences against such turbulence. In the Fairbairnian school, this is seen in terms of ego-splitting (functional and structural divisions within the self) (Fairbairn 1940); and in Kleinian theory, projective mechanisms combined with splitting are held to be a central defence mechanism. (Klein 1946; see Chs 1 and 13). Both theories hold that, as a reaction to emotional stress in infancy and early childhood, the integrity of the self (and, in the Kleinian theory, the view of external experiences as well) is fundamentally altered in order to maintain psychic equilibrium. In Bion's elaboration of Klein's theories (Bion 1962, O'Shaughnessy 1988), he suggests that, in normal mothering, demanding and angry feelings and the anxiety which springs from them, are *contained* and *transformed* (see Ch. 13) by the response of the nurturing environment into which they have been projected. The internalisation of this good experience results in a developing trust of the external world and a gradual lessening of purely omnipotent fantasy to regulate emotional turbulence and preserve psychological equilibrium. Bion (1962) suggests that creative thinking and intuitive imagination result from the development of a mental function, first performed by the mother on the child's behalf, which transforms emotional conflict which would otherwise be projected so that it is not only contained within the self but, as time progresses, initiates and develops a spread of different creative mental functions, especially knowledge and thinking. He gave the name of *alpha function* to this basic mental activity. Feelings that cannot be transformed by alpha function and can only be managed by projection, he called *beta elements* (see Bion 1962). Hence, if the nurturing environment can be receptive to distress, need and anger and be firmly but lovingly responsive, then this is internalised, creating a platform from which normal mental functioning can proceed. Reality will progressively modify fantasy, and the fantasy give meaning and inventiveness to the relationship with the world. Distortions in the internalisation of a good containing experience lead to a variety of malfunctions resulting in neurotic or borderline disorder. When the contained and containing objects are fragmented (as opposed to neurotic distortion) by destructive feelings, this leads to psychotic states of mind (Bion 1957, Rosenfeld 1952).

In the author's view, when the early environment is not only inadequate in its containing functions but frankly retaliatory, so that infantile demands or distress are reacted against with physical abuse, abandonment or collapse, then early projective identification fails both as a defence and a link, and a particular type of malfunction results which differs from both psychotic and neurotic equivalents. The basis of this is not the distortion or fragmentation of containment but the *lack of a container altogether*, with a failure in the functions that spring from it. The result is proliferating turmoil and anxiety without the capacity to use projective identification effectively as a first line of defence to lessen psychic stress. As a result, such an individual when able to do so starts treating the environment as if it were part of his psychic property, in order to achieve equilibrium and avoid fragmentation of the self into psychosis. For those familiar with Bion's work, this can be stated as a failure to establish alpha function, with an accumulation of beta elements that cannot be projected. As a result, the individual coerces or forcibly manages the external world so that it *appears* to him that he has successfully projected them. At the deepest level, this may reproduce in reality the equivalent of the bizarre object formations of psychotic thinking (Bion 1962; see Gallwey 1985 on beta organisations). For example, whereas a patient in a transient borderline state of mind had a nightmare of being surrounded by pieces of pasta, each with a nail embedded in it, a behaviourally disturbed man impaled his transexual partner's pseudo breasts with metal rings at the base of each nipple. The first patient could dream; the second could only undertake his 'dream-work' through *action*.

The delinquent position

Although those in a delinquent state of mind may appear to be alive to the world, in fact they are not relating to the environment as something which needs to be explored and understood in its own right, but, rather, are perceiving it narrowly as if it were no different from their own personal fantasies, to be assembled in such a way that need appears to be assuaged and conflict successfully defended against. This can to some extent be compared with play activity in children. In normal play, however, children are exploring the world as well as their fantasies, and progressively distinguish between toys and non-toys. In the delinquent position, these distinctions are not made. Psychic equilibrium cannot be achieved through play or dreaming, so at its worst, instead of having a nightmare, the individual may construct its equivalent in the world using others as if they were fantasy objects with terrifying social consequences.

Case study 15.1   The management of separation by a violent criminal

In the treatment of a violent criminal, whose job it was to search out individuals who had not paid their debts and then terrify and injure them until they did, the therapist was trying to help manage a forthcoming break. Treatment had concentrated on his fears of abandonment and neglect, to which he had been subjected by his prostitute mother, compounded by fears that his parents would be unable to contain his primitive fury in view of the abuse he had received at the hands of his drunk and violent father. However, in the last session he had asked rather quietly if he could have a milk diet while the therapist was away (he was being treated in prison). The therapist began to interpret this request in terms of the patient's fear that he was going to re-experience starvation and threat to his life by neglect, as he had when he was a child, when the therapist noticed that the patient's face was becoming contorted with fury; he had gone quite white and the therapist felt suddenly very endangered. He realised that any moment he was about to be subject to a very violent attack and, in view of the patient's history of extreme sadistic violence, the therapist reassured him that he would write him up for his milk diet. Had the therapist understood more about the nature of the defensive deficit in criminal states of mind at that time, he might not have abandoned his analytic technique. However, as it was, the therapist realised that to frighten him verbally was not enough, and that the patient might well need to injure him physically, thus proving he could get the better of those on whom he depended, and demonstrate to himself that he really had evacuated his violence, terror and sense of injury into another object.

Obviously acquiring a milk diet doesn't in itself do very much – certainly not heal the wounds of the early traumata, nor bring very much in the way of real satisfactions to the sense of starved deprivation which the patient carried around. It had the appearance of a symbolic requirement, and yet he had no mental functions which would allow him to construct the experience symbolically whether within himself by having a dream, developing a symptom which might assuage it or by involving the environment harmoniously in order to acquire it creatively. He needed actually to terrorise the therapist in order to believe that he could evacuate his anxiety, and in getting the milk diet in this way he could experience himself as being in charge rather than a helpless victim. A psychotic would have done this without necessarily making a move within the environment, by the operation of pure omnipotent fantasy. The neurotic or normal solution would be to use reality to support, often invisibly, the symbolic solution in fantasy.

Case study 15.2   The management of separation by a neurotic patient

Just prior to a weekend break from treatment, a patient arrived in a state which appeared to need urgent medical attention. She told the therapist that she had been unable to contact her general practitioner and felt she must get medical help at once. The symptoms were so convincing that the therapist was anxious for her safety. He stopped trying to understand what she brought analytically, and gave her a note to the local casualty department. In fact, there was nothing physically the matter with her and she used the therapist's temporary abandonment of analysis triumphantly to support the fantasy that she was in charge of him. This in turn supported her narcissistic sense of superiority so that she could avoid contact with the meaning of the break from the point of view of her dependent relationship with the therapist and all that that represented in her internal and external worlds. In fact, she had been very frightened as a child that she would be abandoned by her mother, and that no-one would take action to rescue her. In the therapist's collusion with her in the session, she was able to obtain re-assurance that she could get her object to experience her anxiety and take some action on her behalf. At the same time, she omnipotently proved that she was by comparison much stronger than her object which reinforced her narcissistic isolation and pseudo superiority.

This woman's anxiety in relation to separation was close to that of the criminal patient described above. Whereas she was able to obtain the reassurance she needed and the support for her omnipotent fantasies of superiority by cooperation with the environment, he, because his belief in omnipotent fantasy was deficient, needed to take violent concrete action to make the world fit in with his belief that he was stronger than his object and could completely evacuate his anxiety into it.

This type of failure in defensive organisation and function can be more discreet and intermittent. It can emerge in apparently normal individuals, if the kind of social support that they take for granted and on which they rely to maintain a sense of good containment and management of stress is suddenly removed, when antisocial 'acting out' or the atypical occurrence of frank criminal behaviour can result.

The search for a 'substitute container'

In the author's experience, when individuals feel themselves to be in a containerless state of mind, due to the kinds of deficits that have been described, then the world may be used in two broad ways:

1. by enforced or subversive occupation of a substitute container and/or take-over of its contents
2. by triumph over a substitute container with cruel subjugation or violent annihilation.

These manoeuvres have to be repeated if freedom from anxiety is to be maintained. The first, however, is characterised by more optimism since it expresses the need, however obscured, for a dependent internal relationship. The second is more despairing and pessimistic, and socially more dangerous and destructive. Both can be expressed in a single criminal act or they can happen separately. Sometimes, the person's own body is used and abused as the substitute container. Why this is so is not at all clear, but may be a reflection of an attempt to preserve concern for others and protect the relationship with the environment. This seems more common in women, whose bodies are close to the primary object. Women may arrange forcible occupation or cruel subjugation of their own bodies by using others to do it for them. The area of containerless psychological deficit can be covered over by later, better experience, but will be represented by personality problems or a nascent severe vulnerability.

Acts of social maladjustment do not always arise from severe psychopathology of this kind, but success in treating individuals with problems of social maladjustment depends on an understanding that one may be dealing with psychological disabilities of this profound order of magnitude. Punishment, moral persuasion or psychotherapeutic chats are just not good enough if one is seriously attempting a therapeutic approach. The latter depends very largely on assessing the offender as an individual and taking account of his situation and personality weaknesses.

This chapter offers a scheme based upon differences in personality organisations which the author finds useful in designing treatment and management approaches to individuals with various behavioural difficulties. The categories described are not personality disorders per se, but broad groups with similarities in the organisation of their internal and external relationships. The scheme is a clinical one and relies on careful history-taking of the behavioural difficulties, as well as assessment of the individual in clinical interview.

CLASSIFICATION OF PERSONALITIES FOUND IN PATIENTS WITH BEHAVIOURAL DISORDERS

The following categories can be usefully and fairly straightforwardly identified. They are not mutually exclusive, and overlap is common. The categories represent problems arising from core psychopathology, so that other characteristics and problems may complicate or cloud the clinical presentation.

Category 1   Well-compensated delinquent personalities
Category 2   Poorly-compensated delinquents and frail neurotic
              personalities
Category 3   Over-defended neurotic personalities
Category 4   'Psychotic' personality types, including schizoid, paranoid
              and narcissistic (disguised paranoid) personalities
Category 5   Pseudo-normal and normal personalities
Category 6   Those with a primary psychiatric diagnosis of mental illness
              or organic disorder.

Category 1: Well-compensated delinquent personalities

Patients with well-compensated delinquent personalities pose a very special problem for psychotherapy. There is an identifiable group of individuals who show problems of behaviour from early in their life. They tend to be disobedient and difficult at home and at school. They are often hyperactive as youngsters, are easily distracted and play poorly, show a spread of destructive behaviour, an inability to relate to parents, teachers and other children and go on to develop delinquent lifestyles in their early adolescence. Their social backgrounds, patterns of behaviour and style of social relating are well described by West (1982). The severity of their social maladjustment and the impoverishment of their personal relationships are clearly related to the extent and length of deprivation and the extent of their bad parenting. Psychodynamically speaking, they have been forced to cope in their formative years with excessive amounts of anxiety, psychic pain and aggression, arising from a lack of proper parental support with impoverishment of good internal identifications, leading to the kinds of disturbances described in more detail above. The reason why some individuals with a pattern of faulty parenting deal with it by the development of delinquent strategies, while others become much more frail and neurotic personalities, is not always clear.

The 'successful' delinquents have become immured from feeling by using the world efficiently to manage their anxiety, as already described. As a result, they lack feelings of anxiety or concern for themselves or others. Instead of paranoid fantasies, they develop an alienated way of life in which persecution becomes a reality. Short-term gains from intoxicants, dishonest behaviour and aggression towards others, simulate and support omnipotent fantasies of superiority. Good behaviour is seen as weak; cheating, lying, aggression and self-induced excitement as triumphant, again actualising the illusion of superiority.

Delinquent personalities of this sort are rarely referred directly to psychiatrists. Mostly, they are dealt with by the criminal justice system, and the various penalties that their behaviour attracts fits their fantasy needs (Klein 1934), tending to reinforce the way they organise their emotional and interpersonal lives. Prison culture, particularly in backward prisons, is largely a world manufactured from criminal fantasy, so that the typical penal environment closely resembles the internal world of habitual offenders and can be understood as a more complete realisation of it (see Genet 1964).

The worst period, socially, for individuals in this category is in their mid- and late adolescence, and the situation may improve as they get into their late 20s. However, this is by no means always the case, and some develop into habitually criminal offenders, sometimes with sexual offending as well, and may spend the greater part of their lives in prison. Some really well-organised delinquent personalities seem to escape imprisonment and become 'successful' criminals, manipulating the world around them with repeated occupation and abuse of substitute containers and the realisation of manic fantasies of superiority, resulting in perpetual, ruthless, antisocial behaviour. For them, psychiatrists are only likely to be involved when their condition is complicated by a mental illness. Sometimes, delinquent strategies may fail suddenly under certain kinds of stress, in which case they may either behave catastrophically, often with very violent behaviour such as arson or homicide, or develop a psychotic state which is usually short-lived and highly treatable with supportive containment and neuroleptics.

It is the crack in the armour of the well-compensated delinquent that offers opportunities for a psychotherapeutic response. In a delinquent way of life, the individual has to avoid concern for others; concern decreases the capacity to use others to get rid of conflict, since it threatens the sense of being carefree. 'Successful' delinquents, therefore, are forced to avoid close involvement, and casual, promiscuous and affectionateless relationships are much safer for them psychologically. This is as true for women as it is for men: for instance, the life of many prostitutes appears to be perplexing in its acceptance of affectionlessness and the management of grave hazards, but is understandable within the context of these psychopathological needs. Positive reliance on others gives rise to problems connected with separation, jealousy and frustration which, in the absence of the habitual delinquent solutions, can lead to the outbursts of acute disturbance with violence or catastrophic behaviour.

Case study 15.3   Violence initiated by self-reform

A burglar, with no history of violence, was able to fulfil his wish to give up criminality and settle down when he unexpectedly came across a large quantity of valuable jewels in a house that he had burgled. He had always wanted to retire from crime so he married and with the money he had acquired set up a pet shop and tried to lead a respectable way of life. He expected happiness to follow, but found himself becoming increasingly and perplexedly disturbed, often when his wife was out and sometimes for no reason he could understand. He developed bouts of acute disturbance and fury, and found himself wrecking the pet shop and attacking the animals. On one occasion, he killed a particularly fine parrot. His solution was not consciously devised, but he began once again to break into houses. He found that if he could break into a house at night and sit in the living room, listening to the sounds of the sleeping inhabitants upstairs, it had a calming effect. As he needed no money, he didn't rob the house, but would occasionally take an ashtray or some small object. By returning to his criminal behaviour he was able to control his bouts of acute disturbance. However, he was eventually caught and sent to prison where he was treated for some time with an interpretive and explanatory approach.

The long-term outcome of this, and other such cases is uncertain. It may be possible for such individuals to gain some insight into the nature of their difficulties, but separation problems and the management of frustration, particularly in view of the underlying deprivation, is often too great for any active therapeutic effort to stand much chance of surviving. The uncovering of areas of deprivation and unfulfilled dependency can produce enormous pressure on both therapist and patient, with a speedy move into delinquent acting out, or even violence, when the patient feels let down or abandoned within the therapy. The least hazardous tactic is to contain the individual in a way which minimises the reinforcement of delinquent strategies. This is easier said than done, since such personalities manufacture delinquent cultures and provoke others, especially in penal institutions, into cold and often violent responses towards them. However, from the point of view of psychotherapy, staff support and constant attempts to avoid being pulled into a retaliatory collusive relationship is usually the best that can be managed.

Category 2: Poorly-compensated delinquents and frail neurotic personalities

Category 2 patients represent a spectrum of disorder, ranging from delinquent personalities who are decompensating fairly regularly at one end, to groups of neurotically frail but basically non-delinquent personalities at the other, who may be pushed into delinquent acts, often as a result of drug-taking or alcoholism, or when faced with situations with which they cannot cope. Many sexual offenders, especially those who abuse children or who expose their genitals in public, as well as those who engage in non-criminal behaviour, such as cross-dressing, belong in this category.

A conceptual model for stress management

Elsewhere (Gallwey 1990), the author has described a model based on management of stress which is intended to give a conceptual framework for assessment and deciding on the type of psychotherapeutic input for individuals within this group. The model is based upon a conceptualisation of the ideal management of stress, and the diagrammatic representations are set out below.

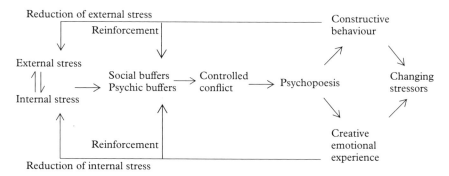

Fig. 15.1   The ideal management of stress.

As Figure 15.1 shows, stress is divided into internal and external stress. Internal stress partly derives from instinctual pressure, but is linked with cyclical patterns of internal fantasy and is inevitably bound up with external stress, although often in ways that are obscure and subtle. Perhaps the most common situation is one in which a figure in the individual's environment evokes an exacerbation of a recurring pattern of conflict because of their historical significance in the individual's life. Authority figures may be very powerful in this way, as will figures on whom individuals are dependent. An understanding of the factors which have triggered such an exacerbation of internal stress may be difficult to establish, but a working hypothesis can often be constructed from the knowledge of an individual's history and an examination of events prior to significant episodes.

Stress is *buffered* by positive social support and through flexible psychic defences which derive from the internalisation of good nurturing experiences, including a good container as described above. This gives the individual a chance to come to terms with the initial impact of stress, and an opportunity not just for its management but also for the creative use of conflict, which the author has termed *'psychopoesis'*. By this, is meant not only those psychological factors which help a person to understand the nature of stress and the things which have led to it, and to devise strategies to overcome it, but also psychological growth under the stimulus of stress, including the changes described by Klein in her concept of the depressive position (Segal 1964). These include the capacity for self-appraisal and the appraisal of others, with the positive identification of good experiences and the discovering of good and bad aspects of the self and of others. The metabolising of stress deriving from the presence of an internal container, as described above, often discernable in dreams, plays a central part in the process of psychopoesis (Bion 1970).

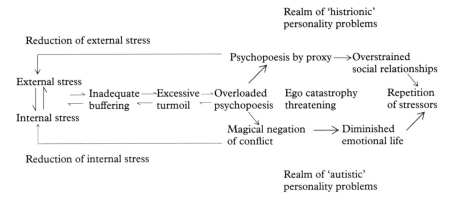

Fig. 15.2   The neurotic management of stress.

In the neurotic positions, stress is not managed in this way. There is a poverty of buffering so that emotional turbulence is not controlled, and psychopoetic activity, which already may be deficient, becomes severely limited or impossible. In the face of this, the individual will endeavour to use others to carry out psychopoetic functions on his behalf – psychopoesis by proxy. This regressive use of others leads to an impoverishment of social relationships, as individuals thus recruited eventually tire of being used in this way, which in turn weakens the availability of social buffers. The alternative pathway leads to omnipotent or 'magical' solutions.

The two types of solution overlap, since to a greater or lesser extent other people will be experienced as part of the magical solutions and may unconsciously or willingly collude. From this perspective, projective identification can be seen as a central magical fantasy.

A combination of the regressive use of others through psychopoesis by proxy, and the utilisation of magical mental mechanisms is generally effective in reducing the stress in the neurotic and in some borderline positions, although it fails to establish the kind of learning and growth that follows from psychopoesis proper. It tends to weaken social relationships and social buffers, and makes the individual over-reliant on purely magical solutions to conflict and stress. Preference for the type of solution in the neurotic position between the regressive use of others and magical mechanisms tends to dictate the personality as either autistic or histrionic.

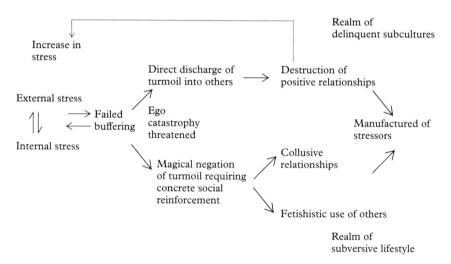

Fig. 15.3   The delinquent management of turmoil.

Figure 15.3 sets out the situation in which stress is managed by delinquent manoeuvres. Here, the buffering is so inadequate and the resources of the personality so impoverished that neither psychopoesis by proxy nor internal magical solutions acting on their own are available.

As described above, habitual delinquents have been unable to build a repertoire of magical solutions in fantasy, and will need to reinforce attempts at such magical solutions by concrete manufacturing of them in the external world in order to defend themselves against the impact of annihilatory anxiety. Individuals can move from an habitually neurotic position into a delinquent one if stress is strong enough or if social or internal buffers fail.

Psychotherapy with frail personalities

A neurotic position provides a window for psychotherapy. It is, however, very important to bear in mind the problem of over-dependency. Most severely deprived people have found ways of coping with their deep sense of need, and it may be a serious disservice to increase contact with their deprivation. Many such individuals become somewhat frantically attached to their therapist, and over-dependency may lead to sudden rejection and cessation of treatment. This in turn could lead to catastrophic behaviour and a worsening in the risk of offending. This is almost always a problem to be considered in the psychotherapy of delinquents and frail person- alities.

Treatment approaches can be directed either at the magical solutions or via the need for psychopoesis by proxy. Both require help with buffering.

The psycho-analytic approach and the modification of omnipotence

The unconscious mental mechanisms described by the various schools of psychoanalysis are all magical solutions, in that they rely on alterations in the experience of external and internal truth. This is as true of the ego defences (Freud A 1937) as it is of the more primitive defences of splitting, projective identification and the manic defence (Segal 1981).

In psychoanalytic technique, except for attempts to replicate primitive containing functions in the transference, psychopoesis by proxy is deliberately withheld (the technique of abstinence; see Freud 1915). Reassurance, advice, moral coercion, direct support or demonstrations of affection or disapproval are tactically avoided, with the result that there is an increase in the pressure toward magical solutions. The aim is to facilitate their discovery and elucidation so that the patient can become aware of the real nature of his unresolved problems, as well as the illusory, pseudo-solutions based upon omnipotent fantasies. Clearly, such an approach demands a great deal both from patient and therapist. The therapist has the problem of attempting to identify the magical solutions, which are elusive and subtly muddled with real external difficulties and creative fantasies, as well as trying to avoid the imposition of his own moral prejudices, emotional shortcomings and conceptual dogmas onto the patient. On the patient's side, psychoanalytic work demands a real wish to get better, a need for truth, a capacity to manage pain and an ability to learn through revelation (see Auden 1973 on the Socratic dialectic and psycho-analysis). Letting go of illusory magical solutions is not at all easy, particularly when they appear to support self-esteem, a sense of superiority and even freedom from conflict. However, the aim is to increase both psychopoetic capacity and internal buffering, making the individual both more creative and more self-sufficient. Many disturbed and frail personalities find it very difficult to cope without psychopoesis by proxy, and where this is unavailable, then it is futile to attempt the psychoanalytic approach. Psychoanalytical patients have to survive between sessions and be sufficiently able to manage their lives without continual direct support.

Treatment based on 'psychopoesis by proxy'

The immediate advantage of providing psychopoesis by proxy is to lessen the reliance on magical solutions so that the patient may become more approachable interpersonally and may feel quickly better. It is used quite spontaneously as a tactic in almost all hospital admissions for inpatient treatment, and is a very valuable tool for creating a therapeutic alliance, either for chemotherapy or for beginning a more direct psychological approach. Behavioural treatments (Perkin 1990), direct psychological techniques, occupational therapy and social training should be aimed at progressively lessening psychopoesis by proxy, and at increasing a person's skills and capacity to manage both his external relationships and his internal conflicts.

Successful direct approaches can often revive an individual's psychopoetic capacity so that he can begin to take up the management of his own conflicts. They have limited effect on fundamental magical solutions which have persisted since infancy and childhood – particularly when they have given rise to personality structures which rely very heavily on such magical solutions as splitting, projective identification and the manic defence. Although such approaches may increase opportunities for creating social buffers, internal buffering will only be minimally improved. Purely cognitive treatments do not usually address directly magical solution in fantasy, but can explore the implications of them indirectly. Art and drama therapy, however, can do so, and when skillfully used may lessen an individual's reliance on magical solutions.

Many individuals in the frail neurotic category benefit from long-term supportive psychotherapy (see Ch. 9), and the use of outpatient groups (see Ch. 3) can be a good way of providing this type of social buffering and encouragement to psychopoesis. These patients may very well relapse during breaks in treatment, and the author's practice is to encourage patients to meet as a group while he is on holiday, or to work with a co-therapist and take holidays at different times. The other alternative is to have junior doctors take such groups as part of their training, and to keep the group going through changes of doctors but with some continuity of approach provided by supervision. Formal psychotherapy groups can form part of a range of supportive help, and community health teams may be very well equipped to provide the combination social buffers, a degree of active psychological help and much long-term support which these patients need.

Category 3: Over-defended neurotic personalities

Category 3, that of over-defended neurotic personalities, obviously overlaps with the previous one. However, individuals in this group have personalities which are manifestly neurotically organised, rather than being frail individuals with bouts of neurotic turbulence. Social maladjustment, as with the other categories, may arise in two ways, either as an expression of the personality problem itself, or as a result of decompensation. Two major subgroups emerge in this category – hysterical personality disorders and obsessional ones.

Hysterical personalities use magical fantasies but, with the over-involvement of others, try to evade having to grapple with their conflicts and this can lead to frank maladjustment. They may move into the delinquent position during containerless episodes, and the disturbed relationship with the world that results can give rise to florid 'psychopathic' behaviour.

The second group, patients with obsessional disorders, are more autistic in the sense that the disturbances are managed more internally and often by symptom formation which is highly personal, such as rituals, circular thinking, phobias, and so on. Such obsessional personalities, because their main psychic pre-occupation is the sado-masochistic control of their internal figures, can be equivalently controlling, cruel and even sadistic in their interpersonal relationships. Sometimes, they will need support from the environment in order to check their obsessional controlling, and although this may be done through inanimate objects, sometimes there can be the overt fetishistic use of others. The degree of cruel controlling and the amount of destructive and violent feelings being managed by the magical obsessional fantasies, results in good parts of the self reacting with depressive bouts and much sense of guilt. Such personalities can show pathological honesty when their sense of guilt becomes attached to some small misdemeanour, real or imagined; they can suffer periods of great unhappiness with ruminative worrying about some piece of behaviour, and this can escalate into depressive illness. When obsessional personalities decompensate, either during a depressive bout or as a result of some other interpersonal stress, then the resulting emotional disturbance can lead to offending behaviour, such as stealing. When the disturbance contains very large quantities of fury then sadistic, violent behaviour or even homicide can result.

The treatment of the hysterical personality disorders is very difficult. Because of their manipulative needs and great problem in managing psychic truth, any insight-giving treatment is very hard. Some intelligent and well-motivated people can use psychoanalytic psychotherapy to produce major change, but the treatments are usually prolonged.

Psychoanalytic treatment of obsessional individuals tends to be very static. Behavioural treatment of obsessionalism has little impact upon individuals in this category because of the associated personality problems. When the conflicts behind the obsessional defences do not contain a great degree of violence, but the controlling has arisen as a result of deprivation of affection by rigid parents, then the prognosis can be much better. Neurotic individuals of the obsessional/depressive variety, sometimes begin to shoplift or commit minor sexual misdemeanours, such as genital exposing, when social pressures or the anxiety of ageing break through the pattern of an over-controlling morality. Cognitive psychotherapy and support, and protection from the consequences of the offending behaviour through expert evidence in mitigation to the Courts, is very worthwhile in these cases.

Category 4: 'Psychotic personality' types

The author prefers to use the term 'psychotic' rather than 'borderline' personality types (see Ch. 14), since the word 'borderline' is used so haphazardly and has so many different meanings that it is best avoided. It has been suggested (Gallwey 1985) that the DSM III 'borderline personality disorder' is unsound, and that the term should only be used descriptively where an individual's mental state is such that he is on the borderline of psychosis, without having a frank mental illness. Used in this way, the individuals in this category, and some of the individuals in the next, are often in a borderline state of mind. In the present category, is included those paranoid, schizoid and narcissistic individuals who have not made a habitual delinquent adjustment but whose reliance on ego splitting, projective identification and manic defences have led them into harmful interpersonal behaviour, or who when they decompensate can become dangerous. The different subtypes have in common a degree of grandiosity which is a reflection of the success of their omnipotent strategies. They are usually socially very limited, although in some occupations where authority over other people is part of the job, their psychopathology can find a legalised outlet and may help them succeed in it. However, they are likely to go too far, abuse their position and, if unable to maintain it, collapse into catastrophic behaviour or psychosis. The extent of manifest paranoia in the sense of being suspicious, despising or victimised by others will depend upon the amount of hostility that is projected.

More passive, schizoid, socially isolated and enclosed personalities may not manifest persecutory anxiety or paranoid ideation because of the limitations in their interpersonal contact. Narcissistic superiority may be maintained by occupations which bring exhibitionistic gratification or popular acclaim, or by more discreet strategies often appearing as sexual deviations which support the grandiosity, such as paedophilia.

Case study 15.4   Too grand to be aroused by others

A middle-aged man was referred because he had been stealing underwear to support a longstanding fetishistic interest in which he put on ladies' knickers and spontaneously ejaculated. He was anorgasmic with his wife, but had maintained a relationship with her as well as running a moderately successful business. He had no other criminal history or behaviour. A period of behavioural psychotherapy had brought no change. He presented as a mildly mannered, somewhat remote individual, who seemed to want some help to change, both to avoid his criminal behaviour and to be more satisfactory as a husband. He had a self-effacing and passive manner, and although there were intimations of grandiosity in the way he spoke of himself and of others, there seemed no paranoia or manifest persecutory fears. He was very lacking in vitality in treatment, usually professed an absence of any thoughts and rarely responded to the therapist's interventions except to imply, usually indirectly, that they were meaningless.

During one session the therapist was interested to note that he made no reference to the fact that a woman in a house opposite the consulting rooms, which could be seen clearly both from where the therapist was sitting and from where the patient was lying on the couch, had begun to undress and was walking around with very little on having left the window of her room open. Most people would have thought the episode worth mentioning, and considering the patient's interest in underwear, his silence and reiteration that he had nothing on his mind needed investigation; however, in view of the shortage of time left in the session the therapist had to leave it unchallenged. The patient made no reference next time he came, so the therapist raised the issue, saying that he thought he could not have failed to notice something the day before across the way. The patient said that yes of course he had, and was not altogether surprised that the therapist should go to the trouble to hire a room and persuade a colleague to take off her clothes in order to try and get him to talk (and this on the National Health Service!). There was no hesitation whatsoever in his belief that the therapist had arranged the matter, and he concluded that the therapist must be desperate to make a success of his treatment of him. As a result of this startling evidence of the patient's grandiosity, the therapist was able to challenge it more, and a great deal of material emerged which indicated how paranoid he was. The patient constantly read the newspapers to see if there was a report of a girl having been knifed, in which case he wouldn't go out, being convinced that he would be accused of it. He also had a longstanding claustrophobic persecutory fear of being trapped.

Some lessening in his grandiosity, narcissistic remoteness, and persecutory anxieties led to an improved emotional and sexual relationship with his wife although, like so many longstanding deviant symptoms, his fascination with dressing in women's knickers continued episodically, albeit in a safer way.

Category 5: Normal and pseudo-normal personalities

Any individual who has sufficient ego capacity to hide both personality defects and behavioural problems falls into the category of normal and pseudo-normal personalities. Such individuals can be in groups 2 or 3, yet be able to achieve a normal adjustment because of areas of good ego functioning. The shortcomings and problems within their lives will emerge if they come to treatment, or may remain undiscovered until some sudden life crisis occurs, they are apprehended for a criminal offence or, sometimes, because spouse or family turn for help and their adjustment is threatened.

The pseudo-normal group is represented by those whose normality is not an indication of a degree of health. The individuals concerned have severe pathology which is covert, and their mental health is as a consequence very precarious. Three types can be identified: those with an encapsulated containerlessness, parasite personalities and the disguised narcissists.

(i) Encapsulated containerlessness

Individuals may have an encapsulated containerless area of themselves with much destructive content (Gallwey 1985). The encapsulation in these cases is sufficiently complete to enable them to mobilise a presenting personality which appears normal. Because of the lack of aggressivity within their presenting personality, they tend to be mild, unassertive individuals, but some 'leakage' of pathology may be managed by an often rather refined or esoteric sexual deviation, or by a degree of neurotic symptomatology, such as a phobia, hypochondriasis or unexplained attacks of anxiety. If encapsulation does break down, then catastrophic behaviour or episodes of psychosis may ensue. These are usually short-lived, with the personality organisation being reinstated after the crises. Their apparent normality and the obscurity of their pathology, together with their capacity for compliance, makes these individuals hard to assess. Adults with normal personalities who commit acts of violence when apparently sleepwalking may well fall into this subgroup.

Case study 15.5   A spectacle fetish that decompensated

An individual was caught carrying a knife, wearing a hood over his head, having attacked a woman and snatched her spectacles. He was a mild mannered, passive man, who had practised a secret fetishism when he would snatch spectacles from the faces of passers-by in the street. He had employment which took him out and about, and he had managed to pursue this criminal behaviour for years without being apprehended and without hurting any of his victims, although of course they were frightened and perplexed when they suddenly lost their spectacles. The thicker the spectacles, the greater their significance, and he would run off and later masturbate while holding the spectacles. He had a store of such spectacles hidden in a wood, and would go and look at them and masturbate over them. He was married and his wife had no inkling of his double life and his fetishistic needs. Stresses within his marriage created a breakdown in encapsulation which led to a rapid escalation, so that he went out hooded carrying a knife; had he not been apprehended, some ghastly, bizarre act of violence might well have followed.

Probably only a small percentage of such cases can be helped with long-term exploratory analytical psychotherapy in which the encapsulated pathology can be brought into the transference and integrated. Williams (1964) has described the treatment of such encapsulated pathology in a series of sexual murderers, in which encapsulation had broken down with the resulting homicide. He used a psychoanalytic technique combined with abreaction and subsequent analysis of written material. All his cases were treated in prison.

(ii) Parasitic personalities

Parasitic personalities are those with hollow eggshell egos who disguise this behind a parasitic dependence on another person or institution (Gallwey 1985). When they are abandoned by the 'host', which may occur after their discharge from the army or prison, or when their long-suffering spouse is eventually freed from them, then depression, psychotic illness or criminal behaviour of one kind or another can ensue. Whole varieties of behaviour are possible, from mild delinquent acts to spiralling disturbance ending in homicide. Many individuals seen in prison fall into this category. They appear perfectly normal in prison, do not express paranoid or delinquent attitudes, and may cooperate fully with attempts at rehabilitation and psychological treatment; yet, within a short time of discharge, they have reverted to the sort of criminal behaviour that has resulted in recurrent imprisonment. Even with years in penal practice, it can be terribly difficult to differentiate between those who have a more genuine capacity to be helped, and those who have essentially hollow egos and are unable to cope with the stresses of independent existence but who present as normal while hosted by an institution or spouse. These individuals pose an obvious problem of over-dependency in psychotherapy (Winnicott 1955) and easily become institutionalised. Catastrophic reactions when therapeutic support is removed is a real risk in these cases.

(iii) The disguised narcissists

The way in which paranoid feelings and persecutory anxiety can be defended against by narcissistic strategies of superiority supported by positions of authority or social prominence has been described earlier. In this present group, the narcissism is both disguised and more benign (Rosenfeld 1971). In fact, the individuals may appear to lead a life socially very dedicated to others, or to the talents and capacities which they may have developed to a high degree of social usefulness. Nevertheless, their social position supports a covert narcissistic position which protects them against major disturbance. Some individuals in the caring professions project collapsed, disturbed and ill parts of themselves into their clients or patients, and look after them sometimes in an extremely over-dedicated way. Their sense of superiority is hidden behind their dedication, the narcissism resting on identification with good but idealised internal objects. They are unable to see that they are themselves ill, and as long as they have someone to look after, they seem normal or even heroic individuals. The collapse of this proxied personality organisation for one reason or another can lead to decompensation into mental disorder, often severe depression or behavioural disturbance including criminal activity, such as shoplifting, sudden unexplained genital exposure, sexual assaults or destructive angry behaviour. Such cases are not uncommon in the entertainment industry, where both the narcissistic superiority and the disturbance that it hides can be disguised behind a lively, sensitive, aesthetically appreciative presenting personality, in which apparent interest in others and a rich store of experience can be captivating and convincing. Often, such individuals secretly support this benign pseudo-normality with drugs or alcohol, which gradually weakens their defence against their hidden conflicts until they finally break through. Catastrophic behaviour, from unexpected suicides to 'breakdowns', is often the outcome of such decompensation. Behavioural problems, often some form of illegal sexual deviance, such as paederism can also result from the need to bolster their grandiosity.

Case study 15.6   A disturbed comedian

A bisexual man with a developed interest in the wellbeing of a socially disadvantaged group on a charitable basis, who was an exceptional comedian and impersonator and able to convey a degree of charm and sensitivity to others, became during periods of depression a habitual visitor to public lavatories and public parks, where he indulged in activities of a patently infantile kind. He particularly enjoyed being fallated by anonymous individuals, which supported his flagging narcissistic superiority which was normally sustained by his real care for others or his capacity to win applause. Analysis of these episodes of infantile behaviour suggested that in his mind he was both feeding someone with his penis and at the same time had changed the male mouth into a female vagina. These magical fantasies reflected his fear of his father's mouth, which was cruel and shouting, as well as his panic about the frailty of his mother as a container and provider of his own needs. Before coming into psychoanalytic treatment, these fantasies had sometimes failed to hold up his increasing depression and paranoid anxiety, and he had been hospitalised and given ECT. In psychoanalysis, his pseudo-normal personality gave way to frequent paranoid furies, frantic attempts at superiority and devaluation of his therapist, with episodes of physical violence during which the therapist was worried for his safety. However, he persisted in treatment, and finally overcame his infantile homosexuality, made considerable further professional achievement and found personal happiness in a heterosexual relationship. There is little doubt that his intelligence, his positive identifications, his natural aesthetic capacity, his sense of humour and other positive qualities were major factors in his successful treatment.

By and large, this group does offer the possibility of being considerably helped. Their personalities have many positive attributes, and rest in part on a narcissistic identification with idealised internal figures. As a result, they have many resources to mobilise in the service of their treatment; they are often good candidates for psychoanalytical treatments, including full analysis, so it is important to be able to identify them.

Category 6: Those with a primary psychiatric diagnosis of mental illness or organic disorder

In Category 6 patients, obviously the priority is to treat the mental illness, but when the previous personality has been of a type in which social maladjustment has played a part then it is very well worth-while trying to assess it in terms of the previous categories.

Rehabilitation needs to take account of the personality weaknesses, since cooperation with after-care, including the management of medication in the long term, may depend upon organising the appropriate form of psychological help.

Case study 15.7   Social maladjustment in a brain-damaged man

A man who had been mildly delinquent in his younger days developed a variety of behaviour problems as a result of extensive brain injury following a road traffic accident. He had made an apparent improvement after repeated hospital admissions, but his de-institutionalisation and community care had been disastrous for him and had caused considerable anxiety in the community because of his sinister and frightening behaviour towards young children. His previous personality and organic deficit resulted in a grave impoverishment of internal buffers so that he had an excessive need for social ones. In an institution, with the skilled and constant supervision and help of staff, he was able to achieve a degree of psychopoetic activity leading to a useful and reasonably happy way of life for him. However, if this input was lessened, he became manipulative and delinquent, and when it was inevitably reduced during his community care, and with the increase in interpersonal stress that social contacts brought him, his behaviour deteriorated so that bizarre offending behaviour and the threat of more serious criminality to children resulted in arrest and a Hospital Order. His mental state and behaviour improved rapidly with containing management and 'psychopoesis by proxy'.

CONCLUSION

The theoretical models and categorisation offered in this chapter aim to provide a framework for the broad understanding of various psycho-pathological causes of social maladjustment. They are meant to facilitate the organisation of psychotherapeutic treatment and management of individuals with a tendency to destructive or dangerous behaviour who are so difficult to contact and to maintain in therapy. The whole area is largely unexplored and awaits more detailed clinical research. It is to be hoped this contribution may make some bad behaviour more understandable and reduce the obstacles, including the emotional ones, to exploring it.

FURTHER READING

Bion W R 1962 Learning from experience. Heinemann, London
Gallwey P 1990 The psychopathology of neurosis and offending. In: Bluglass R, Bowden P
    (eds) The principles and practice of forensic psychiatry. Churchill Livingstone, Edinburgh
West D J 1982 Delinquency: its roots, careers and prospects. Heinemann, London
Winnicott D W 1984 In: Winnicott C, Shepherd R, Davis M (eds) Deprivation and
    delinquency. Tavistock, London

16. Psychosomatic disorders

P. J. Shoenberg

'In other words, my body is not a hero.' (Roland Barthes)

INTRODUCTION

This chapter is concerned with the ways in which psychotherapy may be helpful to patients suffering from psychosomatic disorders. These are the physical conditions in which psychological factors significantly contribute to the genesis of the symptoms. This distinguishes them from the somatisation disorders, which are neurotic disorders in which the hysterical mechanism of conversion operates. In general practice, McWhinney (1981) has observed that a physical illness may present for five different reasons: firstly, because the patient's symptoms have become intolerable; secondly, because of the psychological implications of the symptoms to the patient, (i.e. they are causing anxiety); thirdly, because · the symptoms are being used as a way of presenting a problem of living; fourthly for administrative reasons; and finally, for preventative reasons. In the second category is to be found hypochondriacal anxiety and realistic anxiety about symptoms. In the third category, the doctor will encounter illness that is being used by the patient for primary and secondary gain (as in the hysterical conversion symptom), and illness that has been produced partly by the effects of psychological stress on the body. It is this last group of illnesses that is loosely described as being psychosomatic.

Most of our understanding of the psychogenesis of psychosomatic illness has been derived from observations made in this century. The term, 'psychosomatic' was coined at the beginning of the 19th century by the German physician, Heinroth (Bynùm 1983), and it was the patient and poet Samuel Taylor Coleridge who, in referring to his physical condition, spoke of his 'Psychosomatic Ology' at this time. However, most patients, as Barthes' comment implies, would rather regard their body than their mind as the uncourageous one. Only a few patients are as insightful as Coleridge. In some respects, our modern understanding of medicine and psychosomatics support Barthes' view, in that we now recognise that in order for a psychosomatic illness to occur, the body itself must be as vulnerable as the mind. Thus, we now tend to think of the psychosomatic illness as a psychobiological disorder.

The psychotherapist who attempts to do psychotherapy with patients suffering from physical disorders is bound to feel a conflict between his desire to find meaning in his patient's symptoms, and his need to comprehend any psychobiological mechanisms contributing to the condition. He is also to some extent at the mercy of his patient's physical suffering. These three factors – namely, the search for symbolic meaning, the need for scientific understanding, and the reality of the patient's physical experiences – have given the practice of psychotherapy in psychosomatic medicine a complex development and history.

Although we now recognise that psychological factors may play a part in all physical illness, we know that this role may be more significant in certain medical conditions. In some of these, there are gross changes in structure, such as in essential hypertension, bronchial asthma, peptic ulceration, ulcerative colitis and eczema. In others, there are changes in physiology leading to disturbances of function alone, such as in irritable bowel syndrome, migraine and tension headaches. Each illness is also likely to involve a variety of psychological reactions depending on the personality of the sufferer, especially when the illnes is prolonged or life-threatening. There are also important cultural variables, both in the ways in which physical illness is perceived, and in the ways in which the patient is likely to expect the doctor to deal with his condition (Pouillon 1972). The purpose of this chapter is to explore the scope for psychotherapy in psychosomatic disorders. There are various reviews of the psycho-biological aspects of individual psychosomatic disorders (Weiner 1977, Cheren 1989, Kaplan & Sadock 1989, Wolff & Shoenberg 1990).

HISTORICAL ASPECTS: THEORIES OF PSYCHOPATHOLOGY

Physical symptoms as symbolic communication

Psychotherapeutic work with psychosomatic disorders began in the early years of the 20th century, with Groddeck, a German physician and friend of Freud. He considered that all illness was determined by an unconscious factor which he called the 'It'; for him, this meant that all illnesses had psychological significance and might be amenable to psychotherapy (Groddeck 1925). The psychoanalyst, Ferenczi argued that in certain medical disorders where the autonomic nervous system was involved (such as ulcerative colitis), a psychosomatic mechanism was involved in producing the illness. This mechanism was that of conversion, as in hysteria. This led to the view that the psychosomatic disorders were essentially neurotic disorders whose symptoms could be interpreted symbolically, as in conversion hysteria.

Concept of psychosomatic specificity of intrapsychic conflict for given psychosomatic disorders

In the 1930s and 1940s, a group of psychoanalysts, including Alexander, Deutsch and Sperling, began to use psychoanalysis to treat patients with some of the medical disorders which were regarded as psychosomatic. These included bronchial asthma, peptic ulcer, essential hypertension, ulcerative colitis, rheumatoid arthritis, eczema and thyrotoxicosis. These psychotherapists also believed that the psychological vulnerability to disease was based on neurotic psychopathology, but that the aetiology of each condition was nevertheless multifactorial, and included physical factors. In Alexander's model of disease, he argued that a specific intrapsychic conflict could be activated by a stressful life event. This then led to psychobiological interaction with a vulnerable target organ, thus producing specific somatic changes and symptoms. So, for example in duodenal ulceration, a threat to a person's dependency needs was thought to activate a repressed conflict over oral instinctual needs, which then interacted with elevated blood pepsinogen levels to result in peptic ulceration in the duodenum (Alexander et al 1968).

Many of these theories have been questioned in the light of subsequent discoveries in medicine and psychobiology. Firstly, all these diseases were found to be more complex than had been realised at the time of Alexander's work. For example, the concept of ulcerative colitis was seen as part of inflammatory bowel disease, thus including the newly discovered Crohn's disease which has a different physical pathology. Secondly, in many cases no intrapsychic conflict could be found that was specific for a given psychosomatic condition. Thirdly, the clinical results of Alexander's approach were often disappointing. Although many patients did change psychologically as a result of psychoanalysis, the illness did not necessarily improve (Taylor 1989).

Concept of life events and object loss as stressful

In the 1960s, Engel and Schmale began to emphasise the role of life events in the development of disease. They noted that some individuals would respond to important losses by developing feelings of helplessness and hopelessness, which were accompanied by a physiological conservation-withdrawal response. The resultant 'giving-up-given-up' complex could lead to changes in the immune system, autonomic nervous system and endocrine system, so lowering the body's resistance to disease (Engel 1968). Thus, psychotherapy shifted from an interpretive to a rather more supportive approach, in which ego support was provided in an attempt to restore the patient's disrupted object relationships. Engel found, however, that the medically ill patients often transferred their dependency needs onto their psychotherapist. He then often had to function as a permanently supportive figure. Consequently, a disruption in the psychotherapy could trigger a recurrence of the illness, for example, ulcerative colitis (Taylor 1989).

Concept of 'Pensée Operatoire': Alexithymia

In the 1960s and 1970s, with increasing interest in ego functions, the observation that many medical patients show difficulty in expressing emotions, led to a new model of the psychosomatic personality. Marty and de M'Uzan proposed that there was a particular type of thinking in psychosomatic patients which they called 'la Pensée Operatoire' (de M'Uzan 1974). Sifneos and Nemiah later spoke of the 'Alexithymic personality' (Nemiah 1977). Both groups of psychoanalysts agreed that the psychosomatic patient had a particular difficulty in finding words for his feelings; they noticed that he suffered from an impoverished dream and fantasy life, either, they speculated, because of his very early experiences with the mother or because of structural defects in the brain. This had implications for psychotherapeutic technique. One group of analysts argued that this disturbance made for major limitations on the analysability of these patients. Another group, (McDougall 1974), argued that this deficit demanded greater emotional responsiveness from the psychotherapist toward the patient, so as to help him to get in touch with his feelings.

Taylor (1987), has introduced the ideas of Self Psychology, together with concepts about the early psychobiological regulatory functions of the mother. His book on the psychoanalytic approaches to medical disorders provides a unique coverage of this subject. In it, he explores the effects of potential psychological disturbances of the early maternal environment on the psychosomatic patient. He draws upon new research into the psychobiological regulatory aspects of the mother-baby relationship, and proposes ways in which emotional disturbances in the relationship may influence both these regulatory functions of the mother and the baby's growing sense of self. In this way, he suggests a developmental schema for the subsequent appearance of the Alexithymic personality with its potential for psychosomatic disorder.

In general, there is no consensus of opinion about either the psychopathology, or the most appropriate way of working psycho-therapeutically, with these patients. However, there is general agreement that these are difficult patients to work with in psychotherapy. The therapy is limited by their lack of transference readiness, and by their poor capacity to use interpretations. These difficulties may relate to real deficits in the early mother-infant relationship, which have made later objects relationships precarious, threatening the patient with a psychosomatic breakdown in the face of their disruption. However, not all patients suffering from psychosomatic disorders are emotionally disturbed, and it would be false to assume there must always be significant accompanying psychopathology.

THE SCOPE FOR PSYCHOTHERAPY IN THE TREATMENT OF PSYCHOSOMATIC DISORDERS

There is some irony in the fact that in the District General Hospital-based Psychotherapy department relatively few patients with psychosomatic disorders are referred to the psychotherapist. The level of referrals depends not only on the goodwill and the understanding built up between the psychotherapist and his medical and surgical colleagues, but also upon the willingness of such patients to be referred in the first place. The psychosomatic predicament is one in which real bodily illness is often used as a defence against intolerable anxiety or depression.Not unnaturally, these patients regard a referral to a psychotherapist with suspicion and resistance, fearing that it represents a rejection by their physician or surgeon. If they do accept the idea of going to see a psychotherapist, it is often with a measure of ambivalence.

ORGANISATION OF PSYCHOTHERAPY SERVICES IN THE HOSPITAL CARE OF PSYCHOSOMATIC DISORDERS

In some hospitals, special multidisciplinary teams with an interest in the psychotherapeutic management of psychosomatic disorders have been developed. At the Presbyterian Hospital at Columbia University in New York, a team of physicians and psychoanalysts combined forces to treat patients with ulcerative colitis. In Paris, a similar team under the leadership of a consultant gastroenterologist was created at the Hospital Bichat so as to treat patients with a variety of gastrointestinal disorders. The work of these teams has deepened our understanding of the personality of the psychosomatic patient. For example, a study by Karush, a psychoanalyst, and his colleagues gave rise to a deeper understanding of how to select patients with ulcerative colitis for psychotherapy (Karush et al 1977). Work from Paris team led to fundamental changes in our thinking about the personality of all psychosomatic patients, with their idea of operatory thinking, or 'Pensée Operatoire' (de M'Uzan, 1974). In Germany, a good deal of hospital psychosomatic work has been done in special inpatient psychosomatic units staffed by physicians who are also trained as psychotherapists (Stephanos 1975).

In Britain the inpatient and outpatient care of psychosomatic disorders is not so highly developed. Only a handful of the patients referred to a psychotherapy department will have psychosomatic disorders. Some have been referred from within the hospital, and some from local general practitioners. The commonest of these disorders are the eating disorders (see Ch.18), anorexia nervosa, bulimia nervosa or psychogenic obesity.

After this, there will be a few patients with gastrointestinal disturbances, such as irritable bowel syndrome, ulcerative colitis and peptic ulceration. Some patients are referred with bronchial asthma with or without associated eczema. The psychotherapist may also see essential hypertension and some patients with locomotor disorders such as rheumatoid arthritis, as well as a variety of tension disorders, including psychogenic vomiting, hyperventilation and tension headaches. Some patients seen by the liaison psychiatrists will be referred for psychotherapy: these include patients with chronic psychogenic pain.

Psychotherapy assessment

In the first place a careful assessment of each of these psychosomatic patients must be made. Often, such an assessment is prolonged over several interviews because it is very hard to decide how motivated the patient really is and how much insight he has. Here is an example:

Case study 16.1   Need for prolonged psychotherapy assessment

The author was recently asked by a rheumatologist colleague to see a young woman with a severe, band-like, frontal headache which had troubled her continuously for about three years. Her general practitioner had spent a good deal of time trying to understand these headaches, which he suspected had no organic cause. However, his efforts had been unrewarded as this patient had turned to another general practitioner in the practice who had referred her to the hospital. Here, she had initially been seen by a consultant neurologist who had fully investigated her for a neurological disorder, with no positive findings. He had then referred her to the consultant rheumatologist who, after some further investigations, had found some minimal evidence of an immune disorder, systemic lupus erythematosis. He now referred this young woman to an immunologist, who, however, could not confirm this diagnosis of systemic lupus. At this point she was referred for a psychological opinion.

Elysa came across as a rather tense, highly intelligent young woman; she was very tall with rather heavy features. On the one hand she was preoccupied with her headache, and yet on the other hand she seemed curiously unaffected by it. Each day she carried out demanding research into the genesis of strokes in rabbits. At night, she returned home where she still lived with her mother. Her background pointed to various significant psychological factors in the causation of her headache: her parents had separated when Elysa was twelve years old, and at around this time she became frightened of going to school. She was treated for this with behaviour therapy which helped her symptomatically. She changed her school to a private tutorial college, where she became very attached to a male teacher. Some time later, one of her brothers had a schizophrenic breakdown. She was deeply affected by his illness, which had frightened her. Soon after his mental breakdown she developed the headache. Her relationship to her teacher now deepened into a love affair, but was never consummated.

The telling of this story, while revealing much about Elysa's past life, did not allow her to unburden any great emotion or relieve her of her headache. The therapist saw her on a number of occasions. Each time she complained that her headache was no better, being mistrustful of his approach and feeling that she had been abandoned by her physician. She retained the view that there really was an organic cause for her pain. One day, she told the therapist that not only was her headache worse but also that she had recently repeatedly felt sick. Now the therapist too began to doubt the psychogenicity of her headache, examined her for an organic cause and convinced himself that she needed urgent neurological attention. He referred her to the neurologist, who could find nothing wrong with her and started her on a course of antidepressants. He sent her back to the rheumatologist who then referred her back to the psychotherapist. As there was no evidence of any depression in Elysa by the time she returned to him, the therapist stopped the antidepressants and continued his now prolonged psychotherapy assessment. Finally, she did decide to have psychotherapy. Maybe this was more from exhaustion than from any deeper motivation; however it turned out to be a good decision; her psychotherapy, (undertaken by a colleague in the department), helped her to express and feel much deeper feelings, and her headache left her.

There are various points about this story. Firstly, a series of assessment interviews may help one arrive at some sense of motivation in the patient. Secondly, the possibility that there may be an underlying physical cause is often a persistent anxiety for the psychotherapist, who should usually share the care of his patient with a good physician. Often, there is additional physical pathology which requires investigation and care by a physician. Thirdly, Elysa's progress through so many doctors is very typical, as Balint (1957) first noted.

Collaboration and conflict between carers: 'scatter of therapeutic agents'

The psychotherapy of the psychosomatic patient has to be a shared enterprise from its outset, involving the psychotherapist, the hospital physician and often a general practitioner as partners. This partnership may break down if the patient splits off important feelings and projects these onto his different carers, encouraging destructive rivalries between them. These splits may be related to older conflicts between the parents during the patient's childhood, and this seems particularly characteristic of anorexia nervosa. These splits may mirror aspects of the self at odds with each other, for example the psyche with the soma, good and bad parts, and so on. The following case provides another example, in which the patient was suffering with ulcerative colitis (Shoenberg 1986).

Case study 16.2   Provocation of conflicts between carers in a case of ulcerative colitis

Caroline suffered from ulcerative colitis, with a fairly mild form of proctocolitis of some years duration; she had been in once-weekly psychotherapy for some months. When she first came to see the new therapist, she had been taking propranolol, as an anxiolytic agent for phobic symptoms. By now she was less anxious, and the therapist discussed with her the idea that she might discontinue her medication. She seemed quite happy with this idea, and he said that he would write to her physician and her general practitioner to let them know this plan. A week later, when she came for her next session, she began by asking: 'What shall I do? My G P has just advised me to increase my dose of propranolol'. The therapist reflected and then said, 'Well, I suppose you would find it interesting to see me and him fight it out over the propranolol'. She laughed and in fact stopped taking the drug.

Winnicott (1966), the psychoanalyst and paediatrician, noticed that very often psychosomatic patients needed to find more than two or three carers: he described patients who accumulated even a whole range, including hypnotherapists, acupuncturists, masseurs and priests, in addition to the psychotherapist and his medical colleagues. He referred to this phenomenon as the 'scatter of therapeutic agents', and interpreted it as reflecting the patient's fear of dependence on one person alone. These patients, who have great dependency needs, have a real difficulty in developing a transference to the one psychotherapist. They use this 'scatter of therapeutic agents' to contain many of their unconscious anxieties. They tend to treat the psychotherapeutic setting with reserve, and behave very passively towards psychotherapy.

Case study 16.2 (contd)   Passivity and vulnerability in psychosomatic cases

Caroline, the woman with ulcerative colitis discussed above, would sometimes say that she was 'taking psychotherapy' as if it were another pill. The therapist found her passive attitude very difficult, and felt that his role in her affairs was sometimes more supportive than interpretive. This was compounded by his sense that she was physically so vulnerable, which made him reluctant to be too vigorous in his interpretations. Caroline's psychotherapy permitted her some relief from her unpleasant attacks of diarrhoea, and also helped her to become a more independent person. However, the ending of this therapy was heralded by a major attack of rectal bleeding.

Shame and anger in psychosomatic patients: the role of interpretation

Psychotherapists working with asthmatic patients have observed that an interpretation made in too provocative or confrontative a way may trigger a severe or even fatal asthmatic attack. However, this need for gentleness with these patients can lead the therapist to collude with his patient by becoming too protective, and so avoid facing the patient's denied hostility.

Case study 16.2 (contd)   Anger in ulcerative colitis

Caroline, after attending psychotherapy for some two years, began to turn up later and later for her sessions. Not wishing to provoke her or confront her, the therapist never commented on her latenesses. However, one day when, yet again, she turned up 20 minutes late, he exasparatedly asked her why. She replied, 'Why should I tell you? I feel when I come here I am doing you a favour'. The therapist became angry with her. In the ensuing discussion, she told him of her secret pleasure in teasing various people, including him, and this discussion led her to express her aggression and hostility more openly.

These patients do have a real physical illness which is an essential part of their psychosomatic predicament. We cannot ignore the extent to which it is felt by the patient to be a handicap and stigma, even if at times it may be used defensively. The patient may feel an acute sense of shame about the symptoms. Nowhere is this truer than with eczema, an unsightly and irritating skin condition, where from early on the mother may at times have withdrawn from holding her infant or child at the sight of his eczematous patches. Her later guilty attempts to overcome this by comforting her child with his sore skin may only be met with rage or anger by a child who feels shamed and hurt by this exposure of his humiliation and neediness. This may re-occur in the therapeutic relationship with these eczematous patients, and also with other psychosomatically ill people (Pines 1980). In order to get closer to them, the psychotherapist must not only try to identify with their physical suffering and sense of stigma, but also permit them enough psychological distance to explore feelings of rejection and rage.

Case study 16.2 (contd)   Sense of stigma in ulcerative colitis

Caroline told of a dream in which she was at a dance where all the men were dressed in dinner jackets but had floppy legs as if they were puppets. One man came up to her. She said he could have been the therapist or her lover. He asked her for a dance and she woke at this point. She recalled that the previous morning she had been lying in bed with her lover who had advised her that she should take out a special insurance policy for herself against a worsening of her colitis. She had felt humiliated and insulted by him but had said nothing. Now, in the session with the therapist, she remembered how as a teenager she had helped as a volunteer at parties for physically handicapped children. Thus, it could be seen how, in her dream, she had reversed her anger at the therapist and her boyfriend for being well and had made *them* the handicapped ones whom *she* was looking after.

ROLE OF PSYCHOANALYSIS VERSUS ONCE-WEEK PSYCHOTHERAPY: LIMITS ON RECONSTRUCTION/TRANSFERENCE

Sifneos and Nemiah's concept of Alexithymic personality may not describe all patients with psychosomatic disorders, but it can help us understand some of the real difficulties in the the therapeutic encounter with these patients; they find dependency very difficult to establish, and a transference may only develop very slowly. Intensive psychoanalytic work may allow one to arrive at a reconstruction of the early maternal environment, but often in a once-weekly psychotherapy this can be difficult. With some conditions, such as the irritable bowel syndrome, later fixation points in emotional development may emerge, suggesting a more neurotic psychopathology which can be tackled in less intensive psychotherapy, where a transference neurosis can then develop.

For example, in work with patients with irritable bowel disease, control of feelings is often a significant feature in the underlying psychopathology. In psychotherapy, conflicts over control with the psychotherapist may well emerge in the transference. This may lead to reconstruction of those conflicts in the 'anal' phase of development. With many psychosomatic patients, working face to face as opposed to using a couch may be essential, thereby acknowledging their need for mirroring and their difficulty in allowing dependency to take place.

PSYCHOTHERAPEUTIC OUTCOME

Can psychotherapy cure these psychosomatic disorders? Certainly, it can be extremely helpful in functional disorders, such as psychogenic vomiting, tension headache and hyperventilation. There is evidence that psychotherapy may improve the physical symptoms of patients with irritable bowel syndrome (Svedlund & Sjodin 1986). With eating disorders, mild cases may respond to long-term outpatient psychotherapy. The severe disturbances need a combined team approach in a properly organised inpatient psychosomatic unit. Some of the skin disorders may have a mild underlying psychopathology, but others, such as trichotillomania, may be associated with profound and potentially untreatable personality problems. Where there is definite evidence of a structural pathology in a psychosomatic disorder – as with asthma, eczema, rheumatoid arthritis, ulccrative colitis, peptic ulcer and essential hypertension – we are much less clear about the efficacy of long-term psychotherapy. The study by Karush et al (1977) of a three-month period of individual weekly psychotherapy of patients with chronic ulcerative colitis matched for age and sex with controls, did suggest that a psychoanalytic psychotherapy even for this very short time could lead to improvement in the physical symptoms and physical prognosis in some of the patients. These patients were described as having 'individuated' personalities. They did better than those with 'symbiotic' personalities, who required a more supportive approach. However, such detailed studies have not been repeated either for ulcerative colitis or for the other structural disorders. Clearly, it is possible for some patients, who are motivated and do have insight, for a physical as well as psychological improvement to occur, but very often a significant tendency to somatise can be expected to remain. We must also bear in mind that, in a few cases, psychotherapy may actually produce a decompensated and very fragile personality. This may be too high a price to pay for the loss or improvement of somatic pathology. In other cases, the journey from somatic pain to psychic pain can be rewarding:

Case study 16.1 (contd)   Shift from somatic to psychic pain

Elysa, the patient with tension headaches, found that the ending of her psychotherapy was painful and depressing. During this therapy, she had lost her headache and had begun to explore the meaning of her underlying depression, which had a great deal to do with her early relationship with her mother. Now, in the psychotherapy, she reported a growing sense of guilt at a wish to be more separate from her mother, who had herself been quite emotionally disturbed during the patient's childhood. Just before the therapy ended, Elysa told the therapist a dream in which she was with her mother who was unwell and they were surrounded by groups of people. Gradually, the people disappeared; she asked her mother, 'Do you love me?' Her mother replied 'I shall need to think about it'. In the dream, Elysa and her therapist had to face the loss of the therapist who had been a barrier between her and her inner tendency to compulsively care for this mother and for her schizophrenic brother. But this therapy had at least made Elysa aware that she could find more of herself as a person now and in the future, without having to defend herself with a somatic illness.

CONCLUSION

Some of the practical difficulties associated with the long-term psychotherapy of the psychosomatic patient in a hospital setting can be summarised as follows:

1. the problem of the way in which the patient has been referred and the patient's potential sense of rejection by the referring agent

2. problems in the initial assessment to do with the patient's motivation to have psychotherapy
3. a continuing ambivalence towards psychotherapy in the psychotherapeutic alliance
4. neurotic and non-neurotic splitting of the caring agencies with a need for containment by a wide initial 'scatter' of carers
5. concomitant physical illness, and the associated fear for the therapist and the patient that it is being missed
6. the patient's passivity in relation to the therapist
7. physical fragility in the patient giving rise to a need for gentleness by the therapist who must then not become too overprotective and miss the negative transferences
8. recognition by the psychotherapist of the stigma of physical illness
9. difficulties in attempting a reconstruction in once-weekly psychotherapy
10. problems to do with chronicity of symptoms and secondary gain
11. difficulties in some patients in thinking symbolically and in developing a transference neurosis.

The irony that in a busy general hospital a psychotherapist may receive only a small number of referrals of psychosomatic patients has already been referred to. Although the hospital has the resources for safe and effective therapy, it is in the general practice setting that psychosomatic patients are most frequently met and they are then also at an earlier stage in the development of their disease. There is evidence of increasing interest and awareness of the emotional aspects of physical illness among general practitioners. It is an urgent task for the psychotherapist to extend this understanding to the hospital setting. The psychodynamic understanding of the personality of the psychosomatic patient has enriched medicine, especially through the appreciation of the significance of the doctor-patient relationship; this chapter has tried to show it can also lead to more effective cures in those physical illnesses where stress plays a significant role.

FURTHER READING

Cheren S 1989 Psychosomatic medicine: theory, physiology and practice, vol I/II. International Universities Press, Madison
Kaplan H I, Sadock B J 1989 Comprehensive textbook of psychiatry, ch. V: Psychosomatic disorders. Williams and Wilkins, Baltimore
Taylor G J 1987 Psychosomatic medicine and contemporary psychoanalysis. International Universities Press, Madison
Weiner H 1977 Psychobiology and human disease. Elsevier, New York
Wolff H H O, Shoenberg P J 1990 Individual psychosomatic disorders. In: Wolff H H O, Bateman A, Sturgeon D A (eds) The U C H textbook of psychiatry. Duckworth, London

17. Anorexia nervosa

C. Dare

INTRODUCTION

'There are no cures for anorexia nervosa even though it has been well recognised for over a hundred years and probably has occurred for many centuries.' (Parry Jones 1985)

'There are strong suggestions that the incidence of the disorder is increasing as is its geographical distribution. The anorexic condition can be long enduring and it causes considerable morbidity and significant mortalities.' (Theander 1985, Ratnasuriya et al 1990)

A considerable proportion of patients with anorexia nervosa are admitted to adolescent units or adult psychiatric wards. Those units that specialise in eating disorders can achieve good results, especially in helping the patient's physical condition, but post-discharge relapse is all too common (Morgan & Russell 1975, Russell 1985). It is striking that anorexia nervosa is one of the few conditions within psychiatry for which pharmacological treatments are unavailing. Moreover, the results of specific psychological treatments derived from learning theory have been very unsatisfactory. This is so despite the apparent phenomenological similarity to other severe neurotic disorders of adolescents and young adults, such as obsessive compulsive disorders, which are susceptible to systematic behavioural therapy. Cognitive therapy has been thought to produce beneficial effects in the related problem – normal weight bulimia (Fairburn 1985) – for which antidepressant medication has also been shown to be helpful, at least in the short term (Treasure 1988). Neither formal cognitive therapy nor tricyclic antidepressants have been shown to be effective in anorexia nervosa, although the condition appears to be so similar in much of its phenomenology to that of the low– and normal weight bulimic patients.

The treatment of anorexia nervosa, therefore, remains largely within the province of psychotherapy (see Garner & Garfinkel 1985). The purpose of this chapter is to describe some aspects of psychotherapy with anorexic patients derived from the author's work at the Maudsley and the Bethlem Royal Hospital.

The clinical and research background

The author first had contact with anorexic patients early in general psychiatric training (Dare 1967) within a team that at that time pursued the hypothalamic-pituitary hypothesis. During subsequent training in child and adolescent psychiatry, I began to be interested in the psychological and systems theory approaches. The therapeutic setting was of anorexic patients referred in the course of routine outpatient child and adolescent psychiatric practice. Rather quickly I gave up individual therapy with the adolescent patients, and focused on family therapy with this age group. By 1979, a sufficient number of patients had been seen to conduct a retrospective survey of this group of patients (Nitz 1987, Nitz & Dare 1984). Clinical circumstances enabled a retrospective comparison between a fortuitously matched group treated in outpatient family therapy and a group managed as inpatients in the adolescent unit at the Bethlem Royal Hospital (Dare 1983). This comparison was flawed by its retrospective format, but nevertheless its results suggested the possibility that outpatient family therapy was as effective as long-term inpatient treatment in the management of anorexia nervosa in adolescent patients.

This clinical experience led to a formal, prospective controlled trial in which the effects of outpatient family therapy were compared with outpatient individual, supportive, elective psychiatry, in a large group (80 patients) who had all been first admitted for a re-feeding programme.

This controlled trial (Russell et al 1987, Dare et al 1990) had assigned patients to one of four prognostic categories before random allocations to the outpatient psychotherapies. This design produced a clear and important differential finding: one category of patients alone showed marked benefits from treatment – the young-onset (before the age of 18 years), short duration (less than three years) anorexic patients. In this category, 90% of the patients in family therapy were placed in the good or intermediate class of outcome at one year. Of those patients in this prognostic category treated by individual therapy, 90% were assessed at follow-up as in the poor class of outcome. In none of the other prognostic categories were there statistically significant differences between the effects of the family and individual therapies. However, in one prognostic category of patients – those with late-onset (after 19 years of age) anorexia – there was a significant advantage in the individually treated group of patients over those in family treatment. In that group, during the year of outpatient treatment, better levels of bodyweight were achieved and maintained.

The results of this trial (the 'first MRC trial') led the research in two directions. The first was to try to explore the possibility of developing a more effective individual therapy for the older-onset anorexia patients. This trial (the 'second MRC trial') is continuing. Again, the patients, all seriously undernourished young adults with longstanding anorexia, are admitted for the weight restoration inpatient programme. At discharge, they are randomly assigned to either (1) family therapy (2) supportive individual psychotherapy or (3) focal psychoanalytic psychotherapy. So far, 38 patients have been allocated, 12 or 13 in each treatment group. This trial is, as yet, incomplete, so no formal results are available.

The second direction in which the first MRC trial led the research, was to explore the nature of the effective elements in the family therapy. In a pilot trial, 18 patients with young (12–17 years of age)-onset, short (7–28 months)-duration anorexia nervosa were randomly assigned to two forms of outpatient family treatment: either (1) formal family therapy; or (2) family counselling (a therapy which resembles a traditional 'child guidance' approach to the management of adolescent disorder, within which the parents are seen as a couple and the patient is seen on her own; whole family sessions are rigorously excluded from the treatment). Assessment of this pilot trial showed that good results were possible with both treatments, and so a definitive comparative trial of these therapies is now being undertaken: 'the third MRC trial'. Again, this is a trial in progress and no results are yet available. The pilot trial has led to certain clear findings about the nature of individual and family progress, and changes in family and individual therapy (Dare et al 1990). It has also increased our experience of individual psychotherapy with adolescent anorexic patients.

In addition to the patients within the treatment trials, many other cases of anorexia have been seen or supervised in clinical practice. The patients seen in the controlled trials and in the course of routine clinical practice constitute the case material basis for this description of psychotherapy with anorexia nervosa.

THE STRUCTURE OF PSYCHOTHERAPY WITH ANOREXIA NERVOSA

Psychotherapists often appear to believe that the nature of the exchanges between therapist and patient are largely determined by: (1) the patients' experiences of their condition; (2) the nature of that condition; and (3) the therapists' preferred conceptual framework. In contrast, the author believes that the therapists' ideological/intellectual viewpoint has less effect, and that the therapy is more determined by: (1) the nature and urgency of the patients' problems; (2) what the patient (or couple or family or group of patients) ostensibly *want* from treatment; and (3) the *number* of people in the room.

Psychotherapy with anorexia nervosa is strictly determined by the anorexic psychological organisation. However, a number of other determinants of the form of a psychotherapy can be described.

The effect of the age of the patient and the view she has of the condition

A pre-pubertal child's attitude to therapy for anorexia nervosa is strongly affected by the curious concrete quality and lack of introspection in pre-adolescent thinking. This controls psychotherapeutic strategies.

A young adolescent usually lacks an ability to accept any responsibility for dietary control or for participation in her therapy.

A young adult, on the contrary, is often eager to find a way to be autonomously active in therapy, however difficult this may be for her.

The effect of the 'power' of the symptom

One of the overwhelming paradoxes of psychotherapy with anorexia nervosa is the overwhelming influence of the illness itself on the nature of psychotherapy, despite the importance of life-cycle influences described above. The paradox derives from the *power* of the symptom. Being anorexic, or being able to be anorexic, has an enormous pull once the symptoms have been experienced. The intensity with which anorexic symptoms can become a way of life is highly seductive. The symptoms, then, whatever their origin, can be incorporated into an apparent 'solution' to developmental tasks or personal relationship problems. In this sense, it has been suggested (Szmukler & Tantum 1985) that anorexics become 'addicted' to their symptoms. The state of being anorexic appears, usually, to have much more appeal than being without the symptom. This is analogous to chemical dependence, in which the addicted person believes that life without heroin or alcohol is impossible.

The effect of the severity of the physical threat to life

The level of threat to life dramatically controls the therapists' state of mind and practical responses to the patient. Sudden weight loss, compulsive vomiting or laxative abuse, present as an immediate or medium-term threat to life. The spectre of the patient dying alarms therapists, threatening to distort their treatment plan, however sensible and well performed it may be. Alternatively, the patient's need to deny illness or life threat may be so strong, and the therapeutic relationship so close, that the therapist is induced to accompany the patient in her denial. An outside supervisor or consultant is then needed to insert appropriate anxiety into the patient, through the therapist. It is often necessary to have regular checks on the patient's weight and serum electrolytes made by a doctor in a 'managing' role. In our practice, we cope with the dangers of patient/therapist collusive denial by the psychotherapist weighing the patient at the beginning of the treatment session. The weight chart is literally displayed in the therapy room, and is then incorporated as a continuous communication from patient to therapist. This routine is a striking feature of our work. On videotape records of an individual therapy session, the psychotherapist is often seen, indicating the weight chart, assimilating the weight loss, gain or plateau into an interpretation by the gesture.

The effect of the number of people in the room

Individual and family therapies have striking differences, and these are largely determined by the phenomenon of transference. A single patient in the room is likely to pay some attention to the therapist. After a while, if the patient perceives the therapist as potentially helpful, that attention will always become quite intense. This leads to the patient's repertoire of relationship needs and patterns (especially those deriving from earlier dependencies) being replayed with the psychotherapist. If a couple or a family is being treated, the psychotherapist may become an important figure, and transference processes become observable. However, members of a couple or a family have pre-existing, intense relationships that are already imbued with the qualities of transference. There is a much lower level of automatic availability for therapeutic work of the transferences experienced towards the therapist on the part of the couple or family members, than is the case in individual therapy.

The effects of the motivation for treatment

What the patient wants from treatment can vary. It can be: (1) almost nothing; (2) immediately and solely the reduction of symptoms; (3) a wish for self-exploration and understanding.

These wants are in part age-determined, but are also to some extent determined by culture and personality.

TRANSFERENCE AND COUNTER-TRANSFERENCE IN ANOREXIA NERVOSA

The psychological organisations of anorexia – the highly ambivalent wish for distance and yet an intense longing for intimacy, the insistent demand for autonomy and the great thrust for, and yet anxiety about, adult independence and sexuality, influence the anorexic person's short- and long-term presence in psychotherapy. In particular, this dynamic has a strong effect on the emotional distance that the patient needs to have with the psychotherapist. Her ill, undernourished physical state constitutes an appeal for intimate nurturance. Complementing, and additional to, this appeal which has its origins in the patient's physical state, is a 'psychological' demand for close dependence. An anorexic patient often has a strong belief, at a conscious or, more often, an unconscious level, about what she sees as being demanded of her by her parents. She believes that she has not been wanted for herself, as she believes her self to be. Her actual qualities, she believes, have been unnoticed or unwanted by the parents. She is convinced that her parents have wanted a cipher: an idealised and 'unreal' child. She has tried to conform to this by taking on well-behaved, striving and perfectionistic qualities. However, she has been left with the conviction that her real self is messy, greedy, sexy and selfish. This 'real' self has not been acceptable and, therefore, not looked after. The fervour to be 're-babied', to be adored and cared for simply as she is, can exert a powerful influence on the therapist (as it has upon nurse's, friends, school teachers, family doctors and, above all, upon her parents). At the same time, the anorexic has feared care and nurturance as if it would constitute a demand to be what the other person, the prospective carer, wants her to be, not what she herself feels she is. She may feel so unpractised at 'being herself', that being anorexic is felt to be her sole authenticity.

The fear that receiving care will compromise the patient's control of her own personal qualities leads her to oppose, to fend off, the loving, nurturant help that is simultaneously evoked by her. This quality dominates the initial as well as the evolving transferences and counter-transferences in the relationship between the therapist and patient. This is true regardless of the mode of treatment the therapist is choosing to adopt, or of the model to which he has theoretical and intellectual commitment. Any form of therapy constitutes an offer of care. The anorexic patient fears that the proposition will be part of a plan that the therapist has for her good, and that it will be a straitjacket controlling and organising *her* to be what *he* wants. The therapy will take away her true self which is, or includes, the capability of being anorexic. Fortunately for the development of a therapeutic alliance, there is also a part of the patient that knows that the anorexia is a frightening, obsessive and crazy way of life. That part of her wants to give in to the therapist, to become his patient and conform to his therapeutic suggestions or demands.

An important advantage of working with anorexic patients, both in individual and family therapy, is the extent to which the processes observable within the patient's individual psychopathology mirror identifiable family process. However, it is important that the therapist does not believe that there is any simple causative link between the one and the other – the family process and individual psychology.

The presence of a physically ill, psychologically obsessed patient inevitably has effects upon parents and other family members. Firstly, the self-starvation is a serious challenge to the parents' sense of competence. The capacity to feed children is an elemental role of a family. To fail in that, undermines a basic sense of effectiveness. To fail because the child *refuses* to eat is bewildering and demoralising. Secondly, most parents secretly fear that whatever happens to their offspring is in some way *their* responsibility. It is frighteningly easy for parents to believe that it is the family's fault that a self-destructive, apparently psychological process is causing their daughter to opt out of growing up. Given that many professional helpers openly or covertly share that belief, it is not surprising that parents blame themselves and fear that they will be blamed as 'the cause' of their anorexic daughter's symptoms. Thirdly, most parents of an anorexic have tried desperately hard to use their resources to influence their daughter to give up her symptoms. They have failed, and their failure inspires their expectations of what mental health professional will think of them.

The family of an anorexic patient has also, commonly, particular qualities that are by no means only a result of the anorexic patient's symptomatic presence. There are aspects of family life that appear to be rather frequently present in anorexic families. It is difficult to determine whether or not these antedate the development of symptoms. The relationship between these attributes and the cause of the symptoms is equally unclear. Some of the qualities appear to handicap the family in firmly opposing and reversing the disorder. Whatever their relationship to the origin and perpetuation of the symptoms, the family organisation shapes the relationship that the family make with helping agencies, including the family or individual psychotherapist.

FAMILY QUALITIES

There have been many accounts of the particular qualities of the family of an anorexic patient, from the point of view of the general psychiatrist, the psychoanalyst and the family therapist (Dare 1985, Yager 1982, Yager & Strober 1985). Here, the subject will be reviewed to cover those qualities that affect the psychotherapist's work with the patient or family, or become the subject matter of therapy.

There have been no studies that have demonstrated differences in matched groups between families containing an anorexic patient, and those that do not. We (Dare et al 1990) have used the measures 'Expressed Emotion' (EE) (Leff & Vaughn 1983) and the Family Adaptability Cohesion Evaluation Scales of Olson (FACES) (Olson et al 1979). The former measure, derived from the Camberwell Family Interview (Brown & Rutter 1966) has not been standardised with relevant, matched, 'normal' families. The only comparisons that can be made are with the families of other psychiatric patients (for example, with families containing an identified patient with schizophrenia or depression). In schizophrenic patients' families, the levels of EE are strongly culturally dependent (Leff & Vaughn 1983). Levels of criticism ('Critical Comments'), one element of EE, are higher in families of schizophrenic patients in California, London and Copenhagen than in our sample of families containing an anorexic patient. In Bangalore (India), levels of EE in families of schizophrenic patients (Leff et al 1987) are similar to those in our London samples of anorexic patients' families (Szmukler et al 1985, 1987; Dare et al 1990). We tentatively suggest that, certainly in the families of short-history, early-onset, anorexic patients, there are low levels of EE for Criticism, Emotional Over-involvement, Warmth and Positive Remarks.

Our results match the clinical observations of Minuchin and his colleagues (Minuchin 1975, 1978). This group identified the great problems of managing conflict that occur in families containing an anorexic patient. Our own clinical observations confirm Minuchin's descriptions. We think that the majority of families containing a young anorexic patient do have a great fear of quarrels becoming interminable. They cope with this fear by avoiding conflict. This is accompanied by a tendency to have a low level of communication of any intense affects.

In psychotherapy with individuals and families, there appears to be a close parallel between the intolerance of conflict and the apparent avoidance of intense affective communications, be they positive or negative in quality. These features have to be taken into account because of the influence they have on the therapeutic relationships and the content of the patient's communications. Individual patients and their families hate confrontation, and become very anxious if the therapist is believed to be fostering conflict. Confrontation between patient and therapist is as disliked as that between family members. Such confrontation easily leads individual patients to leave psychotherapy. In family therapy, families become very uncomfortable when a therapist is incautious in demonstrating implicit conflicts within the family, or appears to be encouraging confrontation. Families avoid experiencing confrontations between themselves, and often unite to attack the therapist. Usually, they do this by expressing anger and dissatisfaction with the treatment. Our studies have shown that in anorexic families in which one or other parent expresses two or more Critical Comments about the patient, there is a significant risk of drop-out from family therapy, but not individual therapy (Szmukler et al 1985). We have also shown that this criterion has prognostic implications for the outcome of therapy. In those families in which parental Critical Comments are two or more, the outcome of family therapy is poor, *if the level of parental criticism is not reduced.*

In individual therapy, the fear on the patient's part of confronting the parents is striking, and has to be handled with sympathy. The lack of ready communication of strong feelings between family members often seems to be associated with a sense of having experienced loneliness and emotional coldness from the family.

The FACES (Olson et al 1979) measures have not been standardised with a British population and one for which social class is controlled. In contrast with Olson's 'normal' population in North America (Olson 1986), most anorexic families in Britain complete the questionnaires within the normal range for 'cohesions' (the family members' experience of emotional distance between themselves) and 'adaptability' (the family members' experience of the rigidity or flexibility of the family rules and controls). However, the FACES scoring also allows for a measurement of satisfaction or dissatisfaction with the level of cohesions and adaptability. Unlike the 'normal' families in Olson's studies, most members of anorexic families in our series (Le Grange 1989, Dare et al 1990) fill in the questionnaire as though there is a big difference between how they see the family and how they would like it to be. This dissatisfaction score suggests that the patient, her parents and her siblings all see the family as not close enough and, to a lesser extent, too controlled and hierarchical in its structure. The dissatisfaction seems to account, in part, for the families' belief that there is something wrong with them that has caused or contributed to the development in their daughters of anorexia nervosa. The family members' vulnerability to the guilty fear that they have 'caused' the anorexia can also provide them with motivation for therapy – provided the family therapist does not augment their potential for guilt.

In this section, an attempt has been made to draw attention to the particular qualities of the anorexic experience of the individual, and the nature of the family life in families containing an anorexic patient. The intention has been to show how these qualities structure the work of the psychotherapist.

The chapter is predicated on the belief that:

1. Family therapy and individual psychotherapy are complementary, not contradictory activities.
2. There is a clear relationship between the psychopathology of the individual and the family process in anorexia nervosa.
3. There are consistent principles of structure that determine the conduct of psychotherapy. This underlying consistency is modified by the nature and urgency of the patient's condition, the type of treatment, and the cultural context of the patient and family. The latter determine the family and individual expectations as to what constitutes 'treatment' for the condition.

AN OUTLINE OF THE CONDUCT OF PSYCHOTHERAPY

The course of psychotherapy conforms, to a greater or lesser extent, to the following elements or stages.

Developing a specific setting for a specific therapy, and concerning the people who are to be involved in therapy

All therapies require a specific setting. Freud invented a setting for a confidential, reflective psychotherapy (see Khan 1974). Some psychological treatments, for example, require a psychological laboratory (e.g. for the multiple, simultaneous recording of psycho-physiological parameters). Family therapy requires a one-way screen or other observations setting, to provide team back-up for the therapist at the beginning and at crucial stages of the therapy. Therapies that must focus intensively on the generalisation of therapeutic change into daily life may require that the therapist gains access to the family home.

The therapist decides what setting he needs for his particular treatment and then must invite the patient, couple, family, extended family, professional network or whoever to attend. The meeting must be arranged somewhere, in the home or territory of the patient or referral context, or in the therapist's professional set-up. With anorexic patients, a psychotherapist will usually want to conduct the therapy in the therapist's own setting, for example, to do family therapy with the appropriate technology. A hospital will often be the best place because the patient's condition requires the back-up of medical monitoring and laboratory facilities. Occasionally, other settings have to be accepted, for example, a home visit for an intransigently home-bound parent or child, or a consultation in a general practice surgery to facilitate communications with fellow professionals involved in the management of a difficult case.

Whenever an anorexic is seen, a psychotherapist must decide how to manage the physical aspects of the patient's condition, to consider who will be responsible for decisions about life-threatening crises and physical danger, such as severe inanition, hypokalaemia, hypoproteinaenaemia with oedema, osteoporosis, suicide attempts, and so on. For some therapies and for many medical psychotherapists, the psychotherapist may use the management decisions strategically as an integral part of the psychotherapy. Non-medical psychotherapists may want a medical manager to be actively involved or available on request. In psychodynamic psychotherapy, it is usual to separate the management and psychotherapeutic roles. In our setting, psychoanalytic psychotherapy is best carried out with a medical manager available to make crucial decisions about the level of physiological hazard and the necessity of admission. However, an exception is made to this in that the psychotherapist is always advised to have the patient's current weight as part of the therapy. Therefore, the setting should include a weighing machine and, for younger patients, a measure of height. The psychotherapist records the patient's weight on a chart which is visible during the therapy, so that its trajectory, stability, gaining or losing weight constitutes a readily available piece of information. The rationale for this is: firstly, that the therapist may otherwise lose sight of the fact that the patient is losing weight rapidly or has achieved autonomous control to the extent of gaining weight; secondly, we have come to appreciate that the patient's shape and weight is consistently a crucial non-verbal communication from the patient to other people, but also to the patient's internal objects. This latter fact may seem curious, but, often, a young adult patient seems to see herself, her thinness or fatness, from the viewpoint of a parent or parents with whom she is having a dialogue, even though she may never or rarely see them, or they are on another continent, or are dead.

Joining and engaging

In the chosen setting, the therapist meets the patient, couple or family and begins to establish the rules for the conduct of the treatment. The therapist must develop a professional activity that is not simply a response and that will have the effect of incorporating him into the anorexic patient's psychopathology and family system. To this end, the therapist begins to make clear statements as to what he is and does. These are said in words, but his non-verbal conduct is more important. The therapist must establish whether he is going to be an active conductor, directing the psychotherapy, or a reflective, sympathetic observer and so make greater demands on the patient to initiate and maintain the treatment. It is especially important in short-term, non-intensive therapies (and most family therapy is such a therapy) that the therapist demonstrates the *style* of his therapy as soon as possible, in an unambiguous way, propelling the therapy accurately in the direction it will take. Longer-term therapies may commence in a more leisurely way, the patient and therapist finding out each other's ways. However, there is always the risk that the joining occasion has set patterns contrary to the proper needs of the therapy. The engagement of the patient, couple or family into the psychotherapy, requires that the therapist shows the participants that he understands his business, and that he wants to hear about the problem in great detail, is sympathetic to the predicament, and will be helping the patient, couple or family find a way to get out of the affliction. Often, anorexics have been seen by many professionals. The patient and her family will have had some contradictory experiences and advice. The psychotherapist will have to attend to the patient's and the family's account of those things and must show (and say) how *his* therapy is going to be the same or different. The *demonstration* of the therapeutic style is more important than the spoken explanations, which may not be heard or understood as convincingly as they can be demonstrated. The psychotherapist should show his differences from previous professionals with respect for the point of view of other approaches, but also displaying a strong commitment to his own style and orientation.

Assessing the problem for the particular form of therapy

Different therapies relate to different subject matters. It is not simply that different therapies use different languages to formulate the problem, but that different therapies are concerned with different aspects of the patient's and family's experience. Each particular mode of psychotherapy requires that the therapist, whilst joining with and engaging the patient, couple or family, is also making an assessment in the terms that are necessary and appropriate for his chosen therapeutic modality. The patient and family want to know that such assessment is being made, although they may be extremely impatient with the process. They may see the problem as simple: 'She doesn't eat! She's got anorexia nervosa!'; or: 'There's nothing wrong with me. *They* say I've got anorexia nervosa.' However, most people are grateful to have their story listened to, even more so if the therapist actively relates to and reflects upon the story. The way the story is told, the emphasis and emotional colouring are observed, but even more important is the assessment of the relationship within which the story is imparted. When the consultation is with an individual, the relationship is that which is revealed and unfolds with the therapist. The psychotherapist is assessing what sort of relationship the patient seems to be wanting to establish with him. He will observe what she is doing to him emotionally; what particular state of mind is being set up in the therapist by the encounter; what role she is assigning to herself and to the therapist. Likewise, when the story is told by a family, a relationship pattern is also being assessed. But although what the family is doing to the therapist is important, what goes on between the family members is more so. The family reveal the structure of their relationship as a two-generational group. The essential subject matter of the individual psychotherapist and the family therapist is the same – the relationship pattern in the therapist's presence: in family therapy, the relationships between family members; in individual therapy it is the patient/therapist relationship. However, although the subject matter being assessed is the same, the focus of the therapist's assessment is different in the two modalities.

The common theme in the underlying assumptions determining the assessment of the interpersonal pattern created during the recounting of the problem is that psychotherapy, if it helps problems, does so through the medium of personal relationships. A psychiatric problem – the anorexia nervosa – is not *defined* as being a relationship problem. Psychiatric problems are assumed to cause relationship difficulties. It is assumed that the relationships set up with the patient reveal processes that maintain the symptom in so far it provides a sort of solution to the patient's interpersonal needs. The psychiatric symptoms gain a central and controlling place in the patient's life.

Despite the regressive pull of the symptoms, an anorexic patient is growing up. The family also grows and moves through the life-cycle, so that the patient and her family establish changing patterns of relationship, appropriate to the changing phase of the life-cycle. Specifically, anorexia develops before, or shortly after puberty, or in early adulthood. Most cases begin when the patient is still strongly involved with the family of origin, at a time when the normal development process would require a marked increase in physical and emotional autonomy. The phase of life within which anorexia nervosa develops is one dominated by the moves towards a sense of having a personal, separate and therefore a unique sense of identity. The identity will be linked to, but will differ from, that of her parents, siblings and friends. This process ('individuation/separation') that is occurring in the adolescent or young adult establishes her as a somewhat different person to the one she has been. The family members change their style of relating to this new person. The parents too, however, are changing and growing, emotionally, and so the adolescent or young adult has to change her relationships to them. Describing the changes in relationships as individuals and families grow and change is difficult because of the complementarity of the interactions. The child changes, so the adult changes, but now the adult has changed, so the child's responses must change, but now the child is different so the adult changes. But the adult is changing too; as mothers and fathers are moving through their own life cycles, so the children have to adapt to new interests, jobs, physical states, marital partners or whatever.

Having anorexia may be 'a solution' to the demands for change of adolescence and young adulthood. The patient, for example, literally avoids becoming a sexual person. She can, whilst anorexic, remain or return to an apparently pre-pubertal state. Likewise, the parents need not take into account their daughter as an adult or incipiently adult sexual being, if she becomes anorexic. This may have, at least partially, some relationship advantages. Father keeps his 'little girl' whom it is safe for him to love and in whose physical state he can have a legitimate interest; mother and father continue to have a little child, and, moreover an ill one, to care for. They can go on being parents.

The anorexia nervosa often seems to be allocated a function: it inhibits the process of the life-cycle transition, restricting the normal relationship changes between the growing child and the family that are the typical accompaniment of this transition. Both individual and family therapists make an assessment of the patterns of relationship that appear to maintain the patient in her anorexia. These patterns must change if she is to find a way to relate to people as a non-anorexic. Interpersonal relationships are attended by, evoke, and arise from beliefs, attitudes, thoughts, and conscious and unconscious fantasies. Personal relationships are both a manifestation of psychological processes and determinants of the qualities of subjective experience.

In individual therapy, the assessment of the inner pattern, revealed in relationship with the therapist, is assessed. In family therapy, the relationship pattern is directly demonstrated as the family discuss and interact around their anorexic daughter.

Making the interventions specific to the therapy

The process whereby the therapy has been convened, the patient/ couple/family engaged, the appropriate assessment made, all have one aim: the making of specific and effective interventions. Effective interventions can also be engaging. However, because effective interventions facilitate change, they also have a potential for putting the patient and her family into a new situation. This is, naturally, hoped for and welcomed by the patient and family. But change is also feared, for its strangeness and novelty, and also because it has been long feared.

Case study 17.1   The awful adolescent

One young woman put all her wonderful, obstinate, stubborn defiance into being an anorexic from the age of 10 years. As the parents learned to make it impossible for her to starve, she began to grow and become pubertal. She now began to be stubborn and awkward about clothes, getting up, going to bed, going to school, when to do homework, and so on – like many adolescents. Her mother said: 'I always knew she was going to be an awful adolescent'. As an anorexic, the 'awful adolescent' was avoided.

Case study 17.2   The oedipal anorexic

Another adolescent had a deeply religious faith that also kept her close to her father who had died when she was eleven years. She consciously hated and feared sexuality. She passionately believed that her starvation, asexuality and ascetism kept her more faithful and close to her dead father than her mother, a sister and brother. She had a conscious fantasy of dying and having a glorious reunion in heaven with her father. Her anorexia nervosa had become incorporated into this manifestly oedipal fantasy, and there was an obvious use of the symptoms to protect her from any sexuality getting into the fantasy. There are usually processes in individuals and the family as a whole that resist change – as well as those processes and wishes mobilising development.

For these reasons, interventions must always be made that aim to circumvent, undermine or overpower resistance and blocks to change. There continues to be debate within psychoanalytic circles as to whether psychotherapeutic interventions are 'strategic'. Freud's original attitude (1900) was that the therapeutic effects of interpretations derived from the insight produced; insight being defined as an emotionally charged, intellectual awareness that reduced the power of unconscious mental processes by rendering them conscious. This relatively intellectualised, cognitive view has not been entirely superseded. Elements of cognitive behavioural therapy seem to share the same trust in the power of cognitive mediators over the emotionally charged behavioural/mental sequences that constitute symptoms (see Chs 1 and 11). There is a power for change to be gained by the alteration of a person's beliefs and attitudes, within personal relationships. The extent of that power is, at least in part, culturally and life-cycle determined. Children, up to mid-adolescence, rarely have a capacity to change their behaviour by the acquisition of insight as communicated in verbal interpretations (see Ch. 15). However, even in children, the sorting out of confusions about their own origins, the relationships of people around them, and to them, can be liberating under special circumstances. The careful opening out of 'closed secrets' (Pincus & Dare 1978) is useful. This circumstance is one in which there are events in the history of the individual that are known by some family members and are believed to be secret but are actually revealed in a confusing, incomplete and therefore ambiguous way to other family members. These secrets are of previous unhappy marriages, illegitimacy, imprisonment, incest and so on. From time to time, the tactful facilitation of the revelation and discussion of such a secret can be obviously and dramatically therapeutic. But in most individual and family therapies there is a place for sorting out the facts of personal and family history, for clarifying origins and relationships, for understanding the meanings that have become attached to the symptoms, for allaying fears and misapprehensions.

In family therapy, such interventions are achieved during the development of a history of the family, for example, by drawing up a family tree ('geneogram') (see Ch. 5). Byng-Hall has drawn attention to the process of 're-editing family myths' (Byng-Hall 1973, 1979). The Milan systems therapists describe this process as that of 'second order change' – the alteration of attitudes underlying current relationships, by identifying their role in maintaining patterns of inter-generational, historical localities and connections (Selvini Palazzoli, 1988).

For some adults, especially those who come from cultures that value 'personal awareness' and insight, the therapy must always include interpretations and constructions that add to and alter their beliefs and perceptions about themselves. Convincing and consistent re-evaluations and reorganisations of the person's view of themselves are sought and used therapeutically to achieve change. In individual therapy, this is realised in part by the therapist and patient combining their knowledge – the one personal, specific and subjective, the other emphatic, generalised and external – to investigate the patient's history as it evolves incidentally and relate it to the flow of the patient's thoughts, memories, current crises, dreams and symptomatic behaviour. The therapist also keeps careful track of how he is feeling, responding and fantasising about the patient, and how the patient is relating to him. From these elements, he can construct a history of the patient's relationship experience. The assumption is that although the therapist is, in some ways, giving the patient a novel relationship, she is bound, in part, to imbue it with qualities of her own past experiences. These include a tendency to repeat relationship patterns.

Some repetitions will be based upon gratifying experiences which she will attempt to re-establish for their pleasure. Other relationship patterns, which had been frustrating, are re-evoked in therapy as part of an attempt to master the painful feelings that persist in order to try to 're-write history'. The therapist attempts to identify these transference patterns in order to see which are the most persistently reinstated. In family therapy, the therapist can observe processes like transference and counter-transference structuring the inter-parental relationship, and in the attitude of the parents to children and children to parents. Such observations constitute part of the therapist's assessment of the attitudes and meaning of the interactive relationship patterns of the family. He may choose to share this understanding with the family, and many parents of an anorexic offspring welcome such observations. The information can be used to produce some alteration in the family's relationship pattern.

Overall, however, it is not obvious that the relatively intellectual quality of such insights is a particularly powerful tool for therapy. The therapist's sympathetic understanding based on such observations can be engaging for the family, can enhance their belief that the therapist really knows and understands them, and can thereby empower other types of interventions. A more powerful potential for change is achieved by using the obser-vations about relationship systems in different ways.

In individual therapy, this power is 'working with the transference'. The therapist uses his perception of the relationship between himself and the patient to create hypotheses, 'constructions' which postulate possible historical origins for the types of behaviour in relationships that characterise the patient and her eating disorder. By this means, the therapist and patient together develop a view as to how relationships in the current world are also coloured by repetitive and replicative patterns. The role of the symptom, in particular, in organising and maintaining these patterns is identified as accurately as possible. The therapist is especially concerned to identify his own emotionally charged responses to the patient – either those that he feels he could enact or those that he has, inadvertently, enacted.

The therapist aims to establish a level of responsiveness that is sufficiently human, warm and interested for the patient to have no real grounds to feel rejected, intruded upon, swamped or neglected. But there is an ambiguity about the therapist's beliefs, values and personal responsiveness to the patient. Under the impact of this relatively neutral mode of relating, the anorexic patient has little opportunity to be quite sure of what she is grappling with in the therapeutic relationship. The relative ambiguity gives her the chance to 'invent' her own therapist, the sources for her invention being mostly herself. In consequence, the nature of her inventions are informative about her basic propensities for evolving relationships. But these are not revealed in a neutral way, because of the patient's relative neediness and dependence. This causes her, as time passes, to put into the relationship important aspects of her problems; in particular, the peculiar mixture, already described, of asking for intense care by her physical state, her often quite childlike dependence and vulnerability, and at the same time treating any apparent offer of help as carrying a dangerous likelihood of controlling her and of taking away her essential individuality.

The therapist tries hard to identify and to experience the contradictions and multiplicities in the patient's feelings towards and need of him. He neither encourages nor rejects any of the elements, but simply comments upon them. This style, 'working with the transference', has a number of effects. Firstly, it is an unusual experience for the patient. The patient finds herself getting a quite different response to that which she has normally evoked. The therapist is involved and interested but does not act, he hears and feels and reports upon what is happening. The onus for action is put onto the patient not in a punitive, rejecting way, but in a way that accords with the reality that parents, teachers, nurses and friends have not been able to show to her. The novelty of the relationship must be nurtured by the therapist in a straightforward, undemonstrative way. Being in a new sort of relationship gives the patient an opportunity to practise new aspects of herself.

Secondly, the therapist's attitude of benign responsive interest in the different ways that the patient has of treating him is, to some extent, taken over by the patient. She develops a parallel capacity to observe herself a bit more dispassionately, and learns to assess what is happening before going overboard emotionally. For example, she may observe the repetitive tendencies she has to make contradictory demands, and it may thus come to be more under the patient's conscious control. She may learn to 'catch herself at it' as she rages at the therapist for not offering help when she has just told him that she certainly would not do anything that he asked.

The specific intervention here is an attitude offered by the therapist towards exploring the relationship between patient and therapist. Interpretations, reflecting what is going on between them, are helpful in letting the patient know what is going on, but are not thought by their content, by the information they contain, to be the crucially effective element. It is the fact that they are *made*, and the *conducting of a relationship by recounting the nature of the relationship* that creates and maintains the unique psychoanalytic intervention.

Much of the conceptualisation as to what induces and maintains change in individual therapy holds true for family therapy. In family therapy, the therapist attempts to identify patterns of relationships that seem to be maintained by and which maintain the symptom. The therapy aims to disrupt these patterns in order to give the members of the family a space within which new patterns can be developed, practised and so established. The means by which this is achieved does not depend upon the relationship *with* the therapist presenting a problem requiring a changed pattern. Nonetheless, the therapist *does* relate to the family in such a way that its members are faced with different solutions to established patterns of behaviour.

The therapist's main tools are two-fold. The first is that he makes a verbal account to the family that commands attention because it demonstrates a view of what is going on that is ungainsayable. He articulates their dilemma: they wish to save their daughter's life and health; at the same time they wish to be in a close, loving and non-conflictual relationship with her. It is impossible. The symptom does not allow it. The therapist explores the logical possibilities open to the family: they can go on the same way and await their daughter's deterioration with trepidation. They can make her eat by being more ruthless in their insistence, as their daughter is in her determination to starve. The constraints imposed by the family's fear and love and by the therapist's implacability in holding their concentrated attention upon their dilemma often produces changed behaviour in the parents of adolescent patients. They begin to make their daughter eat.

The second tool that the therapist mobilises is his interest in the practical effects of their behaviour. The therapist listens with great care to the way they set about feeding their daughter, coaching them and encouraging them to join with each other rather than to heed their daughter's great anger and panic. As the parents become successful in beginning to feed her, the family enters a novel situation: they have faced and achieved a confrontation with their daughter's life-threatening behaviour. They can now attend to the therapist's suggestions about the existence of a need now to guide their daughter into those parts of adolescent activities and experiences that her anorexic state precluded. This means dealing with issues of independence, control, conformity and freedom usual to teenagers.

With an adult daughter, it is not predictable, nor even is it usually appropriate, for the parents to take control of eating behaviour in this way. More often, the task is to help the daughter find a way to reduce the extent to which her eating problems dominate her relationship with her parents. Again, this is achieved by facing the family with the contradiction implicit in their dilemma: they want a 'normal' relationship with their daughter. This is impossible if they are made constantly aware of her self-starvation and its consequence. But in being aware, they are not allowed any power to do anything about the terrible situation. They are helpless, even if sympathetic, bystanders. The therapist hears how in many ways the daughter involves the parents in hearing of her suffering with her symptoms, constantly and unavailingly. They are encouraged to explore ways of avoiding the eating problem as the medium of communication and relationship with their daughter, and to insist on other contents – those more appropriate to their general interests and activities.

In family therapy with all ages, the aim is to eliminate the self-starvation having a pervasive control over the family relationships. As this is achieved, it becomes possible for a wider repertoire of experiences to be included in their transactions, replacing the infantile interest in food, weight and nutrition, and giving the possibility for both generations to explore age-appropriate interests.

The repetitive middle phase: continuing re-assessment, generalising and working through

In both individual and family therapies, it is important to develop and maintain a focus. Clinical experience suggests that in cases in which treatment is going to be successful, the focus established early on will be the major guideline for the duration of therapy. Unsuccessful therapies are often much longer lasting, as therapist and patient or patient's family struggle to find a way through the pain. Such a struggle is usually attended by changes of focus for treatment, and changes in strategy and style of treatment. Such alterations may be deliberate, or they may be stumbled into as the symptoms remain the same or worsen. Sometimes, prolonged treatments become successful either with or without a major change in strategy.

Case study 17.3   Anorexia and the non-acrimonious divorce

A 14-year-old adolescent, Sonia, developed anorexia nervosa shortly after her parents, having been divorced, established themselves in new partnerships. Neither of her parents' new partners had had children. Sonia had an older brother who set about becoming independent with energy and pleasure. In her anorexic state, Sonia was quiet, confined herself largely to school and home, and was solicitously cared for by both sets of parents – mother plus stepfather, and father plus stepmother. The initial hypothesis was that the illness provided all parents with the opportunity to have a child needing nurturance; further children would not be conceived, helping the children maintain the fantasy that re-union of the former marriage could be achieved. The anxiety of the shared worry about Sonia eliminated acrimony from the post divorce relationships. All four parents came to therapy with total regularity and conversed harmoniously but anxiously about Sonia. The therapy began as a family therapy involving the four adults and two children. The parents were set the task of establishing a clear and totalitarian feeding regime within which Sonia had no say, until such time as she was gaining weight without protest. Sonia and her brother were encouraged to talk together about the severity and unreasonable rigidity of the parental regime. Sonia gained sufficient weight, soon, to be quite out of physical danger, but then progress ceased. She remained a thin, amenorrhoeic, socially inhibited young woman. The therapy dragged from months into years. She moved from one set of parents to another, neither pair being successful in setting up sufficient control of her eating for her to achieve a reasonable target. Whatever set or combination of parents was seen, the therapist could not help the separated couples separate more completely, and Sonia seemed equally stuck. When she was 17 years old, she asked for some individual help. Granted this opportunity, she came a few times to complain of her parents having divorced and seeming to want her to hang around them whilst her brother had so much freedom. She rapidly improved to social freedom and physical health.

The early hypotheses was never substantially discarded. The content of the final few individual sessions, begun without hope of success because all attempts at family therapy with three separate therapists has seemed so useless, pursued the same theme as the first hypothesis. It appeared strikingly productive as well as effective.

The working-through phase seems often to be simply going over the same ground, the same transferences in individual therapy, the same attempts at structural change in family therapy. In either form of therapy, food and weight will dominate the content whilst the patient is thin and diet-preoccupied. In that state, other topics are pursued desultorily and ineffectively. Apart from the state of thinness, the other topics in individual and family therapy are also similar – the establishment of age-appropriate distance from the parents for both the parents and the children, and the attainment of a way of life that is not so centred on the across-generation family membership, but is more concerned with the peer age-related interests and commitments.

Ending treatment

The psychotherapeutic management of the end of treatment depends upon symptomatic changes. A lack of symptomatic alleviation does not mean that the therapy has not benefited the anorexic patient and her relatives. An improved feeling of independence with an enhanced sense of closeness can occur in a patient in her marriage and/or her family, whilst at the same time the patient knows that she is still in the thrall of her food and shape preoccupation.

However, symptomatic change determines the success or failure of the psychotherapy, and therefore the state of mind and personal relationships of the participants in the therapy. The point at which an aneroxic person achieves a normal bodyweight is a crucial indicator in therapy. Below that weight, it is very unusual for the constant food preoccupation to go away. Without this achievement, there it is also unlikely that there will be a return of menstruation (or normal sexual function in anorexic males). If this physical state is reached by psychotherapy outside an in-patient setting and without, at that point, the patient being on medication, then it is likely that the patient will remain free from anorexic symptomatology. This combination of nutritional health and a level of sex hormone production that allows normal sexual function must be the prime aim of psychotherapy, and allows for the possibility of therapy ending whether or not the interpersonal or psychological aims of therapy have been achieved. This is not to say that these wider aims are unimportant or irrelevant to termination. It is simply that some discussions about the goals of psychotherapy (especially psychoanalytic psychotherapy) are predicated upon the idea that these psychological and transactional qualities can be reached *before* a reversal of the disordered attitude towards eating and sexuality. This wish is also one often incorporated into the change-resisting beliefs of families and anorexic young women. When they are very aware of psychological and family difficulties, participants in psychotherapy often say that it makes irrefutable sense for them to expect that the psychological changes or family relationships must change for the symptoms to improve. There is, however, an indubitable improvement in the psychological sense of wellbeing and in participation in social activities as a result of 'passive' weight gain, that is, that accomplished by a rigorous programme in hospital. But such changes do not usually endure. In the author's experience, as psychotherapy proceeds, physiological, inter-personal and psychological changes tend to go hand in hand, without one clearly preceding the other. The conduct of psychotherapy and its outcome becomes much more uncertain once a patient has lost 15% or more of her usual body weight.

These matters are of great importance in setting the end for psychotherapies in successful treatments. While the patient remains incapable of autonomous regulation of nutritional health herself the ending of psychotherapy is very difficult to manage. It is likely that in such cases termination will occur by default. The patient or family will stop coming, or the therapist leaves for another agency and re-engagement is impossible. The psychotherapist may then have as an aim for the ending of treatment that the possibility of therapy in the future remains. This is sought by the therapist being open and generous in acknowledging his own failures and lapses. The therapist has to identify the strengths in the patient, her marriage and her family. He must be careful to attribute goodwill, as much as possible, and not to convey a blaming attitude.

As the symptomatic patient becomes able to maintain a normal bodyweight, without external coercion although not yet without great personal effort (because of the pain of eating that ensues from continuing anorexic thinking), then a successful end to psychotherapy can be expected and cultivated. The manner of working on the ending is very much determined by the mode of treatment, and especially, by the role of transference in the treatment. In individual, psychoanalytically orientated psychotherapy within which the relationship between patient and therapist has been a central focus, there will have been, in all likelihood, an acknowledgement of the intense dependence of the patient on the therapist. Under those circumstances, a great deal of therapeutic time will have been spent on anticipating the ending. This work, which has the quality of preparatory mourning or grief work, is necessary to facilitate the growth towards and acceptance of psychological separation from the parents. Interpretation of fears of separation about leaving the therapist are rarely necessary in family and couple therapy, where the separation and dependency issues will have been addressed and worked out between the couple or family members. From the clinical viewpoint of the psychoanalytically aware psychotherapist, it is inevitable that the management of the end of therapy of an anorexic patient will be preoccupied with the struggle, the panic, the pain and anger of separation.

WHEN TO DO WHAT SORT OF PSYCHOTHERAPY

Throughout this chapter, it has been assumed that psychotherapy is a treatment whereby a therapist and a family, a couple or an individual face each other over a problem and attempt, *by conversation*, to produce some sort of change that satisfies all participants as a solution to the original problem. As a rule, in psychotherapy, the encounter is 'bare-handed' in that the therapist does not make use of medication or instrumentation to intervene between himself and the patient participants. It is also assumed that there are no necessarily crucial distinctions between psychotherapy that is conducted with an individual, or with a group of family-related or unrelated people. There are many methods of psychotherapy, varying from ad hoc idiosyncratic styles to defined schools, but there are no a priori 'right' ways. Moreover, it seems likely that it is unusual for a particular therapy to be as 'pure' as the practitioner might wish to claim. Both successful and unsuccessful therapies on close inspection would reveal elements of disparate and perhaps apparently ideologically contradictory elements. These assumptions are not an advocacy of 'eclectic' practice, but simply represent what the author believes he observes in casual and formal scientific discourse, in supervision, through the one-way screen and in video recordings.

The crucial decision concerns whether to do individual, couple or family work, or some combination of all three. Formal controlled trials of psychotherapy are unlikely to ease decisions about combined treatments. By their nature, controlled trials require adherence to rigid protocols. A flexible integration of different modalities is impossible. It is clear that individual therapy of school-age patients does not work if the parents are not seen, and this favours family therapy with this age group. However, the success of family therapy with anorexia nervosa in adolescent patients does not prove that family therapy is the most effective method of gaining full parental participation in the management of eating disorder in adolescence. We are currently comparing whole family therapy with a form of 'family counselling', in which the identified adolescent anorexic patient is seen on her own and the parents are seen as a couple for 'parent guidance'. There are as yet no results from this study, but a pilot trial

(Dare et al 1990) showed that the parent counselling mode was successful in a sufficient number of cases to establish the ethics of a larger comparative evaluation. Even if this form of family therapy were shown to be more effective than the control treatment, it certainly would not show that there are no other more effective forms of family therapy.

Family therapy with older anorexic patients was not shown to be any more effective than supportive individual psychotherapy (Russell et al 1987, Dare et al 1990). Supportive psychotherapy has a number of elements, including dietary instruction, exploration of relationship problems, strategic interventions and interpretation of the symbolic meaning of the symptom and its role in the conduct of the patient's life and the management of relationships. As practised by the author and his colleagues, the only psychotherapeutic ingredients absent from supportive psychotherapy were transference interpretations and strict behavioural programming. In a study confined to adult patients (over 18 years of age) supportive psychotherapy, as defined above, is being compared with a focal psychodynamic psychotherapy. There is an additional treatment group of family therapy supervised by family therapists specialising in work with families containing an adult psychiatric patient. This trial may elucidate more precisely a form of psychotherapy suitable for the management of adult anorexic patients.

CONCLUSION

Outside of the formal treatment trials of psychotherapy, it is necessary to intervene in ways that make sense clinically. In the author's clinic, there is a clear strategy of beginning with a family therapy whose initial aim is, paradoxically, *not* the alleviation of the eating disorder. Sometimes, it is possible to begin by allowing the family to try to find ways of taking control of the eating problem. Rarely, they succeed, and then the therapy can move to working to overcome the previous regressed pattern of parent/child relationship. More usually, because the patient and the family are so pessimistic about their ability to manage the symptoms the therapy is specifically shaped, from the beginning, to encourage the evolution of a different style of family relationships, in which eating, weight and the patient's physical state are eliminated as far as is possible from her discourse with the parents. This may even include encouraging the patient to simulate health, as best as she can. The explicit aim is to get the parents and patient to relate to each other age-appropriately, rigorously excluding discussions as though her parents could take responsibility for the eating disorder. When such a state is reached, and it may take months of therapy, *then* the patient is taken into an individual therapy in which dietary advice is combined with interpretative psychotherapy.

This chapter has not referred to the problems of male anorexia, or to the treatment of couples, one of whom is aneroxic. It is clear that there is no evidence from controlled trials that couple therapy is an effective therapy, on its own, for anorexia nervosa. Nonetheless, it is frequently observable that there is a close tie between the marital patterns and the eating problem. For example, in one couple, if an inpatient regime successfully restored the patient's weight, she became sexually active, disenchanted with her husband and sought satisfaction in affairs. As she lost weight, she lost sexual interest and became faithful to her forgiving and relieved husband. A married man or woman who has been anorexic since courtship is likely to have established a marriage within which the eating disorder has an important role. Change in the patient then threatens the relationship's established patterns, and concomitant couple therapy seems indicated. However, it is a very difficult task, and the seeming logicality of the approach does not guarantee efficacy. Combined individual and couple therapy is the best current strategy that we have, but the results are often poor.

FURTHER READING

Dare C, Eisler I, Russell G F M, Szmukler G I 1990 Family therapy for anorexia nervosa: implications from the results of a controlled trial of family and individual therapy. Journal of Marital and Family Therapy 16: 1-26

Garner D M, Garfinkel P E (eds) 1985 Handbook of psychotherapy for anorexia nervosa and bulimia nervosa. Guilford Press, New York

18. Addiction

A. Read

INTRODUCTION: GENERAL PRINCIPLES

Problem drug use can be a paradigm for the whole range of substance abuse since, despite differences, there are many parallels between it, alcoholism, and other dependencies. All involve the use of a substance as intermediary between the user and the environment and the user is commonly ambivalent both about the substance and his or her use of it. Similarly, psychotherapy with problem drug users and other addicts necessarily has much in common with any other psychotherapeutic work, but there are also many differences which pose particular problems for both client and therapist. This chapter will draw on the author's experience of working in the field of chemical dependency including the use of individual and group psychotherapy and psychodrama. In addition, the societal context of drug use and its meaning both for the individual and for society will be explored. The focus will be on psychodynamic psychotherapy since, in the author's view, this mode best explores the meaning of drug use and works towards its resolution. Cognitive and behavioural therapies are also extremely useful tools, particularly in developing strategies for dealing with the recognition of stimuli for drug use, and for working towards relapse prevention. For information on these methods, the reader is referred to Marlatt & George (1984), and Rawson et al (1979).

It is remarkable how much publicity and strong emotion are generated by problem drug users. They are a very small group when compared with heavy alcohol or nicotine users, or people with eating disorders. They have much in common with these groups and many of the themes followed through the chapter are germane to all, but there are also marked differences, the most obvious being that, in the use of an illicit drug, the individual is of necessity setting him or herself outside the law. However, in the United Kingdom, the number of deaths per annum is in absolute terms minute (up to 18 per 100 over 10 years; Gordon 1983), and it can be argued that the damage done to society at large, at least in the United Kingdom, is relatively small. Nonetheless, even before the beginning of the HIV epidemic, the image of 'the drug addict' had become a stereotype for much that is outcast and rejected by society. For this reason, it is preferable to use the term 'problem drug user', since 'drug abuser' implies that the abuse is of the drug rather than of the individual and 'drug mis-user' suggests an alternative, appropriate use which is inapplicable in the context of treating addiction. This choice of words implies that the individual has a problem or problems related to the use of illicit drugs, which have contributed to his or her reasons for becoming addicted, or which have developed as a result of, or concomitantly with, the addiction. The existence of illicit drug users who do not perceive their drug use as a problem, or who are not perceived as having a problem although using drugs, is allowed for in this terminology.

An important issue is whether those who come for treatment are a representative sample or whether they are in some ways different from the other members of the drug scene. The latter is more probable, since Home Office notifications indicate that only between 10% and 20% of addicts present to a doctor at some point in their drug-using lives. The existence of a treatment service in an area will markedly increase the number of identified problem drug users, although there will remain many users who choose not to present. As far as outcome is concerned, recent studies suggest that about half of those entering a service will become abstinent. Gordon's (1983) 10-year follow-up study of patients seen at a London drug clinic in 1970 gives an abstinence rate of a little under 50% and Gossop et al (1989) showed 45% abstinent at six months after treatment.

Who presents for treatment and why?

It would seem appropriate to consider drug users presenting for treatment (a smaller number than the total of *notifications*, since it is incumbent on all doctors meeting a person whom they reasonably suppose to be using a notifiable drug to inform the Home Office under the Misuse of Drugs Act) as a group with at least some particular needs and characteristics. Despite their wide range of origins, ages and life histories, this does seem to be the case. This is not necessarily to postulate an addictive personality type, but rather to draw out a number of themes and experiences that problem drug users appear to share. Drug users have a higher than average incidence of psychopathology, mainly anxiety and depression. Strang (1985) cites psychiatric disorders as among the causative and perpetuating factors in drug use.

Many come seeking not abstinence, but a prescription of a legal form of their drug of choice. But even this contains a psychological aspect: drugs are, after all, an important token of exchange in both material and emotional terms. Abstinence may or may not be in their minds, but they may well believe that they need to offer such an intention in order to 'earn' their prescription, while at the same time believing themselves incapable of bearing their lives without the drug. They are imbued with their own myths and their view of their identity is that of being an addict or junkie. There will inevitably be great ambivalence and distrust. In one psychodrama group, a role-play was taking place and the therapist was offering a therapeutic 'exchange' of personality traits so that the group members could experiment with different modes of behaviour. One member was raising the stakes by asking for the impossible:

'I'm offering a straight deal,' said the therapist.

'A straight dealer; you must be joking!' responded the drug user.

Who should be the psychotherapist?

Ideally, therapist and prescriber should not be the same person. However, drug treatment units and psychotherapy departments are seldom rich in staff and, pragmatically, there may be no choice. The dual role is beset with difficulties and conflicts, but also has many advantages. It requires a peculiar mixture of ruthlessness and compassion, the ability to reach behind the defence of drug use, respecting the person while not being awed or antagonised by the junkie persona and language. It is necessary to enter the client's world in a non-judgemental way without falling into the trap of collusion with its glamorised aspect, viewing the client neither as a helpless victim nor as a 'dope fiend'. Over-involvement and the rescuer mode are as unhelpful as the expectation that the individual need only be adequately motivated to be weaned off the drug, and will thereafter either be cured or have failed. Recognition of the centrality of ambivalence for the user is essential. Ex-drug-users will say that 'motivation is something that we all have on some days of the week' and, equally, that 'pain is not the monopoly of someone who shoots drugs up their arm'.

The life-style

Assessment for treatment, although this may not include psychotherapy, will involve a decision as to whether or not a prescription is necessary, and this will depend both on the drugs used and the type of use. The two major types of drugs in common use are the sedatives and the stimulants. Hallucinogens rarely produce the same degree of dependency. The sedatives include the opiates, such as heroin, opium, morphine and methadone, and the benzodiazepines, such as diazepam, temazepam, and lorazepam. They tranquillise, sedate and, by making physical and emotional pain seem not to matter, provide a sense of distance from it. The stimulants include the amphetamines, cocaine and the appetite suppressants. They raise mood, confidence, energy levels and gregariousness, and decrease the need for sleep and food.

All these drugs can be bought on the illegal market of the drug scene, and, therefore, their user must have enough money to buy them. Some can afford their supply from their wages, but many fund themselves through drug dealing, prostitution and crime, notably highly efficient shoplifting. This, together with the purchase and use of the drug, can quite adequately fill a day and, at the same time, produce a sense of excitement and risk because of the chances of getting caught, the possibility of a good deal and the feelings of success in getting away with something. Many drug users form quite tightly-knit groups, and this can contribute to their sense of identity. The drug itself serves as a token of exchange symbolising feelings of caring and concern, is used to celebrate special occasions as well as being part of daily life, and may be a retreat from discomfort and pain. In a therapy group, a client once spoke of being released from prison and being met by some friends in their car with a syringe drawn up ready for him.

'Some friends?' said the still-naïve therapist.

'Wouldn't your friends offer you a drink if you'd just come out of the nick?' was the answer.

Psychodynamic themes

While psychotherapy may be judged to be indicated at the initial assessment or early in treatment, the client may *not* see it as a possibility, or see any reason for it at all. Nonetheless, insight-orientated work frequently has a place. Even if it never achieves the status of psychotherapy, treatment should be psychotherapeutic and, indeed, should underlie every encounter with a drug-using client, alongside the addressing of practical areas of need.

Those with whom more intensive psychotherapeutic work is possible will be people who at some point in their lives have learned that their needs seem to be more reliably satisfied by a drug with a predictable effect than they can be by people, and who have some recognition of this as a problem which needs to be tackled. They may have been scapegoated, abused, let down or emotionally denied, and almost invariably dislike themselves. Psychological reasons for drug-use are various. They may be the black sheep of the families for whom the enactment of a self-fulfilling prophecy is less frightening that the challenging of a role. Many of the women and some of the men have been sexually abused, and others have suffered an early bereavement. Drug users may, through their own dependency needs, have chosen a drug-using partner and adopted their partner's life-style and identity through a lack of or weakness in their own. Another, rather different, group are those who have grown up in areas where drug use is a norm among the youth; for them to change is thus to challenge a set of assumptions, attitudes and needs based on peer group behaviour and belonging. These groupings approximate to those identified by Rounsaville et al (1982). For all of them drug use can be seen as a defence, an attempt to express and gratify needs, to establish a sense of belonging and to build relationships, and thus as a means of survival. Drugs can also be an emotional anaesthetic, being used to deny or avoid mental discomfort and pain.

The meaning of the prescription

When a drug user comes for help, he or she is making an admission that these defences are falling. They are often angry, always afraid and will test the therapist repeatedly. A prescription can help them face the myth of the terror of withdrawal and his or her fear of a lack of a buffer between her or himself and the issues that they will have to meet. It serves the purpose of stabilisation, and can actually assist the therapist in setting the boundaries of treatment by providing a container between sessions while a therapeutic alliance is becoming established. Gradually, then, the dependency is transferred from the drug to the therapist enabling the growth of trust and the development of the transference. The first task is the establishment of trust. Much of this is done in practical ways, and the therapist's reliability is essential; he or she has to be 'a straight dealer'. As prescriber, the author has more than once been referred to as 'the man', i.e. the dealer! This epithet contains many messages, including references to her power, her gender, her role as potential provider or witholder, the clients' resentment and their need, as well as an only semi-joking attempt to disable her. The boundaries must be clear in terms both of the length and frequency of the sessions and of the prescribing rules. The work is with a person, not with an illness; thus the therapy can be available without the prescription or co-exist with it, but is not tied to it. Dependency is being addressed psychologically as well as pharmacologically, so that gradually, with the utmost consistency on the part of the therapist, she or he may come to be perceived as reliable enough for the drug gradually to be let go of.

For these reasons, psychotherapy often needs to begin before reduction of and weaning from the drug. The two proceed most effectively in tandem. Woody et al (1983) showed that the inclusion of individual psychotherapy in treatment programmes produced significant benefit, including a lower number of drop-outs. An image that can be useful to the therapist comes directly from the actual meaning of the word dependency – a 'hanging from'. The therapist needs to be aware of his or her own dependencies and the importance of these. They are among the things that give individuals their sense of identity, of belonging and of the reliability of their lives. They can be pictured as a series of strings attaching the individual to life as he or she knows it: work; a car; relationships; activities; hobbies; creative pursuits. The severing of even one of these connections produces disorientation and a sense of loss commensurate with its importance. If, then, many or all of these attachments are mediated through a drug or drugs, cessation of use or unavailability may well produce a sense of hopelessness, despair or panic. Concepts of motivation and cooperation, or the expectation that the goal from the onset must be abstinence, may easily become barriers between therapist and client, and may lead to punitiveness in the therapist. This punitiveness can then ally with the self-abusing facet of the client's personality. This is particularly clear when working with those who have been sexually or physically abused in childhood and have internalised both functions, but an internal abused/abuser dichotomy is often present in the emotionally abused as well. It is necessary to respect the client's perceived need for the drug as the string from which he or she hangs as well as the wish, intermittent and often resented, to find other strings in order to be able to let go of it. To maintain the client's own optimism, therefore, the therapist does well to view drug dependency as a chronic relapsing condition of frequently long duration, but with an often positive outcome.

GENERAL PSYCHOTHERAPEUTIC PRINCIPLES

Crises

In the author's experience, individual therapy with an addict often begins almost accidentally. It is well-accepted that counselling is a more significant factor in treatment than is the prescription, when the treatment needed is of long duration. Once the client begins to understand drug use in terms of his or her personal experience of the world in childhood and adolescence, and the bearing that this has upon adult attitudes and behaviour, and if the therapist is responding with interpretations which can be used by the client, then counselling can be safely said to have moved into psychotherapy. If the therapist is psychotherapeutically orientated, this may begin at the assessment interview or soon after, as crises occur in the client's life due either to drug use or to the difficulties caused by no longer participating in the drug scene. Crises due to drug use may involve illness, arrest, or major relationship difficulties, as the client appears unconsciously to engage in a last-ditch attempt to affirm an addict identity.

Moving away from the drug scene may precipitate a crisis in the inner world of the addict as they begin to realise the effects they have had on themselves and on others; or the crisis may occur in the outer world, as the inner changes and his or her life-style evoke resentment or confusion in those around. These episodes may cause the client to avoid the psychotherapeutic approach or to be unable to use it for a while until practical difficulties are resolved. This can give therapy a very staccato feeling, but the therapist will often find that the client returns after such a break and that the experiences can then be put to good psychotherapeutic use. It is as though the resistances were being acted out in an extreme manner and indeed, if interpreted, a crisis can often lead to a major breakthrough in insight and to behaviour change. An example of this is the sudden missing of a series of appointments by a client when he or she has asked for a reduction in his or her prescription. On his return, often in chaos, it may be elucidated with the therapist in terms of not yet being ready for that step. More realistic goals can then be set and, in therapy, the addict may be ready to explore his or her propensity to set him or herself up to fail with tasks that seem impossible.

Often, this disjointed process will continue through a large part of treatment if not all of it; in other cases, the therapy can be more or less continuous. At some point, the psychotherapeutic component in treatment is usually recognised and acknowledged as such by the client, and it can then be explicitly structured into the treatment plan, although the therapist still needs to be prepared for many breaks in the process.

Starting therapy

At the beginning, the clients' view of themselves is often limited to their self-definition as addicts. Judgements tend to be stark, and they may have great ambivalence about the therapist and the process of therapy. They see themselves as anti-authoritarian, very different from 'straight' (i.e. conventional and conforming) society, often victimised and stigmatised, while at the same time in a way glorying in this. Their actual life experience is in reality often one of rejection, dislike and distancing by professionals and family. An *internalised* abused/abuser dichotomy has trapped the addict in a repetition-compulsion of drug use and its ritualisation; a perpetuation which mirrors his internal world. His or her self-esteem is so low that he or she perceives themselves as unable to change. At the same time, there may be an erotic attachment to the habit. The use of a drug may produce sensual gratification which is often described as ecstatic, and the ritual of self-injecting or mutual injection may be a major dependency in itself as well as a quasi-sexual experience. The drug and its use offer both self-punishment and self-gratification. The inner and outer world of the drug user is split in many ways. The drug chosen may reflect his or her inner state (Khantzian 1985). Opiates are often chosen by aggressive, fragmented individuals, and provide a container as well as sedative and emotional analgesia which will enable the suppression of the individual's aggression.

These strong aggressive feelings are dealt with in ways that maintain an essentially paranoid position. The client projects either abuser or victim, judge or sinner, destroyer or destroyed, rage or fear of pain. Opiates may also cocoon them from self-dislike, self-blame and guilt, as they become depressed at the harms caused or the pain that was suffered, but they fail endlessly to achieve the reparative stage of the depressive position.

Stimulants are often chosen at this stage, for their antidepressant, energising effect, and are used by lonely or depressed individuals with low self-esteem for the sense of confidence and gregariousness which they impart. Some individuals alternate between the two types of drug, and it may be that this reflects the movement of their inner world at the time, with one drug serving as protection from the after-effects of the other.

The language and words of the drug scene give some insight into how the drug users view both it and themselves. Drugs are gear, dope, whizz, speed, ecstasy. Injecting encompasses shooting-up, jacking-up, works (the equipment); and the experience includes being stoned, wrecked, smashed, 'out of my head', turned on, out of it. It constitutes a self-mythologising with strong erotic and escapist undertones.

As therapy progresses, an intense relationship with the therapist grows. This has periods of intense hostility alternating with desperate needs for approval which can make the drug user seem like Jekyll and Hyde. Trust feels terrifying and they expect betrayal. Wurmser (1984) explores this in his discussion of therapy with a young polydrug user who 'loved to hate and hated to love' and who, being certain that trust would lead to betrayal, was acutely ambivalent. This is often the presentation of an abused person and, indeed, many such individuals have histories of extreme neglect and abuse which may take years to emerge. Many of the women are likely to have been sexually abused, and there is often a history of alcohol – or medication – abuse in the parents.

The therapist will be tested repeatedly with: missed appointments; dire needs for an increased prescription (whether or not the therapist is the prescriber); threats that the client will be driven back to illicit use if the required response is not forthcoming; demands for immediate appoint-ments; and with statements that, as a well-adjusted and therefore totally happy and competent 'straight', he or she cannot possibly understand how the client feels. A non-punitive, flexible consistency is the only appropriate response to these tests, and the agreed boundaries must be maintained on most occasions. The limits of prescribing and therapist availability must be clearly stated at the outset and reviewed regularly. The client can then rage and despair in the safety of the knowledge that he or she is unlikely to be discharged from treatment, but that the therapist is not a soft touch. It is the therapist's responsibility not to be manipulated, rather than to label the client as manipulative. Even though therapy often breaks down for a period, each episode can stand in its own right and be built on in later ones. The strength of the container, which is really what the client is seeking in acting out, can develop until the exchanges focus less on drug use and more on the client's feelings about him or herself.

SOME EXAMPLES OF PSYCHOTHERAPEUTIC WORK WITH ADDICTS

Case study 18.1   Looking after the hurt child

James presented in a failing marriage and did not engage in therapy until the couple had split up and his wife had taken the children away from the area to go home to her family. He was on prescription for a long time, and had over 10 years of opiate addiction, unbroken by abstinence, behind him. He always needed to appear to be coping and had, indeed, an unbroken work record because of a skill that allowed him to fund his and his wife's habits without recourse to much crime. He therefore had no legal history, but neither had he anything in life more important than drugs. For many months, James came and went in treatment, each time getting to know the staff a little better and each time haltingly disclosing a little more. It was not, however, until a further relationship had broken down that he embarked on therapy, as he began to realise that, without someone to look after, he found life pointless. He then used individual therapy and psychodrama as well as the mandatory group work of his treatment package.

James' parents had been untrustworthy from the start. They fought each other, and his father was violent to his mother and to him. Long before James was 10 years old he dreaded returning from school lest he should yet again need to call the neighbours and the ambulance because of another suicide attempt on his mother's part. His father made him work for his living; his only, but useful, gift to him was his skill with his hands. James found a positive role in protecting his sister, who does seem to have survived relatively well and has since been very supportive to him.

As he began to move away from drug use, James found himself unable to cope as he had been accustomed to. He left work, drifted through various squats and bedsits and became clinically depressed. He became very dependent on the treatment unit, and spoke of it once as 'the only place, for some weeks, where I knew, without looking, where the light switches were'. At times, James dropped in almost daily. The secretary, older than himself, became a mother figure while his therapist bore the brunt of his ambi-valence. Thus, James' early splitting of his mother into idealised and treacherous could be expressed, and it was safe for him to express his rage and feelings of betrayal and to see how drugs had been a seemingly safer substitute. Later, he could also see how they allowed him to gamble with his wish for death.

At the time of the second anniversary of the loss of his wife and child, and shortly after the tragic death of a child in his extended family, James began to value the hurt child in himself as he grieved those that had been lost. He found that, with support, he could bear the intensity of his sadness, regret and anger, and that his therapist could bear them with him. He started to engage in creative activities again, and found a girlfriend who, though quite a hurt person herself, could sustain a career without using drugs. He looked for work. He was still on a low maintenance prescription, but was not supplementing it and was finding his pleasure and his challenges in other areas.

James had learned at an early age to split and project, and thus looked after others instead of himself. His grief was too much to bear without support and trust. Since his childhood relationships had betrayed him, James became totally self-supporting and terrified of trusting anyone, but the cost of this was that he was cut off from his own creativity. His drug use both compensated for this and gave him the support that he could not take from people.

Case study 18.2   The imprisoned princess

Daisy was beautiful. She always had been and she had always been able to find men to look after her. However, she had no sense of self or self-worth, and so believed that she had to pay for her care. Her pimp paid her with drugs and these enabled her to bear working as a prostitute. Daisy earned well and so her pimp was able to buy more drugs. When he was impri- soned, she was free, but very much afraid. She was brought to treatment by another drug user. Daisy was wearing very tight trousers and was painfully thin; she showed many features of anorexia, being bright, controlled and busy. She was also intelligent, and used her intelligence in self-defence. She found talking about her feelings hard, but it gradually emerged that her father and brother were alcoholics and that her mother had been dependent on tranquillisers for some time. In her family there had been money and many presents, but no feelings. Daisy engaged in intermittent bouts of psychotherapy with bouts of chaos in between. Each episode, however, led to gains in trust that could be built on in the next. After over a year, Daisy spoke of an uncle who had cared about her. She had responded to this and had been sexually abused. Nonetheless, his warmth drew her back. Her much older brother guessed, and threatened her with disclosure if she did not let him abuse her also. It took a long time and many absences before Daisy could believe that her therapists could care for her without being placated, but then she was able to cease drug use. She also put on weight, came to see her many pretty clothes as adornment of herself and not as coverings for shame, and embarked on a college course.

Daisy's drug use enabled her to buy what seemed to her, with her materia- listic home, to be love. The abuse that she had suffered in childhood had deprived her of self-worth and left her extremely needy. At the same time, drugs defended her from feeling this, and thus enabled her to survive her life-style of continued abuse.

Case study 18.3   The sick child

Sean grew up in a city area where crime and drugtaking were the norm. His family were not unkind, but his role was that of the sick child and their worries focused on him. His health improved but he became a chronic worrier. He grew into drug use with his peers and gained self-confidence. Sean became over-confident, contracted hepatitis, became drug-free in hospital but returned to drugs on discharge. Now he worried about his drug use because of the risk of infection. He was trapped; worried if he used, worried if he abstained. In the sick role, Sean knew himself but was unhappy; and, though still using drugs, he was coming to see that the confidence which they brought him did not last. He did not want to die. He developed a stomach ulcer which perforated, and the surgeons referred him for treatment. There, while on prescription, he learned in therapy that people liked to see him healthy and enjoyed his company. Sean's confidence grew. He liked his new appearance. However, he also still liked his criminal life and its excitement, and this was a problem because it was for him inextricable from the drug world. As he came to realise this, he began to seek excitement elsewhere. He was intelligent and found a niche for himself in an 'alternative' venture which allowed him to use his organising skills without having to see himself as a conformist. He could be well, find excitement and be liked.

Therapy with Sean raised the issue of the roles that a child may have to carry for his family; Sean had had to bear his family's sickness and could not be himself. He could be said to have been in an 'addictogenic' relationship with his family (see Little & Pearson 1966), where their need for his sickness was a major factor in perpetuating his addiction.

Case study 18.4 Dying of shame

Carla's case is a prime example of the necessity for consistency in therapy with addicts. Abused as a child by her sister after her mother's early death, Carla was very attached to her tinker father, travelled with him and formed no roots. She felt ugly and dirty, and needed constant reassurance in the form of devotion which she obtained from damaged men, always returning to her father when these relationships ended.

Very gradually, Carla began to engage in treatment. For her, detoxification held few fears as she saw her drug use as evidence of her ugliness and dirtiness, was used to feeling awful in a way that withdrawal could not approach, and was desperately ashamed of her habit. She saw it as dirty and had always been fanatically clean. Drugs epitomised the bad side of herself, and as Carla gained reassurance from the affection in which she was held, she could begin to let go of them. They had never symbolised mother for her; they were the bullying sister. Nonetheless, if the reassurance became too much to bear, Carla would binge on drugs and self-distaste. These episodes became less frequent as she came to understand them and gained the confidence to establish a circle of non-drug-using friends. In therapy, Carla could vent her rage against her sister and have her experiences believed.

Sadly, Carla's treatment unit was closed. Later meetings with other drug users brought the information that she had become increasingly depressed and had withdrawn from nearly all social contact. Then she injected herself with a massive dose of heroin and died. Her peers saw it as suicide and her ex-therapist saw no reason to disagree.

This example highlights the strong need for consistency in therapy where there has been none in life. For Carla, drugs were both her 'bad' self and her childhood persecutors, but she still clung onto them, albeit with ambivalence, because of their emotional analgesic effect. Carla's story emphasises the depth of shame found in many drug users.

GROUP THERAPY

This section is drawn from the author's 3-year experience of working with opiate users in psychodynamic psychotherapy groups as part of an overall treatment package (Cartwright et al 1987; see also Ch. 3 for further discussion of group therapy). Receiving a prescription was contingent upon group attendance, and the result of this was that attendance was much higher than it would have been had the choice been a free one. Inevitably, therefore, there was much resentment initially on the part of many group members at having to attend, and some would certainly have been excluded as unsuitable had there been a selection process as in the orthodox mode of selecting clients for group therapy. Nonetheless, more than half of the group members reported themselves as surprised and pleased by the effects upon them of the group process, and felt they had gained both in their understanding of themselves and in their ability to relate to others outside the group as well as those within it. The greatest single reported gain was in self-confidence, which would be unusual in a cohort of people on reducing prescriptions aiming at abstinence. The majority of the groups lasted six months, a few three months; all were closed and all lasted 90 minutes per session and had two therapists. Group members who arrived intoxicated were asked to leave; this recurrently emerged as a group decision. The use of groups for treatment is economical in therapist time, and allows clients to help each other and to meet each other directly without the use of a drug as a token of exchange in any way other than in discussion of it. The style of the groups was consistent with Cartwright's (1987) recommendations that the focus be determined by the group rather than imposed by the leader, and that group members learn from each other. As Cartwright says, it was found to be important that the leaders had expertise in the practical issues which arose, as well as in the psychotherapeutic ones.

The groups differed from conventional psychotherapy groups in that, inevitably, members often already knew each other from the drug scene (couples were not allocated to the same group, however). Thus, they brought their reputations with them, and this heightened the difficulty of achieving trust. Naturally, they also brought a shared culture, perceiving themselves and each other, part-defensively and part-defiantly, as 'junkies', i.e. untrustworthy and unpleasant.

Blame

Often, the clients blamed the drug; there was always a need to find somewhere to place blame. They frequently saw themselves as powerless and dependent on others, particularly dealers, and the therapists would often accept this dependency, at least in part because of their power to negotiate a prescription. Often, these group leaders would be stereotyped as 'normal'; this implied that they knew how to be successful, to cope, to always be happy and never to feel inadequate. They were seen as unable to understand the need for drug use; not being understood was a frequent theme, and understanding themselves was often a very frightening prospect for the clients, particularly as they confused responsibility with blame.

Feedback in and after the groups included such comments as: 'I don't talk like this anywhere else'; 'You realise that you are not the only one to feel this way'; 'The group and the unit are safe because drugs are not allowed here'; 'I'm not just a junkie here'; and 'I gain a feeling of worth'. These comments indicate that members felt enabled to give each other care and support without sharing drugs, and thus began to establish new patterns in their relationships and life-styles.

The group process was recorded using Tuckman's (1965) model of stages – of 'forming', 'storming', 'norming' and 'performing' – with the addition of a pre-stage of 'arriving', since attendance was mandatory and time was needed to come to terms with this. Naturally, the stages did overlap, but they could be clearly recognised in each group.

Arriving

The themes were drawn from the culture from which the members came, and served to establish their identity or, as it were, present their credentials. Members often expressed feelings of powerlessness to change, hopelessness at their situation, and resentment at being expected to attend. In expression of these feelings, they would stereotype the therapists, talk about being falsely arrested by police in the past or unjustly sentenced in the Courts, and state how useless other treatment attempts had been. Resistance was also shown by late arrival, whispering, giggling and mockery, and the therapists' interventions would frequently be treated with hostility. By way of compensation, group members would attempt to raise their self-esteem and impress each other, while perhaps trying to shock the therapists. They would talk about outwitting the police; successful crime; glorious drug-taking experiences; the boredom and conformity of non-drug-users. Overdoses and the closeness of death were themes which seemed to glamorise them in their own eyes, hint at the need for a symbolic rite of passage, and indicate the sense of trappedness and despair that for many of them underlay their dependency.

It became apparent that it was necessary for the therapists to go along with this stage, whereupon the group members themselves began to move from it to the next stage by beginning to find it tedious and 'not what we are really here for'.

Forming

The need for an acceptance of being in the group led to a few members (on average three out of ten) dropping out, and the rest beginning to change the way in which they related to each other and to the therapists. As they began to wonder how it would be to live without dependence on drugs, they began to recognise the need for a long-term perspective. Memories were shared of ambitions from school and members began to consider their talents and abilities. This raised the issue of regret and they could become angry with themselves over wasted opportunities. In this they found that they could help each other to be less judgemental and this in turn led to discussion of families and upbringing. The therapists were now less 'the dealers' and more the potentially punitive parents who were to be placated. From fear, anger began to emerge and so ambivalence became more apparent.

Storming

In the 'storming' stage, as group members gained the confidence to express their feelings, conflict could emerge. The therapists were challenged and their knowledge and competence put in doubt. Confidentiality became a major issue, and was a particularly important one for these people who found themselves sharing feelings and information that they had often not focused on before, let alone voiced, while being likely to meet each other in their daily lives on the drug scene. The groups often took it upon themselves at this stage to reset the group ground rules, and it was very important that they found the therapists consistent. From challenging the therapists, they moved to confronting each other. They were naturally extremely accurate in their perceptions of each others' rationalisations and defences, and a great deal of anger and pain could be generated. It was the therapists' task to begin to interpret these while keeping the group safe and preventing scapegoating. As scapegoats arose, which they usually did, the therapists had the opportunity to help the group examine the process and see what they were rejecting in themselves.

Norming

As the group members began to recognise their ability to feel intensely and in safety, they increasingly developed a sense of cohesion and trust in which they could explore their changing identities. They recognised both their common goal and their personal differences, and thus had both a sense of belonging and an increasing ability to accept themselves. Hostility, judgement and punitiveness lessened and so they could take more responsibility for themselves and begin to believe in the possibility of a life without drugs. Looking at this could cause a great deal of pain and fear, and there were many crises and relapses which were now less likely to lead to drop-out than to be brought to the group and worked on. Grief and regret for the past, both for things suffered and acts committed, were now much safer, and tears were more frequent than rage. Exploring the future meant facing the fear of failure and developing an internal permission to make mistakes. The therapists were increasingly treated as real people, and the group members showed concern and care for them and for each other more openly.

Performing

The group members could now actively recognise the possibility of living without drugs, but they had also to face the emptiness that this entailed. The themes were a mixture of grieving and celebration, and the group often had the sensation of witnessing rites of passage as one member reported the repairing of family relationships, another finding a job, another better accommodation, another an opportunity of training or a new relationship. The group reviewed itself and also focused on strategies for the future. There were many crises; for some these were too much to resolve at this time (although of these many returned later for further help); but for others these were tests that they set themselves and from which they emerged with more confidence and realism. Normal life was no longer the unknown, feared or despised, but was seen more as a journey on which they were beginning a new stage. Their drug-using life could be integrated into it, not denied or rejected but accepted as part of themselves. The group experience had, for those who completed it (between 50% and 70%) enabled them to achieve a sense of self-confidence and self-esteem at a more realistic level of expectation.

PSYCHODRAMA

One of the basic psychodramatic maxims is, 'Show me, don't tell me', and hence it is often very effective with inarticulate people. Because of its immediacy, it is useful with the emotionally frozen or inhibited. As a group process it involves members in playing roles in each others' dramas, and because it is client-centred and yet structured it is safe from the point of view both of drug users' need for autonomy and their fear of new situations. It gives group members the opportunity to enact what does happen in their lives as well as what does not, whether from past, present, or future. Thus, it gives the opportunity for corrective experiences in a concrete as well as a symbolic form. It is particularly helpful in increasing confidence and self-esteem and in working with people whose intellectual and emotional functioning are split, and it is also useful for work on specific problem areas or situations. It has been called a 'rehearsal for living', indicating that group members can test various behaviours and explore the consequences before taking these alternative possibilities into real life. Emotional catharsis is an essential element of many psychodramas, and the energy freed in this way can be channelled into insight-orientated work and the practice of change. Drug users often expect not to be believed, and the chance to show what has happened to them and what they have done can be valuable. In the reversed role or spectator position, they can see themselves through the eyes of others and gain new insights into and compassion for themselves and significant others (see also Ch. 6 for a fuller discussion of psychodrama).

There can be difficulties, however, particularly with addicts' refusal of anything remotely whimsical and their fear of making fools of themselves. In this they resemble adolescents, with their prickly sensitivity and precarious self-esteem and with their desperate fear that they will not be taken seriously or treated with respect. It is essential that the therapist be aware of this and, if not familiar with work with drug users, be aware also of the frequency of childhood abuse and early damage that will be met, and therefore of the level of fear that may be evoked. Psychodrama is not acting out; drug-using behaviour often is. The group, then, should work towards reality testing and accurate mirroring and be firmly grounded in reality at all times. The final stage of a psychodrama group, the sharing, in which group members focus on points of identity and feelings aroused in themselves, is particularly necessary in such a group. Winding down and deroling must be fully completed, and the protagonist must be reintegrated into the group.

Group members must be highly motivated to attend these sessions as, though attractive in theory, they can be very threatening. A group composed of drug users will contain people from many origins, classes and upbringings and with a rich range of experience. The author has found it particularly useful to bring a small number of drug users into conventional groups thus introducing them to the 'straight' world and its difficulties, and offering them acceptance by it as ordinary, wounded human beings.

The following are some examples taken from drug users' psychodramas.

Case study 18.1 (contd)   Filling the toolbox

James began with a scene in which he and his wife and children were hiding beneath the kitchen table in terror of the people hammering on the door. The latter were some men to whom he owed money from drug dealing. He was amazed at the intensity of the re-evoked feelings.

These took him, by association, to a childhood scene in which his parents were fighting in the kitchen. James was then a terrified child. His younger sister was also there and he felt the need to protect her. Despite his anger with both parents, he managed to grab a knife from his mother to prevent anyone coming to harm. He wanted to die himself but could not bear to leave his sister unprotected.

James realised that he had viewed the drug dealers as if they were adults and he a child, and that this was no longer the case. He saw how the drugs he used had masked the fear and anger which he had felt unable to contain. His next psychodrama was one in which he symbolically (he was a skilled craftsman) filled a toolbox with which to be equipped for a drug-free life.

Case study 18.5   The latch-key child

Pete was a latch-key child and stood at his parents' door, not knowing that they had parted and that neither would be coming home. In the role of himself as a child he dared not confront them with his feelings at this stage of the group, and so he was brought back to his adult self to meet each of them in turn. First in the reversed role with a group member playing himself, and then as himself with group members playing the parents, Pete was enabled to begin to feel that his pain could be met and understood by people, as an alternative to containing it with drugs. His sense of invisibility, requiring large quantities of amphetamine to give him self-confidence, was gradually replaced by a sense of himself as someone who was a better father than his own had been, and who could give to his children what he only knew in himself by its absence.

Case study 18.4 (contd)   Corrective role-playing

Carla had lost her mother in early childhood and had been humiliated and abused by her older sister. She could not bear to enact the scenes that had taken place in the cellar of her home when she was still a pre-school child, but she was able to describe the cellar, stand 'in' it and state how bad and ugly she had felt.

Carla's next scenes were corrective. In one, she played her first communion, this time in a beautiful dress with her hair elaborately dressed and, in the reversed role, she saw and said how lovely she was. In another she was a model, as she had been before her involvement with drugs, and lay on the edge of a swimming pool being adored by her ex-husband. She began to see what he had seen in her. Later, she also began to recognise the abuser and the victim in him, both of which had been part of her attraction to him.

Case study 18.6   Grieving the past

Angela had never been able to compete with her sick sister until drugs made her sick too. By then, her rejecting mother was dead. In a mourning scene, she could tell her mother what had happened and, using role reversal, grieve for what all three of them had missed. She could then take this love to her son and begin to set realistic limits to his behaviour and her mothering.

THEMES IN THERAPY

For the individual, drug use has many functions. To work with it psychotherapeutically, there must be recognition that it stems from the impulse to health as well as from more destructive impulses. It will represent a different constellation of needs in each patient, and these must be elucidated individually. Many themes recur, however, and this recognition allows a passage to the possibility of their being expressed in ways which do not necessitate drug use.

The internalised abused/abuser dichotomy

Problem drug use is, par excellence, a repetition compulsion. The user can give him or herself a gratification which is within his or her own power to control, satisfying, as Fenichel (1946) observes, an archaic longing, but needing as a result constantly to repeat the sensation which always fades. At the same time, the addict abuses him or herself, identifying either with the abuser part of him or herself and feeling guilty at the harm which he or she has caused, or with the abused part of him or her, thus feeling him or herself to be the victim. Feeling helpless in his dependency, he or she is the victim both of the drug and of him or herself. If the drug is blamed, it becomes the abuser and the patient the abused one. There is a repeated cycle of self-punishment which they feel they deserve, while also seeing themselves as victims of a persecution that they cannot prevent. The abuser/abused roles are mutually dependent, and the recognition of this in therapy can be the first step towards integrating and going beyond the internalised abused/abuser split. Recognition of the need for self-gratification through the experience of drug use can also lead to exploration of the unmet needs that are being gratified in this way.

Fusion and splitting

An alcoholic was once asked by the author what drink meant to him. 'Mother', came the immediate response, made in a self-mocking tone which could not disguise the serious pain and need underlying it. The 'rush' of drug use often brings a temporary sense of merging, of losing personal boundaries, which seems similar to the very early stages of the mother-child relationship. Often, there is a persistent search for the pleasure of the 'first fix', i.e. the first experience of using the drug, which can be likened to myths of the Golden Age, or the idealised primal mother experience where the reward is immediate (Rado 1957). Here, there is comfort, reliability, security, a sense of belonging, acceptance and self-worth. From it comes self-confidence and self-esteem. To keep the painful opposites at bay, splitting occurs, and the persecuting aspect of the dichotomy is projected either onto the drug or onto the people attempting to prevent its use. The drug user and his fellows form an in-group with its own identity, rituals and a sense of belonging, and this again defends the drug user against feelings of loneliness and of being outcast and worthless. The theme in this pattern is that of the unmothered child and his or her attempt to heal the pain of the loss of something he or she never had or had only inadequately. The need is for unconditional self-acceptance, in order to gain a viable identity. As drug users they assert their idealised group identity in a reaction against the rest of society which they see, usually accurately, as threatened by and hostile to them.

Transition and the rite of passage

By being a member of the drug scene, the internal split within the drug user is mirrored externally. The patient is the victim and the drug either the persecutor or the rescuer from society's persecution. The latter leads to the users being able to see themselves as a hero or, more accurately, an anti-hero. The game becomes cops and robbers or Robin Hood. Survival on the drug scene can be interpreted as outwitting the forces of convention, the enormous odds stacked against the user who becomes the glamorised rebel. There is the sense of being a scapegoat and so blameless, and this can have, of course, the truth in it of the individual's history. At the same time, the impulse to health carries a need for transition which is endlessly defeated by the circularity of the drug use. Yet this very circularity can be seen as an attempt at initiation into a new stage of becoming which turns out always to carry the seed of its own failure. There is an enormous myth among drug users of the awfulness of withdrawal. What this can mask is the fear of facing the stage that comes after, when there is a need for transition, for initiation into a drug-free life. Repeated drug use serves as a repeated attempt at a rite of passage which always fails as the effect of the drug wears off, leaving the situation unchanged.

Purposelessness versus transcendence

For many drug users, life has had little or no meaning or purpose, and drug use has been a refuge from this or a manufacture of it. There is an often inarticulate but intense need for change, for transcendence. Taking drugs is risky, most of all because it can be deadly, and so there is a repeated dance with death. Each cycle carries the symbol of death (the use and its effect), descent (the aftermath) and the hope, ever unrealised, of a rebirth. It is this rebirth that cessation of use needs to achieve. Otherwise the obverse is risked, for drug use is also a repeated gamble with overdosage – a death that is, ultimately, not perceived as the individual's fault or responsibility but, rather, as the ultimate victimisation or punishment. So, while drug use may have been the best defence at the user's command against his or her inability to feel adequate in life, cessation must be a choice of life, with all the risks that entails.

Countertransference in the therapist

The therapist will be seen by the client as a representative of society and, indeed, will know him or herself to some degree to be so. Society, however, tends to have very stereotyped views of drug users with, at one extreme, the concept of the depraved 'dope fiend' and, at the other, that of the poor victim in need of rescue. The therapist must therefore be aware of his or her own position, otherwise he or she is in danger of working from a combination of fascination and distaste and living vicariously through the client, or of setting out to rescue his or her own projected victim. Either may lead the therapist to attempt to gratify his or her own needs by helping his client, and it can then be easy for him or her to become unintentionally punitive if the client is unable or unwilling to comply. Because he or she will be tested repeatedly, the therapist needs to be comfortable in him or herself with the boundaries of the work; if this is not the case, he or she is liable to feel victimised especially when the client is projecting the internalised abuser.

The rescuer, the reformer and the authority figure are all role-traps into which the therapist can fall if unaware of his or her reasons for and attitudes in the work that he or she is doing.

Countertransference in society

More than is the case with other substance abusers, illicit drug users are beyond society's pale. They appear on the surface to be challenging the protestant work ethic of society, and so elicit a harsh and punitive response. Yet western society is deeply consumerist and materialistic, and the addict caricatures this, taking it to an extreme at which the drug, the token of exchange, is involved in almost all exchanges. The hedonism of consumerism is also highlighted, as drug use is perceived by non-users as an endless pursuit of pleasure, which they view with disapproval while denying its similarity to their own use of alcohol, tobacco, food or other gratifying activities. The onlooker's denial of his or her own dependency makes the drug user dangerous by projection.

Also caricatured is the use of medication. Doctors prescribe multitudes of psychotropic drugs in a society which believes in a pill for every ill. This implies that pain, unhappiness, anger, grief and fear are symptoms which can and should be treated. Death is similarly an area of life which is inadequately addressed and avoided as much as possible. In hospitals, it is often seen as equivalent to failure. By gambling with death, the addict challenges society's wish to ignore it, just as, by self-administered analgesia and oblivion, he or she caricatures society's fear of 'negative' feelings of anger and pain.

It may be that drug users perform a function for society as scapegoats, carrying some of its shadow. At the same time, they highlight the lack of ritual and disregard for the need for transcendence that are features of a materialistic society. Drug use has been a feature of most societies, and when they are in transition this can, as in the instances of alcohol use among Eskimos, American Indians and Australian Aborigines, become chaotic and destructive. By contrast, when it has a place in ritual, it is symbolic of transcendence and mediates transition, as does the wine in the Eucharist.

EPILOGUE

In conclusion, a paradigm of society's projections onto the drug addict comes from the case of a patient, treated by the author, who was not a junkie, but who saw himself as one. He had a painful, chronic illness with periods of acute exacerbation. The treatment of the illness itself, with medication, was something he coped with expertly. He saw himself as on perfectly acceptable terms with his illness and its implicit life-sentence. He believed that he felt no need to rage, grieve or fear; things were as they were and had to be accepted as such with no fuss. However, he could not accept his intermittent, acute need for pain relief, and so his analgesia was in chaos. To him, his need for strong painkillers made him an addict, which meant that he was dirty, out of control, weak and despicable. He felt that he should not feel pain, or that if he did he should be able to cope with it without needing any help. Therapy involved the need to re-own the frightened, angry, helpless parts of himself that he had projected onto his need for the drugs, and to allow them expression. On the practical side, he had to learn how to treat his medication as a necessary tool, and not as a pandering to a rejected aspect of himself. His use of it then ceased to be chaotic and, as he lost his need to punish his own weakness, so he could accept a much lessened amount of pain as his due. As this process took place, so he gradually became able to care for himself not only clinically, but as a whole person.

FURTHER READING

Blaine J D, Juluis D A, 1977 Psychodynamics of drug dependence. NIDA Research Monograph 12, United States Department of Health, Education and Welfare, Public Health Service, Washington
Gossop M 1987 Living with drugs, 2nd edn. Wildwood House, Aldershot
The Royal College of Psychiatrists 1987 Drug scenes. Alden Press, Oxford
Zoja L 1989 Drugs, addiction and initiation: the modern search for ritual. Sigo Press, Boston

Psychotherapy with special groups

19. Psychotherapy with adolescents

P. Wilson

'Who are *you*?' said the Caterpillar.

This was not an encouraging opening for a conversation. Alice replied, rather shyly, 'I – I hardly know, Sir, just at present – at least I know who I *was* when I got up this morning, but I think I must have changed several times since then.'

'What do you mean by that?' said the Caterpillar, sternly. 'Explain yourself!'.

'I can't explain *myself*, I'm afraid, Sir,' said Alice, 'because I'm not myself, you see.'

'I don't see,' said the Caterpillar.

'I'm afraid I can't put it more clearly,' Alice replied, very politely, 'for I can't understand it myself, to begin with; and being so many different sizes in a day is very confusing.'

'It isn't,' said the Caterpillar.

'Well, perhaps you haven't found it so yet,' said Alice; 'but when you have to turn into a chrysalis – you will some day, you know – and then after that into a butterfly, I should think you'll feel it a little queer, won't you?'

(Lewis Carroll *Alice's Adventures in Wonderland*)

INTRODUCTION

Adolescence is well known as a time of major growth and change. It is by definition transitional: it is 'The Age Between' (Miller 1983) – an unsettled position both Beyond and yet Not Yet. It is neither one thing nor the other. Childhood has passed; adulthood, yet to happen. Past certainty, however false, has faded; adult sureness, however illusory, has yet to be acquired. The adolescent wants to be cared for as a child and respected as an adult. Like Alice, the adolescent 'changes several times' and has 'so many different sizes in a day'. It is a very indeterminate and contradictory state of affairs. The adolescent is confused, the adult perplexed. So too the psychotherapist.

Winnicott, in inimitable form, summed up the problem. He introduced the image of the 'doldrums' to describe the state of adolescence:

'A few years in which the individual has no way out except to wait and to do this without awareness of what is going on. In this phase the child does not know whether he or she is homosexual, heterosexual or narcissistic.

There is no established identity and no certain way of life that shapes the future and makes sense of graduating exams. There is not yet a capacity to identify with parent figures without loss of personal identity.' (Winnicott 1966b)

Much of the essence of adolescence is captured in this statement – not least its unclear identity, its curious state of awareness and fear of submission. What is conveyed is a time of waiting, an inevitable ennui, in which things might or might not happen. But the notion of the doldrums, oceanic, equatorial, 'where calm and baffling winds prevail', is apposite. Adolescence is a time of unpredictability. It is not surprising that Winnicott concludes: 'There is only one cure for adolescence and this is the passage of time and the passing on of the adolescent into the adult state.... We hold on, playing for time, instead of offering distractions and cures' (Winnicott 1966b).

Faced with the weight of this sigh, it is tempting to conclude that adolescents are inherently untreatable, best kept out of sight until adult and recognisable. There is, indeed, little doubt that many psycho-therapists steer a wide berth, or at best keep a tight ration of adolescent patients on their caseloads – preferring the greater stability and conformity of the motivated and self-observant adult, or the relatively greater compliance and charm of the younger child. In brief, neither the child nor the adult, regardless of individual idiosyncrasy, presents such ambiguity or ambivalence as does the adolescent.

It is, nevertheless, clear that adolescence is a critical phase of development, in which fundamental solutions are found and decisions made affecting the future life of the individual. It is a unique period of life, in which childhood experience is reawakened in an especially powerful way by the impact of puberty. 'The individual recapitulates and expands in the second decennium of life, the development he passed through during the first five years' (Freud 1905c). The possibility arises in adolescence of reviewing and rearranging past experience in the light of present and future requirements. By virtue of being a time of change and reformulation, adolescence is a potentially optimal time for intervention.

It is also a time of considerable energy and remarkable cognitive development. This may not necessarily lead to clarity of understanding or vision, but it nevertheless augments the adolescent's inherent curiosity and fascination in himself and others. Most adolescents spend hours in private preoccupation – about their bodies, families, friendships, achievements and fantasies. All of this is new and intense, frequently bewildering and potentially overwhelming. Most cope well enough by themselves with their friends. Others, however warily and uncertainly, need and seek adult help.

Thus, despite forebodings and undoubted difficulties, there is much in the maturing adolescent – in terms of capacity and motivation – that can be brought into the service of making good use of psychotherapy.

ADOLESCENT DEVELOPMENT AND DISTURBANCE

Adolescent development

Adolescence is fundamentally concerned with the negotiation of two specific developmental tasks. The first has to do with adjusting to the impact of puberty and the changing body (Laufer M 1968). This is primary, and involves the adolescent's preoccupation with questions of control, adequacy, mutuality in relationships and sexual orientation. The second concerns the problem of separation and individuation (Blos 1967) – the adolescent struggling to differentiate himself from those upon whom he has implicitly depended as a child, and to establish a degree of autonomy and self-resource, sufficient to accept the dependance of others as an adult. The two tasks are interrelated, each essentially referring to the growing capacity and readiness of the individual to take responsibility for his body and self.

There is undoubted excitement in this development. And yet always there is the prospect of failure, the fear of the unknown, the peril of disintegration and loss of control. Throughout, there is an essential narcissistic concern with coherence, identity and value. Much depends on the extent to which the adolescent can keep hold of a realistic and positive sense of himself, and achieve a degree of self-assurance and integration of the disparate parts of his personality.

The fears of adolescence and the confusions that surround them cannot be minimised. There is, above all, a brooding sense of increasing unbridled power and of limitless destructive possibility. There is also increasing disquiet in the shifting relationships within the family. Childhood assumptions of care and protection no longer stand so firm. The adolescent perceives his parents in new and more critical ways and becomes more acutely aware that he is on his own. The internal and external demand for self-reliance, though exhilarating, is daunting. Friends and groups clearly play a crucial part – but again there is here no certain comfort or panacea. Issues of identity, of sexuality and intimacy and of belonging become highlighted in this group context. The adolescent may well be part of the group, but frequently he feels very different, oddly exceptional and uncomfortably isolated. The adolescent thus lives in an internal world of considerable apprehension, with major questions about whether he will ever 'make it' in the broadest sense of the term. There can be no immediate solutions, and the adolescent is left in limbo, as it were, awaiting adulthood for the answers. Adolescence is, in more ways than one, the 'meantime'.

It can be of little surprise that, in response to so much anxiety and uncertainty, there should be a significant force within the adolescent to retreat in behaviour and fantasy to the actual or illusory comforts of childhood. There are few adolescents who do not yearn at times to be Peter Pan. Indeed it is this regressive pull back, counterpointing so dramatically with its opposite, that accounts for much of the exasperating inconsistency and variable maturity of so many adolescents.

The capacity and freedom to regress is clearly an essential part of growth – to replenish and draw on past experience in order to move forward. At the same time, regression can also draw the adolescent towards the sheer rawness of childhood experience, and effectively undermine his striving for control and coherence. However benign or favourable childhood once was, the revival of intense infantile feelings – of greed, rage, possessiveness, fears of annihilation, of loss of love and approval – can be very disturbing. This regressive force, though necessary in the process of integration, also threatens the capacity to integrate. The more vulnerable adolescent is caught in a quite desperate tangle – both wanting to escape from the demands of growing up, and yet terrified, excited and confused by the return of childhood experience.

Clearly, these internal developmental issues take place in the context of the 'adolescent family' (Berkowitz 1979; Shapiro 1978). Current and past parental attitudes and family dynamics are crucial to the facilitation of the adolescent's development. Adolescents carry within them, from child-hood, parental values and expectations and, in addition, face ongoing parental responses to their growing autonomy. The ease with which the adolescent can achieve separation and individuation depends on the parents' ability to relinquish their implicit parental control and revise their assumptions and requirements of their child as a growing adult. As the adolescent increasingly differentiates himself, so the parents have to face difficult feelings of loss, disappointment and envy. They also have to confront their own sexuality and marriage, as their children develop adult bodies and enter into sexual relationships.

The 'adolescent family' is notoriously in a state of turbulence, and it is not surprising that, in many families, tolerance of the adolescent's curious and variable state, with its inevitable secrecy, rebellion and ingratitude is severely strained. In the more vulnerable family, the adolescent may well find his moves towards independence restricted and opposed; or construed as proof of his badness with convenient grounds for scape-goating. Optimally, an adolescent needs relative stability around him in order to find his own bearings; families and parents who are immersed in their own disturbance do little to foster healthy adolescent development.

Adolescent disturbance

Given that there is inevitable anxiety and inherent vulnerability in the state of adolescence itself, the question is often raised as to what can be considered 'normal', and what 'disturbed' development. Most adoles-cents, after all, are likely to act at various times in impulsive, shocking, even dangerous ways. There can be no conventional pathway to adult-hood. In appreciation of this, Anna Freud wrote:

'In general, the adolescent upset and its manifestations are not predictable... Adolescence by definition is an interruption of peaceful growth. The adolescent manifestations come close to symptom formation of the neurotic, the psychotic or dissocial order and verge almost imperceptibly into borderline states and initial, frustrated or fully fledged forms of almost all mental illness.' (Freud A 1958).

There is an undoubted difficulty in gauging what is within the range of normality and what falls within the category of established disturbance. At what point, for example, does adolescent risk-taking and recklessness (for example, staying out late, in dubious company, where delinquent activity and drug taking are prevalent) become a significant manifestation of pathological self-destructiveness?

There are no precise guidelines. Perhaps the most distinguishing mark of adolescent disturbance, however, is the element of *compulsivity* – that is, where adolescents are engaged persistently and repeatedly, as if driven from within, in extreme forms of self-destructive behaviour, invariably against their better judgement. These are adolescents who have fundamentally failed adequately to negotiate the developmental tasks. They are unable to draw stimulus from the tensions of their life, and cannot find ways of mastering anxiety in the service of creativity. Their development is essentially restricted by internal preoccupations and conflict, and by lack of family support and encouragement. They are overwhelmed by demands made upon them, both internally and externally. They are especially frightened of being alone, and have limited capacity to tolerate depression. Equally, in relationships, they are frightened of losing their precarious sense of identity or of being dominated, humiliated or rendered useless. They find relationships confusing and have difficulty in tolerating their disappointments and the frustration of their need for closeness. The power of their emotions, of their aggressive and sexual feelings and desires is particularly terrifying to them.

These young people have invariably experienced various extreme forms of trauma and deprivation in their childhood. They have not grown up in an atmosphere of order and cohesion, and have frequently been over-looked or abused. It is not surprising that they lack any sure internal sense of structure or of organisation. By virtue of their past environmental circumstances, they have not been equipped with the means of controlling impulse, testing reality or developing any sense of value in themselves or in others. They are especially vulnerable to the anxiety engendered in adolescence by the revival of past disturbing childhood experiences.

The disturbance in these adolescents can be understood in terms of *unmanageable anxiety, poor ego capacity* and *inadequate defensive responses*. Much of their behaviour and symptomatology can be seen as a kind of panic reaction, a blind defensive flinch to avoid feeling left, forgotten or attacked. Their delinquency is often an attempt to avoid the experience of loss or emptiness by grabbing supplies felt to have been withheld. It can also represent an attempt to avert fears of submission or helplessness by exerting false dominance over others. Their self-harming is frequently a desperate measure to avoid mental anguish, by substituting physical pain. Their promiscuity is not uncommonly a way of pre-empting abandonment through seductive control and active leaving.

Other adolescents, with less severe but nevertheless disturbing experiences in their background, may respond to the complexities of relationships and emerging independence by retreating into social isolation (often retaining firm but ambivalent links to their parents), in an insulated dream world or in obsessive bodily preoccupation. The anorexic girl is clearly in hiding from the sensations and implications of her growing sexual body. The under-achieving, drug-abusing boy, is often in retreat from the power of his destructive and sexual fantasies and the feared consequences of his triumphs or successes. In many of these cases, the picture is not so much of limited ego capacity to control impulse, as of *excessive conscience* and *omnipotent ideals*. These necessarily derive from severe standards, prohibitions and pressures to achieve, internalised in childhood. They continue to exert impossible demands in adolescence, leaving the young person unable to tolerate imperfection of any sort and thus unable to play, make mistakes or enjoy ordinary relationships.

PSYCHOANALYTIC PSYCHOTHERAPY WITH ADOLESCENTS

Whether or not psychoanalysis is to be recommended for adolescents is a debateable issue. Certainly, there is much in the nature and complexity of adolescent disturbance that requires firm containment and detailed attention and understanding. There are many psychoanalysts who believe that only through the re-experiencing of earlier trauma in the transference, can there be any true possibility of enabling the adolescent to achieve a satisfactory degree of integration. The Laufers (1989), for example, forcefully argue for the necessity of psychoanalysis as a treatment of choice for certain severely disturbed adolescents who have undergone an adolescent breakdown: 'Not to undertake psychoanalytic treatment of such vulnerable adolescents is a chance lost and... would leave them open to more severe and crippling pathology in early adulthood.'

Such intensive psychoanalytic treatment, however, should not be undertaken without very careful consideration of the capacities of adolescents to make use of it and the abilities of psychoanalysts to conduct it. For such treatment to be effective, it requires above all the commitment and experience of trained psychoanalysts. These, of course, are in short supply and, in the ordinary course of events in ordinary psychiatric settings, psychoanalysis is not practicable and should not be attempted. There is also the question of whether or not psychoanalysis is in any case, suitable. Many adolescents are unready to make such a major commitment, and are frightened by the intensity of the psychoanalytic relationship. The psychoanalytic re-awakening of the past fits, as it were, too closely to the adolescent's internal processes of recapitulation of the past. The adolescent is wary of his precarious controls and bids for independence being undermined. The very containment and continuity that psychoanalysis fundamentally provides may in fact be counter-productive – its embrace only serving to consolidate and prolong dependency, in substitution for the parental relationship, at a time when progressive processes of detachment need to be under way.

There is undoubtedly considerable tension inherent in the relationship between the psychoanalytic pursuit and the spirit of adolescence and its disturbance. The challenge of psychotherapy with adolescents is to find ways, at any given time, of resolving this tension (Wilson 1986).

Of critical issue in the psychoanalytic psychotherapy of adolescents is the interest and preparedness of the psychotherapist to adapt technique and expectations to the particular developmental state of affairs that characterises this period of life. At a practical level, this invariably means offering a less intensive psychotherapeutic experience – usually once or twice weekly. It also involves a certain realism on the part of the psychotherapist with regard to the aims of psychotherapy. Young people seek help because they are unable to work, study or form or sustain satisfying relationships. Others are troubled because they are caught in some obsessive compulsive preoccupation or activity. They are fundamentally seeking symptomatic relief, and it is important in the psychotherapy of adolescents to hold this as a legitimate aim – not simply to relieve immediate difficulties and distress, but more substantially to enable young people to get back onto the path of normal development, so that, for example, they can actually begin to enjoy study or find that they can hold a job down or that they have found the courage to join a group. At a more urgent level, the aim of therapy may be to help and support a young person through a crisis, and prevent or forestall extreme behaviour that could disrupt family life or endanger their own lives.

In approaching the adolescent, the psychotherapist has to be prepared to encounter certain resistances that are specific to adolescence and derive essentially from the adolescent's immaturity and conflict in relation to his dependency. Clearly there are differences according to the age and developmental level of individual adolescents (Esman 1985). Older adolescents, by virtue of their greater independence and more developed capacity for self-observation, tend to show a greater readiness to make use of psychotherapy than do young adolescents. The characteristics that apply in early adolescence, however, pervade most of the adolescent period in varying degrees. What is at issue is a developmental, rather than an individual or pathological, problem. This concerns both the adolescent's attitude to, and capacity to make use of, psychotherapy.

Anna Freud (1958) has succinctly clarified the nature of the adolescent's resistance to psychotherapy, in terms of characteristic defences against dependency on his parents. In his struggle to detach and separate from his parents, the adolescent turns his investment and energy towards activities and people outside the home. He withdraws within himself, away from his parents; additionally, he reverses affect, turning loving childhood passive feelings into their opposites – the essence of rebellion. In psychotherapy, the psychotherapist is experienced in one way or another as a parent, and the same defences are redeployed. The adolescent, in order to avoid being dominated by the therapist/parent (James 1964) averts his gaze and keeps on guard against the psychotherapist's concern and potential control.

The adolescent, in short, is mistrustful of adults – he is suspicious that they will take over or control or misunderstand. He has a need to keep himself to himself. Privacy is essential, and the keeping of secrets often vital. Telling the truth is not always possible. The adolescent needs his own time to experience and find out things – and he has to do things which adults and parents would ordain not good for him.

It is crucial that the psychotherapist appreciates this state of affairs – and does not punish or fight against it. It is essential, too, that the psychotherapist gives the adolescent time and space to encounter and secure his own impressions and experience before being expected to give account of them publicly. Many of these experiences and feelings are baffling to the adolescent, difficult to articulate and in many respects embarrassing and frightening. Some concern sexual and bodily preoccupations, and are couched in shame, guilt and uncertainty. Some involve ideas and fantasies that are unexpectedly intense, frightening and best not mentioned. Others concern observations and impressions of family and parental life which the adolescent may feel unable, out of loyalty, to disclose outside the family.

The psychotherapist thus needs to be sensitive to and respectful of the adolescent's caution in approaching psychotherapy. He needs, too, to be tolerant of the adolescent's difficulty in making use of help. The adolescent's capacity for, for example, self-observation is relatively limited, still in the process of formation. Young adolescents in particular have difficulty in containing anxiety, and are more prone to relieve tension through action rather than thought. Their excitement is in the doing of things in the here and now, rather than in reflection. Moreover, their typical defences tend to be more rigid and concrete than in the older adolescent. They are inclined to dissociate themselves from their mental distress, and project and put responsibility elsewhere. And, of course, often they simply do not have the words to formulate or express what is on their minds.

Therapeutic setting

The primary task of a psychotherapist is to ensure conditions of work that facilitate communication, and enable both psychotherapist and patient to observe and think about what is happening within and between them.

The concept of a therapeutic setting refers to everything that forms the background in which psychotherapy takes place. At a basic level, it refers to the actual *place* and physical surroundings. In terms of procedure, it is built on an agreed set of *ground rules*. Particularly with children and adolescents, it exists in the context of the *family*. Ultimately, it is determined by the *presence* of the psychotherapist – his orientation and personal style and, in relation to the adolescent, his specific counter-transference and general attitude.

Place

The importance of providing a place which is pleasant and comfortable, and which ensures privacy and safety cannot be emphasised enough. Such a provision serves as a fundamental communication – far better than any words can convey – to the adolescent that he is worthwhile and respected. This is frequently overlooked, especially in services for adolescents, who are mistakenly seen as bejeaned and dishevelled and not warranting such attention to detail. It is important, too, that the waiting room is welcoming and not bare, and that receptionists are friendly, without being intrusive. Care should also be given to the size and arrangement of the therapy rooms. They should not be too large or imposing, nor too small and enclosing; and where possible, they should not be cluttered with desk top paraphernalia or diverting pictures (such as of the psychotherapist's family). Where psychotherapy takes place in institutions or in hospital wards, care should be taken to locate psychotherapy rooms separate from the everyday hurly-burly, and sufficiently distant not to excite curiosity or envy from other patients.

Ground rules

The ground rules laid down by the psychotherapist in the beginning sessions set the tone and define the boundaries of the therapeutic setting. Adolescents, at first, are often not at all sure what they are doing with a psychotherapist, and even less clear what is expected of them. Hill puts this quite directly: 'It is only too easy to assume that the adolescent understands the ground rules ... that he is supposed to volunteer suitable information, refrain from prying into the psychotherapist's private life and recognise this sort of confidential conversation as treatment' (Hill 1989).

It is important, therefore, that the psychotherapist is as straightforward as possible about what he understands of the adolescent's problem, and how he thinks psychotherapy can be of help. This, of course, is not always possible to convey nor easy for the adolescent to hear in the inevitable tension and confusion of early meetings. Nevertheless, the psychotherapist should endeavour to make a statement, at some point during the course of the first session or so, that registers something of his position and understanding.

Case study 19.1   Jim, a 17-year-old: the chance to talk

The following statement includes some of the major points that need to be covered. This was made towards the end of the first session with a 17-year-old boy who had been urged by his mother to see someone in an outpatient setting. For illustration purposes, this statement is written as if given without interruption. This, of course, was not the case in actuality.

'What I understand so far is that you have been feeling miserable for some time. You are bored at school and, although you say that exams don't matter, you think you are a failure and you're feeling hopeless about the future. You tell me you feel bad about your mother – because you have let her down. In fact, you are here because of her. She wanted you to get some help and she fixed it here with me. I wonder what you think about that? Not much, maybe. I think you think it is all a bit pointless and you cannot see what on earth I can do for you.

Well, right now, nor do I. I hardly know you. My guess is that you are feeling that you are not worth much and that you are frightened of what is going to happen to you. I also think you're very dissatisfied and angry about something. If I am to be of any help, I am going to need some more time to get to know you. And you are going to have to decide whether you think it's worth coming here.

I would like to help you – but you have to know now that I have no magic. I have no tricks or quick cures. The best I can do is to offer you the chance to talk over what's on your mind; about what is happening and has happened in your life. It would be good too, to find out what you want to do. At the moment it's all a bit of a mystery. We may be able to make some sense of it – and you may begin to feel you can do things differently or do some things that you want to do that you think you cannot do. A lot is up to you – whether you really want to change anything. You cannot possible know right now how talking can help – you will just have to give it a try.

I should also say that what we talk about here is private and confidential. There is no reason why you should believe that – it's a matter of trust. All I can say is that I shall not talk or communicate with anybody about you without your consent. Similarly, if I hear about you from other people, I shall do my best to let you know what I know. This is the only way we can work.

Having said that, I have to tell you that your mother did in fact telephone me before the session. She wanted me to know that you are taking a lot of drugs. She also said you are not getting up until the middle of the afternoon. You are missing a lot of school and you treat her like a doormat. She said she cannot make you out any more and you are throwing your life away. It sounded as if you are driving her crazy.

You haven't said much about all that so far today. I suppose you'd prefer not to think about it. The only reason I've raised it is because it was what

your mother told me – you need to know what I know. She has quite a lot to
say, doesn't she? It sounds as if she could do with some help – but my job is
not to be her right hand man. I am here for you. But let me say just one
thing about what I think, before we go any further. It may be that your
mother has got it all wrong about the drugs – but if there is any truth to
what she says, then I have just four words 'Drugs are Bad News'. I cannot
stop you taking them. I won't be your nanny but I can tell you straight to cut
them out. They are not going to help you or me to help you.

I suggest that we meet for another six sessions until Easter – each week
for an hour each time. We can see at the end of that time where we have
got to. It may be that you will think enough has been done by that time. Or
it may be that you will want to carry on and find out more about yourself
–in which case we can arrange that.

So, see you next week.'

A statement such as this contains a number of important messages. It puts into words what the psychotherapist understands of the adolescent's problem and of the anxiety that lies behind it. It clarifies the reason for meeting, the concern of the mother and the role of the psychotherapist. It emphasises the importance of talking and of trust, and pays respect to the adolescent's independence. The statement also indicates a readiness to help but not a promise of cure; it conveys a sense of authority and expectation but not of excessive omnipotence. Finally, it conveys with some force the psychotherapist's concern (hence the unequivocal statement on drugs) – but also leaves open whether or not the adolescent chooses to commit himself to change and to psychotherapy.

One aspect that is not included in this statement concerns the behaviour of the adolescent in therapy sessions. Clearly, standards of acceptable behaviour will vary from one psychotherapist to another and in different settings. An adolescent unit or a therapeutic community may be prepared to allow more aggressive behaviour than can an individual psychotherapist in an outpatient setting. In individual psychotherapy, it is essential that the psychotherapist is clear within himself what he can and cannot tolerate. In one way or another, it is important to convey to the adolescent that there are limits to what is permissable – for example, that the patient is not to damage property or to attack the psychotherapist. Laying down these ground rules is often difficult in initial meetings without arousing unnecessary alarm or seeming overly combative. With the majority of adolescents, this is not necessary. However, there are some adolescents whom the psychotherapist may believe to have poor impulse control or be unclear about boundaries, in which case it is important that he be explicit from the outset.

Finally, it is important that the psychotherapist expects the adolescent to attend sessions punctually and regularly. The psychotherapist, paradoxically, may well anticipate that the adolescent will forget or miss sessions or be late – but he should never expect it. He should let the adolescent know that he cares about this boundary of time as much as any other, and be as clear and unequivocal about the time of ending sessions as of beginning them.

The family

Psychotherapy with adolescents always takes place in the context of the adolescent's relationship to his parents or caretakers. It is important that consideration is given to how and where the parents are placed in relationship to the adolescent's psychotherapy. With older adolescents, this is generally not a major issue since, by and large, they seek and receive psychotherapy in their own right. With younger patients, however, who are more dependent on their parents, the position is quite different. In most cases, parental consent to and sanction of psychotherapy for their children is necessary. Without this, there is little hope of success – the parents effectively sabotaging the adolescent's attendance and the adolescent feeling unable to make a commitment out of loyalty to his parents.

In principle, where there are parents who feel responsible or concerned, they should be seen by the psychotherapist at some point in the initial stages of psychotherapy. This may include parents of older adolescents if they have been influential in one way or another in persuading the adolescent to seek help. Some adolescents, of course, are suspicious of the psychotherapist's contact with their parents, and feel that their own space and privacy are being invaded. Older adolescents may not agree to any such contact, and this simply has to be respected. Others, however, particularly younger adolescents, often feel reassured that their parents and psychotherapist are in contact with each other – relieved that the psychotherapist has bothered to see their parents and that there is a sense of shared concern around them. Whereas there is some danger of the parents exerting pressure on the psychotherapist to exact compliance from the adolescent to meet their requirements, there is general overall advantage in having the opportunity to assess the adolescent in the context of his family and, indeed, to have actual sight of the parents and vice-versa.

In general, with young adolescents, it is most useful in the first instance to see them together with their parents or families, and then, if need be, to move onto individual psychotherapy. The parents may subsequently be seen periodically for review or in the event of crisis. If they have significant problems in their own right, they should be referred for help elsewhere. With older adolescents, it is more advisable to insist on offering the adolescent individual interviews in the first instance, to be followed, if necessary, with interviews with the parents – either together with or separately from the adolescent, according to the adolescent's preference.

The older adolescent is more concerned to establish his own separateness and individuality, and it is generally inadvisable for the psychotherapist to have on-going contact with the parents. Clearly, again, if the parents are very concerned about developments, or in the event of a crisis, it should be agreed that they have some right of access to the psychotherapist.

Confidentiality is inevitably a major issue in these various arrangements with parents and family. Clearly, the basic principle of confidentiality should be upheld, and parents encouraged to respect their adolescent's privacy in psychotherapy. Where confidentiality is likely to be threatened – for example, arising out of parental discussions, telephone calls – the psychotherapist can do no more than try to be as open as possible with the adolescent about what has been said. It is often helpful, where the psychotherapist has arranged to meet the parents during the course of the therapy, to ask the adolescent what he would like and not like to have discussed. The adolescent ultimately has to trust that the psychotherapist will honour the agreement that has been made.

There may arise situations in which the psychotherapist judges it necessary to inform parents and others who are responsible for the adolescent of intentions, for example, to commit suicide. The therapist may have to act in this way without the adolescent's consent – but always with his or her knowledge (Wilson 1986).

The psychotherapist

Ultimately, the general tone and atmosphere of the therapeutic setting will be determined by the personality and style of the psychotherapist – for it is he who provides the place, lays out the ground rules and makes the arrangements with the parents. The question of who the psychotherapist is and what he brings to the situation is crucial.

In general, it is to be hoped that the psychotherapist is someone who carries within him a level of personal authority and integrity that enables him to deal with anxiety and confusion without losing control or the ability to listen. Similarly, it is to be hoped that the psychotherapist brings to the therapeutic situation a high degree of self-awareness and a reasonably coherent conceptual framework that can serve to regulate and structure his feelings, perceptions and thoughts – in the interest of offering some clarity to the patient.

These general characteristics are essential to all psychotherapists, but perhaps more so in relationship to adolescents who, above all else, need to have a sense of being contained within clear boundaries and who are quick to sense weakness, prevarication and dishonesty in others.

A very basic requirement of any psychotherapist is the capacity and readiness to be receptive. In practical terms, this simply means that the psychotherapist ensures that he has time and space to see and hear his patients – that he can ensure regular times of meeting and that he can be present in the session without undue preoccupation elsewhere or intrusions of telephones or bleeps. In emotional terms, it means a relative freedom from intrusive irrational feelings and prejudices. In relation to the adolescent, it is important that the psychotherapist is alert to the influence of his counter-transference, as well as positive in his attitude towards young people in general.

Counter-transference. Counter-transference refers to the wide range of irrational feelings and thoughts, expectations and attitudes that are evoked, largely unconsciously, in the psychotherapist in response to the presence of the patient (Money-Kyrle 1956, Moehler 1977). Continuous situations arise in psychotherapy in which the psychotherapist feels at different times helpless, stupid, powerful, persecuted, humiliated, rejected, desired, seduced, punitive and so on. These feelings may well mirror the way in which the patient has felt as a child and/or how he has experienced his parents.

The psychotherapist is thus forced back into areas of his own personal vulnerability. The danger arises of the psychotherapist, by force of the patient's transference, being drawn into ways of reacting that are excessive and unhelpful to the therapeutic needs of the patient. Thus, the past can all too easily repeat itself in the therapeutic situation, to no avail and without understanding. The therapist finds himself reacting, in effect, in the same way as the parents – and the possibility of reflection and of change is lost. All that happens, in accordance with the dictates of transference, is further repetition.

Counter-transference can present more of a major problem in the psychotherapy of adolescents than in that of children or adults. Adolescents' emotions are often very powerful and poorly defended against. Moreover, they bring into the therapeutic situation experiences and attitudes revived and re-enacted both from the past and from current family relationships. If the therapist is to be open to the disturbance within the adolescent, it is inevitable that he will feel the pressure of many of these confusing feelings. What is crucial is that this is monitored and not blindly acted upon. In so many subtle and indirect ways, counter-transference reactions can disturb the sense of stability and of continuity that is the foundation of the therapeutic setting, and is so important to the adolescent patient. Interpretations can easily be made, for example, not so much to improve understanding as to control or excite or punish the adolescent patient.

It is essential that adequate supervision and/or consultation is provided as part of the overall therapeutic setting – to help the psychotherapist clarify, amongst other things, what feelings belong to the adolescent and what belong to him as an individual.

Attitude to adolescents. Beyond the specific feelings of the psychotherapist's counter-transference to an individual adolescent, there reside in all psychotherapists certain fundamental attitudes towards the state of adolescence itself. These relate to the psychotherapist's own experiences of adolescence and to his current predicament as an adult. Psychotherapists have all, of course, been through their own adolescence. Some have been rebellious, others compliant. Some have experienced breakdown, others have enjoyed success. Some remember their adolescence with anguish and hostility towards their parents and authority, whilst others look back with affection and a sense of fun and achievement. As a result, some psychotherapists are excited by the lives of their adolescent patients, and tend to be permissive in their judgements. Others look upon their adolescent patients with alarm and envy, and are inclined to control or even rebuke them in their quest for independence. These feelings are additionally compounded by others related to the psychotherapist's current life as an adult; for example, they may be burdened with family responsibilities, and so resent the adolescent's greater freedom and irresponsibility.

These diverse elements shape the psychotherapist's attitude towards young people in general, and influence his approach to the uniquely transitional and tentative state of the adolescent patient. If left unacknowledged and uncontained, they can easily impede the psychotherapist's capacity to tolerate the adolescent's unpredictability with patience, sympathy and forbearing. Above all, the psychotherapist has to be sensitive enough to appreciate the adolescent's equivocal relationship to dependency, and to hold the balance between respecting the adult and caring for the child in the adolescent. The psychotherapist has, on the one hand, to trust the adolescent's pursuit of independence, allowing space for the adolescent to find his own way and make his own mistakes; on the other hand, the psychotherapist has to be alert to adolescent self-destructive and impulsive tendencies, and be ready to intervene, keep on asking questions, and to set boundaries when needed.

The psychotherapist's task is difficult and fundamentally relies upon his enjoyment and respect of the adolescent state. Without this, he will be unable to be sufficiently flexible or adaptive to make sense of the inherent contradictions in his adolescent patient.

The working alliance

The most difficult task of all in the psychotherapy of adolescents is to establish a working alliance. Much of the art and skill of the psychotherapist resides in the process of forging, often against the odds, a relationship in which the adolescent becomes interested both in understanding his difficulties and in the possibility of change, and in which a spirit of cooperation and enquiry prevails. Many adolescents, despite a potential to be helped, are lost through a failure on the part of the psychotherapist to establish such an alliance – whether it be because of the psychotherapist's inept introductions, inappropriate expectations or sheer inability to understand and respect the adolescent's inherent equivocation. The adolescent usually enters into therapy in a confused and ambivalent state. He is mistrustful, frightened and frequently in resistance to those who have suggested he come to therapy in the first place. There is much that he wants to keep to himself. He knows that he is troubled and that there is something wrong, but he prefers to disown his problem and put blame elsewhere. At the same time, he is curious about himself and about the possibility of help. There is often an overwhelming wish to be understood and to find someone who can magically offer salvation or certitude. There is in most adolescents a readiness for new experience and possibility.

The overriding initial therapeutic task is for the psychotherapist to appreciate this ambivalence, and to find ways of exciting the young person's curiosity about himself and of engaging with that part of the adolescent that is worried about his normality or adequacy. The extent to which this can be achieved depends as much on the attitude of the psychotherapist as on any particular technique or procedure. There is usually a certain element of urgency in the beginning sessions of psychotherapy with an adolescent, for the adolescent is half ready to leave unless reassured by the psychotherapist's manner and level of understanding. The adolescent needs to feel that the psychotherapist is taking him seriously and can grasp the gist of what is worrying him, without knowing too much about him or trying to take him over.

The psychotherapist has to adopt an essentially paradoxical position – conveying, as it were, both interest and disinterest. On the one hand, the psychotherapist needs to be active and positive in expressing concern about the adolescent – inviting dialogue and conversation, and generally trying to capture the adolescent's imagination. On the other hand, he has to be careful not to be too forceful – he must hold back, keep things open and not press the adolescent for commitment. Miller (1983) has argued that, with certain adolescents, it is sometimes necessary to take on a certain larger-than-life, omnipotent manner – answering their request for somebody to take command and prevent them from engaging in further self-destructive behaviour, such as suicide or different forms of delinquency, that could preclude any further help. It is clear, however, that the adolescent also needs to be reminded that the psychotherapist is not omnipotent and cannot bring about magical change, for such an approach inevitably brings its own disenchantments and arouses intolerable anxieties of domination. The opposite position is well described by Anthony (1975) who suggests a 'preparatory course of inaction' in the early phases of treatment, in which the psychotherapist exercises a 'negative capability' to allow for the adolescent's ambiguities before any therapeutic commitment is decided.

The psychotherapist has to live with the paradox that the adolescent wants and does not want to be treated as a child; that he wants and does not want to have his problems taken care of. The psychotherapist in turn finds himself having to be both active and omnipotent, and laid back and laissez faire. The unifying factor has to reside in the psychotherapist's tolerance of the essentially contradictory nature of adolescent. The psychotherapist *holds* the opposites, and thereby prevents psychotherapy ending prematurely, either because the adolescent is unimpressed or bored, or because he is overwhelmed and frightened.

In the example which follows, an account is given of the fifth session with the 17-year-old adolescent introduced earlier. In this session, the adolescent and therapist were still occupied in forming some kind of working alliance. It was all very much at a delicate and uncertain stage. He was clearly drawn by the prospect of the therapist's interest and attention, and yet he was frightened and resistant. Much of how he behaved in the session was typical of adolescent resistance, but clearly it also reflected significant transference currents to do with his fear of humilitation and rejection. The account gives some indication of the therapist's attempt to play both lightly and seriously with the adolescent's assertion of independence, whilst at the same time engaging with the part of him that was lost and very troubled by the intensity and confusion of his feelings. The therapist was all the time trying – both explicitly and through his attitude and behaviour – to convey what psychotherapy was and could be about.

Case study 19.1 (contd)   'I don't talk about problems to anyone'

In this session, the main question was whether or not Jim could be bothered with psychotherapy. After all, he maintained, there was little wrong with him. There was nothing unusual in being miserable – everyone was. As for school, well, exams were irrelevant. There was no point in learning all that stuff – the teachers could not teach and what they did was boring. He could learn better by himself. He had better things to do.

The therapist said he was glad about that. What were they? At first, Jim said he had not come here to talk about 'pleasure'. The therapist said they could talk about anything that mattered to him. He then talked at length about his fascination with radio, hi-fi and TV. He spent hours working on them. He reckoned that within a year or so, he would have built a completely new and unique system. He would then market this and become rich.

The therapist listened, showed interest and asked questions. For a while Jim was animated. He enjoyed impressing me. The therapist said he had an image of a kind of super DJ – Jim at the top, super controls and flashing lights, turning the world in and on. He was amazed. How did I know? That was exactly it. He already did a few gigs. It was great. He felt like a king, they would get better and better.

Suddenly, he said that the therapist was taking the piss. 'You probably like Mozart and opera and all that junk. You're a phoney – just egging me on. You don't care at all – you just say all this because you're paid'. The therapist said, 'Pow – what's all that about? One minute we're talking about what interests you, the next minute you are more or less kicking me out'. For a while he went on about how all 'you psychiatrists' are all alike – clever, devious, just in it for themselves. And anyway, talking was a waste of time. 'I don't talk about problems to anybody – I'm not giving my secrets away. I have all the understanding I need, thank you very much.'

The therapist said that right now he felt at the end of a very strong radio transmission that was saying loud and clear 'Keep Off', to put it mildly. If that is what he really meant, then of course he would. He was not there to frog march him into anything. If what he was telling him was that he really believed that he had no particular problem, that he was fully occupied and that he understood enough of what he needed to know then clearly there was no point in being there at all. Jim said the only reason he was there was to keep his mother quiet. The therapist asked whether she was quiet, and he said he did not know, he did not care. 'If you don't care, why are you bothering to keep her quiet?' He laughed and said: 'Because I can't stop her nagging – she's always putting her big nose in my business. She's always barging into my room. Why doesn't she keep out? She doesn't care anyway. Whatever I do she puts it down. And anyway, she's out half the time with her bloke. I hate her – she's a whore'.

He was suddenly close to tears and for a moment looked furious at the therapist. They sat in silence. The therapist said he knew there was a bit of Jim that would rather not be there. But at the same time, he knew things were not right and he was telling him. He was not upset for nothing – clearly there was a lot that was difficult in his relationship with his mother and no doubt he had a lot of feeling about her bloke – not to mention his father. The gist of it all, the therapist said, seems to be that Jim felt badly let down – by his parents, by adults, by psychiatrists. Nobody can be depended on. No wonder, he said, he was giving him the business earlier on – no way would he trust him yet.

Jim listened but appeared not to be immediately receptive. He reasserted that he knew the therapist didn't care. 'Nobody does'. There was no point in talking about it; 'There is nothing to talk about'. He insisted that he was quite able to take care of himself. The therapist said that no doubt he was right – at 17 he was going to have to take more care of himself. Maybe he didn't like that – it could leave him feeling very alone. He immediately assured the therapist that he liked his own company best, he didn't need anyone else – anyway he had his radios and hi-fi. He was quick then to warn the therapist off 'analysing' anything about his radio. The therapist said once again that Jim was on the alert – wary that the therapist would put him down or dismiss what was important to him.

The therapist made it quite clear that, however Jim saw him, he was not there to diminish him. Nor was he there to deceive him, or to extract his secrets. He was there to help him sort out something that was clearly troubling his mind, and that was getting in the way of what he wanted to do. The therapist added, rather forcibly, that he was not too convinced that Jim could take care of himself yet, and told him that he had not forgotten about the drugs, even though he had not mentioned it. the therapist also disagreed that Jim 'had nothing to talk about'.

As the session ended, Jim grumbled about how difficult it was to travel there. The therapist simply said, 'I hope to see you next week'. He said, 'Do you want to see me?'. The therapist said, 'Yes'. His response was 'Perfectly understandable – it's your job'. The therapist said something like 'It ain't going to be easy to convince you otherwise. How about you – do you want to see me?' He smiled and reminded the therapist about 'my mother's nose'. The therapist said 'Let's talk about it'. He said 'OK – have a good weekend'.

Therapeutic process

Once a working alliance is more or less established – it can never be taken for granted – psychotherapy can take on a life of its own. A therapeutic process is set in motion in which all the various elements of a therapeutic interaction become active in one way or another. In psychotherapy with adults, the predominant activity revolves around the patient verbally bringing experiences and memories to the therapist for thought and understanding. This generally proceeds in an orderly fashion, in which the psychotherapist can retain a degree of distance and objectivity and focus his interest primarily on interpreting the unconscious meaning of what is being said in relation to the transference.

With some adolescents, particularly late adolescents, this model of practice is also possible; and if it is not, it remains a reference point to which to aspire or return. With many adolescents, however, it is rare that psychotherapy can take place in such a straightforward or settled fashion. Most cannot be relied on to talk freely or honestly in a sustained spirit of introspection. Many have difficulty in expressing themselves in words. Their mood and sense of themselves is often extremely variable, they have difficulty just sitting, and they remain typically resistant, as adolescents, to the scrutiny and dependency implicit in psychotherapy.

Throughout treatment, as in establishing a working alliance, the psychotherapist has to maintain a flexible attitude (Steinberg 1987). Much more so than with the adult, the psychotherapist has to take responsibility for attracting and holding the adolescent in therapy, especially at times of resistance and disillusionment. He has to be more prepared to be adaptable. Winnicott's (1971) simple definition of psycho-therapy – 'Psychotherapy has to do with two people playing together' – rings especially true in work with adolescents. The psychotherapist has to be ready to be playful in response to the changeable nature of the adolescent – and to do so seriously and with humour.

Evans (1982) has addressed the significance of play in adolescent life and in psychotherapy. He sees many aspects of adolescent behaviour as a form of play, in which the adolescent enacts various roles that actively express different aspects of himself and of his relationship to others. This role-playing is only partly under the adolescent's conscious control, and is essentially a transitional phenomenon as the adolescent 'works out a new identity'. In psychotherapy sessions, for example, the adolescent may present himself at times as a defiant, insolent layabout who does not care about anything; or as a helpless, hopeless, ingenue who does not know what to do next; or as a sharp, smooth operator who knows all the answers; and so on. These are not simply superficial postures, but substantial modes of communication – dramatised no doubt in order to feel the more real and to see the more clearly. The psychotherapist must be ready to receive them as such and to react accordingly.

Similarly, Eissler (1958) has recognised how variably adolescents can present themselves and how, in effect, each presentation requires different responses from the psychotherapist. His view is that in adolescence psychopathology is in a state of flux, and the adolescent manifests many different clinical conditions and levels of ego capacity. Because of this:

'we encounter technical problems specific to puberty. In many instances, psychopathology switches from one form to another, sometimes in the course of weeks or months but also from one day to another and even within the same psychoanalytic hour. The symptoms manifested by such patients may be neurotic at one time and almost psychotic at another. Then sudden acts of delinquency may occur only to be followed by a phase of perverted sexually activity... the frequency of symptomatic changes manifested by many adolescent patients makes it evident that no one technique can fulfil the requirements for the treatment of adolescents.' (Eissler 1958)

It is clear that, faced with such a variable picture, the psychotherapist cannot sustain the classical analytic position of neutrality. In Eissler's (1958) terms the psychotherapist needs to be in a constant state of alertness and adaptation, seeking always the correct timing of a change in technique to meet the adolescents varying clinical manifestations. He gives a hypothetical illustration in which at times the psychotherapist is predominantly: interpretive in relation to the neurotic aspect of the adolescent; limit setting and authoritative in relationship to the delinquent; gratifying and reassuring in relation to the acute schizophrenic; and actively anxiety arousing and conflict generating in relation to the perverse.

Evans (1982) sees the role of the psychotherapist as 'a transitional object, a substitute authority who is only partially real and with whom the adolescent can "play" through the assumption of temporary roles in relationship to the therapist'. Implicit in his view is the psychotherapist's preparedness to participate in this play – both standing, as it were, for reality and boundary, and also reacting to the adolescent's role-play, by adopting corresponding roles. This is a complex process, which borders closely and dangerously on the psychotherapist becoming embroiled in and lost in the adolescent's transference re-enactments. Evans makes it clear that the therapist must 'simultaneously' be 'able to stand back and observe what is happening'.

Important in this emphasis on the psychotherapist's conduct and manner is the idea that the psychotherapist conveys meaning not only through his words, but through the way he behaves. Osorio (1977) has recognised how adolescents 'express themselves through a language of action', and suggests that the psychotherapist needs to respond in a corresponding way to the symbolic meaning of the adolescent's behaviour. He refers to the concept of 'behavioural interpretation' – the psychotherapist communicating to the adolescent through posture, gesture or manner. Such behaviour is based on and fashioned by the psychotherapist's understanding; it serves to highlight this understanding in action, in counter-response to that of the adolescent. For many adolescents, this can carry far greater weight than words alone. If, for example, an adolescent is dismissive of the psychotherapist, and provocative in his sessions, what he may be primarily expressing is his fear of humiliation and yet need for some boundary and care. If the psychotherapist is able to remain calm, be firm and show humour, he is in effect conveying an awareness of this adolescent's concern. The psychotherapist is not trying to make the adolescent feel 'better' through some form of corrective emotional experience; what he is doing is 'answering', through his way of being, the adolescent's call for understanding.

It would be misleading, however, to suggest that verbal communications are of no significance, for, clearly, within the context of the therapeutic relationship there is ample opportunity and much need for thoughts and ideas to be shared and understood. Much of the work with adolescents is spent in helping the adolescent find words for his feelings and ways of thinking that help him make sense of his relationship and difficulties. Often, the psychotherapist has to be quite active, asking questions if need be to keep things going, offering ideas and perspectives to stimulate and clarify thinking, and at times, where necessary, putting quite openly and honestly his views of the adolescent's behaviour (for example, with regard to drug or alcohol abuse, or attempted suicide). In many respects, this level of activity, which is often quite concrete and down-to-earth, has an educational function, appealing to the adolescent's developing cognitive capacities and growing interest in himself (McAdam 1986).

The focus of this kind of work is close to the adolescent's conscious awareness. It is more about clarifying reality than interpreting what the adolescent is unaware of. Interpretation, in the sense of elucidating unconscious processes particularly in relationship to the transference, refers to a different level of psychotherapeutic activity. This, clearly, is at the heart of all psychodynamic psychotherapy, and undoubtedly plays an important part in psychotherapy with adolescents. It must be remembered, however, that such interpretations are often experienced by adolescents as invasive and controlling. They are strenuously resisted and frequently misconstrued. The danger is that they can so easily be merely complied with or defied, rather than received and assimilated with interest. It is important for the psychotherapist not to be carried away with interpretative zeal nor, indeed, with the belief that verbal understanding alone is effective (Wilson & Hersov 1985). Interpretations need to be given clearly, in the language of the adolescent, and with good evidence. The adolescent must understand how the psychotherapist arrives at his perceptions and must always be allowed room for disagreement and manoeuvre. The effectiveness of interpretations depends as much on their timing as on their accuracy and the way the psychotherapist conveys them. Interpretations can so easily be used by the psychotherapist, out of his negative counter-transference, as tools of control and censure, rather than as levers for self-discovery, and may awaken the adolescent's dread of passive surrender (Balint 1959, Khan 1974, Stewart 1989).

For transference to be an effective therapeutic tool, it is essential that the patient has the capacity to sustain a split between what Greenson (1978) has called 'the experiencing, subjective, irrational ego' and the 'reasonable, observing, analysing ego'. This is fundamental; the patient has to be able to experience the psychotherapist both as a transference object and as an actual psychotherapist. Intense feelings, revived from the past, need to be allowed to emerge whilst contact with the reality of the therapeutic situation is securely held. Without this capacity, transference can be an overwhelming and confusing experience. Many disturbed adolescents do not possess this capacity, nor do they have adequate impulse control, capacity for reality testing or the ability to differentiate between self and object. Their hold over themselves is precarious, and they frequently fail to appreciate the metaphorical nature of transference. They see the psychotherapist as more or less real, and cannot make sense of transference interpretations. They frequently become frustrated and angry that the psychotherapist does not directly fulfil their needs and desires. For some adolescents, the therapeutic relationship and the transference that evolves can be an excrutiating tease.

Case study 19.1 (contd) Understood and withstood

The following account gives some impression of the process of once-weekly psychotherapy over a period of a year with the 17-year-old mentioned earlier. This continued to carry much of the tension present from the beginning, and there was similarly little sense of reliability or predictability. A working alliance was, however, achieved so that, despite his various attacks on the therapist and on understanding, Jim did hold on to an agreement to meet regularly and persist with the concerns that he initially brought.

During the initial six months of psychotherapy, he showed much of the defensiveness and arrogance that had characterised his earlier sessions. His moods were variable. At times he could be light-hearted and ready to share feelings with the therapist. At other times, without any apparent reason, he could be extremely morose, fraught and critical.

In his better moods, he enjoyed talking about his achievements and his cleverness in the world of radio and hi-fi. It was clear that he felt at ease, safe within this knowledge. His purpose in talking about it to the therapist – apart from diverting him from more troubling matters – was to capture his interest and admiration. He demanded the therapist's audience – who for the most part played along, implicitly acknowledging Jim's need for control and time in which to preserve distance from him. The therapist was particularly struck at such times by Jim's narcissistic vulnerability, his fear of humiliation and denigration. The therapist was concerned not to prematurely challenge this for fear of producing some form of forced compliance or, indeed, outright rejection of psychotherapy. His going along with the role assigned to him was not so much a collusive giving in to Jim's imperious demands, as a form of behavioural communication of acceptance and respect for his vulnerability. Occasionally, when feeling less threatened, Jim was able to extend his interest beyond his own self-preoccupation and show interest in the therapist as somebody separate from him and with whom he could learn rather than impress. At such times, they shared interest in the connection between Jim's technology and the therapist's music, and moved on to some reflection on various songs and their lyrics that bordered on his own feelings.

There were sessions, however, in which Jim seemed full of fury and malice. He was blatantly contemptuous and quick to contradict and denigrate anything the therapist might say. In all this, his overriding complaint was that the therapist didn't listen, that he was prejudiced and only interested in himself, and disdainful of anything Jim might think important. He was at times almost beside himself with rage, tearful with clenched fists. The therapist was filled with a kind of impotent fury. In so many ways, Jim seemed hell-bent on provoking a powerful explosion or the therapist's rejection of him.

What mattered above all else for the therapist in this situation was to hold on to some understanding for himself of what was happening, based on Jim's evident feelings and those engendered within the therapist himself. In brief, what made sense to him was that Jim was reliving some earlier painful fight, intensified in puberty, with his mother, whom he perceived as both overwhelmingly controlling and seductive. This transference situation needed to be managed, held within bounds and not further complicated with words. As far as possible, the therapist drew from his understanding some sense of Jim's fear of abandonment and explosive denigration, and managed to behave in a relatively calm, firm and unprovoked manner. Of course at times Jim caught the therapist's exasperation and anger, and almost seemed relieved that he had touched him in this way as well as remorseful that he had hurt him. But for the most part, the therapist tried to meet Jim's anxiety with a behaviour that reflected and conveyed appreciation of this anxiety. At a fundamental level, the therapist survived his attacks. Jim felt both understood and withstood.

During the first six months of psychotherapy, there was a great deal of variability both in Jim's moods and, indeed, in the therapist's responses.

As is so often the case in work with adolescents, a turning point was reached when he felt reassured, out of his testing, of the therapist's implicit understanding of him and capacity to hold some limit. The last six months settled, with periodic eruptions, to a level of psychotherapeutic work that was more orderly and reflective. He became more ready to acknowledge his sense of failure and futility in ever being able to 'get somewhere'. He could also see his loneliness as a reflection of his inability to 'get on with anybody' – he quickly felt sensitive to any possibility of being stood up or criticised. His acceptance of such vulnerability within himself contrasted with the way he had dominated in earlier sessions. He and the therapist were able to draw on some of their memories of how it had been between them and began to make some sense of what mattered to him in his family life. It became increasingly clear how very divided he was in his feelings towards his mother – both very attached, almost obsessively jealous of her boyfriends, and very angry both at her betrayal and the way in which she had ridiculed and frightened him as a child.

The therapist was able to make sense of his moods, his drug-taking and failure at school, in terms of this anger which found so many ways of effectively thwarting and punishing his mother. His life, it seemed, was set to refuse to comply with her wishes – or indeed those of anybody with power. It has been seen how this had found expression in his attitude towards the therapist – he too had felt frustrated and ridiculed, as both Jim and, no doubt, his mother had in various ways. Putting this into words in the form of an interpretation had meaning, and was of use to Jim because of the inescapable evidence provided by what had happened between them in the therapeutic relationship.

Psychotherapy ended after a year, when he moved away to start working. Clearly, there was much that was left incomplete. The understanding that he had gained needed consolidation and there were many other areas, not least his sexuality, and feelings for his father, that had not been adequately covered. Enough, however, had been done to enable Jim to become unstuck, less held back in his revenge against his mother. He was less miserable and less reliant on drugs. He was planning to study again. He found himself better able to tolerate other people without fear of humiliation or of disappointment. He was beginning to allow himself to join the mainstream of normal development, albeit with much idiosyncrasy left intact.

SUMMARY

Throughout this chapter, the main question has been about the possibility, or otherwise, of creating a relationship out of very different interests: on the one side, psychoanalytic therapy with its essential scrutiny and call for reflection; on the other, adolescence, with its essential privacy and preference for action. Both tug away or against each other, and for the two to come together each has to be prepared for at least some partial inversion of what they stand for. The adolescent, by dint of his disturbance, agrees to come to therapy and thereby compromises his independence. The psychotherapist in turn agrees to be flexible and foregoes something of his 'adult' discipline.

Effective psychotherapy with adolescents is a question not so much of specific technique or accurate interpretation as of the development and maintenance of a therapeutic attitude which is sensitive to and respectful of the adolescent state. The psychotherapist has to understand and contend with a mass of contradictions that exist at the centre of the adolescent predicament – sometimes an adult, sometimes a child and always neither. The adolescent needs to find his own way and not be called too much to account; yet he needs attention, guidance and someone to care about him. He does not want to be understood; and yet he does. He wants licence; and yet he needs boundaries.

In response, the psychotherapist's position has to be inevitably and likewise contradictory. At one and the same time, the psychotherapist needs to be ready to be flexible, to play roles and change posture – and yet remain essentially a firm and reliable presence. He has to retain faith in the usefulness of words and yet remind himself that much of what he does non-verbally is crucial. He has at times to be active and involved, sometimes even larger than life and directorial – and yet never lose his fundamental capacity to listen and observe, and tolerate the adolescent's confusion, failure to respond and, at times, sheer silence. Winnicott (1966) suggested that adolescents 'eschew psychoanalytic treatment, though they are interested in psychoanalytic theories' because their 'preservation of personal isolation is part of the search for identity'. Of importance here is Winnicott's concern with the development of the core of true self, uncompromised or intruded upon by the external world. In adolescence, this core self is in a state of delicate and partial formation, and requires both protection and leaving be. Phillips (1988), in his account of Winnicott's work, summarises succinctly the contradiction that characterises so much of psychotherapy of adolescents: 'The paradox that he [Winnicott] had begun to formulate was that the infant – like the adolescent... – was an isolate who needed the object, above all, to protect the privacy of his isolation'.

FURTHER READING

Evans J 1982 Adolescent and pre-adolescent psychiatry. Academic Press, London
Laufer M, Laufer E 1989 Developmental breakdown and psychoanalytic treatment in adolescence. Yale University Press, London
Miller D 1983 The age between: adolescence and therapy. Jason Aronson, London
Wilson P, Hersov L 1985 Individual and group therapy. In: Rutter M, Hersov L (eds) Child and adolescent psychiatry, 2nd edn. Blackwell, Oxford

20. Psychotherapy with the elderly

R. Porter

INTRODUCTION

Geriatrics begins at 65, according to United Kingdom Statute (Chronically Sick and Disabled Persons Act 1970). At around this age, changes such as retirement occur and we start on a new phase in our lives. Whatever has preceded this, life will be different from now on.

The two stages of these last decades of life were first delineated by Neugarten (1975). She described a 'young-old' period when we are still active physically and mentally, may hope to enjoy not having to work for a living and having time for other activities; and an 'old-old' stage, when bodily and mental frailty becomes more evident and physical disabilities are inevitable. This chapter focuses on the author's experience as a psychoanalytic psychotherapist working in a Geriatric Unit with old-old individuals who are frail and also medically ill.

Neugarten's two groups are not clearly delineated, and actual chronological age does not neatly separate individuals into the two categories. However, the age range for the young-old period may be said to be from around 60 to 65 to the early 70s, and for the old-old from the early 70s until death. Numbers in both groups, and especially in the latter, are increasing rapidly in the western world.

There are different intrapsychic tasks at these two stages of life. The young-old are adjusting to a different place in society. Their children have left home and are no longer dependent on them (the empty-nest syndrome) and employment becomes less important. But they have more time. A husband and wife may need to adjust to having more time to spend with each other. And there is time for other, often aesthetically creative, activities. Famous individuals who worked creatively in later life include Beethoven, Tolstoy and Yeats; Simone de Beauvoir and Martha Graham; and Freud and Jung. But it is not necessary to be a genius for later-life creativity. Apparently ordinary individuals in their later years may take up new activities and derive much satisfaction from developing this creative, and until now dormant, part of themselves.

Less happily, adaptations to changes in the body, in sexuality and in internal self-image are also needed; the old-old, in addition, must adapt to the increasingly unpleasant bodily and mental changes of ageing, to dependence on others and to the imminence and inevitability of death.

ADAPTATIONAL TASKS

Erikson (1959), in *Identity and the Life Cycle*, proposed a continuous development of identity through eight stages of life. At each stage, a different set of psychosocial factors precipitates a particular identity crisis, and different intrapsychic adaptations and tasks are needed to adjust to these external and internal pressures (see also Sandler A-M 1984). Erikson describes the crisis at the stage of mature age, the eighth stage, as between integrity on the one hand and despair and disgust on the other. Integrity, the positive component of this dyad, is a sense of the value of one's life experiences and therefore of oneself, as an antidote to the negative component – potentially overwhelming despair. What Erikson calls the 'related element of social order' at this stage is 'wisdom', and the tasks are 'to be, through having been' and 'to face not being' (p. 128 and Appendix: Worksheet). At this time, an individual relinquishes the threads connecting him to his objects and relationships (internal and external), recognises the nearness of death and prepares for this.

Jaques (1965), in his paper 'Death and the mid-life crisis', also defines two critical phases in life when particular transitions and adaptations are needed. One is the crisis occurring in the mid-30s, and the second '... at full maturity around the age of 65.' (p. 502). Jaques writes that creative activity at and during the decades after the mid-life crisis leads to the adaptations that are needed at the second crisis when '... preparation for the final phase in reality-testing has begun – the reality-testing of the end of life.' (p. 513).

Carl Jung also thought and wrote about adaptations towards the end of life. '... for the ageing person, it is a duty and a necessity to devote serious attention to himself.' (1931, p. 399); and '... the life of an older person is characterized by a contraction of forces, by the affirmation of what has been achieved and by the curtailment of further growth.' (1933, p. 67).

The aim of psychoanalytic psychotherapy with the elderly is to help with these internal age-specific adaptations through the understanding of the individual's internal world. In this way, psychological development can continue until death.

Major adaptational tasks are concerned with loss, discontinuity, disorder and chaos, and sexuality.

LITERATURE REVIEW

'When you were young you fastened your belt about you and walked where you chose; but when you are old you will stretch out your arms, and a stranger will bind you fast and carry you where you have no wish to go.' (Blythe 1981, p. 286)

This is Ronald Blythe's (1981) beautifully worded paraphrase into modern English of a verse from the final chapter of St John's Gospel. The quotation embodies some of the features of old age; dependency, helplessness and loneliness. For some, and perhaps eventually for everyone, this is true. But the emotional appeal of these words suggests that old age is always like this and that nothing can be done about it.

Another well-known quotation contains a prejudice against anyone over the age of 50, and presents a stereotype of an elderly person as someone who is stuck:

'The age of patients has this much importance in determining their fitness for psycho-analytic treatment, that, on the one hand, near or above the age of fifty the elasticity of the mental processes, on which the treatment depends, is as a rule lacking – old people are no longer educable – and, on the other hand, the mass of material to be dealt with would prolong the duration of the treatment indefinitely.' (Freud 1905b, p.264)

It took a long time for psychoanalysts to shake free from this prohibition. Pearl King (1974) drew attention to the valuable work that can be done and the intrapsychic changes that are possible with elderly individuals. Reports of psychoanalytic psychotherapy with the elderly are now appearing more often. Peter Hildebrand has worked, taught and written extensively on this subject (Hildebrand 1982, 1985, 1986). Some other publications to note are by Segal (1958); A-M Sandler (1978, 1984); Verwoerdt (1981); Cohen (1982); Pollock (1981, 1982); Achté & Tuulio-Henriksson (1982); and Newton et al (1985). Volume III in the US Department of Health and Human Services' series, 'The course of life; psychoanalytic contributions toward understanding personality development' (Greenspan & Pollock 1981), 'The race against time' (Nemiroff & Colarusso 1985) and 'treating the elderly with psychotherapy' (Sadavoy & Leszcz 1987) are three multi-author volumes from the United States on psychotherapy and psychoanalysis in the second half of life. In all these publications, the authors draw attention to the intrapsychic developmental work that is needed at this stage of life when external life circumstances are changed and the psychological strategies that have been used to cope with external problems and internal conflicts are no longer effective.

PSYCHOTHERAPIES

Psychotherapy in its broadest sense includes all forms of psychological treatment. Psychoanalytic psychotherapy forms the main focus of this chapter. Some other types of psychotherapy that have been used with the elderly are described first.

Supportive psychotherapy

Supportive psychotherapy (see Ch. 9) has no definition, or rather it has many definitions, ranging from a friendly chat and advice on practical problems to support through insight. In supportive therapy, although the therapist may interpret what is said for his own use, interpretations are not passed on verbally.

Crown (1988) maintains that supportive and psychoanalytic psychotherapy are mutually exclusive because in the latter negative emotions which are the opposite of supporting are mobilised. Enid Balint, however, in an unpublished paper given at a Royal College of Psychiatrists' quarterly meeting in London in 1986, commented that it is impossible to provide support without understanding the whole person and that this will of necessity include understanding of unconscious as well as conscious mechanisms and problems.

The support given by non-judgemental listening is a major part of all forms of psychotherapy for the elderly, but support with practical, external issues can distract from the work with internal – and unconscious – problems and should be avoided as far as possible.

Cognitive therapy

Cognitive therapy (CT) with the elderly is based on Aaron Beck's theory and practice of CT in depression (Beck et al 1979; see Ch. 11). Although Beck's earlier work was with younger age-groups, he has recently completed a small, randomised clinical trial of CT, nortriptyline, and CT with nortriptyline in older depressed adults (Gottlieb & Beck 1990). The authors conclude from this careful study that CT may be an important treatment, especially for medically frail geriatric patients who cannot tolerate antidepressants.

Behaviour therapy

The literature on behaviour therapy (see Ch. 4) in the elderly is sparse, although good results with individual cases are described in general texts on psychogeriatrics (for example, Woods 1982). Behavioural techniques are useful in the elderly (as with younger adults) in phobic conditions, including agoraphobia and panic attacks (Marks 1989). Non-specific behavioural techniques, such as the encouragement of activities in which the person can increase his skill, are certainly used by psychotherapists who are not strictly behavioural.

Projective therapies (see Ch. 6)

Music therapy

Music therapy uses the language of music (melody, rhythm and harmony) in a non-threatening way to break through the patient's isolation and communication barrier. In long-term music therapy, the depth of meaning within the music assists the development of confidence and self-awareness, increases independence as far as is possible, and helps severely damaged individuals to relate to the therapist and to others (Sandler F 1989). A major text for music therapists is Nordoff & Robbins (1977). (See also Gloag 1989.)

Art therapy

Art therapy today is based on psychoanalytic principles as well as on the use of art materials (Dalley 1984). It can provide a remarkable short-cut to the unconscious. The textures as well as the colours of paints and ink, paper and clay, help an elderly patient to experience feelings that he may be unable to talk about (Wilkinson 1989).

Music and art therapy may 'touch the depths without stirring the surface' (Bachelard 1969, quoted by Cox & Theilgaard 1987 in the context of archaic language).

Group therapy

Gilewski (1986) reviews the literature and describes his work with cognitively impaired older adults. He suggests that group therapy (see Ch. 3) may be expected to improve morale, reduce symptoms and increase discharge rate in these patients.

In the United Kingdom, studies using psychoanalytic principles with groups of elderly persons are now being reported. Kapur & Pearce (1987) treated five elderly psychiatric patients over a one-and-a-half year period; Hunter (1989) notes that, in her experience, patients with severe medical and cognitive defects can benefit from psychoanalytically based group therapy. Ezquerro (1989) described psychoanalytic therapy with a group of nine individuals between the ages of 55 and 67. He notes intrapsychic change, support amongst the members of the group and adjustments in the external world. He remarks on the strength of the counter-transference (especially sadness when therapy is completed) for therapists who work with the elderly. As a result of his experience, he considers that 'late middle-age is a specific developmental phase in the life-span' and 'a critical period suitable for group psychotherapy.' (p. 275).

It is the author's impression that therapists in the United Kingdom and elsewhere are now working psychoanalytically with groups of elderly patients but much of this work has not yet been published.

ADAPTATIONS AND PSYCHOANALYTIC PSYCHOTHERAPY

Psychological development continues throughout life. The internal developmental adaptations in old age are different from those at other ages because of different internal and external demands and pressures. When psychotherapy releases a person from some of their internal restrictions, they become freer to deal more effectively with external circumstances.

Psychotherapy helps the elderly person with these internal adaptations in five separate although overlapping areas:

1. *Loss.* When sadness in the face of so many losses is admitted, despair and hopelessness diminish; mourning can begin and life as it is now can be lived as fully as possible.
2. *Anger.* Patients may react with anger to their losses and to the threat of helplessness, dependence and death. Anger can be destructive, both internally and externally, or healthy and protective.
3. *Discontinuity.* The elderly feel separated from earlier parts of their lives. They need to remember and to re-establish connections between past and present.
4. *Disorder and chaos.* The degree of internal confusion in old age ranges from mild disorder with transitory memory lapses, to chaotic disintegration. The need here is to find and support whatever internal controls are available.
5. *Sexuality.* The elderly are adapting not only to changes in, but also the continuing presence of, their sexuality and sexual needs. Internal gender shifts (towards masculinity in women and femininity in men) also take place and need attention.

Loss

Psychotherapy for the elderly has been called the psychotherapy of what might have been. The conviction that everything is possible has to be given up. Hopes are extinguished. Choices become fewer. If these losses are not mourned, despair (and destructive anger) may take over.

Old-old individuals have sustained many losses during their lives. As well as parents, spouses and siblings, other relations, friends and even children are dead; houses and streets have been pulled down and disappeared; pets have grown old and died. Bodily losses are inevitable: loss of mobility, speech, hearing and sight; loss of a limb following amputation; and loss (shortness) of breath. The expression 'I've lost heart' economically combines the idea of physical and emotional loss. Short-term memory impairment, which usually precedes other memory defects, is another loss. Financial security may be lost. The loss of status and of a place in society, beginning at the young-old stage, continues, as do anxieties about loss of sexual potency. An elderly woman (or man) who has spent her life attending to the needs of others grieves when she can no longer do this. Perhaps the most painful loss of all is the loss of independence. Finally, there is loss of life itself.

These losses are also experienced intrapsychically as the loss of objects in the internal world, and are accompanied by frightening feelings of fragmentation. Memories of past events are often vivid and mostly accurate but they, also, are broken-up. Memory for recent events is poor: large parts of the person's past life seem to have disappeared. As the real body ages, a healthy body image is lost and replaced by a damaged one. The loss of external hopes and choices is reflected in a sense that the internal world is diminished. Many individuals have had neither time nor opportunity to mourn these losses until now.

Death and dying

The very old do not fear being dead in the way the middle-aged do. But they may very much fear the actual process of dying. They may picture themselves falling and unable to reach the telephone after a stroke; or being found on the floor, incontinent and dirty, in a pool of vomit. Ideas about these external events may not have been voiced before, and can be dealt with practically by, for example, installing a telephone alarm system. Simply to be able to put these fears into words helps.

Conscious and unconscious fears and fantasies surround the idea and the reality of death. Hildebrand (1986) writes about '...the notion of a primary fantasy to do with one's own extinction and that of one's objects.' (p.27); he feels that '...for many of the older patients, their personal death and the deaths of those close to them, whether parents, spouses or children, form a major preoccupation, often unspoken and hard to express in words, which the therapist has to recognise and help the individual to cope with.' (p. 28). But many old-old individuals, who have indeed lost their 'objects', feel that there is little or nothing left to lose. Simone de Beauvoir (1970) has written that in old age there remains nothing that death can destroy. But in the author's view, there *is* something more to be destroyed: death takes away our past.

Despair or sadness

Through psychotherapy, hopeless despair can change to appropriate sadness. When a patient can experience his sadness, despair and anger decrease. The knowledge that there has been something in his life that was worth losing helps him to feel that he is worth something too.

Case study 20.1   From despair to sadness in an elderly man

A depressed man in his late 70s had many medical problems, including hypertension and a residual hemiparesis following a stroke. He could only walk with a frame. He had plenty to be depressed about. His way of dealing with his problems was to grumble incessantly, constantly complaining about the community services and about help he received from informal sources. Although these were real difficulties, his constant complaints antagonised everyone who tried to help him.

He had had a lonely life. His parents were dead and he had not married. He had few friends and had never been able to sustain an emotional relationship nor to have a sexual relationship of any sort. His father had seemed remote, his mother demanding, and family contacts had been superficial and unsatisfying. One of his few happy childhood memories was of helping his father on his allotment and learning gardening skills from him.

After six months of weekly therapy, and during the penultimate session before a two-month break, he talked about his anger with his parents, and with the therapist because of the coming break, and his despair and suicidal thoughts because he could not prevent this. He then – for the first time – expressed sadness, saying: 'the thing I miss most is my allotment. I can hardly bear to see it now, so overgrown and uncared-for.' He was no longer complaining, but was in touch with his sadness about the loss of his father, and the therapist, and with the self that would feel so uncared-for during the therapist's absence.

Anger

In psychotherapy, the patient can express anger without punishment. At the very least, the therapist can deflect anger onto himself and away from others. Anger that is not released outwardly turns inwards, damaging the patient's internal world. The external release of anger relieves this internal persecution. As the internal world becomes more merciful, real people who have been perceived as enemies can be forgiven. Until anger is acknowledged, mourning and forgiveness cannot take place.

Case study 20.2   Working with anger

An angry 90-year-old man with multiple severe medical problems, including diabetes and necrotic leg ulcers, shouted continually on the ward. In spite of a successful life in business, he had constantly been let down by business associates, including members of his family. His marriage had been loveless and unhappy. He had tyrannised his family for many years and, since admission to hospital, he had been cruelly critical of the nursing staff.

The therapist saw him once weekly over a period of five months until he died. He talked easily during the early sessions, expressing his fury against others; next he told the therapist about his marriage and his sexual guilts and difficulties, and then suddenly he turned his anger onto the therapist. He shouted at her when she was there and about her when she was not.

The man's medical condition deteriorated and his left leg was amputated. He survived the operation and could feel that this had been a good experience, because there were doctors, including the therapist, who took care of him; in other words, he was worth caring for. His anger now alternated with quiet periods; he became altogether gentler, and less abusive to the therapist. A loved grand-daughter returned from another country. He finally died reconciled to his family and surrounded by children, grandchildren and great-grandchildren.

Constructive anger

Anger can be constructive. Complaining about conditions in an institution (the food for example) can actually get something done about it. Even a small success promotes optimism and a sense of mastery of the environment. These positive feelings have an internal effect, reinforcing hope and counteracting helplessness.

Sheldon Tobin and his colleagues have studied elderly individuals who enter institutions (Tobin & Lieberman 1976, Lieberman & Tobin 1983). They set up and tested predictors of adaptation to this stress. In *The Experience of Old Age* (1983), they report the results from four such studies. Patients were tested before and one year after the move. The authors found that aggressiveness predicted successful adaptation to the change. Individuals who grumbled and were generally unpleasant survived significantly longer than those who behaved well and did not complain. The authors suggest that this 'grouchy' behaviour prolongs survival through preserving the persons' narcissism – their healthy selfishness – and sense of their own worth.

Discontinuity

Continuity with the past: reminiscence

For an elderly person, to remember their past life and stay in contact with it supports the idea of a constant internal self. The value of reminiscence is to bring memories from the past into the present, and to recognise the child, the adolescent and the mature adult still existing internally. Memories of past happiness and of what *has* been achieved, as well as what has not, enhance the value of the past.

Case study 20.3   'I haven't laughed like that since I was a child'

A woman in her late 80s became depressed following the death of a niece. She had had many losses during her life. She spent her working life as a nanny, looking after children who then grew up and left her. She had never married. The therapist saw her every week or two weeks over the space of one year. At the end of a session in the mid-part of her therapy, she said: 'I hope I've helped you today.' Then she laughed and looked embarrassed. At the beginning of the next session she talked freely about this, saying: 'I haven't laughed like that since I was a child.'

These two sessions, containing laughter as well as positive transference and counter-transference, changed her relationship with the therapist. She treated him less as an authority figure. She had brought happiness from her childhood into the session. She felt that she could indeed still help somebody, and that she was still worth something herself.

Continuity and the future

A sense of continuity with the future is also possible. Religious faith strengthens the idea of immortality and a life after death. A sense of immortality can also be reached through belief in the continuing existence of a world in which some part of oneself can be left. We can live on in children and grandchildren, in the memories of others or in our created objects – our works. We may feel that we continue through our written words – poetry, prose and letters; in art and painting; or in music. A garden implies faith in a future to which we have contributed. Quite simple objects – photographs and home videos for example – can provide this sense of continuity. Cremation is necessary for social reasons, but it is likely that many of the old-old regret there is no plot, and will be no gravestone, for their relations to visit.

Disorder and chaos

Confusion

In helping to control confusion, the reliability of the therapist in relatively simple matters such as the regular timing of sessions, in the same room and with chairs in the same position, is as important as insightful interpretations. If the external world is orderly and manageable, memories can fit into place and the internal world become less unruly.

Case study 20.4   The handbag and the internal world

An 80-year-old patient was nearly blind. She was not demented, but her short-term memory was poor and she was confused at times. During the sessions, she would turn out her handbag looking for keys, appointment cards and so on, but also searching for old photographs and letters to show the therapist. She came to realise that the disorder in her handbag was connected with the confusion in her mind, and that she wanted the therapist to help her in sorting out this internal chaos. Her flat was full of objects from her past life: heavy furniture, old clothes. ornaments – the accumulations of a lifetime. After she had finished regular sessions she took up an offer of sheltered accomodation and moved into a very small flat. She gave away or stored everything that would not fit into this flat. She has made friends with some of her neighbours and, although sad, is managing to live a reasonably ordered life.

Primitive emotions

Regression to child-like emotions and childish behaviour occurs in old age when previous (normal) inhibitions weaken. The disruption of neuronal pathways caused by cerebral damage contributes to this loss of control, but a loosening of emotional restrictions also takes place. In Freudian terms, the id escapes from the control of the ego and super-ego; according to Kleinian formulations, the balance between depressive and paranoid-schizoid positions shifts towards the latter. This loosening of controls, together with confusing alterations in the external environment, frightening bodily changes and cognitive defects, all add to the internal chaos and disorder. Primitive emotions emerge unhindered.

Some old-old individuals become emotionally labile, laughing and crying easily, and fierce bouts of anger can occur for apparently trivial reasons. Inhibitions on sexual behaviour may also be relaxed. Through psychotherapeutic work, some understanding of these primitive feelings can be reached, so that rather than taking charge of the individual and overwhelming him, they can be understood, controlled and even used constructively. (The patient described in Case study 20.2 as an example of working with anger was also releasing uncontrollable primitive emotions.)

Sexuality

Sexuality is as complicated in old age as in youth. The topic has been avoided, presumably because sexuality, even in normal old people, is still an embarrassing subject. It disturbs society. Peter Hildebrand is one of the psychoanalysts who has demolished the myth that an asexual old age is inevitable because of endocrine and physical changes. In discussing sexual functions and needs in the elderly, Hildebrand (1986) describes the persistence of both into extreme old age. He notes that, with age, sexuality can become less a matter of discharge of hormonal tensions and more an expression of tenderness, affection and trust.

Sexual potency, however, does decline with ageing, for psychological as well as physiological reasons, and elderly persons do fear loss of potency and sexual drive. They are therefore dealing with expectations of disapproval of their sexual needs on the one hand, and fears about their potency and diminished sexual attractiveness on the other. They hope to be more attractive to others if they suppress their sexuality.

Gender shifts

Gutmann (1988) has described an internal gender shift in later life. He notes that the post-parental period gives back to women their covert masculinity, and to men their covert femininity. Such changes can be uncomfortable to those who feel they should be 100% male or 100% female.

There is yet another problem. Elderly individuals may evince uninhibited sexual behaviour, including exhibitionism, unwanted sexual advances and masturbation in public. This can be distressing for others, although, apparently, not for the individuals themselves.

The therapist's task is to pick up all these strands. It is important to accept the patient's sexuality and discuss these matters openly in individual sessions with him.

The therapist can also help nursing staff and others through opening up discussion of sexual problems with them.

TECHNICAL ISSUES IN PSYCHOANALYTIC THERAPY WITH THE ELDERLY

Psychoanalytic psychotherapy with the elderly has much in common with, but also some differences from, psychoanalytic work with younger adults.

Similarities

The work is based on understanding the unconscious processes behind the patient's difficulties and symptoms, and deals with areas that are inaccessible to conscious and intellectual understanding. By this approach, an individual can make sense of at least some of the confusion in his life and get in touch with deep feelings. Although access to these feelings will be painful, it encourages the sense of integrity that Erikson (1959) has described.

Transference and counter-transference and the psychological mechanisms of splitting, projection and introjection are as important at this as at other ages. Psychotherapists use whatever theoretical base they are comfortable with, according to their training and experience. The relationship with the therapist, in reality as a professional and caring person and through the transference and counter-transference, is as important as at other life stages. It is belittling to the elderly to assume that they cannot work in this way.

Differences

Communication

To establish rapport with elderly individuals it is necessary to work at their pace, which will usually be slow. A setting for unhurried listening is crucial. Physical handicaps, such as impaired sight or hearing, dysphasia or dementia, are often present. A deaf patient with speech difficulties following a stroke may be labelled as demented. As his speech improves with speech therapy, and his deafness and the anxieties that accompany not being able to hear properly are recognised, his true mental capacity can emerge. The use of a simple device such as a speech amplifier helps the therapist as well as the patient. It is a positive experience for both when rapport is established in spite of such difficulties.

Touch

Old people may never be touched with affection, confirming their sense that their bodies are not only no longer desirable but actually repulsive. Something as simple as shaking hands at the beginning and end of a session helps to counteract these feelings.

Practical problems

Patients usually try to draw the therapist into helping them with their practical difficulties. Invitations to advise on financial or administrative problems can be declined relatively easily, but some practical help may be needed. The act of physically helping a chair-bound individual to the consulting room is sometimes necessary; during the session, the meaning of this help – conscious and unconscious, and for the therapist as well as the patient – can be explored.

Practical arrangements

The author usually sees old-old patients once weekly. Sessions last for 45 minutes, but patients often ask to finish earlier; they time their own sessions and finish when they are tired.

The psychotherapist, whilst preserving confidentiality, can give and receive information and support from other health workers. It helps to learn about the patients' improvement (or otherwise) outside the therapy sessions. Their behaviour in social groups, response to other therapies and use of community services, for example, are useful pieces of information. This two-way exchange is valuable for everyone, not least for the patients.

DEFENCE AND DENIAL

Loneliness, helplessness and dependency become increasingly threatening with age, and the elderly, even more than the young, habitually defend themselves against their panic at these threats. Some defence is necessary and healthy, but when feelings are completely denied pathological defence mechanisms come into play, at serious cost to the patient.

The strength of denial depends not only on the power of the threats but also on the previous personality. An individual who has not been able to grieve for other losses copes with the assaults of ageing with more difficulty than a previously emotionally healthy person.

Individuals whose early narcissism has persisted are especially vulnerable to the attacks of ageing. Throughout their lives they have focused all their attention and love on themselves; externally on their bodies and appearance, and internally on their own feelings and fantasies, conscious and unconscious. They still relate everything and everybody to themselves. This self-centredness is a normal phase in development, but if it continues into adulthood, loving and relating to others are impossible (see Rycroft 1968).

Mechanisms associated with denial include a pathological response to narcissistic injury; somatisation; and focus on practical and external issues.

Narcissistic injury

Pearl King (1980) described ageing as an experience of narcissistic injury, associated with shame and humiliation. Ageing also contains the threat of utter helplessness, and Hess (1987), amongst others, has described narcissistic tyranny as a defence against the anxiety provoked by this. A degree of healthy narcissism can reduce stress in the elderly (Verwoerdt 1981); but a person whose pathological narcissism has previously had an acceptable outlet through the exercise of power during adulthood, at work or towards a submissive spouse, finds that in old age this pattern of behaviour is no longer effective. These individuals continue to act in a superior way, particularly towards those who, by trying to help them, remind them of their helplessness. They become increasingly enraged and despairing; damage to the psyche gives rise to depression and confusion.

King Lear is an example of a man who throughout his life had sustained his narcissistic image of himself through the exercise of power (Hess 1987). When he gives away this power, he cannot mourn the loss but defends himself against increasing helplessness by increasingly tyrannical behaviour. His attempts to control his daughters and sons-in-law are useless, and he goes mad. He cannot regain his sanity until he accepts his helplessness and sadness and can grieve for Cordelia.

Somatisation

Some patients focus on bodily pain to the exclusion of painful feelings. They have a physical condition which causes pain, arthritis or post-herpetic neuralgia for example, and concentrate entirely on this. All suggestions that painful *feelings* may also be present are repulsed or seem not to be heard at all. The bodily pain is the only problem; if it were relieved, life would be perfect. Many remedies – painkillers, anti-rheumatic medication, acupuncture, attendance at a pain-relief clinic, anxiolytics – have been tried and failed, and now psychotherapy is failing too. These patients draw their doctors and other health workers, as well as friends and relations, into their pain: everyone shares it and no-one can relieve it. Treatment fails. Everyone feels helpless. The patient and his pain are in control. When the premise that the pain is not solely in the body is challenged, the doubter is dismissed. These patients are depressed and may respond to antidepressants. Unfortunately, psychotherapy, in the author's experience, does not help them either (see Ch. 16).

Focus on practical issues

Patients transfer their emotional pain not to their bodies, as with somatisation, but to practical problems. They will only talk about day-to-day issues: pensions, transport, prescriptions; or about other patients and their difficulties; or about their therapists. This defence may sound trivial, but it may be impossible to deflect these (usually) talkative patients away from external issues and towards their inner problems.

Healthy defence

Healthy defence should also be recognised. Sometimes, after a number of sessions when the work is proceeding well – losses have been admitted, some mourning accomplished and past conflicts aired – the patient suddenly comes to a full stop. If this halt is a resistance, it can be worked with in therapy; but it may be a healthy and necessary protection against unbearable internal injury and, if so, should be respected as such.

Case study 20.5   The patient who came to a full stop

A depressed man in his late 70s had been chair-bound for many years following a stroke. He was born in another country and had served in the British Air Force during World War II. Many of his relatives had died in concentration camps. He told of the joy with which he and his compatriots bombed enemy territory, but he also revealed his guilt about the bombing, guilt which he had felt but could not admit to at the time. He talked freely during early sessions about his childhood and his wartime experiences. He described recurrent nightmares from which he awoke shouting in the night. Then, suddenly, following a holiday break in treatment, he stopped. He would talk only of practical matters. He told the therapist he was better, that he had no dreams, no fears, and that everything was fine. He tried to get out of the room, he asked to see another doctor, anything to get away from her. He could not face the anxiety and anger stirred up by the therapist's absence. The therapist continued to see him for a few weeks, when they talked of daily matters. It was important to show him that the therapist could survive, but psychoanalytic work could not continue.

Case study 20.6   A toe in the water

Another patient, a woman in her 80s, talked easily during three sessions about childhood memories of her mother and sisters. She also described excursions to the public swimming bath with her grandchildren, and connected these present trips with visits to the public baths when she was a child. She said that although it was all right for her grandchildren now, and her sisters then, to go into the water, her mother had told her that this would always be too dangerous for her. At this clear instruction the therapist stopped psychoanalytic work with her.

PROBLEMS FOR THE THERAPIST

Age, transference and counter-transference

For psychotherapists in the second half of their own lives, age differences do not seem to present any old-age-specific problems. The therapist knows that in the transference he may be perceived as child, or even grandchild, as well as spouse, parent and/or authority figure. These different transferences also affect the counter-transference, and may be more difficult for the young therapist.

Ageism

Ageism is a different problem altogether. Prejudice against the elderly is widespread, and exists not only in 'everyone else' but also in psychotherapists and in the elderly themselves. The therapist has to recognise his own conscious and unconscious prejudices.

Projections

One of the reasons that psychoanalysts delayed working with the elderly for so long must have been the painful nature of what, by the process of projective identification (see Chs 1, 13 and 21), is transferred from the inner world of the patient to that of the analyst. This is especially so with the old-old, when control of primitive and violent feelings is breaking down for organic (cerebral degeneration) as well as psychological reasons. In such danger areas as death, helplessness, bodily losses and physical disease, the patient's and the therapist's anxieties, which are conscious and unconscious for both, have to be disentangled. Supervision helps to clarify what is happening.

Death

The patients project their fears of death and dying into the therapist. The therapist is dealing with his own and the patient's fears and anxieties.

Helplessness

A therapist will often feel helpless (and hopeless) in the face of so many problems. It helps to recognise that he is containing the patient's helplessness as well as his own.

Body image

The patient with a stroke or an amputated leg is dealing not only with what has happened to his body externally, but also with a changed and damaged internal body image. The therapist's fears about physical ill-health and decrepitude, and the patient's damaged internal body image need to be clearly distinguished.

Frustration

Irritation at the slow pace of the work is, for the therapist, another real external problem, which also contains the patients' frustration at their own bodily and mental slowness.

Dependence

Dependence is inevitable. It is valuable, as at other ages, in establishing the therapist/patient relationship. But it can create difficulties when the patient is in reality physically dependent.

Dependent patients become anxious about the duration of therapy. In the author's view, if psychoanalytic psychotherapy is successfully established, the contract should be for as long as the patient wishes and the therapist lives (or is available in that job and place). In practice, this ideal is usually not possible. However, the sense that someone is alive and available to care for the patient for as long as he needs him can be transferred to another individual; or to a group of individuals, such as the nurses for a patient in hospital; or even to an institution, for example the hospital itself (Martindale 1989). Patients with repeated strokes or advancing dementia may be unable to continue to work psychoanalytically because of cerebral damage. In these circumstances, it is important for the therapist to continue brief, regular contacts and stay alive for the patient. In some way, even a severely brain-damaged patient seems able to sense that the therapist contains life.

Envy

Unconscious envy is mobilised in psychotherapy with the elderly, as with other age groups. But envy that is appropriate to the therapist in real life is also present. The therapist's life is more satisfying than the patient's. He is likely to be more sexually active, less mentally confused and with a healthier body than the patient. The therapist is mobile. He can get up and go home after a session – the patient cannot. On the other hand, a therapist may also envy the looking-after that a bedridden and helpless patient receives.

Sympathy

The lives of many of these patients are in reality so difficult and sad that it is a temptation to offer sympathy. We have our own needs, including our wish to comfort. The safety which patients feel in the knowledge that their experience of sadness and helplessness can be spoken about is more help than expressions of sympathy.

Failure

The therapist is at times in danger of being overwhelmed by the extent and number of the problems. There is so much that cannot be done for medically ill, old-old individuals. Psychotherapy does fail. When a therapist really experiences this depression – their own and the patient's – supervision provides support and understanding.

CONCLUSIONS

Psychotherapy helps the elderly to live the final part of their lives, however limited, as fully as possible. George Pollock (1982), in his paper 'On ageing and psychopathology', describes the goal of psychoanalytic treatment at any age as 'to make more of people available to themselves for present and future creative and satisfying life experiences' (p. 280). When old-old patients understand something of their internal world, and can let go of the pathological defences they use to protect themselves from their feelings of helplessness and sadness, they become more available not only to their internal selves but also to relationships in the external world. The relationship with the therapist, too, becomes in itself a satisfying experience.

The work is full of contradictions. Privacy, attention to oneself and withdrawal from one's objects exist alongside the need for satisfying relationships in the external world; there is at times a need for solitude and privacy, and at times for activity and engagement with the environment. But privacy can drift into isolation and loneliness, and healthy activity escalate into manic and omnipotent behaviour.

Internal and external worlds mingle in old age. A failing body and mind, the many losses already described, dependence and helplessness, and the threat to life itself all exist internally and externally. For the very old, the boundaries between internal and external worlds seem unclear. Laurens van der Post's comment, although about a troubled young man, is apposite: 'my mind is on a slant and I see outside me only what is already in me.' (van der Post 1934, p.125).

Although there is so much that *cannot* be done, psychotherapy with the very old is satisfying work. Positive indicators for therapy are said to be motivation, psychological awareness, a previously healthy personality and recent onset of problems – the death of a spouse or physical illness, for example (see Chs. 1 and 8). But worthwhile intrapsychic change can also take place in elderly, socially disadvantaged and psychologically naïve individuals. None of the patients described in this chapter is psychologically sophisticated; they had never heard of psychotherapy; but they are survivors. They have come through two world wars. Their lives have been hard. Their minds are tough although their bodies are frail. Their internal worlds are teeming with life, and with ideas, dreams and fantasies that may not have had the chance of expression until now. The realisation that time is short because of the nearness of death is an incentive to work, rather than the opposite. A real deadline serves to concentrate the mind. It is not surprising that psychotherapists who embark on this work enjoy it.

FURTHER READING

Erikson E H 1959 Identity and the life cycle. Norton, New York
Hanley I, Gilhooly M (eds) 1986 Psychological therapies for the elderly. Croom Helm, London

21. Psychotherapy with people who have been sexually abused

S. Grant

INTRODUCTION

Freud shocked the scientific and medical establishment by suggesting that childhood sexual abuse was an aetiological factor in adult neurosis. He later put greater emphasis on childhood sexuality itself and 'wishful phantasies' rather than on environmental reality (Freud 1925). This shift led to the foundations of psychoanalysis and to an understanding of the complexities of the human mind. It has also left him open to the serious charge that generations of children have suffered because the reality of their abuse has been denied (Masson 1985).

Within psychoanalysis, the interaction between subjective and objective reality remains an important discussion point (for example, Schimiek 1975, Spence 1982, Hayman 1989). For the psychiatrist, research and clinical experience reveals that childhood sexual abuse is a common occurrence. It causes not only immediate distress but can lead to long-term psychological damage. In the words of one woman, sexually abused by her mother over several years, 'what she did to my body I can sort of cope with. I never liked my body very much anyway. What she did to my mind is unforgivable: it affected my ability to learn and to have relationships and it made me mad'; (she suffered from a schizo-affective psychosis).

THE PREVALENCE OF CHILD SEXUAL ABUSE

Forty years ago, Kinsey's pioneering and monumental survey of male sexual behaviour in America revealed that 60% of men sampled had had pre-adolescent homosexual activity, 17% of them to the extent of anal intercourse. 40% of his sample had had heterosexual activity before adolescence, half of them involving penetration or attempted penetration. He construed this as 'sex play'. When he went on to investigate the female population, he appeared more concerned and recorded the age discrepancy between the girl and the other person. Of the 4441 women interviewed, 24% had been sexually approached before puberty by boys or men at least five years older. Just under 1% of the whole sample said that they had experienced coitus before adolescence (Kinsey 1948, 1953).

More recent studies provide a range of prevalence figures. This reflects different sample populations, different definitions of sexual abuse (e.g. including or excluding exhibitionism), different age limits for the children and different definitions of abuser (to exclude mutual childhood exploration and distinguish between intra-familial and extra-familial abuse). Under-reporting may result from the inherent secrecy of incest, repression and failure to remember the abuse, and refusal to participate in such a survey. As media attention continues, an opposite trend may develop as childhood sexual abuse becomes 'respectable' and 'fashionable'. As one patient put it: 'If only I could remember having been sexually abused it would make such sense of all I'm going through now'.

Whatever the true prevalence is, it is undoubtedly high. In America, Herman found that one in four women had been sexually abused by the age of 18, and in one in ten of these the perpetrator was a close family member (Herman 1983). Russell's figure for sexual abuse was even higher, 54% (Russell 1983, 1986). In Britain, a survey of 1049 women found a lower prevalence of 12%, using a cut-off age of 16 and a broad definition of abuse (Baker & Duncan 1985).

There is evidence also that boys are sexually abused, although the figures tend to be less than for girls. In the clinical setting, it is apparent that many women are now able to come forward directly for help. The identity of having been a victim provides some relief, giving temporary legitimacy to symptoms whilst sufferers attempt to resolve their problems. In the present culture, for men to be seen as victims appears to imply weakness or failure, so that it becomes more difficult for men to seek direct help for feelings of guilt and shame about abuse.

To reflect present clinical experience, patients will be referred to as 'she', although many of the features apply also to men who have been abused.

Given the large numbers of people in the general population who have been sexually abused, it is not surprising that surveys of psychiatric populations reveal very large numbers. Friedman & Harrison found that 60% of schizophrenic inpatients had been sexually abused (Friedman & Harrison 1984). A survey of drug abusers by Benward & Densen-Gerbet (1975) showed that 44% had been abused. 51% of patients with eating disorders, surveyed by Oppenheimer et al (1985) described childhood sexual abuse. Baisden & Baisden (1979) reviewed 240 patients with sexual dysfunction and found that 90% had been abused. Associations have also been drawn between childhood sexual abuse and psychogenic pelvic pain (Gross et al 1980), and incest and trichotillomania (Singh & Maguire 1989). A disturbance in mood is frequently seen. Jehu (1988) noted that 70% of his adult sample of sexually abused women had had depressive episodes. It becomes a matter of clinical judgement to decide whether the abuse was instrumental in leading to the psychiatric disorder, whether it was a factor in impairing the person's ability to cope, or whether it is irrelevant. To be able to put the sexual abuse in perspective requires a knowledge of the patterns of behaviour and the subjective experience of those who have been abused.

THE NATURE OF CHILD SEXUAL ABUSE

The most common age of onset of sexual abuse as reviewed by Finkelhor & Baron (1986) was 10 to 13 years. In clinical work, it can be difficult for patients to recall the age of onset. 'It just seemed to be always happening.' Sometimes, the dates are obvious because they are linked to when an abuser enters or leaves the household. 'It was when Mum's boyfriend came to live with us when I was seven.'

The patients describe a range of sexual activity from fondling to vaginal and anal intercourse. The severity of the abuse may be hidden until the patient has tested whether the therapist can cope with the revelation (or whether she herself can). Jehu (1988) found that nearly 62% of his patients had had childhood experience of full intercourse.

Commonly, the abuse is done under threat: 'If you tell anyone I shall kill you'; 'No one will believe you'; 'I will be put in prison'; 'You will be put into care'; 'It will kill your mother'. These children live in a state of fear, helplessness and constant vigilance, especially if the abuser lives with them.

To cope with the physical aspects of the experience, the child oftens resorts to dissociation, consciously fostered, for example, by concentrating attention on a door-knob or staring at the ceiling. 'I would put all my thoughts into the rose on the wallpaper and I would't feel the pain at all.' Denial, and ignorance, helps them also. 'I didn't like it but I didn't know it was wrong until I was a teenager and then I felt sick when I realised.'

Not only do such girls feel betrayed by their father, if he is the abuser, they frequently feel abandoned and betrayed by their mother if she fails to recognise what is going on. Sometimes, it seems that mother encouraged the activity. 'She would tell me to go to bed with Daddy after lunch and keep him happy.' In other situations, there is a desperate attempt to protect mother, who is also seen as a victim. 'He would beat her unless I let him do what he wanted with me and I couldn't bear that.' There is often an aura of precocious maturity and role reversal about these women. They may have had to do the housework and raise younger children, as well as being the father's sexual partner. Their mother may be grateful and offer support. Alternatively she may ignore the situation, or, worse, she may condemn her daughter as a dangerous rival. Whatever the mother's role, it should not be forgotten that the criminal abusive act is perpetuated by the man. (The less researched area of female sexual abuse is acknowledged, but not discussed in this chapter.)

One of the most frequent questions asked is why such children do not tell the truth and seek help. In such families, it is as if the taboo against incest has been perverted into a taboo against putting incest into words. This is fostered by the threats. It is enabled also by an intense fear of family break-up, and by the actual experience of attempts at disclosure. One girl had sexual intercourse with her father and two elder brothers, and suffered associated physical abuse. By her teens she had a severe anxiety state. In her early 20s she tried to explain to the rest of the family what was wrong. They closed ranks and ostracised her. She continues to experience real anguish about being excluded from the intense family network, however pathological it is.

For those who do disclose in childhood, the deserved support may be sadly lacking. They may face disbelief, blame and anger. 'She called me a whore and a dirty slut.' The literature indicates that such responses are common (Jehu 1988). Even a potentially appropriate response may be experienced by the child as negative. One girl repulsed the repeated advances of her alcoholic father. She told her mother, who immediately separated from him. The girl was horrified. 'If only I had let him do it and kept my mouth shut we would still be a family.' Within six months she had developed severe Crohn's disease, then later endometriosis. Now in her mid-20s, with an ileostomy and facing a hysterectomy, she views the destruction of her body as retribution for not having given in. Even if disclosure in vindicated by a trial, conviction and prison sentence, the girl may face subsequent abuse by her father on his release. She may find his role taken over by a brother or uncle. 'He said that if I could do it for Dad then I could do it for him.'

LONG-TERM SEQUELAE

Clinical and research evidence suggests that the degree and nature of later disturbance mirrors not only the extent of the abuse but also the extent of ameliorating and supportive factors. Coincident emotional and physical abuse or deprivation compounds the likelihood of developmental failure and subsequent pathology. The longer and more frequent the abuse, the more severe the damage. If the abuser is a father or father substitute, or if there are multiple offenders, subsequent difficulties are likely to be more serious (Finkelhor & Browne 1986). One would anticipate that the younger the age of onset, the more disturbed the adult, but this is not yet proven. It is important to note that the pubertal and adolescent child, struggling with her own emerging sexual drives and identity, is also particularly vulnerable.

Re-enactment and repetition

Self-inflicted abuse

The child who has experience of her body not being treated with respect may grow up to continue to mistreat it. The dissociative mechanisms and the depersonalisation which helped her cope with the original trauma continue in a maladaptive way to enable her to treat her body as if it were inanimate and belonged to someone else. Once the self-body boundary has been breached in one way, the process is liable to be repeated in other ways.

The repetition of abuse in the form of self-harm may have a variety of meanings. One teenager who had suffered prolonged sexual abuse from her father and brother took repeated overdoses. For her, this was not an expression of suicidal intent but of her rage. 'When I feel angry I can't say anything, I just take an overdose.' A woman in her 30s sought help because she feared her son would notice the repeated lacerations she made on her legs 'for no reason'. In therapy, she realised that the triggers were related to reminders of the anal and vaginal rape she had endured from her father as a young girl. At that time she would cope partly by picking at scabs on her leg to make them bleed. Concentrating on the pain in her leg, which was under her control, helped her to tolerate the greater pain over which she had no control. In adulthood, she continued to use this method to block out her psychological pain.

The perpetual victim

The person habituated to abuse may enter a cycle of repeated abuse, even when she is consciously only desperately seeking affection. One woman, sexually abused by a family friend, maintained a strict moral code against physical adornment or expression of sexuality, linked to religious beliefs. Nevertheless she willingly tolerated a humiliating and degrading sexual exploitation by her boyfriend. 'That is all I have to offer.' Some women become promiscuous, or perceive themselves as such (Fromuth 1986). Other become prostitutes (Silbert & Pines 1983, Welldon 1988). Most tragic is when such women become rape victims. Many writers discuss the reasons for the greater risk of rape in women who have been sexually abused as children (e.g. Mezey 1985, Russell 1986, McCormack et al 1986). Because of her inappropriate early sexualisation, the girl may grow up feeling unable to protect herself appropriately, and unwittingly give an impression of available sexuality. At an unconscious level, there may also be a tendency to repeat in order to master the trauma. For the woman herself, the complexities of a situation to which she is an unconscious contributor may be hard to face, especially if they serve to confirm her guilt and self-disgust. 'Once is a coincidence, three times is a pattern. I turn men into monsters.' It is a matter of considerable therapeutic skill to help such women tolerate their feelings and learn to express their anger towards the offender and not themselves. What is often required is an unambiguous statement that there is no condoning or excusing the offence.

The victim turned abuser

The abused child has an internalised relationship modelled on abuse. She may grow up to repeat the pattern in a form of 'identification with the aggressor'. She may directly abuse her own children or marry a man who does. For both male and female victims, their fears and doubts about the capacity to be parents can cause considerable distress. The repetition of the trauma through generations is another cogent reason for active professional intervention at an early stage (Oliver 1988, Steele & Alexander 1981).

Relationship difficulties

For children who have been sexually abused, especially by a trusted parental figure, there may lie ahead decades of struggle to achieve an intimate caring relationship. Some women resolve never to trust again and withdraw emotionally and sexually, denying the need for closeness or sexual desires. Some deliberately make themselves unattractive, both as a protective device and as a challenge. 'He has to prove he loves me for myself and not for my body.'

Others move towards a degree of intimacy but cannot take the final step towards sexual closeness and responsiveness, even when they want to. At the other end of the spectrum is a person over-sexualised, who gets involved in multiple relationships, but cannot commit herself to one partner. The early experience of intergenerational boundary confusion and denial of social taboos may be repeated. Some women get into a pattern of repeated relationships with married men, often older authority figures, with tragic consequences. Another aspect of repetition within a close relationship is the fact that abused women are more prone to marital discord and domestic violence (Russell 1986, Jehu 1988).

Problems of self-esteem

Women who have been abused are left with feelings of guilt and shame. Such self-denigration and sense of worthlessness may be more striking than anger against the abuser. This is another facet of the distorted family dynamics where the girl is made to carry responsibility way beyond her years. She feels even worse if she was very passive or was bribed. 'I started getting used to the money and didn't want to give it up, even though I loathed what he did.' Even if she comes to accept the reality that children are not responsible for adult misbehaviour, this fragile security may be lost if she experiences some repetition in adulthood.

Additional sources of guilt are aroused if the family splits up, if she discovers younger siblings have been abused after she has left the family, or if the abuser kills himself.

The survivors

Working in a psychiatric setting one sees those people most traumatised and affected. It is impossible at the same time not to respect the resilience and resourcefulness of many of these patients. The legacy of vigilance may be turned into self scrutiny and sensitivity towards others. The prematurely responsible nurturing role they have played can be appropriately utilised (or exploited) in adulthood. Some people may well choose to work in a caring profession. Such a solution may be adaptive and useful to society and to the survivor. By looking after others she can achieve status and assuage guilt by reparative behaviour. Usually, the personal pain is split off, denied or projected. Unfortunately, such an individual, if she has not dealt with her own trauma, may be vulnerable to becoming over-identified with clients or patients. She may find it especially difficult in situations where she is in reality powerless to help.

THERAPY

Clinical presentation

As a direct result of the abuse

The change in public awareness and sympathy has enabled some people to break the secret for the first time, seeking professional help and recognition for their resulting difficulties. For many, consultation with their general practitioner will be adequate. Some will require secondary referral (Douglas 1988).

The same publicity that is liberating for some may be disturbing for others, breaking through rigidly maintained defences and precipitating a psychological crisis. When denial and dissociation break down, the person may be flooded with previously repressed memories and pain. Significant regression may occur. 'I always avoid programmes about sex or sexual abuse but this was a preview and I heard one sentence about them not feeling loved and that was enough. I haven't been able to cope since.' Sometimes, the disturbance may be sufficiently incapacitating to require admission to hospital.

Indirect presentation

When the patient does not present with an overt history of sexual abuse, clinical acumen is required to alert one to suspicious signs. In a psychiatric history, attention should be paid to mysterious difficulties such as a deterioration in school performance, or delinquent behaviour, without any other evident explanatory trigger. The question of sexual abuse should always be considered when treating eating disorders, addictions, sexual perversions, sexual dysfunction, mood disorders and borderline personality disorders. In practice, therefore, it is wisest to consider the question of sexual abuse in childhood as a routine part of history taking.

Assessment interview

Given the potency of the taboo on disclosure, it is clearly important that when sexual abuse is suspected, the interview is conducted in as sensitive a manner as possible.

Occasionally, the psychiatrist is the very first person to hear the disclosure, for example when it is elicited in a routine history. Even if the story has been told to several people along the path to referral, the psychiatrist has a special significance as an authority figure who is in a position of power. He or she is seen as being able to judge the sanity and the veracity of the patient. It may be difficult for the interviewer if the patient recounts her abuse in a detached manner. As one colleague said: 'How do I know it really happened – it sounds as if she is making it up'. It is imperative that the psychiatrist recognise that this dissociated hysterical presentation is more likely to be a product of genuine abuse than of lying. The aim would be to get in touch with the underlying affect. The psychiatrist may point out that the patient has described upsetting and frightening things yet appears detached from them. Perhaps that means that it is difficult for her to let the psychiatrist know how hurt she is. She may even be unable to let herself know. Commenting in this way may result in an emotional shift and encourage some contact between interviewer and patient.

Having acknowledged and accepted the fact of the sexual abuse, the psychiatrist may feel pressured into making premature supportive remarks. Immediately to point out the patient's positive qualities may appear patronising and dismissive. Equally, to stress a patient's anger about what happened is only effective if the therapist is tuned empathically into the patient's anger. It may well be that the anger is the therapist's own reaction. If the patient actually blames herself or misses positive aspects of the relationship with the abuser, then such a remark is unhelpful. It is usually safest to say in an open-ended way, 'What do you feel about that?' than to presume that one actually knows.

Emotional experience is not necessarily one sided in such an interview, and psychiatrists may have to cope with personal feelings. If he or she was raised in a secure and orderly background, there may be a sense of horror at the account of a chaotic, disorganised family where partners seem to be interchangeable. Even more threatening may be learning of such experiences within outwardly successful middle-class academic or medical families. Another component of the psychiatrist's feelings may be the result of his or her capacity to tune in to feelings the patient has but cannot face. Projective identification is a ubiquitous defence mechanism, most pervasive in childhood and when primitive defences remain in operation. The patient expels her painful feelings into the psychiatrist, both as a way of easing her own pain, and as a means of communication. This projection reverberates with the psychiatrist's own experiences, and comes to his or her attention as a feeling of anger, disgust, arousal, etc. The psychiatrist experiences what the patient cannot bear to experience (Sandler 1988, Hinshelwood 1989). Such experiences often go unrecognised, but they are familiar and form the basis of empathy. The task is to tolerate such bombardment of feelings without being too defensive. It is well to remember that these patients have sensitive antennae to the moods of those in authority. But it is better to be honest than to be stony-faced. 'I find it hard to take in all the painful things you are telling me, can you slow down and let me catch up.'

A psychotherapy assessment interview is not only the briefest form of therapy, it has a primary task of assessing what the problem is, what needs to be done and the best way to do it. The psychiatrist must determine whether the sexual abuse is of direct relevance to the presenting problems, and if so whether it should be tackled directly, left alone, or delayed until other problems are more under control. These are individual clinical judgements, and guidelines cannot be drawn covering the multiple factors in such a decision.

Important features to consider will be:

1. whether the presenting symptoms can be understood as directly bearing on the sexual abuse
2. whether the patient has clear areas of competence and healthy functioning
3. whether she has an effective support network in the family or socially.

The latter two factors are important. If a decision is made to proceed with some form of psychotherapy, then account must be taken of the fact that this will be disturbing and distressing for the patient and possibly her family. If it does not seem wise or appropriate to focus on the sexual abuse at this point in time, or if the patient does not wish to do so, then an awareness of the sexual abuse can still be useful in understanding her and can lead to sensitive management.

Treatment settings

If the psychiatrist decides that psychotherapeutic intervention is appropriate, then a range of settings are available.

The psychiatric setting

There is always the risk that the patient will construe being referred elsewhere as a rejection and a sign that she is too hard to handle. Yet there are limitations to the psychiatrist's time, skills and inclinations. If the psychiatrist does decide to continue treating such a patient, or if there is little alternative option, it may prove to be a disturbing but enlightening experience both professionally and personally.

In addition to elective psychotherapeutic treatment, discussed below, the psychiatrist can be faced with the management of such patients in acute crisis when admitted to hospital. There may be escalating self-mutilation or para-suicidal behaviour, which is severely trying. The staff may start out as 'rescuers', feel themselves becoming 'victims' and ultimately become 'persecutors' themselves in a form of interpersonal enactment of the patient's problems. It becomes hard to remember that the patient who seems to demand so much, and be so powerful, actually feels utterly powerless inside. The sense of fragmentation and splitting inside the patient may be transferred to the ward team. Staff conflicts and multidisciplinary rivalries become heightened. As the staff feel increasingly impotent in the face of the patient's despair and regression, different disciplines or different specialists may be called in.

The psychiatrist has to recognise this process happening to enable staff to free themselves from such projections in order to work more effectively with the patient. Key attention should be placed on the need for setting boundaries, acknowledging limitations, and respecting the patient's autonomous adult functioning.

The voluntary sector and self-help organisations

There are a range of facilities available in Britain to help the adult who has been sexually abused, including Women's Aid, Rape Crisis, RSPCC and Relate. The local facilities may vary. For some patients, such a setting may feel less threatening. For others, the fact that they have already crossed the boundary into a psychiatric setting may lead them to wish to continue being a 'patient', which feels more secure.

The psychiatrist should be careful not to refer a patient on to a group without some personal knowledge of its reputation, competence and skills. The patient should have information about the approach that will be taken. Psychotherapy can be dangerous as well as helpful, although this, of course, applies within the psychiatric setting as well as elsewhere. The referring psychiatrist should be alert to problems that may occur when the therapy setting, albeit with the best of intentions, appears to reinforce some of the difficulties inherent in being sexually abused. For example, therapists may cross professional boundaries and become personally involved with clients. They may fail to set limits to the amount of time available. Sometimes, encouraging the client to express anger and rage against the offender is extended into an ideology that all men are bad, which may be counterproductive.

The statutory sector

Social work agencies may provide counselling services through such facilities as a Women's Resource Centre. They also have a vital statutory responsibility to investigate and protect children still at risk.

Specialist psychotherapy services

The specialist services are sufficiently under-resourced that it is impossible for them routinely to offer individual long-term therapy for all such patients. What may usually be available is a service for assessment, consultation and brief therapy. This can underpin the existing network of outpatient, day patient, group therapy, marital therapy and sex therapy facilities.

A special sexual abuse team working in a psychotherapy setting will optimally include or liaise with colleagues working in psychology, social work, forensic psychiatry and child and adolescent psychiatry.

The task of therapy

Many different theoretical models may be used to conceptualise the process of therapy. The one to be described here is based on psychoanalytic theory. Some aspects of the treatment approach may be similar to those adopted by therapists from non-psychoanalytic backgrounds. The terminology used can be translated into other frames of reference, although there are clear areas of divergence. Jehu gives a good summary of a cognitive and behavioural approach (Jehu 1988).

One of the unique features of a dynamic approach is the attention paid to the therapist as well as to the patient and to the interaction between them. It is assumed that aspects of the abusive situation will re-emerge within the transference-countertransference matrix. This has been described in an inpatient setting, but applies even if the therapy is brief and task oriented. Such an emotional re-enactment within the therapy relationship give an opportunity for understanding the essence of the problem.

To appreciate the task of therapy with these patients requires a knowledge of the nature of trauma. An experience is traumatic if the emotional pain that results cannot be dealt with. This mean not only that the normal defensive barriers against psychic pain are breached, but that the very capacity for dealing with such pain is lessened and the person becomes flooded with unmanageable and unimaginable feelings. She then has to resort to more primitive defences.

Bion developed Klein's notion that the baby projects his raw emotions into the mother (Bion 1962). She would 'contain' them and metabolise them so they could be tolerated again by the baby. This abstract metaphor is better understood with a concrete example related to a slightly older age. A toddler falls off a swing and bangs his head and screams. The mother feels intense fear as if it is she herself who is wounded. She will rush up and calm the child by her authority, her soothing manner and her use of his own familiar imagery to describe what is happening. At the same time, she will be dealing with her own feelings and thinking what needs practically to be done. She 'contains' his panic and distress. Another mother may be able only to convey her sense of the catastrophe, fuelling the child's own terror. The 'containing' capacity of the mother will be internalised and forms the basis of the child's own capacity to convert raw emotions into thought. He or she acquires an 'internalised container'.

A psychological trauma such as sex abuse is seen as damaging this internalised container itself (see Ch. 22). The pain cannot be metabolised or worked through, and cannot be thought about. The recourse for survival is primitive defences such as splitting, dissociation, denial and projection. The trauma is unthinkable, a situation which is reinforced by a public (family) context where it is unspeakable. The primary task of therapy is therefore to provide a setting where the abused person is able to face the pain (Joseph 1976) and to think about it. This requires a therapist who can set appropriate, secure boundaries to the therapeutic session, and who can tolerate intense disturbing feelings inside himself or herself.

With this basic task achieved, the therapist and patient can explore together the specific patterns of re-enactment and distorted thinking. Although the focus is on historical and current social relationships and on self-esteem, the therapist should be alert to potential re-enactment in the therapy setting. He or she should be able to interpret both the experience that the patient feels abused by therapy and that the patient may herself be treating the therapist in an abusive manner.

The delivery of therapy

Brief therapy

Brief therapy may be the optimum approach, at least in the first instance when many patients lack sufficient trust to embark on an open-ended therapy. Five to ten sessions of therapeutic work, although constituting mainly a prolonged assessment, may produce sufficient shift to enable the patient to continue working through the same issues on her own. When a brief therapy approach is employed, it is important to follow this up with continuing reviews of the patient. The opportunity for long-term therapy should be available if it is necessary. (For discussion of very brief therapy, see Barkham 1989.)

Long-term individual therapy

In practice, long-term individual therapy is available in few treatment settings due to scarcity of resources, in terms of both numbers of staff and the level of their training. For the disturbed patient, long-term therapy will mean many years of work at least once a week. This remains the preferred treatment for patients with severe disturbance who also have ego strengths and external support.

Case study 21.1   Long-term individual therapy with a sexual abuse survivor

Janet sought therapy at the age of 28 after her four-year-old daughter was taken into care. Janet had been systematically physically abusing the child. A second child had died at one year from obscure causes. She has always denied harming that child.

Her own background was unhappy. She was conceived in an extra-marital relationship and her mother married another man when Janet was two. Janet's stepfather sexually abused her until the age of five when her father took her back. At six, she was placed in a children's home and remained there until she was 16. Between the ages of eight and 12 she was further sexually assaulted in a particularly perverse and degrading way by a female care assistant. She attempted to describe this at the time but was ridiculed, and did not mention it for many years thereafter.

On leaving the home, she sought reunion with her mother, but this broke down due to her mother's jealousy of her stepfather's attention. After several suicide attempts, Janet received treatment in an adolescent unit which was one of the first good experiences she can recall. From then on, however, began a continuing pattern of sexual relationships with those in a professional caring relationship with her. Her first marriage, after a whirlwind romance, did not prove to be the 'Little House on the Prairie' she longed for. It broke up after their child was taken into care. Janet once more sought support from her mother, but fled when her stepfather again raped her.

She has been in therapy weekly for five years. There have been episodes of self-mutilation, depression and anxiety, but overall improvement.

The approach taken has been influenced by the work of Kernberg (1975) on borderline states. The major aim has been to provide support and concentrate on present-day realities. This has been done from a firm dynamic standpoint, being alert to the dangers of regression and acting out. Throughout, the transference relationship has been interpreted.

Janet has re-established herself in work. She has found considerable support from an Evangelical Church movement. She has remarried, to someone who had previously been in a caring role towards her, but had left this profession. The sexual difficulties that arose in this relationship brought to the surface more details of her earlier abuse. This remains one of the discussion points of her continuing therapy. She continues to be denied any access to her daughter, who remains in foster care.

Boundaries. Janet's primary caretakers did not respect her basic right to the privacy of her body. One of the reasons for her referral to a female psychotherapist was anxiety about the continuing sexual relationships she had with men looking after her. The failure to keep appropriate boundaries can be re-enacted in more subtle ways. Thus, for a considerable time, her therapist allowed the therapy sessions to run for 60 minutes instead of her usual 50 minutes, rationalising this as being due to the distance she had to travel. It took some time for recognition that this was a version of over-involvement.

Another area where boundaries had to be maintained was in terms of her longing for physical contact which at times was intense. She found it hard to tolerate being a patient with a therapist as opposed to the idealised mother she keeps seeking. At times of stress, she could not bear sitting in her chair and would wander around the room, often going to stand out of sight. She had thrown her arms around the therapist, or knelt at her feet, sobbing and clutching her legs. Extricating one's self from such predicaments in a firm but humane way is a difficult but essential task!

An area common in such cases, where boundaries do have to be breached for legal reasons, is the question of psychiatric reports. There was a continued monitoring of her progress via Child Abuse Case Conferences. It would be tempting for the psychiatrist to collude with a splitting, in which the psychiatrist is the apparently good object on the patient's side whereas the social work department and legal services are left to be seen as punitive and judgemental. In this instance, the fact that the psychiatrist did *not* deny her sense that the patient was potentially dangerous, and felt obliged to say so in a report, caused considerable distress. Ultimately, however, it meant that the patient herself could face exploring such awareness and the intense guilt that surfaced. She knew her therapist had already faced it and took it seriously. The therapist has to guard against idealising the 'victim' while ignoring the 'abuser' when the same patient has played both roles.

Transference. There was an apparent rapid development of trust, as is familiar when working with those who have spent considerable time in institutions. They have become accustomed to relating superficially to roles rather than individuals. Her new therapist became fused with her previous therapist in adolescence, with whom she remains in intermittent written contact. Behind this apparent therapeutic alliance, there was considerable censoring of certain feelings and testing of limits. The therapist was predominantly maintained as her fantasy idealised mother/therapist, who was an extension of herself. There would be anxiety and attack when the therapist's autonomy became evident, as when boundaries were set or her distorted perceptions were interpreted rather than colluded with. Rapidly, the therapist would switch from being seen as ideal to being seen as a self-interested, exploitative and aggressive person.

It took four years for Janet to be able fully to face the sexual abuse in the children's home. She no longer had her striking capacity for denial and splitting, and when she remarried she experienced neurotic symptoms. She suffered from vaginismus and felt phobic about sex. This was seen as her therapist's fault: 'I knew I shouldn't have told you anything'. Quite concretely the psychiatrist came to be viewed as the perverse, sadistic abuser of her childhood, triumphing over her humiliation. At the same time, the patient herself felt, the personification of evil, with the devil inside her. Her symptoms were neurotic, but the transference relationship had developed into a near-psychotic one. There is continuing gradual resolution of this phase.

Counter-transference. Faced with such borderline pathology, the counter-transference response was intense and at risk of being acted out in terms of excessive friendliness or the reverse, withdrawal. The real horror of some of Janet's experiences evoked not just concern and pity, but also disgust and rage. Hardest to contend with were feelings of impotence, fear, disbelief, hate and sexual arousal. Behind this was a growing sense of respect for Janet's resilience and capacity to survive. She has been able to face disturbing and painful aspects of herself.

Summary. This condensed account of work with a young woman who was sexually abused throughout childhood demonstrates some of the features commonly found. In adulthood, she found herself repeating some of her earlier experiences in terms of her relationships with men and her abuse of herself and her child. Within the therapeutic relationship, the therapist had to face being seen as an abuser and to encounter a range of disturbing feelings.

Group therapy

Group therapeutic approaches on a focal basis for these patients may have significant advantages over individual therapy. The patient no longer feels unique, and recognises that others have endured similar circumstances, with similar results. Things she is blind to in herself she can see in others. There may be considerable social support and cohesion.

In the first instance, it is often the therapist who can see these advantages rather than the patient. Most of the published surveys acknowledge some difficulty in accumulating patients either because of patient resistance or therapist exclusion criteria (Herman & Schatzow 1984, Goodman & Nowak-Scibelli 1985, Bergart 1986, Douglas & Matson 1989). It may well be that to enable the patients to gain maximum benefit from this modality they should have previous or concurrent individual therapy.

Family therapy

Most adult psychiatrists are less familiar with family approaches than are child and adolescent psychiatrists. When working with adult survivors of childhood sexual abuse, it is imperative to consider both the family of origin and the present family. The major factors to consider in the family of origin include the impact of potential disclosure on the patient's parents and siblings, and the possibility that other children are at risk. For a mother to learn that her daughter has been sexually abused can be a devastating blow, leading to tremendous guilt and anxiety. If the offender himself is still within the family, he may for the first time have to face his own behaviour. Non-abused siblings are also troubled, feeling guilty or even excluded. Sisters may wonder if it will happen to them – and even feel jealous. Brothers become troubled because they have not protected their sister, and if the father is the offender they worry that they may turn out like him. They often experience considerable anger towards the father which may erupt into violence.

Within the patient's current family, if she is married, the reaction of her spouse may be anger, revulsion, incomprehension or even guilt. If he experiences some revulsion not only towards the act itself, but also towards his wife, he often knows also that such feelings would be potentially damaging if they were expressed. Another issue for such families is how to raise their own children appropriately and protect them from sexual abuse, without being over-protective.

When taking an adult into therapy focusing on her sexual abuse as a child, provision should be made available for other family members, including her husband, to have direct access to therapy either individually or as part of family therapy. It should also be considered that the perpetrator may seek help. This is rarely provided in the same setting, but alternatives should be available. The serious matter of children still at risk is addressed later.

Sex therapy

Many patients who have been sexually abused understandably have difficulties with sexuality in adulthood. In these cases, the traditional modified Masters & Johnston approach to sex therapy, which ignores the historical antecedents, may be ineffective. There is often a degree of phobic formation. For instance, if a woman has been inappropriately fondled in childhood, she may not be able to tolerate foreplay, rushing to intercourse before she is aroused. Typically, sexually abused women report flashbacks during sexual activity in which they recall the experience in childhood while their partner engages in similar activity. Some women do not feel anxious, but continue to experience the dissociation they learnt long ago, remaining cold and detached. To facilitate sex therapy, some preliminary individual psychotherapy to explore the sexual abuse may be required. A particularly difficult issue for the sex therapist is if the woman has confided the sexual abuse to him or her but not to her partner, and the dynamic of secrecy is alive once more in the therapy setting (Jehu 1988, Tsai & Wagner 1978). The therapist should advise the patient that this is a dilemma, and have her at least acknowledge to her husband that something bad happened in childhood that she cannot yet talk about.

Special problems

Children at risk

It is crucial that the psychiatrist be alert to the possibility that the abuser is continuing to offend. The patient should be questioned about young children in contact with the perpetrator. In the first instance, the patient herself may feel able to alert relatives and investigate the situation. It is incumbent on the psychiatrist, however, to alert the social services if the risk appears significant, even when the patient herself wishes confidentiality to be preserved. If in doubt, the psychiatrist should discuss the case with colleagues and with his or her defence union.

The person who has been abused by a therapist

Working in the field of sexual abuse, one learns that the re-enactment occurs even with professional colleagues. This is especially disturbing, both when the patient gives hints about who the person is, and when she actually reveals the truth and it is someone known to the psychiatrist. It is inconsistent to assume that patients are telling the truth about domestic abuse, but lying about professional abuse. Therapists do occasionally abuse patients. It is also true that psychotic transferences occur and patients distort reality. Each instance has to be dealt with in an appropriate professional manner, seeking information where feasible, and eschewing both collusion and minimisation of the offence, or condemnation and witch-hunting.

CONCLUSION

Psychotherapy with people who have been sexually abused is a difficult area of work which may lead to considerable professional stress, often exacerbated by the insufficiency of resources to meet the increasing demand for help. Much remains to be learnt about the outcome of psychotherapeutic intervention, both in childhood and in later adult life. Long-term prospective research is required.

FURTHER READING

Jehu D 1988 Beyond sexual abuse. Therapy with women who were childhood victims. Wiley, Chichester
Porter R (ed) 1984 Child sexual abuse within the family. Tavistock Publications, London

22. External disasters and the internal world: an approach to psychotherapeutic understanding of survivors

Caroline Garland

INTRODUCTION

Since the fire in the football stadium at Bradford in May 1985, Britain has had an extraordinary run of major public disasters: the capsizing of the *Herald of Free Enterprise* in March 1987, the Kings Cross fire in November 1987, the massacre at Hungerford in August 1988, the Clapham train crash, and the sabotaged aircraft at Lockerbie, both in December 1988. 1989 was no better. In January came the air-crash on the M1, and in April the Hillsborough football stadium disaster; in July, the Piper Alpha oil-rig exploded. The list is not complete, because it is not the task of this chapter to speculate about the economic, sociological and psychological factors that contribute to the creation of an 'accident', but it needs to be acknowledged that the way all of us ignore disaster warnings is well-documented: foam-filled furniture, unstable ferries, bombs on aeroplanes, the nuclear threat. It implies a universal acquiescence, even a faint but hideously seductive unconscious pull towards the idea of an accident *over there*, not here. The fantasy is that intolerable states of helplessness can be projected on a massive scale, followed by a dedicated repairing of that state of affairs, a determination to see it will never happen again, both in the individual and in the larger group. Disasters of this kind have a tremendous and lasting impact on those caught up in them – survivors, the bereaved, the emergency services, relief workers, social services, local psychiatric and psychological services, the community at large, in ever widening if diminishing waves of disturbance. This is implicitly acknowledged in the way disasters are named after their location. It implies an effect upon an entire social network, not just a large number of individuals.

These major public events draw attention forcibly to the effects of sudden and violent death upon those who have escaped, but they also serve as a reminder of the thousands of similar private disasters that get no more than a paragraph in a local paper. The terrible and endless toll of road accidents; the nightmare of house fires; drownings; accidents on building sites. The survivors and the bereaved suffer the same conse-

507

quences with less public attention and support. They may form a considerable part of the population at a general practice surgery, or in the outpatient sector of many departments of psychiatry.

In this chapter, some features of the response to a 'traumatic' event will be discussed. It is hoped that through conceptualising what happens to the internal world of the survivor of an identifiable external disaster, a paradigm will evolve for understanding something of what happens to the mind, and its struggle to adapt, in other kinds of personal private traumata. The impact may be less public, dramatic or sudden, but the processes are essentially the same whether the cause is physical or sexual abuse, abandonment by a parent, the death of one's child, sexual betrayal, divorce, loss of employment, loss of one's country. The response to each of these has its own characteristic profile, but they also have something in common: the breaking down of established defences which are found to be inadequate to deal with the intensity of the event, the releasing of primitive horrors (Winnicott 1974) and the consequent disruption and disintegration of existing mental organisation, with long-lasting consequences for the personality. An external disaster, therefore, provides an extreme, sudden, speeded-up and highly visible version of processes that are part of the experience of being alive: the constant balancing act, the feats of adjustment needed to sustain an equilibrium in the face of a changing and unpredictable environment.

As an example, the psychological impact on the survivors of the experience of an industrial accident, a fire in which there were a number of deaths, will be examined. This paper is less about the immediate aftermath, which is increasingly well organised and provided for by local emergency and social services (McCready 1989), than about something more unpredictable, the longer-term outcome for the individual. The argument is based on the following hypothesis: although the initial impact of a disaster, in the first weeks, does indeed produce a 'normal' response in everyone (the phrase one hears quoted constantly to survivors is: 'This is a normal response in a normal person to an abnormal event'), what happens later on is, by contrast, unique to that individual. In that sense, it loses its average or ordinary quality, precisely because the traumatic event in the present will link up quite specifically and in a peculiarly locked-in and intractable way with whatever is already damaged or flawed from the survivor's own past. The presentation of the trauma in the present will increasingly come to incorporate features and take on some of the emotional colouring of the trauma of the past, which up to that point may have been more or less invisible and, indeed, unknown.

The hypothesis raises difficult issues. Why should being the survivor of a disaster in which others died appear to have such a lasting and radical effect on the personality? What is the nature of the interaction between event and personality that lodges it so securely and so centrally in the mind? One of its most noticeable consequences is that the event appears to *alter the survivor's capacity for symbolic thinking*; at its simplest, it alters the capacity to 'imagine' something quite vividly, while simultaneously knowing that the event is not taking place in external reality. Of course, in both conscious and (far more importantly) unconscious phantasy, fears of one's own annihilation and omnipotent wishes for the destruction of others exist in everyone. It seems as though once such phantasies have been actualised, made flesh, whether or not one bore any actual responsibility for their happening, then thought, imagination and phantasy can no longer be experienced confidently as distinct from the external reality. The thought itself becomes the agent of the event, and the memory *is* the event itself. This may be a crucial factor when it comes to the difficult area of treatment, since the capacity for symbolisation, and for thinking 'about' something (an event which itself is over) is a necessary part of working through – of dealing with, of laying to rest – a psychically painful experience.

TRAUMA

Trauma is a Greek word meaning 'to pierce'. We hear it used most often of physical injuries where the skin is broken – where something once intact has been breached. It suggests that the event which creates the breach is of a certain intensity, or violence – and the consequences for the organisation of the organism are long-lasting. From there, it is a small step to the metaphorical use of the concept, to the sense of an event which in the same intense or violent way ruptures the protective layer that surrounds the mind, with equally long-lasting consequences for psychic organisation. Freud (1920) wrote: 'We describe as "traumatic" any excitations from outside which are powerful enough to break through the protective shield...the concept of trauma necessarily implies a connection...with a breach in an otherwise efficacious barrier against stimuli.' The breach in the stimulus barrier has profound economic consequences: it presents the mind 'with an increase of stimulus too powerful to be dealt with or worked off in the normal way, and thus must result in permanent disturbances of the manner in which the energy operates.'

Although he never abandoned the sense of a trauma as an event which overwhelmed the mind through its magnitude, its quantity rather than quality, in other ways Freud's thinking on psychic trauma evolved over the years. In the 1880s, a traumatic event in an individual's past could be inferred from symptomatic behaviour in the present. The two were causally linked but in a dissociated form. The implication was that if the event were recalled and worked through, the symptoms would resolve. The realisation that reported events often turned out to have been imagined, led Freud to an understanding of the importance of fantasy in psychic functioning and psychosexual development. The trauma was seen to be connected with unacceptable levels of excitation from primarily internal sources. Ideas about treatment concerned the reconstruction of the event in such a way that it could be assimilated and integrated into psychic functioning in a consciously acknowledged form, instead of remaining split off and compulsively repeated. The model implied here involves a more or less discrete event, lodged as a foreign body in the mind, whose vestigial memory traces, or finger-prints, could be followed like clues until the causative event was recovered.

Nearly forty years later, in Beyond the Pleasure Principle (1920) – and, significantly, just after the end of 'the terrible war' – Freud is using a different model: that of a mental apparatus, the ego, whose proper functioning depends upon the filtering, distribution and effective management of the quantities of stimulation that flow into it, from both external and internal sources. At this point, the notion of trauma implied an organisation, that of the mind, invaded by stimulation so intense that normal psychic activity is devastatingly 'paralysed and reduced', since the mind's overriding task is to muster all its available energy to bind or immobilise the unmanageable quantities of excitation pouring through the breach in the protective shield. By now, Freud is giving due importance to the shattering effect of certain life-threatening *external* events.

In spite of the rather old-fashioned terminology, this description by Freud remains a vivid and accurate evocation of the states of mind encountered in the survivors of any of the recent major disasters. There is a terrible sameness about the effect of their immediate impact, whatever the cause and however varied the long-term outcome. The things that happen to people and what they say about the helplessness and confusion and loss is, because of the almost audible struggle with the limitations of language at such a moment, deeply poignant. 'It was like a battlefield. It was absolutely awful – I was so helpless. Unless you were there you couldn't imagine it. It was awful – and there was nothing you could do.' Through the very inarticulacy created by the scale of the breach in the protective shield, one experiences a projected fraction of the helplessness that overwhelmed the survivor: the blasting away of his normal psychic systems of mastery, control and defence, to leave him unprotected, dis-integrated, and suffering acute mental pain in the struggle to restore some kind of equilibrium.

Freud's description also encompasses the collection of symptoms that constitute the diagnostic criteria in DSM-III-R for Post-Traumatic Stress Disorder (PTSD). It offers a theory of why those particular symptoms should exist, a rationale for their relation to each other, and an argument for their sequential development over time.

Post-Traumatic Stress Disorder (DSM-III-R)

A. The person has experienced an event that is outside the range of usual human experience and that would be markedly distressing to almost anyone, e.g. serious threat to one's life or physical integrity; serious threat or harm to one's children, spouse, or other close relative and friends; sudden destruction of one's home or community; or seeing another person who has recently been, or is being, seriously injured or killed as the result of an accident or physical violence.

B. The traumatic event is persistently re-experienced in at least one of the following ways:

1. recurrent and intrusive distressing recollections of the event (in young children, repetitive play in which themes or aspects of the trauma are expressed)
2. recurrent distressing dreams of the event
3. sudden acting or feeling as if the traumatic event were recurring (includes a sense of reliving the experience, illusions, hallucinations, and dissociative (flashback) episodes, even those that occur upon awakening or when intoxicated
4. intense psychological distress at exposure to events that symbolise or resemble an aspect of the traumatic event, including anniversaries of the trauma.

C. Persistent avoidance of stimuli associated with the trauma or numbing of general responsiveness (not present before the trauma), as indicated by at least three of the following:

1. efforts to avoid thoughts or feelings associated with the trauma
2. efforts to avoid activities or situations that arouse recollections of the trauma
3. inability to recall an important aspect of the trauma (psychogenic amnesia)
4. markedly diminished interest in significant activities (in young children, loss of recently acquired developmental skills such as toilet training or language skills)
5. feeling of detachment or estrangement from others
6. restricted range of affect, e.g. unable to have loving feelings
7. sense of a foreshortened future, e.g. does not expect to have a career, marriage or children, or a long life.

D. Persistent symptoms of increased arousal (not present before the trauma), as indicated by at least two of the following:

1. difficulty falling or staying asleep
2. irritability or outbursts of anger
3. difficulty concentrating
4. hypervigilance
5. exaggerated startle response
6. physiologic reactivity upon exposure to events that symbolise or resemble an aspect of the traumatic event (e.g. a woman who was raped in an elevator breaks out in a sweat when entering any elevator).

E. Duration of the disturbance (symptoms in B, C, and D) of at least one month.

If, as I hope to show, one adds to this formulation of Freud's an understanding of Bion's (1962, 1970) theory on the development of the capacity for thought (coherent directed mental activity), and Segal's (1957) thinking on the capacity to symbolise, one has a way not just of understanding the existence of the symptoms themselves, but also a rationale for their alleviation.

Many later psychoanalysts – Fenichel (1937), Kris (1956), Sandler (1967), Greenacre (1967), Furst (1967, 1978), Anna Freud (1967), Yorke (1986), Goldschmidt (1986) and others – have continued to explore the concept of psychic trauma. Their aim has been to clarify and develop the central issues – the interplay of external and internal forces, objective and subjective factors, that contributes to the nature and severity of the trauma, to the possibility of re-integration, and so to the eventual outcome for a given individual.

Even holding constant the nature of the external event, there are obvious sources of profound individual difference: for example, in constitutional factors, such as differences in pain or sensory thresholds; in earliest experiences, such as the mother's capacity to function as an auxiliary ego, a protective shield suited to her particular baby's temperament and needs; in the timing of the trauma in relation to the stage of psychic development and its associated phantasies. At one extreme, these predisposing factors, vividly revealed through psychoanalytically-based treatment, can sometimes seem to diminish the decisive quality of the traumatic event itself. And, of course, in one way questions about the relative contributions of external and internal factors in a trauma are only an extreme version of perennial questions about the relation between perception and experience, and its connection with development – about the nature of mind itself. As I have already suggested, a disaster presents us with an acute and dramatically visible version of this problem.

The alternative position, one that seems the more pressing the closer we are in time and space to the event itself, is that the overwhelming nature of the disaster over-rides individual differences to create a homogenous traumatised response. Throughout the literature (Yorke 1986, Cooper 1986, Hamilton 1988), we can detect a sort of gentleman's agreement that there are some events whose shocking and horrific nature could not be expected to leave intact even the most integrated and sturdy of psychic organisations. Freud (1920) writes, 'where the strength of a trauma exceeds a certain limit this factor (namely a well-prepared system) will no doubt cease to carry weight.' The remarkable and detailed work on the survivors of the Nazi concentration camps (Krystal 1968, Pines 1986) are among the best documented accounts of the permanent and irreversible effects on mental functioning of events more systematically, intentionally and perversely horrific than anything in recorded history.

INTERVIEWING SURVIVORS

A technique of interviewing will now be described, developed in the Unit for the Study of Trauma and its Aftermath in the Tavistock Clinic, as a result of seeing many individuals referred for assessment several months, or even years after a traumatic event. It is worth noting that the effects of traumatic events may be managed through repression for years, and break through only after a further incident that may in itself seem trivial; or after a life-event, such as retirement, a bereavement, or moving house, which disrupts a precarious equilibrium. Routine psychiatric history-taking might therefore include enquiry about previous accidents and traumatic losses. We have concentrated on the understanding and treatment of the survivors, rather than the bereaved, whom we felt were already better understood and presented different, though related problems. Of course, many survivors are both, and the sequelae of survival are compounded by those of bereavement and vice-versa, leading sometimes to the classical picture of melancholia described by Freud in his great paper, 'Mourning and Melancholia' (1917).

All survivors seen four months or more after a traumatic event have been offered the same interview procedure. Some time needs to elapse following the event before an interview of this kind can usefully be conducted: earlier on, something slightly different is needed (discussed below in the section on Treatment). Offered too soon or too eagerly, the interview could compound the disturbance where the passage of time, support from family, friends and the local general practitioner or bereavement counsellor might have been successful on their own. However, if symptoms persist, and personal relationships and work deteriorate, such an interview can have a considerable therapeutic value, as well as a potential assessment and research function.

Survivors are interviewed for between two and two-and-a-half hours each (it is essential to provide a long initial appointment), and then offered at least two follow-up appointments, the first of which is two to four weeks later. The intention is to explore the interaction between event and individual as fully as possible, given the framework of an open-ended interview. Although there are a number of questions to which, by the end of the interview, answers are wanted, in practice they rarely have to be asked systematically: a long and deep interview makes it possible for the material to emerge in a natural way. However, by the end of the interview, the therapist hopes to have material on family background and childhood history; early illnesses, accidents or separations; dreams before as well as after the event; early memories of each parent; work experience; current family status and, most importantly, some sort of feel for the development of, and capacity for, significant relationships both past and present. This last emerges, as in all psychodynamic interviewing, through a careful use of the interviewer's counter-transference, as well as from the historical facts.

The interview with a survivor begins with the invitation to talk about what seems most pressing at that moment. Some immediately give an account of their experience in the disaster. Others prefer to begin by talking about their background and early history, knowing from the appointment letter that the therapist has an interest in this and that over two hours are available for the meeting. These interviews are not assessments for psychotherapy, in that the implicit contract does not focus on interpretations in the transference; but neither is it avoided when it seems important. It is often useful to make links between the past and the present as the story progresses.

Although a recent research project has made use of both tape recordings and questionnaires, the Unit's most usual technique involves only a highly attentive and inevitably involved listener. Nevertheless, and not surprisingly, it takes a while in each case for 'the story' to begin. By 'story' is meant less a formal account of events in an orderly progression, minute by minute (as it might be for an official public enquiry) but, instead, a narrative in which what is recounted, and the way in which it is told – the details given special attention, their order, the way they are linked in time, the associated emotions, the mood that pervades the telling – has a profound personal meaning. Several interviewees gave their first version of events in just such a formal 'public enquiry' manner, repeating the words they had used to countless interviewers, both official and unofficial, beforehand. The state of affairs in which 'the story' could begin took over when the interviewee seemed to feel the interviewer had made contact at a deeper, more personal level, and that (perhaps above all) there was going to be enough time to think and reflect together on events and their significance. Sometimes, this meant that the 'official' version of event given at the outset was elaborated later in the interview with quite a different feeling and colour to it: it was told to a particular person in a particular way, with the intention of making contact rather than fending it off.

THE DISASTER

In February 1987, a fire occurred in an industrial complex on the edges of a small manufacturing town in the north-east of England. It took place in a factory undergoing modernisation of its plant while attempting at the same time to continue normal production. There were, at that time, difficulties in the management which compounded the degree of disorganisation that provided the context for the fire, which began with an electrical fault in a small enclosed storage space underground. The fire quickly developed an intense ferocity as it built up within an enclosed space, erupting into a large underground area with which various sectors of the manufacturing process connected, and which was temporarily being used as storage for drums of chemicals, as well as recently disused machinery, thousands of litres of oil paint, and oil waste, all awaiting disposal elsewhere. The factory was at the point at which the day and the night shifts were exchanging, and there were larger numbers of people than usual in the corridors leading off the central area. At first, the fire seemed small and easily containable with existing fire-fighting equipment, but as the word spread that there was trouble, panic began, which became acute as the lighting system failed. The heat built up rapidly, the oil waste ignited, and within minutes a fireball exploded, killing eight people who had already failed to find their way back out of the central area to alternative exits.

From this event, the author has chosen to present individuals who were either not at all physically injured or only slightly so, in order to focus on trauma that has its origin in mental structures, and their disruption.

Case study 22.1   The clerical assistant who survived

This is the case of a woman who has not worked since the fire, and who has remained virtually housebound, suffering from depression and anxiety. Miss A, a woman in her early 30s, a clerical assistant, had been in the ladies' washroom off the central area getting ready for a meeting with her boyfriend. She remained trapped there for some four hours, that is to say for the duration of the fire. Once she saw and smelt smoke seeping through a ventilator grille, she tried to leave; she briefly opened the door into the central area and become instantly aware of the impossibility of escape through the inferno, the choking black smoke and utter absence of visibility. She was extremely frightened. She saw no way out. Taking some evasive action (covering the ventilator grille and wedging her coat along the bottom of the door) she retreated as far back from the door as possible, sometimes weeping, sometimes calling for help through another small grille at the back of the washroom that seemed to have fresh air coming through it, and so perhaps gave onto an area of safety. Overwhelming during the four hour period was her sense of utter helplessness, of being trapped in a hopeless situation in which she was bound to die in a peculiarly horrible way, and from which no-one could save her. She spent that time, she said, 'waiting to die', and she meant it quite literally. Some hours later, things seemed to be quiet and still enough outside to risk opening the door a fraction – and eventually she picked her way out through the pitch dark, smoking, devastated and sodden storage area to the outside.

Miss A then went on to talk about her background, the most relevant parts of which are given here. She was born in the North of England, one of nine children very few of whom had the same father. She herself had had a black father, and it showed, though for years her mother denied that there was any difference between any of her children. When she was four, and again at a later age, she and a sibling were put into care while younger children were born, and this was for her a terrible experience. This interview turned out to be the first time she had spoken about these events to anyone other than the sister with whom she had shared them. Two of the care assistants in this home systematically physically abused the two small girls, in a way that horrifies but no longer surprises us. Threats of being killed altogether made them terrified to tell anyone of what was happening, and, most significant for our purposes today, Miss A described in a bemused way her own passivity and compliance, her lack of protest, as night after night the children would be woken and taken to the bathroom for these rituals to be enacted.

Also crucial in her childhood were the deaths of two of her siblings from muscular dystrophy, one at the age of 11 when Miss A was eight, and one at 13 when Miss A was one year older at 14, and was very involved in the care of her dying sibling. This second death was particularly painful: the child had her sisters sleeping in the bed with her to keep her warm as she grew iller and iller, but Miss A felt that even before her sister died she had become like a corpse. The dying child developed pneumonia and was so frightened she would not lie down to sleep any more; she got her sisters to stay up with her night after night. After a week she was exhausted, and with the pneumonia raging in her she died one afternoon, held up by her sisters, with her head in her mother's lap. Miss A remembers her mother crying for two years after this second death, though she herself never cried.

After one has done a number of these interviews, one can begin to sense that for each individual involved there was a moment – perhaps a sight, perhaps a sound, sometimes the memory of an effort that failed – that formed a kind of focus for mental activity around the topic of the trauma and on which the memory would home-in repeatedly. It often represented to the survivor something that he or she recognised as 'the worst moment', and there can be a point in the interview at which, if the answer is not already apparent, it becomes possible to say, 'What was the worst moment for you?' It is always a difficult question to ask. It is also often unnecessary and is not being recommended as an invariable point of technique. For the survivor, it can be highly intrusive; for the interviewer, it is risky because if one cannot remain truly open to the answer, whatever it may be, the contact is lost and the interview slips away at the most important level.

Case study 22.1   (contd)

However, at a certain moment the interviewer put that question to Miss A. She was silent for while, looking at her hands in her lap, and then she began to cry. She apologised and said she had done no crying about the fire, she had just felt numb; she couldn't see why she should be crying now. She then said, repeating the interviewer's words, that the worst moment had been when, sitting helplessly on a chair trapped in this little room, knowing if she opened the door she would die too, she had heard two of her colleagues choking to death in the smoke outside. They were coughing, choking and vomiting, and calling out, 'Oh God, oh God', and choking some more. And she had sat on the other side of the door rooted to the spot, feeling a deathly lethargy invading her body and mind, listening. It was not as if, she said, she could have saved them. She knew if she tried to go out there to bring them in she too would die. But, she said, very thoughtfully and painfully, she knew that that was not the real reason why she hadn't moved. She had felt paralysed; she couldn't have moved even if she'd wanted to. Eventually, there was silence, and she knew they were dead. She wept for some time, scrubbing at her face with a Kleenex, continuing to apologise for crying now when she never had done before.

Such a moment, for some characterised as 'the worst moment', represents perhaps the opening stages in the development of an adult version of a screen memory (Freud 1899); that is to say, the compressing, concentrating and focusing of a series of events into a single sight, sound or even smell which comes to stand, sometimes indirectly, for the whole. The Unit's experience of these interviews has been that when whatever has lodged most vividly with the survivor is looked at in detail, is as it were unpacked, it is found to link with indelible but repressed childhood memories. These may be conscious memories from which the accompanying affect has been repressed, as I think was the case with Miss A; while, for some survivors, the link may be beyond that, through every defence, to the situation described by Winnicott (1974) in which a state of breakdown had existed before it was capable of being recognised for what it was.

The specificity of the link between Miss A's childhood feelings of paralysis when terrible things were happening both to her and to others, her conviction that there was absolutely no-one who would hear and help (no helpful object), her helplessness over her siblings' choking deaths, and her experiences in the fire must be immediately obvious. She herself was unusually in touch with painful and complicating feelings of rivalry with the dead siblings, both those at home and those in the fire, and the sort of guilt that this produced. Miss A went on to describe her current difficulties: on a visit to the one member of her family with whom she is still in touch, she became uncontrollably panicky when it grew foggy outside. The fog was 'known' to be fog, but could not be experienced as anything other than smoke. All the doors and windows had to be tightly shut to ward it off, and she did not recover until the fog cleared. The capacity to distinguish reality from fantasy had been obliterated in all but a very small, split-off area of the mind; in the larger part, symbolisation had gone and concrete thinking predominated. She described as 'weird' her experience of holding in a small part of her conscious mind the thin and insubstantial knowledge that this was indeed fog, and harmless, while her overwhelming experience, her real conviction, was that she was in intense danger from the 'smoke' that surrounded her.

THE THEORETICAL FRAMEWORK

Bion and containment

A framework will now be offered for thinking about the problem of trauma as it has come to be seen in the survivors interviewed by the author and co-workers – about the interaction between external event and internal world. This framework is based on the work of Wilfred Bion (1962, 1970). Bion's understanding of what happens during the course of development between two people, a mother and an infant, involves most crucially the notion of containment and, through containment, transformation of what is unthinkable into what can be thought about. The raw sense-perceptions that form the primary material of the infant's experience cannot in their original state be thought about, they can only be got rid of, through projective identification.

Projective identification is the name first given by Melanie Klein (1946) to an intra-psychic process whereby unwanted feelings, perceptions, attitudes, thoughts and fantasies are projected out of the self and perceived to be situated in the object. The object then becomes, in the mind of the projector, identified with those same feelings, attitudes, thoughts or fantasies. Although it was described as an omnipotent fantasy in that it paid very little attention to the actual properties of the object, by some process still not yet fully understood (but recognised in current psychoanalytic practice to be at the heart of much that goes on between people), the external object can be induced to feel or think or behave as though he or she did indeed possess these attributed properties – in other words, the object can get caught up in the reciprocal and complementary state of *introjective identification*.

Thus, although projective identification is, indeed, primarily an omnipotent fantasy in which the actual properties of the external object are ignored, it can be seen that something less omnipotent and more in touch with the object's own reality must be going on when the object is successfully induced to act as host to the projected or evacuated states of mind. For them to be taken in and (effectively) adopted, there must be some degree of fit with something already present in the object. Bion's view is that projective identification is not only the infant's primary way of dealing with unmanageable levels of distress, through getting rid of them wholesale, but it is also his earliest means of communication. It is how he lets his mother know what he is feeling like at a stage before other means of communication are available. The parent's capacity to contain the infant's anxieties without being overwhelmed by them – to know what sort of state of affairs exists in the infant without becoming too identified with it through introjection – enables the infant to begin to order and make sense of his own experience.

Since an external disaster plunges the survivor back into a position of extremity, into the prolonged helplessness that characterises the earliest stages of infancy, inevitably projective identification becomes the primary means of managing it. The survivor is making a desperate and unconscious attempt to rid himself of intolerable states of terror and helplessness, and at the same time to let the object know about the condition of his internal world so that something can be done about it. Part of what is characterised as a 'state of shock' involves the loss of the ability to communicate effectively through any means other than projective identification (see the section below on Treatment).

An individual's permeability to attempts by others to communicate through projective identification varies; in some, it can be part of a formalised professional defence to avoid it. In psychoanalysis, or psychoanalytic therapy, however, its reception, its understanding and its use form an essential part of the struggle to work effectively. Some understanding of the nature of this process is helpful for anyone working in any capacity with survivors, since their inevitable resort to projective identification as a means of communicating and evacuating intense anxiety can be seen operating vividly in the relationships that may develop between survivors and front-line helpers, for example the emergency services. It plays a major part in the way that rescue workers are so at risk of becoming 'secondary casualties' themselves.

Bion develops Klein's ideas about projective identification in his own attempt to formulate what goes on between the infant and its mother that results in the baby's beginning to develop its own thought processes. A mother who is capable of containing her baby's projection into her of its intolerable states, its being filled with something unthinkably awful, and in particular the fear of annihilation, can by holding these projections inside her without being impelled to action, do something with them that, in Bion's word, 'detoxifies' them; transforming them into something manageable and meaningful. Moreover, a baby with a more or less successfully containing parent eventually takes into itself that very 'capacity to contain' that is the parent's own. The development of this internal container, a space in which thoughts and thinking can happen, is the development of an apparatus (to use Bion's word) for doing something with thoughts, for making sense of an experience, using it to learn from, and managing it progressively through symbolisation. Bion is talking about the development of mind itself. Bion's formulation, even in such a condensed form, seems highly relevant to the understanding and treatment of survivors, in whom the renewed experience of the fear of dying has breached and flooded not just the external stimulus barrier, not just the internal barrier between unconscious and conscious, stirring up again the most primitive horrors about annihilation, but the structure of the internal container, the thinking apparatus itself.

SEGAL AND SYMBOLISATION

What we see in the survivor, therefore, is a breakdown. It is imposed by a massive upheaval in the external environment which is followed by an equally massive upheaval and disruption in the internal world. Something unmanageable has happened, and a state of extreme helplessness ensues. All the survivor's defences have been overwhelmed and he is flooded by persecutory anxiety of a quite overwhelming kind and degree. It is a forcible return to a position in which the world seems an entirely dangerous and hostile place, and where such feelings are confirmed by external reality. There is no potential for waking up from the nightmare. Hanna Segal, whose work on symbol formation (1981) is basic to this chapter, writes, 'If the anxieties are too strong, a regression to the paranoid-schizoid position can occur at any stage of the individual's development and projective identification may be resorted to as a defence against anxiety'.

Although her paper predates Bion's, Segal's work provides an essential link between Bion's theory of an apparatus for dealing with thoughts, and the development of the depressive position: the recognition of the object as separate from the self, no longer under one's omnipotent control, and consequently capable of generating both loving and hating feelings towards itself. Segal views as an essential corollary of the depressive position the development of proper symbolisation, a movement forward from the kind of concrete thinking (characteristic of the paranoid/schizoid position) that results in symbolic equations: that is to say, the creation of something that is not a symbol proper, but which, although a substitute for the original object, *is treated as and felt to be no different from it.* In the example given earlier, fog no longer stands for smoke, it *is* smoke. The original object, the mother who is also the fog, is no longer merely foggy (obscuring the reality, the truth), she is the danger itself, a thoroughly bad object, undifferentiated from, *the same as* the danger from which she failed to protect her child. The original disturbance in the relation between the ego and its object, the developing child and the mother, is recreated most vividly in the events of the fire, in the 'waiting to die', and in the unhelped and unhelpable siblings, the paralysed sitting by as they choke to death. Segal points out that where there is only a partial attainment of the depressive position, and of whole-object relations, the result can be a split-off area in which earlier, unintegrated ego experiences are retained in a sealed-off pocket of vulnerability whose existence forms a 'constant threat to stability. At worst a mental breakdown occurs and earlier anxieties and split-off symbolic equations invade the ego'.

Can we assume that any parent has been able to function as a perfect container? Isolated pockets of disturbance, of madness, of raw untransformed primitive experience, inhabit us all. We can be skilful, or we can be just lucky, and they may never emerge fully into the light of day; but whatever the nature of the degree of failure in the original relationship with the primary object, the experience of an external disaster will seek it out and give it fresh life and fresh significance.

Thus, the suggestion is that the breakdown, the gross disruption of mental functioning occurring in a disaster, taps directly into, and joins up with, what Bion would call the psychotic part of the personality, or Segal would call an 'isolated pocket of schizophrenia'. Healthy and necessary splits are broken down, and pre-existing structures and functions arc rendercd uselessly chaotic. Thinking (the ability to do something constructive with thoughts) is lost; the mind is invaded by raw sense data *both from without (the disaster) and within (untransformed raw elements of experience)*. Segal's view is that the infant introjects the transforming adult, the maternal object, in the form of a container, the internal space in which the infant's own thinking can develop. In a disaster, the internal container is lost, its walls are breached, and what space there was is filled with the raw data of the disaster itself: images of death, disintegration, sounds and smells of destruction, all accompanied by the most intense fear – that of annihilation.

Not surprisingly, there comes a moment for many who actually survived when the balance between the wish to go on living, and the wish to let go, if only to end the seeing and experiencing of what was happening, is on a knife edge. And this is a struggle that can continue long after the actual event has been survived. The experience of 'the flashback' is the repetition of the loss of the container. The sense of being taken over once more by unmanageable experience is exceedingly powerful. Thinking is obliterated again; it is the disaster itself that is creating the mental activity, running the mind, filling every space, until the subjective experience of possession by the event is absolute.

Thus, to understand fully the nature of the breakdown that is imposed on mental functioning by a disaster, and its long-term consequences, it is suggested that it is necessary to link these three formulations – Freud's notion of the sudden breaking down of the stimulus barrier, Bion's theory of the development of an apparatus for thinking, and (intimately related to it) Segal's understanding of the development of a capacity to symbolise.

Binding

I should like to add to the above a brief consideration of what Freud (1920) called 'binding'. Freud described binding as what the mind struggles to do in order to restrict the free flowing of extreme influxes of excitation, as for example in a disaster. By creating links with what is already there, by joining up what pours in with an existing feature or function of the mind, the ego is attempting to create once more structures of some permanence in which ego functioning is possible. In Freud's final theory of instincts, binding was felt to be a part of the life instincts ('the aim of Eros is to establish even greater unities'), unlike its opposite, unbinding or the breaking of links, leading to disintegration and destruction (Freud 1940). The central difficulty with a disaster lies, I believe, right here: the very intensity of the struggle to deal with the flood of unmanageable material *in the absence of the apparatus for thinking itself* locks that material powerfully and precisely to whatever has been released by the breaking down of internal barriers and structures. A disaster *is* a failure of the maternal object, and it links with the failure of the maternal object (however fleeting) that was the original disaster. Devastating material from the external world gets locked into devastating material from the internal world, and becomes bound or fixed; and because of the intense emotional charge associated with both the internal and the external material, these connections are hard to undo. There seems to be a simple rule that the more intense the traumatic event, the greater and more lasting the emotional loading (cathexis) that it carries, and correspondingly the harder it is to disengage from the freshly released or aroused, and equally highly charged material to which it gets bound.

The example of Miss A is one where events in the history, a pre-existing disaster, had a specific parallel with the disaster in the present. Following the thinking outlined above, one would expect Miss A to have poor prognosis without treatment.

Case study 22.2   The manager who survived

Mr B presents a slightly different picture. He was one of the factory's management team, a modestly successful man in his 40s, with a stable, if quite strict family background: he had a tough father, and a rather depressed mother who used her youngest son's tendency to develop coughs and colds to keep him away from school for weeks at a time, and in the house with her. He now has a growing family of his own which he takes much satisfaction in providing for well. Like Miss A, Mr B had a number of pre-existing features in his experience and personality which would link readily to the fire. He presented himself as very much in control, charming and affable, putting me at my ease, and quite anxious to be seen to be not making a fuss in spite of his burnt hands, and a number of troublesome sequelae following smoke inhalation. He came, he reminded me, from the North, where you didn't fuss about things that went wrong, you just made the best of them and got on with it. Yes, he'd been in one or two scrapes before: there was an incident in a neighbour's hay-field where he, as a boy of seven – 'silly chump', he said with a grin – had climbed on top of the baling machine at harvest time, and would have been well and truly baled himself if the tractor driver hadn't noticed the boy in the nick of time, jamming the machine to a stop. His father was furious with him for being such an idiot. Then there was another time a few years later – as a matter of fact he'd never told his parents about this one, they'd have been so angry – when running across a wet wooden level-crossing to catch the train to school, he'd slipped and fallen, and had to lie there frozen as the express to Leeds had thundered by nine inches from his head. Sometimes, at night, he wakes with a jump and sees the giant wheels spinning past him on the pillow. Pretty silly of him really, to have been running on a wet crossing in front of the express; he must be like a cat, with a few lives to spare.

Mr B's explicit belief that if you get into an accident it's your own fault, and that people will only be angry with you, made sense of his behaviour in the fire itself. He was caught in one of the passages leading to the central storage area when the fireball exploded. He was knocked to the ground with the force of the explosion, and was filled with an immense lethargy, quite drained of life and energy, feeling as he had done, he said, only once before in his life, when he'd been very ill as a small child with a high temperature; he simply assumed he would be burned to death. He remembered thinking he hoped it wouldn't take long, and he said (laughing) he'd hoped, like the early Christian martyrs who had prayed for green wood, that it would be the smoke that would kill him before the fire did. He felt his scalp beginning to blister in the heat; with a supreme effort he tried as hard as he could to cross the passage to reach the stairs and exit, but realised he couldn't make it. Instead he turned and blundered back the way he'd come. Eventually, he found his way back through an alternative route, and was one of the first to get taken to the local hospital's Casualty Unit. He told Casualty, who put him under a cold tap, that they could expect more severely damaged people shortly; and after 45 minutes on his own, phoned his wife to tell her he'd be a bit late home. His words were: 'I'm afraid silly old James had gone and got himself burned...'. But, he added to the therapist, he hadn't asked her to come and get him, she'd decided that off her own bat; he was jolly glad, as it happened, because do you know, he didn't think he'd have had the energy to walk home at that point, he might even have asked for a taxi.

What was the moment that seemed to sum it all up for him? It was when he felt so drained of energy, the heat had sucked it all out of him, and he thought only with great pain that he hadn't taken care of his family properly, he hadn't provided for them sufficiently, should he, the breadwinner, be killed as he was now going to be. That had been the worst moment, that feeling that it was now too late and that he was cut off from his family for ever, and how would they manage? Just visible in that moment is the small boy's defensively omnipotent conviction of being essential to his mother's well-being, that it was he who was responsible for her, rather than vice-versa.

To some extent, the omnipotent belief that if you get into trouble it's your own fault allowed this survivor to retain a sense of control. He may feel he's an idiot but at least he wasn't put there by a power greater than himself, as happened to Miss A. Mr B, a more robust personality with the advantage of a currently stable home life, apparently clung to that sense of control through everything that happened to him subsequently, making powerful use of repression and denial in order to retain his belief in his own indispensibility. It seemed in the interview that to be reminded of the moments in which he felt helpless, cut off from his family and powerless to help them, was something he wished quite explicitly to avoid. The system to which he struggled to bind the floods of incoming stimuli was his own area of psychotic thinking (Bion 1970, Segal 1981) in which, single-handed, he was responsible for keeping all his objects alive and in good shape. This is visible in the outcome. Unlike Miss A, Mr B refused psycho-therapy ('I come from the North'), but agreed to return for periodic check-ups. He has deployed his compensation in a way that could be reparative, by putting it straight into a fund for the family. But his anxiety is growing. At first, it was limited to feelings of panic when unexpectedly he saw the Company's logo on its products in the shops: this was the symbolic equivalent of being caught helplessly in the fire. By now, he is unwilling to use that or any related product from other manufacturers, and feels highly anxious when he knows any of his children do. It makes him withdrawn, irritable and preoccupied, and, he feels, has changed him. When he lit the first fire in their living room for the autumn of 1988, he was quite overwhelmed with a panic that he couldn't put into words and he went away and hid upstairs. All fires have become concretised, the same fire, in this area of regressed and primitive thinking, and they all, I suggest, join up with the fire that was the burning fever, the mother's failure to protect him from the fear of his own annihilation. Any and all of them have the capacity to obliterate his own maternal function, the containing space in which thought and symbolisation can occur.

But they do something else as well. In Miss A's case, the darkness and obscurity and the choking to death, and in Mr B's case, the burning fire were at one time available, however tenuously, as *symbols* for the bad object: for the mother that kept you in the dark and let your siblings die, and for the mother that left you burning helplessly with a fever. These versions of the internal mother are a result of actual but survivable experience infused with phantasy. While smoke and fire are symbols, they are available for internal work: for dreaming, and for unconscious phantasy. But what happens when life is endangered by real smoke and by real fire, and others are seen and heard being destroyed by their actuality? The external reality locks in to the phantasy and traps it, renders it earthbound. Phantasy is no longer freely available to be used as a means of working through anxieties because it has been over-ridden and incorporated into the intensity of the imagery – the sights, sounds and smells – of the actual event. By the time this process is complete, perhaps many weeks or months after the traumatic event, outside help is needed if it is to change. The containment of the analytic/therapeutic process can prevent the development of a permanently split-off area of inferno. It can help to restore, in a necessarily modified form, depressive position functioning: a capacity for the containment of grief as opposed to being overwhelmed by feelings, for symbolic as opposed to concrete thinking, and for working through as opposed to stasis.

TREATMENT

The work of treatment is to restore, in some cases in a more workable form, the survivor's capacity to manage his own experience, so that once again he can begin to think about and make sense of it, integrating it into the rest of his functioning. The timing of this process, judging the moment at which an entry into a mind possessed by unmanageable stimuli can be effected without aggravating, exacerbating or prolonging the existing problems, is an important issue. Immediately following a disaster, there is a period when what is needed is the very best kind of nursing: a physical, containing, stable presence, which stays put and holds on through grim death. In one way, this is a description of the internal good object, but in this chapter it has been suggested that it is precisely this which is overwhelmed by the encounter with the actuality of one's own death in an unpremeditated or violent form. There is an immediate and deep need for a good *external* object with which the fragmented elements of earlier good experiences can begin to connect, and be held by, while the survivor is at his most regressed or broken-down.

Although many individuals will recover a more or less workable equilibrium following their survival of a disaster, particularly with the support of family, friends and other helpers, the breach in the stimulus shield (to return to Freud's metaphor) can represent an area of permanent vulnerability. Later losses, ill health, a further accident, and the individual is at risk again. Each traumatic event has the potential to reactivate those of earlier years which have not been worked through and integrated. The more life-threatening and catastrophic the present event, the deeper and more buried the vulnerabilities it will unearth. What kind and degree of treatment can be offered, and in what sort of sequence, to counterweight the insidious ability of a traumatic event to disrupt normal functioning in a chronic way?

Stage one. Speed of response: the first 48 hours

In the first 48 hours after a disaster, the survivor's overwhelming need and wish will be to find something or someone he can perceive, even temporarily, as offering primary maternal care. For many, this will be a pressing need to return 'home', if the degree of injury permits it. Home may be a person, or it may amount to no more than the survivor's own bed, but it represents the setting which is most familiar, safest and most containing to an extremely regressed level of functioning. The degree of shock is variable but always present, however rational the presentation. The initial euphoria at having survived means the full impact of events may not be experienced until hours or even days later. At this early stage, what is needed are blankets, holding, warmth, the presence of another human being within physical reach and, above all, one who is in a state to sit and simply be with the survivor, rather than bustling about in a busy way. This is an area in which volunteer help is invaluable, provided that volunteers can manage the impact of the fear and distress of the survivor without becoming overwhelmed themselves.

As described earlier, regression to a primitive level of functioning in which the world has become a dangerously unpredictable and hostile place involves a regression to concrete thinking. It is very difficult for the survivor, certainly in the earliest stages, to hear or to use language in a sophisticated way. Words may become blunt instruments, at a level of abstraction not far removed from cries and groans; they are not at this point carrying their full freight of symbolic and associative import, however rational the survivor may sound. Although there is often a compulsive need to speak about the disaster, this regression and the accompanying breakdown in depressive-position functioning may make it difficult for the survivor to feel that he can reach or make contact with his object. The outcome can be a long period when his driving need to feel heard and understood will mean an insistent unconscious attempt to pull his object into a position where he can see the object is feeling as affected, even overwhelmed, as he has been by the disaster. This frantic (though still unconscious) need to stir up the external object with projections of helplessness and dread is about re-establishing links; about the flight from the terror of solitude in the fact of death. Some toleration by the external object of this projective identification may be necessary before the survivor can feel the experience has been communicated to another in all its awfulness. The very process of communication, however primitive, is about the beginning of recovery.

The survivor's wish to affect the helper with the intensity of his internal experience is a complex business. Firstly, it is an expression of the need to communicate and to be understood, which in itself may feel like the first glimpse of a meaningful world once more. Secondly, it represents an attempt to be rid of the intolerable nature of the experience, through an intense evacuation of the feelings stirred up into the nearest available object; and thirdly, and this should not be underestimated, it can be accompanied by a kind of rage engendered by helplessness itself, and the utter dependence that accompanies it. It creates a profound and often hidden conflict between extreme need, and a deep silent resistance to those who appear or claim to have some professional capacity to help contain the anxieties of others without rushing about and being busy. Thus, as well as generating the most profound dependence, helplessness may also generate a repressed resentment and mistrust of those who are not also helpless. Because it is of the essence of trauma that it overwhelms and fragments the individual, opening up primitive feelings about good and bad in their most raw and split form, a 'helper' who is not perceived to be helping in an active and practical way can feel very persecuting to those who are overwhelmed. Formal psychotherapy, therefore, belongs at a later stage of treatment, when the symbolic level of functioning can be tolerated once more without exacerbating feelings of persecution in the survivor. In the earliest stage, containment and management may need to be actual and concrete, as in infant care, establishing the basis for others to engage later in more structured forms of treatment.

Planning ahead for a disaster should include some preparation for those who will be working in the front-line, through teaching and training programmes. It should make a distinction between primary and secondary stages of treatment; and should prepare a coordinated service for the care of the front-rank helpers (emergency services and volunteers) themselves. This would include daily debriefing sessions (Dyregrov 1989) at a regular time and place for all staff and volunteers, with the aim of providing containment for those who themselves are required to contain and process massive amounts of extremely painful material.

Stage two: 48 hours – 3 months

It is important to remain in touch with survivors who want and are able to return home. In some, the wish to deny the impact of the event may be strong, leading to a rejection of help, but the evidence is accumulating (Thompson & Rosser 1990) that those who talk about it recover their equilibrium more effectively than those who do not. 'No go' areas in the mind (created through denial, or the wholesale repression of undigested material) restrict its full emotional and intellectual functioning, and such areas can grow rather than diminish when there is no treatment. A train accident, for instance, can enlarge to a fear of travelling in any form.

Probably the most effective setting for treatment in this second stage, when circumstances allow for it, is a group (Van der Kolk 1987). A group would consist of 4–15 members. Survivors of the same experience provide support and containment for each other simply by virtue of their shared experience. There is less need on the part of each to overwhelm the other with the impact of his feelings (the use of projective identification for either communication or evacuation of intolerable feeling), because the often-heard statement, 'You couldn't know what it was like unless you were there', does not apply. The fact that there are others present who *were* there, and do know what it was like, enables the survivor to feel heard and believed – an essential step in treatment.

Groups are, of course, only possible when an accident involves a number of people who can be brought together after the event. A different phenomenon can happen after an accident involving only one or two individuals, in that each may remain silent about his experience. To follow the argument presented earlier, if traumatic experience taps directly into the psychotic part of the personality where *only* seeing is believing, an individual who cannot resort to massive projective identification as a means of communication is at a real risk of being isolated by his experience if he is the only one to have suffered it.

Nevertheless, for those who can and do talk following an event, the wish to go on doing so may diminish quite rapidly, and after a while, groups may be felt to be stirring up painful feelings rather than helping to resolve them. Group meetings might, therefore, take place over four or five weeks, once-weekly for an hour and a half, within a stable setting, in which the parameters of day of the week, time, duration, room, chairs, group leader and (as far as possible) members are held constant. Two later follow-up sessions after a gap of three or four weeks might be planned.

In the author's view, it is important to make clear at the outset the task and the number of sessions that will be available for that particular piece of work. The outcome can be reviewed at the end of that number of sessions, but they must then be brought to a close; and, if necessary, a new task defined. Thus, the original task might be: '*To talk with each other about what happened to each of us in the disaster, and how we are managing in the aftermath*'. Individuals in the group, knowing at the outset the number of sessions available, will unconsciously plan their internal work to accord with the time allotted. A subsequent task, if circumstances lead the group leader to decide that another batch of sessions would be helpful, might be: '*to talk with each other about the changes this disaster has made in our lives, short and longer-term, and about how we and our families/friends/colleagues are adapting to them*'.

These group sessions need a leader who was *not* present at the event, but who has some knowledge and experience of the kinds of processes that take place in all small closed groups, and some understanding of the counter-tranference – the kinds of thoughts and feelings that are stirred up in the therapist by the patients' unconscious phantasies (at a group – as well as at an individual level) as well as conscious behaviour. The same leader must take all the sessions with a particular group. The focus is on the event itself, its associations, and its outcome for each individual. Any death, for example, will stir up memories of earlier deaths, and it is important that these links should be explicit; but the overall purpose of these groups is to provide a containing environment in which the survivors can begin to work at the process of thinking about their experiences for themselves, and with each others' help.

Members can be encouraged to bring dreams to these sessions, and to see them as internal work on the processing of the event. A dream brought by someone will trigger memories and associations in others, in the present as much as from the event itself. Once a group has established a modus operandi, something that almost always happens between the second and third sessions, a considerable degree of trust and mutual dependence develops between members. Unlike in a normal therapy group, it is almost inevitable that members will meet each other outside sessions. If and when this happens, it needs to be acknowledged explicitly by the leader, particularly if one or two members for any reason are not included in extra-group meetings. Becoming aware of their feelings about this state of affairs is a proper part of the treatment. There can be a tendency for members to form intensely emotional or sexualised relationships, in part as a defence against the recognition of separation and loss, in part as a reassertion of life in the face of death. Some recognition by the leader of the feelings that are being defended against in this way can help to hold them without their needing to be acted out.

Sometimes, the configuration produced within a group, for example by inclusion/exclusion splits, echoes some feature of the disaster itself: perhaps the proportion of saved to not-saved. Interpretation of this sort of material will depend on circumstances – the speed with which the group develops a capacity to reflect on events, and the level of training of the group leader. In general, with groups of this kind, focused on a problematic event, members can be allowed to develop their own way of helping each other, held by the therapist's close and thoughtful attention. However, silent members may need to be asked if they feel comfortable remaining quiet for the moment; or offered some such opening for them to use when they feel ready.

Case study 22.3   Group therapy following a disaster

Members of a group formed at the survivors' own request after the fire in the Sheraton-owned hotel in Cairo (February 1990), and run in the Trauma Study Unit at the Tavistock, found by the third session that they had moved on from the events of the fire itself. A major focus of their attention became the shared difficulties they found in handling the reactions of friends, partners and colleagues. It led to a general recognition that at that point in time they were all in the sort of rattled state where 'no-one could get it right' – neither overt sympathy nor tactful avoidance felt satisfactory – and the identifying and sharing of common frustrations and distress produced relief, and even some humour. This group was unusual, and also fortunate, in that it included the daughter of an older survivor, who, although she had not been in Cairo at the time, attended in order to assist her injured father. The dialogue that eventually developed in the room between father and daughter was immensely useful to the other members, in that it demonstrated in vivo the difficulties that many of them had experienced with their own relatives and partners. The young daughter wanted to help, but was concerned lest her assistance was felt to be intrusive or over-concerned or just of the wrong sort; the parents very much needed help, but felt anxious that they were taking the young woman away from the things she really wanted to be doing. She experienced their struggle to be independent as rejecting – 'I want to be *allowed* to help!' For them, it was a product of guilt, and the wish to have survived intact, undamaged. Each was able to say to the other in the room, and with the understanding and encouragement of the other members, what neither would have broached in the privacy of the home; about the difficulties both of needing and of giving help after a life-threatening situation.

As so often happens in group treatment, the members working at the understanding and helping may have benefited quite as much as the helped (Garland 1982). Taking an active part in alleviating another's distress acts powerfully on the process of restoring an individual's sense of control after a period of acute helplessness.

Although members can be encouraged explicitly to attend all group sessions, many will not do so, and this has to be accepted. The fact of the group's existence at a known place and time is in itself helpful; individual members will then titrate their own dose level. For those that use dissociation or depersonalisation as defences, a degree of group treatment can be helpful – others can be observed to be feeling something strongly as a result of what has happened, and even envied for their ability to cry about it – but too much can be threatening. My own view is that such members can be left to find their own level of catharsis. Others will, in any case, encourage one another to 'talk it out', something that is by now part of a generally accepted view of the best way to deal with tragedy. Often, individuals will find feelings stirred more by others' accounts of their ordeals and feelings than by their own, part of the value of group treatment for a group event.

After five or even fewer sessions, there will be a tendency for the group to bring current difficulties, not necessarily directly stemming from the disaster, into the session. At this point, the therapist needs to acknowledge their sense that life has continued in spite of everything and is moving on, but to remind members of the task of this particular series of meetings. Once a group becomes a general-purpose therapy group, and there will invariably be a pull for it to do so, it could continue indefinitely in a half-cocked way. It is important, as said before, to end a group convened for a particular purpose at the point at which the end was originally planned. Members will then be relieved to see that the therapist does not believe they need to be in treatment for the rest of their lives as a result of the disaster.

However, there is no doubt that a small proportion of individuals will need to go further, and one of the functions of the group is to provide a chance for the group leader to see who is beginning to recover and who is not. There will be some for whom a third stage of treatment will be important.

Stage three: the longer term

Patients who continue to feel overwhelmed by unmanageable aspects of their experience, showing in a prolonged way the symptoms now collected under the heading of Post-Traumatic Stress Disorder, may be helped in various ways. Stress clinics which offer behavioural techniques for the management of anxiety are one possibility; cognitive therapy is available in some areas. Although the outlook for all survivors suggests at best an increased vulnerability to stressful events which no form of treatment can avoid altogether, the risk with 'stress management' is that the survivor can develop a horizontal split in the mind as a solution to his difficulties. Superficially, normal functioning is re-established, work may be resumed, but below the surface remains a fundamental preoccupation with the disaster and its sequelae. Survivors mentally check out the positions of exits, of electric sockets, of the distance of windows from the ground, of the stairs rather than lifts. While actually in the process of talking about something apparently unrelated, another part of the mind is filled and occupied with images of the event, and with the need to keep these under control. It is as though, in the example given, the fire is still burning underground. Effectively, so much of the ego's available energy is occupied with fire-fighting, that its other functions become shrunken and restricted ('ego-shrinkage'; see Cooper 1986).

In the author's view, the work of psychoanalytic psychotherapy is ultimately the restoration of reasonably sustained 'depressive position functioning' (see Chs 1 and 13) with its accompanying capacity for symbolic thinking. Experiences are not avoided, but are worked through repeatedly until they can be integrated into the overall picture. In the case of a disaster, this is a complicated procedure, involving as it does a degree of mourning for the pre-disaster self (Menzies-Lyth 1989), and a working-through of the guilt about having survived where others died. Beyond the experience of the actual disaster, and the separating out of conscious and unconscious phantasy from reality, there is the need to rework the original trauma locked into, and given fresh life by, the present catastrophe. Taking a survivor into psychotherapy will inevitably involve the treatment of the past through the present, and often the past in its own right, from the beginning.

It is the experience of the Trauma Study Unit that there are particular issues that arise in the longer-term treatment of patients who present after a disaster. On the one hand, the treatment may find itself lodged on the traumatic event or events, and around the patient's conception of himself as a victim. On the other hand, there is the risk of leaving the disaster out altogether; allowing it to get buried, or, particularly with child patients, be covered over by a defensive organisation that is so all-pervasive that the specificity of its relationship to the traumatic event can be overlooked.

It is a necessary part of treatment of such patients that it involves the recognition, exploration and re-introjection of the patient's own destructiveness, both actual and in phantasy. To have been caught up in an external event of real destructiveness links up with the earliest and most primitive phantasies. The work of separating out what belongs to the survivor from what belongs to the event itself is central to psychoanalytic psychotherapy of a patient who presents following a traumatic event.

An external disaster can link up with the survivor's own destructiveness in several ways. Inevitably, it will connect with scenes of psychic devastation from the infant's own history, when the infant perceived himself to have been responsible for that state of affairs and was overwhelmed with its consequences. At a more conscious level, the disaster will release considerable amounts of hatred, rage and anger in return. Some of this will be justified in terms of revenge or retribution – it can be disguised as a determined litigiousness, which may or may not be appropriate. However, prolonged anger can also have a defensive function. States of chronic persecutory or depressive breakdown may be avoided by organising the tattered fragments of the ego around a state of rage, or righteous indignation, which then has to be sustained to avoid the breakdown. This is a precarious state of affairs which treatment will inevitably disrupt; there will then be a need for a treatment setting in which the consequences of the eventual breakdown, which has almost certainly been avoided in this way for years, can be worked through and recovered from. Then, too, following a disaster there are the long-term future consequences for defensive organisation to be attended to. The difficult issue of the unconscious gratification of holding on to the painful nature of the event must be looked at. For some, an identification with the aggressor may seem psychically preferable to becoming the victim. For others, the existence of an identifiable external enemy can be incorporated into a defensive strategy involving in a chronic way the stance of victim. The hope is that treatment would allow for a better defensive solution than either of these.

which, although important in all treatment, seem particularly relevant to survivors. But even with psychotherapy, even with analysis, I suspect there is a limit to the possibilities following a major external catastrophe. It cannot restore the survivor to a pre-disaster state: things will have shifted inside and, perhaps as with all experience, they will reform themselves differently. They may even in some respects improve, though the survivor's own experience is of increased vulnerability. Yet Aesop's reed did better in the storm than the oak; and if, through a fresh experience of containment, we can restore the ability to think, then at least we can be, like Pascal, a thinking reed. This is not the same as believing in getting over it. There may only be getting on with it: facing the changes, knowing something more about one's own destructiveness, knowing something more, too, about the chronically vulnerable areas; and remaining connected to the rest of the world in a turning back from death towards life.

FURTHER READING

Furst S 1967 Psychic trauma: a survey. In: Furst S (ed) Psychic trauma. Basic Books, New York
Krystal H (ed) 1976 Massive psychic trauma. International Universities Press, New York
Parkes C M 1972 Bereavement. Reprinted 1976 Penguin Books, London
Van der Kolk B 1987 Psychological trauma. American Psychiatric Press, Washington, D C
Wolfenstein M 1976 Disaster: a psychological essay. Routledge & Kegan Paul, London

References

Abend S M, Porder M S, Willick M S 1983 Borderline patients: Psychoanalytic perspectives. I U P, Connecticut

Abraham K 1924 A short study of the development of the libido, viewed in the light of mental disorders. In: Abraham K 1949 Selected papers. Hogarth, London

Achté K, Tuulio-Henriksson A 1982 On the psychotherapy of geriatric patients. Psychiatrica Fennica International Edition: 13–27

Aguilera D C, Messick J M 1978 Crisis intervention: theory and methodology, 3rd edn. Mosby, St Louis

Ahrenfeldt R H 1968 Military psychiatry in medical services in war. HMSO, London

Akiskal H S, Chen E S, Davis G C et al 1985 Borderline: an adjective in search of a noun. Journal of Clinical Psychiatry 46: 41–48

Alanen Y, Rakkolainen V, Laakso J 1986 Towards need-specific treatment of schizophrenic psychoses. Springer, London

Alexander F, French T M 1946 Psychoanalytic psychotherapy. University of Nebraska Press, Lincoln

Alexander F, French T M, Pollock G H 1968 Psychosomatic specificity, Vol. 1. University of Chicago Press, Chicago

Alvin J 1983 Music therapy. Hutchinson, London

Alladin W 1988 Cognitive-behavioural group therapy. In: Aveline M, Dryden W (eds) Group therapy in Britain. Open University Press, Milton Keynes

Allyon T, Azrin N H 1968 The token economy. Appleton-Century-Crofts, New York

American Psychiatric Association 1987 Diagnostic and statistical manual, 3rd edn. (revised version). Washington D C

Anderson C M, Hogarty G, Reiss D J 1981 The psycho-educational family treatment of schizophrenia. In: Goldstein M J (ed) New developments in interventions with families of schizophrenics. Jossey, San Francisco

Andrews G, Pollock C, Stewart G 1989 The determination of defence style by questionnaire. Archives of General Psychiatry 46: 455–460

Anthony E J 1975 Between yes and no: the potentially neutral area where the adolescent and his therapist can meet. In: Feinstein S C, Giovachini P L (eds) Adolescent psychiatry: developmental clinical studies, Vol. IV. Jason Aronson, New York

Archer J Jnr, Kagan N 1973 Teaching interpersonal relationship skills on campus: a pyramid approach. Journal of Counselling Psychology 20: 535–541

Arieti S 1974 Interpretation of schizophrenia. Basic Books, New York

Armstrong D 1890 Madness and coping. Sociology of Health and Illness 2(3): 293–316

Asch S 1980 Suicide, and the hidden executioner. International Review of Psycho-Analysis 7: 57–60

Ashbach C, Schermer V L 1987 Object relations, the self, and the group: a conceptual paradigm. Routledge & Kegan Paul, London

Assagioli R 1975 Psychosynthesis. Tavistock, London

Auden W H 1973 The Greeks and us. In Forwards and Afterwards. Faber & Faber, London

Aveline M 1980 Making a psychodynamic formulation. Bulletin of the Royal College of Psychiatrists December: 192–193

Aveline M O 1988 The relationship of drug therapy and psychotherapy. Current Opinion in Psychiatry 1: 309–313

Aveline M, Dryden W 1988 Group therapy in Britain. Open University Press, Milton Keynes
Aveline M 1990 The training and supervision of individual therapists. In: Dryden W (ed) Handbook of individual therapy in Britain. Open University Press, Milton Keynes (In press)
Aveline M O, Fowlie D G 1980 Surviving ejection from military aircraft: psychological reactions, modifying factors and intervention. Stress Medicine 3: 15–20
Bachelard G 1969 The poetics of space. Beacon Press, Boston
Bachrach H M 1980 Analyzability: a clinical research perspective. Psychoanalysis and Contemporary Thought 3: 6–11
Baisden M J, Baisden J R 1979 A profile of women who seek counselling for sexual dysfunction. American Journal of Family Therapy 7: 68–76
Baker A W, Duncan S P 1985 Child sexual abuse: a study of prevalence in Great Britain. Child Abuse and Neglect 9: 457–467
Baker H S, Baker M N 1987 Heinz Kohut's self psychology: an overview. American Journal of Psychiatry 144: 1–9
Balint M 1957 The doctor, his patient and the illness. Pitman Medical, London
Balint M 1959 Regression in the analytic situation. In: 1952 Thrills and regression. Hogarth Press, London pp.91–100
Balint M 1964 Primary love and psychoanalytic technique. Tavistock, London
Balint M 1968 The basic fault. Tavistock, London
Balint M, Balint E 1961 Psychotherapeutic techniques in medicine. Tavistock, London
Balint M, Ornstein P, Balint E 1972 Focal psychotherapy. Tavistock, London
Bancroft J 1986 Crisis intervention. In: Bloch S (ed) An introduction to the psychotherapies, 2nd edn. Oxford University Press, Oxford
Bandler R, Grinder J 1979 Frogs into princes. Real People Press. Moab, Utah
Bandura A 1977 Self-efficacy – towards a unifying theory of behavioural change. Psychological Review 84: 191–215
Bandura A, Ross D, Ross S A 1963 Vicarious reinforcement and imitative learning. Journal of Abnormal Social Psychology 67: 601–607
Barkham M 1989 Exploratory therapy in two-plus-one sessions: I – Rationale for a brief psychotherapy model. British Journal of Psychotherapy 6(1) 81–88
Barkam M J, Hobson R F 1989 Exploratory therapy in two-plus-one sessions: II – a single case study. British Journal of Psychotherapy 6 (1): 87–98
Bateman A W 1989 Borderline personality in Britain: a preliminary study. Comprehensive Psychiatry 30: 385–390
Bateson G, Jackson D, Haley J, Weakland J 1956 Toward a theory of schizophrenia. Behavioural Science 1: 251–254
Bateson G 1972 Steps to an ecology of mind. Ballantine Books, New York
de Beauvoir S 1970 Old age. Editions Gallimard, Paris. (1977 Penguin, London)
Beck A T 1976 Cognitive therapy and the emotional disorders.International University Press, New York
Beck A T, Rush A J, Shaw B F, Emery G 1979 Cognitive therapy of depression. International University Press, New York
Beezley Mrazek P, Kempe C H (eds) 1981 Sexually abused children and their families. Pergamon Press, Oxford
Beitman B D, Goldfried M R, Norcross J C 1989 The movement toward integrating the psychotherapies: an overview. American Journal of Psychiatry 146: 138–147
Bellack A S, Hersen M, Himmelhoch J M 1983 A comparison of social skills training, pharmacotherapy and psychotherapy for depression. Behaviour, Research and Therapy 21: 101–107
Bennett M J 1983 Focal psychotherapy – terminable and interminable. American Journal of Psychotherapy XXXVII 3: 365–375
Benward J, Densen-Gerber J 1975 Incest as a causative factor in antisocial behaviour: an exploratory study. Contemporary Drug Problems 4: 323–340
Bergart A M 1986 Isolation to intimacy: incest survivors in group therapy social casework. The Journal of Contemporary Social Work May: 266–275
Bergin A E, Lambert M J 1978 The evaluation of therapeutic outcomes. In: Garfield S L, Bergin A E (eds) Handbook of psychotherapy and behaviour change: 2nd edn. John Wiley, New York

Berkowitz D A 1979 The disturbed adolescent and his family: problems of individuation. Journal of Adolescence 11: 27–39

Berkowitz R 1984 Therapeutic intervention with schizophrenic patients and their families: a description of a clinical research project. Journal of Family Therapy 3: 211–233

Betcher R W, Zinberg N E 1988 Supervision and privacy in psychotherapy training. American Journal of Psychiatry 145 (7): 796–803

Bettleheim B 1982 Freud and man's soul. Knopf, New York

Beutler L, Mitchell R 1981 Differential psychotherapy outcome among depressed and impulsive patients as a function of analytic and experiential treatment procedures. Psychiatry 44: 297–306

Binder J L, Henry W P, Strupp H H 1987 An appraisal of selection criteria for dynamic psychotherapies and implications for setting time limits. Psychiatry 50: 154–166

Bion W R 1957 Differentiation of the psychotic from the non-psychotic personalities. In: 1967 Second thoughts. Heinemann, London

Bion W R 1962 Learning from experience. Heinemann, London

Bion W R 1970 Attention and interpretation. Tavistock, London

Bion W R, Rickman J 1943 Intra-group tensions in therapy. Lancet 27: 678–681

Blackburn I M, Bishop S, Glen A I M, Whally L J, Christie J F 1981 The efficacy of cognitive therapy in depression: a treatment trial using cognitive therapy and pharmacotherapy, both alone and in combination. British Journal of Psychiatry 139: 181–189

Blackburn I M, Bishop S 1983 Changes in cognition with pharmacotherapy and cognitive therapy. British Journal of Psychiatry 143: 609–617

Blackburn I M, Ennson K M, Bishop S 1986 A two-year naturalistic follow-up of depressed patients treated with cognitive therapy, pharmacotherapy and a combination of both. Journal of Affective Disorders 10: 67–75

Blatner H 1973 Acting in – practical application of psychodramatic methods. Springer, New York

Bloch S 1982 Psychotherapy. In: Granville-Grossman K (ed) Recent advances in clinical psychiatry. Churchill Livingstone, Edinburgh

Bloch S 1986 Supportive psychotherapy. In: Bloch S (ed) An introduction to the psychotherapies, 2nd edn. Oxford Medical Publications, Oxford

Bloch S, Crouch E 1985 Therapeutic factors in group psychotherapy. Oxford University Press, Oxford

Blos P 1967 The second individuation process of adolescence. The Psychoanalytic Study of the Child. 22: 162–186

Blythe R 1981 The view in winter. Penguin, London

Chronically Sick and Disabled Persons Act 1970 Department of Health and Social Security SBN 105444707. HMSO, London

Boll T E M 1962 Mary Sinclair and the Medico-Psychological Clinic of London. Proceedings American Philosophical Society 106: 310–326

Bolton J S 1926 The myth of the unconscious mind. Journal of Mental Science January 25

Book H E 1987 The resident's countertransference: approaching an avoided topic. American Journal of Psychotherapy 41: 555–562

Bowlby J 1951 Maternal care and mental health. World Health Organization, Geneva

Bowlby J 1965 Child care and the growth of love. Penguin, London

Bowlby J 1969 Attachment and loss. Volume I: attachment. Hogarth, London

Bowlby J 1973 Attachment and loss. Volume II: separation. Hogarth, London

Bowlby J 1979 The making and breaking of affectional bonds. Tavistock, London

Bowlby J 1980 Attachment and loss. Volume III: sadness and depression. Hogarth, London

Bowlby J 1988 Developmental psychiatry comes of age. American Journal of Psychiatry 145: 1–10

Boyer L B 1987 Regression and countertransference in the treatment of a borderline patient. In: Grotstein J S, Solomon M F, Lang J A (eds) The borderline patient. The Analytic Press, Hillsdale, N.J.

Boyle H A 1922 The ideal clinic for the treatment of nervous and borderline cases. Programme of the Royal Society of Medicine (Section of Psychiatry): 39–48

Bramley W 1990 Sensitivity groups: a conductor's field experience. Group Analysis 23: 301–316

Brandes D 1982 Gamesters handbook two. Hutchinson, London

Brandes D, Phillips H 1978 Gamesters handbook. Hutchinson, London

Breuer J, Freud S 1893 On the psychical mechanisms of hysterical phenomena: preliminary communication. Strachey J (ed) The standard edition of the complete psychological works of Sigmund Freud. Vol 2. Hogarth, London

British Medical Association / British Medical Journal (suppl) 1929 Report on psychoanalysis 29: 6

Britton R 1981 Re-enactment as an unwitting professional response to family dynamics. In: Box S (ed) Psychotherapy with families: an analytic approach. Routledge, London

Brockman B, Poynton A, Ryle A, Watson J P 1987 Effectiveness of time-limited therapy carried out by trainees. Comparison of two methods. British Journal of Psychiatry 151: 602–610

Brome V 1979 Havelock Ellis, Philosopher of Sex. Carcanet, London

Brown D, Peddler J 1979 Introduction to psychotherapy. Tavistock, London

Brown G, Rutter M 1966 The measurement of family activities and relationships: a methodological study. Human Relations 19: 241–263

Brown G W, Harris T O 1978 Social origins of depression. Tavistock, London

Brown G W, Andrews B 1986 Social support and depression. In: Appley M H, Turnbill R (eds) Dynamics of stress: physiological, psychological and social perspectives. Plenum, New York

Brudenell P 1987 Dramatherapy with people with a mental handicap. In: Jennings S 1987 Dramatherapy: theory and practice for teachers and clinicians. Croom Helm, Beckenham

Buss A H, Plomin R 1986 The EAS approach to temperament. In: Plomin R, Dunn J (eds) The study of temperament: changes, continuities and challenges. Lawrence Erlbaum, Hillsdale, N.J.

Byng-Hall J 1973 Family myths used as defence in conjoint family therapy. British Journal of Medical Psychology 46: 239–249

Byng-Hall J 1979 Re-editing family mythology during family therapy. Journal of Family Therapy 1: 103–116

Bynum W F 1983 Psychosomatic. In: Shepherd M, Zangwill O L (eds) Handbook of psychiatry: general psychopathology. Cambridge University Press, Cambridge

Cade B 1984 paradoxical techniques in therapy. Journal of Child Psychology and Psychiatry 25 (4): 509–516

Caine T M, Smail D J 1969 The treatment of mental illness. University of London Press, London

Caparotta L, Marrone M 1981 Staff responses to patients with a primary disturbance of the self. Group Analysis 14: 50–56

Cartwright A 1987 Group work with substance abusers: basic issues and future research. British Journal of Addiction 82(9): 951–953

Cartwright S, Read A, Wilks J, Dodds E, Reeves R 1987, Avon drug research and rehabilitation project: final report to the DHSS. HMSO, London

Carvhallo R 1988 Supervision. Paper presented at Psychotherapy Section of the Royal College of Psychiatrists Trainers and Trainees Forum.

Casement P 1985 On learning from the patient. Tavistock, London

Cawley R H 1977 The teaching of psychotherapy. Association of University Teachers of Psychotherapy Newsletter

Cheren S 1989 Psychosomatic medicine: theory, physiology and practice. Vol. I/II International Universities Press, Madison

Clark D H 1965 The therapeutic community: concept, practice and future. British Journal of Psychiatry III: 947–954

Clark D M, Salkovskis P M, Chalkley A J 1985 Respiratory control as a treatment for panic attacks. Journal of Behaviour Therapy and Experimental Psychiatry 16: 23–30

Clark M J 1981 The rejection of psychological approaches to mental disorder in late nineteenth century British psychiatry. In: Scull A (ed) Madhouses, mad-doctors and madmen. Athlone Press, London

Cobb J P, Liebermann S 1987 The grammar of psychotherapy: a descriptive account. British Journal of Psychiatry 151: 589–594

Cobb S 1976 Social support as a moderator of life stress. Psychosomatic Medicine 38: 300–314

Cohen M B, Baker G, Cohen R A et al 1963 An intensive study of twelve cases of manic-depressive psychosis. Psychiatry 17: 103–137

Cohen N A 1982 On loneliness and the ageing process. International Journal of Psycho-Analysis 63(2): 149–156

Cohen P, Cohen J 1984 The clinician's illusion. Archives of General Psychiatry 41: 1178–1182

Coleman J V 1949 The initial phase of psychotherapy. Bulletin of the Menninger Clinic 13: 189–197

Conte H R, Plutchik R 1986 Controlled research in supportive psychotherapy. Psychiatric Annals 16: 9 September 1986, pp. 530–533

Cooper A M 1986 Towards a limited definition of psychic trauma. In : Rothstein (ed) The reconstruction of trauma. International Universities Press, Connecticut.

Cox A, Hopkinson K, Rutter M 1981a Psychiatric interviewing techniques II: Naturalistic study: eliciting factual information. British Journal of Psychiatry 138: 283–291

Cox A, Holbrook D, Rutter M 1981b Psychiatric interviewing techniques VI: Experimental study: eliciting feelings. British Journal of Psychiatry 139: 144–152

Cox A, Rutter M, Holbrook D 1988 Psychiatric interviewing techniques: A second experimental study: eliciting feelings. British Journal of Psychiatry 152: 64–72

Cox M, Theilgaard A 1987 Mutative metaphors in psychotherapy. Tavistock, London

Crichton-Browne J 1920 Notes on psychoanalysis and psychotherapy. Lancet June 5: 12

Crown S 1988 Supportive psychotherapy: a contradiction in terms. British Journal of Psychiatry 152: 266–296

Dalley T (ed) 1984 Art as therapy; an introduction to the use of art as a therapeutic technique. Tavistock, London

Dalley T (ed) 1987 Images of art therapy: new developments in theory and practice. Tavistock, London

Dare 1967 Glomerular filtration rate in anorexia nervosa. Dissertation, Academic Diploma in Psychological Medicine, University of London

Dare C 1983 Family therapy for families containing an anorectic youngster. In: Understanding anorexia nervosa and bulimia. Report of the Fourth Ross Conference on Medical Research. Ross Laboratories, Columbus, Ohio, pp. 28–34

Dare C 1985 The family therapy of anorexia nervosa. Journal of Psychiatric Research 19: 435–485

Dare C, Eisler I, Russell G F M, Szmukler G I 1990a Family therapy for anorexia nervosa: implications from the results of a controlled trial of family and individual therapy. Journal of Marital and Family Therapy 16: 1–26

Dare C, Le Grange D, Eisler I 1990b Anorexia nervosa and family therapy: a study of the changes in the individual and the family during the process of restoring normal body weight. Unpublished manuscript.

Davanloo H (ed) 1980 Short-term dynamic psychotherapy. Jason Aronson, New York

Davies M H 1988 Psychodrama group therapy. In: Aveline M, Dryden W (eds) Group therapy in Britain. Open University Press, Milton Keynes

Davis J D, Elliott R, Davis M L et al 1987 The development of a taxonomy of therapist difficulties: initial report. British Journal of Medical Psychology 60 (2): 109–120

Dendy R F 1971 A model for the training of undergraduate hall assistants as para-professional counsellors using videotape techniques and Interpersonal Process Recall. Unpublished Doctoral dissertation, Michigan State University

Deutsh H 1942. Some forms of emotional disturbance and their relationship to schizophrenia. Psychoanalytic Quarterly 11: 301–321

Dewhurst K 1982 Hughlings Jackson on psychiatry. Sandford, Oxford

Dicks H V 1970 50 years of the Tavistock Clinic. Routledge & Kegan Paul, London

Douglas A R 1988 Incest – a suitable case for treatment? The Practitioner 232: 547–551

Douglas A R, Matson I 1989 An account of a time-limited therapeutic group in an NHS setting for women with a history of incest. Group 13: 83–94

Dryden W 1984 Individual therapy in Britain. Open University Press, Milton Keynes

Dryden W, Golden W 1986 Cognitive-behavioural approaches to psychotherapy. Harper & Row, London

Dyregrov A 1989 Caring for helpers in disaster situations: psychological debriefing. Paper given at Survival Seminar, Tavistock Clinic, London, March 1989. In press

Eckler-Hart A H 1987 True and false self in the development of the psychotherapist Psychotherapy 24: 683–692

Edinburgh Medical Journal 1920. Review of Stoddart's 'Mind and its disorders'. EMJ 24: 263–264

Eissler K R 1958 Notes on problems of technique in the psychoanalytic treatment of adolescents: with some remarks on perversions. Psychoanalytic Study of the Child 13: 223–254

Eliot T S 1944 Four quartets. Faber and Faber, London

Elkin I, Shea M T, Watkins J T et al 1989 National Institute of Mental Health Treatment of Depression Collaborative Research Programme. Archives of General Psychiatry 46: 971–982

Elliott R 1983 'That in your hands' – a comprehensive process analysis of a significant event in psychotherapy. Psychiatry 46: 113–129

Elliott R, Hill C E, Stiles W B, Friedlander M L, Mahrer A, Margison F R 1987 The eight primary therapist response modes: a comparison of six rating systems. Journal of Consulting and Clinical Psychology 55 (2): 218–223

Elliott R K, Shapiro D A 1988 Brief structured recall: a more efficient method of studying significant therapy events. British Journal of Medical Psychology 61: 141–153

Emery G, Tracy N L 1987 Theoretical issues in the cognitive-behavioral treatment of anxiety disorders. In: Michelson L, Ascher L M (eds) Anxiety and stress disorders; cognitive behavioral assessment and treatment. Guilford, New York

Engel G L 1968 A life setting conducive to illness. The giving-up – given-up complex. Annals of Internal Medicine 69: 293–300

Erikson E H 1959 Identity and the life cycle. Psychological Issues 1(1): 1–173. (1980 Norton, New York)

Erikson E H 1965 Childhood and society. Hogarth, London

Erikson E H 1968 Identity, youth and crisis. Norton, New York

Esman A H 1985 A developmental approach to the psychotherapy of adolescents. In: Feinstein S C (ed) Adolescent psychiatry: developmental and clinical studies Vol XII: 119–133. University of Chicago Press, Chicago

Evans J 1982 Adolescent and pre-adolescent psychiatry. Academic Press, London

Eysenck H J 1983 An analysis of psychotherapy versus placebo studies. Behaviour and Brain Sciences 6: 275–310

Ezquerro A 1989 Group psychotherapy with the pre-elderly. Group Analysis 22: 299–308

Ezriel H A 1950 A psychoanalytic approach to group treatment. British Journal of Medical Psychology 23: 59–74

Fairbairn W R D 1940 Psycho-analytic studies of the personality. Tavistock, London

Fairbairn W R D 1949 Steps in the development of an object-relations theory of the personality. In: Fairbairn W R D 1952 Psychoanalytic studies of the personality. Routledge & Kegan Paul, London

Fairburn C G 1985 Cognitive behavioral treatment for bulimia nervosa. In: Garner D M, Garfinkel P E (eds) Handbook of psychotherapy for anorexia nervosa and bulimia nervosa. Guilford Press, New York, pp.160–192

Falloon I R H (ed) 1988 Handbook of behavioural family therapy. Unwin Hyman, London

Falloon I R H et al 1977 Social skills training in outpatient groups. British Journal of Psychiatry 131: 599–609

Falloon I R H, Boyd J L, McGill C W, Razani J, Moss H B, Gilderman A M 1982 Family management in the prevention of exacerbations of schizophrenia. New England Journal of Medicine 306: 1437–1440

Farrell D 1976 The use of active experiential group techniques with hospitalized patients. In: Wolberg L R, Aronsoh M L (eds) Group therapy 1976: an overview. Stratton, New York

Fenichel O 1937 The concept of trauma in contemporary psycho-analytic theory. In: 1954 The Collected Papers of Otto Fenichel, 2nd series. Norton, New York

Fenichel O 1946 The psychoanalytic theory of neuroses. Routledge & Kegan Paul, London

Ferenczi S, Rank O 1925 The development of psychoanalysis. The Nervous and Mental Diseases Publishing Company, New York

Finkelhor D, Baron L 1986 High risk children. In: Finkelhor D (ed) A sourcebook of child sexual abuse. Sage, Beverly Hills, pp. 60–68

Finkelhor D, Browne A 1986 Initial and long-term effects: a conceptual framework. In: Finkelhor D (ed) A sourcebook of child sexual abuse. Sage, Beverly Hills, pp. 180–198

Fleming J 1967 Teaching the basic skills of psychotherapy. Archives of General Psychiatry 16: 416–426

Foerster K 1984 Supportive psychotherapy combined with autogenous training in acute leukaemic patients under isolation therapy. Psychotherapy and Psychosomatics 4 (2): 100–105

Fonagy P 1989 On tolerating mental states: Theory of mind in borderline personality. Bulletin of the Anna Freud Centre 12: 91–115

Fordham M 1979 Analytical psychology in England. Journal of Analytical Psychology 24: 279–297

Foulkes S H 1948 Introduction to group-analytic psychotherapy: studies in the social integration of individuals and groups. Heinemann, London

Foulkes S H 1964 Therapeutic group analysis. George Allen & Unwin, London

Foulkes S H, Anthony E J 1957 Group psychotherapy: the psychoanalytic approach. Penguin, Harmondsworth

Frances A J, Clarkin J, Perry S 1984 Differential therapeutics in psychiatry: the art and science of treatment selection. Brunner/Mazel, New York

Frank J D 1979 What is psychotherapy? In: Bloch S (ed) An introduction to the psychotherapies. Oxford University Press, Oxford

Frank J 1986 Psychotherapy, the transformation of meanings. Journal of the Royal Society of Medicine 79: 341–346

Freeman T 1988 The psychoanalyst in psychiatry. Karnac, London

Freud A 1937 The ego and the mechanisms of defence. Hogarth, London

Freud A 1958 Adolescence. The psychoanalytic study of the child 13: 255–278

Freud A 1967 Comments on trauma. In: Furst S (ed) Psychic trauma. Basic Books, New York

Freud S 1894a On the grounds for detaching a particular syndrome from neurasthenia under the description of 'anxiety neurosis'. Standard edn, Vol 3. Hogarth, London

Freud S 1894b The neuro-psychoses of defence (an attempt at a psychological theory of acquired hysteria, of many phobias and obsessions and of certain hallucinatory psychoses). Standard edn, Vol 2. Hogarth, London

Freud S 1896 Analysis of a case of chronic paranoia. Standard edn, Vol 3. Hogarth, London

Freud S 1899 Screen memories. Standard edn, Vol 3. Hogarth, London

Freud S 1900 Interpretation of dreams. Standard edn, Vols 4 – 5. Hogarth, London

Freud S 1905a Fragment of an analysis of a case of hysteria. Standard edn, Vol 7. Hogarth, London

Freud S 1905b On psychotherapy. Standard edn, Vol 7. Hogarth, London

Freud S 1905c Three essays on the theory of sexuality. Hogarth Press, London

Freud S 1909 Analysis of a phobia in a two year old boy. Standard edn, Vol 10. Hogarth, London

Freud S 1911a Two principles of mental functioning. Standard edn, Vol 12. Hogarth, London

Freud S 1911b Psychoanalytic notes on an autobiographical account of a case of paranoia. Standard edn. Vol 12. Hogarth, London

Freud S 1912 The dynamics of transference. Standard edn, Vol 12. Hogarth, London

Freud S 1913 Recommendations to physicians practicing psychoanalysis. Standard edn, Vol 12. Hogarth, London

Freud S 1914a Remembering, repeating and working-through. Standard edn, Vol 12. Hogarth, London

Freud S 1914b On the history of the psychoanalytic movement. Standard edn, Vol 14. Hogarth, London

Freud S 1915a Introductory lectures on psychoanalysis. Lecture 25. Standard edn, Vol 16. Hogarth, London

Freud S 1915b Observations on transference-love (Further recommendations on the technique of psycho-analysis III). Standard edn, Vol 12. Hogarth, London

Freud S 1917 Mourning and melancholia. Standard edn, Vol 14. Hogarth, London

Freud S 1918 From the history of an infantile neurosis. Standard edn, Vol. 17. Hogarth Press, London

Freud S 1919a Lines of advance in psycho-analytic therapy. Standard edn, Vol 17. Hogarth, London

Freud S 1919b Psychoanalysis and the war neuroses. Standard edn, Vol 17. Hogarth, London

Freud S 1920 Beyond the pleasure principle. Standard edn, Vol 18. Hogarth, London

Freud S 1923 The ego and the id. Standard edn, Vol 19. Hogarth, London

Freud S 1925 An autobiographical study. Standard edn, Vol 20. Hogarth, London

Freud S 1926 The question of lay analysis. Standard edn, Vol 20. Hogarth, London

Freud S 1933 New introductory lectures in psychoanalysis. Standard edn, Vol 22. Hogarth, London

Freud S 1937 Analysis, terminable and interminable. Standard edn, Vol 23. Hogarth, London

Freud S 1940 An outline of psycho-analysis. Standard edn, Vol 23. Hogarth, London

Friedman C T, Yamamoto J, Wolkon G H, David L 1978 Videotape recording of dynamic psychotherapy: supervisory tool or hindrance? American Journal of Psychiatry 135: 1388–1391

Friedman S, Harrison G 1984 Sexual histories, attitudes and behaviour of schizophrenic and 'normal' women. Archives of Sexual Behaviour 13: 555–567

Fromuth M E 1986 The relationship of childhood sexual abuse with later psychological and sexual adjustment in a sample of college women. Child Abuse and Neglect 10: 5–15

Frosch J 1964 The psychotic character: clinical psychiatric considerations. Psychiatric Quarterly 38: 81–96

Frosch J 1983 The psychotic process. International Universities Press, New York

Frosch J 1988 Psychotic character versus borderline. Part 1. International Journal of Psychoanalysis 69: 347–358

Furst S 1967 Psychic trauma: a survey. In: Furst S (ed) Psychic trauma. Basic Books, New York

Furst S 1978 The stimulus barrier and the pathogenicity of trauma. International Journal of Psycho-Analysis 59: 345

Gallwey P L G 1985 The psychodynamics of borderline personality. In: Farrington D P, Gunn J (eds) Aggression and dangerousness. Wiley, London

Gallwey P L G 1990 The psychopathology of neurosis and offending. In: Bluglass R, Bowden P (eds) The principles and practice of forensic psychiatry. Churchill Livingstone, Edinburgh

Ganster D C, Victor B 1988 The impact of social support on mental health and physical health. British Journal of Medical Psychology 61: 17–36

Garfield S 1986 Research on client variables in psychotherapy. In: Garfield S, Bergin A 1986 Handbook of psychotherapy and behaviour change. Wiley, New York

Garfield S L, Bergin A E 1986 Handbook of psychotherapy and behaviour change. Wiley, Chichester

Garland C 1982 Group-analysis: taking the non-problem seriously. Group Analysis XV (1)

Garner D M , Garfinkel P E (eds) 1985 Handbook of psychotherapy for anorexia nervosa and bulimia nervosa. Guildford Press, New York

Gask L, McGrath G 1989 Psychotherapy and general practice. British Journal of Psychiatry 154: 445–453

Gaston E 1968 Music in therapy. MacMillan, New York

Gelder M, Gath D, Mayou R 1989 Oxford textbook of psychiatry, 2nd edn. Oxford University Press, Oxford

Genet J 1964 Our lady of the flowers. Blond, London

Ghosh A, Marks I M, Carr A C 1988 Therapist contact and outcome of self-exposure for phobias: a controlled study. British Journal of Psychiatry 152: 234–238

Gilewski M J 1986 Group therapy in cognitively impaired older adults. In: Brink T L (ed) Clinical gerontology: a guide to assessment and treatment. Haworth Press, New York, p 281–296

Gillett R 1986 Short term intensive psychotherapy – a case history. British Journal of Psychiatry 148: 98–100

Gillieron E 1987 Setting and motivation in brief psychotherapy. Psychotherapy and Psychosomatics 47: 105–112

Glasser M, 1979 Some aspects of the role of aggression in the perversions. In: Rosen I (ed) Sexual deviation, 2nd edn. Oxford University Press, Oxford

Gloag D 1989 Music and disability. British Medical Journal Editorial 298: 402–403

Godbert K 1989 The long term effectiveness of psychotherapy teaching. Unpublished MSc thesis, University of Manchester

Goffman E 1961 Asylums: essays on the social situation of mental patients and other inmates. Penguin, Harmondsworth

Goin M K, Kline F 1976 Countertransference: a neglected subject in clinical supervision. American Journal of Psychiatry 133 (1): 41–44

Goldberg D A 1983 Resistance to the use of video in individual psychotherapy training. American Journal of Psychiatry 140 (9): 1172–1176

Goldberg D P, Hobson R F, Maguire G P et al 1984 The clarification and assessment of a method of psychotherapy. British Journal of Psychiatry 144: 567–580

Goldberg R L, Green S 1985 Medical psychotherapy. American Family Physician 31(1): 173–178

Goldschmidt O 1986 A contribution to the subject of 'psychic trauma' based on the course of a psycho-analytic short therapy. International Review of Psycho-Analysis 13: 181

Goldstein J E 1974 The Woolf's response to Freud. Water spiders, singing canaries and the second apple. Psychoanalytic Quarterly 43: 438–476

Goldstein M J, Rodnick E H, Evans J R, May P R A, Steinberg M R, 1978 Drug and family therapy in the aftercare treatment of acute schizophrenics. Archives of General Psychiatry 35: 1169–1177

Good T S 1927 An attempt to investigate and treat psycho-neuroses and psychoses at an outpatient clinic. British Journal of Medical Psychology 7: 36–71

Good T S 1930 The history and progress of Littlemore Hospital. Journal of Mental Science 76: 602–621

Goodman B, Nowak-Scibelli D 1985 Group treatment for women incestuously abused as children. International Journal of Group Psychotherapy 35 (4): 534–544

Gordon A M 1983 Drugs and delinquency: a ten-year follow-up of drug clinic patients. British Journal of Psychiatry 142: 169–173

Gossop M, Green L, Phillips G, Bradley B 1989 Lapse, relapse and survival among opiate addicts after treatment: a prospective follow-up study. British Journal of Psychiatry 1 54: 348–353

Gottlieb G L, Beck A T 1990 Cognitive therapy and pharmacotherapy in geriatric depressives: a pilot randomized clinical trial. In press

Grant S, Margison F, Powell A 1991 The future of psychotherapy services. Psychiatric Bulletin 15: 174–179

Green H 1964 I never promised a rose garden. Pan Books, London

Greenacre P 1967 The influence of infantile trauma on genetic patterns. In: Furst S (ed) Psychic trauma. Basic Books, New York

Greenberg L S, Safran J D 1987 Emotion in psychotherapy. The Guildford Press, New York

Greenberg J R, Mitchell S A 1983 Object relations in psychoanalytic theory. Harvard University Press, Cambridge, Mass.

Greenson R R 1978 The technique and practice of psychoanalysis. Vol I. Hogarth Press, London

Greenspan S I, Pollock G H (eds) 1981 The course of life: psychoanalytical contributions towards understanding personality development. Vol III Adulthood and the aging process. Publication No. (ADM) 81.1000 US Department of Health and Human Services, Washington DC

Grinder J, Bandler R 1981 Trans-formations-NLP and the structure of hypnosis. Real People Press, Moab, Utah

Grinker R R, Werble B, Drye R 1968 The borderline syndrome. Basic Books, New York

Groddeck G W 1925 The meaning of illness: selected psychosomatic writings. Hogarth Press, London

Gross R J et al 1980 Borderline syndrome and incest in chronic pelvic pain patients. International Journal of Psychiatry in Medicine 10: 79–96

Grosskuth P 1986 Melanie Klein. Hodder & Stoughton, London

Groth N, Burgess W, Holmstrom L L, 1977 Rape: power, anger and sexuality. American Journal of Psychiatry 143: 817–824

Grotstein J 1983 Deciphering the schizophrenic experience. Psychoanalytic Inquiry 3: 37–70

Guidano V F, Liotti G 1983 Cognitive processes and emotional disorders. Guilford, New York

Gunderson J G, Elliott G R 1985. The interface between borderline personality disorder and affective disorder. American Journal of Psychiatry 142: 277–288

Gunderson J G, Kolb J E 1978. Discriminating features of borderline patients. American Journal of Psychiatry 135: 792–796

Gunderson J G, Kolb J E, Austin V 1981 The diagnostic interview for borderline patients. American Journal of Psychiatry 138: 896–903

Gunderson J G, Singer M T 1975 Defining borderline patients: an overview. American Journal of Psychiatry 132: 1–10

Guntrip H 1974a The schizoid personality and the external world. In: Schizoid phenomena, object relations and the self. Hogarth, London

Guntrip H 1974b Ego-weakness, the core of the problem of psychotherapy. In: Schizoid phenomena, object relations and the self. Hogarth, London

Gutmann D 1988 Reclaimed powers: towards a new psychology of men and women in later life. Hutchinson, London

Hafner R J, Marks I M 1976 Exposure in vivo of agoraphobics: contributions of diazepam, group exposure and anxiety evocation. Psychological Medicine 6: 71–88

Hale R 1985 Suicide and the violent act. Bulletin of the British Association of Psychotherapists. July

Haley J 1977 Problem-solving therapy. Jossey Bass, San Francisco

Hamilton V 1988 'The mantle of safety' – transference interpretation and reconstruction of childhood traumas in once-weekly therapy with a 37-year-old woman. Unpublished paper, given at the Tavistock Clinic, London, November 1988

Hardin G, 1969 The cybernetics of competition: a biologist's view of society. In Shepard P, McKinley D (eds) The subversive science: essays toward an ecology of man. Houghton Mifflin, Boston

Hardy G E, Shapiro D A 1985 Therapist verbal response modes in prescriptive versus exploratory psychotherapy. British Journal of Clinical Psychology 24: 235–245

Hart B 1912 The psychology of insanity. Cambridge University Press, Cambridge

Hart B 1927 Psychopathology. Cambridge University Press, Cambridge

Hawton K, Catalan J 1987 Attempted suicide: a practical guide to its nature and management. Oxford University Press, Oxford

Hawton K, Fagg J 1988 Suicide and other causes of death following attempted suicide. British Journal of Psychiatry 152: 359–366

Hayman A 1989 What do we mean by 'phantasy'? International Journal of Psycho-Analysis 70: 105–144

Head H 1922 The diagnosis of hysteria. British Medical Journal, May 27th

Heard D H 1988 Introduction to: Suttie I D The origins of love and hate. Free Association Books, London

Heim F 1980, 'Supportive therapy' P rediscovered? – a plea for adaptive psychotherapies (summary in English). Psychotherapie Medizinische Psychologie Psychother med Psychol 30: 261–273

Heiserman M S 1971 The effect of experiential videotape training procedures compared to cognitive classroom teaching methods on the interpersonal communication skills of juvenile court case workers. Unpublished PhD dissertation, Michigan State University

Henderson D K 1964 The evolution of psychiatry in Scotland. E S Livingstone, Edinburgh

Henry W P 1986 Interpersonal process in psychotherapy. Doctoral thesis, Department of Psychology, Vanderbilt University

Herman J 1983 Recognition and treatment of incestuous families. International Journal of Family Therapy Summer: 81–91

Herman J, Schatzow 1984 Time-limited group therapy for women with a history of incest. International Journal of Group Psychotherapy 34(4): 605–616

Heron J 1975 Six category intervention analysis. University of Surrey, Guildford

Herr M 1978 Dispatches. Pan, London

Hess N 1987 King Lear and some anxieties of old age. British Journal of Medical Psychology 60: 209–215

Hildebrand P 1982 Psychotherapy with older patients. British Journal of Medical Psychology 55: 19–28

Hildebrand P 1985 Object loss and development in the second half of life. In: Nemiroff R A, Colarusso C A (eds) The race against time. Plenum Press, New York, pp. 211–227

Hildebrand P 1986 Dynamic psychotherapy with the elderly. In: Hanley I, Gilhooly M (eds) Psychological therapies for the elderly. Croom Helm, London, pp. 22–40

Hill C E 1978 Development of a counsellor verbal response category system. Journal of Counselling Psychology 25: 461–468

Hill D 1954 Psychotherapy and the physical methods of treatment in psychiatry. Journal of Mental Science 100: 360–374

Hill J 1982 Reasons and causes: the nature of explanations in psychology and psychiatry. Psychological Medicine 12: 501–514

Hill P 1989 Adolescent psychiatry. Churchill Livingstone, London

Hinshelwood R D 1989 A dictionary of Kleinian thought. Free Association Books, London

History of the Great War 1923 Medical Services Diseases of the War, Vol II. HMSO, London

Hobbs M 1984 Crisis intervention in theory and practice: a selective review. British Journal of Medical Psychology 57: 23–34

Hobbs M 1988 The psychological treatments. In: Rose N (ed) Essential psychiatry. Blackwell, Oxford

Hobbs M 1990a Childhood sexual abuse: how can women be helped to overcome its long-term effects? In: Hawton K, Cowen P (eds) Dilemmas and controversies in the management of psychiatric patients. Oxford University Press, Oxford

Hobbs M 1990b The role of the psychotherapist as consultant to inpatient psychiatric units. Psychiatric Bulletin 14: 8–12

Hobbs M, Birtchnell S, Harte A, Lacey H 1989 Therapeutic factors in short-term group therapy for women with bulimia. International Journal of Eating Disorders 8: 623–633

Hobman J B 1949 David Eder: Memoirs of a modern pioneer. Victor Gollancz, London

Hobson R F 1977 A conversational model of psychotherapy. Association of University Teachers of Psychiatry Newsletter, January: 14–18

Hobson R F 1985 Forms of feeling: the heart of psychotherapy. Tavistock, London

Hoch P, Polatin P 1949 Pseudoneurotic forms of schizophrenia. Psychiatric Quarterly 23: 248–276

Hoffman L 1981 Foundations of family therapy. Basic Books, New York

Hogarty G E, Anderson C M, Reiss D J et al 1986 Family psychoeducation: social skills training and maintenance chemotherapy in the aftercare treatment of schizophrenia. Archives of General Psychiatry 43: 633–642

Holmes J 1988 Supportive analytical psychotherapy. An account of two cases. British Journal of Psychiatry 152: 824–829

Holmes J 1990 What can psychotherapy contribute to community psychiatry and vice versa. Bulletin of the Royal College of Psychiatry 14: 213–216

Holmes J, Lindley R 1989 The values of psychotherapy. Oxford University Press, Oxford

Holmes T H, Rahe R H 1967 The social readjustment rating scale. Journal of Psychosomatic Research 11: 213–218

Hopkinson K, Cox A, Rutter M 1981 Psychiatric interviewing techniques III: Naturalistic study: eliciting feelings. British Journal of Psychiatry 138: 406–415

Horney K 1937 The neurotic personality of our time. Norton, New York

Horowitz M 1984 Personality styles and brief psychotherapy. Basic Books, New York

Horowitz M J, 1986 Stress-response syndromes, 2nd edn. Aronson, Northvale, N.J.

Horowitz M J, Marmar C, Weiss D S, De Witt K, Rosenbaum R 1984 Brief psychotherapy of bereavement reactions: the relationship of process to outcome. Archives of General Psychiatry 41: 438–448

Howard K I, Krause M S, Orlinsky D E 1986 The attrition dilemma: toward a new strategy for psychotherapy research. Journal of Consulting and Clinical Psychology 54: 106–110

Howard K I, Kopta S M, Krause M S, Orlinsky D E 1986 The dose-effect relationship in psychotherapy. American Psychologist 41: 159–164

Howard K I, Davidson C V, O'Mahoney M T, Orlinsky D E, Brown K P 1989 Patterns of psychotherapy utilization. American Journal of Psychiatry 146: 775–778

Howlin P 1981 The effectiveness of operant language training with autistic children. Journal of Autism and Developmental Disorders 11: 89–105

Hughes J 1989 Reshaping the psychoanalytic domain. University of California Press, Berkeley

Hunter A J G 1989 Reflections on psychotherapy with ageing people, individually and in groups. British Journal of Psychiatry 154: 250–252

Hutton I 1960 Memories of a doctor in war and peace. Heinemann, London

Hyde K 1988 Analytic group psychotherapies. In: Aveline M, Dryden W (eds) Group therapy in Britain. Open University Press, Milton Keynes

Ivey A, Normington C, Miller C, Morrill C, Morrill W, Haase R 1968 Microcounselling and attending behaviour: an approach to pre-practicum counsellor training. Journal of Counselling Psychology 15 (2): 1–12

Ivey A E, Simek-Downing L 1980 Counselling and Psychotherapy: skills, theories and practice. Prentice-Hall, New Jersey

Jackson M 1985 A psycho-analytical approach to the assessment of a psychotic patient. Psychoanalytic Psychotherapy 1: 11–22

Jackson M 1989a Schizoid mental states. In: Proceedings of 9th International symposium on the psychotherapy of schizophrenia, Turin (In press)

Jackson M 1989b Manic-depressive psychosis: psychodynamics and psychotherapy in a psychodynamic milieu. In: Haugsgjerd (ed) Lines of life: psychiatry and humanism. Tano, Oslo

Jackson M, Pines M 1986 The borderline personality. Neurologia et Psychiatrics 9 (1): 66–68; 9(2): 54–67

Jackson M, Tarnopolsky A 1990 The borderline personality. In: Bluglass R, Bowden P (eds) The principles and practice of forensic psychiatry. Churchill Livingstone, Edinburgh

Jacobson E 1967 Psychotic conflict and reality. Hogarth Press, London

James D C 1984 Bion's 'containing' and Winnicott's 'holding' in the context of the group matrix. International Journal of Group Psychotherapy 34: 201–213

James M 1964 Interpretation and management in the treatment of pre-adolescents. International Journal of Psychoanalysis 45: 499

Jaques E 1955 Social systems as a defence against persecutory and depressive anxiety. In: Klein M, Heimann P, Money-Kyrle R E (eds) New directions in psychoanalysis. Tavistock, London

Jaques E 1965 Death and the mid-life crisis. International Journal of Psycho-Analysis 46: 502–514

Jehu D 1988 Beyond sexual abuse. Therapy with women who were childhood victims. John Wiley, Chichester

Jennings S 1987 Dramatherapy – theory and practice for teachers and clinicians. Routledge, London

Jones E 1959 Memories of a psychoanalyst. Hogarth, London (Reprinted by Free Association Books, London 1988)

Jones M C 1924 The elimination of children's fears. Journal of Experimental Psychology 7: 383–390

Joseph B 1976 Towards the experiencing of psychic pain. In: James S Grotstein (ed) 1983 Do I dare disturb the universe? A memorial to Wilfred R Bion. Karnac, London

Joseph B 1986 Envy in everyday life. Psychoanalytic Psychotherapy 2: 20–32

Judkins M, Margison F R 1988 Learning about supervision: an experiential approach. Paper presented to North Western Regional Health Authority training section conference, 'Supervision in psychotherapy'. Brindle Lodge, Hoghton

Jung C G 1902 The psychology of dementia praecox. Collected Works, Vol 3. Routledge, London

Jung C G 1931 Standard edition of complete works 8: 399, (1960 Routledge and Kegan Paul, London)

Jung C G 1933 Modern man in search of a soul, 9th impression. Kegan Paul, Trench, Trubner, London

Kagan N 1980 Influencing human interactions – eighteen years with IPR. In: Hess A K (ed) Psychotherapy supervision: theory, research and practice. John Wiley, New York

Kanfer F H, Goldstein A P 1986 Helping people change, 3rd edn. Pergamon, New York

Kanfer F, Saslow G 1965 Behavioral analysis: an alternative to diagnostic classification. Archives of General Psychiatry 12: 529–538

Kaplan H I, Sadock B J 1989 Psychosomatic disorders. In: Comprehensive textbook of psychiatry V. Williams and Wilkins, Baltimore

Kapur R, Pearce M 1987 Group psychotherapy with the elderly. British Journal of Psychotherapy 3(4): 289–296

Karasu T B 1982 Psychotherapy and pharmacotherapy: toward an integrative model. American Journal of Psychiatry 139: 1102–1113

Karasu T B 1986 The psychotherapies: benefits and limitations. American Journal of Psychotherapy 40: 324–343

Karon B, Vandenbos G 1981 Psychotherapy of schizophrenia. Aronson, London

Karush A, Daniels G E, Flood C, O'Connor J F 1977 Psychotherapy in ulcerative colitis. Saunders, Philadelphia

Kedward H B, Cooper B 1968 Neurotic disorder in urban practice: a three year follow up. Journal of the Royal College of General Practitioners 1: 148–163

Kempler W 1974 Principles of Gestalt family therapy. The Kempler Institute, Costa Mesa, California

Kennard D 1983 An introduction to therapeutic communities. Routledge & Kegan Paul, London

Kernberg O F 1967 Borderline personality organisation. Journal of the American Psychoanalytic Association 16: 641–685

Kernberg O F 1975a Borderline conditions and pathological narcissism. Aronson, New York

Kernberg O F 1975b A systems approach to priority setting of interventions in groups. International Journal of Group Psychotherapy 25: 251–275

Kernberg O F 1978 Leadership and organisational functioning: organisational regression. International Journal of Group Psychotherapy 28: 3–25

Kernberg O F 1980 Internal world and external reality. Aronson, New York

Kernberg O F 1981 Some issues in the theory of hospital treatment. Tidsskr Nor Loegeroren 14: 101; 837–843

Kernberg O F 1984 Severe personality disorders: psychotherapeutic strategies. Yale University Press, New Haven

Kernberg O F, Burstein E D, Coyne L, Applebaum A, Horowitz L, Bough H 1972 Psychotherapy research project. Bulletin of the Menninger Clinic 36(1): 2751–2755

Kety S S, Rosenthal D, Wender P H, Schulsinger F 1968 The types and prevalence of mental illness in the biological and adoptive families of adopted schizophrenics. In: Rosenthal D, Kety S S (eds) The transmission of schizophrenia. Pergamon Press, Oxford, pp. 345–362

Khan M M R 1974 The privacy of the self. Hogarth Press, London

Khantzian E J 1985 The self-medication hypothesis of addictive disorders: focus on heroin and cocaine dependence. American Journal of Psychiatry 142(11): 1259–1264

King P 1974 Notes on the psychoanalysis of older patients. Journal of Analytic Psychology 19: 22–37

King P 1980 The life cycle as indicated by the nature of the transference in the psychoanalysis of the middle-aged and elderly. International Journal of Psycho-Analysis 61(2): 153–160

King P, Steiner R 1990 The Freud-Klein Controversy 1941–5. Routledge, London

Kingsley R G, Wilson G T 1977 Behavior therapy for obesity: a comparative investigation of long term efficacy. Journal of Consulting and Clinical Psychology 49: 309–319

Kinsey A C, Pomeroy W B, Martin C E 1948 Sexual behaviour in the human male. Saunders, Philadelphia, pp. 162–174

Kinsey A C, Pomeroy W B, Martin C E, Gebhard P H 1953 Sexual behaviour in the human female. Saunders, Philadelphia, pp. 116–122

Klein D F, Zitrin C M, Woerner M G, Ross D C 1983 Treatment of phobias. Behaviour therapy and supportive psychotherapy: are there any specific ingredients? Archives of General Psychiatry 40: 139–145

Klein M 1934 On criminality. In: Kahn M R (ed) Vol I Collected Works. Hogarth, London, p. 258

Klein M 1946 Notes on some schizoid mechanisms. In: Kahn M R (ed) Vol III Collected Works. Hogarth, London, p.1

Klein M 1950 Contributions to psycho-analysis. Hogarth, London

Klein M 1957 Envy and gratitude. Hogarth, London

Klein R H 1977 In-patient group psychotherapy: practical considerations and special problems. International Journal of Group Psychotherapy 27: 201–214

Knight R 1953 Borderline states. Bull Menninger Clin. 17: 1–12

Kohon G 1986 The British school of psychoanalysis: the independent tradition. Free Association Books, London

Kohut H 1977 The restoration of the self. International University Press, New York

Koss M P, Butcher J N 1986 Research in brief psychotherapy. In: Garfield S L, Bergin A E (eds) Handbook of psychotherapy and behaviour change, 3rd edn. Wiley, New York

Kovell J 1976 A complete guide to therapy. Pelican Books, London, Ch. 9

Kraemer S 1988 Splitting and stupidity in child sexual abuse. Psychoanalytic Psychotherapy 3(3): 247–257

Krasner L 1965 The behavioral scientist and social responsibility: no place to hide. Journal of Social Issues 21: 9–30

Kris E 1956 The recovery of childhood memories in psychoanalysis. The Psychoanalytic Study of the Child 11: 54

Krystal H, Niederland W G 1968 Clinical observations on the survivor syndrome. In: Krystal H (ed) Massive psychic trauma. International Universities Press, New York

Laing R D 1960 The divided self. Tavistock, London

Laing R D 1961 The self and others. Tavistock, London

Lake B 1985 Concept of ego strength in psychotherapy. British Journal of Psychiatry 147: 471–478

Lakovics M 1983 Classification of countertransference for utilisation in supervision. American Journal of Psychotherapy 37(2): 245–257

Lambert M J, De Julio S S, Stein D M 1978 Therapeutic interpersonal skills: process outcome and methodological considerations, and recommendations for future research. Psychological Bulletin 85: 467–489

Lambert M J, Shapiro D A, Bergin A E 1986 The effectiveness of psychotherapy. In: Garfield S L, Bergin A E (eds) Handbook of psychotherapy and behaviour change, 3rd edn. Wiley, New York

Langley D M, Langley G E 1983 Dramatherapy and psychiatry. Croom Helm, London

Langs R 1976 The bipersonal field. Aronson, New York

Lankton S 1980 Practical magic – a translation of basic NLP into clinical psychotherapy. Meta Publications, Cupertino, California

Laplanche J, Pontalis J-B 1973 The language of psycho–analysis. Hogarth, London

Laufer M 1968 The body image, the function of masturbation and adolescence. Problems of the ownership of the body. The Psychoanalytic Study of the Child 23: 114–37

Laufer M, Laufer M E 1984 Adolescence and developmental breakdown. Yale University Press, New Haven

Laufer M, Laufer M E 1989 Developmental breakdown and psychoanalytic treatment in adolescence. Yale University Press, New Haven

Lazarus A A 1966 Behavior rehearsal vs nondirective therapy vs advice in effecting behavior change. Behaviour Research and Therapy 4: 301–303

Lazarus A A, Messer S B 1988 Clinical choice points: behavioral versus psychoanalytic interventions. Psychotherapy 25: 59–70

Leff J P 1985 Family treatment of schizophrenia. In: Granville-Grossman K (ed) Recent advances in clinical psychiatry, Vol 5. Churchill Livingstone, Edinburgh

Leff J P, Kuipers L, Berkowitz R, Eberlein-Fries R, Sturgeon D 1982 A controlled trial of intervention in the families of schizophrenic patients. British Journal of Psychiatry 141: 121–134

Leff J, Vaughn C 1983 Expressed emotion in families. Guilford Press, New York

Leff J, Wig N N, Ghosh A et al 1987 Influence of relatives' expressed emotion on the course of schizophrenia in Chandigarh. British Journal of Psychiatry 151: 166–173

Le Grange P D 1989 Anorexia nervosa and family therapy: a study of changes in the individual and family during the process of body weight restoration. Ph.D thesis, University of London

Lempa W, Poets C, Arnold M A et al 1985 Effectiveness of supportive psychotherapy for medically ill inpatients: empirical findings and practical consequences. Psychotherapie Medizinische Psychologie 30: 315–319

Leuner H 1978 Guided affective imagery. In: Singer J, Pope K 1978 The power of human imagination. Plenum Press, New York

Levi P 1988 The drowned and the saved. Michael Joseph, London

Levine H B 1980 Milieu biopsy: the place of the therapy group on the in-patient ward. International Journal of Group Psychotherapy 30: 77–93

Lewis A 1979 Edward Mapother and the making of the Maudsley Hospital. In: Later Papers. Oxford University Press, Oxford

Lewis G, Appleby L 1988 The patients psychiatrists dislike. British Journal of Psychiatry 153: 44

Lieberman M, Yalom I, Miles M 1973 Encounter groups: first facts. Basic Books, New York

Lieberman M A, Tobin S S 1983 The experience of old age: stress, coping and survival. Basic Books, New York

Lieberman S, Cobb J P 1987 The grammar of psychotherapy: interactograms: three self-monitoring instruments for audiotape feedback. British Journal of Psychiatry 151: 594–601

Lieberman S, Cobb J P, Jackson C H 1989 Study of the 'grammar of psychotherapy' course using a student and control population. Some results, trends and disappointments. British Journal of Psychiatry 155: 842–845

Line W 1934–5 Some impressions of British psychiatry. American Journal of Psychiatry 91: 1059–1077

Liotti G 1986 Structural cognitive therapy. In: Dryden W, Golden W (eds) Cognitive-behavioural approaches to psychotherapy. Harper & Row, London

Little R B, Pearson M M 1966 The management of pathologic interdependency in drug addiction. American Journal of Psychiatry 123(5): 554–560

London N 1983 Psychoanalytic psychotherapy of schizophrenia: a psychoanalytic view from without. Psychoanalytic Inquiry 3: 91–104

Lorion R P, Felner R D 1986 Research on mental health interventions with the disadvantaged. In: Garfield S L, Bergin A E (eds) 1986 Handbook of psychotherapy and behaviour change. Wiley, Chichester

Lovaas O I et al 1966 Establishment of social reinforcers in two schizophrenic children on the basis of food. Journal of Experimental Child Psychology 4: 109–125

Lowen A 1975 Bioenergetics. Penguin, London

Luborsky L 1984 Principles of psychoanalytic psychotherapy: a manual for supportive-expressive treatment. Lippincott, Philadelphia

Luborsky L, Chandler M, Auerbach A H, Cohen J, Bachrach H M 1971 Factors influencing the outcome of psychotherapy: a review of quantitative research. Psychological Bulletin 75: 145–185

Luborsky L, Singer B, Luborsky L 1975 Comparative studies of psychotherapies: is it true that 'everyone has won and all must have prizes'? Archives of General Psychiatry 37: 471–481

Luborsky L, Crits-Cristoph P 1988 Measures of psychoanalytic concepts – the last decade of research from 'The Penn Studies'. International Journal of Psychoanalysis 69 (1): 75–86

Luborsky L, Crits-Christoph P, Mellon J 1989 Psychotherapy: who will benefit and how? Factors influencing the outcomes of psychotherapy. Basic Books, New York

Lucas R 1985 On the contribution of psychoanalysis to the management of psychotic patients in the N H S. Psychoanalytic Psychotherapy 1: 3–17

McAdam E K 1986 Cognitive behaviour therapy and its application with adolescents. Journal of Adolescence 9: 1–15

Macaskill N D 1980 The narcissistic core as a focus in the group therapy of the borderline patient. British Journal of Medical Psychology 53: 137–143

Macaskill N D 1982a Therapeutic factors in group therapy with borderline patients. International Journal of Group Psychotherapy 32: 61–73

Macaskill N D 1982b The theory of transitional phenomena and its application to the psychotherapy of the borderline patient. British Journal of Medical Psychology 55: 349–360

McCormack A, Janus M D, Burgess A W 1986 Runaway youths and sexual victimisation: gender difference in an adolescent runaway population. Child Abuse and Neglect 10: 387–395

McCready K F 1987 Milieu countertransference in treatment of borderline patients. Psychotherapy 24: 720–728

McCready K F 1989 The Lockerbie air disaster. One psychiatrist's experience. Psychiatric Bulletin 13: 120–122

MacCurdy J 1923 Problems in dynamic psychiatry. Cambridge University Press, Cambridge

McDougall J 1974 The psychosoma and the psychoanalytic process. International Review of Psychoanalysis 1: 437–459

McFarlane A C 1989 The treatment of post-traumatic stress disorder. British Journal of Medical Psychology 62: 81–90

McGrath G, Lowson K 1986 Assessing the benefits of psychotherapy: the economic approach. British Journal of Psychiatry 150: 65–71

Mackie A J 1981 Attachment theory: its relevance to the therapeutic alliance. British Journal of Medical Psychology 54: 203–212

McWhinney I R 1981 An introduction to family medicine. Oxford University Press, New York

Madanes C 1981 Strategic family therapy. Josey Bass, San Francisco

Madanes C 1984 Behind the one-way mirror. Advances in the practice of strategic therapy. Josey Bass, San Francisco

Maguire P, Goldberg D, Hyde C, Jones D, O'Dowd T, Roe P 1978 The value of feedback in teaching interviewing skills to medical students. Psychological Medicine 8: 695–704

Main T F 1957 The ailment. British Journal of Medical Psychology 30: 129–145

Main T F 1983 The concept of the therapeutic community: variations and vicissitudes. In: Pines M (ed) The evolution of group analysis. Routledge & Kegan Paul, London

Main T F 1989 The ailment and other psychoanalytic essays. Free Association Books, London

Malan D H 1963 A study of brief psychotherapy. Tavistock, London

Malan D H 1976a The frontier of brief psychotherapy. Plenum, New York

Malan D H 1976b Toward the validation of dynamic psychotherapy. Plenum, New York

Malan D H 1976c A study of brief psychotherapy. Plenum, New York

Malan D H 1979 Individual psychotherapy and the science of psychodynamics. Butterworth, London

Maltzberger J G, Buie D H 1980 The devices of suicide. International Review of Psycho-Analysis 7: 6–22

Mann J 1973 Time limited psychotherapy. Harvard University Press, Cambridge, Mass.

Mann J, Goldman R 1982 A casebook of time-limited psychotherapy. McGraw Hill, New York

De Mare P B 1983 Michael Foulkes and the Northfield Experiment. In: Pines M (ed) The evolution of group analysis. Routledge & Kegan Paul, London

Margison F R 1989 'Countertransference'. Current Opinion in Psychiatry 2(3): 357–361

Margison F R, Allen R T, Hobson R F 1986 Teaching psychotherapy skills to post-graduate trainees in the Region. Unpublished report to North Western Regional Health Authority Research Committee

Marlatt G A, George W H 1984 Relapse prevention: introduction and overview of the model. British Journal of Addiction 79: 261–275

Marks I M 1975 Behavioral treatments of phobic and obsessive-compulsive disorders: a critical appraisal. In: Hersen M, Eisler R, Miller P (eds) Progress in Behavior Modification: Vol 1. Academic Press, New York

Marks I M 1987 Cure and care of neurosis. Wiley, Chichester

Marks I 1989 Personal communication

Martindale B 1989 Becoming dependent again: the fears of some elderly persons and their younger therapists. Psychoanalytic Psychotherapy 4(1): 67–75

Marzillier J S 1989 Special review of: Michelson L, Ascher L M (eds) 1987 Anxiety and stress disorders; cognitive-behavioral assessment and treatment. Guilford, New York. Behaviour Research and Therapy 27: 211–212

Maruyama M 1988 The second cybernetics: deviation–amplifying mutual casual processes. In: Buckley W (ed) Modern systems research for the behavioural scientist. Aldine, Chicago

Masson J M 1985 The assault on truth: Freud's suppression of the seduction theory. Penguin, Harmondsworth

Matarazzo R G, Patterson D R 1986 Methods of teaching therapeutic skill. In: Bergin A E, Garfield S C Handbook of psychotherapy and behaviour change, 3rd edn. John Wiley, New York

Mathews A M, Gelder M G, Johnston D W 1981 Agoraphobia: nature and treatment. Tavistock, London

May R 1958 Contributions of existential psychotherapy. In: May R, Angel E, Ellenberger H F (eds) Existence. Basic Books, New York

Maxmen J S 1973 Group therapy as viewed by hospitalized patients. Archives of General Psychiatry 28: 404–408

Maxmen J S 1978 An educative model for in-patient group therapy. International Journal of Group Psychotherapy 28: 321–338

Meares R A, Hobson R F 1977 The persecutory therapist. British Journal of Medical Psychology 50: 349–359

Meichenbaum D H, Cameron R 1973 Training schizophrenics to talk to themselves: a means of developing attentional controls. Behavior Therapy 4: 515–534

Meltzoff J, Kornreich M 1970 Research in psychotherapy. Atherton Press, New York

Menninger K A 1933 Psychoanalytic aspects of suicide. International Journal of Psycho-Analysis 14: 376–390

Menninger K A 1958 Theory of psycho-analytic technique. Basic Books, New York

Mental outpatient clinics 1931. Discussion at annual meeting of RMPA Journal of Medical Science 77: 22–52

Menzies Lyth I E P 1959 The functioning of social systems as a defence against anxiety: a report on a study of the nursing service of a general hospital. Human Relations 13: 95–121. Reprinted in: Menzies Lyth I E P 1988 Containing anxiety in institutions. Free Association Books, London

Menzies Lyth I E P 1989 The aftermath of disaster: survival and loss. In: The dynamics of the social. Free Association Books, London

Mercier C A 1916 Psycho-analysis. British Medical Journal, December: 897–900

Mezey G C 1985 Rape – victiminological and psychiatric aspects. British Journal of Hospital Medicine March: 152–158

Michelson L, Ascher L M (eds) 1987 Anxiety and stress disorders; cognitive-behavioral assessment and treatment. Guilford, New York

Miller A 1983 The drama of being a child. Faber and Faber, London

Miller D 1983 The age between: adolescence and therapy. Aronson, London

Mintz J 1981 Measuring outcome in psychodynamic psychotherapy: psychodynamic vs symptom assessment. Archives of General Psychiatry 38: 503–506

Mintz J, Luborsky L, Christolph P 1979 Measuring the outcomes of psychotherapy: findings of the Penn Psychotherapy Project. Journal of Consulting and Clinical Psychology 47: 319–334

Minuchin S 1974 Families and family therapy. Tavistock, London

Minuchin S, Baker L, Rosman B L, Liberman R, Milman L, Todd T C 1975 A conceptual model of psychosomatic illness in children: family organization and family therapy. Archives of General Psychiatry 32: 1031–1038

Minuchin S, Rosman B L, Baker L 1978 Psychosomatic families. Harvard University Press, Cambridge, Mass.

Minuchin S, Fishman H C 1981 Family therapy techniques. Harvard University Press, Cambridge, Mass.

Mitchell J (ed) 1985 The selected Melanie Klein. Penguin, London

Moehler M L 1977 Self and object in countertransference. International Journal of Psychoanalysis 58: 365–374

Mohl P C 1988 Brief supportive psychotherapy by the primary care physician. Texas Medicine 84: 28–32

Molnos A 1984 The two triangles are four: a diagram to teach the process of dynamic brief psychotherapy. British Journal of Psychotherapy 1: 112–25

Molnos A 1986 Anger that destroys and anger that heals: handling hostility in group analysis and in dynamic brief psychotherapy. Group Analysis 19: 207–221

Money-Kyrle R E 1956 Normal counter-transference and some of its deviations. International Journal of Psychoanalysis 37: 360–366

Moos R H, Schaffer J A 1986 Life transitions and crises. In: Moos R H (ed) Coping with life crises: an integrated approach. Plenum, New York

Moreno J L 1946 Psychodrama Vol I. Beacon, New York

Moreno J L Psychodrama. In: Arieti S (ed) American handbook of psychiatry, Vol II. Basic Books, New York

Morgan H G, Russell G F M 1975 Value of family background features and clinical features as predictors of long-term outcome in anorexia nervosa: four year follow-up study of 41 patients. Psychological Medicine 5: 355–371

Morse S 1973 The after-pleasure of suicide. British Journal of Medical Psychology 46: 227–238

Muench G A 1965 An investigation of the efficacy of time-limited psychotherapy. Journal of Counselling Psychology 12: 294–298

de M'Uzan M 1974 Psychodynamic mechanisms in psychosomatic symptom formation. Psychotherapy Psychosomatics 23: 103–110

Nemiah J C 1977 Alexithymia: theoretical considerations. Psychotherapy Psychosomatics 28: 199–206

Nemiah J C 1980 Anxiety state (anxiety neurosis). In: Kaplin H I, Fredman A M, Sadock B J (eds) Comprehensive textbook of psychiatry Vol 1, 3rd edn. Williams & Wilkins, Baltimore

Nemiroff R A, Colarusso C A (eds) 1985 The race against time. Plenum Press, New York

Neugarten B, 1975 The future of the young-old. The Gerontologist 15: 4–9

Neustatter W L 1935 The result of fifty cases treated by psychotherapy. Lancet, April: 796–99

Newcombe N, Lerner J C 1982 Britain between the wars: the historical content of Bowlby's theory of attachment. Psychiatry 45: 1–12

Newton N A, Brauer D, Gutman D L, Grunes J 1985 Psychodynamic therapy with the aged: a review. In: Brink T L (ed) Clinical gerontology: a guide to assessment and intervention. Haworth Press, New York, pp. 205–229

Nitz H 1987 Anorexia Nervosa bei Jugendlichen. Springer Verlag, Berlin

Nitz H, Dare C 1984 A retrospective survey of outcome in the family of therapy of anorexia nervosa. Unpublished paper presented at the International Conference on Anorexia Nervosa and Related Disorders, University College, 5th September

Nordoff P, Robbins C 1977 Creative music therapy: individualized treatment for the handicapped child. John Day, New York

Noyes R, Kathol R G, Crowe R, Hoenk P R, Slymen D J 1978 The familial prevalence of anxiety neurosis. Archives of General Psychiatry 35: 1057–1059

O'Dowd T C 1988 Five years of heartsink patients in general practice. British Medical Journal 297: 20–27

Ogden T H 1980 On the nature of schizophrenic conflict. International Journal of Psychoanalysis 61: 513–531

Ogden T H 1985 On potential space. International Journal of Psychoanalysis 66: 129–142

Oldham J M, Russakoff L M 1987 Dynamic therapy in brief hospitalisation. Aronson, New York

Oliver J E 1988 Successive generations of child maltreatment: the children. British Journal of Psychiatry 153: 543–553

Olson D H 1986 Circumplex model VII: validation studies and FACES III. Family Process 25: 337–351

Olson D H, Sprenkle D H, Russell C S 1979 Circumplex model of marital and family systems: I Cohesion and adaptibility dimensions, family types, and clinical application. Family Process 18: 3–28

Oppenheimer R, Howells K, Palmer R L, Chaloner D A 1985 Adverse sexual experience in childhood and clinical eating disorders: a preliminary description. Journal of Psychosomatic Research 19: 357–361

Orlinsky D E, Howard K I 1986 Process and outcome in psychotherapy. In: Garfield S L, Bergin A E (eds) 1986 Handbook of psychotherapy and behaviour change. Wiley, Chichester

O'Shaughnessy E 1988 W R Bion's theory of thinking and new techniques in child analysis. In Spillius E B (ed) Melanie Klein Today Vol 2: Mainly practice. Routledge, London

Osorio L C 1977 The psychoanalysis of communication in adolescents. In: Feinstein S C, Giovacchini P L (eds) Adolescent psychiatry: developmental and clinical studies, Vol 5. Aronson, New York, pp 442–448

Pao P-N 1979 Schizophrenic disorders. International Universities Press, New York

Parkes C M 1975 Bereavement. Penguin, Harmondsworth

Parry G, Shapiro D A, Firth J 1986 The case of the anxious executive: a study from the research clinic. British Journal of Medical Psychology 59: 221–233

Parry-Jones W L 1985 Archival exploration of anorexia nervosa. Journal of Psychiatric Research 19: 95–100

Passons W 1975 Gestalt approaches in counselling. Holt, Rinehart and Winston, New York

Patterson G R 1982 Coercive family process. Castalia Publishing Company, Eugene, Oregon

Paul G L 1967 Strategy of outcome research in psychotherapy. Journal of Consulting Psychology 31: 109–118

Paul G L, Lentz R J 1977 Psychosocial treatment of the chronic mental patient. Harvard University Press, Cambridge, MA

Paxton R, Rhodes D, Crooks I 1988 Teaching nurses therapeutic conversation: a pilot study Journal of Advanced Nursing 13: 401–404

Paykel E S 1989 Treatment of depression – the relevance of research for clinical practice. British Journal of Psychiatry 155: 754–763

Pedder J 1982 Failure to mourn and melancholia. British Journal of Psychiatry 141: 329–337 329–337

Pedder J 1986 Reflections on the theory and practice of supervision. Psychoanalytic Psychotherapy 2(1): 1–12

Pedder J 1989 How can psychotherapists influence psychiatry? Psychoanalytic Psychotherapy 4: 43–54

Pekala R J, Siegel J M, Farrar D H 1985 The problem-solving support group: structured group therapy with psychiatric in-patients. International Journal of Group Psychotherapy 35: 391–409

Perkin D 1990 Behavioural psychotherapy for conduct disorders. In: Bluglass R, Bowden P (eds) The principles and practice of forensic psychiatry. Churchill Livingstone, Edinburgh

Perls F 1973 The Gestalt approach/eye witness to therapy. Science and Behaviour Books, Palo Alto

Perls F, Hefferline R, Goodman P 1973 Gestalt therapy: excitement and growth in the human personality. Pelican, London

Perris C 1988 Cognitive psychotherapy and Milieu therapeutic processes in psychiatric inpatient units. Journal of Cognitive Psychotherapy 2: 35–50

Perry S, Cooper A, Michels R 1987 The psychodynamic formulation. American Journal of Psychiatry 144: 543–550

Phillips A 1988 Winnicott. Fontana, London

Pincus L, Dare C 1978 Secrets in the family. Faber and Faber, London

Pines D 1980 Skin communication: early skin disorders and the effect on transference and countertransference. International Journal of Psychoanalysis 61: 315–323

Pines D 1986 Working with women survivors of the holocaust: affective experiences in transference and counter-transference. International Journal of Psycho-analysis 67: 29

Pines M 1980 What to expect in the psychotherapy of the borderline patient. Group Analysis 13: 168–177

Pines M (ed) 1983 The evolution of group analysis. Routledge & Kegan Paul, London

Pines M 1989. Borderline personality disorder and its treatment. Current Opinion in Psychiatry 2: 362–367

Plutchik R 1980 Emotion: a psychoevolutionary synthesis. Harper & Row, New York

Polanski N A, Harkins E B 1969 Psychodrama as an element in hospital treatment. Psychiatry 32: 74–87

Pollock G H 1981 Ageing or aged: development or pathology. In: Greenspan S I, Pollock G H (eds) The course of life: psychoanalytic contributions towards understanding personality development. Vol III: Adulthood and the aging process. Publication No (ADM) 81,1000. US Department of Health and Human Services, Washington DC, pp. 549–585

Pollock G H 1982 On ageing and psychopathology. International Journal of Psycho-Analysis 63(3): 275–281

Polster E, Polster M 1973 Gestalt therapy integrated. Brunner Mazel, New York

Pope H G, Jonas J M, Hudson J I, Cohen B M, Gunderson J G 1983 The validity of DSM-III borderline personality disorder. Archives of General Psychiatry 46: 41–48

Porter R (ed) 1984 Child sexual abuse within the family. Ciba Foundation, Tavistock, London

Pouillon J 1972 Doctor and patient: same and/or the other? (ethnological remarks). The Psychoanalytic Study of Society 5: 9–32. International Universities Press, New York

Powell A 1986 Object relations in the psychodramatic group. Group Analysis 19(2): 125–133

Priestley M 1975 Music therapy in action. Constable, London

Prince G S 1963 Jung's psychology in Britain. In: Fordham M (ed) Contact with Jung. Tavistock, London

Prioleau L, Murdoch M, Brody B 1983 An analysis of psychotherapy versus placebo studies. The Behavioural and Brain Sciences 6: 275–285

Psychoanalytic treatment 1933 Editorial, British Medical Journal December 23: 1175

Rachman S J, Hodgson R, Marks I M 1971 The treatment of chronic obsessional neurosis. Behaviour Research and Therapy 9: 237–247

Rachman S J 1973 The effects of psychological treatment. In: H J Eysenck (ed) Handbook of abnormal psychology Basic Books, New York

Racker H 1968 Transference and countertransference. Reprinted 1982 Maresfield Library, Karnac, London

Rado S 1957 Narcotic bondage. American Journal of Psychiatry 114(165): 165–170

Rank O 1924 (reissued 1973) The trauma of birth. Harper & Row, New York

Rapoport R 1960 Community as doctor. Tavistock, London

Ratigan B, Aveline M 1988 Interpersonal group therapy. In: Aveline M, Dryden W (eds) Group therapy in Britain. Open University Press, Milton Keynes

Ratnasuriya R H, Eisler I, Szmukler G I, Russell G F M 1990 Anorexia nervosa: outcome and prognostic factors. In press

Rawson R A, Glazer M, Callaghan E J, Liberman R Paul 1979 Naltrexone and behaviour therapy for opiate addicts. NIDA Research Monograph 25, United States Department of Health, Education and Welfare, Public Health Service, Washington

Rayner F 1986 Human development, 3rd edn. Allen and Unwin, London

Rees W L 1976 Stress, distress and disease. British Journal of Psychiatry 128: 3–18

Reid W J, Schyne A W 1969 Brief and extended casework. Columbia University Press, New York

Rey H 1975 Liberte et processus de pensee psychotiques. La vie Medicale au Canada Francais 4: 1046–60

Rey H 1977 The schizoid mode of being and the space time continuum. Unpublished paper read to the British Psychoanalytical Society

Rey J H 1979 Schizoid phenomena in the borderline patient In: Le Boit J, Capponi A (eds) Advances in psychotherapy of the borderline patient. Aronson, London

Rice C A, Rutan J S 1981 Boundary maintenance in in-patient therapy groups. International Journal of Group Psychotherapy 31: 297–309

Rice C A, Rutan J S 1987 Inpatient group psychotherapy: a psychodynamic perspective. Macmillan, New York

Rice L N 1980 A client-centered approach to the supervision of psychotherapy In: Hess A K Psychotherapy supervision: theory, research and practice. John Wiley, New York

Rice L N, Wagstaff A K 1967 Client voice quality and expressive style as indexes of productive psychotherapy. Journal of Consulting Psychology 31: 557–563

Rice L N, Greenberg L S (eds) 1984 Patterns of change. Guilford Press, New York

Rickman R 1950 Obituary. International Journal of Psycho-Analysis 31: 286–8

Rivers W H R 1923 Conflict and dream. Kegan Paul, London

Roberts J P 1982 Foulkes' concept of the matrix. Group Analysis 15: 111–126

Robertson J 1958 Young children in hospital. Tavistock, London

Robbie E 1988 Neuro linguistic programming. In: Rowan J, Dryden W (eds) 1988 Innovative therapy in Britain. Open University Press, Milton Keynes

Rogers C R 1951 Client-centred therapy. Constable, London

Rogers C R 1957 Training individuals to engage in the therapeutic process. In: Strother C R (ed) Psychology and mental health. American Psychological Association, Washington

Rorty R 1989 Contingency, irony, and solidarity. Cambridge University Press, Cambridge

Rosen J N 1962 Direct psychoanalytic psychiatry. Grune and Stratton, New York

Rosenfeld H A 1952 Transference-phenomena and transference-analysis in an acute catatonic schizophrenic patient. International Journal of Psycho-Analysis 33: 457

Rosenfeld H A 1965 Psychotic states: a psycho-analytical approach. Hogarth, London

Rosenfeld H A 1971 A clinical approach to the psycho-analytic theory of the life and death instincts: an investigation into the aggressive aspects of narcissism. International Journal of Psychoanalysis 52: 169–178

Rosenfeld H A 1978 Notes of the psychopathology and psychoanalytic treatment of some borderline patients. International Journal of Psychoanalysis 59: 215–221

Rosenfeld H A 1979 Transference psychosis in the borderline patient. In: Le Boit J, Capponi A (eds) Advances in psychotherapy of the borderline patient. Jason Aronson, New York

Rosenfeld H A 1987 Impasse and interpretation. Hogarth, London

Rosenthal R 1983 Assessing the statistical and social importance of the effects of psychotherapy. Journal of Consulting and Clinical Psychology 51: 4–13

Ross T A 1923 The common neuroses. Edward Arnold, London

Ross T A 1932 Introduction to analytic psychotherapy. Edward Arnold, London

Rosser R M, Birch S, Bond H, Denford J, Schacter J 1987 Five year follow-up of patients treated with in-patient psychotherapy at the Cassel Hospital for Nervous Diseases. Journal of the Royal Society of Medicine 80: 549–555

Rounsaville B J, Weissman M M, Wilber C H, Kleber H D 1982 Pathways to opiate addiction: an evaluation of differing antecedents. British Journal of Psychiatry 141: 437–446

Rowan J, Dryden W 1988 Innovative therapy in Britain. Open University Press, Milton Keynes, Chs. 7, 8, 9, 12

Rows R G 1920 Functional mental illness. The Morrison Lectures 1920. Edinburgh Medical Journal 25: 228–242

Rundell J R, Ursano R J, Holloway H C, Silberman E K, 1989 Psychiatric responses to trauma. Hospital and Community Psychiatry 40: 68–74

Rush A J, Beck A T, Kovacs M, Hollon S 1977 Comparative efficacy of cognitive therapy and pharmacotherapy in the treatment of depressed outpatients. Cognitive Therapy and Research 1: 17–37

Russell D E 1983 The incidence and prevalence of intra-familial and extra-familial sexual abuse in female children. Child Abuse and Neglect 7: 133–146

Russell D E H 1986 The secret trauma: incest in the lives of girls and women. Basic Books, New York

Russell G F M 1985 Anorexia and bulimia nervosa. In: Rutter M, Hersov L (eds) Child and adolescent psychiatry: model approaches. Blackwell, Oxford, pp. 625–637

Russell G F M, Szmukler G, Dare C, Eisler I 1987 An evaluation of family therapy in anorexia nervosa and bulimia nervosa. Archives of General Psychiatry 44: 1047–1056

Russell R L, Stiles W B 1979 Categories for classifying language in psychotherapy. Psychological Bulletin 84: 404–419

Rutan J S, Stone W N 1984 Psychodynamic group psychotherapy. Macmillan, New York

Rutter M 1981 Stress, coping and development: some issues and some questions. Journal of Child Psychology and Psychiatry 22: 323–356

Rutter M 1985 Resilience in the face of adversity: protective factors and resistence to psychiatric disorder. British Journal of Psychiatry 147: 598–611

Rutter M 1987a The role of cognition in child development and disorder. British Journal of Medical Psychology 60: 1–16

Rutter M 1987b Temperament, personality and personality disorder. British Journal of Psychiatry 150: 443–458

Rutter M, Cox A 1981a Psychiatric interviewing techniques I: methods and measures British Journal of Psychiatry 138: 273–282

Rutter M, Cox A, Egert S, Holbrook D, Everitt B 1981b Psychiatric interviewing techniques IV: experimental study: four contrasting styles. British Journal of Psychiatry 138: 456–465

Rycroft C 1971 Reich. Fontana, London

Rycroft C 1972 A critical dictionary of psychoanalysis. Penguin, Harmondsworth

Rycroft C 1985 Psychoanalysis and beyond. Chatto & Windus, London

Ryle A 1979 The focus of brief psychotherapy: dilemmas, traps and snags as target problems. British Journal of Psychiatry 174: 46–64

Ryle A 1982 Psychotherapy: a cognitive integration of theory and practice. Academic Press, London

Ryle A 1984 How can we compare different psychotherapies? Why are they all effective? British Journal of Medical Psychology 57: 261–264

Ryle A 1990 Cognitive analytic therapy: active participation in change. John Wiley, Chichester

Sadavoy J, Leszoz M (eds) 1987 Treating the elderly with psychotherapy: scope for change in later life. International Universities Press, Madison, Connecticut

Sampson H, Weiss J 1986 Testing hypotheses: The approach of the Mount Zion psychotherapy research group. In: Greenberg L S, Pinsof W (eds) The psychotherapeutic process: a research handbook. Guilford Press, New York, Ch. 17

Samuel A 1985 Jung and the post-Jungians. Routledge, London

Sandler A-M 1978 Problems in the psychoanalysis of an aging narcissistic patient. Journal of Geriatric Psycho-Analysis 11: 5–36

Sandler A-M 1984 Problems of development and adaptation in an elderly patient. Psychoanalytic Study of the Child 39: 471–489

Sandler F 1989 Personal communication

Sandler J (ed) 1988 Projection, identification, projective identification. Karnac, London

Sandler J 1967 Trauma, strain and development. In: Furst S (ed) Psychic trauma. Basic Books, New York, ch. 5

Schimiek J G 1975 The interpretations of the past: childhood trauma, psychical reality and historical truth. Journal of the American Psycho-Analytic Association 23: 845–865

Schulz C G 1983 Technique with schizophrenic patients. Psychoanalytic Inquiry 3: 105–124

Searles H F 1965 Collected papers on schizophrenia and related subjects. Hogarth, London

Sechehaye M A 1951 Symbolic realisation. International Universities Press, New York

Segal H 1958 Fear of death: notes on the analysis of an old man. International Journal of Psycho-Analysis 39(1): 178–181

Segal H 1964 Introduction to the work of Melanie Klein. Heinemann, London

Segal H 1981 The work of Hanna Segal. Aronson, London

Selvini Palazzoli M 1988 The family of the anorexic patient: a model system. In: Selvini M (ed) The work of Mara Selvini Palazzoli. Jason Aronson, New York, pp. 183–197

Selvini Palazzoli et al 1978 Paradox and counter-paradox. Aronson, New York

Selvini Palazzoli M, Cecchin G, Prata G, Boscolo L 1980 Hypothesising – circularity – neutrality. Family Process 19: 3–12

Selvini Palazzoli M, Cirillo S, Selvini M, Sorrentino A M 1989 Family games. Karnac, London

Shapiro D A 1989 Outcome research. In: G Parry , F N Watts (eds) Behavioural and mental health research: a handbook of skills and methods. Lawrence Erlbaum Associates, London & Hove, Ch. 9

Shapiro D A, Firth J A 1987 Prescriptive vs exploratory therapy: outcomes of the Sheffield Psychotherapy Project. British Journal of Psychiatry 151: 790–799

Shapiro R L 1978 The adolescent, the therapist and family: the management of external resistances to psychoanalytic therapy of adolescents. Journal of Adolescence 1: 3–10

Sharp D J, King M B 1989 Classification of psychosocial disturbance in general practice. Journal of the Royal College of General Practitioners 39: 356–358

Shepherd M 1979 Psychoanalysis, psychotherapy and health services. British Medical Journal 3: 1157–1559

Shoenberg P J 1986 The Psychotherapist's anxiety about bodily processes and some ways in which this anxiety may affect the long-term psychotherapy of psychosomatic disorders. In: Lacey J H, Sturgeon D A (eds) Proceedings of the 15th European Conference on Psychosomatic Research. J Libbey, London, pp. 54–58

Sifneos P 1972 Short-term psychotherapy and emotional crisis. Harvard University Press, Cambridge, Mass.

Sifneos P 1979 Short-term dynamic psychotherapy: evaluation and technique. Plenum, New York

Silbert M H, Pines A M 1983 Early sexual exploitations as an influence in prostitution. Social Work 28: 285–289

Simons A D, Garfield S L, Murphy G E 1984 The process of change in cognitive therapy and pharmacotherapy for depression. Archives of General Psychiatry 41: 45–51

Singer J, Pope K 1978 The power of human imagination. Plenum Press, New York

Singh A N, Maguire J 1989 Trichotillomania and incest. British Journal of Psychiatry 155: 108–110

Skinner B F 1938 The behaviour of organisms. Appleton-Century-Crofts, New York

Skinner B F 1971 Beyond freedom and dignity. Knopf, New York

Slater E, Shields J 1969 Genetical aspects of anxiety. In: Lader M H (ed) Studies of anxiety. British Journal of Psychiatry Special Publication No. 3

Sloane R B, Staples F R, Cristol A H, Yorkston N J, Whipple K 1975 Psychotherapy versus behaviour therapy. Harvard University Press, Cambridge, Mass.

Slobodin R 1978 W H R Rivers. Columbia University Press, New York

Smith M L, Glass G V, Miller T I 1980 The benefits of psychotherapy. John Hopkins Press, Baltimore

Solnit A J 1988 Foreword to Freeman T 1988 The psychoanalyst in psychiatry. Karnac, London

Soloff P A, George A, Nathan S et al 1986 Progress in pharmacotherapy of borderline disorders. Archives of General Psychiatry 43: 691–697

Spence D P 1982 Narrative truth and historical truth. Meaning and interpretation in psychoanalysis. Norton, New York

Spillius E (ed) 1988 Melanie Klein today. Routledge, London

Spitzer R L, Endicott J, Gibbon M 1979 Crossing the border into borderline personality and borderline schizophrenia. Archives of General Psychiatry 36: 17–24

Stanton A H, Schwartz M S 1954 The mental hospital. Basic Books, New York

Steele B F, Alexander H 1981 Long-term effects of sexual abuse in childhood. In: P Beezley Mrazek , Kempe C H (eds) Sexually abused children and their families. Pergamon Press, Oxford

Steinberg D 1987 Basic adolescent psychiatry. Blackwell Scientific Publications, Oxford

Steiner J 1979 The border between the paranoid-schizoid and the depressive positions in the borderline patient. British Journal of Medical Psychology 52: 385–391

Steiner J 1985 Psychotherapy under attack. Lancet 1: 266–267

Stekel W 1910 On suicide with particular reference to young students. In: Friedman P (ed) 1967 Discussions of the Munich Psychoanalytic Society 1910. International Universities Press, New York

Stephanos S 1975 The object relations of the psychosomatic patient. British Journal of Medical Psychology 48: 257–266

Stern A 1938 Psychoanalytic investigation and therapy in the borderline group of neuroses. Psychoanalytic Quarterly 7: 467–489

Stern D N 1985 The interpersonal world of the infant. Basic Books, New York

Stevens J 1971 Awareness: exploring, experimenting, experiencing. Real People Press, Moab, Utah

Stewart H 1989 Technique at the basic fault/regression. International Journal of Psychoanalysis 70: 221–230

Stierlin H 1968 Short-term versus long-term psychotherapy in the light of a general theory of human relationships. British Journal of Medical Psychology 41: 357–367

Stiles W B, Shapiro D, Elliott R 1986 Are all psychotherapies equivalent? American Psychologist 41: 165–180

Stiles W B, Shapiro D A, Firth-Cozens J A 1988a Verbal response mode use in contrasting psychotherapies: a within subjects comparison. Journal of Consulting and Clinical Psychology 56: 727–733

Stiles W B, Shapiro D A, Firth-Cozens J A 1988b Do sessions of different treatments have different impacts? Journal of Counselling Psychology 35: 391–396

Stiles W B, Shapiro D 1989 Abuse of the drug metaphor in psychotherapy process: outcome research. Clinical Psychology Review 9: 521–543

Stock Whitaker D 1985 Using groups to help people. Routledge & Kegan Paul, London

Stoddart W H P 1915 The new psychiatry. Lancet, March 20 and 27

Stoller R J 1984 Psychiatry's mind-brain dialectic, or the Mona Lisa has no eyebrows. American Journal of Psychiatry 141: 554–558

Stone M H 1983 Psychotherapy with schizotypal borderline patients. Journal of the American Academy of Psychoanalysis 11(1): 87–111

Stones M 1985 Shellshock and the psychologists. In: Bynum W F, Porter R, Shepherd M (eds) The anatomy of madness, Vol 2. Tavistock Press, London

Storr A 1979 The art of psychotherapy. Secker and Warburg, London

Storr A 1983 A psychotherapist looks at depression. British Journal of Psychiatry 143: 431–435

Storr A 1988 Freud. Oxford University Press, Oxford

Strachey J 1934 The nature of the therapeutic action of psychoanalysis. International Journal of Psychoanalysis 15: 127–159

Straker M 1958 Clinical observations of suicide. Canadian Medical Association Journal 79: 473–479

Strang J 1985 The generalist's guide to the assessment and treatment of the problem drug-taker. Update: 979–989

Strupp H H 1979 Specific versus non-specific factors in psychotherapy: a controlled study of outcome. Archives of General Psychiatry 36: 1125–1136

Strupp H H 1980 Success and failure in time limited psychotherapy. Archives of General Psychiatry 36: 1125–1136

Strupp H H 1983 Are psychoanalytic therapists beginning to practice cognitive behaviour therapy or is behaviour therapy turning psychoanalytic? British Journal of Cognitive Psychotherapy 1: 17–27

Sutherland J D 1980 The British object relations theorists: Balint, Winnicott, Fairbairn, Guntrip. Journal of the American Psychoanalytic Association 28: 829–860

Suttie I D 1988 The origins of love and hate. Free Association Books, London

Suttie I D, Suttie J 1932 The mother: agent and objects, Parts 1 and 2. British Journal of Medical Psychology 12: 91–108, 199–233

Svedlund J, Sjodin I 1986 The psychosomatic approach to treatment in the irritable bowel syndrome. In: Lacey J K, Sturgeon D A (eds) Proceedings of the 15th European Conference on Psychosomatic Research. J Libbey, London pp. 314–318

Symington N 1986 The analytic experience. Free Association Books, London

Szmukler G I, Tantum T 1985 Anorexia nervosa: starvation dependence. British Journal of Medical Psychology 57: 303–310

Szmukler G, Eisler I, Russell G F M, Dare C 1985 Anorexia nervosa, parental 'Expressed Emotion' and dropping out of treatment. British Journal of Psychiatry 147: 265–271

Szmukler G I Berkowitz R, Eisler I, Leff J, Dare C 1987 A comparative study of parental 'Expressed Emotion' in individual and family settings. British Journal of Psychiatry 151: 174–178

Tahka V A 1978 On some narcissistic aspects of self-destructive behaviour and their influence on its predictability. Psychiatrica Fennica Supplementum, pp. 59–62

Tarnopolsky A, Berelowitz M 1987 Borderline personality – a review of recent research. British Journal of Psychiatry 151: 724–734

Taylor G J 1989 Symposium on 'Psychoanalytic Therapy with Medical Patients' (Introduction). International College of Psychosomatic Medicine, 10th World Congress. (Personal communication)

Taylor G J 1987 Psychosomatic medicine and contemporary psychoanalysis. International Universities Press, Madison

Tennant C, Bebbington P, Hurry I 1981 The short-term outcome of neurotic disorders in the community: the relation of remission to clinical factors and 'neutralizing' effects. British Journal of Psychiatry 139: 213–220

Theander, S 1985 Outcome and prognosis in anorexia nervosa and bulimia: some results of previous investigations, compared with those of a Swedish long-term study. Journal of Psychiatric Research 19: 493–508

Thoma H, Kachele H 1986 Psycho-analytic practice. Springer Verlag, London

Thompson J, Rosser R 1990 In preparation

Tillett R 1984 Gestalt therapy in theory and in practice. British Journal of Psychiatry 145: 231–235

Tillett R 1986 Providing therapy for therapists: residential groups for helping professionals. Bulletin of the Royal College of Psychiatrists 10: 27–18

Tobin S S, Lieberman M A 1976 Last home for the aged: critical implications of institutionalization. Jossey-Bass, San Francisco

Treasure J 1988 Psychopharmoacological approaches to anorexia and bulimia. In: Scott D (ed) Anorexia and bulimia nervosa: practical approaches. Croom Helm, London, pp. 123–134

Trower P, Bryant B, Argyle M 1978 Social skills and mental health. Methuen, London

Truax C B, Carkhuff R R 1967 Toward effective counselling and psychotherapy: training and practice. Aldine, Chicago

Tsai M, Wagner N N 1978 Therapy groups for women sexually molested as children. Archives of Sexual Behaviour 7: 417–428

Tuckman B W 1965 Developmental sequence in small groups. Psychological Bulletin 63(6): 384–399

Turquet P M 1974 Leadership: the individual and the group. In: Gibbard G S, Hartman J J, Mann R D (eds) Analysis of groups. Josscy-Bass, San Francisco

Tyrer P 1985 Neurosis divisible? Lancet 1: 685–688

Tyrer P 1989 Treating panic. Editorial, British Medical Journal 298: 201

Ugelstad E 1979 Possibility of organising psychotherapeutically oriented treatment programmes for schizophrenia within sectorised psychiatric service. In: Muller C (ed) Psychotherapy of schizophrenia. Excerpta Medica, Amsterdam

Valliant 1977 Adaptation to life. Little and Brown, Boston

van der Kolk B 1987 The role of the group in the origin and resolution of the trauma response. In: Psychological trauma. American Psychiatric Press, Washington, DC, Ch. 7

van der Post L 1984 In a province. Penguin, London (First published 1934 Hogarth Press, London)

Verwoerdt A 1981 Psychotherapy for the elderly. In: Arie T (ed) Health care of the elderly. Croom Helm, London, pp. 118–139

Waldinger R J 1987 Intensive psychodynamic therapy with borderline patients : an overview. American Journal of Psychiatry 144: 267–275

Wallace C J, Liberman R P 1985 Social skills training for schizophrenics. A controlled clinical trial. Psychiatry Research 5: 239–247

Wallace E R 1989 The philosophy of psychiatry. Current Science 2(5): 667–675

Wallerstein R S 1989 Psychoanalysis and psychotherapy: an historical perspective. International Journal of Psychoanalysis 70: 563–591

Watson J B, Rayner R 1920 Conditioned emotional reactions. Journal of Experimental Psychology 3: 1–14

Watzlawick P, Weakland J, Fish R 1974 Change: principles of problem formation and problem resolution. Norton, New York

Weiner H 1977 Psychobiology and human disease. Elsevier, New York

Weissman M M, Klerman G L, Prusoff B A, Sholomskas D, Padian N 1981 Depressed outpatients one year after treatment with drugs and/or interpersonal psychotherapy (IPT). Archives of General Psychiatry 38: 51–55

Welldon E 1988 Mother, madonna, whore: the idealisation and denigration of motherhood. Free Association Books, London

Werman D S 1984 The practice of supportive psychotherapy. Bruner-Mazel, New York

West D J 1982 Delinquency: its roots, careers and prospects. Heinemann, London

West D J, Roy C, Nichols F L 1978 Understanding sexual attacks. Heinemann, London

Whiteley J S 1986 Sociotherapy and psychotherapy in the treatment of personality disorder: discussion paper. Journal of the Royal Society of Medicine 79: 721–725

Whiteley J S, Gordon J 1979 Group approaches in psychiatry. Routledge & Kegan Paul, London

Will D 1984 The progeny of positivism: the Maudsley school and anti-psychiatry. British Journal of Psychotherapy 1: 50–67

Williams A H 1964 Psychopathology and treatment of sexual murderers. In: Rosen I (ed) Psychology and treatment of sexual deviation. Oxford University Press, London

Wilkinson C 1989 Personal Communication

Wilson P 1986 Individual psychotherapy in a residential setting. In: Steinberg D (ed) The adolescent unit: work and teamwork in adolescent psychiatry. John Wiley, Chichester

Wilson P 1986 Psychoanalytic therapy and the young adolescent. Maladjustment and Therapeutic Education 4(2): 19–32

Wilson P 1987 Psychoanalytic therapy and the young adolescent. Bulletin of Anna Freud Centre 110: 51–59

Wilson P, Hersov L 1985 Individual and group psychotherapy. In: Rutter M, Hersov L (eds) Child and adolescent psychiatry. Modern approaches, 2nd edn. Blackwell, Oxford, Ch. 52

Winnicott D W 1949 Hate in the counter-transference. International Journal of Psychoanalysis 30: 69–74

Winnicott D W 1955 Clinical varieties of transference. In: Collected papers. Tavistock, London

Winnicott D W 1957 Direct child observation. In: Winnicott D W 1965 The maturational process and the facilitating environment. Hogarth Press, London

Winnicott D W 1958 The depressive position in normal emotional development. In: Collected papers. Tavistock, London

Winnicott D W 1960 Ego distortion in terms of true and false self. In: Winnicott D W 1965 The maturational process and the facilitating environment. Hogarth Press, London

Winnicott D W 1960 The theory of the parent-infant relationship: In: Winnicott D W 1965 The maturational processes and the facilitating environment. Hogarth, London

Winnicott 1965 The development of the capacity for concern. In: Winnicott D W 1965 The maturational process and the facilitating environment. Hogarth Press, London

Winnicott D W 1966a Psycho-somatic illness in its positive and negative aspects. International Journal of Psychoanalysis 47: 510–516

Winnicott D W 1966b Adolescence: struggling through the doldrums. In: 1985 The family and individual development. Tavistock Publications, London, pp. 79–87

Winnicott D W 1968 Communicating and not communicating leading to a study of certain opposites. In: Winnicott D W 1965 The maturational process and the facilitating environment: studies in the theory of emotional development. Hogarth Press, London, pp. 179–92

Winnicott D W 1971 Playing and reality. Tavistock Publications, London

Winnicott D W 1974 Fear of breakdown. International Review of Psycho-Analysis 1: 103

Winnicott D W 1984 In: Winnicott C, Shepherd R, David M (eds) Deprivation and delinquency. Tavistock, London

Winston A, Pinsker H, McCullough L 1986. A review of supportive psychotherapy. Hospital and Community Psychiatry 37: 93–99

Wolberg L R 1988 Supportive therapy. In: The techniques of psychotherapy, 3rd edn, Pt. 1. Academic Press, London

Wolff H H 1971 The therapeutic and developmental functions of psychotherapy. British Journal of Medical Psychology 44: 117–130

Wolff H H O, Shoenberg P J 1990. Individual psychosomatic disorders. In: Wolff H H O, Bateman A, Sturgeon D A (eds) The UCH textbook of psychiatry. Duckworth, London

Wolpe J 1958 Psychotherapy by reciprocal inhibition. Standard University Press, Palo Alto

Wolpe J 1977 Inadequate behavior analysis: the Achilles heel of outcome research in behavior therapy. Journal of Behavior Therapy and Experimental Psychiatry 8: 1–3

Woods R 1982 The psychology of ageing: assessment of defects and their management. In: Levy R, Post F (eds) The psychiatry of later life. Blackwell Scientific Publications, Oxford, pp.68–111

Woodmansey A 1988 Are psychotherapists out of touch? British Journal of Psychotherapy 5(1): 57–65

Woody G E, Luborsky L, McClellan A et al 1983 Psychotherapy for opiate addicts. Archives of General Psychiatry 40: 639–645

World Health Organization 1988 International classification of diseases, injuries and causes of death. WHO, Geneva

Wurmser L 1984 More respect for neurotic process: comments on the problem of narcissm in severe psychopathology, especially the addictions. Journal of Substance Abuse Treatment 1: 37–45

Wynther G, Sorensen T 1989 Group therapy with manic-depressives. Group Analysis 22: 19–30

Yager J 1982 Family issues in the pathogenesis of anorexia nervosa. Psychosomatic Medicine 44: 43–60

Yager J, Strober M 1985 Family aspects of eating disorder. American Psychiatric Update 4: 481–502

Yalom I D 1980 Existential psychotherapy. Basic Books, New York

Yalom I D 1983 In-patient group psychotherapy. Basic Books, New York

Yalom I D 1985 The theory and practice of group psychotherapy, 3rd edn. Basic Books, New York

Yalom I D, Vinogradov S 1988 Bereavement groups: techniques and themes. International Journal of Group Psychotherapy 38: 419–446

Yorke C 1986 Reflections on the problem of psychic trauma. Psycho-Analytic Study of the Child 41: 221

Yorke G, Wiseberg S, Freeman T 1989 Development and psychopathology. Studies in psychoanalytic psychiatry. Yale, London

Young J E, Beck A T 1982 Cognitive therapy: clinical applications. In: Rush A J (ed) Short term psychotherapies for depression. Guilford Press, New York

Young-Bruhl E 1988 Anna Freud. Macmillan, London

Zilboorg G 1941 Ambulatory schizophrenia. Psychiatry 4: 149–156

D'Zurilla T J, Goldfried M R 1971 Problem solving and behavior modification. Journal of Abnormal Psychology 78: 107–126

Index